Business Management Economics

Mgt 352

Instructor

J. Shannon Neibergs

Authors

Powell • Samuelson

To order books or for customer service please,

call 1-800-CALL WILEY (225-5945).

Printed in the United States of America 10 9 8 7 6 5 4 3 2 1

Printed in the United States of America
ED-11-17-11

List of Titles

Table of Contents

MANAGERIAL ECONOMICS
SIXTH EDITION

To Our Families

W. F. S
S. G. M

MANAGERIAL ECONOMICS
SIXTH EDITION

William F. Samuelson
Boston University

Stephen G. Marks
Boston University

WILEY

JOHN WILEY & SONS, INC.

ASSOCIATE PUBLISHER	Judith Joseph
ASSOCIATE EDITOR	Jennifer Conklin
EDITORIAL ASSISTANT	Sarah Vernon
EXECUTIVE MARKETING MANAGER	Amy Scholz
MARKETING ASSISTANT	Alana Filipovich
SENIOR MEDIA EDITOR	Allison Morris
PRODUCTION EDITOR	Janet Foxman
PRODUCTION MANAGEMENT	Ingrao Associates
PRODUCTION ASSISTANT	Matt Winslow
DESIGNER	Jeof Vita
COVER PHOTO	Corbis Digital Stock

This book was set in 10/12 New Baskerville by Prepare, Inc. and printed and bound by RRD Crawfordsville. The cover was printed by RRD Crawfordsville.

This book is printed on acid-free paper. ∞

To order books or for customer service, please call 1-800-CALL WILEY (225-5945).

Library of Congress Cataloging-in-Publication Data

Samuelson, William.
   Managerial economics / William F. Samuelson, Stephen G. Marks.—6th ed.
      p. cm.
   Includes index.
   ISBN 978-0-470-28242-7 (cloth)
1. Managerial economics.   2. Decision making.   I. Marks, Stephen G.
(Stephen Gary)   II. Marks, Stephen G.   III. Title.
   HD30.22.S26 2009
   338.5024'658—dc22   2008029114

Printed in the United States of America

10 9 8 7 6 5 4 3 2 1

2

Optimal Decisions Using Marginal Analysis

Government and business leaders should pursue the path to new programs and policies the way a climber ascends a formidable mountain or the way a soldier makes his way through a mine field: with small and very careful steps.

ANONYMOUS

The rapid growth in franchising during the last three decades can be explained in large part by the mutual benefits the franchising partners receive. The franchiser (parent company) increases sales via an ever-expanding network of franchisees. The parent collects a fixed percentage of the revenue each franchise earns (as high as 15 to 20 percent, depending on the contract terms). The individual franchisee benefits from the acquired know-how of the parent, from the parent's advertising and promotional support, and from the ability to sell a well-established product or service. Nonetheless, economic conflicts frequently arise between the parent and an individual franchisee. Disputes even occur in the loftiest of franchising realms: the fast-food industry. In the 1990s, there were ongoing conflicts between franchise operators and parent management of McDonald's and Burger King.

Conflict in Fast-Food Franchising[1]

These conflicts were centered on a number of recurring issues. First, the parent insisted on periodic remodeling of the premises; the franchisee resisted. Second, the franchisee favored raising prices on best-selling items; the parent opposed the change and wanted to expand promotional discounts. Third, the parent sought longer store hours and multiple express lines to cut down on lunchtime congestion; many franchisees resisted both moves.

[1]We begin this and the remaining chapters by presenting a managerial decision. Your first job is to familiarize yourself with the manager's problem. As you read the chapter, think about how the principles presented could be applied to this decision. At the chapter's conclusion, we revisit the problem and discuss possible solutions.

25

How does one explain these conflicts? What is their economic source? What can the parent and the franchisee do to promote cooperation? (At the conclusion of the chapter, we will revisit the franchising setting and offer explanations for these conflicts.)

This chapter introduces the analysis of managerial decision making that will occupy us for the remainder of the book. The chapter is devoted to two main topics: The first is a simple economic model (i.e., a description) of the private, profit-maximizing firm; the second is an introduction to marginal analysis, an important tool for arriving at optimal decisions. Indeed, it is fair to say that the subsequent chapters provide extensions or variations on these two themes. The present chapter employs marginal analysis as a guide to output and pricing decisions in the case of a single product line under the simplest demand and cost conditions. In Chapters 3 and 4, we extend marginal analysis to the cases of complex demand conditions, multiple markets, and price discrimination. In Chapters 5 and 6, we apply the same approach to settings that involve more complicated production technologies and cost conditions, multiple production facilities, and multiple products. In Chapters 7, 8, and 9, we analyze the key market environments—competition, oligopoly, and monopoly—in which the profit-maximizing firm operates. Together, these chapters demonstrate the great power of marginal analysis as a tool for solving complex decisions. Consequently, it is important to master the logic of marginal analysis at the outset. We start with a simple example before turning to the model of the firm.

SITING A SHOPPING MALL

A real-estate developer is planning the construction of a large shopping mall in a coastal county. The question is where to locate it. To help her in the decision, the developer has gathered a wealth of information, including the stylized "map" of the region in Figure 2.1. The county's population centers run from west to east along the coast (these are labeled A to H), with the ocean to the north. Since available land and permits are not a problem, the developer

FIGURE 2.1

Locating a Shopping Mall

At what site along the west–east coast, running from towns A to H, should a developer locate a shopping mall?

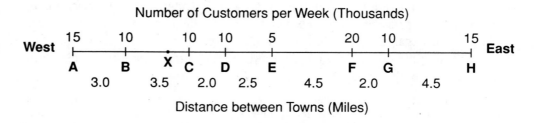

Number of Customers per Week (Thousands)

Distance between Towns (Miles)

judges that she can locate the mall anywhere along the coast, that is, anywhere along line segment AH. In fact, the mall would be welcome in any of the towns due to its potential positive impact on the local economy.

According to an old adage, "The three most important factors in the real-estate business are location, location, and location." Accordingly, the developer seeks a site that is proximate to as many potential customers as possible. A natural measure of locational convenience is the total travel miles (TTM) between the mall and its customer population. Thus, Figure 2.1 notes the distances between towns in the county. It also shows the potential number of customers per week in each town. Thus, the developer's key question is, Where along the coast should the mall be located to *minimize* the total travel miles?

To start, suppose that the developer considers one site at a time, computes its TTM, and selects the site that has the lowest TTM. For example, the TTM at the possible site labeled X (1 mile west of town C) is

$$(5.5)(15) + (2.5)(10) + (1.0)(10) + (3.0)(10)$$
$$+ (5.5)(5) + (10.0)(20) + (12.0)(10) + (16.5)(15) = 742.5.$$

The TTM is found by multiplying the distance to the mall by the number of trips for each town (beginning with A and ending with H) and summing.

We could try to solve the problem by enumeration. However, the method requires a good deal of computational brute force; it also offers no guarantee that an optimal location (i.e., one that has the lowest TTM of all possible candidates) will be found. The method only claims that its choice is the best of the limited number of candidates for which TTMs have been computed.

Fortunately, we can use a basic decision-making method, called marginal analysis, to identify the optimal site with much less computational effort. **Marginal analysis** is the process of considering small changes in a decision and determining whether a given change will improve the ultimate objective. Because this definition is a mouthful, let's see how the method works in siting the mall.

Let's begin with an arbitrary location, say, point X. It is *not* necessary to compute its TTM. Instead, we consider a small move to a nearby site, such as town C. (The direction of the move, east or west, is unimportant.) Then we ask, What is the *change* in the TTM of such a move? The clear result is that the TTM must have declined. The eastward move means a 1-mile reduction in travel distance for all customers at C or farther east (70,000 trip-miles in all). Therefore, the TTM is reduced by this amount. Of course, travel distances have increased for travelers at or to the west of X. For these customers, the TTM increase is 25,000 trip-miles. Therefore, the net overall change in TTM is $-70,000 + 25,000 = -45,000$ trip-miles. Total TTM has declined because the site moved toward a greater number of travelers than it moved away from. Town C, therefore, is a better location than site X.

Next, because the original move was beneficial, we try moving farther east, say, to town D. Again, the move reduces the TTM. (Check this.) What about a move east again to town E? This brings a further reduction. What about a move to town F? Now we find that the TTM has increased. (By how much?) Moreover, any further moves east would continue to increase the TTM. Thus, town E is the best site.

It is worth noting the simple but subtle way in which we found the optimal site. The simple maxim of marginal analysis is as follows:

> Make a "small" move to a nearby alternative if and only if the move will improve one's objective (in this case, reduce TTM). Keep moving, always in the direction of an improved objective, and stop when no further move will help.

The subtlety of the method lies in its focus on changes. One need never actually calculate a TTM (or even know the distances between towns) to prove that town E is the optimal location. (We can check that town E's TTM is 635.) One requires only some simple reasoning about the effects of changes.

Of course, on the tip of your tongue may be the declaration, "This problem is too simple; that is the only reason why the method works." This protest is both right and wrong. It is true that this particular location problem is special and therefore somewhat artificial. (Two-dimensional siting problems are both more realistic and more difficult.) But the simplicity of the setting was not the key to why marginal analysis worked. The method and its basic reasoning can be used in almost any optimization problem, that is, in any setting where a decision maker seeks to maximize (or minimize) a well-defined objective.

A SIMPLE MODEL OF THE FIRM

The decision setting we will investigate can be described as follows:

1. A firm produces a single good or service for a single market with the objective of maximizing profit.
2. Its task is to determine the quantity of the good to produce and sell and to set a sales price.
3. The firm can predict the revenue and cost consequences of its price and output decisions with certainty. (We will deal with uncertainty in Chapters 12 and 13.)

Together these three statements fulfill the first four fundamental decision-making steps described in Chapter 1. Statement 1 specifies the setting and objective, statement 2 the firm's possible decision alternatives, and statement 3 (along with some specific quantitative information supplied shortly) the link between actions and the ultimate objective, namely profit. It remains for the firm's manager to solve and explore this decision problem using marginal analysis (steps 5 and 6).

Before turning to this task, note the simplifying facts embodied in statement 1. Typically, a given firm produces a variety of goods or services. Nonetheless, even for the multiproduct firm, examining products one at a time has significant decision advantages. For one thing, it constitutes an efficient managerial division of labor. Thus, multiproduct firms, such as Procter & Gamble, assign product managers to specific consumer products. A product manager is responsible for charting the future of the brand (pricing, advertising, promotion, and production policies). Similarly, most large companies make profit-maximizing decisions along product lines. This product-by-product strategy is feasible and appropriate so long as the revenues and costs of the firm's products are independent of one another. (As we shall see in Chapters 3 and 6, things become more complicated if actions taken with respect to one product affect the revenues or costs, or both, of the firm's other products.) In short, the firm can maximize its total profit by separately maximizing the profit derived from each of its product lines.

A Microchip Manufacturer

As a motivating example, let's consider a firm that produces and sells a highly sophisticated microchip. The firm's main problem is to determine the quantity of chips to produce and sell (now and in the immediate future) and the price. To tackle this problem, we begin by examining the manager's basic objective: profit. A simple accounting identity states that profit is the difference between revenue and cost. In algebraic terms, we have $\pi = R - C$, where the Greek letter pi (π) stands for profit. To see how profit depends on the firm's price and output decisions, let's examine the revenue and cost components in turn.

REVENUE   The analysis of revenue rests on the most basic empirical relationship in economics: the law of demand. This law states:

> All other factors held constant, the higher the unit price of a good, the fewer the number of units demanded by consumers and, consequently, sold by firms.

The law of demand operates at several levels. Consider the microchip industry as a whole, consisting of the manufacturer in question and a half-dozen major competitors. Suppose the leading firms raise their chip prices due to the increased cost of silicon. According to the law of demand, the industry's total sales of chips will fall. Of course, the law applies equally to a single-chip manufacturer. An individual firm competes directly or indirectly with the other leading suppliers selling similar chips. Let's suppose that currently there is a stable pattern of (different) prices and market shares for the leading firms in the industry. Consider what would happen if one of the firms unilaterally instituted a significant reduction in the price of its chips. The law of demand predicts that its microchip sales would increase. The sources of the increase are threefold: (1) increased sales to the firm's current customers, (2) sales gained from competing suppliers, and (3) sales to new buyers. Of course, each of these factors might be important to a greater or lesser degree.

Figure 2.2 graphically illustrates the law of demand by depicting the individual firm's downward-sloping **demand curve**. The horizontal axis lists the quantity of microchips demanded by customers and sold by the firm each week. For convenience, the quantity of chips is measured in lots consisting of 100 chips. The vertical axis lists the price per lot (measured in thousands of dollars) charged by the firm. Three particular points along the downward-sloping demand curve are noted. Point A corresponds to a quantity of 2 lots and a price of $130,000; this means that if the firm charges $130,000 per lot, its weekly

FIGURE 2.2

The Demand Curve for Microchips

The demand curve shows the total number of microchips that will be demanded (i.e., purchased) by buyers at different prices.

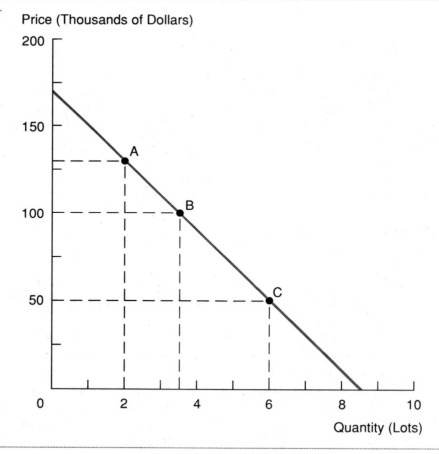

sales will be 2 lots (or 200 chips). If the firm cut its price to $100,000, its sales would increase to 3.5 lots (point B). A dramatic reduction to a price of $50,000 would increase sales to 6 lots (point C). Thus, the demand curve shows the firm's predicted sales over a range of possible prices. The downward slope of the curve embodies the law of demand: A lower price brings forth an increased quantity of sales.

Demand curves and demand equations have a wide variety of uses in economics. Predicting the profit consequences of selective fare discounts by airlines, the impact of higher oil prices on automobile travel, and the effect of government day-care subsidies for working mothers all require the use of demand curves. The properties of demand curves and the ways of estimating demand equations are important topics in Chapters 3 and 4. At present, we will focus on the firm's main use of the demand relationship:

> The firm uses the demand curve as the basis for predicting the revenue consequences of alternative output and pricing policies.

Quite simply, the demand curve allows the firm to predict its quantity of sales for any price it charges. In turn, revenue can be computed as the product of price and quantity. The most useful way to begin the revenue estimation task is to work with the mathematical representation of the demand curve. An algebraic representation of the demand curve in Figure 2.2 is

$$Q = 8.5 - .05P, \qquad [2.1]$$

where Q is the quantity of lots demanded per week and P denotes the price per lot (in thousands of dollars). In this form, the demand equation predicts the quantity of microchips sold at any given price. For instance, if P equals $50 thousand, then, according to Equation 2.1, Q equals 6 lots (point C in the figure); if P equals $130 thousand, Q equals 2 lots, and so on. *For any price the firm charges, the demand equation predicts the resulting quantity of the good that will be sold.* Setting different prices and computing the respective quantities traces out the demand curve in Figure 2.2.

With a bit of algebraic rearrangement, we can derive an equivalent version of Equation 2.1, namely,

$$P = 170 - 20Q. \qquad [2.2]$$

This equation generates exactly the same price-quantity pairs as Equation 2.1; thus, the two equations are equivalent. The only difference is the variable chosen for placement on the left-hand side. Note the interpretation of Equation 2.2. For any quantity of microchips the firm plans to sell, Equation 2.2 indicates the price needed to sell exactly this quantity. For instance, setting Q = 3.5 lots in Equation 2.2, we find that P equals $100 thousand (point

B in Figure 2.2). This price equation usually is referred to as the firm's **inverse demand equation.**[2]

Equation 2.1 (or the equivalent, Equation 2.2) contains all the information the firm needs to predict revenue. However, before launching into the revenue analysis, we should pause to make two points. First, the demand equation furnishes a quantitative snapshot of the *current* demand for the firm's product as it depends on price. Of course, many other factors, including competing firms' products and prices and the general strength of the computer industry, affect the firm's chip sales. The demand prediction of Equation 2.1 is based on the current state of these factors. If economic conditions change, so too will the firm's sales at any given price; that is, Equation 2.1 would no longer be a valid representation of the new demand conditions. Keep in mind that our use of the demand equation takes other demand-relevant factors as *given,* that is, unchanged. (Chapters 3 and 9 take up the effects of changing market conditions and competitor behavior on a firm's demand.)

The second point is that we view the demand curve as **deterministic**; that is, at any given price, the quantity sold can be predicted with certainty. For a given price, Equation 2.1 furnishes a precise sales quantity. Conversely, for any targeted sales quantity, Equation 2.2 provides a precise market-clearing price. We acknowledge that such certainty is hardly the norm in the real world. Nonetheless, the demand equation representation remains valid so long as the margin of error in the price-quantity relationship is relatively small. To become comfortable with the demand equations, think of a product with a long and stable history, allowing sales predictions to be made with very little error. (A deterministic demand equation would be inappropriate in the case of a new product launch. Other methods, discussed in Chapters 12 and 13, would be used to provide probability forecasts of possible sales levels.)

Let's use Equation 2.2 to predict the revenues generated by alternative sales policies of the microchip manufacturer. Figure 2.3 contains the pertinent information and provides a graph of revenue. Column 1 of the tabular portion lists a spectrum of possible sales quantities ranging from 0 to 8.5 lots. It will be convenient to think of the sales quantity, Q, as the firm's decision variable, that is, the variable it explicitly chooses. For each alternative choice of Q, column 2 lists the corresponding sales price obtained from Equation 2.2. (Be sure you understand that the firm *cannot* set both Q and P independently. Once one is set, the other is determined by the forces of demand embodied in the demand equation.) Finally, column 3 lists the resulting revenue earned by the firm, where revenue is defined as $R = P \cdot Q$. From the table, we observe that

---

[2]An important special case occurs when the firm produces for a perfectly competitive market. (An extensive discussion appears in Chapter 7.) There the firm faces a horizontal demand curve instead of a downward-sloping curve. For example, suppose the inverse demand equation is $P = 170$. The firm can sell as much or as little output as it wishes at $170,000 per lot, the competitive price, and its actions will have no effect on this price.

FIGURE 2.3

Revenue
from Microchips

The table and graph show the amount of total revenue the firm will earn for different quantities of microchips that it sells.

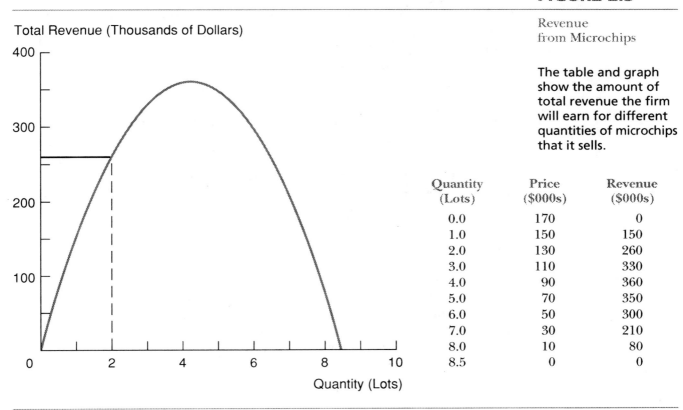

Total Revenue (Thousands of Dollars)

Quantity (Lots)

Quantity (Lots)	Price ($000s)	Revenue ($000s)
0.0	170	0
1.0	150	150
2.0	130	260
3.0	110	330
4.0	90	360
5.0	70	350
6.0	50	300
7.0	30	210
8.0	10	80
8.5	0	0

revenue is zero when sales are zero (obviously). Then as Q increases, revenue initially rises, peaks, and eventually begins to fall, finally falling to zero at Q = 8.5 lots. (Note that to sell 8.5 lots, the requisite sales price from Equation 2.2 is zero; that is, the lots would have to be given away.) In short, the law of demand means that there is a fundamental trade-off between P and Q in generating revenue. An increase in Q requires a cut in P, the former effect raising revenue but the latter lowering it. Operating at either extreme—selling a small quantity at high prices or a large quantity at very low prices—will raise little revenue.

The revenue results in Figure 2.3 can be obtained more directly using basic algebra. We know that R = P·Q and that the market-clearing price satisfies P = 170 − 20Q from Equation 2.2. Substituting the latter equation into the former yields the **revenue function:**

$$R = P \cdot Q = (170 - 20Q)Q = 170Q - 20Q^2. \qquad [2.3]$$

Figure 2.3 also shows the graph of revenue as it depends on the quantity of chips sold. At the sales quantity of two lots, the market-clearing price is

$130,000; therefore, revenue is $260,000. The graph clearly indicates that the firm's revenue rises, peaks, then falls as the sales quantity increases. (Some readers will recognize Equation 2.3 as a quadratic function. Therefore, the graph in Figure 2.3 is a simple parabola.)

CHECK STATION 1   Let the inverse demand function be P = 340 − .8Q. Find the revenue function.

COST   To produce chips, the firm requires a plant, equipment, and labor. The firm estimates that it costs $380 (in materials, labor, etc.) for each chip it produces; this is $38,000 per lot. In addition, it incurs fixed costs of $100,000 per week to run the plant whether or not chips are produced. These are the only costs. (Remember that we are constructing a highly simplified example.) The total cost of producing a given quantity of output is given by the equation

$$C = 100 + 38Q, \qquad [2.4]$$

where C is the weekly cost of production (in thousands of dollars) and Q is the number of lots produced each week. This equation is called the **cost function**, because it shows how total cost depends on quantity. By substituting in a given quantity, we can find the resulting total cost. Thus, the cost of producing Q = 2 lots is $176 thousand. Other quantities and costs are listed in Figure 2.4,

FIGURE 2.4

The Cost of Microchips

The table and graph show the firm's total cost of producing different quantities of microchips.

Quantity (Lots)	Cost ($000s)
0.0	100
1.0	138
2.0	176
3.0	214
4.0	252
5.0	290
6.0	328
7.0	366

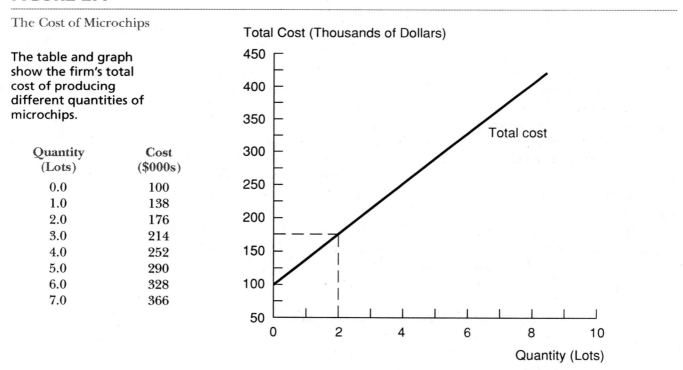

which also shows the graph of cost versus output. As the graph shows, in this simple example the firm's total cost of production increases with output at a steady rate; that is, the slope of the cost function is constant.

PROFIT   From the preceding analysis of revenue and cost, we now have enough information to compute profit for any given output of microchips the firm might choose to produce and sell. These profit calculations are listed in Figure 2.5, where the profit column is computed as the difference between the revenue and cost columns reproduced from earlier figures. The graph in Figure 2.5 shows profit (on the vertical axis) as it varies with quantity (on the horizontal axis). Observe that the graph depicts the level of profit over a wide range of output choices, not just for the round-lot choices listed in the tabular portion of the figure. In effect, the graph allows us to determine visually the profit-maximizing, or optimal, output level from among all possible sales plans. In this case, the optimal output appears to be about 3.3 lots (or 330 microchips) per week.

FIGURE 2.5

Profit from Microchips

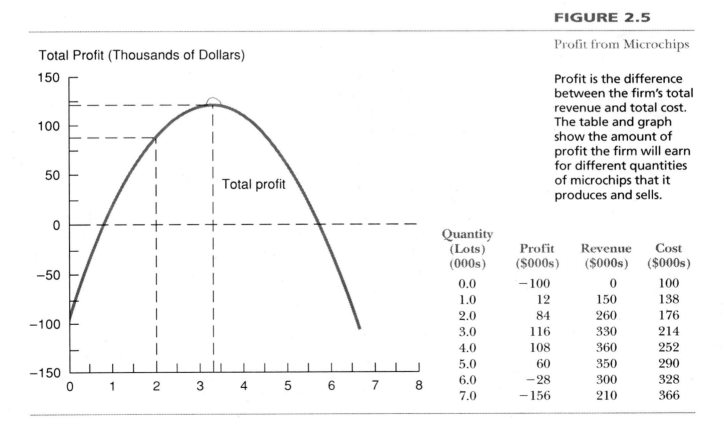

Profit is the difference between the firm's total revenue and total cost. The table and graph show the amount of profit the firm will earn for different quantities of microchips that it produces and sells.

Quantity (Lots) (000s)	Profit ($000s)	Revenue ($000s)	Cost ($000s)
0.0	−100	0	100
1.0	12	150	138
2.0	84	260	176
3.0	116	330	214
4.0	108	360	252
5.0	60	350	290
6.0	−28	300	328
7.0	−156	210	366

How were we able to graph the profit curve in Figure 2.5 so precisely? The graph was constructed from the following basic profit equation, often called the **profit function:**

$$\pi = R - C \hspace{3cm} [2.5]$$
$$= (170Q - 20Q^2) - (100 + 38Q)$$
$$= -100 + 132Q - 20Q^2.$$

In the second line, we have substituted the right-hand sides of the revenue and cost equations to express profit in terms of Q, the firm's decision variable. In the third line, we have collected terms. The important point about the profit equation is that it provides a numerical prediction of profit for any given quantity Q. To check that the equation is correct, simply substitute in a value for Q, say, 2 lots, and calculate profit: $\pi = -100 + (132)(2) - (20)(4) = \$84$ thousand, the same result as in Figure 2.5.

CHECK STATION 2   Suppose the inverse demand function is $P = 340 - .8Q$ and the cost function is $C = 120 + 100Q$. Write down the profit function.

MARGINAL ANALYSIS

Consider the problem of finding the output level that will maximize the firm's profit. One approach is to use the preceding profit formula and solve the problem by *enumeration,* that is, by calculating the profits associated with a range of outputs and identifying the one with the greatest profit. Enumeration is a viable approach if there are only a few output levels to test. However, when the number of options is large, enumeration (and the numerous calculations it requires) is not practical. Instead, we will use the method of *marginal analysis* to find the optimal output level.

Marginal analysis looks at the change in profit that results from making a small change in a decision variable. To illustrate, suppose the firm first considers producing 3 lots, forecasting its resulting profit to be $116,000 as in Figure 2.5. Could it do better than this? To answer this question, the firm considers increasing production slightly, to, say, 3.1 lots. (One-tenth of a lot qualifies as a *small* change. The exact size of the change does not matter as long as it is small.) By substituting Q = 3.1 into Equation 2.5, we see that the new profit is $117,000. Thus, profit has increased by $1,000. The *rate* at which profit has changed is a $1,000 increase per .1 lot increase, or $1,000/.1 = $10,000 per lot.

Here is a useful definition: **Marginal profit** is the change in profit resulting from a small increase in any managerial decision variable. Thus, we say that the marginal profit from a small (.1 lot) increase in output starting from 3.0 lots is $10,000 per lot. The algebraic expression for marginal profit is

$$\text{Marginal profit} = (\text{Change in profit})/(\text{Change in output})$$
$$= \Delta\pi/\Delta Q = (\pi_1 - \pi_0)/(Q_1 - Q_0),$$

where the Greek letter delta (Δ) stands for "change in" and Q_0 denotes the original output level and π_0 the associated profit. The variables Q_1 and π_1 denote the new levels of output and profit. We abbreviate marginal profit by the notation $M\pi$.

Using the profit function you found in Check Station 2, find the marginal profit of increasing output from 99 to 100 units.

CHECK STATION 3

In Table 2.1, we have calculated marginal profits for various output levels. The marginal profit associated with a given change in output is calculated based on a .1 lot increase from the next lowest output. Thus, the $M\pi$ for an increase in output from 2.9 to 3.0 lots is ($116,000 - $114,600)/.1 = $14,000.

TABLE 2.1

Marginal Profit

Marginal profit is the extra profit the firm earns from producing and selling an additional unit of output.

Quantity	Profit	Marginal Profit (per Lot)
2.5	$105,000	
		$30,000
2.6	108,000	
		26,000
2.7	110,600	
		22,000
2.8	112,800	
		18,000
2.9	114,600	
		14,000
3.0	116,000	
		10,000
3.1	117,000	
		6,000
3.2	117,600	
		2,000
3.3	117,800	
		-2,000
3.4	117,600	
		-6,000
3.5	117,000	
		-10,000
3.6	116,000	
		-14,000
3.7	114,600	

How can the decision maker use profit changes as signposts pointing toward the optimal output level? The answer is found by applying the maxim of marginal analysis:

> Make a small change in the level of output if and only if this generates an increase in profit. Keep moving, always in the direction of increased profits, and stop when no further output change will help.

Starting from a production level of 2.5 lots, the microchip firm should increase output to 2.6 because marginal profit from the move ($30,000) is positive. Marginal profit continues to be positive up to 3.3 lots. Therefore, output should be increased up to and including a final step going from 3.2 to 3.3 lots. What about increasing output from 3.3 to 3.4 lots? Since the marginal profit associated with a move to 3.4 is negative (−$2,000), this action would decrease profit. Having reached 3.3 lots, then, no further profit gains (positive marginal profits) are possible. Note that the final output, 3.3, could have been reached starting from a high output level such as 3.7 lots. As long as marginal profit is negative, one should reduce output (i.e., reverse field) to increase profit.

Marginal Analysis and Calculus

The key to pinpointing the firm's optimal quantity (i.e., the *exact* output level at which maximum profit is attained) is to compute marginal profit *at* any given level of output rather than *between* two nearby output levels. At a particular output, Q, marginal profit is given by the slope of the *tangent* line to the profit graph *at* that output level. Figure 2.6 shows an enlarged profit graph with tangent lines drawn at outputs of 3.1, and 3.3 lots. From viewing the tangents, we draw the following simple conclusions. At 3.1 lots, the tangent is upward sloping. Obviously, marginal profit is positive; that is, raising output by a small amount increases total profit. Conversely, at 3.4 lots, the curve is downward sloping. Here marginal profit is negative, so a small reduction in output (not an increase) would increase total profit. Finally, at 3.3 lots, the tangent is horizontal; that is, the tangent's slope and marginal profit are zero. Maximum profit is attained at precisely this level of output. Indeed, the condition that marginal profit is zero marks this point as the optimal level of output. Remember: If Mπ were positive or negative, total profit could be raised by appropriately increasing or decreasing output. Only when Mπ is exactly zero have all profit-augmenting opportunities been exhausted. In short, when the profit function's slope just becomes zero, we know we are at the precise peak of the profit curve.[3] Thus, we have demonstrated a basic optimization rule:

---

[3]In some cases, the Mπ = 0 rule requires modification. For example, suppose demand and cost conditions are such that Mπ > 0 for all output quantities up to the firm's current production capacity. Clearly, the rule Mπ = 0 does not apply. However, the marginal profit message is clear: The firm should increase output up to capacity, raising profit all the while. (For further discussion, see the appendix to this chapter and Problem 5 at the end of the chapter.)

FIGURE 2.6

A Close-Up View
of Profit

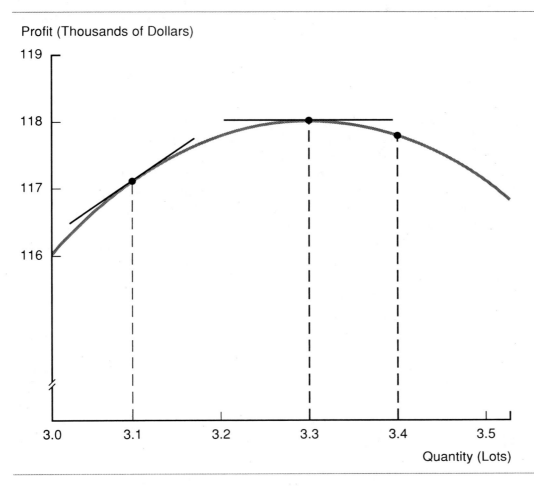

Maximum profit occurs
at an output where
marginal profit is zero;
that is, the slope of the
tangent line is zero.

Maximum profit is attained at the output level at which marginal profit is zero ($M\pi = 0$).

A practical method for calculating marginal profit at any level of output is afforded by the simple rules of differential calculus. (For a thorough review, read the appendix to this chapter.) Consider once again the firm's profit equation:

$$\pi = -100 + 132Q - 20Q^2 \qquad [2.6]$$

Marginal profit (the slope of the corresponding profit graph) is found by taking the derivative of this equation with respect to Q. The result is

$$M\pi = d\pi/dQ = 132 - 40Q. \qquad [2.7]$$

With this formula in hand, we can find the marginal profit at any output level simply by substituting the specified quantity into the equation. For example, the marginal profit at Q = 3.0 is $12 thousand per lot.[4] In turn, we can immediately determine the firm's profit-maximizing level of output. Using Equation 2.7, we simply set Mπ = 0 and solve for Q:

$$M\pi = 132 - 40Q = 0.$$

Therefore, we find that Q = 132/40 = 3.3 lots. At 3.3 lots per week, the firm's marginal profit is zero. This is the output that maximizes profit.

Figure 2.7 graphs the firm's total profit in part (a) as well as the firm's marginal profit in part (b). Note that at the optimal output, Q = 3.3 lots, total profit reaches a peak in Figure 2.7a, whereas marginal profit is exactly zero (i.e., the marginal profit graph just cuts the horizontal axis) in Figure 2.7b.

A complete solution to the firm's decision problem requires two additional steps. We know the optimal quantity is Q = 3.3 lots. What price is required for the firm to sell this quantity? The answer is found by substituting Q = 3.3 into Equation 2.2: P = 170 − (20)(3.3) = $104 thousand. What is the firm's final profit from its optimal output and price decision? At this point, we can separately compute total revenue and total cost. Alternatively, we can compute profit directly from Equation 2.5 (with Q = 3.3). Either way, we arrive at π = $117,800. This completes the algebraic solution.

CHECK STATION 4 Once again consider the inverse demand curve P = 340 − .8Q and the cost function C = 120 + 100Q. Derive the formula for Mπ as it depends on Q. Set Mπ = 0 to find the firm's optimal output.

MARGINAL REVENUE AND MARGINAL COST

The concept of marginal profit yields two key dividends. The general concept instructs the manager that optimal decisions are found by making small changes in decisions, observing the resulting effect on profit, and always moving in the direction of greater profit. A second virtue of the approach is that it provides an efficient tool for calculating the firm's optimal decision. The discussion in this section underscores a third virtue: Marginal analysis is a powerful way to identify the factors that determine profits and, more important, profit changes. We will look once again at the two components of profit—revenue and cost—and highlight the key features of *marginal revenue* and *marginal cost*.

[4]The difference between Equation 2.7 and Table 2.1 is that the latter lists marginal profit over small, discrete intervals of output, whereas the former lists marginal profit *at* particular output levels. When we use a very small interval, the discrete marginal profit between two output levels is a very close approximation to marginal profit at either output. For example, with an interval of .01, the discrete marginal profit at Q = 3 is the slope of the line connecting the points Q = 2.99 and Q = 3.00. This line is nearly identical to the tangent line (representing marginal profit) *at* Q = 3. Thus,

Using a .01 interval: Mπ = $12,200
Via calculus (Equation 2.7)   Mπ = $12,000

FIGURE 2.7

Total Profit
and Marginal Profit

The point of maximum total profit in part (a) corresponds to the point at which marginal profit is zero in part (b). In each case, the firm's optimal output is 3.3 lots.

(a)   Total Profit (Thousands of Dollars)

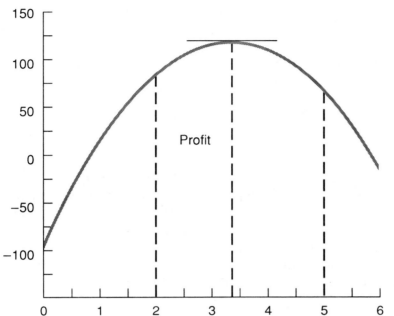

(b)   Marginal Profit

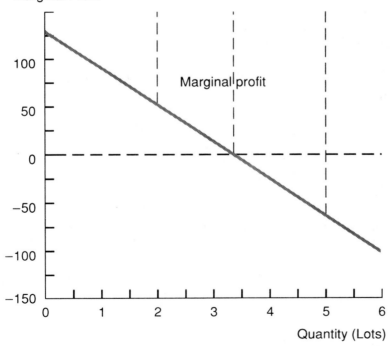

Quantity (Lots)

Marginal Revenue

Marginal revenue is the amount of additional revenue that comes with a unit increase in output and sales. The marginal revenue (MR) of an increase in unit sales from Q_0 to Q_1 is

$$\text{Marginal revenue} = (\text{Change in revenue})/(\text{Change in output})$$
$$= \Delta R/\Delta Q = (R_1 - R_0)/(Q_1 - Q_0).$$

For instance, the MR earned by increasing sales from 2.0 to 2.1 lots is

$$(268.8 - 260.0)/(2.1 - 2.0) = \$88 \text{ thousand per lot,}$$

where 268.8 is the revenue from selling 2.1 lots and 260.0 is the revenue from selling 2.0 lots. The graphic depiction of the MR between two quantities is given by the slope of the line segment joining the two points on the revenue graph.

In turn, MR *at* a given sales quantity has as its graphic counterpart the slope of the tangent line touching the revenue graph. To calculate the MR at a given sales output, we start with the revenue expression (Equation 2.3), $R = 170Q - 20Q^2$, and take the derivative with respect to quantity:

$$MR = dR/dQ = 170 - 40Q. \qquad [2.8]$$

We can use this formula to compute MR at any particular sales quantity. For example, marginal revenue at $Q = 3$ is $MR = 170 - (40)(3) = \$50$ thousand; that is, at this sales quantity, a small increase in sales increases revenue at the rate of $50,000 per additional lot sold.

A SIMPLIFYING FACT Recall that the firm's market-clearing price is given by Equation 2.2:

$$P = 170 - 20Q.$$

Note the close similarity between the MR expression in Equation 2.8 and the firm's selling price in Equation 2.2. This similarity is no coincidence. The following result holds:

| For any linear (i.e., straight-line) demand curve with an inverse demand equation of the form $P = a - bQ$, the resulting marginal revenue is $MR = a - 2bQ$.

In short, the MR equation has the same intercept and twice the slope as the firm's price equation.[5]

---

[5] If $P = a - bQ$, it follows that $R = PQ = aQ - bQ^2$. Taking the derivative with respect to Q, we find that $MR = dR/dQ = a - 2bQ$. This confirms the result described.

Marginal Cost

Marginal Cost (MC) is the additional cost of producing an extra unit of output. The algebraic definition is

$$\text{Marginal cost} = (\text{Change in cost})/(\text{Change in output})$$
$$= \Delta C/\Delta Q = (C_1 - C_0)/(Q_1 - Q_0).$$

The computation of MC is particularly easy for the microchip manufacturer's cost function in Equation 2.4. From the cost equation, $C = 100 + 38Q$, it is apparent that producing an extra lot (increasing Q by a unit) will increase cost by $38 thousand. Thus, marginal cost is simply $38 thousand per lot. Note that regardless of how large or small the level of output, MC is always constant. The cost function in Equation 2.4 has a constant slope and thus also an unchanging marginal cost. (We can directly confirm the MC result by taking the derivative of the cost equation.)

Profit Maximization Revisited

Given that $\pi = R - C$, it should not be surprising that

$$M\pi = MR - MC. \qquad [2.9]$$

In other words, marginal profit is simply the difference between marginal revenue and marginal cost.

The logic of this relationship is simple enough. Suppose the firm produces and sells an extra unit. Then its change in profit is simply the extra revenue it earns from the extra unit net of its additional cost of production. But the extra revenue is MR and the extra cost is MC, so $M\pi = MR - MC$.

Thus far, we have emphasized the role of marginal profit in characterizing the firm's optimal decision. In particular, profits are maximized when marginal profit equals zero. Thus, using the fact that $M\pi = MR - MC$, an equivalent statement is $MR - MC = 0$. This leads to the following basic rule:

> The firm's profit-maximizing level of output occurs when the additional revenue from selling an extra unit just equals the extra cost of producing it, that is, when MR = MC.

There are a number of ways to check the logic of the MR = MC decision rule. Figure 2.8 provides a graphic confirmation. Part (a) reproduces the microchip manufacturer's revenue and cost functions (from Equations 2.3 and 2.4) in a single graph. The graph of profit also is shown in Figure 2.8a and,

FIGURE 2.8

Marginal Revenue
and Marginal Cost

In part (a), total profit
is shown as the
difference between
total revenue and total
cost. In part (b), the
firm's optimal output
occurs where the
marginal revenue and
marginal cost curves
intersect.

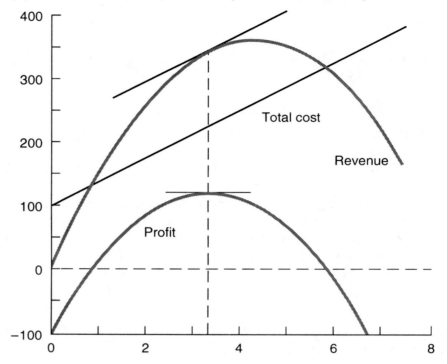

(a) Total Revenue, Cost, and Profit (Thousands of Dollars)

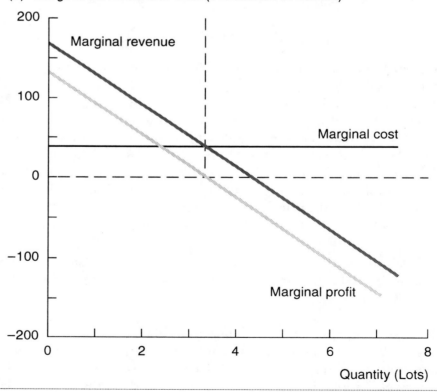

(b) Marginal Revenue and Cost (Thousands of Dollars)

44

except for scale, is identical to Figure 2.5. (Note that, for any level of output, the firm's profit is measured as the vertical distance between the revenue and cost curves.) The firm's break-even outputs occur at the two crossings of the revenue and cost curves. At these outputs, revenue just matches cost, so profit is zero. Positive profits are earned for quantities between these two output levels. Of course, the firm incurs losses for very high or very low levels of production, outside the break-even output levels. From the figure, we observe the profit peak at an output of $Q = 3.3$ lots.

Using the MR = MC rule, how can we confirm that the output level $Q = 3.3$ is profit maximizing? A simple answer is provided by appealing to the revenue and cost curves in Figure 2.8a. Suppose for the moment that the firm produces a lower quantity, say, $Q = 2$ lots. At this output, the revenue curve is steeper than the cost line; thus, MR > MC. Hence, the firm could increase its profit by producing extra units of output. On the graph, the move to a greater output widens the profit gap. The reverse argument holds for a proposed higher quantity, such as 4 lots. In this case, revenue rises less steeply than cost: MR < MC. Therefore, a reduction in output results in a greater cost saved than revenue sacrificed. Again profit increases. Combining these arguments, we conclude that profit always can be increased so long as a small change in output results in *different* changes in revenue and cost. Only at $Q = 3.3$ is it true that revenue and cost increase at exactly the same rate. At this quantity, the slopes of the revenue and cost functions are equal; the revenue tangent is parallel to the cost line. But this simply says that marginal revenue equals marginal cost. At this optimal output, the gap between revenue and cost is neither widening nor narrowing. Maximum profit is attained.

It is important to remember that the Mπ = 0 and MR = MC rules are exactly equivalent. Both rules pinpoint the *same* profit-maximizing level of output. Figure 2.8b shows this clearly. At $Q = 3.3$ lots, where the profit function reaches a peak (and the profit tangent is horizontal) in part (a), we note that the MR line exactly intersects the MC line in part (b). This provides visual confirmation that profit is maximized at the output level at which marginal revenue just equals marginal cost.

The MR = MC rule often is the shortest path to finding the firm's optimal output. Instead of finding the marginal profit function and setting it equal to zero, we simply take the marginal revenue and marginal cost functions and set them equal to each other. In the microchip manufacturer's problem, we know that MR = $170 - 40Q$ and MC = 38. Setting MR = MC implies that $170 - 40Q = 38$. Solving for Q, we find that $Q = 3.3$ lots. Of course, this is precisely the same result we obtained by setting marginal profit equal to zero.

Once again let us consider the price equation $P = 340 - .8Q$ and the cost equation $C = 120 + 100Q$. Apply the MR = MC rule to find the firm's optimal output. From the inverse demand curve, find its optimal price.

CHECK STATION 5

SENSITIVITY ANALYSIS

As we saw in Chapter 1, sensitivity analysis addresses the basic question: How should the decision maker alter his or her course of action in light of changes in economic conditions? Marginal analysis offers a powerful answer to this question:

> For any change in economic conditions, we can trace the impact (if any) on the firm's marginal revenue or marginal cost. Once we have identified this impact, we can appeal to the MR = MC rule to determine the new, optimal decision.

Figure 2.9 illustrates the application of this rule for the microchip firm's basic problem. Consider part (a). As before, the firm's decision variable, its output quantity, is listed on the horizontal axis. In turn, levels of MR and MC are shown on the vertical axis, and the respective curves have been graphed. How do we explain the shapes of these curves? For MC, the answer is easy. The marginal cost of producing an extra lot of chips is $38,000 regardless of the starting output level. Thus, the MC line is horizontal, fixed at a level of $38,000. In turn, the graph of the MR curve from Equation 2.8 is

$$MR = 170 - 40Q.$$

We make the following observations about the MR equation and graph. Starting from a zero sales quantity, the firm gets a great deal of extra revenue from selling additional units (MR = 170 at Q = 0). As sales increase, the extra revenue from additional units falls (although MR is still positive). Indeed, at a quantity of 4.25 lots (see Figure 2.9) MR is zero, and for higher outputs MR is negative; that is, selling extra units causes total revenue to fall. (Don't be surprised by this. Turn back to Figure 2.3 and see that revenue peaks, then falls. When volume already is very large, selling extra units requires a price cut on so many units that total revenue drops.)

In part (a) of Figure 2.9, the intersection of the MR and MC curves establishes the firm's optimal production and sales quantity, Q = 3.3 lots. At an output less than 3.3 units, MR is greater than MC, so the firm could make additional profit producing extra units. (Why? Because its extra revenue exceeds its extra cost.) At an output above 3.3 units, MR is smaller than MC. Here the firm can increase its profit by cutting back its production. (Why? Because the firm's cost saving exceeds the revenue it gives up.) Thus, profit is maximized only at the quantity where MR = MC.

Asking What If

The following examples trace the possible effects of changes in economic conditions on the firm's marginal revenue and marginal cost.

FIGURE 2.9

Shifts in Marginal
Revenue and Marginal
Cost

(a) Marginal Revenue and Cost (Thousands of Dollars)

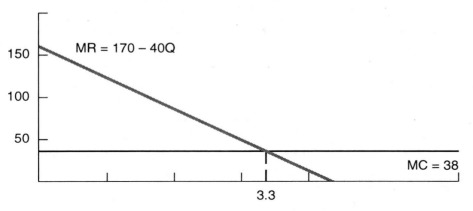

Part (b) depicts an
increase in marginal
cost as an upward shift
in the marginal cost
curve. As a result, the
firm's optimal output
level declines. Part (c)
shows an upward
(rightward) shift in
marginal revenue
resulting from an
increase in demand. As
a result, the firm's
optimal output level
increases.

(b) Marginal Revenue and Cost (Thousands of Dollars)

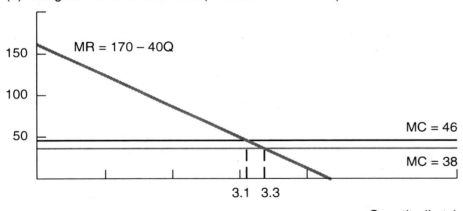

(c) Marginal Revenue and Cost (Thousands of Dollars)

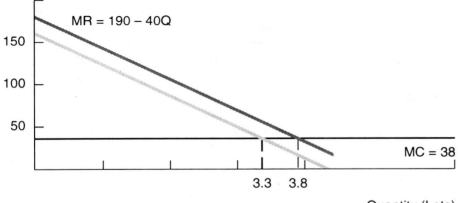

INCREASED OVERHEAD   Suppose the microchip manufacturer's overhead costs (for the physical plant and administration) increase. Fixed costs were $100,000 per week; now they are $112,000. How will this affect the firm's operating decisions? The simple, albeit surprising, answer is that the increase in fixed costs will have no effect whatsoever. The firm should produce and sell the same output at the same price as before. There are several ways to see this.

First, note that the firm's profit is reduced by $12,000 (relative to its profit before the cost increase) *whatever its level of output.* Thus, whatever output was profit-maximizing before the change must be profit-maximizing after it. Second, the revenue and cost graphs in Figure 2.8a provide a visual confirmation of the same reasoning. An increase in fixed cost causes the cost line to shift upward (parallel to the old one) by the amount of the increase. At any output, the revenue-cost gap is smaller than before. But note that the point of equal slopes—where MR = MC and the profit gap is maximized—is unchanged. Profit is still maximized at the same output as before, Q = 3.3. Finally, the MR and MC curves in Figure 2.9a make the same point. Has the increase in fixed cost changed the MR or MC curves? No! Thus, the firm's optimal output, where the MR and MC lines intersect, is unchanged.

INCREASED MATERIAL COSTS   Silicon is the main raw material from which microchips are made. Suppose an increase in the price of silicon causes the firm's estimated cost per lot to rise from $38,000 to $46,000. How should the firm respond? Once again the answer depends on an appeal to marginal analysis. In this case, the firm's MC per chip has changed. In Figure 2.9b, the new MC line lies above and parallel to the old MC line. The intersection of MR and MC occurs at a lower level of output. Because producing extra output has become more expensive, the firm's optimal response is to cut back the level of production. What is the new optimal output? Setting MR = MC, we obtain $170 - 40Q = 46$, so Q = 3.1 lots. In turn, the market-clearing price (using Equation 2.2) is found to be $108,000. The increase in cost has been partially passed on to buyers via a higher price.

INCREASED DEMAND   Suppose demand for the firm's chips increases dramatically. At the higher demand, the firm could raise its price by $20,000 per lot ($200 per chip) and still sell the same quantity of chips as before. The old price equation was P = 170 − 20Q. The new price equation is P = 190 − 20Q. What should be the firm's response? Here the increased demand raises the marginal revenue the firm obtains from selling extra chips. In fact, given the new price equation, the new MR equation must be MR = 190 − 40Q. Thus, the new MR curve in Figure 2.9c has a larger intercept than the old one, although the slope is the same. The upward parallel shift in the MR curve means the new intersection of MR and MC occurs at a higher output. What is the new optimal output? Setting MR = MC, we find that $190 - 40Q = 38$, so

Q = 3.8 lots. The corresponding market-clearing price (using the *new* price equation) is $114,000. The firm takes optimal advantage of the increase in demand by selling a larger output (380 chips per week) at a higher price per lot.

Domestic steel producers have long competed vigorously with foreign steel manufacturers for shares of the U.S. market. Given the intensity of price competition, global steel producers constantly strive to trim production costs to maintain profits. Over the last five years, the competitive playing field has been buffeted by large swings in foreign exchange rates. For instance, between 2002 and 2005, the dollar's value fell (depreciated) from a high of about 132 Japanese yen per dollar to a level of about 102 yen per dollar. But, from 2005 to the summer of 2007, the dollar rose in value (appreciated) back to 123 yen per dollar before falling again to 107 yen by the beginning of 2008.

Responding to Exchange Rate Changes

What was the effect of the dollar's 2005–2007 appreciation on the competition for the domestic market between Japanese and U.S. steel producers?

The dollar appreciation (the fall in the value of the yen) conferred a relative cost advantage on Japanese producers to the detriment of domestic producers.

To see this, suppose that based on its current costs, a Japanese steel maker sets its 2005 price for a unit of specialty steel at 10,200 yen. When it sells to U.S. buyers, the company quotes a dollar price of $100 (based on the 102 yen per dollar exchange rate). Two and a half years later, suppose that the Japanese supplier's costs and targeted price in yen are unchanged. However, with an exchange rate of 123 yen per dollar, the equivalent dollar price of its steel is now 10,200/123 = $82.93. Of course, the Japanese firm need not set its U.S. price this low. Perhaps, it will settle on $85 to $90, thereby increasing its yen-denominated price and profits while reaping a significant increase in demand from the 10 to 15 percent dollar price reduction.

Now let's turn our attention to U.S. steel producers. The effect of dramatically lower prices of imported steel is to shift the demand curve of a typical domestic firm inward, that is, downward and to the left. What is the domestic firm's profit-maximizing response to this adverse demand shift? Turning around the example of increased demand displayed in Figure 2.9c, we find that the domestic firm should plan to cut its output as well as to cut its price to meet the increase in foreign competition.

Suppose that with lower foreign prices, the domestic firm's demand curve experiences a parallel downward shift of $15. That is, in 2007 the firm would have to cut its price by $15 to maintain the same level of demand and sales as in 2005. Is such a price cut optimal?

CHECK STATION 6

Conflict in Fast-Food Franchising Revisited

The example that opened this chapter recounted the numerous kinds of conflicts between fast-food parents and individual franchise operators. Despite the best intentions, bitter disputes have erupted from time to time at such chains as McDonald's, Burger King, Wendy's, and Subway. A key source for many of these conflicts is the basic contract arrangement between parent and individual franchisee. Virtually all such contracts call for the franchisee to pay back to the parent a specified percentage of revenue earned. This total *royalty* comprises a base percentage plus additional percentages for marketing and advertising and rent (if the parent owns the outlet). Thus, the franchisee's profit begins only after this royalty (typically ranging anywhere from 5 to 20 percent depending on the type of franchise) and all other costs have been paid.

Thus, a key source of conflict emerges. Under the contract agreement, the parent's monetary return depends on (indeed, is a percentage of) the revenues the franchisee takes in. Thus, the parent wants the franchisee to operate so as to maximize revenue. What does the pursuit of maximum revenue imply about the franchisee's volume of sales? Suppose the revenue and cost curves for the franchisee are configured as in Figure 2.8a. (Ignore the numerical values and reinterpret the quantity scale as numbers of burgers sold rather than microchips.) We observe that the revenue-maximizing output is well past the franchisee's optimal (i.e., profit-maximizing) output. The range of economic conflict occurs between these two outputs—the franchisee unwilling to budge from the lower output and the parent pushing for the higher output.

The same point can be made by appealing to the forces of MR and MC. The parent always wants to increase revenue, even if doing so means extra costs to the franchisee. Thus, the parent wishes to push output to the point where MR is zero. (Make sure you understand why.) But the franchisee prefers to limit output to the point where extra costs match extra revenues, MR = MC. Past this point, the extra revenues are not worth the extra costs: MR < MC. In Figure 2.8b, the franchisee's preferred output occurs where MR = MC and the parent's occurs at the larger output where MR = 0.

The conflict in objectives explains each of the various disputes. In the parent company's view, all its preferred policies—longer operating hours, more order lines, remodeling, lower prices—are revenue increasing. In each case, however, the individual franchisee resists the move because the extra cost of the change would exceed the extra revenue. From its point of view (the bottom line), none of the changes would be profitable.

To this day, conflicts between parent and individual franchisees continue. The Quiznos sandwich shop chain has experienced repeated franchisee revolts. Dunkin Donuts franchisees have strongly opposed its parent's deals to allow Procter & Gamble, Sara Lee Foods, and Hess gas stations to sell the chain's branded coffee, reporting that this has cut into their own stores' coffee sales. Even McDonald's Corp., long considered the gold standard of the franchise business, is feeling the heat. McDonald's diverse efforts to increase market share have been fiercely resisted by a number of franchisees. What's good for the parent's market share and revenue may not be good for the individual franchisee's profit. Franchise owners have resisted the company's efforts to enforce value pricing (i.e., discounting). McDonald's strategy of accelerating the opening of new restaurants to claim market share means that new outlets inevitably cannibalize sales of existing stores. Such conflicts are always just below the surface. Indeed, before Burger King went public in 2006, it worked hard to repair relationships with its storeowners.

SUMMARY

Decision-Making Principles

1. The fundamental decision problem of the firm is to determine the profit-maximizing price and output for the good or service it sells.
2. The firm's profit from any decision is the difference between predicted revenues and costs. Increasing output and sales will increase profit, so long as the extra revenue gained exceeds the extra cost incurred. Conversely, the firm will profit by cutting output if the cost saved exceeds the revenue given up.
3. If economic conditions change, the firm's optimal price and output will change according to the impact on its marginal revenues and marginal costs.

Nuts and Bolts

1. The basic building blocks of the firm's price and output problem are its demand curve and cost function. The demand curve describes (1) the quantity of sales for a given price or, conversely, (2) the price needed to generate a given level of sales. Multiplying prices and quantities along the demand curve produces the revenue function. The cost function estimates the cost of producing a given level of output. Combining the revenue and cost functions generates a profit prediction for any output Q.
2. The next step in finding the firm's optimal decision is to determine the firm's marginal profit, marginal revenue, and marginal cost.
   a. Marginal profit is the extra profit earned from producing and selling an additional unit of output.
   b. Marginal revenue is the extra revenue earned from selling an additional unit of output.
   c. Marginal cost is the extra cost of producing an additional unit of output.
   d. By definition, marginal profit is the difference between marginal revenue and marginal cost: $M\pi = MR - MC$. The $M\pi$, MR, and MC expressions can be found by taking the derivatives of the respective profit, revenue, and cost functions.
3. The firm's optimal output is characterized by the following conditions: (1) $M\pi = 0$ or, equivalently, (2) $MR = MC$. Once output has been determined, the firm's optimal price is found from the price equation, and profit can be estimated accordingly.

Questions and Problems

1. A manager makes the statement that output should be expanded so long as average revenue exceeds average cost. Does this strategy make sense? Explain.

2. The original revenue function for the microchip producer is $R = 170Q - 20Q^2$. Derive the expression for marginal revenue, and use it to find the output level at which *revenue is maximized*. Confirm that this is greater than the firm's profit-maximizing output, and explain why.

3. Because of changing demographics, a small, private liberal arts college predicts a fall in enrollments over the next five years. How would it apply marginal analysis to plan for the decreased enrollment? (The college is a nonprofit institution, so think broadly about its objectives.)

4. Suppose a firm's inverse demand curve is given by $P = 120 - .5Q$, and its cost equation is $C = 420 + 60Q + Q^2$.
   a. Find the firm's optimal quantity, price, and profit (1) by using the profit and marginal profit equations and (2) by setting MR equal to MC. Also provide a graph of MR and MC.
   b. Suppose instead that the firm can sell any and all of its output at the fixed market price $P = 120$. Find the firm's optimal output.

5. a. As in Problem 4, demand continues to be given by $P = 120$, but the firm's cost equation is linear: $C = 420 + 60Q$. Graph the firm's revenue and cost curves. At what quantity does the firm break even, that is, earn exactly a zero profit?
   b. In general, suppose the firm faces the fixed price P and has cost equation $C = F + cQ$, where F denotes the firm's fixed cost and c is its marginal cost per unit. Write down a formula for the firm's profit. Set this expression equal to zero and solve for the firm's break-even quantity (in terms of P, F, and c). Give an intuitive explanation for this break-even equation.
   c. In this case, what difficulty arises in trying to apply the MR = MC rule to maximize profit? By applying the logic of marginal analysis, state the modified rule applicable to this case.

6. A television station is considering the sale of promotional DVDs. It can have the DVDs produced by one of two suppliers. Supplier A will charge the station a set-up fee of $1,200 plus $2 for each DVDs; supplier B has no set-up fee and will charge $4 per DVD. The station estimates its demand for the DVDs to be given by $Q = 1,600 - 200P$, where P is the price in dollars and Q is the number of DVDs. (The price equation is $P = 8 - Q/200$.)
   a. Suppose the station plans to give away the videos. How many DVDs should it order? From which supplier?

    b. Suppose instead that the station seeks to maximize its profit from sales of the DVDs. What price should it charge? How many DVDs should it order from which supplier? (Hint: Solve two separate problems, one with supplier A and one with supplier B, and then compare profits. In each case, apply the MR = MC rule.)

7. The college and graduate school textbook market is one of the most profitable segments for book publishers. A best-selling accounting text, published by Old School Inc (OS), has a demand curve: $P = 150 - Q$, where Q denotes yearly sales (in thousands) of books. (In other words, $Q = 20$ means 20 thousand books.) The cost of producing, handling, and shipping each additional book is about $40, and the publisher pays a $10 per book royalty to the author. Finally, the publisher's overall marketing and promotion spending (set annually) accounts for an average cost of about $10 per book.

    a. Determine OS's profit-maximizing output and price for the accounting text.

    b. A rival publisher has raised the price of its best-selling accounting text by $15. One option is to exactly match this price hike and so exactly preserve your level of sales. Do you endorse this price increase? (Explain briefly why or why not.)

    c. To save significantly on fixed costs, OS plans to contract out the actual printing of its textbooks to outside vendors. OS expects to pay a somewhat higher printing cost per book, than in part (a), from the outside vendor (who marks up price above its cost to make a profit). How would outsourcing affect the output and pricing decisions in part (a)?

8. Modifying a product to increase its "value added" benefits customers and can enhance supplier profits. For example, suppose an improved version of a product increases customer value added by $25 per unit. (In effect, the demand curve undergoes a parallel upward shift of $25.)

    a. If the redesign is expected to increase the item's marginal cost by $30, should the company undertake it?

    b. Suppose instead that the redesign increases marginal cost by $15. Should the firm undertake it, and (if so) how should it vary its original output and price?

9. Firm Z is developing a new product. An early introduction (beating rivals to market) would greatly enhance the company's revenues. However, the intensive development effort needed to expedite the introduction can be very expensive. Suppose total revenues and costs associated with the new product's introduction are given by

$$R = 720 - 8t \quad \text{and} \quad C = 600 - 20t + .25t^2,$$

where t is the introduction date (in months from now). Some executives have argued for an expedited introduction date, 12 months from now (t = 12). Do you agree? What introduction date is most profitable? Explain.

10. A producer of photocopiers derives profits from two sources: the immediate profit it makes on each copier sold and the additional profit it gains from servicing its copiers and selling toner and other supplies. The firm estimates that its additional profit from service and supplies is about $300 over the life of *each copier sold.*

    There is disagreement in management about the implication of this tie-in profit. One group argues that this extra profit (although significant for the firm's bottom line) should have no effect on the firm's optimal output and price. A second group argues that the firm should maximize total profit by lowering price to sell additional units (even though this reduces its profit margin at the point of sale). Which view (if either) is correct?

11. Suppose the microchip producer discussed in this chapter faces demand and cost equations given by $Q = 8.5 - .05P$ and $C = 100 + 38Q$. Choosing to treat price as its main decision variable, it writes profit as

$$\pi = R - C$$
$$= [P(8.5 - .05P)] - [100 + (38)(8.5 - .05P)]$$
$$= -423 + 10.4P - .05P^2.$$

Derive an expression for $M\pi = d\pi/dP$. Then set $M\pi = 0$ to find the firm's optimal price. Your result should confirm the optimal price found earlier in the chapter.

12. As the exclusive carrier on a local air route, a regional airline must determine the number of flights it will provide per week and the fare it will charge. Taking into account operating and fuel costs, airport charges, and so on, the estimated cost per flight is $2,000. It expects to fly full flights (100 passengers), so its marginal cost on a *per passenger* basis is $20. Finally, the airline's estimated demand curve is $P = 120 - .1Q$, where P is the fare in dollars and Q is the number of passengers per week.
    a. What is the airline's profit-maximizing fare? How many passengers does it carry per week, using how many flights? What is its weekly profit?
    b. Suppose the airline is offered $4,000 per week to haul freight along the route for a local firm. This will mean replacing one of the weekly passenger flights with a freight flight (at the same operating cost). Should the airline carry freight for the local firm? Explain.

13. Suppose a firm's inverse demand and cost equations are of the general forms $P = a - bQ$ and $C = F + cQ$, where the parameters a and b

denote the intercept and slope of the inverse demand function and the parameters F and c are the firm's fixed and marginal costs, respectively. Apply the MR = MC rule to confirm that the firm's optimal output and price are Q = (a − c)/2b and P = (a + c)/2. Provide explanations for the ways P and Q depend on the underlying economic parameters.

*14. Under the terms of the current contractual agreement, Burger Queen (BQ) is entitled to 20 percent of the revenue earned by each of its franchises. BQ's best-selling item is the Slopper (it slops out of the bun). BQ supplies the ingredients for the Slopper (bun, mystery meat, etc.) at cost to the franchise.

  The franchisee's average cost per Slopper (including ingredients, labor cost, and so on) is $.80. At a particular franchise restaurant, weekly demand for Sloppers is given by P = 3.00 − Q/800.

  a. If BQ sets the price and weekly sales quantity of Sloppers, what quantity and price would it set? How much does BQ receive? What is the franchisee's net profit?

  b. Suppose the franchise owner sets the price and sales quantity. What price and quantity will the owner set? (Hint: Remember that the owner keeps only $.80 of each extra dollar of revenue earned.) How does the total profit earned by the two parties compare to their total profit in part (a)?

  c. Now, suppose BQ and an individual franchise owner enter into an agreement in which BQ is entitled to a share of the franchisee's profit. Will profit sharing remove the conflict between BQ and the franchise operator? Under profit sharing, what will be the price and quantity of Sloppers? (Does the exact split of the profit affect your answer? Explain briefly.) What is the resulting total profit?

  d. Profit sharing is not widely practiced in the franchise business. What are its disadvantages relative to revenue sharing?

15. Suppose a firm assesses its profit function as

$$\pi = -10 - 48Q + 15Q^2 - Q^3.$$

  a. Compute the firm's profit for the following levels of output: Q = 2, 8, and 14.

  b. Derive an expression for marginal profit. Compute marginal profit at Q = 2, 8, and 14. Confirm that profit is maximized at Q = 8. (Why is profit not maximized at Q = 2?)

Discussion Question As vice president of sales for a rapidly growing company, you are grappling with the question of expanding the size of your direct sales force (from its current level of 60 national salespeople). You are considering hiring from 5 to 10 additional personnel.

*Starred problems are more challenging.

How would you estimate the additional dollar cost of each additional salesperson? Based on your company's past sales experience, how would you estimate the expected net revenue generated by an additional salesperson? (Be specific about the information you might use to derive this estimate.) How would you use these cost and revenue estimates to determine whether a sales force increase (or possibly a decrease) is warranted?

Spreadsheet Problems[6]

S1. A manufacturer of spare parts faces the demand curve,

$$P = 800 - 2Q,$$

and produces output according to the cost function,

$$C = 20,000 + 200Q + .5Q^2.$$

a. Create a spreadsheet modeled on the example shown. (The only numerical value you should enter is the quantity in cell B7. Enter appropriate formulas to compute all other numerical entries.)

b. What is the firm's profit-maximizing quantity and price? First, determine the solution by hand, that is, by changing the quantity value in cell B7. (Hint: Keep an eye on MR and MC in finding your way to the optimal output.)

c. Use your spreadsheet's optimizer to confirm your answer to part (a).

	A	B	C	D	E	F	G
1							
2			THE OPTIMAL OUTPUT OF SPARE PARTS				
3							
4							
5		Quantity	Price	Revenue	Cost	Profit	
6							
7		20	760	15,200	24,200	−9,000	
8							
9							
10				MR	MC	Mprofit	
11							
12				720	220	500	
13							

[6]This chapter's special appendix reviews the basics of creating, using, and optimizing spreadsheets.

S2. Your firm competes with a close rival for shares of a $20 million per year market. Your main decision concerns how much to spend on advertising each year. Your rival is currently spending $8 million on advertising. The best estimate of your profit is given by the equation

$$\pi = 20[A/(A + 8)] - A,$$

where A is your firm's advertising expenditure (in millions of dollars). According to this equation, the firms' shares of the $20 million market are in proportion to their advertising spending. (If the firms spend equal amounts, A = 8, they have equal shares of the market, and so on.)

a. Create a spreadsheet modeled on the example shown. Determine the firm's optimal advertising expenditure. Refer to the appendix of this chapter, if you are unsure about finding MR, that is, taking the derivative of the quotient, A/(A + 8).

b. Use your spreadsheet's optimizer to confirm your answer in part (a). Is matching your rival's spending your best policy?

	A	B	C	D	E	F
1						
2		AN OPTIMAL ADVERTISING BUDGET				
3						
4						
5		Advertising	Revenue	Cost	Profit	
6						
7		8.00	10.00	8.00	2.00	
8						
9						
10			MR	MC	Mprofit	
11						
12			0.625	1.000	−0.375	
13						

Suggested References

The following references provide advanced treatments of marginal analysis using differential calculus.

Baldani, J., J. Bradford, and R. Turner. *Mathematical Economics*. Fort Worth, TX: Cengage Learning, 2004.

Besanko, D., and W. R. Braeutigam. *Microeconomics: An Integrative Approach*. New York, NY: John Wiley & Sons, 2007.

Valuable references on optimization methods include:

Fourer, R., and J.-P. Goux. "Optimization as an Internet Resource." *Interfaces* (March–April 2001): 130–150.

Fylstra, D. et al. "Design and Use of the Microsoft Excel Solver." *Interfaces* (September–October 1998): 29–55.

Can a disastrous decision result from mistaking a minimum for a maximum? For a dramatic example, see

Biddle, W. "Skeleton Alleged in the Stealth Bomber's Closet." *Science,* May 12, 1989, 650–651.

A guide to optimization software and resources on the World Wide Web is provided by H. D. Mittelmann "Decision Tree for Optimization Software." http://plato.asu.edu/guide.html, 2007.

CHECK STATION ANSWERS

1. The revenue function is $R = 340Q - .8Q^2$.

2. The profit function is $\pi = R - C = -120 + 240Q - .8Q^2$.

3. At $Q = 100$, $\pi = -120 + (240)(100) - .8(100)^2 = 15,880$.

   At $Q = 99$, $\pi = -120 + (240)(99) - .8(99)^2 = 15,799.2$.

   Thus, $M\pi = (15,880 - 15,799.2)/(100 - 99) = 80.8$.

4. Marginal profit is $M\pi = d\pi/dQ = 240 - 1.6Q$. Setting this equal to zero implies that $240 - 1.6Q = 0$, or $Q = 150$.

5. Setting $MR = MC$ implies that $340 - 1.6Q = 100$. Therefore, $Q = 150$. Substituting $Q = 150$ into the price equation implies that $P = 340 - .8(150) = 220$.

6. Cutting price the full amount to maintain sales at the same level is not optimal. A downward shift in the steel producer's demand curve implies a similar downward shift in the MR curve. Absent any other changes, the new intersection of the MR and MC curves is now at a lower output. Thus, the firm's profit-maximizing response in the face of lower prices from competing Japanese suppliers is to reduce its target level of output and to undertake a partial price cut.

Calculus and Optimization Techniques

The study of managerial economics emphasizes that decisions are taken to maximize certain objectives. Although the precise objective may vary, the key point is that the manager should be able to quantify his or her ultimate goals. For instance, if the manager's objective is to maximize profit, he or she must be able to estimate and measure the profit consequences of alternative courses of action (such as charging different prices). This appendix introduces and reviews the use of calculus in optimization problems. These techniques will be applied throughout the book. Let's begin with an example.

MAXIMIZING PROFIT   A manager who is in charge of a single product line is trying to determine the quantity of output to produce and sell to maximize the product's profit. Based on marketing and production studies, she has estimated the product's profit function to be

$$\pi = 2Q - .1Q^2 - 3.6. \qquad \text{[2A.1]}$$

where π is profit (thousands of dollars) and Q is quantity of output (thousands of units). Here the level of output, Q, is identified as the manager's *decision variable,* the item the decision maker controls. The profit function shows the relationship between the manager's decision variable and her objective. (For this reason, it often is referred to as the *objective function.*)

59

FIGURE 2A.1

The Firm's Profit
Function

Marginal profit at a
particular output is
determined by the
slope of the line drawn
tangent to the profit
graph.

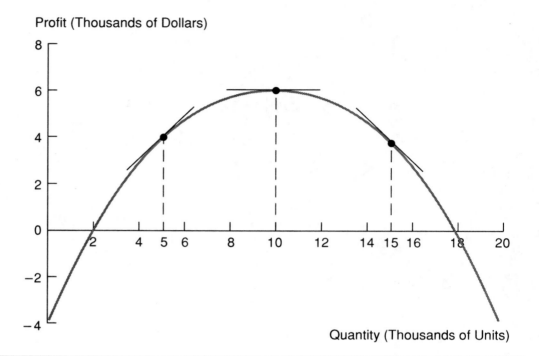

Quantity (000s)	Profit ($000s)
0.0	−3.6
2.0	0
4.0	2.8
6.0	4.8
8.0	6.0
10.0	6.4
12.0	6.0
14.0	4.8
16.0	2.8
18.0	0
20.0	−3.6

An equation is the most economical way to express the profit function, but it is not the only means. Figure 2A.1 presents a table listing the profit consequences of different output choices and graphs the profit function. (The graph plots profits across a continuum of possible output levels. Remember that output is measured in thousands of units. Thus, Q = 6.123 and Q = 6.124 are both legitimate output candidates.) According to convention, the graph plots the decision variable (also commonly referred to as the *independent* variable) on the horizontal axis and the objective (or *dependent* variable) on the vertical axis.

From either the table or the graph, we see that at very low output levels profit is negative. As the level of output increases, profit rises, becomes positive, and peaks. For still higher outputs, profit declines and eventually turns negative. The goal of management is to set production to generate positive profits—in particular, to attain maximum profit.

Marginal Analysis

The marginal value of any variable is the change in that variable per unit change in a given decision variable. In our example, marginal profit is the change in profit from an increase in output. A direct way to express marginal profit is to find the slope of the profit function at a given level of output. The graph in Figure 2A.1 shows how this is done. We start by specifying a particular level of output, say, Q = 5. Next, we draw a tangent line that just touches the profit graph at this output level. Finally, we find the slope of the tangent line. By careful measurement (taking the ratio of the "rise over the run" along the line), we find the slope to be exactly 1 (i.e., the tangent happens to be a 45° line). Thus, the marginal profit at Q = 5 is measured as $1,000 per additional 1,000 units or, equivalently, $1 per unit.

The upward-sloping tangent shows that profit rises as output increases. Marginal profit measures the steepness of this slope, that is, how quickly profit rises with additional output. In the graph in Figure 2A.1, tangents also are drawn at output levels Q = 10 and Q = 15. At Q = 15, profit falls with increases in output; marginal profit (the slope of the tangent) is negative. At Q = 10, the tangent line is horizontal; marginal profit (again its slope) is exactly zero.

Marginal analysis can identify the optimal output level directly, dispensing with tedious enumeration of candidates. The principle is this:

> The manager's objective is maximized when the marginal value with respect to that objective becomes zero (turning from positive to negative).

To maximize profit, the marginal principle instructs us to find the output for which marginal profit is zero. To see why this is so, suppose we are considering an output level at which marginal profit is positive. Clearly, this output cannot be optimal because a small increase would raise profit. Conversely, if marginal profit is negative at a given output, output should be decreased to raise profit. In Figure 2A.1, profit can be increased (we can move toward the revenue peak) if current output is in either the upward- or downward-sloping region. Consequently, the point of maximum profit occurs when marginal profit is neither positive nor negative; that is, it must be zero. This occurs at output Q = 10 thousand, where the tangent's slope is flat, that is, exactly zero.

DIFFERENTIAL CALCULUS   To apply the marginal principle, we need a simple method to compute marginal values. (It would be tedious to have to compute rates of change by measuring tangent slopes by hand.) Fortunately, the rules of differential calculus can be applied directly to any functional equation to *derive* marginal values. The process of finding the tangent slope commonly is referred to as *taking the derivative of* (or *differentiating*) the functional equation.[1] To illustrate the basic calculus rules, let y denote the dependent variable and x the independent variable. We write y = f(x), where f(x) represents the

---

[1] The following are all equivalent statements:
     1. The slope of the profit function at Q = 5 is $1 per unit of output.
     2. The derivative of the profit function at Q = 5 is $1 per unit of output.
     3. The marginal profit at Q = 5 is $1 per unit of output.
     4. At Q = 5, profit is rising at a rate of $1 per unit of output.

(unspecified) functional relationship between the variables. The notation dy/dx represents the derivative of the function, that is, the rate of change or slope of the function at a particular value of x. (The d in this notation is derived from the Greek letter delta, which has come to mean "change in.") We list the following basic rules:

- *Rule 1.*   The derivative of a constant is zero. If $y = 7$, for example, $dy/dx = 0$. Note that $y = 7$ is graphed as a horizontal line (of height 7); naturally this has a zero slope for all values of x.

- *Rule 2.*   The derivative of a constant times a variable is simply the constant. If $y = bx$, then $dy/dx = b$. For example, if $y = 13x$, then $dy/dx = 13$. In words, the function $y = 13x$ is a straight line with a slope of 13.

- *Rule 3.*   A power function has the form $y = ax^n$, where a and n are constants. The derivative of a power function is

$$dy/dx = n \cdot ax^{n-1}.$$

For instance, if $y = 4x^3$, then $dy/dx = 12x^2$.

It is important to recognize that the power function includes many important special cases.[2] For instance, $y = 1/x^2$ is equivalently written as $y = x^{-2}$. Similarly, $y = \sqrt{x}$ becomes $y = x^{1/2}$. According to Rule 3, the respective derivatives are $dy/dx = -2x^{-3} = -2/x^3$ and $dy/dx = .5x^{-1/2} = .5/\sqrt{x}$.

- *Rule 4.*   The derivative of a sum of functions is equal to the sum of the derivatives; that is, if $y = f(x) + g(x)$, then $dy/dx = df/dx + dg/dx$. This simply means we can take the derivative of functions term by term. For example, given that $y = .1x^2 - 2x^3$, then $dy/dx = .2x - 6x^2$.

- *Rule 5.*   Suppose y is the product of two functions: $y = f(x)g(x)$. Then we have

$$dy/dx = (df/dx)g + (dg/dx)f.$$

For example, suppose we have $y = (4x)(3x^2)$. Then $dy/dx = (4)(3x^2) + 4x(6x) = 36x^2$. (Note that this example can also be written as $y = 12x^3$; we confirm that $dy/dx = 36x^2$ using Rule 3.)

- *Rule 6.*   Suppose y is a quotient: $y = f(x)/g(x)$. Then we have

$$dy/dx = [(df/dx)g - (dg/dx)f]/g^2.$$

---

[2] Notice that Rules 1 and 2 are actually special cases of Rule 3. Setting $n = 0$ implies that $y = a$, and therefore $dy/dx = 0$ (Rule 1). Setting $n = 1$ implies that $y = ax$, and therefore $dy/dx = a$ (Rule 2).

For example, suppose we have $y = x/(8 + x)$. Then

$$dy/dx = [1 \cdot (8 + x) - 1 \cdot (x)]/(8 + x)^2 = 8/(8 + x)^2.$$

Let's derive an expression for marginal profit (denoted by $M\pi$) applying these calculus rules to our profit function:

$$\pi = 2Q - .1Q^2 - 3.6.$$

From Rule 4, we know we can proceed term by term. From Rule 2, the derivative of the first term is 2. According to Rule 3, the derivative of the second term is $-.2Q$. From Rule 1, the derivative of the third term is zero. Thus,

$$M\pi = d\pi/dx = 2 - .2Q.$$

Notice the elegance of this approach. By substituting specific values of Q, we can find marginal profit at any desired level of output. For instance, at $Q = 5$, we find that $M\pi = 2 - (.2)(5) = 1$; at $Q = 12$, $M\pi = -.4$; and so on.

To determine the firm's optimal output level, we set $M\pi = 0$. Thus,

$$2 - .2Q = 0.$$

Solving this equation for Q, we find $Q = 10$. This confirms that the profit-maximizing level of output is 10 thousand units.

THE SECOND DERIVATIVE   In general, one must be careful to check that a maximum, not a minimum, has been found. In the previous example, the graph makes it clear that we have found a maximum. But suppose the profit expression is more complicated, say,

$$\pi = 1.8Q^2 - .1Q^3 - 6Q - 10. \qquad [2A.2]$$

Figure 2A.2 shows the associated profit graph. Notice that there are two quantities at which the slope is zero: One is a maximum and the other is a minimum. It would be disastrous if we confused the two. Taking the derivative of the profit function, we find

$$M\pi = d\pi/dx = 3.6Q - .3Q^2 - 6.$$

Substitution confirms that marginal profit is zero at the quantities $Q = 2$ and $Q = 10$. The graph shows that $Q = 2$ *minimizes* profit, whereas $Q = 10$ *maximizes* profit.

There is a direct way to distinguish between a maximum and a minimum. At a maximum, the slope of the profit function changes from positive to zero

FIGURE 2A.2

A Second Profit
Function

The manager must be
careful to distinguish a
maximum from a
minimum.

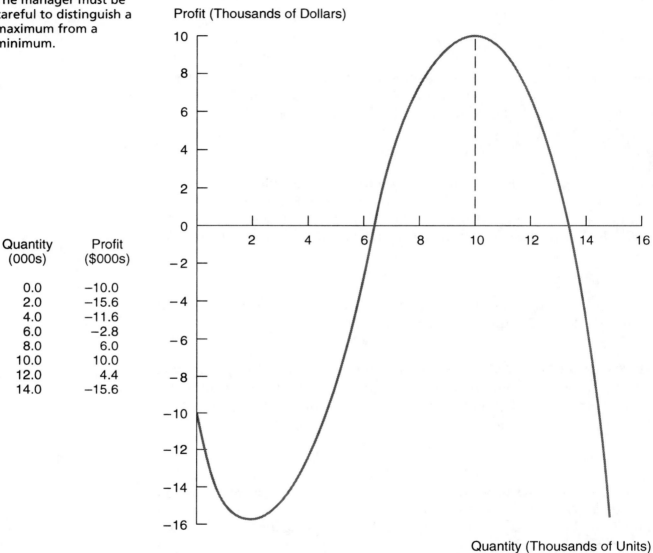

Quantity (000s)	Profit ($000s)
0.0	−10.0
2.0	−15.6
4.0	−11.6
6.0	−2.8
8.0	6.0
10.0	10.0
12.0	4.4
14.0	−15.6

to negative as output increases; that is, the slope of the profit function decreases
as output increases around the maximum. In contrast, at a minimum, the slope
changes from negative to zero to positive; the slope is increasing. Because of
this difference, the *second* derivative of the profit function can be used to distinguish between the two cases. The second derivative is found by taking the

derivative of $d\pi/dt$. If the second derivative is negative (i.e., the slope is decreasing), the point in question is a local maximum; if the second derivative is positive, the point is a local minimum. Taking the derivative of $d\pi/dQ$, we find the second derivative to be

$$d^2\pi/dQ^2 = d(d\pi/dQ)/dQ$$
$$= dM\pi/dQ = d(3.6Q - .3Q^2 - 6)/dQ$$
$$= 3.6 - .6Q$$

In finding the second derivative, we start from the original profit function and take the derivative *twice*. At $Q = 2$, we find that $d^2\pi/dQ^2 = 3.6 - .6(2) = 2.4$. Since this is positive, $Q = 2$ represents a local minimum. At $Q = 10$, we find that $d^2\pi/dQ^2 = 3.6 - .6(10) = -2.4$. Since this is negative, $Q = 10$ represents a local maximum.

MARGINAL REVENUE AND MARGINAL COST We have seen that maximum profit is achieved at the point such that marginal profit equals zero, $d\pi/dQ = 0$. The same condition can be expressed in a different form by separating profit into its two components. Profit is defined as the difference between revenues and costs. Thus, the profit function can be written as

$$\pi(Q) = R(Q) - C(Q),$$

the difference between revenues and costs. In turn, the condition that marginal profit equal zero is

$$d\pi/dQ = dR/dQ - dC/dQ = MR - MC = 0.$$

In short, profit is maximized when marginal revenue equals marginal cost.

Maximizing Multivariable Functions

Frequently, the manager must determine optimal values for several decision variables at once, for instance, a product's price and its associated advertising budget. In this case, the product's profit would be expressed by the function, $\pi = \pi(P, A)$, where P is the product's price and A is its advertising budget in dollars. Here the key to maximizing profit is to apply a double dose of marginal reasoning. Marginal profit with respect to each decision variable should be equated to zero. The optimal value of P is found where the *partial* derivative of profit with respect to P equals zero. This partial derivative is denoted by $\partial\pi/\partial P$ and is found by taking the derivative with respect to P, holding A (the other decision variable) constant. Similarly, the optimal value of A is found where $\partial\pi/\partial A = 0$.

PRICE AND ADVERTISING   Suppose the firm's profit function is

$$\pi = 20 + 2P - 2P^2 + 4A - A^2 + 2PA.$$

The partial derivative of profit with respect to P is

$$\partial\pi/\partial P = 2 - 4P + 2A$$

Notice that when we take the partial derivative with respect to P, we are treating A as a constant. Thus, 4A and A^2 disappear (Rule 1) and 2PA becomes 2A (Rule 2). The partial derivative of profit with respect to A is

$$\partial\pi/\partial A = 4 - 2A + 2P.$$

Setting each of these expressions equal to zero produces two equations in two unknowns. Solving these simultaneously, we find that P = 3 and A = 5. Thus, profit is maximized at these values of P and A.

Constrained Optimization

In the previous examples, the decision variables were unconstrained, that is, free to take on any values. Frequently, however, decision variables can be changed only within certain constraints. Consider the following example.

A SUPPLY COMMITMENT   A firm is trying to identify its profit-maximizing level of output. By contract, it already is committed to supplying at least seven units to its customer. Suppose that its predicted profit function is given by $\pi = 40Q - 4Q^2$. The firm seeks to maximize π subject to $Q \geq 7$. Setting marginal profit equal to zero, we have $d\pi/dQ = 40 - 8Q = 0$ so that $Q = 5$. But this value is *infeasible;* it violates the contract constraint. The constrained maximum occurs at $Q = 7$, where $d\pi/dQ = -6$. Note that, since marginal profit is negative, profit would decline if Q were increased. Thus, the firm would like to raise profit by decreasing Q, but this is impossible due to the binding contract constraint.

A different kind of constrained optimization problem occurs when there are multiple decision variables.

PROFITS FROM MULTIPLE MARKETS   A firm has a limited amount of output and must decide what quantities (Q_1 and Q_2) to sell to two different market segments. For example, suppose it seeks to maximize total profit given by

$$\pi = \left(20Q_1 - .5Q_1^2\right) + \left(40Q_2 - Q_2^2\right),$$

subject to $Q_1 + Q_2 \leq 25$. Setting marginal profit equal to zero for each quantity, we find that $Q_1 = 20$ and $Q_2 = 20$. But these desired quantities are infeasible; the total (40) exceeds the available supply (25). The manager must cut back one or both outputs. But how should she do this while maintaining as high a level of profit as possible? To answer this question, observe that if output is cut back in each market, the marginal profit in each market will be positive. What if the manager chose outputs such that marginal profit differed across the two markets, say, $M\pi_1 > M\pi_2 > 0$? If this were the case, the manager could increase her total profit by selling one more unit in market 1 and one less unit in market 2. She would continue to switch units so long as the marginal profits differed across the markets. At the optimal solution, marginal profits must be equal. Thus, $\partial\pi/\partial Q_1 = \partial\pi/\partial Q_2$ must hold as well as $Q_1 + Q_2 = 25$. Taking derivatives, we find the first condition to be $20 - Q_1 = 40 - 2Q_2$. Solving this equation and the quantity constraint simultaneously, we find that $Q_1 = 10$ and $Q_2 = 15$. This is the firm's optimal solution.

THE METHOD OF LAGRANGE MULTIPLIERS   The last two problems can be solved by an alternative means known as the *method of Lagrange multipliers*. To use the method, we create a new variable, the Lagrange multiplier, for each constraint. In the subsequent solution, we determine optimal values for the relevant decision variables and the Lagrange multipliers. For instance, in the supply commitment example, there is one constraint, $Q = 7$. (We know the constraint is binding from our discussion.) To apply the method, we rewrite this constraint as $7 - Q = 0$, create a new variable, call it z, and write

$$L = \pi + z(7 - Q)$$
$$= 40Q - 4Q^2 + z(7 - Q).$$

In short, we have formed L (denoted the Lagrangian) by taking the original objective function and adding to it the binding constraint (multiplied by z). We then find the partial derivatives with respect to the two variables, Q and z, and set them equal to zero:

$$\partial L/\partial Q = 40 - 8Q - z = 0;$$
$$\partial L/\partial z = 7 - Q = 0.$$

Solving these equations simultaneously, we find that $Q = 7$ and $z = -16$. The value of Q is hardly surprising; we already know this is the best the manager can do. The interpretation of the Lagrange multiplier, z, is of some interest. The value of the multiplier measures the marginal profit ($M\pi = -16$) at the constrained optimum.

To apply the method in the multiple-market example, we write

$$L = \left(20Q_1 - .5Q_1^2\right) + \left(40Q_2 - Q_2^2\right) + z\left(25 - Q_1 - Q_2\right),$$

where the binding constraint is $Q_1 + Q_2 = 25$ and z again denotes the Lagrange multiplier. Setting the appropriate partial derivatives equal to zero, we find

$$\partial L/\partial Q_1 = 20 - Q_1 - z = 0;$$
$$\partial L/\partial Q_2 = 40 - 2Q_2 - z = 0;$$
$$\partial L/\partial z = 25 - Q_1 - Q_2 = 0.$$

Notice that the third condition is simply the original constraint. We now find values that satisfy these three equations simultaneously: $Q_1 = 10$, $Q_2 = 15$, and $z = 10$. The values for Q_1 and Q_2 confirm our original solution. In addition, note that the first two equations can be written as $z = 20 - Q_1 = 40 - 2Q_2$, or $z = M\pi_1 = M\pi_2$. In other words, the multiplier z represents the common value of marginal profit (equalized across the two markets). The actual value of $M\pi$ in each market is $z = 10$. Thus, if the manager could increase total sales (above 25), he would increase profit by 10 per unit of additional capacity.

To sum up, the use of Lagrange multipliers is a powerful method. It effectively allows us to treat constrained problems as though they were unconstrained.[3]

Questions and Problems

1. The economist Arthur Laffer has long argued that *lower* tax rates, by stimulating employment and investment, can lead to *increased* tax revenue to the government. If this prediction is correct, a tax rate reduction would be a win-win policy, good for both taxpayers and the government. Laffer went on to sketch a tax revenue curve in the shape of an upside-down U.

   In general, the government's tax revenue can be expressed as $R = t \bullet B(t)$, where t denotes the tax rate ranging between 0 and 1 (i.e., between 0 and 100 percent) and B denotes the tax base. Explain why the tax base is likely to shrink as tax rates become very high. How might this lead to a U-shaped tax revenue curve?

2. The economic staff of the U.S. Department of the Treasury has been asked to recommend a new tax policy concerning the treatment of the foreign earnings of U.S. firms. Currently the foreign earnings of U.S. multinational companies are taxed only when the income is returned to

---

[3]It is important to note that the method of Lagrange multipliers is relevant only in the case of binding constraints. Typically, we begin by seeking an unconstrained optimum. If such an optimum satisfies all of the constraints, we are done. If one or more constraints are violated, however, we apply the method of Lagrange multipliers for the solution.

the United States. Taxes are deferred if the income is reinvested abroad. The department seeks a tax rate that will maximize total tax revenue from foreign earnings. Find the optimal tax rate if

a. $B(t) = 80 - 100t$

b. $B(t) = 80 - 240t^2$

c. $B(t) = 80 - 80\sqrt{t}$,

where $B(t)$ is the foreign earnings of U.S. multinational companies returned to the United States and t is the tax rate.

3. A firm's total profit is given by $\pi = 20x - x^2 + 16y - 2y^2$.
    a. What values of x and y will maximize the firm's profit?
    b. Repeat part (a) assuming the firm faces the constraint $x + y \leq 8$.
    c. Repeat part (a) assuming the constraint is $x + .5y \leq 7.5$.

SPECIAL APPENDIX
TO CHAPTER 2

Optimization Using Spreadsheets

We have already encountered several quantitative approaches to optimizing a given objective: enumeration, graphic solutions, and (in the preceding appendix) calculus. To these we can add a fourth approach—spreadsheet-based optimization. Over the past 25 years, spreadsheets have become powerful management tools. Modeling a quantitative decision on a spreadsheet harnesses the power of computer calculation instead of laborious pencil-and-paper figuring. Besides helping to define and manage decision problems, spreadsheets also compute optimal solutions with no more than a click of a mouse. There are many leading spreadsheet programs—Excel, Calc, Google Docs, Lotus 123, Quattro Pro, to name a few—and all work nearly the same way. To review the fundamentals of spreadsheet use, let's revisit the microchip example.

Table 2A.1 shows this example depicted in an Excel spreadsheet. The spreadsheet consists of a table of cells. Besides the title in row 2, we have typed labels (Quantity, Price, MR) in rows 5 and 10. We have also entered the number 2.0 in cell B7 (highlighted in colored type). This cell houses our basic decision

Optimizing a
Spreadsheet

	A	B	C	D	E	F	G
1							
2		THE OPTIMAL OUTPUT OF MICROCHIPS					
3							
4							
5		Quantity	Price	Revenue	Cost	Profit	
6							
7		2.0	130	260	176	84	
8							
9							
10				MR	MC	Mprofit	
11							
12				90	38	52	
13							
14							

variable, output. For the moment, we have set microchip output at 2.0 lots. Cells C7 to F7 show the price, revenue, cost, and profit results of producing 2.0 lots. These cells are linked via formulas to our output cell. For instance, consider cell C7 showing a price of 130. When we created the spreadsheet, we typed the formula

$$= 170 - 20*B7,$$

into cell C7 (and then pressed return). This formula embodies the price equation, P = 170 − 20Q. By entering the preceding spreadsheet formula, we are telling the computer to subtract 20 times the value of cell B7 from 170 and to enter the resulting numerical value in cell C7. (Note: We typed a formula, *not* the number 130, into this cell.)

The other numerical values are similarly determined by formulas. Thus, in cell D7, we entered the formula = B7*C7, instructing the spreadsheet to compute revenue as the product of the price and quantity cells. In cell E7, we entered this cost formula: = 100 + 38*B7. In cell F7, we computed profit by entering = D7 − E7, and in cell D12, we computed MR by entering = 170 − 40*B7. Indeed, to gain experience with the ways of spreadsheets, we suggest that you start with a blank spreadsheet and recreate Table 2A.1 for yourself—that is, type in labels, numerical values, and formulas as indicated. (Note: Typing in cell addresses is not the only way to enter formulas. The quickest way is to mouse click on the cell that is part of the formula.)

With the spreadsheet in hand, there are several ways to determine the microchip firm's profit-maximizing output. The most primitive way is to try various numerical values in cell B7, observe the resulting profit results in cell F7, and thereby identify the optimal output. This represents solution by enumeration. A second, more expeditious approach uses MR and MC as guides. Again, values in cell B7 are varied by hand, but this time systematically. Output should be increased as long as MR exceeds MC; it should be cut if MC exceeds MR. When MR equals MC, the profit-maximizing level of output has been attained.

A third approach is to direct the computer to optimize the spreadsheet. The top menu in Table 2A.2 illustrates Excel's optimizer, called "Solver," which is called by clicking on the "Solver" listing found under the "Tools" menu. By completing the menu in Table 2A.2, one instructs the computer to optimize the spreadsheet. In the menu, we have (1) entered target cell F7 (the profit cell), (2) to be maximized, (3) by varying cell B7. Then, after one clicks on the solve box, the computer finds a new numerical value in cell B7 that maximizes cell F7. (The value one starts with in cell B7 does not matter; the computer will replace it with the optimal value it finds.) Using an internal mathematical algorithm, Solver finds the optimal level of output, 3.3 lots, places this value in cell B7, and the other cells (price, revenue, cost, etc.) change accordingly.

This simple example illustrates but does not do full justice to the power of spreadsheet optimization. In fact, optimizers are designed to solve complex problems involving many decision variables and multiple constraints. For instance, the firm's profit might well depend on several decision variables: output, advertising spending, and the size of its direct sales force. Here, in order to maximize profit, the manager would specify multiple variable cells in the solver menu. In addition, the firm might face various constraints in its quest for maximum profit. For instance, suppose the microchip producer was quite sure that setting a price greater than $91,000 per lot would attract a cutthroat competitor whose sales of "cloned" chips would decimate the firm's own profit. In this case, management's *constrained* optimization problem would include the requirement that the value in price cell C7 should not exceed 91. The bottom menu in Table 2A.2 includes this new constraint. The spreadsheet's new optimal solution (not shown) becomes 3.95 lots, implying exactly a $91,000 price and a reduced profit of $109,350.

To sum up, the beauty of any spreadsheet-based optimization program is that, upon execution, it instantly computes all optimal values consistent with satisfying all constraints.

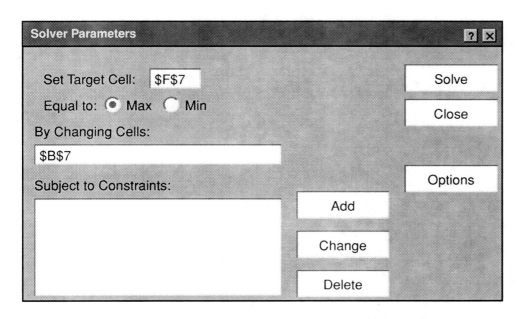

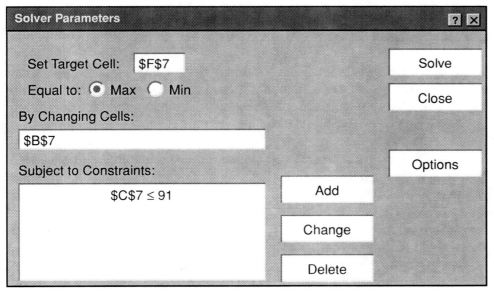

CHAPTER 3

Demand Analysis and Optimal Pricing

There's no brand loyalty so strong that the offer of "penny off" can't overcome it.

A MARKETING APHORISM

Airline Ticket Pricing

Anyone who has traveled via commercial airline, even on an infrequent basis, knows there is a bewildering plethora of fares for the same route. Besides the standard first-class and coach fares, there are discount fares for round-trip travel and for travelers who book two or more weeks in advance, leave during the week, stay over Saturday night, or fly standby. The fare structure is daunting not only for travelers but also for the airlines. In determining the standard coach fare on a particular route, the airline has to consider (1) the cost of the flight (including fuel, labor, and administrative costs), (2) the historical pattern of business and leisure use on the route, (3) overall economic conditions (which affect travel demand), and (4) the prices charged by competing airlines. Together the airlines mount some 31,000 domestic flights each day, and they repeatedly alter prices on their computerized reservation systems as conditions change.

Among airlines, the name of the game is yield management: how to price seat by seat to generate the greatest possible profit. For instance, airlines typically sell higher-priced tickets to business travelers who cannot take advantage of supersaver and other discount fares. At the same time, they sell other seats on the same flight at sharply lower prices to attract price-sensitive vacation travelers. A classic example of yield management is the competitive route between Los Angeles and Kennedy Airport in New York.[1]

[1] These fares are reported in "Equalizing Air Fares," *Wall Street Journal*, August 17, 2004, B1.

74

During June 2004, the cabin of a 158-seat aircraft along this route featured scores of fares, ranging from first-class roundtrip tickets at $2,400 and greater to discount tickets below $250. On average, half the tickets sold for fares below $400, some 20 percent of tickets were priced above $800, with the remainder priced in between. Some travelers cashed in frequent flier miles. Some purchased at discounts from third-party providers; others received lower fares for restricted tickets requiring Saturday stayovers. In general, early buyers paid less, but fares fluctuated day-to-day depending on demand.

The question here is: How can demand analysis help the airlines win the game of yield management?

In Chapter 2, we presented a simple model of profit maximization. There the manager began with demand and cost functions and used them to determine the profit-maximizing price and output level for a given product or service. In this chapter, we will take a closer look at demand and the role it plays in managerial decision making.

The notion of demand is much richer than the simple formulation given in Chapter 2. For instance, up until now we have studied the dependence of demand on a single factor: price. We begin this chapter by considering the *multiple* determinants of demand. Next, we look more closely at the responsiveness of demand to these factors, a concept captured in the basic definition of *elasticity*. In the remaining sections, we present a richer formulation of demand and show how it can be used to guide managers in their goal of maximizing profits. Toward this end, we will refine our optimization techniques to account for more complicated demand conditions—those that include the possibilities of market segmentation and price discrimination.

DETERMINANTS OF DEMAND

The Demand Function

To illustrate the basic quantitative aspects of demand, let's start with a concrete example: the demand for air travel.[2] Put yourself in the position of a manager for a leading regional airline. One of your specific responsibilities is to analyze the state of travel demand for a nonstop route between Houston, Texas, and a rapidly growing city in Florida. Your airline flies one daily departure from each city to the other (two flights in all) and faces a single competitor that offers two daily flights from each city. Your task is complicated by the fact that the number of travelers on your airline (and therefore the revenue your company earns) has fluctuated considerably in the past three years. Reviewing this past experience, you realize the main determinants of your airline's traffic are your

---

[2]We are not ready yet to analyze the complicated problem of setting multiple fares described in the opening of this chapter. That must wait until the concluding section.

own price and the price of your competitor. In addition, traffic between the two cities was brisk during years in which the Texas and Florida economies enjoyed rapid expansion. But, during the slowdown of 2001, air travel fell between the two cities.

Your immediate goal is to analyze demand for coach-class travel between the cities. (The small aircraft used on this route does not accommodate first-class seating.) You begin by writing down the following demand function:

$$Q = f(P, P°, Y). \tag{3.1}$$

This expression reads, "The number of your airline's coach seats sold per flight (Q) depends on (is a function of) your airline's coach fare (P), your competitor's fare (P°), and income in the region (Y)." In short, the **demand function** shows, in equation form, the relationship between the quantity sold of a good or service and one or more variables.

The demand function is useful shorthand, but does not indicate the exact quantitative relationship between Q and P, P°, and Y. For this we need to write the demand function in a particular form. Suppose the economic forecasting unit of your airline has supplied you with the following equation, which best describes demand:

$$Q = 25 + 3Y + P° - 2P. \tag{3.2}$$

Like the demand equations in Chapter 2, Equation 3.2 predicts sales quantity once one has specified values of the explanatory variables appearing on the right-hand side.[3] What does the equation say about the present state of demand? Currently your airline and your competitor are charging the same one-way fare, $240. The current level of income in the region is 105.[4] Putting these values into Equation 3.2, we find that

$$Q = 25 + 3(105) + 1(240) - 2(240)$$
$$= 100 \text{ seats.}$$

A comparison of this prediction with your airline's recent experience shows this equation to be quite accurate. In the past three months, the average number of coach seats sold per flight (week by week) consistently fell in the 90- to 105-seat range. Since 180 coach seats are available on the flight, the airline's load factor is $100/180 = 55.5$ percent.

---

[3]Methods of estimating and forecasting demand are presented in Chapter 4.

[4]This value is an *index* of aggregate income—business profits and personal income—in Texas and Florida. The index is set such that *real* income (i.e., after accounting for inflation) in 1998 (the so-called base year) equals 100. Thus, a current value of 105 means that regional income has increased 5 percent in real terms since then. In the depth of the Texas recession, the index stood at 87, a 13 percent reduction in real income relative to the base year.

The demand equation can be used to test the effect of changes in any of the explanatory variables. From Equation 3.2, we see that

1. For each point increase in the income index, 3 additional seats will be sold.
2. For each $10 increase in the airline's fare, 20 fewer seats will be sold.
3. For each $10 increase in the competitor's fare, 10 additional seats will be sold.

Each of these results assumes the effect in question is the *only* change that occurs; that is, all other factors are held constant. In fact, the *total change* in demand caused by simultaneous changes in the explanatory variables can be expressed as

$$\Delta Q = 3\Delta Y + 1\Delta P^\circ - 2\Delta P, \qquad [3.3]$$

where (Δ means "change in." Thus, if income increases by 5 index points while both airline prices are cut by $15, we find $\Delta Q = 3(5) + 1(-15) - 2(-15) = 30$ seats. Your airline would expect to sell 30 additional seats on each flight.

Use Equation 3.3 to compute the change in sales, ΔQ, that will result from $\Delta Y = -8$, $\Delta P^\circ = 12$, and $\Delta P = 20$.

CHECK STATION 1

The Demand Curve and Shifting Demand

Suppose that, in the immediate future, regional income is expected to remain at 105 and the competitor's fare will stay at $240. However, your airline's fare is not set in stone, and you naturally are interested in testing the effect of different possible coach prices. Substituting the values of Y and P° into Equation 3.2's demand function, we find that

$$\begin{aligned} Q &= 25 + 3(105) + 1(240) - 2P, \qquad [3.4] \\ &= 580 - 2P. \end{aligned}$$

Like the basic demand equation facing the microchip producer in Chapter 2, Equation 3.4 relates the quantity of the good or service sold to its price. Here, however, it is important to remember that, in the background, all other factors affecting demand are held constant (at the values Y = 105 and P° = 240). Of course, it is a simple matter to graph this demand equation as a demand curve. (Do this yourself as practice.) As usual, the demand curve is downward sloping.[5]

[5]We can graph the demand *curve* (by putting quantity and price on the respective axes), but we cannot graph the demand *function* (because this involves four variables and we do not have four axes). Thus, graphing a particular demand curve requires holding all other factors constant.

Starting from an initial price, by varying the coach fare up or down, we move *along* (respectively up and down) the demand curve. A higher price means lower sales. But what happens if there is a change in one of the other factors that affect demand? As we now show, *such a change causes a shift in the demand curve*. To illustrate, suppose that a year from now P° is expected to be unchanged but Y is forecast to grow to 119. What will the demand curve look like a year hence? To answer this question, we substitute the new value, Y = 119 (along with P° = 240), into the demand function to obtain

$$Q = 622 - 2P, \qquad\qquad [3.5]$$

Now compare the new and old demand equations. Observe that they are of the same form, with one key difference: The constant term of the new demand curve is larger than that of the old. Therefore, if your airline were to leave its own fare unchanged a year from now, you would enjoy a greater volume of coach traffic. Figure 3.1 underscores this point by graphing both the old and new demand curves. Note that the new demand curve constitutes a parallel shift to the right (toward greater sales quantities) of the old demand curve. At P = $240, current demand is 100 seats per flight. At the same fare, coach demand one year from now is forecast to be 142 seats (due to the increase in

FIGURE 3.1

A Shift in Demand

Due to growth in regional income, the airline's demand curve in one year's time lies to the right of its current demand curve. At an unchanged price a year from now, it expects to sell 42 additional seats on each flight.

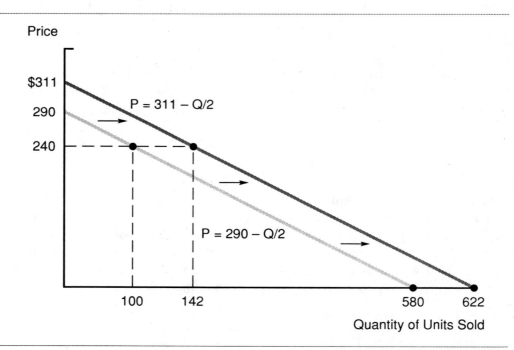

regional income), a gain of 42 seats. In fact, for *any* fare your airline might set (and leave unchanged), demand a year from now is predicted to grow by 42 seats. Thus, we confirm that there is a 42-unit rightward shift in the demand curve from old to new demand.

Another way to think about the effect of the increase in regional income is to write down the equations for the market-clearing price for the old and new demand curves:

$$P = 290 - Q/2 \text{ (old)} \qquad\qquad [3.6]$$
$$P = 311 - Q/2 \text{ (new)}$$

Thus, if your airline seeks to sell the same number of seats a year from now that it does today, it can do so while raising the coach ticket price by $21 (the difference between 311 and 290). To see this in Figure 3.1, fix the quantity and read the higher price off the new demand curve.

General Determinants of Demand

The example of demand for air travel is representative of the results found for most goods or services. Obviously, the *good's own price* is a key determinant of demand. (We will say much more about price later in the chapter.) Close behind in importance is the *level of income* of the potential purchasers of the good or service. A basic definition is useful in describing the effect of income on sales: A product is called a **normal good** if an increase in income raises its sales. In our example, air travel is a normal good. For any normal good, sales vary directly with income; that is, the coefficient on income in the demand equation is positive. As an empirical matter, most goods and services are normal. Any increase in consumer income is spread over a wide variety of goods and services. (Of course, the extra spending on a given good may be small or even nearly zero.) Likewise, when income is reduced in an economy that is experiencing a recession, demand falls across the spectrum of normal goods. For a small category of goods (such as certain food staples), an increase in income causes a reduction in spending. These are termed **inferior goods**. For instance, an individual of moderate means may regularly consume a large quantity of beans, rice, and ground meat. But, after experiencing an increase in income, the individual can better afford other foods and therefore reduces his consumption of the old staples.

A third set of factors affecting demand are the prices of *substitute* and *complementary* goods. As the term suggests, a **substitute good** competes with and can substitute for the good in question. In the airline example, travel on one airline serving the same intercity route is a very close substitute for travel on the other. Accordingly, *an increase in the price of the substitute good or service causes an* *increase in demand for the good in question* (by making it relatively more attractive to purchase). Note that substitution in demand can occur at many levels. For instance, the airline's sales along the route are affected not only by changes in competing airline fares but also by train and bus fares and auto-operating costs. To a greater or lesser degree, these other modes of transportation are substitutes for air travel.

A pair of goods is **complementary** if an increase in demand for one causes an increase in demand for the other. For instance, an increase in the sales of new automobiles will have a positive effect on the sales of new tires. In particular, tire manufacturers are very interested in the prices car manufacturers announce for new models. They know that discount auto prices will spur not only the sales of cars but also the sales of tires. The price of a complementary good enters negatively into the demand function; that is, *an increase in the price of a complementary good reduces demand for the good in question.* For example, Florida resort packages and travel between Houston and Florida are to some extent complementary. Thus, the price of resort packages would enter with a negative coefficient into the demand function for travel along the route.[6]

Finally, a wide variety of other factors may affect the demand for particular goods and services. Normal *population* growth of prime groups that consume the good or service will increase demand. As the populations of Houston and the Florida city grow, so will air travel between them. The main determinant of soft-drink sales is the number of individuals in the 10–25 age group. Changes in preferences and tastes are another important factor. Various trends over the past 20 years have supported growth in demand for new foods (diet, natural, organic), new electronic products (cell phones, digital cameras, MP3 players, CD and DVD players), new recreation services (exercise, travel, tanning salons, and so on). The list is endless.

ELASTICITY OF DEMAND

Price Elasticity

Price elasticity measures the responsiveness of a good's sales to changes in its price. This concept is important for two reasons: (1) Knowledge of a good's price elasticity allows firms to predict the impact of price changes on unit sales; and (2) price elasticity guides the firm's profit-maximizing pricing decisions.

---

[6]Although we say that autos and tires are complementary goods, the cross-price effects need not be of comparable magnitudes. Auto prices have a large impact on tire sales, but tire prices have a very minor impact on auto sales because they are a small fraction of the full cost of a new car.

Let's begin with a basic definition: The **price elasticity of demand** is the ratio of the percentage change in quantity and the percentage change in the good's price, all other factors held constant. In algebraic terms, we have

$$E_P = \frac{\% \text{ change in Q}}{\% \text{ change in P}} \tag{3.7}$$

$$= \frac{\Delta Q / Q}{\Delta P / P} = \frac{(Q_1 - Q_0)/Q_0}{(P_1 - P_0)/P_0},$$

where P_0 and Q_0 are the initial price and quantity, respectively. For example, consider the airline's demand curve as described in Equation 3.4. At the current \$240 fare, 100 coach seats are sold. If the airline cut its price to \$235, 110 seats would be demanded. Therefore, we find

$$E_P = \frac{(110 - 100)/100}{(235 - 240)/240} = \frac{10.0\%}{-2.1\%} = -4.8.$$

In this example, price was cut by 2.1 percent (the denominator), with the result that quantity increased by 10 percent (the numerator). Therefore, the price elasticity (the ratio of these two effects) is -4.8. Notice that the change in quantity was due solely to the price change. The other factors that potentially could affect sales (income and the competitor's price) did not change. (The requirement "all other factors held constant" in the definition is essential for a meaningful notion of price elasticity.) We observe that there is a large percentage quantity change for a relatively small price change. The ratio is almost fivefold. Demand is very responsive to price.

Price elasticity is a key ingredient in applying marginal analysis to determine optimal prices. Because marginal analysis works by evaluating relatively small changes taken with respect to an initial decision, it is useful to measure elasticity with respect to an infinitesimally small change in price. In this instance, we write elasticity as

$$E_P = \frac{dQ / Q}{dP / P}. \tag{3.8a}$$

We can rearrange this expression to read

$$E_P = \left(\frac{dQ}{dP}\right)\left(\frac{P}{Q}\right). \tag{3.8b}$$

In words, the elasticity (measured at price P) depends directly on dQ/dP, the derivative of the demand function with respect to P (as well as on the ratio of P to Q).

The algebraic expressions in Equations 3.7 and 3.8a are referred to as *point elasticities* because they link percentage quantity and price changes *at a price-quantity point on the demand curve.* Although most widely used, point elasticity measures are not the only way to describe changes in price and quantity. A closely related measure is *arc* price elasticity, which is defined as

$$E_P = \frac{\Delta Q / \overline{Q}}{\Delta P / \overline{P}},$$

where $\overline{Q}$ is the average of the two quantities, $\overline{Q} = (Q_0 + Q_1)/2$, and $\overline{P}$ is the average of the two prices, $\overline{P} = (P_0 + P_1)/2$. In the airline example, the average quantity is 105 seats, the average price is \$237.50, and the arc price elasticity is $(10/105)/(-5/237.5) = -4.5$.

The main advantage of the arc elasticity measure is that it treats the prices and quantities symmetrically; that is, it does not distinguish between the *initial* and *final* prices and quantities. Regardless of the starting point, the elasticity is the same. In contrast, in computing the elasticity via Equation 3.7, one must be careful to specify P_0 and Q_0. To illustrate, suppose the initial airfare is \$235 and 110 seats are filled. The elasticity associated with a price hike to \$240 (and a drop to 100 seats) is $E_P = (-10/110)/(5/235) = -4.3$. Thus, we see that the elasticity associated with the change is -4.8 or -4.3, depending on the starting point.

The overriding advantage of point elasticities (Equation 3.8a) is their application in conjunction with marginal analysis. For instance, a firm's optimal pricing policy depends directly on its estimate of the price elasticity, $E_P = (dQ/Q)/(dP/P)$. In this and later chapters, we will focus on point elasticities in our analysis of optimal decisions.[7]

Elasticity measures the sensitivity of demand with respect to price. In describing elasticities, it is useful to start with a basic benchmark. First, demand is said to be **unitary elastic** if $E_P = -1$. In this case, the percentage change in price is exactly matched by the resulting percentage change in quantity, but in the opposite direction. Second, demand is **inelastic** if $-1 < E_P < 0$. The term *inelastic* suggests that demand is relatively unresponsive to price: The percentage change in quantity is less (in absolute value) than the percentage change in price. Finally, demand is **elastic** if $E_P < -1$. In this case, an initial change in price causes a larger percentage change in quantity. In short, elastic demand is highly responsive, or sensitive, to changes in price.

The easiest way to understand the meaning of inelastic and elastic demand is to examine two extreme cases. Figure 3.2a depicts a vertical demand curve representing **perfectly inelastic** demand, $E_P = 0$. Here sales are constant (at $Q = 100$) no matter how high the price charged. Thus, for any price change,

---

[7]So long as the price change is very small, the point elasticity calculated via Equation 3.7 will vary little whether the higher or lower price is taken as the starting point. Furthermore, this value will closely approximate the exact measure of elasticity given by Equation 3.8a.

FIGURE 3.2

Two Extreme Cases

The vertical demand curve in part (a) represents perfectly inelastic demand, $E_P = 0$. The horizontal demand curve in part (b) represents perfectly elastic demand, $E_P = -\infty$.

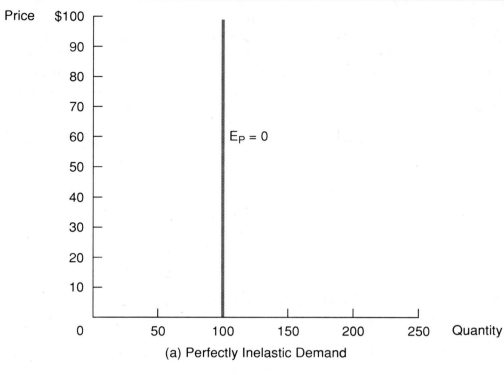

(a) Perfectly Inelastic Demand

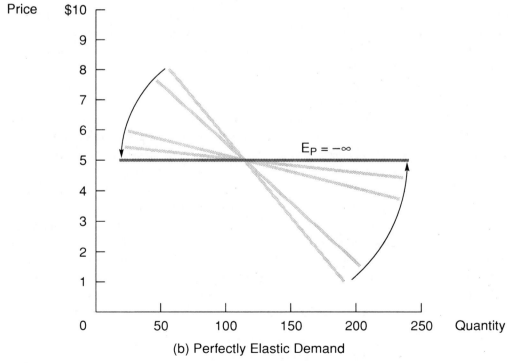

(b) Perfectly Elastic Demand

the quantity change is zero and therefore so is the elasticity.[8] Figure 3.2b depicts the opposite extreme: a horizontal demand curve where demand is **perfectly elastic**, $E_P = -\infty$. The horizontal curve indicates that the firm can sell as much output as it likes at the given price; whether it sells a large or small output quantity will have no effect on its price. In this case, we say that the *market* determines the firm's price. (Note also that the firm can sell nothing at a higher-than-market price.) Demand is called perfectly elastic because sales are infinitely sensitive to price. To see this, consider the nearly horizontal demand curve in Figure 3.2 and observe that any small price change causes a very large quantity change in the opposite direction. For horizontal demand, the quantity change becomes infinite for any price change, even one approaching zero; thus, the elasticity ratio becomes infinite, $E_P = -\infty$.

CHECK STATION 2 "The demand for automobiles must be less elastic than the demand for CD players because a $50 reduction in the price of cars does not affect the number sold nearly as much as a $50 reduction in the price of CD players." Is this statement correct? Explain.

FACTORS AFFECTING PRICE ELASTICITY   What determines whether the demand for a good is price elastic or price inelastic? Here are four important factors.

A first factor is the degree to which the good is a necessity. If a good or service is not considered essential, the purchaser can easily do without it—if and when the price becomes too high—even if there are no close substitutes. In that case, demand is elastic. If the good is a necessary component of consumption, it is more difficult to do without it in the face of a price increase. Thus, demand tends to be price inelastic.

A second factor is the availability of substitutes. With many substitutes, consumers easily can shift to other alternatives if the price of one good becomes too high; demand is elastic. Without close substitutes, switching becomes more difficult; demand is more inelastic. For this reason, *industry demand tends to be much less elastic than the demand facing a particular firm in the industry.* If one firm's price increases, consumers are able to go to other firms quite easily. Thus, the demand facing a single firm in an industry may be quite elastic because competitors produce goods that are close substitutes. But consider what happens if the *industry* price goes up, that is, all firms in the industry increase their prices in unison. In this case, price-sensitive consumers are limited in their course of action: to do without the good or to find a good in another industry to replace it. If these options are infeasible, the third option is to pay the higher price. Thus, industry demand is less elastic. The same point applies to the case where a single monopolist dominates an industry or product line. Other things being

---

[8]Caution: The strictly vertical demand curve should be thought of as a hypothetical, limiting case, not something that could occur in practice. If it did occur, the firm could raise the good's price as high as it wished, maintaining an unchanged level of sales. By doing so, it would earn unlimited profit. We all know, however, that there is no such "free lunch" in the business world.

equal, the monopolist's demand is less elastic (since it is the sole producer) than the demand facing a particular firm in a multifirm industry.

A third determinant of price elasticity is the proportion of income a consumer spends on the good in question. The issue here is the cost of searching for suitable alternatives to the good. It takes time and money to compare substitute products. If an individual spends a significant portion of income on a good, he or she will find it worthwhile to search for and compare the prices of other goods. Thus, the consumer is price sensitive. If spending on the good represents only a small portion of total income, however, the search for substitutes will not be worth the time, effort, and expense. Thus, other things being equal, the demand for small-ticket items tends to be relatively inelastic.

Finally, time of adjustment is an important influence on elasticity. When the price of gasoline dramatically increased in the last five years, consumers initially had little recourse but to pay higher prices at the pump. Much of the population continued to drive to work in large, gas-guzzling cars. As time passed, however, consumers have begun to make adjustments. Some commuters switched from automobiles to buses or other means of public transit. Gas guzzlers have been replaced by smaller, more fuel-efficient cars including hybrids. Some workers moved closer to their jobs, and when jobs turned over, workers found new jobs closer to their homes. Thus, in the short run, the demand for gasoline is relatively inelastic. But in the long run, demand appears to be much more elastic as people are able to cut back consumption by a surprising amount. Thus, the time of adjustment is crucial. As a general rule, demand is more elastic in the long run than in the short run.

Other Elasticities

The elasticity concept can be applied to any explanatory variable that affects sales. Many of these variables—income, the prices of substitutes and complements, and changes in population or preferences—have already been mentioned. (An additional important variable affecting sales is the firm's spending on advertising and promotion.) To illustrate, consider the elasticity of demand with respect to income (Y). This is defined as

$$E_Y = \frac{\% \text{ change in } Q}{\% \text{ change in } Y} = \frac{\Delta Q / Q}{\Delta Y / Y}$$

in a manner exactly analogous to the earlier price elasticity definition.[9] **Income elasticity** links percentage changes in sales to changes in income, *all*

[9]If an infinitesimal change is considered, the corresponding elasticity expression is $E_Y = (dQ/Q)/(dY/Y)$. In addition, when multiple factors affect demand, the partial-derivative notation emphasizes the separate effect of income changes on demand, all other factors held constant. In this case, we write $E_Y = (\partial Q/Q)/(\partial Y/Y)$.

other factors held constant. For example, the income elasticity of demand for spending on groceries is about .25; that is, a 10 percent increase in income results in only about a 2.5 percent increase in spending in this category. In other words, a household's consumption of groceries is relatively insensitive to changes in income. In contrast, restaurant expenditures are highly sensitive to income changes. The income elasticity for this type of spending is about 3.0.

A main impact on the sales outlook for an industry, a firm, or a particular good or service is the overall strength of the economy. When the economy grows strongly, so do personal income, business profits, and government income. Gains in these income categories generate increased spending on a wide variety of goods and services. Conversely, when income falls during a recession, so do sales across the economy. Income elasticity thus provides an important measure of the sensitivity of sales for a given product to swings in the economy. For instance, if $E_Y = 1$, sales move exactly in step with changes in income. If $E_Y > 1$, sales are highly *cyclical*, that is, sensitive to income. For an inferior good, sales are *countercyclical*, that is, move in the opposite direction of income, and $E_Y < 0$.

CROSS-PRICE ELASTICITIES   A final, commonly used elasticity links changes in a good's sales to changes in the prices of related goods. **Cross-price elasticity** is defined as

$$E_{P^\circ} = \frac{\Delta Q / Q}{\Delta P^\circ / P^\circ},$$

where P° denotes the price of a related good or service. If the goods in question are substitutes, the cross-price elasticity will be positive. For instance, if a 5 percent cut in a competitor's intercity fare is expected to reduce the airline's ticket sales by 2 percent, we find $E_{P^\circ} = (-2\%)/(-5\%) = .4$. The magnitude of E_{P° provides a useful measure of the substitutability of the two goods.[10] For example, if $E_{P^\circ} = .05$, sales of the two goods are almost unrelated. If E_{P° is very large, however, the two goods are nearly perfect substitutes. Finally, if a pair of goods are complements, the cross-price elasticity is negative. An increase in the complementary good's price will adversely affect sales.

Table 3.1 provides estimated price and income elasticities for selected goods and services.

---

[10]We could also examine the effect of a change in the airline's fare on the competitor's ticket sales. Note that the two cross-price elasticities may be very different in magnitude. For instance, in our example the airline flies only half as many flights as its competitor. Given its smaller market share and presence, one would predict that changes in the airline's price would have a much smaller impact on the sales of its larger rival than vice versa.

TABLE 3.1

Good or Service	Price Elasticity	Income Elasticity	
Air travel:			Estimated Price and Income Elasticities for Selected Goods and Services
Business	−.18	1.1	
Nonbusiness	−.38	1.8	
Automobiles:		1.9	
Subcompact	−.81		
Luxury	−2.1		
Beef	−.5	.51	
Cigarettes:			
All smokers	−.7		
Ages 15–18	−1.4		
Gasoline (1 year)	−.32	.20	
Housing		.34	
Telephone calls			
Long distance	−.5	1.0	

Source: Elasticities were compiled by the authors from articles in economic journals and other published sources.

Price Elasticity and Prediction

Price elasticity is an essential tool for estimating the sales response to possible price changes. A simple rearrangement of the elasticity definition (Equation 3.7) gives the predictive equation:

$$\Delta Q / Q = E_P (\Delta P / P) \qquad [3.9]$$

For instance, in Table 3.1, the short-term (i.e., one-year) price elasticity of demand for gasoline is approximately −.3. This indicates that if the average price of gasoline were to increase from $2.50 to $3.00 per gallon (a 20 percent increase), then consumption of gasoline (in gallons) would fall by only 6 percent (−.3 × 20%). The table also shows that the price elasticity of demand for luxury cars is −2.1. A modest 5 percent increase in their average sticker price implies a 10.5 percent drop in sales. (Caution: Equation 3.9 is exact for very small changes but only an approximation for large percentage changes, over which elasticities may vary.)

How does one estimate the impact on sales from changes in two or more factors that affect demand? A simple example can illustrate the method. In Table 3.1, the price and income elasticities for nonbusiness air travel are estimated to be $E_P = -.38$ and $E_Y = 1.8$, respectively. In the coming year, average airline fares are expected to rise by 8 percent and income by 5 percent. What will be the impact on the number of tickets sold to nonbusiness travelers? The answer is found by adding the separate effects due to each change:

$$\Delta Q/Q = E_P(\Delta P/P) + E_Y(\Delta Y/Y) \qquad [3.10]$$

Therefore, $\Delta Q/Q = (-.38)(8\%) + (1.8)(5\%) = 6\%$. Sales are expected to increase by about 6 percent.

DEMAND ANALYSIS AND OPTIMAL PRICING

In this section, we put demand analysis to work by examining three important managerial decisions: (1) the special case of revenue maximization, (2) optimal markup pricing, and (3) price discrimination.

Price Elasticity, Revenue, and Marginal Revenue

What can we say about the elasticity along any downward-sloping, linear demand curve? First, we must be careful to specify the starting quantity and price (the point on the demand curve) from which percentage changes are measured. From Equation 3.8b, we know that $E_P = (dQ/dP)(P/Q)$. The slope of the demand curve is dP/dQ (as it is conventionally drawn with price on the vertical axis). Thus, the first term in the elasticity expression, dQ/dP, is simply the inverse of this slope and is constant everywhere along the curve. The term P/Q decreases as one moves downward along the curve. Thus, along a linear demand curve, moving to lower prices and greater quantities reduces elasticity; that is, demand becomes more inelastic.

As a concrete illustration of this point, consider a software firm that is trying to determine the optimal price for one of its popular software programs. Management estimates this product's demand curve to be

$$Q = 1,600 - 4P,$$

where Q is copies sold per week and P is in dollars. We note for future reference that $dQ/dP = -4$. Figure 3.3a shows this demand curve as well as the associated marginal revenue curve. In the figure, the midpoint of the demand curve is marked by point M: $Q = 800$ and $P = \$200$. Two other points, A and B, along the demand curve also are shown.

The figure depicts a useful result. Any linear demand curve can be divided into two regions. *Exactly midway along the linear demand curve, price elasticity is unity.* To the northwest (at higher prices and lower quantities),

FIGURE 3.3

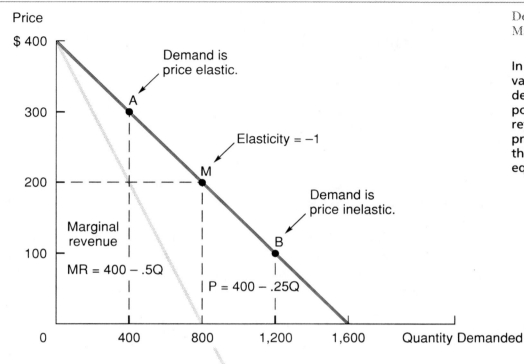

(a)

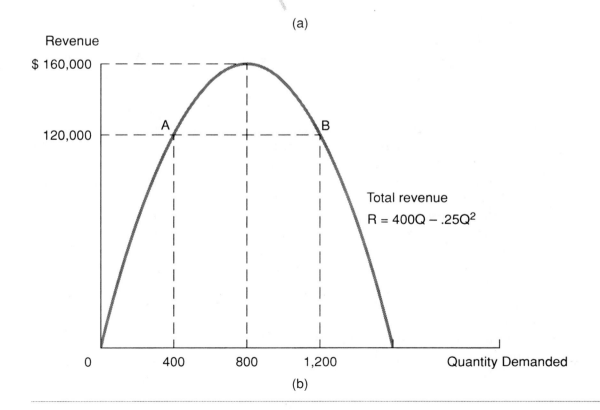

(b)

Demand, Revenue, and Marginal Revenue

In part (a), elasticity varies along a linear demand curve. The point of maximum revenue occurs at a price and quantity such that MR = 0 or, equivalently, $E_P = -1$.

demand is elastic. To the southeast (at lower prices and greater quantities), demand is inelastic. Consider a point on the inelastic part of the curve such as B: P = \$100 and Q = 1,200. Here the point elasticity is $E_P = (dQ/dP)(P/Q) = (-4)(100/1,200) = -.33$. Conversely, at a point on the elastic portion of the demand curve such as A (P = \$300 and Q = 400), the point elasticity is $E_P = (-4)(300/400) = -3.0$.

CHECK STATION 3   Compute the price elasticity at point M. Show that the elasticity is unity. This result holds for the midpoint of any linear demand curve.

Figure 3.3b depicts the firm's total revenue curve for different sales volumes. It displays the familiar shape of an upside-down U. Total revenue increases as quantity increases up to the revenue peak; at still higher quantities, revenue falls.

Let's carefully trace the relationship between changes in revenue and price elasticity. Suppose management of the software firm is operating at point A on the demand curve in Figure 3.3a. Its price is \$300, it sells 400 copies of the software program, and it earns \$120,000 in revenue per week. Could the firm increase its revenue by cutting its price to spur greater sales? If demand is elastic, the answer is yes. Under elastic demand, the percentage increase in quantity is greater than the percentage fall in price. Thus, revenue—the product of price and quantity—must increase. The positive change in quantity more than compensates for the fall in price. Figure 3.3b shows clearly that starting from point A, revenue increases when the firm moves to greater quantities (and lower prices). Starting from any point of elastic demand, the firm can increase revenue by reducing its price.

Now suppose the software firm is operating originally at point B, where demand is inelastic. In this case, the firm can increase revenue by raising its price. Because demand is inelastic, the percentage drop in quantity of sales is smaller than the percentage increase in price. With price rising by more than quantity falls, revenue necessarily increases. Again, the revenue graph in Figure 3.3b tells the story. Starting from point B, the firm increases its revenue by reducing its quantity (and raising its price). So long as demand is inelastic, revenue moves in the same direction as price. By raising price and reducing quantity, the firm moves back toward the revenue peak.

Putting these two results together, we see that when demand is inelastic or elastic, revenue can be increased (by a price hike or cut, respectively). It follows that revenue is maximized when neither a price hike nor a cut will help; that is, when demand is unitary elastic, $E_P = -1$. In the software example, the revenue-maximizing quantity is Q = 800 (see Figure 3.3b). This quantity (along with the price, P = \$200) is precisely the point of unitary elasticity (in Figure 3.3a).

Our discussion has suggested an interesting and important relationship between marginal revenue and price elasticity. The same point can be made mathematically. By definition, $MR = dR/dQ = d(PQ)/dQ$. The derivative of this product (see Rule 5 of the appendix to Chapter 2) is

$$MR = P(dQ/dQ) + (dP/dQ)Q \qquad [3.11]$$
$$= P + P(dP/dQ)(Q/P)$$
$$= P[1 + (dP/dQ)(Q/P)]$$
$$= P[1 + 1/E_P].$$

For instance, if demand is elastic (say, $E_P = -3$), MR is positive; that is, an increase in quantity (via a reduction in price) will increase total revenue. If demand is inelastic (say, $E_P = -.6$), MR is negative; an increase in quantity causes total revenue to decline. If elasticity is precisely -1, MR is zero. Figure 3.3a shows clearly the relationship between MR and E_P.

Maximizing Revenue

As we saw in Chapter 2, there generally is a conflict between the goals of maximizing revenue and maximizing profit. Clearly, maximizing profit is the appropriate objective because it takes into account not only revenues but also relevant costs. In some important special cases, however, the two goals coincide or are equivalent. This occurs when the firm faces what is sometimes called a **pure selling problem**: a situation where it supplies a good or service while incurring *no* variable cost (or a variable cost so small that it safely can be ignored). It should be clear that, without any variable costs, the firm maximizes its ultimate profit by setting price and output to gain as much revenue as possible (from which any *fixed* costs then are paid). The following pricing problems serve as examples.

- A software firm is deciding the optimal selling price for its software.
- A manufacturer must sell (or otherwise dispose of) an inventory of unsold merchandise.
- A professional sports franchise must set its ticket prices for its home games.
- An airline is attempting to fill its empty seats on a regularly scheduled flight.

In each of these examples, variable costs are absent (or very small). The cost of an additional software copy (documentation and disk included) is trivial. In the case of airline or sports tickets, revenues crucially depend on how many tickets are sold. The cost of an additional passenger or spectator is negligible once the flight or event has been scheduled. As for inventory, production costs are sunk; selling costs are negligible or very small. Thus, in each case the firm maximizes profits by setting price and output to maximize revenue.

How does the firm determine its revenue-maximizing price and output? There are two equivalent answers to this question. The first answer is to apply Chapter 2's fundamental rule: MR = MC. In the case of a pure selling problem, marginal cost is zero. Thus, the rule becomes MR = 0, exactly as one would expect. This rule instructs the manager to push sales to the point where there is no more additional revenue to be had—MR = 0—and no further.

From the preceding discussion, we have established a second, equivalent answer: Revenue is maximized at the point of unitary elasticity. If demand were inelastic or elastic, revenue could be increased by raising or lowering price, respectively. The following proposition sums up these results:

> Revenue is maximized at the price and quantity for which marginal revenue is zero or, equivalently, the price elasticity of demand is unity (-1).

Note that this result confirms that the point of unitary elasticity occurs at the midpoint of a linear demand curve. For the sales quantity at the midpoint, marginal revenue is exactly zero (since the MR curve cuts the horizontal axis at the midpoint quantity). But when MR = 0, it is also true that $E_P = -1$.

CHECK STATION 4   The management of a professional sports team has a 36,000-seat stadium it wishes to fill. It recognizes, however, that the number of seats sold (Q) is very sensitive to average ticket prices (P). It estimates demand to be $Q = 60,000 - 3,000P$. Assuming the team's costs are known and do not vary with attendance, what is management's optimal pricing policy?

Pricing the Olympics Telecasts and Online Access

It is not easy to estimate the state of demand for a new product or one with a very short track record of sales. One famous example of overestimating demand involved Triplecast, NBC and Cablevision's pay-per-view cable coverage of the 1992 Summer Olympics in Barcelona. Based on extensive surveys of potential demand, the partners hoped to raise $250 million in revenue by attracting some 2 million subscribers for three channels of nonstop Olympics coverage over 15 days. Accordingly, NBC set the average package price at $125 for complete coverage and offered a separate price of $29.95 per day. However, as the games began, fewer than 300,000 homes had subscribed, and even with aggressive price cutting no more than 500,000 sports fans tuned in.

America Online (AOL) experienced the opposite problem when it instituted a radical pricing shift in November 1996. In a bid to increase its customer base, it replaced its old monthly fee of $9.95 (good for five free hours) and $2.95 for each additional hour by a fixed monthly fee of $19.95 for unlimited access. The results should have been predictable. AOL's customer base did increase, but, more important, current customers more than doubled their daily time online. Constrained by a fixed capacity, AOL's system overloaded. Customers received busy signals and experienced interminable waits for access. One commentator likened the new pricing policy to offering a perpetual all-you-can-eat buffet to food lovers, who once seated would eat through breakfast, lunch, and dinner, fearing they would not get back in if they gave up their table. Customers were disaffected, and AOL was forced by regulators to give widespread refunds while it scrambled to increase its network capacity at a cost of $350 million.

What are the lessons from these examples? In the case of Triplecast, it appears that management faced a pure selling problem, the marginal cost of each additional subscriber being insignificant. Unfortunately, management dramatically misjudged its demand curve as well as the point of maximum revenue along it. Once it recognized the depressed state of demand, management instituted a dramatic price cut—its best course of action to capture what revenue was available. Over time, the cable companies reduced their package price from $125 to $99 to $79 and the daily price from $29.95 to $19.95 to $11.95. However, these actions at best were able only to stem large losses.

For AOL, there appears to be a happier ending. Despite the high monetary and reputation cost of its one-price policy, the company achieved a key objective: raising its customer base over 18 months from 8 million to some 11 million subscribers. Fueled by revenues from retailers, advertisers, and publishers, who would pay for access to AOL's customers, the company earned its first quarterly profits in 1998. It has since raised its monthly fee to $25.90 while continuing to expand its network capacity.

Optimal Markup Pricing

There is a close link between demand for a firm's product and the firm's optimal pricing policy. In the remainder of this chapter, we will take a close and careful look at the trade-off between price and profit. Recall that in Chapter 2, the focus was squarely on the firm's quantity decision. Once the firm determined its optimal output by weighing marginal revenue and marginal cost, it was a simple matter to set price in order to sell exactly that much output. Now we shift our focus to price and consider a somewhat different trade-off.

To illustrate this trade-off, we can write the firm's contribution as

$$\text{Contribution} = (P - MC)Q,$$

where, for simplicity, MC is assumed to be constant. How should the firm set its price to maximize its contribution (and, therefore, its profit)? The answer depends on how responsive demand is to changes in price, that is, on price elasticity of demand. Raising price increases the firm's contribution per unit (or margin), P − MC. But to a greater or lesser degree, a price hike also reduces the total volume of sales Q. If sales are relatively unresponsive to price (i.e., demand is relatively inelastic), the firm can raise its price and increase its margin without significantly reducing quantity. In this instance, the underlying trade-off works in favor of high prices.

Alternatively, suppose demand is very elastic. In this instance, a price increase would bring a large drop in sales to the detriment of total contribution. Here, the way to maximize contribution (and profit) is to play the other side of the trade-off. The firm should pursue a policy of discount pricing to maximize profitability. As we shall see, the correct pricing policy depends on a careful analysis of the price elasticity of demand. Indeed, when the firm has the ability to segment markets, it may benefit by trading on demand differences. As noted in this chapter's opening example, airlines set a variety of different ticket prices—charging high fares to less price-sensitive business travelers and discounting prices to economy-minded vacation travelers.

In Chapter 2, we focused on the application of the MR = MC rule as a way to determine the firm's optimal level of output. It is possible to write down and apply a modified (but exactly equivalent) version of the MR = MC rule to derive a simple rule for the firm's profit-maximizing *price*. The firm's optimal price is determined as follows:

$$\frac{P - MC}{P} = \frac{1}{-E_P}.$$

[3.12]

This equation, called the **markup rule**, indicates that

> The size of the firm's markup (above marginal cost and expressed as a percentage of price) depends inversely on the price elasticity of demand for a good or service.

The markup is always positive. (Note that E_P is negative, so the right-hand side is positive.) What happens as demand becomes more and more price elastic (i.e., price sensitive)? The right-hand side of the markup rule becomes smaller, and so does the optimal markup on the left-hand side. In short, the more elastic is demand, the smaller is the markup above marginal cost.[11]

The markup rule is intuitively appealing and is the most commonly noted form of the optimal pricing rule. Nonetheless, to make computations easier, it is useful to rearrange the rule to read

$$P = \left(\frac{E_P}{1 + E_P}\right)MC.$$

[3.13]

Using this formula, Table 3.2 lists optimal prices by elasticity. Again, we see that greater elasticities imply lower prices.

CAUTION   The markup rule is applicable only in the case of *elastic* demand. Why not inelastic demand? The simple fact is that *the firm's current price cannot be profit maximizing if demand is inelastic.* Under inelastic demand, the firm could

---

[11] Here is how the markup rule is derived. From Equation 3.11, we know that MR = $P[1 + 1/E_P]$. Setting MR = MC, we have $P + P/E_P = MC$. This can be written as $P - MC = -P/E_P$ and, finally, $[P - MC]/P = -1/E_P$, the markup rule. Thus, the markup rule is derived from and equivalent to the MR = MC rule.

TABLE 3.2

Elasticities and
Optimal Prices

The markup of price
above marginal cost
varies inversely with
the elasticity of
demand.

	Elasticity	Markup Factor $E_P/(1 + E_P)$	MC	Price
	−1.5	3.0	100	300
	−2.0	2.0	100	200
	−3.0	1.5	100	150
	−5.0	1.25	100	125
	−11.0	1.1	100	110
	−∞	1.0	100	100

raise its price and increase its revenue. Because it would sell less output at the higher price, it also would lower its production cost at the same time. Thus, profit would increase. In short, the firm should never operate on the inelastic portion of its demand curve. It should increase profit by raising price and moving to the elastic portion; the optimal markup rule tells it exactly how far it should move into the elastic region of demand.

Business Behavior —Pricing in Practice

The markup rule is a formal expression of the conventional wisdom that *price should depend on both demand and cost*. The rule prescribes how prices should be determined in principle. In practice, managers often adopt other pricing policies. The most common practice is to use *full-cost pricing*. With this method, price is

$$P = (1 + m)AC, \qquad [3.14]$$

where AC denotes total average cost (defined as total cost divided by total output) and m denotes the markup of price above average cost.

Our study of optimal managerial decisions suggests two points of criticism about full-cost pricing. First, full-cost pricing uses average cost—the incorrect measure of relevant cost—as its base. The logic of marginal analysis in general and the optimal markup rule (Equation 3.13) in particular show that optimal price and quantity depend on marginal cost. Fixed costs, which are counted in AC but not in MC, have no effect on the choice of optimal price and quantity.[12] Thus, to the extent that AC differs from MC, the full-cost method can lead to pricing errors.

[12]Fixed costs obviously are important for the decision about whether to produce the good. For production to be profitable in the long run, price must exceed average cost, $P \geq AC$. If not, the firm should cease production and shut down. Chapter 6 provides an extensive discussion of this so-called shut-down rule for firms producing single and multiple products.

Second, the percentage markup should depend on the elasticity of demand. There is considerable evidence that firms vary their markups in rough accord with price elasticity.[13] Gourmet frozen foods carry much higher markups than generic food items. Inexpensive digital watches ($15 and under) have lower markups than fine Swiss watches or jewelers' watches. Designer dresses and wedding dresses carry much higher markups than off-the-rack dresses. In short, producers' markups are linked to elasticities, at least in a qualitative sense. Nonetheless, it is unlikely that firms' full-cost markups exactly duplicate optimal markups. Obviously, a firm that sets a fixed markup *irrespective* of elasticity is needlessly sacrificing profit.[14]

CHECK STATION 5 The U.S. cigarette industry has negotiated with Congress and government agencies to settle liability claims against it. Under the proposed settlement, cigarette companies will make fixed annual payments to the government based on their historic market shares. Suppose a manufacturer estimates its marginal cost at $1.00 per pack, its own price elasticity at −2, and sets its price at $2.00. The company's settlement obligations are expected to raise its average total cost per pack by about $.60. What effect will this have on its optimal price?

Price Discrimination

Price discrimination occurs when a firm sells the same good or service to different buyers at different prices.[15] As the following examples suggest, price discrimination is a common business practice.

- Airlines charge full fares to business travelers, while offering discount fares to vacationers.

- Firms sell the same products under different brand names or labels at different prices.

---

[13]In evaluating the practice of full-cost pricing, the real issue is how close it comes to duplicating optimal markup pricing. Even if firms do not apply the optimal markup rule, they may price as though they did. For instance, a firm that experiments with different full-cost markups may soon discover the profit-maximizing price (without ever computing an elasticity). In contrast, a rival firm that retains a suboptimal price will earn a lower profit and ultimately may be driven from the highly competitive market. So-called natural economic selection (elimination of less profitable firms) means that the surviving firms are ones that have succeeded in earning maximum profits.

In some circumstances, full-cost pricing is a lower-cost alternative to the optimal markup rule. Estimating the price elasticities necessary for setting optimal markups is sometimes quite costly. Accordingly, the firm may choose to continue its current pricing policy (believing it to be approximately optimal) rather than generating new and costly elasticity estimates and setting a new markup.

[14]For an instance of an entrepreneur suboptimally operating on the inelastic portion of the demand curve, see S. Leavitt, "An Economist Sells Bagels: A Case Study in Profit Maximization," Working Paper 12152, National Bureau of Economic Research (March 2006).

[15]Here, we are discussing legal methods of price discrimination, that is, we are using the term *discrimination* in its neutral sense. Obviously, the civil rights laws prohibit economic discrimination (including unfair pricing practices) based on gender, race, or national origin. The antitrust statutes also limit specific cases of price discrimination that can be shown to significantly reduce competition.

- Providers of professional services (doctors, consultants, lawyers, etc.) set different rates for different clients.

- Manufacturers introduce products at high prices before gradually dropping price over time.

- Publishers of academic journals charge much higher subscription rates to libraries and institutions than to individual subscribers.

- Businesses offer student and senior citizen discounts for many goods and services.

- Manufacturers sell the same products at higher prices in the retail market than in the wholesale market.

- Movies play in "first-run" theaters at higher ticket prices before being released to suburban theaters at lower prices.

When a firm practices price discrimination, it sets different prices for different market segments even though its costs of serving each customer group are the same. Thus, price discrimination is purely demand based. Of course, firms may also charge different prices for the "same" good or service because of cost differences. (For instance, transportation cost may be one reason why the same make and model of automobile sells for significantly different prices on the West and East coasts.) But cost-based pricing does not fall under the heading of price discrimination.

Price discrimination is a departure from the pricing model we have examined up to this point. Thus far, the firm has been presumed to set a *single* market-clearing price. Obviously, charging different prices to different market segments, as in the examples just listed, allows the firm considerably more pricing flexibility. More to the point, the firm can increase its profit with a policy of optimal price discrimination (when the opportunity exists).

Two conditions must hold for a firm to practice price discrimination profitably. First, the firm must be able to identify market segments that differ with respect to price elasticity of demand. As we show shortly, the firm profits by charging a higher price to the more inelastic (i.e., less price-sensitive) market segment(s). Second, it must be possible to *enforce* the different prices paid by different segments. This means that market segments receiving higher prices must be unable to take advantage of lower prices. (In particular, a low-price buyer must be unable to resell the good or service profitably to a high-price buyer.) The conditions necessary to ensure different prices exist in the preceding examples. Sometimes the conditions are quite subtle. Business travelers rarely can purchase discount air tickets because they cannot meet advance-booking or minimum-stay requirements. First-run moviegoers pay a high ticket price because they are unwilling to wait until the film comes to a lower-price theater.

How can the firm maximize its profit via price discrimination? There are several (related) ways to answer this question. The markup rule provides a ready explanation of this practice. To illustrate, suppose a firm has identified two market segments, each with its own demand curve. (Chapter 4 discusses the means by which these different demand curves can be identified and estimated.) Then the firm can treat the different segments as separate markets for the good. The firm simply applies the markup rule twice to determine its optimal price and sales for each market segment. Thus, it sets price according to $P = [E_P/(1 + E_P)]MC$ (Equation 3.13) separately for each market segment. Presumably the marginal cost of producing for each market is the same. With the same MC inserted into the markup rule, the difference in the price charged to each segment is due solely to differences in elasticities of demand. For instance, suppose a firm identifies two market segments with price elasticities of -5 and -3, respectively. The firm's marginal cost of selling to either segment is \$200. Then, according to the markup rule, the firm's optimal prices are \$250 and \$300, respectively. We see that the segment with the more inelastic demand pays the higher price. The firm charges the higher price to less price-sensitive buyers (with little danger of losing sales). At the same time, it attracts the more price-sensitive customers (who would buy relatively little of the good at the higher price) by offering them a discounted price. Thus, by means of optimal price discrimination, the firm maximizes its profit.[16]

Like the method just described, a second approach to price discrimination treats different segments as distinct markets and sets out to maximize profit separately in each. The difference is that the manager's focus is on optimal sales quantities rather than prices. The optimal sales quantity for each market is determined by setting the extra revenue from selling an extra unit in that market equal to the marginal cost of production. In short, the firm sets MR = MC in each market.

Multinational Production and Pricing Revisited

In the first example in Chapter 1, an automobile producer faced the problem of pricing its output at home and abroad. We are now ready to put demand analysis to work to determine the firm's optimal decisions. The facts are as follows: The producer faces relatively little competition at home; it is one of the most efficient domestic producers, and trade barriers limit the import of foreign cars. However, it competes in the foreign market with many local and foreign

[16]Here is another way to make the same point. Suppose the firm initially made the mistake of charging the same price to both market segments. The markup rule says it can increase its profit by raising one price and lowering the other. Let's check that this is the case. At the common price, let the first segment's demand be more elastic. Now suppose the firm lowers the price charged to the first segment and raises the price charged to the second in just the right amounts to maintain the same *total* sales. Given the differences in elasticities, it can do so while increasing the *average* price at which it sells units. With a higher average price and the same total number of units sold, the dual-pricing strategy has increased revenue. (The revenue gained from the first segment exceeds the revenue lost from the second.) With total output unchanged, profit has increased.

manufacturers. Under these circumstances, demand at home is likely to be much more inelastic than demand in the foreign country. Suppose that the price equations at home (H) and abroad (F) are, respectively,

$$P_H = 30{,}000 - 50Q_H \text{ and } P_F = 25{,}000 - 70Q_F,$$

where price is in dollars per vehicle and quantities are annual sales of vehicles in thousands. Automobiles are produced in a single domestic facility at a marginal cost of $10,000 per vehicle. This is the MC relevant to vehicles sold in the domestic market. Shipping vehicles to the foreign market halfway around the world involves additional transport costs of $1,000 per vehicle. What are the firm's optimal sales quantities and prices?

Addressing this question is straightforward, but the answer may come as a surprise. The quantities of cars sold to the respective markets are determined by the conditions $MR_H = MC_H$ and $MR_F = MC_F$. Therefore, $30{,}000 - 100Q_H = 10{,}000$, and $25{,}000 - 140Q_F = 11{,}000$. The optimal quantities and prices (after substituting back into the demand curves) are $Q_H = 200$ thousand and $P_H = \$20{,}000$ in the domestic market and $Q_F = 100$ thousand and $P_F = \$18{,}000$ in the foreign market. The surprise comes when we compare domestic and foreign prices. Even though the marginal cost of vehicles sold in the foreign market is 10 percent higher than that of cars sold domestically, the foreign price is *lower*—by some 10 percent—than the domestic price. Why is it profitable for the company to sell on the foreign market at a much lower price than at home? It must be because demand is much more elastic abroad than it is domestically. Accordingly, the company's pricing policy is a textbook case of an optimal dual-pricing strategy.

DEMAND-BASED PRICING   As these examples indicate, the ways in which firms price discriminate are varied. Indeed, there are many forms of demand-based pricing that are closely related to price discrimination (although not always called by that name). For instance, resorts in Florida and the Caribbean set much higher nightly rates during the high season (December to March) than at off-peak times. The difference in rates is demand based. (The resorts' operating costs differ little by season.) Vacationers are willing to pay a much higher price for warm climes during the North American winter. Similarly, a convenience store, open 24 hours a day and located along a high-traffic route or intersection, will set premium prices for its merchandise. (Again, the high markups are predominantly demand based and only partly based on higher costs.) Likewise, golf courses charge much higher prices on weekends than on weekdays. Each of these examples illustrates demand-based pricing.

FORMS OF PRICE DISCRIMINATION   Finally, it is useful to distinguish three forms of price discrimination. The practice of charging different prices to different market segments (for which the firm's costs are identical) is often referred to as **third-degree price discrimination**. Airline and movie ticket pricing are examples. Prices differ across market segments, but customers within a market segment pay the same price.

Now suppose the firm could distinguish among different consumers within a market segment. What if the firm knew each customer's demand curve? Then it could practice perfect price discrimination. **First-degree (perfect) price discrimination** occurs when a firm sets a different price for each customer and by doing so extracts the maximum possible sales revenue. As an example, consider an auto dealer who has a large stock of cars for sale and expects 10 serious potential buyers to enter her showroom each week. She posts different model prices, but she knows (and customers know) that the sticker price is a starting point in subsequent negotiations. Each customer knows the maximum price he or she is personally willing to pay for the car in question. If the dealer is a shrewd judge of character, she can guess the range of each buyer's maximum price and, via the negotiations, extract almost this full value. For instance, if four buyers' maximum prices are $6,100, $6,450, $5,950, and $6,200, the perfectly discriminating dealer will negotiate prices nearly equal to these values. In this way, the dealer will sell the four cars for the maximum possible revenue. As this example illustrates, perfect discrimination is fine in principle but much more difficult in practice. Clearly, such discrimination requires that the seller have an unrealistic amount of information. Thus, it serves mainly as a benchmark—a limiting case at best.

Finally, **second-degree price discrimination** occurs when the firm offers different price schedules, and customers choose the terms that best fit their needs. The most common example is the offer of quantity discounts: For large volumes, the seller charges a lower price per unit, so the buyer purchases a larger quantity. With a little thought, one readily recognizes this as a form of profitable price discrimination. High-volume, price-sensitive buyers will choose to purchase larger quantities at a lower unit price, whereas low-volume users will purchase fewer units at a higher unit price. Perhaps the most common form of quantity discounts is the practice of *two-part pricing*. As the term suggests, the total price paid by a customer is

$$P = A + pQ,$$

where A is a fixed fee (paid irrespective of quantity) and p is the additional price per unit. Telephone service, electricity, and residential gas all carry two-part prices. Taxi service, photocopy rental agreements, and amusement park admissions are other examples. Notice that two-part pricing implies a quantity discount; the average price per unit, $P/Q = A/Q + p$, declines as Q increases. Two-part pricing allows the firm to charge customers for access to valuable services (via A) while promoting volume purchases (via low p).

Information Goods

In the last decade, we have witnessed explosive growth in the provision of **information goods and services**. The business press speaks of Internet industries and e-business markets. The *information* label is meant to be both more broad based and more precise. An information good could be a database, game cartridge, news article (in electronic or paper form), piece of music, or piece of software. Information services range from e-mail and instant messaging, to electronic exchanges and auctions, to brokerage and other financial services, to job placements. Of course, information services also include all manner of Internet-based transactions, such as purchasing airline tickets, selling real estate, procuring industrial inputs, and gathering extensive data on potential customers.[17]

Although the information category is broad, all of the preceding examples share a common feature: *Information is costly to produce but cheap (often costless) to reproduce.* In short, any information good or service is characterized by high fixed costs but low or negligible marginal costs. With marginal costs at or near zero, the firm's total costs vary little with output volume, so that average cost per unit sharply declines as output increases. (Creating a $1 million database to serve 1,000 end-users implies an average cost of $1,000 per user. If, instead, it served 500,000 end-users, the average cost drops to $2 per user.) Moreover, with marginal costs negligible, a supplier of an information good once again faces a pure selling problem: how to market, promote, and price its product to maximize revenue (and thereby profit).

Not surprisingly, the early history of e-business activities has been characterized by high up-front costs and the pursuit of customers, revenues, and profits, in that order. In 1999 and 2000, Internet start-ups were the beneficiaries of enormous capital infusions by investors and spectacular market valuations, sometimes before a trace of revenue had been earned. These early Internet ventures are properly regarded as investments, and risky ones at that. Early losses are expected to be balanced by significant future revenues. For instance, strong revenue growth has been the pattern for such information goods as videotapes, CDs, DVDs, MP3 players, and music downloads (once a critical mass of consumers had adopted the new technologies).

In many respects, however, information providers face special revenue issues. First, there are numerous ways in which revenues can be earned. The most familiar is simply setting a price per unit, as in the sale of a music CD, a movie DVD, a piece of software, or content to a Web site. Maximizing total revenue from sales means identifying the unit price such that $E_P = -1$. However, there are myriad other pricing options. When a movie producer sells a DVD to

---

[17]A superb discussion of the economics of information goods can be found in C. Shapiro and H. R. Varian, *Information Rules*, Chapters 1–3, 7 (Boston: Harvard Business School Press, 1999).

Blockbuster for rental, it receives a modest price of $8 per unit, but shares roughly 40 percent of rental revenues with the video chain. Alternatively, software may be sold via site license, allowing group users to enjoy a kind of quantity discount. Internet services are sold by monthly subscription, by pay per use (or per download), or in some combination. Many information services, particularly search engines such as Google and high-traffic Web portals, earn the bulk of their cash flows from advertising revenues. Internet advertising includes banner ads, buttons, pop-up ads, e-mail advertisements, and even Web-page sponsorships to promote brand names. Finally, there are all kinds of indirect revenues. For instance, some information suppliers sell their customer lists to third parties. It is also important to recognize the numerous trade-offs between these different revenue sources. Outright DVD sales compete with DVD rentals. Raising subscription prices lowers traffic and therefore reduces the effectiveness of Web advertising. Obviously, these trade-offs complicate the task of maximizing total revenue. In effect, the information supplier faces multiple, interdependent, and imprecise demand curves.

Second, most information goods exhibit positive **network externalities**. This means that customers of a given information good obtain greater value with a larger network of other connected customers. For instance, wireless telephone customers benefit from the most fully developed nationwide (or worldwide) network, and air travelers benefit from airlines with integrated national and international routes offering multiple daily flights. Teenagers intensively utilize American Online's instant message service. The network need not be physical. For example, the global network of Microsoft's Windows-based operating system and Office applications allows easy file and software transfers among users. By contrast, the separate network of Apple Mac users is much more limited. eBay, the highly successful online auction company, has attracted thousands of sellers and millions of buyers. This enormous network is valuable not only for sellers, who seek the greatest number of potential buyers (and vice versa), but also for eBay, which earns a percentage fee on all auction listings. In all these instances, positive network externalities imply that customer values and, therefore, underlying demand curves shift outward over time as the customer network expands.[18]

What are the strategic implications of network externalities for information providers? Clearly, there is a potential "first-mover" advantage in enlisting the greatest number of users of the information good in question. (We will say more about first-mover strategies in Chapter 10.) Users "in hand" are valuable to the firm not only for the revenue they directly generate, but also because

---

[18] Let there be n members of a network and suppose that each member's value is proportional to the number of other network members $(n - 1)$. Then, according to Metcalf's "law," the total value of the network (summed over all members) is proportional to $(n)(n - 1) = n^2 - n$. In short, network value increases geometrically and rapidly as the square of the number of members. By this reckoning, a mega-network enjoys an enormous value advantage over a smaller network.

they enhance the value of other current and future users (from which the firm also gains revenue). Well aware of this dynamic, e-business firms have aggressively sought customers, not only via advertising and promotions but also by significant price cuts. The extreme cases of cutthroat competition have bred *free* information services of all kinds: electronic greeting cards, e-mail, Internet connections, and online newspapers and magazines. Interestingly, offering free services is a viable business strategy so long as the expanded customer base generates revenue via advertising or from any of the avenues mentioned earlier. In numerous instances, free downloadable versions of stripped-down software or Web content have enticed consumers to trade up to "professional" or "deluxe" versions, for which dollar fees are charged. In other cases, information providers have been locked in savage price wars or battles over free content that have decimated company revenues, thereby degenerating into "wars of attrition." To date, the identities of information suppliers with business plans capable of earning consistent and sustainable revenues are still being sorted out in the market.

CUSTOMIZED PRICING AND PRODUCTS The emergence of electronic commerce and online transactions has greatly expanded the opportunities for market segmentation and price discrimination. From management's point of view, the beauty of information goods and services is that they can be sold over and over again (at negligible marginal cost). Moreover, unlike a traditional good sold at a posted price from a store shelf, the price of an information good (transacted electronically) can be changed minute by minute, customer by customer. Sellers of sophisticated databases—from Reuters to Lexis-Nexis to Bloomberg financial information—set scores of different prices to different customers. As always, prices are set according to elasticities; the most price-sensitive (elastic) customers receive the steepest discounted prices. Consider the ways in which an airline Web site (such as www.delta.com) can price its airline seats. Each time a customer enters a possible itinerary with departure and return dates, the Web page responds with possible flights and prices. These electronic prices already reflect many features: the class of seat, 21-day, 14-day, or 7-day advanced booking, whether a Saturday night stay is included, and so on. By booking in advance and staying a Saturday night, pleasure travelers can take advantage of discounted fares. Business travelers, whose itineraries are not able to meet these restrictions, pay much higher prices. Moreover, the airline can modify prices instantly to reflect changes in demand. If there is a surplus of unsold discount seats as the departure date approaches, the airline can further cut their price or sell them as part of a vacation package (hotel stay, rental car included) at even a steeper discount. (Airlines also release seats to discount sellers, such as Priceline.com, Hotwire.com, and lastminute.com, who sell tickets at steep discounts to the most price-sensitive fliers.) Or, some discount seats might be reassigned as full-fare seats if last-minute business demand for the flight is particularly brisk. Online, the pricing possibilities are endless.

Closely akin to customized pricing is the practice of **versioning**—selling different versions of a given information good or service. Whether it be software, hardware, database access, or other Internet services, this typically means a "standard" version offered at a lower price and a "professional" or "deluxe" version at a premium price. The versions are designed and priced to ensure that different market segments self-select with respect to the product offerings. The inelastic demand segment eagerly elects to pay the premium price to obtain the more powerful version. The more elastic demand segment purchases the stripped-down version at the discounted price. Although customers may not know it, the firm's costs for the different versions are usually indistinguishable. In this respect, versioning is closely akin to third-degree price discrimination. In fact, some software firms begin by designing their premium products and then simply disable key features to create the standard version.

Airline Ticket Pricing Revisited

We are now ready to take a closer look at the pricing policy of the airline in the chapter-opening example and to suggest how it might succeed at yield management. Consider again Equation 3.4, which describes current demand:

$$Q = 580 - 2P.$$

At its present price, \$240, the airline sells 100 coach seats (of the 180 such seats available per flight). Assuming the airline will continue its single daily departure from each city (we presume this is not an issue), what is its optimal fare?

The first step in answering this question is to recognize this as a pure selling problem. With the airline committed to the flight, all associated costs are fixed. The marginal cost of flying 180 passengers versus 100 passengers (a few extra lunches, a bit more fuel, and so on) is negligible. Thus, the airline seeks the pricing policy that will generate the most revenue.

The next step is to appeal to marginal revenue to determine the optimal fare. The price equation is $P = 290 - Q/2$. (Check this.) Consequently, $MR = 290 - Q$. Note: Even at a 100 percent load ($Q = 180$), marginal revenue is positive ($MR = \$110$). If more seats were available, the airline would like to ticket them and increase its revenue. Lacking these extra seats, however, the best the airline can do is set $Q = 180$. From the price equation, \$200 is the price needed to sell this number of seats. The airline should institute a \$40 price cut. By doing so, its revenue will increase from \$24,000 to \$36,000 per flight.[19]

Now let's extend (and complicate) the airline's pricing problem by introducing the possibility of profitable price discrimination. Two distinct market segments purchase coach tickets—business travelers (B) and pleasure travelers (T)—and these groups differ with respect to their demands. Suppose the equations that best represent these segments' demands are $Q_B = 330 - P_B$ and $Q_T = 250 - P_T$. Note that these demand equations are

---

[19] The same point can be made by calculating the price elasticity of demand at $Q = 180$ and $P = 200$. Elasticity can be written as $E_P = (dQ/dP)(P/Q)$. From the demand equation earlier, we know that $dQ/dP = -2$. Therefore, we find that $E_P = (-2)(200/180) = -2.2$. Since demand is elastic, the airline would like to increase revenue by cutting price and increasing the number of coach travelers. But because all its seats are full, the best it can do is set the full-capacity price, \$200.

consistent with Equation 3.4; that is, if both groups are charged price P, total demand is $Q = Q_B + Q_T = (330 - P) + (250 - P) = 580 - 2P$, which is exactly Equation 3.4. The airline's task is to determine Q_B and Q_T to maximize total revenue from the 180 coach seats.

The key to solving this problem is to appeal to the logic of marginal analysis. With the number of seats limited, the airline attains maximum revenue by setting $MR_B = MR_T$. The marginal revenue from selling the last ticket to a business traveler must equal the marginal revenue from selling the last ticket to a pleasure traveler. Why must this be so? Suppose to the contrary that the marginal revenues differ: $MR_B > MR_T$. The airline can increase its revenue simply by selling one less seat to pleasure travelers and one more seat to business travelers. So long as marginal revenues differ across the segments, seats should be transferred from the low-MR segment to the high-MR segment, increasing revenue all the while. Revenue is maximized only when $MR_B = MR_T$.

After writing down the price equations, deriving the associated marginal revenue expressions, and equating them, we have

$$330 - 2Q_B = 250 - 2Q_T,$$

which can be simplified to $Q_B = 40 + Q_T$. The maximum-revenue plan always allocates 40 more seats to business travelers than to pleasure travelers. Since the plane capacity is 180, sales are constrained by $Q_B + Q_T = 180$. Therefore, the optimal quantities are $Q_B = 110$ and $Q_T = 70$. Optimal prices are $P_B = \$220$ and $P_T = \$180$. In turn, if we substitute $Q_B = 110$ into the expression $MR_B = 330 - 2Q_B$, we find that $MR_B = \$110$ per additional seat. (Of course, MR_T is also $\$110$ per seat.) Finally, total revenue is computed as $R = R_B + R_T = (\$220)(110) + (\$180)(70) = \$36,800$. Recall that maximum revenue under a single price system was $\$36,000$. Optimal yield management (price discrimination) has squeezed an additional $\$800$ out of passengers on the flight. As the chapter-opening example suggests, additional revenue can be gained by increasing the number of different fares, from two to as many as 12 or more.

Suppose the airline's management is considering adding an extra flight every second day. Therefore, average daily capacity would increase from 180 to 270 seats. The additional cost of offering this extra flight is estimated at $\$50$ per seat. Show that adding this "second-day" flight would be profitable but that an additional "everyday" flight would not. Determine the new ticket prices for the two classes.

CHECK STATION 6

SUMMARY

Decision-Making Principles

1. Optimal managerial decisions depend on an analysis of demand.
2. In particular, the firm's optimal uniform price is determined by the markup rule. This price depends on marginal cost and the price elasticity of demand.
3. Where the opportunity exists, the firm can increase its profit by practicing price discrimination.

Nuts and Bolts

1. The demand function shows, in equation form, the relationship between the unit sales of a good or service and one or more economic variables.
   a. The demand curve depicts the relationship between quantity and price. A change in price is represented by a movement along the demand curve. A change in any other economic variable shifts the demand curve.
   b. A pair of goods are substitutes if an increase in demand for one causes a fall in demand for the other. In particular, a price cut for one good reduces sales of the other.
   c. A pair of goods are complements if an increase in demand for one causes an increase in demand for the other. In particular, a price cut for one good increases sales of the other.
   d. A good is normal if its sales increase with increases in income.

2. The price elasticity of demand measures the percentage change in sales for a given percentage change in the good's price, all other factors held constant: $E_P = (\Delta Q/Q)/(\Delta P/P)$.
   a. Demand is unitary elastic if $E_P = -1$. In turn, demand is elastic if $E_P < -1$. Finally, demand is inelastic if $-1 < E_P < 0$.
   b. Revenue is maximized at the price and quantity for which marginal revenue is zero or, equivalently, the price elasticity of demand is unity.

3. The optimal markup rule is $(P - MC)/P = -1/E_P$. The firm's optimal markup (above marginal cost and expressed as a percentage of price) varies inversely with the price elasticity of demand for the good or service. (Remember that the firm's price cannot be profit maximizing if demand is inelastic.)

4. Price discrimination occurs when a firm sells the same good or service to different buyers at different prices (based on different price elasticities of demand). Prices in various market segments are determined according to the optimal markup rule.

Questions and Problems

1. During a five-year period, the ticket sales of a city's professional basketball team have increased 30 percent at the same time that average ticket prices have risen by 50 percent. Do these changes imply an upward-sloping demand curve? Explain.

2. A retail store faces a demand equation for Roller Blades given by

$$Q = 180 - 1.5P,$$

where Q is the number of pairs sold per month and P is the price per pair in dollars.

   a. The store currently charges P = $80 per pair. At this price, determine the number of pairs sold.

   b. If management were to raise the price to $100, what would be the impact on pairs sold? On the store's revenue from Roller Blades?

   c. Compute the point elasticity of demand first at P = $80, then at P = $100. At which price is demand more price sensitive?

3. Management of McPablo's Food Shops has completed a study of weekly demand for its "old-fashioned" tacos in 53 regional markets. The study revealed that

$$Q = 400 - 1{,}200P + .8A + 55Pop + 800P°,$$

where Q is the number of tacos sold per store per week, A is the level of local advertising expenditure (in dollars), Pop denotes the local population (in thousands), and P° is the average taco price of local competitors. For the typical McPablo's outlet, P = $1.50, A = $1,000, Pop = 40, and P° = $1.

   a. Estimate the weekly sales for the typical McPablo's outlet.

   b. What is the current price elasticity for tacos? What is the advertising elasticity?

   c. Should McPablo's raise its taco prices? Why or why not?

4. A minor league baseball team is trying to predict ticket sales for the upcoming season and is considering changing ticket prices.

   a. The elasticity of ticket sales with respect to the size of the local population is estimated to be about .7. Briefly explain what this number means. If the local population increases from 60,000 to 61,500, what is the predicted change in ticket sales?

   b. Currently, a typical fan pays an average ticket price of $10. The price elasticity of demand for tickets is −.6. Management is thinking of raising the average ticket price to $11. Compute the predicted percentage change in tickets sold. Would you expect ticket revenue to rise or fall?

   c. The typical fan also consumes $8 worth of refreshments at the game. Thus, at the original $10 average price, each admission generates $18 in *total* revenue for team management. Would raising ticket prices to $11 increase or reduce *total* revenue? Provide a careful explanation of your finding. (Hint: If you wish, you may assume a certain number of tickets sold per game, say 5,000. However, to answer the question the precise number of tickets need not be specified.)

5. a. General Motors (GM) produces light trucks in several Michigan factories, where its annual fixed costs are $180 million, and its marginal cost per truck is approximately $20,000. Regional demand

for the trucks is given by: $P = 30{,}000 - 0.1Q$, where P denotes price in dollars and Q denotes annual sales of trucks. Find GM's profit-maximizing output level and price. Find the annual profit generated by light trucks.

b. GM is getting ready to export trucks to several markets in South America. Based on several marketing surveys, GM has found the elasticity of demand in these foreign markets to be $E_P = -9$ for a wide range of prices (between $20,000 and $30,000). The additional cost of shipping (including paying some import fees) is about $800 per truck. One manager argues that the foreign price should be set at $800 above the domestic price, in part (a), to cover the transportation cost. Do you agree that this is the optimal price for foreign sales? Justify your answer.

c. GM also produces an economy ("no frills") version of its light truck at a marginal cost of $12,000 per vehicle. However, at the price set by GM, $20,000 per truck, customer demand has been very disappointing. GM has recently discontinued production of this model but still finds itself with an inventory of 18,000 unsold trucks. The best estimate of demand for the remaining trucks is

$$P = 30{,}000 - Q.$$

One manager recommends keeping the price at $20,000; another favors cutting the price to sell the entire inventory. What price (one of these or some other price) should GM set and how many trucks should it sell? Justify your answer.

6. Over the last decade, Apple Computer has seen its global share of the personal computer market fall from above 10 percent to less than 5 percent. Despite a keenly loyal customer base, Apple has found it more and more difficult to compete in a market dominated by the majority standard: PCs with Microsoft's Windows-based operating system and Intel's microchips. Indeed, software developers put a lower priority on writing Mac applications than on Windows applications.

a. In the 1980s and 1990s, Apple vigorously protected its proprietary hardware and software and refused to license Mac clones. What effect did this decision have on long-run demand?

b. In the early 1990s, Apple enjoyed high markups on its units. In 1995 Apple's chief, John Sculley, insisted on keeping Mac's gross profit margin at 50 to 55 percent, even in the face of falling demand. (Gross profit margin is measured as total revenue minus total variable costs expressed as a percentage of total revenue.) At this time, the business of selling PCs was becoming more and more "commodity-like." Indeed, the price elasticity facing a particular company was estimated in the neighborhood of $E_P = -4$. Using the markup rule of equation 3.12, carefully assess Sculley's strategy.

c. Recently, Apple has discontinued several of its lower-priced models and has expanded its efforts in the education and desktop publishing markets. In addition, recent software innovations allow Macs to read most documents, data, and spreadsheets generated on other PCs. Do these initiatives make sense? How will they affect demand?

7. As economic consultant to the dominant firm in a particular market, you have discovered that, at the current price and output, demand for your client's product is price inelastic. What advice regarding pricing would you give?

8. A New Hampshire resort offers year-round activities: in winter, skiing and other cold-weather activities; and in summer, golf, tennis, and hiking. The resort's operating costs are essentially the same in winter and summer. Management charges higher nightly rates in the winter, when its average occupancy rate is 75 percent, than in the summer, when its occupancy rate is 85 percent. Can this policy be consistent with profit maximization? Explain.

9. In 1996 the drug Prilosec became the best-selling anti-ulcer drug in the world. (The drug was the most effective available and its sales outdistanced those of its nearest competitor.) Although Prilosec's marginal cost (production and packaging) was only about $.60 per daily dose, the drug's manufacturer initially set the price at $3.00 per dose—a 400 percent markup relative to MC!

   Research on demand for leading prescription drugs gives estimates of price elasticities in the range -1.4 to -1.2. Does setting a price of $3.00 (or more) make economic sense? Explain.

10. Explain how a firm can increase its profit by price discriminating. How does it determine optimal prices? How does the existence of substitute products affect the firm's pricing policy?

11. Often, firms charge a range of prices for essentially the same good or service because of cost differences. For instance, filling a customer's one-time small order for a product may be much more expensive than supplying regular orders. Services often are more expensive to deliver during peak-load periods. (Typically it is very expensive for a utility to provide electricity to meet peak demand during a hot August.) Insurance companies recognize that the expected cost of insuring different customers under the same policy may vary significantly. How should a profit-maximizing manager take different costs into account in setting prices?

12. In what respects are the following common practices subtle (or not-so-subtle) forms of price discrimination?
    a. Frequent-flier and frequent-stay programs
    b. Manufacturers' discount coupon programs
    c. A retailer's guarantee to match a lower competing price

*13. A private-garage owner has identified two distinct market segments: short-term parkers and all-day parkers with respective demand curves of $P_S = 3 - (Q_S/200)$ and $P_C = 2 - (Q_C/200)$. Here P is the average hourly rate and Q is the number of cars parked at this price. The garage owner is considering charging different prices (on a per-hour basis) for short-term parking and all-day parking. The capacity of the garage is 600 cars, and the cost associated with adding extra cars in the garage (up to this limit) is negligible.

   a. Given these facts, what is the owner's appropriate objective? How can he ensure that members of each market segment effectively pay a different hourly price?

   b. What price should he charge for each type of parker? How many of each type of parker will use the garage at these prices? Will the garage be full?

   c. Answer the questions in part (b) assuming the garage capacity is 400 cars.

*14. A golf-course operator must decide what greens fees (prices) to set on rounds of golf. Daily demand during the week is $P_D = 36 - Q_D/10$, where Q_D is the number of 18-hole rounds and P_D is the price per round. Daily demand on the weekend is $P_W = 50 - Q_W/12$. As a practical matter, the capacity of the course is 240 rounds per day. Wear and tear on the golf course is negligible.

   a. Can the operator profit by charging different prices during the week and on the weekend? Explain briefly. What greens fees should the operator set on weekdays and how many rounds will be played? On the weekend?

   b. When weekend prices skyrocket, some weekend golfers choose to play during the week instead. The greater the difference between weekday and weekend prices, the greater are the number of these "defectors." How might this factor affect the operator's pricing policy? (A qualitative answer will suffice.)

Discussion Question The notion of elasticity is essential whenever the multiplicative product of two variables involves a trade-off. (Thus, we have already appealed to price elasticity to maximize revenue given the trade-off between price and output.) With this in mind, consider the following examples:

a. Why might a bumper crop (for instance, a 10 percent increase in a crop's output) be detrimental for overall farm revenue?

b. Court and legal reforms (to speed the process of litigation and lower its cost) will encourage more disputants to use the court system. Under what circumstances, could this cause an *increase* in total litigation spending?

*Starred problems are more challenging.

c. Despite technological advances in fishing methods and more numerous fishing boats, total catches of many fish species have declined over time. Explain.

d. Predict the impact on smoking behavior (and the incidence of lung disease) as more and more producers market low-tar and low-nicotine cigarettes.

Spreadsheet Problems

S1. Let's revisit the maker of spare parts in Problem S1 of Chapter 2 to determine its optimal price. The firm's demand curve is given by $Q = 400 - .5P$ and its cost function by $C = 20,000 + 200Q + .5Q^2$.

a. Treating price as the relevant decision variable, create a spreadsheet (based on the example shown) to model this setting. Compute the price elasticity in cell B12 according to $E_P = (dQ/dP)(P/Q)$.

b. Find the optimal price by hand. (Hint: Vary price while comparing cells E12 and F12. When $(P - MC)/P$ exactly equals $-1/E_P$, the markup rule is satisfied and the optimal price has been identified.)

c. Use your spreadsheet's optimizer to confirm the optimal price.

	A	B	C	D	E	F	G
1							
2		\multicolumn{5}{c}{THE OPTIMAL PRICE FOR SPARE PARTS}	
3							
4							
5		Price	Quantity	Revenue	Cost	Profit	
6							
7		780	10	7,800	22,050	−14,250	
8							
9							
10		Elasticity	MC		$(P - MC)/P$	$-1/EP$	
11							
12		−39.0	210		0.7308	0.0256	
13							

S2. On a popular air route, an airline offers two classes of service: business class (B) and economy class (E). The respective demands are given by

$$P_B = 540 - .5Q_B \quad \text{and} \quad P_E = 380 - .25Q_E.$$

Because of ticketing restrictions, business travelers cannot take advantage of economy's low fares. The airline operates two flights daily.

Each flight has a capacity of 200 passengers. The cost per flight is $20,000.

a. The airline seeks to maximize the total revenue it obtains from the two flights. To address this question, create a spreadsheet patterned on the example shown. (In your spreadsheet, only cells E2, E3, E4, C9, and D9 should contain numerical values. The numbers in all other cells are computed by using spreadsheet formulas. For instance, the total available seats in cell E5 is defined as the product of cells E2 and E3.)

b. What fares should the airline charge, and how many passengers will buy tickets of each type? Remember that maximum revenue is obtained by setting MR_B equal to MR_E. After you have explored the decision by hand, confirm your answer using your spreadsheet's optimizer. (Hint: Be sure to include the constraint that the total number of seats sold must be no greater than the total number of seats available—that is, cell E9 must less than or equal to cell E5.)

c. Suppose the airline is considering promoting a single "value fare" to all passengers along the route. Find the optimal single fare using your spreadsheet's optimizer. *Hint:* Simply modify the optimizer instructions from part (b) by adding the constraint that the prices in cells C11 and D11 must be equal.

	A	B	C	D	E	F
1						
2		DUAL AIRFARES			Planes	2	
3					Seats/Plane	200	
4					Cost/Plane	20,000	
5					Total Seats	400	
6						
7				Business	Non-Bus.	Total	
8						
9		Number of Seats		200	200	400	
10						
11		One-way Fare		440	330	—	
12						
13		Revenue		88,000	66,000	154,000	
14		MR		340	280		
15						
16		MC		100	Total Cost	40,000	
17						
18					Total Profit	114,000	
19						

S3. Now suppose the airline in Problem S2 can vary the number of daily departures.

    a. What is its profit-maximizing number of flights, and how many passengers of each type should it carry? (Hint: The optimal numbers of passengers, Q_B and Q_E, can be found by setting $MR_B = MR_E = MC$ per seat. Be sure to translate the \$20,000 marginal cost per flight into the relevant MC per seat.)

    b. Confirm your algebraic answer using the spreadsheet you created in Problem S2. (*Hint:* The easiest way to find a solution by hand is to vary the number of passengers of each type to equate MRs and MC; then adjust the number of planes to carry the necessary total number of passengers.)

    c. Use your spreadsheet's optimizer to confirm the optimal solution. (*Hint:* Be sure to list cell E2 as an adjustable cell.)

Suggested References

The following references illustrate the various uses of demand analysis, including the computation and application of elasticities.

Baye, M. R., D. W. Jansen, and J. W. Lee. "Advertising Effects in Complete Demand Systems." *Applied Economics* 24 (1992): 1087–1096.

Becker, G. S., M. Grossman, and K. M. Murphy. "An Empirical Analysis of Cigarette Addiction." *American Economic Review* 84 (June 1994): 396–418.

Bordley, R. F. "Estimating Automotive Elasticities from Segment Elasticities and First Choice/Second Choice Data." *Review of Economics and Statistics* 75 (August 1993): 455–462.

Gallet, C. A., and J. A. List. "Elasticities of Beer Demand Revisited." *Economics Letters* 61 (October 1998): 67–71.

Hughes, J. E., C. R. Knittel, and D. Sperling. "Evidence of a Shift in the Short-Run Price Elasticity of Gasoline Demand." Working Paper 12530, National Bureau of Economic Research, September 2006.

Hunt-McCool, J., B. F. Kiker, and Y. C. Ng. "Estimates of the Demand for Medical Care Under Different Functional Forms." *Journal of Applied Econometrics* 9 (1994): 201–218.

McCarthy, P. S. "Market Price and Income Elasticities of New Vehicles Demand." *Review of Economics and Statistics* 78 (August 1996): 543–547.

Schaller, B. "Elasticities for Taxicab Fares and Service Availability." *Transportation* 26 (August 1999): 283–297.

Silk, J. I., and F. L. Joutz. "Short- and Long-Run Elasticities in U.S. Residential Electricity Demand: A Co-integration Approach." *Energy Economics* 19 (October 1997): 493–513.

Subramanian, S., and A. Deaton. "The Demand for Food and Calories." *Journal of Political Economy* 104 (February 1996): 133–162.

Pagoulatos., E, and R. Sorenson, "What Determines the Elasticity of Industry Demand?" *International Journal of Industrial Organization* 4 (1986): 237–250.

The following references contain discussions of optimal pricing, price discrimination, and advertising.

"The Price Is Right, but Maybe It's not and How Do You Know?" *Knowledge@Wharton*, October 3, 2007, http://knowledge.wharton.upenn.edu/article.cfm?articleid=1813.

Dolan, R. J. "How Do You Know When the Price Is Right?" *Harvard Business Review* (September-October 1995): 174–183.

Knetter, M. M. "International Comparisons of Pricing-to-Market Behavior." *American Economic Review* 83 (June 1993): 473–486.

Leavitt, S. D. "An Economist Sells Bagels: A Case Study in Profit Maximization." Working Paper 12152, *National Bureau of Economic Research*, March 2006.

Tirole, J. *The Theory of Industrial Organization,* Chapters 2 and 3, Cambridge, MA.: MIT Press, 1989.

Van Dalen, J., and R. Thurik. "A Model of Pricing Behavior: An Econometric Case Study." *Journal of Economic Behavior and Organization* 36 (August 1998): 177–195.

Demand characteristics and selling strategies for information goods and services are analyzed in

Shapiro, C., and H. Varian. *Information Rules,* Chapters 1–3, 7. Boston: Harvard Business School Press, 1999, and at the associated Web site, www.inforules.com.

CHECK STATION ANSWERS

1. $\Delta Q = -24 + 12 - 40 = -52$ seats.

2. The facts in the second part of the statement are correct, but this does not mean that auto demand is less elastic. Elasticity measures the effect of a percentage change in price, not an absolute change. The change in any good's sales is given by $\Delta Q/Q = E_P(\Delta P/P)$; that is, it depends both on the elasticity and the magnitude of the percentage price change. After all, a $50 auto price cut is trivial in percentage terms. Even if auto demand is very elastic, the change in sales will be small. By contrast, a $50 price cut for a CD player is large in percentage terms. So there may be a large jump in sales even if player demand is quite inelastic.

3. $E_P = (dQ/Q)/(dP/P) = (dQ/dP)(P/Q)$. With $dQ/dP = -4$, the elasticity at $P = \$200$ and $Q = 800$ is $E_P = (-4)(200)/800 = -1$.

4. Since costs are assumed to be fixed, the team's management should set a price to maximize ticket revenue. We know that $Q = 60,000 - 3,000P$ or, equivalently, $P = 20 - Q/3,000$. Setting MR $= 0$, we have $20 - Q/1,500 = 0$, or $Q = 30,000$ seats. In turn, $P = \$10$ and revenue $= \$300,000$ per game. Note that management should *not* set a price to fill the stadium (36,000 seats). To fill the stadium, the necessary average price would be $8 and would generate only $288,000 in revenue.

5. Before the settlement, the cigarette company is setting an optimal price called for by the markup rule: $P = [-2/(-2 + 1)](1.00) = \$2.00$. The settlement payment takes the form of a fixed cost (based on past sales). It does not vary with respect to current or future production levels. Therefore, it does not affect the firm's marginal cost and should not affect the firm's markup. Note also that the individual firm faces *elastic* demand (because smokers can switch to other brands if the firm unilaterally raises prices), whereas industry demand (according to Table 3.1) is *inelastic.* If all firms raise prices by 10 percent, total demand will decline by only 7 percent.

6. The new seat allocations satisfy $MR_B = MR_T$ and $Q_B + Q_T = 270$. The solution is $Q_B = 155$ and $Q_T = 115$. In turn, $P_B = \$175$, $P_T = \$135$, and total revenue is $42,650—approximately $6,000 greater than current revenue ($36,800). Since the extra cost of the "second day" is only $4,500 ($90 \times \$50$), this expansion is profitable. Note, however, that the common value of marginal revenue has dropped to $20. (To see this, compute $MR_B = 330 - 2(155) = \$20$.) Because the marginal revenue per seat has fallen below the marginal cost ($50), any further expansion would be unprofitable.

Consumer Preferences and Demand

In this appendix, we provide a brief overview of the foundations of consumer demand—how consumers allocate their spending among desired goods and services. The analysis is important in its own right as a basis for downward-sloping demand curves. Perhaps its greater importance lies in the broader decision-making principle it illustrates. As we shall see, an optimal decision—made either by a consumer or a manager—depends on a careful analysis of preferences and trade-offs among available alternatives.

The Consumer's Problem

Consider an individual who must decide how to allocate her spending between desirable goods and services. To keep things simple, let's limit our attention to the case of two goods, X and Y. These goods could be anything from specific items (soft drinks versus bread) to general budget categories (groceries versus restaurant meals or food expenditures versus travel spending). The consumer faces a basic question: Given a limited amount of money to spend on the two goods, and given their prices, what quantities should she purchase?

INDIFFERENCE CURVES   To answer this question, we will use a simple graphical device to describe the individual's preferences. Imagine that we have asked

115

the consumer what her preferences are for alternative bundles of goods. Which do you prefer, 5 units of X and 10 units of Y, or 7 units of X and 6 units of Y? The answers to enough of such questions generate a preference ranking for a wide range of possible bundles of goods. Figure 3A.1 shows these possible

FIGURE 3A.1

A Consumer's
Indifference Curves

Each indifference curve shows combinations of the goods that provide the consumer with the same level of welfare.

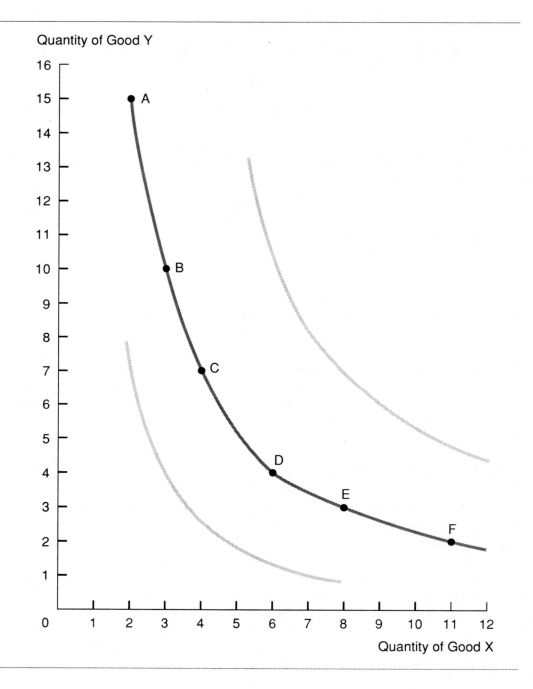

bundles by listing the quantities of the goods on the respective axes. The figure also depicts a number of the consumer's indifference curves as a way of representing her preferences.

As its name suggests, an **indifference curve** shows all combinations of the goods among which the individual is indifferent. The consumer is indifferent between all bundles on the same curve. Using the middle indifference curve in the figure, we see that the consumer is indifferent between the bundle containing 15 units of Y and 2 units of X (point A), 10 units of Y and 3 units of X (point B), and 4 units of Y and 6 units of X (point D). The bundles corresponding to points C, E, and F lie on the same indifference curve and are equally preferred by the consumer.

We can make three observations about the consumer's indifference curves. First, as we move to greater quantities of *both* goods, we move to higher and higher indifference curves. The figure depicts three different indifference curves. The consumer's welfare increases as we move to curves farther to the northeast in the figure.[1] Second, we note that the indifference curve is downward sloping. Since both goods are valued by the consumer, a decrease in one good must be compensated by an increase in the other to maintain the same level of welfare (or utility) for the consumer.

Third, we note that the slope of each curve goes from steep to flat, moving southeast along its length. This means that the trade-off between the goods changes as their relative quantities change. For instance, consider a movement from A to B. At point A, the consumer has 15 units of Y (a relative abundance) and 2 units of X. By switching to point B, she is willing to give up 5 units of Y to gain a single additional unit of X. Thus, the trade-off is five to one. By moving from point B (where Y is still relatively abundant) to point C, the consumer is willing to give up another 3 units of Y to get an additional unit of X. Now the trade-off between the goods (while leaving the consumer indifferent) is three to one. The trade-offs between the goods continue to diminish by movements from C to D to E. Thus, the indifference curve is bowed. This shape represents a general result about consumer preferences:

> The greater the amount of a good a consumer has, the less an additional unit is worth to him or her.

This result usually is referred to as the *law of diminishing marginal utility*. In our example, moving southeast along the indifference curve means going from a relative abundance of Y and a scarcity of X to the opposite proportions. When X is scarce, the consumer is willing to trade many units of Y for an additional

---

[1] One way to think about the indifference curve is to view it as a contour elevation map. Such a map has contour lines that connect points of equal elevation. Theoretically, there is a line for every elevation. Practically, we cannot have an infinite number of lines, so we draw them for only a few elevations. Similarly, we draw a few representative indifference curves for the consumer. Bundles of goods lying on "higher" indifference curves generate greater welfare.

unit of X. As X becomes more abundant and Y more scarce, X's relative value diminishes and Y's relative value increases.

THE BUDGET CONSTRAINT   Having described her preferences, next we determine the consumer's alternatives. The amount of goods she can purchase depends on her available income and the goods' prices. Suppose the consumer sets aside $20 each week to spend on the two goods. The price of good X is $4 per unit, and the price of Y is $2 per unit. Then she is able to buy any quantities of the goods (call these quantities X and Y) so long as she does not exceed her income. If she spends the entire $20, her purchases must satisfy

$$4X + 2Y = 20. \qquad\qquad [3A.1]$$

This equation's left side expresses the total amount the consumer spends on the goods. The right side is her available income. According to the equation, her spending just exhausts her available income.[2] This equation is called the consumer's **budget constraint**. Figure 3A.2 depicts the graph of this constraint. For instance, the consumer could purchase 5 units of X and no units of Y (point A), 10 units of Y and no units of X (point C), 3 units of X and 4 units of Y (point B), or any other combination along the budget line shown. Note that bundles of goods to the northeast of the budget line are infeasible; they cost more than the $20 that the consumer has to spend.

OPTIMAL CONSUMPTION   We are now ready to combine the consumer's indifference curves with her budget constraint to determine her optimal purchase quantities of the goods. Figure 3A.3 shows that the consumer's optimal combination of goods lies at point B, 3 units of X and 4 units of Y. Bundle B is optimal precisely because it lies on the consumer's "highest" attainable indifference curve while satisfying the budget constraint. (Check that all other bundles along the budget line lie on lower indifference curves.)

Observe that, at point B, the indifference curve is tangent to the budget line. This means that at B the slope of the indifference curve is exactly equal to the slope of the budget line. Let's consider each slope in turn. The slope of the budget line (the "rise over the run") is -2. This slope can be obtained from the graph directly or found by rearranging the budget equation in the form $Y = 10 - 2X$. As a result, $\Delta Y/\Delta X = -2$. More generally, we can write the budget equation in the form

$$P_X X + P_Y Y = I,$$

where P_X and P_Y denote the goods' prices and I is the consumer's income. Rearranging the budget equation, we find $Y = I/P_Y - (P_X/P_Y)X$. Therefore,

---

[2]Because both goods are valuable to the consumer, she will never spend *less* than her allotted income on the goods. To do so would unnecessarily reduce her level of welfare.

The Consumer's
Budget Line

The budget line shows
the combinations of
goods X and Y that can
be purchased with the
consumer's available
income.

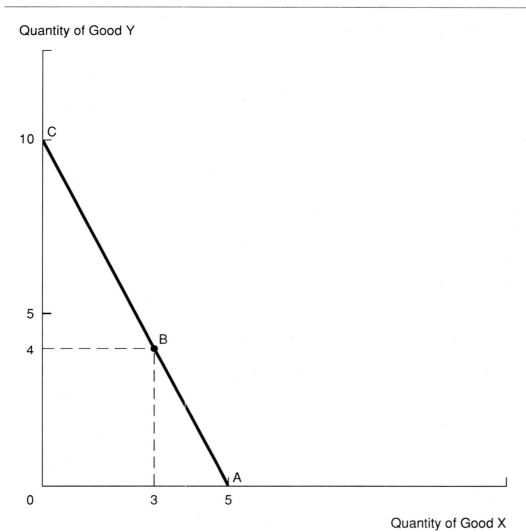

we have $\Delta Y/\Delta X = -P_X/P_Y$. The trade-off between the goods along the budget line is the *inverse* of the ratio of the goods' prices. Since the price of X is twice that of Y, by purchasing one less unit of X, the consumer can purchase two additional units of Y. In short, $\Delta Y/\Delta X = -2$.

We already have commented on the slope of the consumer's indifference curve. Unlike the budget line, the indifference curve's slope is not constant. Rather, it flattens as one moves southeast along its length. The **marginal rate of substitution (MRS)** measures the amount of one good the consumer is willing to give up to obtain a unit of the other good. In other words, MRS measures the trade-off between the goods in terms of the consumer's preferences. To be

FIGURE 3A.3

The Consumer's
Optimal Consumption
Bundle

**The consumer attains
her highest level of
welfare at point B,
where her indifference
curve is tangent to the
budget line.**

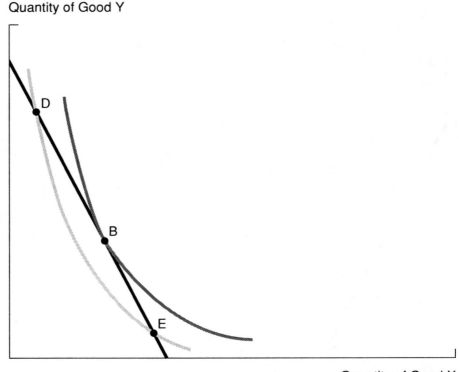

specific, MRS measures the slope of the indifference curve at any bundle, that is, MRS = $-\Delta Y/\Delta X$ along the indifference curve. In the present example, the MRS at point B is 2.

Now we are ready to state a general result:

> The consumer's optimal consumption bundle is found where the marginal rate of substitution is exactly equal to the ratio of the product prices, MRS = P_X/P_Y.

Another way of saying this is that the consumer's preference trade-off between the goods should exactly equal the price trade-off she faces. The MRS represents the *value* of X in terms of Y, whereas P_X/P_Y is the *price* of X in terms of Y. If the relative value of X were greater than its relative price (such as is the case at point D), the consumer would shift to additional purchases of X and thereby move to higher indifference curves. At point E, the situation is reversed. The relative value of X falls short of its relative price, so the consumer would purchase less of X. The consumer's optimal purchase quantities (3 units of X and

4 units of Y) occur at point B. Here, MRS = P_X/P_Y = 2. No change in purchases could increase the consumer's welfare.

Demand Curves

The demand curve graphs the relationship between a good's price and the quantity demanded, holding all other factors constant. Consider the consumer's purchase of good X as its price is varied (holding income and the price of Y constant). What if the price falls from $4 per unit to $2 per unit to $1 per unit? Figure 3A.4 shows the effect of these price changes on the consumer's budget line. As the price falls from $4 to $2, the budget line flattens and pivots around its vertical intercept. (Note: With the price of Y unchanged, the maximum amount of Y the consumer can purchase remains the same.) The figure shows the new budget lines and new points of optimal consumption at the lower prices.

As one would expect, reduction in price brings forth greater purchases of good X and increases the consumer's welfare (i.e., she moves to higher

FIGURE 3A.4

The Price-Consumption Curve

The price-consumption curve shows that the consumer's demand for X increases as its price falls.

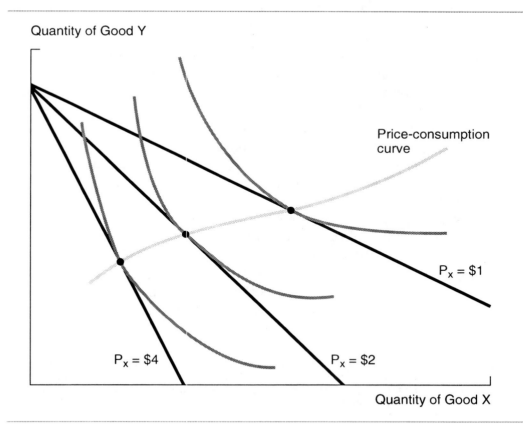

Quantity of Good Y

Price-consumption curve

$P_X = \$1$

$P_X = \$4$

$P_X = \$2$

Quantity of Good X

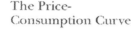

indifference curves). The figure also shows a **price-consumption curve** that passes through the optimal consumption points. This curve shows the consumer's optimal consumption as the price of X is varied continuously. Using this curve, we can record the consumption of X at each price. If we plot the quantity of X demanded versus its price, we arrive at the consumer's demand curve for X; it has the usual downward slope. The consumer increases her optimal consumption of X in response to lower prices.

Of course, different individuals will have varying preferences for goods and varying incomes. For these reasons, they obviously will have different demand curves. How do we arrive at the market demand curve (the total demand by all consumers as price varies)? The answer is found by summing the quantities demanded by all consumers at any given price. Graphically, this amounts to *horizontally* summing the individual demand curves. The result is the market demand curve.[3]

Questions and Problems

1. a. Consider a different consumer who has much steeper indifference curves than those depicted in Figure 3A.1. Draw a graph showing such curves. What do these curves imply about his relative valuation for good X versus good Y?
   b. Using the curves from part (a) and the budget line in Equation 3A.1, graph the consumer's optimal consumption bundle. How does his consumption bundle compare with that of the original consumer? Is it still true that $MRS = P_X/P_Y = 2$?

2. a. Suppose the income the consumer has available to spend on goods increases to $30. Graph the new budget line and sketch a new indifference curve to pinpoint the consumer's new optimal consumption bundle. According to your graph, does the consumer purchase more of each good?
   b. Sketch a graph (with an appropriate indifference curve) in which one of the goods is inferior. That is, the rise in income causes the consumer to purchase less of one of the goods.

3. Suppose that the price of good X rises and the price of good Y falls in such a way that the consumer's new optimal consumption bundle lies on the same indifference curve as his old bundle. Graph this situation. Compare the quantities demanded between the old and new bundles.

[3]Of course, market researchers do not investigate demand individual by individual. Rather, they survey random, representative samples of potential consumers. The main point is that properties of individual demand curves—their downward slope stemming from optimal consumption behavior—carry over to the market demand curve itself.

CHAPTER 5

Production

One-tenth of the participants produce over one-third of the output. Increasing the number of participants merely reduces the average output.

NORMAN AUGUSTINE, AUGUSTINE'S LAWS

To a greater or lesser extent, almost all firms face the task of finding and retaining customers for their goods. For many service-intensive companies, the sales force is as important as—and indeed may outnumber—the production workforce. The deployment of this sales force is thus a type of production decision.

Allocating a Sales Force

Consider an office equipment company that leases copiers, word processors, computers, and various types of office furniture to large and small firms. In this business, equipment leases rarely last more than one year. Thus, the firm's sales force must continually reenlist current customers, and find new customers. A key question faces the company's sales and marketing director: Of the firm's current sales force (18 strong), how many "reps" should specialize in servicing and retaining current leases and how many should devote themselves to new prospective accounts? Could a reallocation of the sales force increase the firm's total sales?

Production and cost are closely linked. The production manager strives to produce any given level of output at minimal total cost and continually seeks less costly ways to produce the firm's goods and services.

We open this chapter by examining the production function, a quantitative summary of the firm's production possibilities. Next, we look closely at production in the short run and examine the impact on output of changing a

179

single input. Then we consider production in the long run, when the firm has the flexibility to vary the amounts of all inputs. Next, we turn to the various types of production functions and discuss the means by which they are estimated. Finally, we consider a number of constrained production decisions involving the allocation of inputs (in fixed supply) to multiple plants or products, or both.

BASIC PRODUCTION CONCEPTS

Production Technology

Production transforms inputs into outputs. For instance, producing automobiles requires a variety of inputs (also called factors of production): raw materials (steel, plastic, rubber, etc.), factories, machines, land, and many different categories of workers. For analysis, it is convenient to refer to two main categories of inputs—labor and materials on the one hand and long-term capital on the other—with each category broadly defined. Labor and materials includes production workers, marketers, and managers at all levels as well as raw materials and intermediate goods, including parts, water, electricity, and so on. Capital includes buildings, equipment, and inventories.

The firm's **production function** indicates the maximum level of output the firm can produce for any combination of inputs. We will start by considering a production function with two inputs: labor and capital.[1] A shorthand description of such a production function is

$$Q = F(L, K). \qquad [5.1]$$

This states that the firm's quantity of output depends on the respective quantities of labor (L) and capital (K). For instance, a major domestic automobile manufacturer might plan to produce 3 million passenger cars per year, using materials (of all kinds) that cost $24 billion, a total nationwide labor force of 80,000 workers, and a total capital stock valued at $100 billion. Note that the firm's production function specifies the *maximum* output for a given combination of inputs. It assumes that managers use inputs efficiently. Obviously, production technologies improve over time, and efficient firms vigorously pursue these improvements.

---

[1]As we have said, production also requires material inputs. For now, we assume that the firm has little or no flexibility with respect to this input. Each part requires a fixed amount of raw materials; producing twice as many parts requires twice as much raw materials and so on. Accordingly, the production function focuses on labor and capital and does *not* list the implicit amount of raw materials associated with each level of output. A more detailed production function might disaggregate materials into scores of categories, separate labor into numerous job descriptions, and disaggregate capital expenditures.

TABLE 5.1

A Production Function
for a Specialty Part

This production func-
tion shows the quan-
tity of output that can
be obtained from vari-
ous combinations of
plant size and labor.

Number of Workers	Plant Size (Thousands of Square Feet)			
	10	20	30	40
10	93	120	145	165
20	135	190	235	264
30	180	255	300	337
40	230	315	365	410
50	263	360	425	460
60	293	395	478	510
70	321	430	520	555
80	346	460	552	600
90	368	485	580	645
100	388	508	605	680

A PRODUCTION FUNCTION FOR AUTO PARTS   Consider a multiproduct firm that supplies parts to several U.S. automobile manufacturers. Table 5.1 tabulates the firm's production function for one such specialty part. The table lists the quantities of output that can be produced using different combinations of two inputs, labor and capital. For instance, the first entry indicates that an output of 93 specialty parts per day can be produced employing 10 workers in a 10,000-square-foot plant.

PRODUCTION WITH ONE VARIABLE INPUT

Short-Run and Long-Run Production

Our analysis of production and cost makes an important distinction between the short run and the long run.

In the **short run** one or more of the firm's inputs is fixed, that is, cannot be varied. In the **long run** the firm can vary *all* of its inputs. There is no universal rule for distinguishing between the short and long run; rather, the dividing line must be drawn on a case-by-case basis. For a petrochemical refinery, the short run might be any period less than five years since it takes roughly this long to build a new refinery. For a fast-food chain, six months (the time it takes to obtain zoning approvals and construct new restaurants) may be the dividing line between short and long run.

Inputs that cannot be changed in the short run are called **fixed inputs**. A firm's production facility is a typical example. In the long run, the firm could vary the size and scale of its plant, whereas in the short run the size of this plant would be fixed at its existing capacity. If a firm operates under restrictive, long-term labor contracts, its ability to vary its labor force may be limited over the contract duration, perhaps up to three years. In this case, labor could be a fixed input in the short run.

MARGINAL PRODUCT   Let's consider the production decisions of the auto parts firm. Currently it is operating with a 10,000-square-foot plant. In the short run, this capital input is fixed. However, labor is a **variable input**; that is, the firm can freely vary its number of workers. Table 5.2 shows the amount of output obtainable using different numbers of workers. (This information is reproduced from the earlier production function and expanded slightly.) Notice that output steadily increases as the workforce increases, up to 120 workers. Beyond that point, output declines. It appears that too many workers within a plant of limited size are counterproductive to the task of producing parts.

TABLE 5.2

Production of Specialty Parts (10,000-Square-Foot Plant)	Number of Workers	Total Product	Marginal Product
	10	93	
The second column shows the amount of total output generated by different amounts of labor. The third column shows the marginal product of labor—the extra output produced by an additional worker.			4.2
	20	135	
			4.5
	30	180	
			5.0
	40	230	
			3.3
	50	263	
			3.0
	60	293	
			2.8
	70	321	
			2.5
	80	346	
			2.2
	90	368	
			2.0
	100	388	
			1.2
	110	400	
			0.3
	120	403	
			−1.2
	130	391	
			−1.1
	140	380	

The last column of Table 5.2 lists the marginal product of labor (abbreviated MP_L). This **marginal product** is the additional output produced by an additional unit of labor, all other inputs held constant. For instance, increasing labor from 20 to 30 workers increases output by $180 - 135 = 45$ units, or $45/10 = 4.5$ units per worker. A further increase from 30 to 40 workers implies an MP_L of 5.0 units per worker. Mathematically, labor's marginal product is $MP_L = dQ/dL$. In other words, labor's marginal product is the change in output per unit change in labor input.

In our example, MP_L first rises (for increases up to 40 workers), then declines.[2] Why does MP_L rise initially? With a small workforce, the typical worker must be a jack-of-all-trades (and master of none). Increasing the number of workers allows for *specialization* of labor—workers devoting themselves to particular tasks—which results in increased output per worker. Furthermore, additional workers can use underutilized machinery and capital equipment.

Figure 5.1a graphs labor's total product. Consider the total product curve for a 10,000-square-foot plant. Initially, the total product curve increases rapidly. As the number of workers increases, the curve's slope becomes less steep, then reaches a peak and declines. This reflects labor's marginal productivity. When MP_L is large (see Figure 5.1b), the total product curve is steep. As MP_L declines, the curve becomes less steep. The product curve peaks when MP_L approaches zero and begins to decline when MP_L becomes negative. Figure 5.1a also displays labor's total product curve for a 20,000-square-foot plant (with output rates taken from Table 5.1). As indicated, the larger plant generates an increased rate of output for the same workforce. Finally, Figure 5.1b graphs labor's marginal product for a 10,000-square-foot plant.

Graph the marginal product of labor if the firm produces output using a 30,000-square-foot plant. Compare this with the MP_L using a 10,000-square-foot plant. Explain the difference.

CHECK
STATION 1

THE LAW OF DIMINISHING MARGINAL RETURNS The declining marginal product of an input (like labor) represents one of the best-known and most important empirical "laws" of production:

> *The Law of Diminishing Marginal Returns.* As units of one input are added (with all other inputs held constant), resulting additions to output will eventually begin to decrease; that is, marginal product will decline.

[2]Indeed, labor's marginal product becomes negative for additional workers beyond 120; that is, total product actually declines when "too many" workers are employed.

FIGURE 5.1

Total Product and
Marginal Product

Part (a) graphs labor's
total product; part
(b) depicts labor's
marginal product.

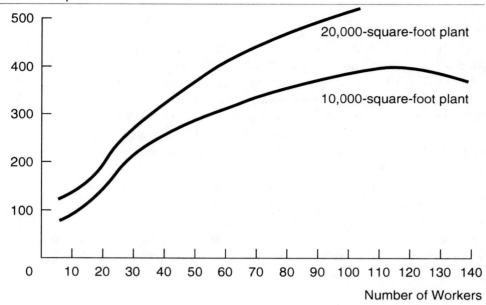

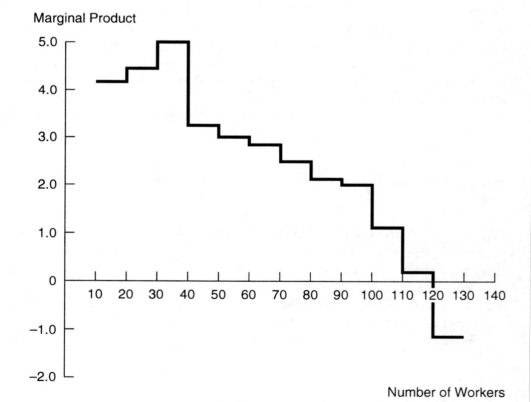

(b) Labor's Marginal Product (10,000-Square-Foot Plant)

In the preceding example, diminishing returns to labor occur beyond 40 workers. At this point the most productive jobs already are filled, specialization is being fully exploited, and the plant and equipment are being used efficiently. Extra workers are assigned to less productive tasks. These workers generate additional output but at a diminishing rate.

Optimal Use of an Input

The law of diminishing returns means that the firm faces a basic trade-off in determining its level of production. By using more of a variable input, the firm obtains a direct benefit—increased output—in return for incurring an additional input cost. What level of the input maximizes profits? As before, we look at the firm's marginal profit, but this time we look at marginal profit *per unit of input*. We increase the input until the marginal profit per unit of input is zero.

In analyzing this input decision, a definition is helpful. Marginal revenue product is the formal name for the marginal revenue associated with increased use of an input. An input's **marginal revenue product** is the extra revenue that results from a unit increase in the input. To illustrate, suppose the auto parts supplier is considering increasing labor from 20 to 30 workers. According to Table 5.2, the resulting marginal product is 4.5 parts per worker. Suppose further that the supplier's marginal revenue per part is constant. It can sell as many parts as it wants at a going market price of $40 per part. Therefore, labor's marginal revenue product (MRP_L) is ($40)(4.5) = $180 per worker. Similarly, the MRP_L for a move from 30 to 40 workers is ($40)(5.0) = $200 per worker. More generally, labor's MRP_L can be expressed as

$$MRP_L = (MR)(MP_L), \qquad [5.2]$$

where MR denotes marginal revenue per unit of output.[3]

Now consider the marginal cost of using additional labor. The **marginal cost of an input** is simply the amount an additional unit of the input adds to the firm's total cost.[4] If the firm can hire as many additional workers as it wishes at a constant wage (say, $160 per day), then the marginal cost of labor is MC_L = $160. (In some cases, however, the firm may have to bid up the price of labor to obtain additional workers.)

Now note that the additional profit from adding one more worker is the revenue generated by adding the worker less the worker's marginal cost:

$$M\pi_L = MRP_L - MC_L.$$

---

[3]In calculus terms, $MRP_L = dR/dL = (dR/dQ)(dQ/dL) = (MR)(MP_L)$.

[4]It is important to distinguish between the marginal cost of an input and the marginal cost of an additional unit of output. Taking labor as an example, MC_L is defined as $\Delta C/\Delta L$, the cost of hiring an extra worker. In contrast, the added cost of producing an extra unit of *output* is $MC = \Delta C/\Delta Q$.

The firm should continue to increase its labor force so long as the amount of additional profit from doing so is positive, that is, so long as the additional revenue (MRP_L) is greater than the additional cost (MC_L). Due to diminishing marginal returns, labor's marginal revenue product eventually will fall. When MRP_L exactly matches MC_L (i.e., when $M\pi_L = 0$), increasing the labor force any further will be unprofitable, which leads to the following principle:

> To maximize profit, the firm should increase the amount of a variable input up to the point at which the input's marginal revenue product equals its marginal cost, that is until

$$MRP_L = MC_L. \tag{5.3}$$

After this point, the marginal cost of labor will exceed the marginal revenue product of labor, and profits will decline.

EXAMPLE 1   The human resources manager of the auto parts firm with a 10,000-square-foot plant estimates that the marginal cost of hiring an extra worker is $P_L = \$160$ per day. Earlier we noted that a move from 20 to 30 workers implies an MRP_L of \$180 per worker (per day). Since this exceeds the daily cost per worker, \$160, this move is profitable. So, too, is a move from 30 to 40 workers ($MRP_L = \$200$). But an increase from 40 to 50 workers is unprofitable. The resulting MRP_L is ($40)(3.3) = \$132, which falls well short of MC_L. After this, MRP_L continues to decline due to diminishing returns. Thus, the optimal size of the firm's labor force is 40 workers.

What would be the firm's optimal labor force if it had in place a 30,000-square-foot plant? From Table 5.1, we see that a move from 50 to 60 workers results in an MRP_L of \$212, a move from 60 to 70 workers an MRP_L of \$168, and a move from 70 to 80 workers an MRP_L of \$128. Given a labor price of \$160 per day, the firm profits by increasing its labor force up to a total of 70 workers (since $MRP_L > MC_L$ in this range). But an increase beyond this level reduces profitability ($MRP_L < MC_L$). The firm would best utilize the 30,000-square-foot plant by using 70 workers and producing 520 parts per day.

CHECK STATION 2   Let MR = \$40 and $MC_L = \$160$ per day. Using the relevant information from Table 5.1, determine the firm's optimal number of workers for a 20,000-square-foot plant. Repeat the calculation for a 40,000-square-foot plant.

EXAMPLE 2   Suppose that a firm's production function is described by

$$Q = 60L - L^2,$$

where Q measures units of output and L is the number of labor hours. Suppose that output sells for \$2 per unit, and the cost of labor is $MC_L = \$16$

per hour. How many hours of labor should the firm hire, and how much output should it produce?

To answer these questions, we apply the fundamental rule

$$MRP_L = MC_L.$$

First, observe that labor's marginal product is $MP_L = dQ/dL = 60 - 2L$. In turn, labor's marginal revenue product is $MRP_L = (\$2)(60 - 2L) = 120 - 4L$. Setting this equal to \$16, we obtain $120 - 4L = 16$. The optimal amount of labor is $L = 26$ hours. From the production function, the resulting output is 884 units. Finally, the firm's operating profit (net of its labor cost) is $(\$2)(884) - (\$16)(26) = \$1,352$.

PRODUCTION IN THE LONG RUN

In the long run, a firm has the freedom to vary all of its inputs. Two aspects of this flexibility are important. First, a firm must choose the proportion of inputs to use. For instance, a law firm may vary the proportion of its inputs to economize on the size of its clerical staff by investing in computers and software specifically designed for the legal profession. In effect, it is substituting capital for labor. Steeply rising fuel prices have caused many of the major airlines to modify their fleets, shifting from larger aircraft to smaller, fuel-efficient aircraft.

Second, a firm must determine the scale of its operations. Would building and operating a new facility twice the size of the firm's existing plants achieve a doubling (or more than doubling) of output? Are there limits to the size of the firm beyond which efficiency drastically declines? These are all important questions that can be addressed using the concept of returns to scale.

Returns to Scale

The *scale* of a firm's operations denotes the levels of all the firm's inputs. A *change in scale* refers to a given percentage change in *all* inputs. At a 15 percent scale increase, the firm would use 15 percent more of each of its inputs. A key question for the manager is how the change in scale affects the firm's output. **Returns to scale** measure the percentage change in output resulting from a given percentage change in inputs. There are three important cases.

Constant returns to scale occur if a given percentage change in all inputs results in an equal percentage change in output. For instance, if all inputs are doubled, output also doubles; a 10 percent increase in inputs results in a 10 percent increase in output, and so on. A common example of constant returns to scale occurs when a firm can easily replicate its production process. For instance, a manufacturer of electrical components might find that it can double its output by replicating its current plant and labor force, that is, by building an identical plant beside the old one.

Increasing returns to scale occur if a given percentage increase in all inputs results in a greater percentage change in output. For example, a 10 percent increase in all inputs causes a 20 percent increase in output. How can the firm do better than constant returns to scale? By increasing its scale, the firm may be able to use new production methods that were infeasible at the smaller scale. For instance, the firm may utilize sophisticated, highly efficient, large-scale factories. It also may find it advantageous to exploit specialization of labor at the larger scale. As an example, there is considerable evidence of increasing returns to scale in automobile manufacturing: An assembly plant with a capacity of 200,000 cars per year uses significantly less than twice the input quantities of a plant having a 100,000-car capacity. Frequently, returns to scale result from fundamental engineering relationships. Consider the economics of an oil pipeline from well sites in Alaska to refineries in the contiguous United States. Doubling the circumference of the pipe increases the pipe's cross-sectional area *fourfold,* allowing a like increase in the flow capacity of the pipeline. As long as there are increasing returns, it is better to use larger production facilities to supply output instead of many smaller facilities.

Decreasing returns to scale occur if a given percentage increase in all inputs results in a smaller percentage increase in output. The most common explanations for decreasing returns involve organizational factors in very large firms. As the scale of the firm increases, so do the difficulties in coordinating and monitoring the many management functions. As a result, proportional increases in output require more than proportional increases in inputs.

Output elasticity is the percentage change in output resulting from a 1 percent increase in all inputs. For constant returns to scale, the output elasticity is 1; for increasing returns, it is greater than 1; and for decreasing returns, it is less than 1. For instance, an output elasticity of 1.5 means that a 1 percent scale increase generates a 1.5 percent output increase, a 10 percent scale increase generates a 15 percent output increase, and so on.

CHECK STATION 3   Reexamine the production function in Table 5.1. Check that production exhibits increasing returns for low levels of input usage and decreasing returns for high levels of usage. Can you find instances of constant returns in the medium-input range?

Returns to Scale in Coal Mining

A study of surface (i.e., strip) coal mining estimated production functions for deposits of different sizes.[5] The study was based on a survey of Illinois mines that included information (for each mine) on the production of coal (in tons), the amount of labor employed (in hours), the quantity of earth-moving capital

---

[5]G. A. Boyd, "Factor Intensity and Site Geology as Determinants of Returns to Scale in Coal Mining," *Review of Economics and Statistics* (1987): 18–23.

(in dollars), and the quantity of other capital (also in dollars). Significant economies of scale were found for most types of mines. The average elasticity of output with respect to inputs was 1.24. (A 20 percent increase in all inputs raised output by about 25 percent.) Typically, economies of scale were not exhausted until an annual output level of 4.8 million tons of coal was reached—a level higher than the actual operating scale of most mines. (Thus, further increases in the scale of mineral extraction would seem to be warranted.) In addition, there was evidence that increased use of large-scale, primary earth-moving equipment greatly enhanced the degree of returns to scale. In short, higher capital intensity implies greater returns to scale in mining.

Least-Cost Production

In the long run, the firm can vary all of its inputs. Because inputs are costly, this flexibility raises the question: How can the firm determine the mix of inputs that will minimize the cost of producing a given level of output? To answer this question, let's return to the case of two inputs, labor and capital. Here the firm's production function is of the form

$$Q = F(L, K),$$

where L is the number of labor hours per month and K is the amount of capital used per month. There are possibly many different ways to produce a given level of output (call this Q_0), utilizing more capital and less labor or vice versa.

The optimal mix of labor and capital in producing output Q_0 depends on the costs and marginal products of the inputs. Let's denote the firm's labor cost per hour by P_L and its cost per unit of capital by P_K. Then the firm's total cost of using L and K units of inputs is

$$TC = P_L L + P_K K.$$

The firm seeks to minimize this cost, subject to the requirement that it use enough L and K to produce Q_0. We now state the following important result concerning optimal long-run production:

| In the long run, the firm produces at least cost when the ratios of marginal products to input costs are equal across all inputs.

For the case of two inputs, we have

$$MP_L/P_L = MP_K/P_K. \qquad [5.4]$$

Equation 5.4 shows that when total cost is minimized, the extra output per dollar of input must be the same for all inputs. To see why this must be true, assume to the contrary that the ratios in Equation 5.4 differ. As an example, let MP_L be 30 units per hour and P_L be \$15 per hour; in turn, let MP_K be 60 and P_K be \$40. Then $MP_L/P_L = 30/15 = 2$ units per dollar of labor, while $MP_K/P_K = 60/40 = 1.5$ units per dollar of capital. Because labor's productivity per dollar exceeds capital's, it is advantageous for the firm to increase its use of labor and reduce its use of capital. The firm could maintain its present output level by using *two extra units of labor* in place of *one fewer unit of capital.* (The 60 units of output given up by reducing capital is exactly matched by $(2)(30) = 60$ units of output provided by the additional labor.) The net savings in total cost is \$40 (the saved capital cost) minus \$30 (the cost of two labor hours), or \$10. If one input's productivity per dollar exceeds another's, the firm can produce the same output at lower cost by switching toward greater use of the more productive input. It should continue to make such switches until the ratios in Equation 5.4 come into equality. At that point, the firm will have found its least-cost input mix.

CHECK STATION 4   Suppose that initially $MP_L/P_L > MP_K/P_K$. Explain why the ratios will move toward equality as the firm switches to more labor and less capital.

EXAMPLE 3   A manufacturer of home appliances faces the production function $Q = 40L - L^2 + 54K - 1.5K^2$ and input costs of $P_L = \$10$ and $P_K = \$15$. Thus, the inputs' respective marginal products are

$$MP_L = \partial Q/\partial L = 40 - 2L$$

and

$$MP_K = \partial Q/\partial K = 54 - 3K.$$

We know that the firm's least-cost combination of inputs must satisfy $MP_L/P_L = MP_K/P_K$. This implies that

$$[40 - 2L]/10 = [54 - 3K]/15.$$

Solving for L, we find $L = K + 2$. This relation prescribes the optimal combination of capital and labor. For instance, the input mix $K = 8$ and $L = 10$ satisfies this relationship. The resulting output is $Q = (40)(10) - (10)^2 + (54)(8) - 1.5(8)^2 = 636$. The firm's total input cost is $TC = (\$10)(10) + (\$15)(8) = \$220$. In other words, the minimum cost of producing 636 units is \$220 using 10 units of labor and 8 units of capital.

Winning in Football and Baseball

The National Football League (NFL) lives by the golden rule of team parity. Large-market teams in New York, Miami, or Dallas command greater revenues from ticket sales, concessions, TV and cable contracts, team products, and promotional deals. But small-market teams in Green Bay, Kansas City, and Cincinnati can nonetheless field winning teams. To achieve parity, the NFL has instituted a cap on team salaries, a system of revenue sharing, and more favorable player draft positions and schedules for weaker teams.[6]

How can a sports franchise construct a winning team with a strictly limited player budget ($74.6 million per team in 2003)? Coach Bill Belichick of the New England Patriots (once an economics major at Wesleyan University) assembled teams that won the Super Bowl in 2002, 2004, and 2005, before losing in the Super Bowl in 2008, by carefully considering not only player performance but also price. The Patriots deliberately avoided superstars (considered to be overpriced) and relied instead on a mix of moderate-priced veterans and undervalued free agents and draft choices. The team traded marquee quarterback Drew Bledsoe and installed young Tom Brady in his place. Lawyer Milloy, an outstanding defensive player, was replaced with free-agent veteran Rodney Harrison, trading a $5.8 million salary for $3.2 million. Although Milloy's marginal product (i.e., ability and winning impact) was likely higher than Harrison's, this gain was not worth the salary price. Harrison was retained because $MP_H/P_H > MP_M/P_M$.

By contrast, major league baseball, lacking a salary cap and having limited revenue sharing, suffers from severe competitive inequalities. The richest large-market teams are able to sign the established top players at gargantuan salaries and, thus, assemble the best teams. Championship teams bring extra revenues, and strong players help bring championships. During the fall of 2007, the Yankees re-signed free-agent superstar Alex Rodriguez for $175 million (plus incentive bonuses) for 10 years. With no salary cap, the signing makes economic sense as long as the player's marginal revenue product is greater than his salary: $MRP_L > P_L$. And since championships produce greater marginal revenues for large-market teams than for small-market teams, the marginal revenue product is much greater for the Yankees than for other teams. Thus the Yankees were probably one of a few teams in baseball willing to pay A-Rod this much money.

In sum, under their respective ground rules, baseball's rich tend to get richer, while football's middle-class teams operate on the same level playing field.

A GRAPHICAL APPROACH   Consider once again the production function of Example 3: $Q = 40L - L^2 + 54K - 1.5K^2$. We saw that the firm could produce $Q = 636$ units of output using $L = 10$ and $K = 8$ units of inputs. The same output, $Q = 636$, can be produced using different combinations of labor and capital: 6 units of labor and 12 units of capital, for instance. (Check this.)

An **isoquant** is a curve that shows all possible combinations of inputs that can produce a given level of output. The isoquant corresponding to $Q = 636$ is drawn in Figure 5.2a. The amounts of the inputs are listed on the axes. Three

---

[6]This account is based in part on L. Zinser, "Path to Super Bowl No Longer Paved with Stars," *New York Times*, February 4, 2004, A1.

input combinations along the Q = 636 isoquant, (L = 6, K = 12), (L = 10, K = 8), and (L = 14.2, K = 6), are indicated by points A, B, and C, respectively. A separate isoquant has been drawn for the output Q = 800 units. This isoquant lies above and to the right of the isoquant for Q = 636 because producing a greater output requires larger amounts of the inputs.

The isoquant's negative slope embodies the basic trade-off between inputs. If a firm uses less of one input, it must use more of the other to maintain a given level of output. For example, consider a movement from point B to point A in Figure 5.2a—a shift in mix from (L = 10, K = 8) to (L = 6, K = 12). Here an additional 12 − 8 = 4 units of capital substitute for 10 − 6 = 4 units of labor. But moving from point B to point C implies quite a different trade-off between inputs. Here 4.2 units of labor are needed to compensate for a reduction of only 2 units of capital. The changing ratio of input requirements directly reflects diminishing marginal productivity in each input. As the firm continually decreases the use of one input, the resulting decline in output becomes greater and greater. As a result, greater and greater amounts of the other input are needed to maintain a constant level of output.

Using the production function, we can obtain a precise measure of the isoquant's slope. The slope of an isoquant is just the change in K over the change in L (symbolically, $\Delta K/\Delta L$), holding output constant. Consider again point B, where 10 units of labor and 8 units of capital are used. Recall from Example 3 that $MP_L = 40 − 2L$ and $MP_K = 54 − 3K$. Thus, at these input amounts, $MP_L = 40 − 2(10) = 20$ and $MP_K = 54 − 3(8) = 30$. This means that a decrease in labor of one unit can be made up by a two-thirds unit increase in capital. Therefore, the slope of the isoquant at point B is

$$\Delta K/\Delta L = [+2/3 \text{ capital units}]/[−1 \text{ labor units}] = −2/3.$$

The general rule is that the slope of the isoquant at any point is measured by the ratio of the inputs' marginal products:

$$\Delta K/\Delta L \text{ (for Q constant)} = −MP_L/MP_K.$$

Notice that the ratio is $−MP_L/MP_K$ and not the other way around. The greater is labor's marginal product (and the smaller capital's), the greater the amount of capital needed to substitute for a unit of labor, that is, the greater the ratio $\Delta K/\Delta L$. This ratio is important enough to warrant its own terminology. The **marginal rate of technical substitution (MRTS)** denotes the rate at which one input substitutes for the other and is defined as

$$MRTS = −\Delta K/\Delta L \text{ (for Q constant)} = MP_L/MP_K.$$

For example, at point B, the MRTS is 20/30 = .667 units of capital per unit of labor. At point A (L = 6, K = 12), the marginal products are $MP_L = 28$ and

FIGURE 5.2

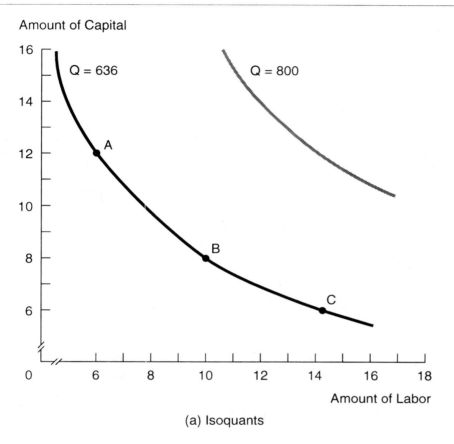

(a) Isoquants

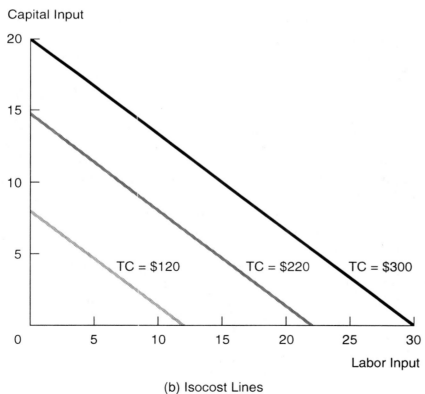

(b) Isocost Lines

Isoquants and Isocost Lines

The two isoquants in part (a) show the different combinations of labor and capital needed to produce 636 and 800 units of output. The isocost lines in part (b) show combinations of inputs a firm can acquire at various total costs.

$MP_K = 18$. At this input combination, the MRTS is $28/18 = 1.55$ and the slope of the isoquant is -1.55 (much steeper).

Suppose the manager sets out to produce an output of 636 units at least cost. Which combination of inputs along the isoquant will accomplish this objective? The answer is provided by portraying the firm's least-cost goal in graphic terms. Recall that the firm's total cost of using L and K units of input is

$$TC = P_L L + P_K K.$$

Using this equation, let's determine the various combinations of inputs the firm can obtain at a given level of total cost (i.e., expenditure). To do this, we rearrange the cost equation to read

$$K = TC/P_K - (P_L/P_K)L.$$

To illustrate, suppose the firm faces the input prices of Example 3, $P_L = \$10$ and $P_K = \$15$. If it limits its total expenditures to TC = \$120, the firm can use any mix of inputs satisfying $K = 120/15 - (10/15)L$ or $K = 8 - (2/3)L$. This equation is plotted in Figure 5.2b. This line is called an **isocost line** because it shows the combination of inputs the firm can acquire at a given total cost. We can draw a host of isocost lines corresponding to different levels of expenditures on inputs. In the figure, the isocost lines corresponding to TC = \$220 and TC = \$300 are shown. The slope of any of these lines is given by the ratio of input prices, $\Delta K/\Delta L = -P_L/P_K$. The *higher* the price of capital (relative to labor), the *lower* the amount of capital that can be substituted for labor while keeping the firm's total cost constant.

By superimposing isocost lines on the same graph with the appropriate isoquant, we can determine the firm's least-cost mix of inputs. We simply find the lowest isocost line that still touches the given isoquant. This is shown in Figure 5.3. For instance, to produce 636 units of output at minimum cost, we must identify the point along the isoquant that lies on the *lowest* isocost line. The figure shows that this is point B, the point at which the isocost line is tangent to the isoquant. Point B confirms Example 3's original solution: The optimal combination of inputs is 10 units of labor and 8 units of capital. Since point B lies on the \$220 isocost line, we observe that this is the minimum possible cost of producing the 636 units.

Note that at the point of tangency, the slope of the isoquant and the slope of the isocost line are the same. The isoquant's slope is $-MP_L/MP_K$. In turn, the isocost line's slope is $-P_L/P_K$. Thus, the least-cost combination of inputs is characterized by the condition

$$MRTS = MP_L/MP_K = P_L/P_K.$$

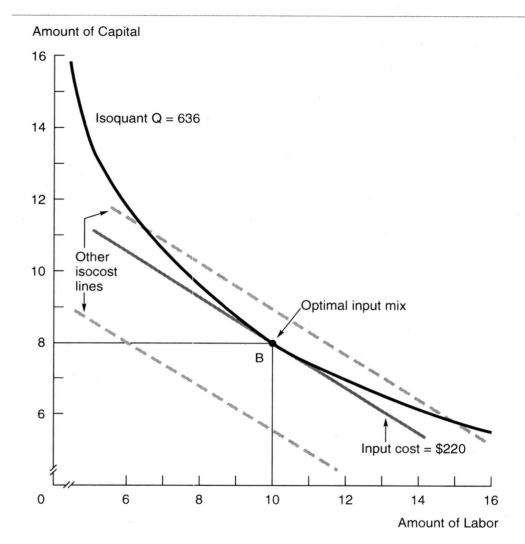

FIGURE 5.3

Producing Output at Minimum Cost

The firm produces 636 units at minimum cost at point B, where the isoquant is tangent to the lowest possible isocost line. Point B corresponds to 10 units of labor and 8 units of capital.

The ratio of marginal products exactly matches the ratio of input prices.[7] (If one input is twice as expensive as another, optimal usage requires that it have twice the marginal product.) This relationship can be rearranged to read

$$MP_L/P_L = MP_K/P_K.$$

[7]The same condition is derived readily using the method of Lagrange multipliers introduced in the appendix to Chapter 2. The problem is to minimize $TC = P_L L + P_K K$ subject to $F(L, K) = Q_0$, where Q_0 denotes a given level of output. The Lagrangian is $\pounds = P_L L + P_K K + z(Q_0 - F(L, K))$. The optimality conditions are $\partial\pounds/\partial L = P_L - z(\partial F/\partial L) = 0$, $\partial\pounds/\partial K = P_K - z(\partial F/\partial K) = 0$, and $\partial\pounds/\partial z = Q_0 - f(L, K) = 0$. Dividing the first condition by the second yields $P_L/P_K - (\partial F/\partial L)/(\partial F/\partial K) = 0$. It follows that $P_L/P_K = MP_L/MP_K$, after recognizing that $MP_L = \partial F/\partial L$ and $MP_K = \partial F/\partial K$.

This is exactly the condition established in Equation 5.4. The marginal product per dollar of input should be the same across all inputs.

MEASURING PRODUCTION FUNCTIONS

In this section, we briefly discuss ways in which managers can estimate and measure production functions based on engineering or economic data. Let us begin by considering four common specifications.

Linear Production

As the term suggests, a **linear production function** takes the form

$$Q = aL + bK + c, \qquad [5.5]$$

where a, b, and c are coefficients that must be estimated from the data. An immediate implication of linearity is that each input's marginal product is constant: $MP_L = a$ and $MP_K = b$. Constant marginal productivity may approximate production over a limited range of input usage, but at sufficiently high levels of inputs, it is at odds with the law of diminishing marginal productivity. In this sense, the linear form is too simple and should be viewed as a somewhat extreme case.

Because of the constant marginal products, the inputs are *perfect substitutes* for one another. Suppose, for example, that the production function is $Q = 20L + 40K$. In this case, one can always substitute two units of labor for one of capital to maintain the same level of production, and vice versa. Given fixed input prices, production will be "all or nothing" in the long run. If the unit cost of capital is less than twice the wage per unit of labor, the firm's least-cost means of production is to use only capital. In contrast, if labor is the less expensive option, production should use labor exclusively. In general, so long as $MP_K/P_K > MP_L/P_L$, the firm should use capital exclusively (and vice versa if the inequality is reversed).

Production with Fixed Proportions

Production with fixed proportions is the opposite extreme from linear production; fixed-proportions production allows no input substitution. Output can only be produced with a fixed proportion of inputs. Simple examples include a taxi and its driver or a construction crane and its operator. In both cases, the required mix of labor to capital is one to one. An excess of either input—a machine without an operator or vice versa—does no good. Expansion of production requires balanced increases in the necessary inputs. Like linear production, fixed-proportions production should be thought of as an extreme case. Rarely is there no opportunity for input substitution. (For example, it is true that a crane needs an operator, but, at a more general level, extra construction workers can substitute for construction equipment.)

However, there is an important implication of fixed-proportions production. In the face of an increase in an input's price, the firm *cannot* economize on its use, that is, substitute away from it. Thus, a petrochemical firm that uses fixed proportions of different chemicals to produce its specialty products is at the mercy of market forces that drive up the prices of some of these inputs.

Polynomial Functions

In the *polynomial form,* variables in the production function are raised to positive integer powers. As a simple example, consider the quadratic form

$$Q = aLK - bL^2K^2,$$

where a and b are positive coefficients. It is easy to check that each input shows diminishing returns. (For example, $MP_L = \partial Q/\partial L = aK - 2bK^2L$, which declines as L increases.) The quadratic form also displays decreasing returns to scale. A more flexible representation is the cubic form,

$$Q = aLK + bL^2K + cLK^2 - dL^3K - eLK^3,$$

where all coefficients are positive. We can show that this function displays increasing returns for low output levels and then decreasing returns for high output levels. The marginal product of an input (say, labor) takes the form

$$MP_L = \partial Q/\partial L = (aK + cK^2 - eK^3) + 2bKL - 3dKL^2.$$

We see that marginal product is a quadratic function in the amount of labor; that is, it is a parabola that rises, peaks, and then falls. Thus, this functional form includes an initial region of increasing marginal productivity followed by diminishing returns.

The Cobb-Douglas Function

Perhaps the most common production function specification is the **Cobb-Douglas function:**

$$Q = cL^\alpha K^\beta, \qquad [5.6]$$

where c, α, and β denote parameters to be estimated. (Furthermore, α and β are between 0 and 1.) The Cobb-Douglas function is quite flexible and has a number of appealing properties. First, it exhibits diminishing returns to each input. To see this, note that $MP_L = \partial Q/\partial L = c\alpha K^\beta L^{\alpha-1}$ and $MP_k = \partial Q/\partial K = c\beta L^\alpha K^{\beta-1}$. Labor's marginal product depends on both L and K. It declines as labor increases, since L is raised to a negative power ($\alpha - 1 < 0$). However, labor's marginal product shifts upward with increases in the use of capital, a complementary input. (Analogous results pertain to capital.)

Second, the nature of returns to scale in production depends on the sum of the exponents, $\alpha + \beta$. Constant returns prevail if $\alpha + \beta = 1$; increasing returns exist if $\alpha + \beta > 1$; decreasing returns exist if $\alpha + \beta < 1$. We can check these effects as follows. Set the amounts of capital and labor at specific levels, say, L_0 and K_0. Total output is $Q_0 = cL_0^\alpha K_0^\beta$. Now suppose the inputs are increased to new levels, zL_0 and zK_0, for $z > 1$. According to Equation 5.6, the new output level is

$$\begin{aligned}
Q_1 &= c(zL_0)^\alpha(zK_0)^\beta \\
&= cz^{\alpha+\beta}L_0^\alpha K_0^\beta \\
&= z^{\alpha+\beta}Q_0,
\end{aligned}$$

after regrouping terms and using the definition of Q_0. If the scale increase in the firm's inputs is z, the increase in output is $z^{\alpha+\beta}$. Under constant returns ($\alpha + \beta = 1$), the increase in output is z; that is, it is identical to the scale increase in the firm's inputs. For instance, if inputs double (so that $z = 2$), output doubles as well. Under increasing returns ($\alpha + \beta > 1$), output increases in a greater proportion than inputs (since $z^{\alpha+\beta} > z$). Under decreasing returns ($\alpha + \beta < 1$), output increases in a smaller proportion than inputs.[8]

Third, the Cobb-Douglas function can be conveniently estimated in its logarithmic form. By taking logs of both sides of Equation 5.6, we derive the equivalent linear equation:

$$\log(Q) = \log(c) + \alpha \log(L) + \beta \log(K).$$

With data on outputs and inputs, the manager can employ the linear regression techniques of Chapter 4 using $\log(L)$ and $\log(K)$ as independent variables and $\log(Q)$ as the dependent variable. The statistical output of this analysis includes estimates of $\log(c)$ (the constant term) and the coefficients α and β.

EXAMPLE 4   Suppose the firm faces the production function $Q = L^{.5}K^{.5}$ and input prices are $P_L = \$12$ and $P_K = \$24$. (The inputs are equally productive,

---

[8]One disadvantage of the Cobb-Douglas function is that it cannot allow simultaneously for different returns to scale. For instance, actual production processes often display increasing returns to scale up to certain levels of output, constant returns for intermediate output levels, and decreasing returns for very large output levels. The Cobb-Douglas function cannot capture this variation (because its returns are "all or nothing").

but capital is twice as expensive as labor.) The optimal input mix satisfies Equation 5.4 so that

$$[.5L^{-.5}K^{.5}]/12 = [.5L^{.5}K^{-.5}]/24.$$

After collecting terms, we get $K^{.5}/K^{-.5} = (12/24)L^{.5}/L^{-.5}$, or

$$K = .5L.$$

As noted, capital is twice as expensive as labor. As a result, for the Cobb-Douglas function, the firm employs half the number of units of capital as it does of labor.

Estimating Production Functions

Data for estimating production functions come in a number of forms. Engineering data can provide direct answers to a number of production questions: On average, how much output can be produced by a certain type of machine under different operating conditions? How many bushels of a particular crop can be grown and harvested on land (of known quality) using specified amounts of labor, capital, and materials (such as fertilizer)? Such information usually is based on experience with respect to similar (or not so similar) production processes. Consequently, the estimated production function is only as accurate as the past production experience on which it is based. The development of new weapons systems is a case in point. Although production and cost estimates are based on the best available engineering estimates (and possibly on tests of prototypes), they nonetheless are highly uncertain.[9]

A second source of production information is production data. For example, in a production time-series analysis, the firm's managers compile a production history, month by month or year by year, recording the amounts of inputs (capital, labor, land, materials, etc.) used in production and the resulting level of output. Alternatively, the economic data may come in the form of a *cross section*. In this case, information is gathered for different plants and firms in a given industry during a single period of time. For instance, by observing production in the auto industry, one can address a number of important questions: For plants of fixed size (possibly employing different degrees of automation), what is the effect on output of expanding the labor force (for instance, adding extra shifts)? Does the industry exhibit economies of scale and, if so, over what range of outputs? (That is, will a 40 percent increase in plant scale deliver more than a 40 percent increase in output?)

Production data, although subject to measurement errors, are very useful to managers. Based on these data, the manager (often with the help of an

[9]Another limitation of engineering data is that they apply only to parts of the firm's activities, typically physical production operations. Thus, such data shed little light on the firm's marketing, advertising, or financial activities.

operations research specialist) can estimate the mathematical relationship between levels of inputs and quantity of output. The principal statistical method for carrying out this task is regression analysis (the most important elements of which were discussed in Chapter 4). The end product of this analysis is a tangible representation of the firm's production function.

OTHER PRODUCTION DECISIONS

Within the limits of its production technology, the firm's managers face a number of important decisions. We have already discussed finding the optimal use of a single input in the short run and choosing the best mix of inputs in the long run. We now consider two other decisions: (1) the allocation of a single input among multiple production facilities and (2) the use of an input across multiple products.

Multiple Plants

Consider an oil company that buys crude oil and transforms it into gasoline at two of its refineries. Currently it has 10 thousand barrels of oil under long-term contract and must decide how to allocate it between its two refineries. The company's goal is to allocate supplies to maximize total output from the refineries. Let M_A and M_B represent the crude input at each refinery and Q_A and Q_B the gasoline outputs. The firm's problem is

Maximize $Q = Q_A + Q_B$, subject to $M_A + M_B = 10$ thousand.

The key to maximizing total output is to compare marginal products at the two refineries. Barrels of crude first should be allocated to the refinery whose marginal product is greater. Let's say this is refinery A. As additional barrels are allocated to this refinery, its marginal product diminishes, and it becomes worthwhile to allocate oil to refinery B as well.

In the final allocation of all 10 thousand barrels, output is maximized if and only if *the marginal products of both refineries are equal,* that is, when

$$MP_A = MP_B.$$

Why must this be the case? If marginal products differed (say, $MP_A < MP_B$), barrels should be shifted from the low-MP plant (refinery A) to the high-MP plant (refinery B).

Let's apply this rule in a specific example. Based on extensive studies, suppose that management has estimated the following production functions for the refineries:

Refinery A: $Q_A = 24M_A - .5M_A^2$
Refinery B: $Q_B = 20M_B - M_B^2,$

where gasoline outputs are measured in thousands of gallons and quantities of crude oils are measured in thousands of barrels. Marginal products are

$$\text{Refinery A:} \quad MP_A = 24 - M_A$$
$$\text{Refinery B:} \quad MP_B = 20 - 2M_B.$$

Figure 5.4 shows the marginal product curve for each refinery and two possible allocations. One is a *naive* allocation calling for an equal split between the two facilities: $M_A = M_B = 5$ thousand barrels. Using the production functions, we find total output to be 182.5 thousand gallons. However, the figure immediately points out the inefficiency of such a split. At this division, the marginal product of the last barrel of crude at refinery A greatly exceeds the marginal product of the last barrel at refinery B (19 > 10). Barrels should be reallocated toward refinery A.

We can readily identify the optimal solution from Figure 5.4: $M_A = 8$ thousand barrels and $M_B = 2$ thousand barrels.[10] At these allocations, each refinery's marginal product is 16. (To check this, refer to the marginal product

FIGURE 5.4

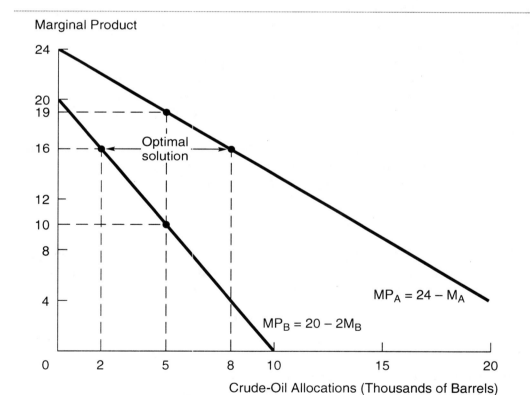

Marginal Product

Crude-Oil Allocations (Thousands of Barrels)

Splitting Production between Two Plants

To produce a given amount of output at least cost, the firm divides output between the plants in order to equate the plants' marginal products.

[10]We can find these allocations directly using the facts that $MP_A = MP_B$ and $M_A + M_B = 10$. Equating marginal products implies $24 - M_A = 20 - 2M_B$. Solving this equation and the quantity constraint simultaneously gives the solution, $M_A = 8$ thousand barrels and $M_B = 2$ thousand barrels.

expressions just given.) The total output of gasoline from this allocation is 196 thousand gallons—a considerable improvement on the naive allocation. Furthermore, no other allocation can deliver a greater total output.

Multiple Products

Firms often face the problem of allocating an input in fixed supply among different products. The input may be a raw material—for instance, DRAM computer chips allocated to the various models of personal computers manufactured by the firm—or it may be capital. Frequently, the input in shortest supply is managerial labor itself. Which products of the firm are in greatest need of managerial attention? Which top-level managers are best suited to improve performance in a given product line?

Consider a variation on the oil company's decision. Suppose two of the company's product managers are engaged in a heated debate. The first manager oversees the company's production and sale of gasoline; the second is responsible for production of synthetic fiber. Both products use crude oil as an essential input. The problem is that the current demands of the managers for this input exceed the firm's available crude oil supply, 20 thousand barrels. Each manager is arguing for a greater share of the input.

How can economic analysis be used to resolve this dispute? Given a limited resource and two products, gasoline and fiber, management's ultimate goal must be to allocate the crude oil to each product (in quantities M_G and M_F) to maximize total profit subject to the constraint of 20 thousand total barrels.

The form of this decision is very similar to that of the multiplant decision. Here total profit is maximized if and only if the input is allocated such that *the products generate identical marginal profits per unit of input.*[11]

$$M\pi_G = M\pi_F$$

If fibers had a higher marginal profit per unit input than gasoline, gallons of crude should be switched from gasoline production to fiber production.

Here is a concrete example. Suppose the production functions are

$$\text{Gasoline:} \quad G = 72M_G - 1.5M_G^2$$
$$\text{Fiber:} \quad F = 80M_F - 2M_F^2$$

Here gasoline output is measured in thousands of gallons, fiber output in thousands of square feet, and crude oil in thousands of barrels. The products' profits

---

[11] Here marginal profit is calculated *per unit input* because input is the appropriate decision variable.

per unit output are $.50 per gallon for gasoline and $.75 per square foot for fiber. Then the respective marginal profits are

$$M\pi_G = (\$.50)MP_G = (\$.50)(72 - 3M_G) = 36 - 1.5M_G$$
$$M\pi_F = (\$.75)MP_F = (\$.75)(80 - 4M_F) = 60 - 3M_F.$$

Setting these equal to each other and rearranging gives

$$M_F = .5M_G + 8.$$

Solving this equation and the constraint $M_G + M_F = 20$ implies $M_G = 8$ thousand barrels and $M_F = 12$ thousand barrels. This allocation generates 480 thousand gallons of gasoline and 672 thousand square feet of fiber. The firm's total profit is $744 thousand (less the cost of the crude).

Find the optimal crude oil allocation in the preceding example if the profit associated with fiber were cut in half, that is, fell to $.375 per square foot.   **CHECK STATION 5**

Final Remarks

With respect to both the plant and product decisions, two comments are in order. First, the appropriate marginal conditions are extended easily to the case of multiple (more than two) plants and decisions. (For instance, if there are three plants, the marginal product condition becomes $MP_A = MP_B = MP_C$.) Second, the decision framework changes significantly if management is able to vary the amount of the input. If management has access to as much crude oil as it wants (at a price) the problem can be dealt with plant by plant or product by product. Indeed, we have already considered the solution to this decision earlier: For each plant or each product, use of the input should be expanded to the point where its marginal revenue product equals its marginal cost per unit input (i.e., the input's price).

Recall that the key issue for the office supply firm was how to divide its 18-person sales force between large accounts (firms already under contract with the company or a competitor) and new accounts (firms without a current rental contract). To address this problem, five senior sales managers have put to paper their best estimate of the profit functions for both types of accounts; these functions are shown in Figure 5.5. There is general agreement that the large accounts are more profitable than the new accounts. In Figure 5.5, the profit function for large accounts is uniformly greater than that for new accounts. (For instance, assigning five salespeople to the former generates $800,000, whereas assigning the same number to new accounts generates only $400,000.) In light of the profit curves, would senior sales managers be justified in allocating all 18 salespeople to large accounts?   **Allocating a Sales Force Revisited**

FIGURE 5.5

Profit Functions for an Office Supply Firm

The optimal division of salespeople is 8 individuals to "large" accounts and 10 to "new" accounts.

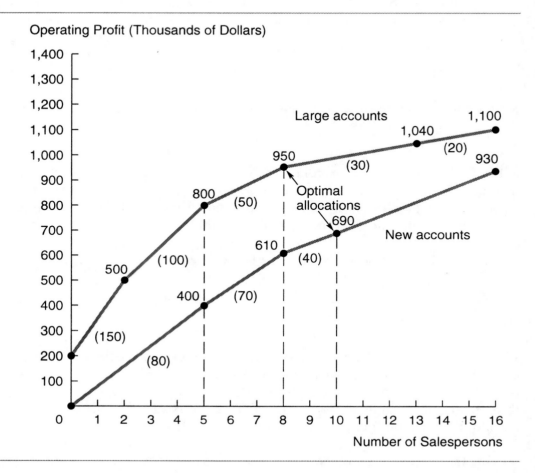

The answer is a resounding no! Management's objective is to assign its sales force to maximize total profit. This is just a fixed-input/multiple-product decision. Thus, the company should assign salespersons to the category of account that generates the greater marginal profit per unit input. For convenience, Figure 5.5 lists marginal profits (in parentheses) for each type of account and for the different sizes of sales force. The profit function for large accounts indicates that a two-person sales force raises profit from $200,000 to $500,000, implying a marginal profit of $150,000 per person (presumably this minimal sales force is essential for retaining the firm's most loyal current clients); going from two to five salespeople increases profit by $100,000 per individual, and so on.

The optimal allocation is 8 salespeople to large accounts and 10 to new accounts. We assign salespersons to accounts in order of marginal profits; that is, the highest marginal profit assignments are made first. The "first" five individuals serve large accounts. (Marginal profit is $150,000 and then $100,000 per person.) The "next" eight individuals serve new accounts. (Marginal profit is $80,000 and then $70,000 per person.) The "next" three individuals go to large accounts (marginal profit is $50,000). The "last" two salespeople serve new accounts (marginal profit is $40,000). By assigning 8 and 10 salespeople to large and new accounts, respectively, the firm earns a total operating profit of $950,000 + $690,000 = $1,640,000.

New accounts have a lower average profit per salesperson but claim a majority of the sales force. The intuitive explanation is that these accounts offer better profit opportunities at the margin. Once five salespeople have been assigned to maintain the large accounts, there is relatively little opportunity to increase profit in this area. In contrast, there is a relatively steady marginal profit to be earned in new accounts. Thus, this is where the majority of the salespeople should be placed.

SUMMARY

Decision-Making Principles

1. Production is the process of turning inputs into outputs.
2. To maximize profit, the firm should increase usage of a variable input up to the point where the input's marginal cost equals its marginal revenue product.
3. To minimize the cost of producing a particular amount of output, the firm should choose an input mix such that the ratio of the marginal product to the input's cost is the same across all inputs.
4. In allocating an input among multiple plants, the firm maximizes total output when marginal products are equal across facilities.
5. In allocating an input among multiple products, the firm maximizes total profit when marginal profits per unit input are equal across products.

Nuts and Bolts

1. The production function indicates the maximum amount of output the firm can produce for any combination of inputs.
2. The short run is a period of time in which the amount of one or more of the firm's inputs is fixed, that is, cannot be varied.
   a. Marginal product (MP) is the additional output produced by an additional unit of an input, all other inputs held constant.
   b. The law of diminishing returns states that, as units of one input are added (with all other inputs held constant), a point will be reached where the resulting additions to output will begin to decrease; that is, marginal product will decline.
   c. An input's marginal revenue product (MRP) is the extra revenue generated by a unit increase in the input. For input A,
   $MRP_A = (MR)(MP_A)$.

3. The long run is an amount of time long enough to allow the firm to vary all of its inputs.
   a. Constant returns to scale occur if a given percentage change in all inputs results in an equal percentage change in output.
   b. Increasing (decreasing) returns to scale occur if a given increase in all inputs results in a greater (lesser) proportionate change in output.

4. Production functions are estimated by specifying a variety of mathematical forms and fitting them to production data derived from engineering studies, economic time series, or cross sections.

Questions and Problems

1. Explain the difference between diminishing returns and decreasing returns to scale.

2. "One-tenth of the participants produce over one-third of the output. Increasing the number of participants merely reduces the average output." If this statement were true, would it be consistent with the law of diminishing returns?

3. Does optimal use of an input (such as labor) mean maximizing average output (per unit of input)? Explain.

4. In November 1990, Chrysler Corporation announced plans to initiate three-shift or nearly continuous (21-hours-per-day) production at a number of its plants. Explain why Chrysler's decision might have been prompted by movements in its wage costs or capital costs, or both. Why would Chrysler have instituted this production change for its most popular (and profitable) vehicles, its minivans and Jeep Cherokee? What risks might such a plan pose?

5. Consider the production function $Q = 10L - .5L^2 + 24K - K^2$ for L and K in the range 0 to 10 units. Does this production function exhibit diminishing returns to each input? Does it exhibit decreasing returns to scale? Explain.

6. a. Suppose the inputs in Problem 5 can be purchased at the same price per unit. Will production be relatively labor intensive or capital intensive? Explain.
   b. Suppose input prices are $P_L = 40$ and $P_K = 80$ and the price of output is 10. Determine the optimal quantity of each input.

7. A 200-pound steer can be sustained on a diet calling for various proportions of grass and grain. These combinations are shown in the table.

Pounds of Grass	Pounds of Grain
50	80
56	70
60	65
68	60
80	54
88	52

a. Plot the isoquant corresponding to the inputs necessary to sustain a 200-pound steer. Comment on its shape.

b. The rancher's cost of grass is $.10 per pound; the cost of grain is $.07 per pound. He prefers a feed mix of 68 pounds of grass and 60 pounds of grain. Is this a least-cost mix? If not, what is? Explain.

c. The rancher believes there are constant returns to scale in fattening cattle. At current feed prices, what input quantities should he choose if he wants to raise the steer's weight to 250 pounds?

8. A trendy French restaurant is one of the first businesses to open in a small corner of a commercial building still under construction. The restaurant has received rave reviews and has lines of diners waiting for tables most nights.

a. In the short run (next few months), what measures should the restaurant take to maximize its profit? Explain.

b. In the long run (next six months and beyond), how can it maximize its profit? (Assume that the impressive state of demand is permanent.)

9. Steel can be produced using three different methods: (1) a basic process using coke that produces steel ingots, (2) continuous casting, or (3) an electric furnace using steel scrap. The following table lists the average cost per ton of steel for each method.

Type of Cost	Basic Process	Continuous Casting	Electric Furnace
Materials	$150	$140	$120
Labor	$ 80	$ 75	$ 70
Capital	$100	$100	$ 60
Energy	$ 20	$ 15	$ 50
Other	$ 45	$ 40	$ 25

a. Production of steel by electric furnace is a relatively new development (beginning in the late 1970s) and accounts for a growing fraction of total steel sold. What is your prediction about the future production share of this method? Explain.

b. If there were a new energy crisis (causing energy prices to triple), how would this affect steelmakers' choices of production methods?

c. Suppose the price of steel scrap is expected to fall significantly over the next five years. What effect would this have on the choice of production method?

10. Making dresses is a labor-intensive process. Indeed, the production function of a dressmaking firm is well described by the equation $Q = L - L^2/800$, where Q denotes the number of dresses per week and L is the number of labor hours per week. The firm's additional cost of hiring an extra hour of labor is about $20 per hour (wage plus fringe benefits). The firm faces the fixed selling price P = $40.

a. How much labor should the firm employ? What is its resulting output and profit?

b. Over the next two years, labor costs are expected to be unchanged, but dress prices are expected to increase to $50. What effect will this have on the firm's optimal output? Explain. Suppose instead that inflation is expected to increase the firm's labor cost and output price by identical (percentage) amounts. What effect would this have on the firm's output?

c. Finally, suppose once again that MC_L = $20 and P = $50 but that labor productivity (i.e., output per labor hour) is expected to increase by 25 percent over the next five years. What effect would this have on the firm's optimal output? Explain.

11. In her last-minute preparations for final exams, a student has set aside five hours to split between studying for two subjects, finance and economics. Her goal is to maximize the average grade received in the two courses. (Note that maximizing the average grade and maximizing the sum of the grades are equivalent goals.) According to her best guesses, grades vary with study as follows:

Study Hours	Finance Grade	Study Hours	Economics Grade
0	70	0	75
1	78	1	81
2	83	2	85
3	88	3	87
4	90	4	89
5	92	5	90

a. List the marginal values of additional hours worked for each subject.

b. How much time should the student spend studying each subject?

c. Suppose the student also is taking an accounting exam and estimates that each hour of studying will raise her grade by three points. She has allotted two hours for studying accounting (in addition to the five hours already mentioned). Is this an optimal decision? Explain. (Assume her objective is to maximize her average grade across the three courses.)

12. Consider the production function $Q = 100L^{.5}K^{.4}$. Suppose $L = 1$ and $K = 1$ so that $Q = 100$.
    a. If L is increased by 1 percent, that is, to $L = 1.01$, with capital unchanged, what is the resulting percentage increase in output?
    b. Describe the nature of returns to scale for this production function.

13. A firm is producing a given amount of output at least cost using a mix of labor and capital (which exhibit some degree of substitutability). Using an isoquant graph, show that if one input price increases, least-cost production calls for the firm to lower the use of that input (and increase the use of the other).

*14. Let $Q = L^{\alpha}K^{\beta}$. Suppose the firm seeks to produce a given output while minimizing its total input cost: $TC = P_L L + P_K K$. Show that the optimal quantities of labor and capital satisfy $L/K = (\alpha/\beta)(P_K/P_L)$. Provide an intuitive explanation for this result.

*15. In a particular region, there are two lakes rich in fish. The quantity of fish caught in each lake depends on the number of persons who fish in each, according to $Q_1 = 10N_1 - .1N_1^2$ and $Q_2 = 16N_2 - .4N_2^2$, where N_1 and N_2 denote the number of fishers at each lake. In all, there are 40 fishers.
    a. Suppose $N_1 = 16$ and $N_2 = 24$. At which lake is the average catch per fisher greater? In light of this fact, how would you expect the fishers to re-deploy themselves?
    b. How many fishers will settle at each lake? (Hint: Find N_1 and N_2 such that the average catch is equal between the lakes.)
    c. The commissioner of fisheries seeks a division of fishers that will maximize the total catch at the two lakes. Explain how he should use information on the marginal catch at each lake to accomplish this goal. What division of the 40 fishers would you recommend?

Spreadsheet Problems

S1. A firm's production function is well described by the equation

$$Q = 2L - .01L^2 + 3K - .02K^2.$$

Input prices are $10 per labor hour and $20 per machine hour, and the firm sells its output at a fixed price of $10 per unit.

* Starred problems are more challenging.

a. In the short run, the firm has an installed capacity of K = 50 machine hours per day, and this capacity cannot be varied. Create a spreadsheet (based on the example that follows) to model this production setting. Determine the firm's profit-maximizing employment of labor. Use the spreadsheet to probe the solution by hand before using your spreadsheet's optimizer. Confirm that $MRP_L = MC_L$.

b. In the long run, the firm seeks to produce the output found in part (a) by adjusting its use of both labor and capital. Use your spreadsheet's optimizer to find the least-cost input amounts. (*Hint:* Be sure to include the appropriate output constraint for cell I3.)

c. Suppose the firm were to downsize in the long run, cutting its use of both inputs by 50 percent, relative to part (b). How much output would it now be able to produce? Comment on the nature of returns to scale in production. Has the firm's profitability improved? Is it currently achieving least-cost production?

	A	B	C	D	E	F	G	H	I
1									
2			OPTIMAL INPUTS						
3								Output	136.0
4								Price	10.0
5		Labor	20.0		Capital	50.0			
6		MP_L	1.600		MP_K	1.000		MR	10.00
7								Revenue	1360.0
8		MRP_L	16.0		MRP_K	10.0			
9		MC_L	10.0		MC_K	20.0		Cost	1200.0
10								Ave Cost	8.8
11									
12								Profit	160.0
13									

S2. A second firm's production function is given by the equation

$$Q = 12L^{.5}K^{.5}.$$

Input prices are $36 per labor unit and $16 per capital unit, and P = $10.

a. In the short run, the firm has a fixed amount of capital, K = 9. Create a spreadsheet to model this production setting. Determine the firm's profit-maximizing employment of labor. Use the spreadsheet to probe the solution by hand before using your spreadsheet's optimizer.

b. Once again, the firm seeks to produce the level of output found in part (a) by adjusting both labor and capital in the long run. Find the least-cost input proportions. Confirm that $MP_L/P_L = MP_K/P_K$.

c. Suppose the input price of labor falls to 18. Determine the new least-cost input amounts in the long run. Provide an intuitive explanation for the change in inputs caused by the lower labor price.

Suggested References

The following reading surveys the use and estimation of production functions.

Gold, B. "Changing Perspectives on Size, Scale, and Returns: An Interpretative Survey." *Journal of Economic Literature* (March 1981): 5–33.

The following references offer case studies of production and economies of scale.

Basu, S., and J. G. Fernald. "Returns to Scale in U.S. Production: Estimates and Implications." *Journal of Political Economy* 105 (April 1997): 249–283.

Boyd, G. A. "Factor Intensity and Site Geology as Determinants of Returns to Scale in Coal Mining." *Review of Economics and Statistics* (1987): 18–23.

Cookenboo, L. "Production Functions and Cost Functions: A Case Study" in E. Mansfield (Ed.), *Managerial Economics and Operations Research.* New York: Norton, 1993.

Noulas, A. G., S. C. Ray, and S. M. Miller. "Returns to Scale and Input Substitution for Large U.S. Banks." *Journal of Money, Credit and Banking* 22 (February 1990): 94–108.

Managers' production strategies are discussed in

Womack, J. P. "From Lean Production to Lean Enterprise." *Harvard Business Review* (March-April 1994): 93–103.

CHECK STATION ANSWERS

1. Labor's marginal product is uniformly greater (i.e., greater for any size of labor force) at a 30,000-square-foot plant than at a 10,000-square-foot plant.

2. At a 20,000-square-foot plant, the optimal labor force is 50 workers. (Here the MRP_L changes from \$180 to \$140.) At a 40,000-square-foot plant, the optimal labor force is 90 workers. (The MRP_L changes from \$180 to \$140.)

3. Doubling scale (starting from 10 workers and a 10,000-square-foot plant) more than doubles output. The same is true starting from 20 workers and a 20,000-square-foot plant. In contrast, doubling scale (starting from 50 workers and a 20,000-square-foot plant) produces less than double the output. Constant returns occur for a doubling of scale starting from 40 workers and a 10,000-square-foot plant or 30 workers and a 20,000-square-foot plant.

4. Given diminishing returns, using additional labor and less capital will lower the marginal product of labor and raise the marginal product of capital. Using extra labor also might bid up the price of labor. These effects move MP_L/P_L and MP_K/P_K into equality.

5. If fiber's profit is \$.375 per square foot, fiber's marginal profit becomes $M\pi_F = 30 - 1.5M_F$. Equating this to $M\pi_G$ implies $M_F = M_G - 4$. Together with $M_F + M_G = 20$, the solution is $M_F = 8$ thousand barrels and $M_G = 12$ thousand barrels. Given the reduced profit from fiber, the allocation of crude oil to this product is lowered (from 12 thousand to 8 thousand barrels).

CHAPTER 6

Cost Analysis

Delete each element of capability until system capability is totally gone and 30 percent of the cost will still remain.

Norman Augustine, Augustine's Laws

Allocating Costs

A sporting goods firm recently experimented with producing a new line of shoes: cross-training shoes for boys 10 to 16 years old. The boys' shoe is very similar to the firm's main product, a best-selling women's athletic shoe. (The sizes are virtually the same; only the colors and logos differ.) Thus, the new line of shoes is easy and inexpensive to produce—indeed, there is excess production-line capacity to do so. Production of the women's shoe runs about 8,000 pairs per week, and the company recently began producing 2,400 pairs of boys' shoes per week. The firm's production managers estimate that the factory overhead cost shared between the two shoe lines comes to about $90,000 per week. (Overhead costs include shared factory space, machines, electricity, and some sales and support staff.) The company's policy is to allocate these shared fixed costs in proportion to the numbers of pairs of each line of shoes.

Currently the company charges an average price of $36 per pair for the boys' shoe. However, the total revenues generated at that price fail to cover the shoe's total costs: its direct cost (primarily materials and labor) and the allocated overhead cost just mentioned. Faced with this apparent loss, top management is considering various options to achieve profitability:

- The firm's chief accountant suggests raising the price on the new line (say, to $40 per pair) to improve margins and better cover production costs.

212

- The marketing manager agrees this might be reasonable but cautions that sales are bound to drop.
- The head of production adds that unit costs will vary with volume as well. He advocates producing at an output level at which direct costs per unit will be minimized.

In light of this conflicting advice, what type of cost analysis could guide the firm in determining its profit-maximizing course of action?

Cost analysis is the bedrock on which many managerial decisions are grounded. Reckoning costs accurately is essential to determining a firm's current level of profitability. Moreover, profit-maximizing decisions depend on projections of costs at other (untried) levels of output. Thus, production managers frequently pose such questions as, What would be the cost of increasing production by 25 percent? What is the impact on cost of rising input prices? What production changes can be made to reduce or at least contain costs? In short, managers must pay close attention to the ways output and costs are interrelated.

In this chapter, we build on Chapter 5's analysis of production to provide an overview of these crucial cost concepts. In the first section, we discuss the basic principles of *relevant costs*—considering the concepts of opportunity costs and fixed costs in turn. Next, we examine the relationship between cost and output in the short run and the long run. Then we turn to economies of scale and economies of scope. Finally, we consider the importance of cost analysis for a number of key managerial decisions.

RELEVANT COSTS

A continuing theme of previous chapters is that optimal decision making depends crucially on a comparison of relevant alternatives. Roughly speaking, the manager must consider the relevant pros and cons of one alternative versus another. The precise decision-making principle is as follows:

In deciding among different courses of action, the manager need only consider the differential revenues and costs of the alternatives.

Thus, the only relevant costs are those that differ across alternative courses of action. In many managerial decisions, the pertinent cost differences are readily apparent. In others, issues of relevant cost are more subtle. The notions of opportunity costs and fixed costs are crucial for managerial decisions. We will consider each topic in turn.

Opportunity Costs and Economic Profits

The concept of opportunity cost focuses explicitly on a comparison of relative pros and cons. The **opportunity cost** associated with choosing a particular decision is measured by the benefits forgone in the next-best alternative. Typical examples of decisions involving opportunity cost include the following:

- What is the opportunity cost of pursuing an MBA degree?
- What is the opportunity cost of using excess factory capacity to supply specialty orders?
- What is the opportunity cost that should be imputed to city-owned land that is to be the site of a public parking garage downtown?

As the definition suggests, an estimate of the opportunity cost in each case depends on identifying the next-best alternative to the current decision. Consider the first example. Suppose the MBA aspirant has been working in business for five years. By pursuing an MBA degree full-time, what is he giving up? Presumably, it is the income he could have earned from the present job. (This opportunity cost is larger or smaller depending on how remunerative the job is and on the chances for immediate advancement.) Therefore, the total cost of taking an MBA degree is the explicit, out-of-pocket tuition cost plus the implicit (but equally real) opportunity cost.[1]

Next, consider the case of excess factory space. Assuming this space otherwise would go unused, its opportunity cost is zero! In other words, nothing is given up if the extra space is used to supply the specialty orders. More realistically, perhaps, one would assign a small opportunity cost to the capacity; committing the space to the specialty order might preclude using it for a more profitable "regular" order that might arrive unexpectedly.

Finally, consider the case of the city-owned land. Here the opportunity cost is whatever dollar value the land could bring in its next-best alternative. This might mean a different, more profitable city project. In general, an accurate estimate of the land's alternative value is simply its current market price. This price reflects what potential buyers are willing to pay for comparable downtown real estate. Unless the city has a better alternative for the land, its next-best option will be to sell the land on the open market.

As the first and third examples illustrate, opportunity costs for goods, services, or inputs often are determined by market prices (assuming such markets exist). For instance, the opportunity cost of the full-time MBA student's time

---

[1]Here are some questions to consider: What is the opportunity cost of pursuing an MBA degree part-time at night while holding one's current job? For a 19-year-old, what is the opportunity cost of pursuing an undergraduate business degree?

is his forgone wage (determined, of course, by labor-market conditions). The cost of the city-owned land is its market price. Note that if the city did not own the land, its cost would be explicit; it would have to pay the market price to obtain it. The fact of ownership doesn't change this cost; opportunity cost is still determined by the market price.[2]

The concept of opportunity cost is simply another way of comparing pros and cons. The basic rule for optimal decision making is this:

Undertake a given course of action if and only if its incremental benefits exceed its incremental costs (including opportunity costs).

Thus, pursuing the MBA degree makes sense only if the associated benefits—acquisition of knowledge, career advancement, higher earnings—exceed the total costs. Likewise, the factory space should be used only if the direct increase in cash flows exceeds the opportunity cost. Finally, the garage should be built only if its total benefits exceed its costs.

How would one estimate the full cost to an airline if one of its planes is held over for 24 hours in a western airport for repair?

CHECK
STATION 1

ECONOMIC PROFIT   At a general level, the notion of profit would appear unambiguous: Profit is the difference between revenues and costs. On closer examination, however, one must be careful to distinguish between two definitions of profit. **Accounting profit** is the difference between revenues obtained and expenses incurred. The profit figures reported by firms almost always are based on accounting profits; it is the job of accountants to keep a careful watch on revenues and explicit expenses. This information is useful for both internal and external purposes: for managers, shareholders, and the government (particularly for tax purposes). With respect to managerial decision making, however, the accounting measure does not present the complete story concerning profitability. In this case, the notion of economic profit is essential. **Economic profit** is the difference between revenues and all economic costs (explicit and implicit), including opportunity costs. In particular, economic profit involves costs associated with capital and with managerial labor. Here is a simple illustration.

STARTING A BUSINESS   After working five years at her current firm, a money manager decides to start her own investment management service. She has

---

[2]Of course, explicit costs and opportunity costs sometimes differ. For example, suppose an individual possesses financial wealth that earns an 8 percent rate of return. If that person were to borrow from a bank, the rate would be no lower than 11 percent. Then the opportunity cost of internally financing payment of MBA tuition is lower than the market cost of obtaining a loan to do so.

developed the following estimates of annual revenues and costs (on average) over the first three years of business:

Management fees	$140,000
Miscellaneous revenues	12,000
Office rent	−36,000
Other office expenses	−18,000
Staff wages (excluding self)	−24,000

From this list, the new venture's accounting profit, the difference between revenues and explicit expenses, would be reckoned at $74,000.

Is going into business on one's own truly profitable? The correct answer depends on recognizing all relevant opportunity costs. Suppose the money manager expects to tie up $80,000 of her personal wealth in working capital as part of starting the new business. Although she expects to have this money back after the initial three years, a real opportunity cost exists: the interest the funds would earn if they were not tied up. If the interest rate is 8 percent, this capital cost amounts to $6,400 per year. This cost should be included in the manager's estimate. Furthermore, suppose the manager's compensation (annual salary plus benefits) in her current position is valued at $56,000. Presumably this current position is her best alternative. Thus, $56,000 is the appropriate cost to assign to her human capital.

After subtracting these two costs, economic profit is reduced to $11,600. This profit measures the projected monetary gain of starting one's own business. Since the profit is positive, the manager's best decision is to strike out on her own. Note that the manager's decision would be very different if her current compensation were greater—say, $80,000. The accounting profit looks attractive in isolation. But $74,000 obviously fails to measure up to the manager's current compensation ($80,000) even before accounting for the cost of capital.

In general, we say that economic profit is zero if total revenues are exactly matched by total costs, where total costs include a normal return to any capital invested in the decision and other income forgone. Here *normal return* means the return required to compensate the suppliers of capital for bearing the risk (if any) of the investment; that is, capital market participants demand higher normal rates of return for riskier investments. As a simple example, consider a project that requires a $150,000 capital investment and returns an accounting profit of $9,000. Is this initiative profitable? If the normal return on such an investment (one of comparable risk) is 10 percent, the answer is no. If the firm must pay investors a 10 percent return, its capital cost is $15,000. Therefore, its economic profit is $9,000 − $15,000 = −$6,000. The investment is a losing proposition. Equivalently, the project's rate of return is 9,000/150,000, or 6 percent.

Although this return is positive, the investment remains unprofitable because its return is well below the normal 10 percent requirement.

Now suppose the investment's return is 12 percent; that is, its accounting profit is $18,000. In this case, the project delivers a 2 percent "excess" return (i.e., above the normal rate) and would be economically profitable. Finally, suppose the project's accounting profit is exactly $15,000. Then its economic profit would be exactly zero: $15,000 − (.1)($150,000) = 0. Equivalently, we would say that the project just earned a normal (10 percent) rate of return.

Fixed and Sunk Costs

Costs that are **fixed**—that is, do not vary—with respect to different courses of action under consideration are irrelevant and need not be considered by the manager. The reason is simple enough: If the manager computes each alternative's profit (or benefit), the same fixed cost is subtracted in each case. Therefore, the fixed cost itself plays no role in determining the relative merits of the actions. Consider once again the recent graduate who is deciding whether to begin work immediately or to take an MBA degree. In his deliberations, he is concerned about the cost of purchasing his first car. Is this relevant? The answer is no, assuming he will need (and will purchase) a car whether he takes a job or pursues the degree.

Consider a typical business example. A production manager must decide whether to retain his current production method or switch to a new method. The new method requires an equipment modification (at some expense) but saves on the use of labor. Which production method is more profitable? The hard (and tedious) way to answer this question is to compute the bottom-line profit for each method. The easier and far more insightful approach is to ignore all fixed costs. The original equipment cost, costs of raw materials, selling expenses, and so on are all fixed (i.e., do not vary) with respect to the choice of production method. The only differential costs concern the equipment modification and the reduction in labor. Clearly, the new method should be chosen if and only if its labor savings exceed the extra equipment cost. Notice that the issue of relevant costs would be very different if management were tackling the larger decision of whether to continue production (by either method) *or shut down*. With respect to a shut-down decision, many (if not all) of the previous fixed costs become variable. Here the firm's optimal decision depends on the magnitudes of costs saved versus revenues sacrificed from discontinuing production.

Ignoring fixed costs is important not only because it saves considerable computation but also because it forces managers to focus on the differential costs that are relevant. Be warned that ignoring fixed costs is easier in principle than in practice. The case of sunk costs is particularly important. A **sunk cost** is an expense that already has been incurred and cannot be recovered. For instance, in the earlier factory example, plant space originally may have been built at a high price. But this historic cost is sunk and is irrelevant to the firm's current decision. As we observed earlier, in the case of excess, unused factory capacity, the relevant opportunity cost is near zero.

More generally, sunk costs cast their shadows in sequential investment decisions. Consider a firm that has spent $20 million in research and development (R&D) on a new product. The R&D effort to date has been a success, but an additional $10 million is needed to complete a prototype product that (because of delays) may not be first to market. Should the firm make the additional investment in the product? The correct answer depends on whether the product's expected future revenue exceeds the total *additional* costs of developing and producing the product. (Of course, the firm's task is to forecast accurately these future revenues and costs.) The $20 million sum spent to date is sunk and, therefore, irrelevant for the firm's decision. If the product's future prospects are unfavorable, the firm should cease R&D.

Perhaps the last word on sunk cost is provided by the story of seventeenth-century warship *Vassa*. When newly launched in Stockholm before a huge crowd that included Swedish royalty, the ship floated momentarily, overturned, and ignominiously (and literally) became a sunk cost.

Business Behavior —Sunk Costs

Sunk costs are easy to recognize in principle but frequently distort decisions in practice. The construction of nuclear power plants in the 1970s and 1980s illustrates the problem. New plant construction was plagued by cost overruns and safety problems. (Indeed, after the Three Mile Island accident in 1979, safety concerns and strict safety regulations contributed to the overrun problem.) At the same time, revenue projections declined due to the low prices of alternative energy sources, oil and natural gas. While no *new* plants were initiated in the 1980s (because of worsening profit prospects), many utilities continued to spend on plants already in progress, despite equally dim profit prospects. In light of uncertain profits and looming losses, making the right decision—to continue construction or abandon the effort—wasn't easy. (As the unrepentant actress Mae West once said, "In a choice between two evils, my general rule is to pick the one I haven't tried yet.") In some cases, utilities abandoned plants that were 85 percent complete after having spent more than $1 billion. Yet looking forward, this might be a perfectly rational decision. By contrast, construction of the Shoreham nuclear plant on Long Island continued to completion despite severe cost escalation and safety concerns. With an accumulated cost bill of $6 billion by 1989, it never received regulatory approval to operate, and the enormous sums spent came to nothing.

Research by psychologists testing decision behavior of individuals, including business managers, clearly shows that sunk costs can adversely affect judgment[3]. For instance, executives will choose rightly to make a substantial initial

[3]For research on decision making and sunk costs, see H. Arkes and C. Blumer, "The Psychology of Sunk Cost," *Organizational Behavior and Human Decision Process*, 1985, 124–140; and W. Samuelson and R. Zeckhauser, "Status Quo Bias in Decision Making," *Journal of Risk and Uncertainty*, 1988, 7–59.

investment in a simulated project, such as new product development, an R&D effort, or a capital investment. Yet, they continue to make cash investments even when new information in the simulation is highly unfavorable. By contrast, executives who enter the simulation only at the second decision with the same information (here, previous management has made the initial decision) are much more likely to pull the plug and write off the investment. The moral is clear; it's difficult to be objective when one is already psychologically invested in the initial decision (the more so the larger the initial sunk cost). Initial investors tend to maintain an overly optimistic outlook (despite the unfavorable new information) and adhere to the status quo established by their initial decision. Sunk costs also have effects in other contexts. For instance, in ongoing business disputes ranging from labor impasses to law suits, the rival parties frequently dig in as costs accumulate and refuse to settle (even when it is in their self-interest), thereby escalating the conflict.

Government spending programs, particularly in energy, defense, and basic science face similar challenges. During the 1980s and 1990s, the U.S. government halted public spending on scores of energy projects, including almost all synthetic-fuel programs ($25 billion spent). In light of changing economics, the Pentagon canceled development of a number of weapons systems. In 1989, Congress authorized the largest pure science project ever undertaken, the Supercollider program. Unhappily, the project's cost estimates obeyed their own law of acceleration, rising over the years from $4.4 billion to $6 billion to $8.2 billion to $11 billion to $13 billion. In 1993, with $2 billion already spent and 15 miles of underground tunnels dug, Congress voted to abandon the program. Despite critics' contentions that government programs, once begun, seem to have lives of their own, the budget axe has been used effectively in scrapping uneconomical programs.

A firm spent $10 million to develop a product for market. In the product's first two years, its profit was $6 million. Recently there has been an influx of comparable products offered by competitors (imitators in the firm's view). Now the firm is reassessing the product. If it drops the product, it can recover $2 million of its original investment by selling its production facility. If it continues to produce the product, its estimated revenues for successive two-year periods will be $5 million and $3 million and its costs will be $4 million and $2.5 million. (After four years, the profit potential of the product will be exhausted and the plant will have zero resale value.) What is the firm's best course of action?

CHECK STATION 2

Profit Maximization with Limited Capacity: Ordering a Best Seller

The notion of opportunity cost is essential for optimal decisions when a firm's multiple activities compete for its limited capacity. Consider the manager of a bookstore who must decide how many copies of a new best seller to order.

Based on past experience, the manager believes she can accurately predict potential sales. Suppose the best seller's estimated price equation is $P = 24 - Q$, where P is the price in dollars and Q is quantity in hundreds of copies sold per month. The bookstore buys directly from the publisher, which charges $12 per copy. Let's consider the following three questions:

1. How many copies should the manager order, and what price should she charge? (There is plenty of unused shelf space to stock the best seller.)

2. Now suppose shelf space is severely limited and stocking the best seller will take shelf space away from other books. The manager estimates that there is a $4 profit on the sale of a book stocked. (The best seller will take up the same shelf space as the typical book.) Now what are the optimal price and order quantity?

3. After receiving the order in Question 2, the manager is disappointed to find that sales of the best seller are considerably lower than predicted. Actual demand is $P = 18 - 2Q$. The manager is now considering returning some or all of the copies to the publisher, who is obligated to refund $6 for each copy returned. How many copies should be returned (if any), and how many should be sold and at what price?

As always, we can apply marginal analysis to determine the manager's optimal course of action, provided we use the "right" measure of costs. In Question 1, the only marginal cost associated with the best seller is the explicit $12 cost paid to the publisher. The manager maximizes profit by setting MR equal to MC. Since $MR = 24 - 2Q$, we have $24 - 2Q = 12$. The result is $Q = 6$ hundred books and $P = \$18$. This outcome is listed in Table 6.1a.

By comparison, what are the optimal order quantity and price when shelf space is limited, as in Question 2? The key point is that ordering an extra best seller will involve not only an out-of-pocket cost ($12) but also an opportunity cost ($4). The opportunity cost is the $4 profit the shelf space would earn on an already stocked book—profit that would be forgone. In short, the total cost of ordering the book is $12 + 4 = \$16$. Setting MR equal to $16, we find that $Q = 4$ hundred and $P = \$20$. Given limited shelf space, the manager orders fewer best sellers than in Question 1. Table 6.1b compares the profitability of ordering 400 versus 600 books. The cost column lists the store's payment to the publisher ($12 per best seller). Forgone profit is measured at $4 per book.

We confirm that ordering 400 books is the more profitable option, taking into account the forgone profit on sales of other books. Indeed, the logic of marginal analysis confirms that this order quantity is optimal, that is, better than any other order size.

Finally, Question 3 asks how the manager should plan sales and pricing of the 400 best sellers already received if demand falls to $P = 18 - 2Q$. The key here is to recognize that the original $12 purchase price is irrelevant; it is a

TABLE 6.1

An Optimal Book Order

The optimal number of books to order and sell depends on demand, sales costs, and opportunity costs.

	Price	Sales Revenue	Cost	Forgone Profit	Final Net Profit
(a) $Q_s = 600$	$18	$10,800	$7,200	$ 0	$3,600
(b) $Q_s = 400$	20	8,000	4,800	1,600	1,600
[$Q_s = 600$]	18	10,800	7,200	2,400	1,200
(c) $Q_s = 200$	14	2,800	4,800	800	−1,600
$Q_r = 200$	6	1,200		0	
[$Q_s = 400$]	10	4,000	4,800	1,600	−2,400
[$Q_r = 0$]	6	0		0	
[$Q_s = 0$]	—	0	4,800	0	−2,400
[$Q_r = 400$]	6	2,400		0	

sunk cost. However, opportunity costs are relevant. The opportunity cost of keeping the best seller for sale has two elements: the $4 profit that another book would earn (as in Question 2) plus the $6 refund that would come if the copy were returned. Therefore, the total opportunity cost is $6 + 4 = \$10$. Setting MR equal to MC implies $18 - 4Q = 10$, or $Q = 2$ hundred. The store manager should keep 200 books to be sold at a price of $18 - (2)(2) = \$14$ each. She should return the remaining 200 books to obtain a $1,200 refund. As Table 6.1 indicates, this course of action will minimize her overall loss in the wake of the fall in demand. The table also shows that selling all 400 copies or returning all copies would generate greater losses.

THE COST OF PRODUCTION

As we noted in Chapter 5, production and cost are very closely related. In a sense, cost information is a distillation of production information: It combines the information in the production function with information about input prices. The end result can be summarized in the following important concept: The **cost function** indicates the firm's total cost of producing any given level of output. The concept of a cost function was first introduced in Chapter 2. In this section, we take a much closer look at the factors that determine costs. A key point to remember is that the concept of the cost function presupposes that the firm's managers have determined the least-cost method of producing any given level of output. (Clearly, inefficient or incompetent managers could contrive to produce a given level of output at some—possibly inflated—cost, but this would hardly be profit maximizing. Nor would the resulting cost schedule foster optimal managerial decision making.) In short, the cost function should always be thought of as a *least-cost function*. It usually is denoted as C = C(Q) and can be described by means of a table, a graph, or an equation.

As in our study of production, our analysis of cost distinguishes between the short run and the long run. Recall that the short run is a period of time so limited that the firm is unable to vary the use of some of its inputs. In the long run, all inputs—labor, equipment, factories—can be varied freely. Our investigation of cost begins with the short run.

Short-Run Costs

In the basic model of Chapter 5, we focused on two inputs, capital and labor. In the short run, capital is a fixed input (i.e., cannot be varied) and labor is the sole variable input. Production of additional output is achieved by using additional hours of labor in combination with a fixed stock of capital equipment in the firm's current plant. Of course, the firm's cost is found by totaling its expenditures on labor, capital, materials, and any other inputs and including any relevant opportunity costs, as discussed in the previous section. For concreteness, consider a firm that provides a service—say, electronic repair. Figure 6.1 provides a summary of the repair firm's costs as they vary for different quantities of output (number of repair jobs completed).

The total cost of achieving any given level of output can be decomposed into two parts: fixed and variable costs. As the term suggests, **fixed costs** result from the firm's expenditures on fixed inputs. These costs are incurred regardless of the firm's level of output. Most overhead expenses fall into this category. Such costs might include the firm's lease payments for its factory, the cost of equipment, some portion of energy costs, and various kinds of administrative costs (payment for support staff, taxes, and so on). According to the table in Figure 6.1, the repair firm's total fixed costs come to $270,000 per year. These costs are incurred irrespective of the actual level of output (i.e., even if no output were produced).

Variable costs represent the firm's expenditures on variable inputs. With respect to the short-run operations of the repair firm, labor is the sole variable input. Thus, in this example, variable costs represent the additional wages paid by the firm for extra hours of labor. To achieve additional output (i.e., to increase the volume of repair jobs completed), the firm must incur additional variable costs. Naturally, we observe that total variable costs rise with increases in the quantity of output. In fact, a careful look at Figure 6.1 shows that variable costs rise increasingly rapidly as the quantity of output is pushed higher and higher. Note that the firm's total cost exhibits exactly the same behavior. (With fixed costs "locked in" at $270,000, total cost increases are due solely to changes in variable cost.) The graph in Figure 6.1 shows that the total cost curve becomes increasingly steep at higher output levels.

FIGURE 6.1

A Firm's Total Costs

Total cost is the sum of fixed cost and variable cost.

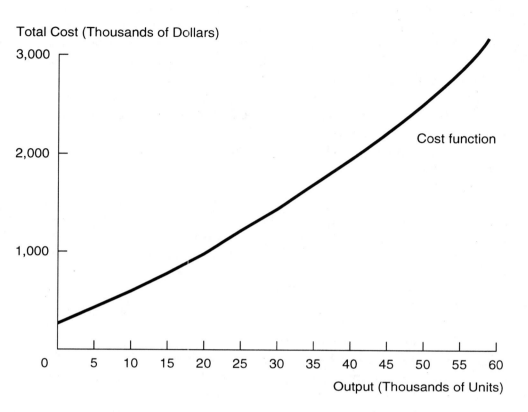

Total Cost (Thousands of Dollars)

Cost function

Output (Thousands of Units)

Annual Output (Repairs Thousands)	Total Cost ($ Thousands)	Fixed Cost ($ Thousands)	Variable Cost ($ Thousands)
0	270.0	270	0.0
5	427.5	270	157.5
10	600.0	270	330.0
15	787.5	270	517.5
20	990.0	270	720.0
25	1,207.5	270	937.5
30	1,440.0	270	1,170.0
35	1,687.5	270	1,417.5
40	1,950.0	270	1,680.0
45	2,227.5	270	1,957.5
50	2,520.0	270	2,250.0
55	2,827.5	270	2,557.5
60	3,150.0	270	2,880.0

Average total cost (or simply **average cost**) is total cost divided by the total quantity of output. Figure 6.2 shows average costs for the repair company over different levels of output. (Check that the average cost values are computed as the ratio of total cost in column 2 of the table and total output in column 1.) The graph displays the behavior of average cost. Both the table and graph show that short-run average cost is U-shaped. Increases in output first cause average cost (per unit) to decline. At 30,000 units of output, average cost achieves a minimum (at the bottom of the U). As output continues to increase, average unit costs steadily rise. (We will discuss the factors underlying this average cost behavior shortly.) Finally, **average variable cost** is variable cost divided by total output. Because it excludes fixed costs, average variable cost is always smaller than average total cost.

Marginal cost is the addition to total cost that results from increasing output by one unit. We already are acquainted with the concept of marginal cost from the analyses of the firm's output and pricing decisions in Chapters 2 and 3. Now we take a closer look at the determinants of marginal cost. The last column of the table in Figure 6.2 lists the repair company's marginal costs for output increments of 5,000 units. For instance, consider an output increase from 25,000 to 30,000 units. According to Figure 6.2, the result is a total cost increase of 1,440,000 − 1,207,500 = \$232,500. Consequently, the marginal cost (*on a per-unit basis*) is 232,500/5,000 = \$46.50/unit. The other entries in the last column are computed in an analogous fashion. From either the graph or the table, we observe that the firm's marginal cost rises steadily with increases in output. Expanding output starting from a level of 40,000 units per month is much more expensive than starting from 20,000 units.

What factors underlie the firm's increasing short-run marginal cost (SMC)? The explanation is simple. With labor the only variable input, SMC can be expressed as

$$SMC = P_L/MP_L, \tag{6.1}$$

where P_L denotes the price of hiring additional labor (i.e., wage per hour) and MP_L denotes the marginal product of labor.[4] To illustrate, suppose the prevailing wage is \$20 per hour and labor's marginal product is .5 units per hour (one-half of a typical repair job is completed in one hour). Then the firm's marginal (labor) cost is 20/.5 = \$40 per additional completed job. According to Equation 6.1, the firm's marginal cost will increase if there is an increase in the price of labor or a decrease in labor's marginal product. Moreover, as the firm uses additional labor to produce additional output, the *law of diminishing returns* applies. With other inputs fixed, adding

---

[4]The mathematical justification is as follows. Marginal cost can be expressed as $MC = \Delta C/\Delta Q = (\Delta C/\Delta L)/(\Delta Q/\Delta L) = P_L/MP_L$. As the notation indicates, here we are looking at discrete changes in output and input. The same relationship holds with respect to infinitesimal changes, (dC/dQ).

FIGURE 6.2

A Firm's Average and
Marginal Costs

Cost/Unit (Thousands of Dollars)

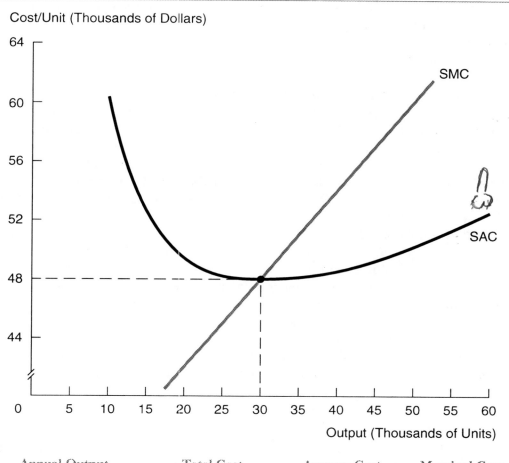
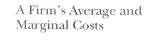

Annual Output (Repairs Thousands)	Total Cost (Thousands of Dollars)	Average Cost (Dollars/Unit)	Marginal Cost (Dollars/Unit)
0	270.0	∞	
			31.5
5	427.5	85.5	
			34.5
10	600.0	60	
			37.5
15	787.5	52.5	
			40.5
20	990.0	49.5	
			43.5
25	1,207.5	48.3	
			46.5
30	1,440.0	48	
			49.5
35	1,687.5	48.2	
			52.5
40	1,950.0	48.8	
			55.5
45	2,227.5	49.5	
			58.5
50	2,520.0	50.4	
			61.5
55	2,827.5	51.4	
			64.5
60	3,150.0	52.5	

increased amounts of a variable input (in this case, labor) generates smaller amounts of additional output; that is, after a point, *labor's marginal product declines.* As a result, marginal cost rises with the level of output. (Clearly, material costs are also variable and, therefore, are included in SMC. However, because these costs typically vary in proportion to output, they do not affect the shape of SMC.)

Now we can explain the behavior of short-run average cost (SAC). When output is very low (say 5,000 units), total cost consists mainly of fixed cost (since variable costs are low). SAC is high because total cost is divided by a small number of units. As output increases, total costs (which are mostly fixed) are "spread over" a larger number of units, so SAC declines. In the graph in Figure 6.2, notice that SAC lies well above SMC for low levels of output. So long as extra units can be added at a marginal cost that is lower than the average cost of the current output level, increasing output must reduce overall average cost. But what happens to average cost as marginal cost continues to rise? Eventually there comes a point at which SMC becomes greater than SAC. As soon as extra units become more expensive than current units (on average), the overall average begins to increase. This explains the upward arc of the U-shaped SAC curve. This argument also confirms an interesting result: *The firm's marginal cost curve intersects its average cost curve at the minimum point of SAC.*

We have described the firm's short-run cost function in tabular and graphic forms. The cost function also can be represented in equation form. The repair company's short-run cost function is

$$C = C(Q) = 270 + (30Q + .3Q^2), \qquad [6.2]$$

where output is measured in thousands of units and costs are in thousands of dollars. (You should check this equation against Figure 6.1 for various outputs.) The first term is the firm's fixed costs; the term in parentheses encompasses its variable costs. In turn, short-run average cost is SAC = C/Q, or

$$SAC = 270/Q + (30 + .3Q). \qquad [6.3]$$

The first term usually is referred to as **average fixed cost** (fixed cost divided by total output); the term in the parentheses is **average variable cost** (variable cost divided by total output). According to Equation 6.3, as output increases, average fixed cost steadily declines while average variable cost rises. The first effect dominates for low levels of output; the second prevails at sufficiently high levels. The combination of these two effects explains the U-shaped average cost curve. Finally, treating cost as a continuous function, we find marginal cost to be

$$SMC = dC/dQ = 30 + .6Q. \qquad [6.4]$$

We observe that marginal cost rises with the level of output.

Long-Run Costs

In the long run, the firm can freely vary all of its inputs. In other words, there are no fixed inputs or fixed costs—*all costs are variable*. Thus, there is no difference between total costs and variable costs. We begin our discussion by stressing two basic points. First, the ability to vary all inputs allows the firm to produce at lower cost in the long run than in the short run (when some inputs are fixed). In short, flexibility is valuable. As we saw in Chapter 5, the firm still faces the task of finding the least-cost combination of inputs.

Second, the shape of the long-run cost curve depends on returns to scale. To see this, suppose the firm's production function exhibits constant returns to scale. **Constant returns to scale** means that increasing all inputs by a given percentage (say, 20 percent) increases output by the same percentage. Assuming input prices are unchanged, the firm's total expenditure on inputs also will increase by 20 percent. Thus, the output increase is accompanied by an equal percentage increase in costs, with the result that average cost is unchanged. *So long as constant returns prevail, average cost is constant.*

Production exhibits **increasing returns to scale** or equivalently **economies of scale** if average cost falls as the firm's scale of operation increases. For instance, a 20 percent increase in inputs now generates a greater than 20 percent increase in output causing average cost per unit to fall. *When increasing returns prevail, average cost falls as output increases.* Finally, we can apply analogous reasoning to show that *decreasing returns to scale* implies *rising average costs as the firm's output and scale increase.*

SHORT-RUN VERSUS LONG-RUN COST   Consider a firm that produces output using two inputs, labor and capital. Management's immediate task is to plan for future production. It has not leased plant and equipment yet, nor has it hired labor. Thus, it is free to choose any amounts of these inputs it wishes. Management knows that production exhibits constant returns to scale. Consequently, the firm's long-run average cost (LAC) is constant as shown by the horizontal line in Figure 6.3. Furthermore, we can show that the firm should plan to use the same optimal *ratio* of labor to capital in production, regardless of the level of output. If the firm plans to double its level of output, it should also double the use of each input, leaving the proportions unchanged. These input proportions (in combination with prevailing input prices) determine the firm's average cost per unit. In Figure 6.3, LAC = C/Q = \$4. The long-run total cost function is $C = 4Q$. Thus, long-run marginal cost (LMC) is also \$4 per unit. As the figure shows, LMC and LAC are constant and identical.

Figure 6.3 also shows the short-run average cost curves for three possible plants of varying sizes. The firm's plant (and equipment therein) represents the total capital input. The left curve is for a 9,000-square-foot plant, the middle curve for an 18,000-square-foot plant, and the right curve for a 27,000-square-foot plant. Notice that the smallest plant is optimal for producing 72,000 units of output.

FIGURE 6.3

Short-Run versus
Long-Run Cost

Under constant returns
to scale, the firm's
LAC is constant.
However, SACs depend
on the size of the firm's
plant and are U-shaped.

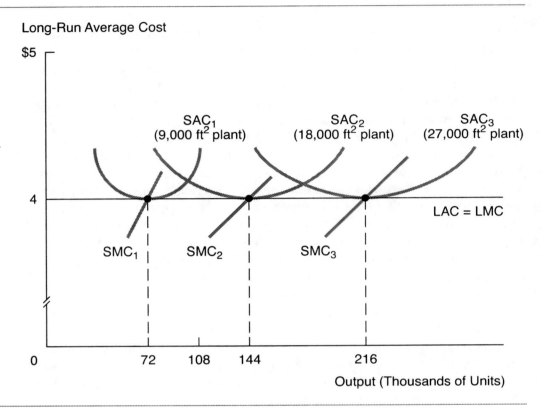

With such a plant in place (and using the right amount of labor), the firm can produce this output level at a minimum average cost of $4. If the firm planned to produce twice the level of output (144,000 units), it would use a plant twice the size (an 18,000-square-foot facility) and twice the labor. Finally, the largest plant is optimal for producing 216,000 units.

Once its plant is in place, however, the firm has considerably less flexibility. In the short run, its plant cannot be varied. Thus, if a 9,000-square-foot plant is in place, production of an output, such as 108,000 units (see Figure 6.3), means an increase in the average cost of production above $4. Why? To produce this output requires expanding the use of labor (since the plant is fixed). Because of diminishing returns, the extra output comes at an increasing marginal cost, and this drives up average cost as well.

Obviously, the firm may have many choices of plant size, not just three. Before its plant is in place, the firm has complete flexibility to produce *any* level of output at a $4 unit cost. (It simply builds a plant of the proper scale and applies the right proportion of labor.) But, once the plant is in place, any change in planned output must be achieved by a change in labor (the sole variable input). The result is a movement either right or left up the U of the relevant SAC curve. In either case, there is an increase in average cost.

In a host of industries, such as electronics, automobiles, computers, aircraft, and agricultural products of all kinds, competition is worldwide. The major industrial countries of the world compete with one another for shares of global markets. For numerous goods, a U.S. consumer has a choice of purchasing a domestically produced item or a comparable imported good made in a far-flung corner of the world—for instance, Europe, East Asia, or South America. Thus, a knowledge of international trade is essential for successful managers in increasingly global industries.

International trade is based on mutually beneficial specialization among countries. Why does one country concentrate on production and exports in certain goods and services, and another country specialize in others? Important reasons for varying patterns of specialization include different resource endowments, differences in the amount and productivity of labor, and differences in capital. For instance, a nation with abundant agricultural resources, predominantly unskilled labor, and little capital is likely to specialize in production of basic foods. By contrast, a nation, such as Japan, with a highly educated population and abundant capital, but with relatively few natural resources, has an advantage in manufactured goods. Many observers believe that the United States' competitive advantage lies in high-tech goods and services. Relying on their research expertise and innovative ability, American firms excel in the development of technologically advanced goods and services. As these markets grow and mature, however, one would expect that high-tech goods will evolve into commodity items, assembled and produced in large-scale facilities. It is not surprising that production of these goods tends to shift to other parts of the world over time.

To understand the basis for mutually beneficial trade, it is important to grasp the notion of comparative advantage. The easiest way to explain this concept is with a simple example. Table 6.2 offers a stylized depiction of trade involving two goods, digital electronic watches and pharmaceutical products, and two countries, the United States and Japan. Part (a) of the table shows the productivity of labor (i.e., output per hour) in each country for each good. For instance, on average U.S. workers produce 4 bottles of pills and 1 digital watch per labor-hour; their Japanese counterparts produce 2 bottles and .8 watches per labor-hour. According to the table, the United States is a more efficient manufacturer of both items; that is, U.S. workers are more productive in both sectors.

However, labor productivity is only one factor influencing the cost of production. The other determinant is the price of the input, in this case, the price of labor. To compute the labor cost per unit of output, we need to know the prevailing hourly wage in each country. To keep things simple, suppose the U.S. wage in both sectors is $15 per hour, whereas the Japanese wage in both sectors is 1,000 yen (¥) per hour. Naturally, the Japanese wage is denominated in that country's currency, the yen. Now consider the labor cost per unit of each good in each country. For the U.S. pharmaceutical sector, this labor cost is simply ($15 per hour)/(4 bottles per hour) = $3.75 per bottle, using Equation 6.1.

Comparative Advantage and International Trade

TABLE 6.2

Relative Costs in the
United States and
Japan

a. Productivity

	Pharmaceuticals	Digital Watches
United States	4 per hour	1 per hour
Japan	2	.8

b. Costs

	Pharmaceuticals	Digital Watches
United States	$3.75 per bottle	$15 per watch
Japan	$5.00	$12.50
	(¥500)	(¥1,250)

Part (b) of the table lists these costs for each country. For Japan, the cost in yen is shown in parentheses. For example, the labor cost per digital watch is $1,000/.8 = ¥1,250$.

Finally, to make cross-country cost comparisons, we need one additional piece of information: the prevailing exchange rate between the two currencies. As its name suggests, the exchange rate denotes the amount of one country's currency that exchanges for a unit of another country's. Again, keeping things simple, suppose the current exchange rate in round numbers is 100 yen per dollar. (Furthermore, we suppose that this rate is expected to remain unchanged.) Using this exchange rate, it is a simple matter to convert the countries' costs per unit into a common currency, in this case the dollar. Japan's labor cost per bottle is ¥500, or $5.00 after dividing by the exchange rate of ¥100 per dollar. Similarly, its cost per digital watch is ¥1,250, or $12.50. Table 6.2b lists these conversions.

Table 6.2 conveys a specific message about the countries' relative costs for the goods. The United States has a unit labor cost advantage in producing pharmaceuticals ($3.75 compared to $5), whereas Japan has an advantage producing watches ($12.50 compared to $15). Thus, one would envision the United States specializing in pharmaceuticals and Japan in digital watches. The predicted pattern of trade would have the United States exporting the former product and importing the latter from Japan. Indeed, actual trade flows in the 1990s between the two countries displayed exactly this pattern.

Table 6.2 also carries a general message: Productivity matters, but it is not the only thing that matters. After all, according to the table, the United States has an absolute productivity advantage in both goods. Yet Japan turns out to have a cost advantage in watches. The cost edge materializes because Japan has a **comparative advantage** in watches. That is, Japan's productivity disadvantage is much smaller in watches (where it is 80 percent as productive as the United States) than in pharmaceuticals (where it is only 50 percent as productive). After taking into account its lower wage rate, Japan indeed is the lower-cost watch producer.

Let us emphasize the point: Besides productivity, the countries' relative wages and the prevailing exchange rate also matter. For instance, if U.S. wages increased more rapidly than Japanese wages over the coming year, the U.S. cost advantage in pharmaceuticals would narrow, and Japan's cost advantage in watches would widen. Alternatively, suppose productivities and wages were unchanged in the two countries, but the exchange rate changed over the year. For instance, suppose the value of the dollar rose to ¥125 per dollar. (We say that the dollar has appreciated or, equivalently, that the yen has depreciated.) At this new exchange rate, Japan's labor costs per unit of output (converted into dollars) become $500/125 = \$4$ and $1,250/125 = \$10$ for the respective goods. With the appreciation of the dollar, Japanese goods become less costly (after converting into dollars). The U.S. cost advantage in pharmaceuticals has narrowed significantly (\$3.75 versus \$4), whereas the Japanese cost advantage in watches has widened. Accordingly, U.S. pharmaceutical exports should decline; these exports simply are not as attractive to Japanese consumers as before. In turn, a more expensive dollar (a cheaper yen) makes Japanese watch exports more attractive to U.S. consumers.

To sum up, relative productivities, relative wages, and the prevailing exchange rate combine to determine the pattern of cost advantage and trade. With respect to the exchange rate, depreciation of a country's currency increases its exports and decreases its imports. A currency appreciation has exactly the opposite effect.

RETURNS TO SCALE AND SCOPE

Returns to Scale

Returns to scale are important because they directly determine the shape of long-run average cost. They also are crucial for answering such questions as, Are large firms more efficient producers than small firms? Would a 50 percent increase in size reduce average cost per unit? Although the exact nature of returns to scale varies widely across industries, a representative description is useful. Figure 6.4 depicts a long-run average cost curve that is U-shaped. This reflects increasing returns to scale (and falling LAC) for low output levels and decreasing returns (increasing LAC) for high levels. In the figure, the minimum level of long-run average cost is achieved at output level Q_{min}. As in Figure 6.3, SAC curves for three plants are shown. Thus, output Q_{min} is produced using the medium-sized plant. If the costs of *all* possible plants were depicted, the lower "envelope" of the many SAC curves would trace out the figure's LAC curve. To sum up, if the firm is free to use *any* size plant, its average production cost is exactly LAC.

FIGURE 6.4

U-Shaped, Long-Run Average Cost

The U shape is due to increasing returns at small outputs and decreasing returns at large outputs.

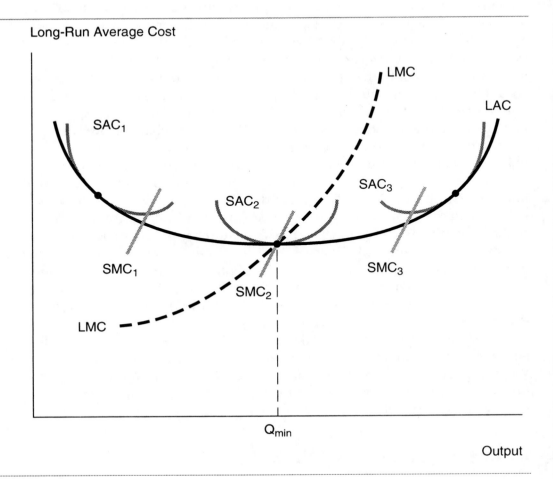

Long-Run Average Cost

As noted in Chapter 5, a number of factors influence returns to scale and, therefore, the shape of LAC. First, *constant average cost* (due to constant returns to scale) occurs when a firm's production process can be replicated easily. For instance, the electronics repair firm may find it can double its rate of finished repair jobs simply by replicating its current plant and labor force, that is, by building an identical repair facility beside the existing one and proportionally increasing its labor force. By duplication, the firm could supply twice the level of service at an unchanged average cost per job.

Second, *declining average cost* stems from a number of factors, including capital-intensive mass production techniques, automation, labor specialization, advertising, and distribution. By increasing scale, the firm may be able to use new production methods that were infeasible at smaller outputs. It also may find it advantageous to exploit specialization of labor at the larger scale. The result of either kind of production innovation is a reduction in long-run average cost.

Fundamental engineering relationships may have the same effect. In the expanding market of the 1990s, operators of Caribbean cruise liners launched ever larger ships (the largest having over 2,000 berths, almost three times the industry average) to take advantage of scale economies. At twice the tonnage, a super–cruise liner can carry significantly more than twice the number of passengers while requiring only a small increase in crew. Accordingly, the cost per passenger declines markedly.

Declining average cost also may be due to the presence of a variety of fixed expenses. Frequently, significant portions of a firm's advertising, promotional, and distributional expenses are fixed or (at least) vary little with the firm's level of output. (For instance, a 30-second television advertisement represents the same fixed cost to a large fast-food chain and a small chain alike. But this expense constitutes a much lower average cost per burger for the large chain.) Similarly, the costs to firms of many government regulations are (in the main) fixed. Accordingly, they represent a smaller average cost for the large firm. The U.S. automobile industry, perhaps the most highly regulated sector in the world, is a case in point.

Finally, *increasing average cost* is explained by the problems of organization, information, and control in very large firms. As the firm's scale increases, so do the difficulties of coordinating and monitoring its many management functions. The result is inefficiency, increased costs, and organizational overload.[5]

A great many studies have investigated the shape of average cost curves for different industries in both the short and long runs. Almost all of these studies use regression techniques to generate equations that explain total cost as a function of output and other relevant explanatory variables (such as wages and other input prices). The data for this analysis can come from either a time series (the same firm over a number of months or years) or a cross section (a cost comparison of different firms within a single time period). Despite difficulties in estimating costs from accounting data and controlling for changing inputs (especially capital), technology, and product characteristics, these studies have produced valuable information about costs.

One general finding is that, for most goods and services, there are significant economies of scale at low output levels, followed by a wide region of constant returns at higher levels. In short, for a great many industries, LAC tends to be L-shaped, as depicted in Figure 6.5b. This is in contrast to the usual textbook depiction of U-shaped LAC shown in Figure 6.5a. A small number of products display continuously declining average costs. This case usually is described under the term *natural monopoly* and includes many (but not all) local utilities, local telephone service, and cable television. Figure 6.5c shows this case.

---

[5]For many goods and services, transportation costs are an important factor in explaining increasing LAC. At a small scale, the firm can efficiently serve a local market. But delivering its good or service to a geographically far-flung market becomes increasingly expensive.

FIGURE 6.5

Three Examples of Long-Run Average Cost

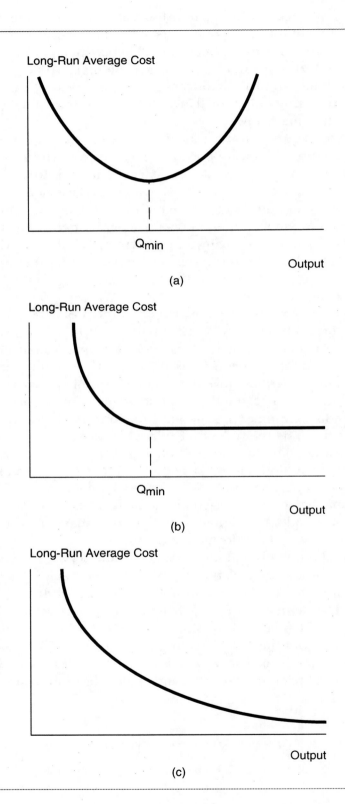

(a)

(b)

(c)

A useful way to summarize the degree of scale economies across industries is provided by the notion of efficient scale. **Minimum efficient scale (MES)** is the lowest output at which minimum average cost can be achieved. In parts (a) and (b) of Figure 6.5, minimum efficient scale is designated by Q_{min}. In part (b), this occurs where the average cost curve first achieves a minimum. In part (c), there is no minimum efficient scale because LAC continuously declines.

Minimum efficient scale is important in determining how many firms a particular market can support. For example, suppose market demand is 10 million units per year. If minimum efficient scale for the typical firm occurs at 100,000 units per year, the market can support 100 firms, each producing at minimum efficient scale. In contrast, if minimum efficient scale is 5 million units, the market can support only two firms producing efficiently. Finally, if average cost declines for all outputs (up to 10 million units), the market may be able to support only one firm efficiently.

As one might expect, estimates of MES vary widely across industries.[6] For instance, in the production of sulfuric acid (a standard chemical), the MES for a plant is about 4 percent of total U.S. consumption. The average cost disadvantage of producing at one-half of MES is only 1 percent. The clear implication is that there is ample room in the market for as many as 25 (1/.04) firms. By comparison, the MES for electric motors is about 15 percent of U.S. consumption, and the cost disadvantage at one-half of MES is 15 percent. For production of commercial aircraft, MES is 10 percent of the U.S. market, and the cost disadvantage at one-half of MES is 20 percent. This suggests that the industry could support as many as 10 manufacturers. Economies of scale would not seem to explain why Boeing and Airbus dominate the worldwide market. Rather, the rise of these two aviation giants and the demise of Lockheed and McDonnell-Douglas more aptly are attributed to differences in the companies' management strategies and technological capabilities.

Economies of Scope

Most firms produce a variety of goods. Computer firms, such as IBM and Toshiba, produce a wide range of computers from mainframes to personal computers. Consumer products firms, such as Procter & Gamble and General Foods, offer myriad personal, grocery, and household items. Entertainment firms, such as Walt Disney Corporation, produce movies, television programs, toys, theme park entertainment, and vacation services. In many cases, the justification for multiple products is the potential cost advantages of producing many closely related goods.

---

[6]Estimates of plant-level economies of scale for different industries are collected in W. Shepherd and J. M. Shepherd, *The Economics of Industrial Organization* (Upper Saddle River, NJ: Prentice Hall, 2003).

A production process exhibits **economies of scope** when the cost of producing multiple goods is less than the aggregate cost of producing each item separately. A convenient measure of such economies is

$$SC = \frac{C(Q_1) + C(Q_2) - C(Q_1, Q_2)}{C(Q_1) + C(Q_2)}.$$

Here, $C(Q_1, Q_2)$ denotes the firm's cost of jointly producing the goods in the respective quantities; $C(Q_1)$ denotes the cost of producing good 1 alone and similarly for $C(Q_2)$. For instance, suppose producing the goods separately means incurring costs of $12 million and $8 million, respectively. The total cost of jointly producing the goods in the same quantities is $17 million. It follows that $SC = (12 + 8 - 17)/(12 + 8) = .15$. Joint production implies a 15 percent cost savings vis-a-vis separate production.

There are many sources for economies of scope. In some cases, a single production process yields multiple outputs. Cattle producers sell both beef and hides; indeed, producing cattle for beef or hides alone probably is not profitable. In other cases, production of a principal good is accompanied by the generation of unavoidable byproducts. Often these byproducts can be fashioned into marketable products. Sawdust is a valuable byproduct of lumber production. Tiny plastic pellets (the byproduct of stamping out buttons) are used in sandblasting instead of sand. After the harvest, leftover cornstalks are used to produce alcohol for power generation. Still another source of economies is underutilization of inputs. An airline that carries passengers may find itself with unused cargo space; thus, it contracts to carry cargo as well as passengers. In recent years, many public school systems have made their classrooms available after hours for day-care, after-school, and community programs.

An important source of economies of scope is transferable know-how. Soft-drink companies produce many types of carbonated drinks, fruit juices, sparkling waters, and the like. Presumably, experience producing carbonated beverages confers cost advantages for the production of related drinks. Brokerage houses provide not only trading services but also investment advising and many bank-like services, such as mutual funds with check-writing privileges. Insurance companies provide both insurance and investment vehicles. In fact, whole-life insurance is a clever combination of these two services in an attractive package.

Scope economies also may be demand related. The consumption of many clusters of goods and services is complementary. For instance, the same company that sells or leases a piece of office equipment also offers service contracts. A select number of firms compete for the sales of cameras and photographic film. Sometimes the delivery of multiple services is so common and ubiquitous that it tends to be overlooked. Full-service banks provide a wide range of services to customers. The leading law firms in major cities provide extensive services in dozens of areas of the law. (Of course, smaller, specialty law firms coexist with these larger entities.) Many large hospitals provide care in all major medical specialties as well as in the related areas of emergency medicine, mental-health care, geriatrics, and rehabilitative therapy.

Toshiba America Information Systems (a subsidiary of the parent Japanese company) sells laptop computers, printers, disk drives, copiers, facsimile machines, and telephone equipment in North America. Would you expect there to be economies of scope in these product lines? If so, what are the sources of these economies?

CHECK STATION 3

E-Commerce and Cost Economies

As noted in Chapter 3, the Internet and the emergence of e-commerce have significant impacts on the structure of firm costs.[7] A wide-ranging research study by Washington's Brookings Institution estimates that across the whole of the U.S. economy, the adoption of information technology and e-commerce methods will produce total annual cost savings as high as $100 billion (about 1 percent of annual gross domestic product). Increased efficiency stems from reengineering the firm's supply chain and from reducing transactions costs of all kinds. The greatest potential savings emerge in information-intensive industries such as health care, financial services, education, and public-sector operations.

Recall that the hallmark of information economics is the presence of high fixed costs accompanied by low or negligible marginal costs. As a result, average costs decline sharply with output. The fixed costs of business capital investments are increasingly found in computers, computing systems such as servers, software, and telecommunications (together constituting over 10 percent of capital expenditure), rather than in the traditional "bricks and mortar" of factories, assembly lines, and equipment. To date, a number of firms—Microsoft, Google, Cisco Systems, Yahoo, Oracle, eBay, Sun Microsystems, and YouTube, to name a few—have taken advantage of information economics to claim increasing shares of their respective markets, thus benefiting from sharply declining average unit costs.

E-commerce also benefits from significant economies of scale in customer acquisition and distribution. In many e-commerce markets there has been a "land rush" to acquire customers (often by offering a variety of free services). These customers come at a high initial fixed cost but have a very low marginal cost of servicing them. In addition, demand-side externalities mean that customers receive greater value as the population of other customers increase. This is true in online sites ranging from job-search to business-to-business commerce to online classified ads. For instance, such economies of scale provide

---

[7]For discussions of e-commerce and cost economies see G. Ellison and S. F. Ellison, "Lessons about Markets from the Internet," *Journal of Economic Perspectives* (Spring 2005): 139–158; S. Borenstein and G. Saloner, "Economics and Electronic Commerce," *Journal of Economic Perspectives* (Winter 2001): 3–12; and R. E. Litan and A. M. Rivlin, "Projecting the Economic Impact of the Internet," *American Economic Review*, Papers and Proceedings, May 2001, 313–317.

eBay and Google with dominant positions in online auctions and search, respectively. In turn, economies of scale in distribution means that at large enough scale, taking orders online, holding inventories in centralized facilities, and shipping direct to customers is cheaper than selling the same item at a retail outlet.

Information economics also provides new sources for economies of scope both in the online and offline worlds. E-commerce firms find it easy to customize the online buying experience. Amazon.com automatically recommends items based on a user's past purchase history. Retailers such as Nordstrom and the Gap offer much more clothing variety at their online sites than in their stores. In manufacturing facilities, computer-aided design and manufacturing (CAD/CAM) systems can quickly switch from one product to another, allowing the production of many products and designs, all using similar inputs. Items ranging from microchips to aircraft are now engineered this way. Micromarketing is the process of differentiating products and targeting more markets. Most Americans are familiar with Nabisco's Oreo cookies. If you liked the original, there are now Fudge Covered Oreos, Oreo Double Stufs, and Oreo Big Stufs—each targeted to a separate junk-food market. Formerly, Procter & Gamble sold one type of Tide laundry detergent; now it sells four. Boeing uses computer-aided design to develop simultaneously several types of sophisticated aircraft for different buyers (domestic and international airlines).

Some experts suggest that relying on economies of scale—producing dedicated systems that are economical but inflexible—is no longer enough. The most successful firms in the future will also exploit the flexibility provided by economies of scope.

COST ANALYSIS AND OPTIMAL DECISIONS

Knowledge of the firm's relevant costs is essential for determining sound managerial decisions. First, we consider decisions concerning a single product; then we examine decisions for multiproduct firms.

A Single Product

The profit-maximizing rule for a single-product firm is straightforward: So long as it is profitable to produce, the firm sets its optimal output where marginal revenue equals marginal cost. Figure 6.6 shows a single-product firm that faces a downward-sloping demand curve and U-shaped average cost curves. The firm's profit-maximizing output is Q* (where the MR and MC curves cross), and its optimal price is P* (read off the demand curve). The firm's economic profit is measured by the area of the shaded rectangle in the figure. The rectangle's height represents the firm's profit per unit (P* − AC), and its base is

FIGURE 6.6

A Firm's Optimal Output

Regardless of the shape of its costs, a firm maximizes its profit by operating at Q*, where marginal revenue equals marginal cost.

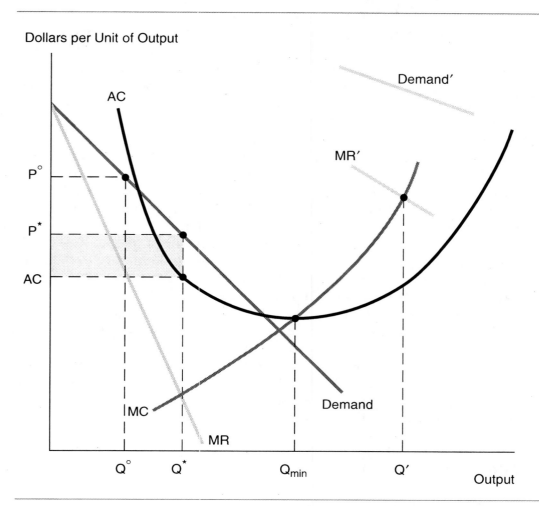

total output Q*. (Remember that the firm's average cost includes a normal return on its invested capital. Therefore, a positive economic profit means that the firm is earning a greater-than-normal rate of return.) No alternative output and price could generate a greater economic profit.

By now, the application of marginal revenue and marginal cost should be very familiar. Nonetheless, it is worth pointing out two fallacies that occasionally find their way into managerial discussions. The first fallacy states that the firm always can increase its profit by exploiting economies of scale. But fully exploiting these economies means producing at minimum efficient scale—the point of minimum average cost. Figure 6.6 shows the problem with this contention: The profit-maximizing output Q* falls well short of Q_{min}. In fact, if the firm were to produce at Q_{min}, it would suffer an economic loss. (The demand line falls below the average-cost curve at Q_{min}.)

The general point is that the firm's optimal output depends on *demand* as well as cost. In Figure 6.6, the level of demand for the firm's product is insufficient to justify exploiting all economies of scale. However, we easily could depict a much higher level of demand—one that pushes the firm to an output well above Q_{min}, that is, into the range of increasing average cost. The figure shows part of a (hypothetical) demand curve and the associated marginal revenue curve that intersects marginal cost at output Q'. For this level of demand, Q' (a quantity much greater than Q_{min}) is the profit-maximizing output.

The second fallacy works in the opposite direction of the first. It states that if the current output and price are unsatisfactory, the firm should raise its price to increase profits. The intuitive appeal of this "rule" is obvious. If price is too low relative to average cost, the remedy is to increase price. However, this contention is not necessarily so. In Figure 6.6, raising price is appropriate only if the current price is lower than P^* (with output greater than Q^*). If price is already greater than P^*, further price increases only reduce profits. In fact, the figure can readily demonstrate the classic fallacy of managing the product out of business. Suppose management makes the mistake of setting its output at $Q°$. Here the firm's price $P°$ is slightly below average cost, so the firm is incurring a loss. As a remedy, the firm raises price. Does this improve profits? No. The increase in price causes a decrease in quantity (which is expected) but also an increase in average cost (perhaps unexpected). At a higher price and lower output, the firm still is generating a loss. If it raises price again, its volume will shrink further and its price still will fail to catch up with its increasing average cost. By using this strategy, the firm quickly would price itself out of the market.

The Shut-Down Rule

Under adverse economic conditions, managers face the decision of whether to cease production of a product altogether, that is, whether to shut down. Although the choice may appear obvious (shut down if the product is generating monetary losses), a correct decision requires a careful weighing of relevant options. These alternatives differ depending on the firm's time horizon.

In the short run, many of the firm's inputs are fixed. Suppose the firm is producing a single item that is incurring economic losses—total cost exceeds revenues or, equivalently, average total cost exceeds price. Figure 6.7 displays the situation. At the firm's current output, average cost exceeds price: $AC > P^*$; the firm is earning negative economic profit. Should the firm cease production and shut down? The answer is no. To see this, write the firm's profit as

$$\pi = (R - VC) - FC = (P - AVC)Q - FC. \qquad [6.5]$$

FIGURE 6.7

Shutting Down

In the short run, the firm should continue to produce at Q* (even if it is suffering a loss) so long as price exceeds average variable cost. In the long run, the firm should shut down if price falls short of average cost.

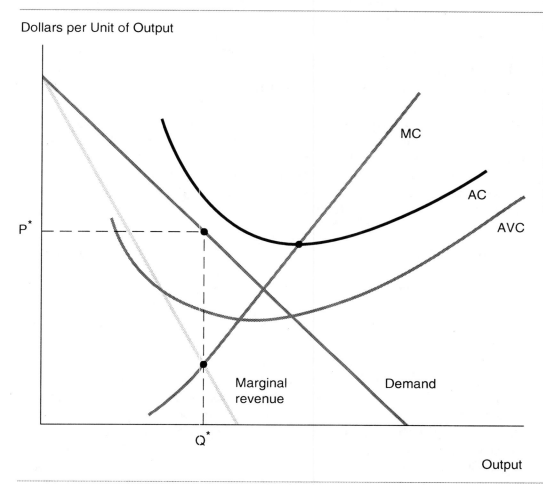

Dollars per Unit of Output

MC

AC

AVC

P*

Marginal revenue

Demand

Q*

Output

The first term, R − VC, is referred to as the product's *contribution*. So long as revenue exceeds variable costs (or, equivalently, P > AVC), the product is making a positive contribution toward the firm's fixed costs. Observe that price exceeds average variable cost in Figure 6.7. (The average variable cost curve is U-shaped, and it lies below the AC curve because it excludes all fixed costs.) Therefore, continuing to produce the good makes a contribution to fixed costs. (In fact, output Q* delivers maximum contribution because MR = MC.) If instead the firm were to discontinue production (Q = 0), this contribution would be lost. In the short run, the firm is stuck with its fixed costs. It will incur these costs whether or not it produces output. If the firm shuts down, its profit will be $\pi = -FC$. (The firm will earn no revenues but will pay its fixed costs.) In sum, the firm should continue production because the product generates a positive contribution, thereby minimizing the firm's loss. The firm suffers an economic loss in the short run; nevertheless, this is better than shutting down. Thus, we have the following general rule:

> In the short run, the firm should continue to produce so long as price exceeds average variable cost. Assuming it does produce, the firm maximizes contribution (and minimizes any losses) by setting marginal revenue equal to marginal cost.

In the long run, all inputs and all costs are variable. (For instance, a firm that leases its plant and equipment can shed these costs if it chooses not to renew its two-year lease. The firm can also downsize its workforce over time.) In the long run, the firm should continue operating only if it expects to earn a nonnegative economic profit. A firm that suffers persistent economic losses will be forced to exit the industry.

CHECK STATION 4   Earlier we noted that the repair firm's cost function is $C = 270 + 30Q + .3Q^2$. Suppose demand is given by $P = 50 - .2Q$. What is the firm's optimal course of action in the short run? In the long run?

Multiple Products

In the previous section, we noted that the prevalence of multiproduct firms is explained by economies of scope. The implication of such economies is that the firm can produce multiple products at a total cost that is lower than the sum of the items' costs if they were produced separately. As we shall see, managers must be careful to pay attention to relevant costs in a multiproduct environment.

To illustrate, consider a firm that produces two products in a common facility. The firm's total cost of production is described as

$$C = FC + VC_1 + VC_2,$$

where FC denotes the total fixed costs shared by the products. The separate variable costs for the products also are included and depend directly on the output levels of each product. The firm's total profit is

$$\pi = (R_1 - VC_1) + (R_2 - VC_2) - FC, \qquad [6.6]$$

where R_1 and R_2 denote the products' revenues. As noted earlier, each term in parentheses is the product's contribution. The firm's total profit is the sum of its products' contributions minus its total fixed costs.

As we saw in the single-product case, the firm should continue producing an item only if $R > VC$ or, equivalently, $P > AVC$. Exactly the same principle applies to the multiproduct case. Furthermore, in the long run the firm should continue in business only if the total profit in Equation 6.6 is nonnegative;

otherwise, it should shut down. The firm's output rule for multiple goods can be stated in two parts:

1. Each good should be produced if, and only if, it makes a positive contribution to the firm's fixed costs: $R_i > VC_i$ or, equivalently, $P_i > AVC_i$.
2. In the long run, the firm should continue operations if, and only if, it makes positive economic profits.

MULTIPLE PRODUCTS: A NUMERICAL EXAMPLE   Suppose a firm's total fixed cost is $2.4 million per year. For the first good, $P_1 = \$10$, $AVC_1 = \$9$, and $Q_1 = 1.2$ million; in turn, $P_2 = \$6.50$, $AVC_2 = \$4$, and $Q_2 = .6$ million. Total profit is $1.2 + 1.5 - 2.4 = \$.3$ million per year. Each product makes a positive contribution, and total contribution exceeds total fixed cost. Thus, the firm should stay in business. What if the second good's price is $5.50? In the short run, both goods continue to contribute toward fixed costs and, therefore, should be produced. In the long run, total contribution ($2.1 million) falls short of total fixed cost, so the firm should shut down. Finally, if the second good's price is $3.50, then $P_2 < AVC_2$. The firm should halt production of the second good immediately and cease operations altogether in the long run.

Sizing up relevant costs for production decisions and measuring costs for accounting purposes are sometimes in conflict. For instance, almost all accounting systems allocate fixed costs across the firm's multiple products. Typically, these allocations are in proportion to the products' volumes. If a product accounts for 20 percent of a firm's output (whether by units, labor costs, or machine-hours), it is assigned 20 percent of these costs. These allocated costs are added to the product's direct unit costs to determine its total cost of production. According to this cost-accounting system, the product is profitable if, and only if, its total revenues exceed its total costs.

Although cost accounting systems are useful in many respects (especially for tax purposes), they can be misleading when it comes to economic decisions. For decision-making purposes, costs that are truly fixed (i.e., don't vary) with respect to products' volumes should not be allocated at all. This is in keeping with the earlier proposition that fixed costs do not matter. According to Equation 6.6, contribution is the only relevant measure of a good's performance. Production should continue if contribution is positive and should cease if it is negative. Note that the good's accounting profit (by including a fixed-cost allocation) understates its contribution. Consequently, when it comes to product decisions, accounting profit can be very misleading.

In the preceding example, a typical accounting allocation would assign the $2.4 million in fixed costs to the products in proportion to output: $1.6 million to the first product and $.8 million to the second. (The first product constitutes two-thirds of total output.) Thus, the first product's accounting profit would be $\pi_1 = (10 - 9)(1.2) - 1.6 = -\$.4$ million. Based on this measure, the product appears to be unprofitable. What if the firm discontinues its production? The firm will no longer earn any contribution from the first good. But there will be no decline in the $2.4 million fixed cost; now the entire fixed cost will be assigned to the second item. Left producing a single good, the firm will be unable to earn a profit (its *loss* will amount to $2.4 - 1.5 = \$.9$ million) and will be forced to shut down. Here, allocating fixed costs leads to a disastrous series of decisions. As we noted earlier, the firm's optimal course of action is to produce both products. To repeat, assigning fixed costs to products is unnecessary (and potentially misleading). Instead, the only relevant long-run issue is whether the firm's total contribution covers these fixed costs in the aggregate.

Allocating Costs Revisited

In the example that opens this chapter, the managers of a sports shoe company were engaged in a debate over what strategy would lead to the greatest profit. Should production of the boys' shoes be increased? Cut back? Discontinued? The correct answers to these questions depend on a careful analysis of relevant costs. To clarify the situation, management has gathered cost information about different sales quantities. The firm's production managers have supplied the data on direct (i.e., variable) costs. Recall that production of women's and boys' running shoes share $90,000 in fixed costs. The firm's accountants allocate this cost to the two lines in proportion to numbers of pairs. The output of women's shoes is 8,000 pairs.

Pairs of Shoes	Price	Revenue	Direct Cost	Allocated Cost	Average Total Cost
1,600	$40	$64,000	$66,400	$15,000	$50.88
2,400	36	86,400	74,400	20,769	39.65
3,200	32	102,400	85,600	25,714	34.79
3,600	30	108,000	92,400	27,931	33.43
4,000	28	112,000	100,000	30,000	32.50

Thus, if the volume of boys' shoes is 4,000 pairs, the product's output is one-third of the total; hence, its allocation is $(1/3)(\$90,000) = \$30,000$. Allocations for other outputs are computed in the same way. Average total cost is the sum of direct and allocated costs divided by total output.

The firm currently is charging a price of $36 per pair and selling 2,400 pairs per week. How would management evaluate the current profitability of this strategy, and how might it improve its profits? First, consider the *wrong* method of approaching these questions. Management observes that when it sells 2,400 pairs, total average cost is $39.65 per pair. This exceeds the $36 selling price. Therefore, management believes its current strategy is unprofitable. What are its other options? An obvious possibility is to increase price to a level above $39.65, say, to $40. The table shows the results of this strategy. Volume drops to 1,600 pairs, but average total cost rises to $50.88. (Because the decline in volume is much greater than the reduction in total cost, average cost rises dramatically.) Price still falls well short of average cost. A price cut will do no better. The other prices in the table tell the same story: Average total cost exceeds price in all cases. Therefore, management concludes that the boys' running shoe cannot earn a profit and should be discontinued.

Let's now adopt the role of economic consultant and explain why management's current reasoning is in error. The problem lies with the allocation of the $90,000 in "shared" costs. Recall the economic "commandment": Do not allocate fixed costs. In a multiproduct firm, contribution is the correct measure of a product's profitability. A comparison of columns 3 and 4 in the table shows that the boys' shoe makes a positive contribution for four of the price and output combinations. Thus, the shoe should be retained. The firm's optimal strategy is to lower the price to P = $32. The resulting sales volume is Q = 3,200. Maximum contribution is $102,400 − $85,600 = $16,800. Beyond P = $32, however, any further price reduction is counterproductive. (The additional cost of supplying these additional sales units exceeds the extra sales revenue.) Thus, the production manager would be wrong to advocate a policy of minimizing direct costs per unit of output. We can check that of the five output levels, average variable cost is minimized at Q = 4,000. (Here AVC is $100,000/4,000 = $25 per pair.) Nonetheless, this volume of output delivers less contribution than Q = 3,200 because the accompanying drop in price is much greater than the decline in average variable cost. To sum up, the firm's correct strategy is to maximize the product's contribution.

SUMMARY

Decision-Making Principles

1. Cost is an important consideration in decision making. In deciding among different courses of action, the manager need only consider the differential revenues and costs of the various alternatives.

2. The opportunity cost associated with choosing a particular decision is measured by the forgone benefits of the next-best alternative.

3. Economic profit is the difference between total revenues and total costs (i.e., explicit costs and opportunity costs). Managerial decisions should be based on economic profit, not accounting profit.

4. Costs that are fixed (or sunk) with respect to alternative courses of action are irrelevant.

5. In the short run, the firm should continue to produce so long as price exceeds average variable cost. Assuming it does produce, the firm maximizes its profit (or minimizes its loss) by setting marginal revenue equal to marginal cost.

6. In the long run, all revenues and costs are variable. The firm should continue production if, and only if, it earns a positive economic profit. A multiproduct firm should continue operating in the long run only if total revenue exceeds total costs. There is no need to allocate shared costs to specific products.

Nuts and Bolts

1. The firm's cost function indicates the (minimum) total cost of producing any level of output given existing production technology, input prices, and any relevant constraints.

2. In the short run, one or more of the firm's inputs are fixed. Short-run total cost is the sum of fixed cost and variable cost. Marginal cost is the additional cost of producing an extra unit of output. In the short run, there is an inverse relationship between marginal cost and the marginal product of the variable input: $MC = P_L/MP_L$. Marginal cost increases due to diminishing returns. The short-run average cost curve is U-shaped.

3. In the long run, all inputs are variable. The firm chooses input proportions to minimize the total cost of producing any given level of output. The shape of the long-run average cost curve is determined by returns to scale. If there are constant returns to scale, long-run average cost is constant; under increasing returns, average cost decreases with output; and, under decreasing returns, average cost rises. Empirical studies indicate L-shaped (or U-shaped) long-run average cost curves for many sectors and products.

4. Many firms supply multiple products. Economies of scope exist when the cost of producing multiple goods is less than the aggregate cost of producing each good separately.

5. Comparative advantage (not absolute advantage) is the source of mutually beneficial global trade. The pattern of comparative advantage between two countries depends on relative productivity, relative wages, and the exchange rate.

Questions and Problems

1. The development of a new product was much lengthier and more expensive than the company's management anticipated. Consequently, the firm's top accountants and financial managers argue that the firm should raise the price of the product 10 percent above its original target to help recoup some of these costs. Does such a strategy make sense? Explain carefully.

2. Comment on the following statement: "Average cost includes both fixed and variable costs, whereas marginal cost includes only variable costs. Therefore, marginal cost is never greater than average cost."

3. A company produces two main products: electronic control devices and specialty microchips. The average total cost of producing a microchip is $300; the firm then sells the chips to other high-tech manufacturers for $550. Currently, there are enough orders for microchips to keep its factory capacity fully utilized. The company also uses its own chips in the production of control devices. The average total cost (AC) of producing such a device is $500 plus the cost of two microchips. (Assume all of the $500 cost is variable and AC is constant at different output volumes.) Each control device sells for an average price of $1,500.
   a. Should the company produce control devices? Is this product profitable?
   b. Answer part (a) assuming outside orders for microchips are insufficient to keep the firm's production capacity fully utilized.
   c. Now suppose $200 of the average cost of control devices is fixed. Assume, as in part (a), that microchip capacity is fully utilized. Should control devices be produced in the short run? Explain.

4. The year 1998 saw an unprecedented number of mega-mergers in the banking industry: NationsBank with BankAmerica, Bank One with First Chicago NBD, and Citicorp with Travelers Group, to name the three largest mergers. These merged entities are hoping to offer one-stop shopping for financial services: everything from savings to home mortgages, investments, and insurance.
   a. In the short run, what are the potential cost advantages of these mergers? Explain.
   b. Is a $300 billion national bank likely to be more efficient than a $30 billion regional bank or a $3 billion state-based bank? What economic evidence is needed to determine whether there are long-run increasing returns to scale in banking?
   c. Do you think the mergers are predicated on economies of scope?

5. An entrepreneur plans to convert a building she owns into a video-game arcade. Her main decision is how many games to purchase for the arcade. From survey information, she projects total revenue per year as $R = 10,000Q - 200Q^2$, where Q is the number of games. The cost for each game (leasing, electricity, maintenance, etc.) is $4,000 per year. The entrepreneur will run the arcade, but instead of paying herself a salary, she will collect profits. She has received offers of $100,000 to sell her building and a $20,000 offer to manage a rival's arcade. She recognizes that a normal return on a risky investment such as the arcade is 20 percent.
   a. As a profit maximizer, how many games should she order?
   b. What is her economic profit?

6. Suppose the manufacturer of running shoes has collected the following quantitative information. Demand for the boys' shoe is estimated to be $Q = 9,600 - 200P$, or, equivalently, $P = 48 - Q/200$. The shoe's direct cost is $C = \$60,000 + .0025Q^2$.
   a. Check that these demand and cost equations are consistent with the data presented in the "Allocating Costs Revisited" section.
   b. Find the firm's profit-maximizing price and output.

7. A firm's long-run total cost function is

$$C = 360 + 40Q + 10Q^2.$$

   a. What is the shape of the long-run average cost curve?
   b. Find the output that minimizes average cost.
   c. The firm faces the fixed market price of $140 per unit. At this price, can the firm survive in the long run? Explain.

8. A firm uses a single plant with costs $C = 160 + 16Q + .1Q^2$ and faces the price equation $P = 96 - .4Q$.
   a. Find the firm's profit-maximizing price and quantity. What is its profit?
   b. The firm's production manager claims that the firm's average cost of production is minimized at an output of 40 units. Furthermore, she claims that 40 units is the firm's profit-maximizing level of output. Explain whether these claims are correct.
   c. Could the firm increase its profit by using a second plant (with costs identical to the first) to produce the output in part (a)? Explain.

9. Suppose you are a theater owner fortunate enough to book a summer box-office hit into your single theater. You are now planning the length of its run. Your share of the film's projected box-office is $R = 10w - .25w^2$, where R is in thousands of dollars and w is the number of weeks that the movie runs. The average operating cost of your theater is AC = MC = $4 thousand per week.
   a. To maximize your profit, how many *weeks* should the movie run? What is your profit?
   b. You realize that your typical movie makes an average operating profit of $1.5 thousand per week. How does this fact affect your decision in part (a), if at all? Explain briefly.
   c. In the last 25 years, stand-alone movie theaters have given way to cineplexes with 4 to 10 screens and megaplexes with 10 to 30 screens (yes, 30 screens!) under one roof. During the same period, total annual movie admissions have barely changed. What cost factors can explain this trend? In addition, what demand factors might also be relevant?
   d. The film's producer anticipated an extended theater run (through Labor Day) and accordingly decided to move back the DVD release of the film from Thanksgiving to January. Does the decision to delay make sense? Explain carefully.

10. Firm A makes and sells motorcycles. The total cost of each cycle is the sum of the costs of frames, assembly, and engine. The firm produces its own engines according to the cost equation:

$$C_E = 250,000 + 1,000Q + 5Q^2.$$

The cost of frames and assembly is $2,000 per cycle. Monthly demand for cycles is given by the inverse demand equation $P = 10,000 - 30Q$.
   a. What is the MC of producing an additional *engine?* What is the MC of producing an additional *cycle?* Find the firm's profit-maximizing quantity and price.
   b. Now suppose the firm has the chance to buy an unlimited number of engines from another company at a price of $1,400 per engine. Will this option affect the number of *cycles* it plans to produce? Its price? Will the firm continue to produce engines itself? If so, how many?

11. As noted in Problem 5 of Chapter 3, General Motors (GM) produces light trucks in its Michigan factories. Currently, its Michigan production is 50,000 trucks per month, and its marginal cost is $20,000 per truck. With regional demand given by $P = 30,000 - 0.1Q$, GM sets a price of $25,000 per truck.
   a. Confirm that setting $Q = 50,000$ and $P = \$25,000$ is profit maximizing.
   b. GM produces the engines that power its light trucks and finds that it has some unused production capacity, enough capacity to build an additional 10,000 engines per year. A manufacturer of sports utility vehicles (SUVs) has offered to purchase as many as 25,000 engines from GM at a price of $10,000 per engine. GM's contribution is estimated to be about $2,000 per engine sold (based on a marginal cost of $8,000 per engine). Should GM devote some of its engine capacity to produce engines to sell to the SUV manufacturer? Does this outside opportunity change GM's optimal output of light vehicles in part (a)?
   c. GM also assembles light trucks in a West Coast facility, which is currently manufacturing 40,000 units per month. Because it produces multiple vehicle types at this mega-plant, the firm's standard practice is to allocate $160 million of factory-wide fixed costs to light trucks. Based on this allocation, the California production manager reports that the average total cost per light truck is $22,000 per unit. Given this report, what conclusion (if any) can you draw concerning the marginal cost per truck? If West Coast demand is similar to demand in Michigan, could the West Coast factory profit by changing its output from 40,000 units?

*12. A firm produces digital watches on a single production line serviced during one daily shift. The total output of watches depends directly on the number of labor-hours employed on the line. Maximum capacity of the line is 120,000 watches per month; this output requires 60,000 hours of labor per month. Total fixed costs come to $600,000 per month, the wage rate averages $8 per hour, and other variable costs (e.g., materials) average $6 per watch. The marketing department's estimate of demand is $P = 28 - Q/20,000$, where P denotes price in dollars and Q is monthly demand.

a. How many additional watches can be produced by an extra hour of labor? What is the marginal cost of an additional watch? As a profit maximizer, what price and output should the firm set? Is production capacity fully utilized? What contribution does this product line provide?

b. The firm can increase capacity up to 100 percent by scheduling a night shift. The wage rate at night averages $12 per hour. Answer the questions in part (a) in light of this additional option.

c. Suppose demand for the firm's watches falls permanently to $P = 20 - Q/20,000$. In view of this fall in demand, what output should the firm produce in the short run? In the long run? Explain.

*13. A manufacturing firm produces output using a single plant. The relevant cost function is $C = 500 + 5Q^2$. The firm's demand curve is $P = 600 - 5Q$.

a. Find the level of output at which average cost is minimized. (*Hint*: Set AC equal to MC.) What is the minimum level of average cost?

b. Find the firm's profit-maximizing output and price. Find its profit.

c. Suppose the firm has in place a second plant identical to the first. Argue that the firm should divide production equally between the plants. Check that the firm maximizes profit at total output Q* such that

$$MR(Q^*) = MC_1(Q^*/2) = MC_2(Q^*/2).$$

Find Q*. Explain why total output is greater than in part (b).

d. In the long run, the firm can produce using as many or as few plants as it wishes (each with the preceding cost function). In this case, what kind of returns to scale hold? What are the firm's optimal output and price in the long run? How many plants will the firm use to produce the good? *Hint*: Refer to the value of minimum AC you found in part (a).

Discussion Question Explain why the cost structure associated with many kinds of information goods and services might imply a market supplied by a small number of large firms. (At the same time, some Internet businesses such as grocery home deliveries have continually suffered steep losses regardless of scale. Explain why.) Could lower transaction costs in e-commerce ever make it easier for small suppliers to compete? As noted in Chapter 3, network

*Starred problems are more challenging.

externalities are often an important aspect of demand for information goods and services. (The benefits to customers of using software, participating in electronic markets, or using instant messaging increase with the number of other users.) How might network externalities affect firm operating strategies (pricing, output, and advertising) and firm size?

Spreadsheet Problems

S1. A firm's production function is given by the equation

$$Q = 12L^{.5}K^{.5},$$

where L, K, and Q are measured in thousands of units. Input prices are 36 per labor unit and 16 per capital unit.

a. Create a spreadsheet (based on the example shown) to model this production setting. (You may have already completed this step if you answered Problem S2 of Chapter 5. An algebraic analysis of this setting appears in this chapter's Special Appendix.)

b. To explore the shape of short-run average cost (SAC), hold the amount of capital fixed at K = 9 thousand and vary the amount of labor from 1 thousand to 2.5 thousand to 4 thousand to 5.5 thousand to 7.5 thousand to 9 thousand units. What is the resulting behavior of SAC? Use the spreadsheet optimizer to find the amount of labor corresponding to minimum SAC. What is the value of SAC_{min}?

	A	B	C	D	E	F	G	H	I	J
1										
2			COST ANALYSIS							
3								Output	36	
4								Price	8.50	
5		Labor	1.00		Capital	9.00				
6		MP_L	18.00		MP_K	2.00		MR	8.00	
7								Revenue	306	
8		MRP_L	144.00		MRP_K	16.00				
9		MC_L	36.00		MC_K	16.00		Cost	180	
10								Avg. Cost	5.00	
11										
12								Profit	126	
13										

c. In your spreadsheet, set L = 9 thousand (keeping K = 9 thousand) and note the resulting output and total cost. Now suppose that the firm is free to produce this same level of output by adjusting both labor and capital in the long run. Use the optimizer to determine the firm's optimal inputs and LAC_{min}. (Remember to include an output constraint for cell I3.)

d. Confirm that the production function exhibits constant returns to scale and constant long-run average costs. For instance, recalculate the answer for part (c) after doubling both inputs.

e. Finally, suppose the firm's inverse demand curve is given by

$$P = 9 - Q/72.$$

With capital fixed at K = 9 in the short run, use the optimizer to determine the firm's optimal labor usage and maximum profit. Then find the optimal amounts of both inputs in the long run. Explain the large differences in inputs, output, and profit between the short run and the long run.

S2. A multinational firm produces microchips at a home facility and at a foreign subsidiary according to the respective cost functions:

$$C_H = 120Q_H \quad \text{and} \quad C_F = 50Q_F + .5Q_F^2.$$

The firm sells chips in the home market and the foreign market where the inverse demand curves are

$$P_H = 300 - D_H \quad \text{and} \quad P_F = 250 - .5D_F,$$

respectively. Here D denotes the quantity *sold* in each market, and Q denotes the quantity *produced* in each facility. Chips can be costlessly shipped between markets so that D_H need not equal Q_H (nor D_F equal Q_F). However, total production must match total sales: $Q_H + Q_F = D_H + D_F$.

a. Create a spreadsheet (based on the accompanying example) to model the firm's worldwide operations. Find the firm's profit-maximizing outputs, sales quantities, and prices. Are chips shipped overseas? (*Hint*: The key to maximizing profit is to find sales and output quantities such that $MR_H = MR_F = MC_H = MC_F$. Also note that MC_H is constant. When using your spreadsheet's optimizer, be sure to include the constraint that cell F9—extra output—must equal zero. That is, total sales must exactly equal total output.)

b. Answer the questions in part (a) under an "antidumping" constraint; that is, the company must charge the *same* price in both markets. (*Hint*: Include the additional constraint that cell F12, the price gap, must equal zero.)

	A	B	C	D	E	F	G	H
1								
2		**WORLDWIDE CHIP DECISIONS**						
3								
4		Set Sales & Output Quantities (000s)						
5								
6			Home	Abroad	Total			
7								
8		Sales	10	10	20		Extra	
9						0	< Output	
10		Output	10	10	20			
11								
12		Price	290	245		45	< Price Gap	
13								
14		Revenues	2,900	2,450	5,350			
15		MR	280	240	—			
16								
17		Costs	1,200	550	1,750			
18		MC	120	60	—			
19								
20		Profit	1,700	1,900	3,600			
21								

Suggested References

The following articles examine the existence of scale and scope economies in a variety of settings.

Clark, J. "The Economies of Scale and Scope at Depository Financial Institutions: A Review of the Literature." *Economic Review* (Federal Reserve Bank of Kansas City, 1988): 16–33.

Koshal, R. K., and M. Koshal. "Do Liberal Arts Colleges Exhibit Economies of Scale and Scope?" *Education Economics* 8 (December 2000): 209–220.

Silk, A. J., and E. R. Berndt. "Scale and Scope Effects on Advertising Agency Costs." National Bureau of Economic Research, Working Paper No. w9965, September 2003.

Sung, N., and M. Gort. "Economies of Scale and Natural Monopoly in the U.S. Local Telephone Industry." *Review of Economics and Statistics* 82 (November 2000): 694–697.

Wholey, D., et al. "Scale and Scope Economies among Health Maintenance Organizations." *Journal of Health Economics* 15 (December 1996): 657–684.

The following article reviews research estimating cost functions.

J. Panzar. "Determinants of Firm and Industry Structure" in R. Schmalensee and R. Willig (Eds.). *Handbook of Industrial Organization.* Amsterdam, North Holland: 1989, 3–59.

The following article describes cost analysis at Bethlehem Steel Corporation.

Baker, G. L., et al. "Production Planning and Cost Analysis on a Microcomputer." *Interfaces* (July–August 1987): 53–60.

**CHECK STATION
ANSWERS**

1. The full cost to the airline of a grounded plane includes explicit costs—repair costs, overnight hangar costs, and the like. It also includes an opportunity cost: the lost profit on any canceled flights.

2. The past profits and development costs are irrelevant. If the firm drops the product, it recovers $2 million. If the firm continues the product, its additional profit is $5 + 3 - 4 - 2.5 = \$1.5$ million. Thus, the firm should drop the product.

3. The related electronics products would exhibit economies of scope for several reasons. First, they have many technological elements in common (expertise in copier technology carries over to facsimile machines, for example). They also have some common components (microchips). Second, customers see the products as complementary. Thus, brand name allegiance gained in computers could carry over to telephone equipment. Third, there are also likely economies in joint advertising, promotion, and distribution. (Toshiba's sales force can pursue sales on any or all of its products.)

4. The repair firm's marginal revenue is $MR = 50 - .4Q$ and its marginal cost is $MC = 30 + .6Q$. Setting MR equal to MC, we find $Q^* = 20$. From the price equation, $P^* = 50 - (.2)(20) = 46$. In turn, profit is $\pi = 920 - 990 = -70$. The firm incurs a loss in the short run, but this is preferable to shutting down ($\pi = -270$). It is earning a maximum contribution toward overhead. In the long run, the firm should shut down unless conditions improve.

Transfer Pricing

In the body of this chapter, we have focused on the production and sale of a firm's products to outside buyers. While this is the most common case, products are also sold among divisions within large firms. For example, major automobile companies consist of many divisions. The division that produces parts will transfer its output to separate assembly divisions responsible for automobiles, trucks, and vans. In turn, assembled vehicles are transferred to different sales divisions and finally to dealers. In the same way, within a major chemical manufacturer, one division may produce a basic chemical that is used as an input in the production of specialty chemicals and plastics, each housed in separate divisions.

The price the selling division charges to the buying division within the company is called the **transfer price**. The firm's objective is to set the transfer price such that the buying and selling divisions take actions that maximize the firm's total profit. Accomplishing this task requires an accurate cost assessment. To illustrate the issues at stake, consider a large firm that sells a variety of office electronics products, such as telephones, printers, desktop computers, and copiers. One division specializes in the production of microchips that serve as the "electronic brains" for many of the firm's final products, including copiers, laser printers, and facsimile machines. For the time being, we assume there is no outside market for the firm's specialty chips; they are produced only for use in the firm's final products. (We relax this assumption in the following section.) What transfer price per unit should the chip division charge the copier (or any other) division?

The answer to this question is that *the firm should set the internal transfer price for the microchip exactly equal to its marginal cost of production.* Figure 6A.1 summarizes the demand and cost conditions associated with the production of copiers. The key point about the figure is understanding the "full" marginal cost of producing copiers. Managers of the copier division are well aware of the direct costs they incur in assembly. This marginal cost is shown as the upward-sloping MC_A curve in the figure. In addition, we must consider the marginal cost of producing the chips that are used in the copier. In Figure 6A.1, this marginal cost (labeled MC_M) is superimposed on the MC_A curve. The total marginal cost of producing copiers is the sum of the chip cost and the assembly cost. In the figure, this total marginal cost curve is denoted by $MC_T = MC_A + MC_M$ and is drawn as the vertical sum of the two curves. (Note

FIGURE 6A.1

Transfer Pricing

In the absence of an external market, the optimal transfer price for an intermediate product equals the item's marginal cost of production. Optimal output of the firm's final product occurs at Q*, where MR equals MC_T. Here MC_T includes the intermediate good's transfer price.

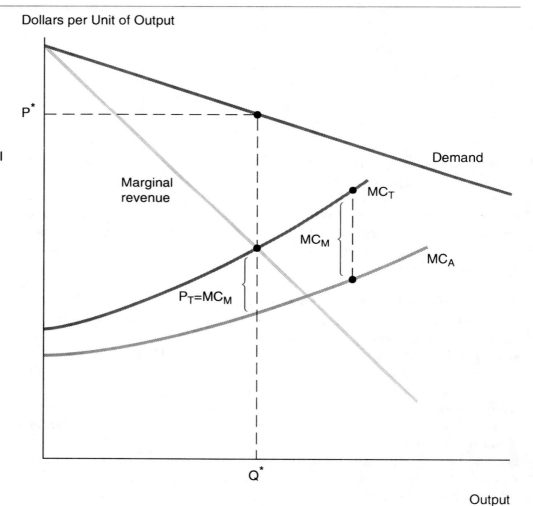

that MC_M is depicted as slightly upward sloping; that is, the gap between MC_A and MC_T steadily increases as output rises.)

The firm maximizes the total profit it earns on copiers by setting the quantity such that marginal revenue equals total marginal cost, $MR = MC_T$. In Figure 6A.1, the optimal quantity occurs at Q^* and the associated optimal selling price for the copier is P^*. What transfer price for chips will lead to this outcome? The appropriate transfer price should be set at $P_T = MC_M$. By paying this transfer price, the copier division incurs an additional cost of $MC_A + P_T = MC_A + MC_M$ for each extra copier it produces. By taking into account the true "full" cost of producing additional output, the copier division automatically maximizes the firm's total profit.

A MARKET FOR CHIPS   If there is an external market in which microchips can be bought and sold, the profit-maximizing analysis must be modified. In this case, *the firm should set the internal transfer price for the microchip equal to the prevailing market price.* The reasoning is straightforward. Let $P^°$ denote the prevailing market price. Obviously, the chip division cannot charge the copier division a transfer price that exceeds $P^°$; the copier division would simply opt to buy chips from the outside market. Nor would the chip division be satisfied with a transfer price below $P^°$; it would prefer to produce and sell chips exclusively for the outside market. Consequently, $P_T = P^°$ is the only price at which internal transfers will occur.

Here is another way to arrive at this conclusion. The correct price to impute to internally produced chips should reflect the firm's true opportunity cost. Each chip that goes into the "guts" of the firm's copiers is a chip that could have been sold on the outside market at price $P^°$. Since it is this market price that the firm gives up, the internal transfer price should be set accordingly.

TRANSFER PRICING: A NUMERICAL EXAMPLE   Let the demand for copiers be given by $P = 4,000 - 3Q$, where Q is the number of copiers demanded per week and P is the price in dollars. The total cost of assembling copiers (excluding the cost of microchips) is given by $C_A = 360,000 + 1,000Q$. The cost of producing microchips is $C_M = 40,000 + 200Q_M + .5Q_M^2$, where Q_M is the quantity of chips. Suppose each copier uses *one* microchip. The total cost of producing copiers is $C_T = C_A + C_M = 400,000 + 1,200Q + .5Q^2$. In turn, the marginal cost of copiers is $MC_T = dC_T/dQ = 1,200 + Q$. Equivalently, $MC_T = MC_A + MC_M = 1,000 + (200 + Q) = 1,200 + Q$. Setting $MR = MC_T$ implies $4,000 - 6Q = 1,200 + Q$. Thus, $Q^* = 400$ and $P^* = 4,000 - (3)(400) = \$2,800$. At a production rate of 400 microchips per week, marginal cost is $MC_M = 200 + 400 = \$600$. Thus, in the absence of an external market for microchips, the appropriate transfer price is $P_T = MC_M = \$600$. At an output of 400 chips, the average cost per chip is $AC_M = C_M/Q = \$500$. Thus, by selling its output to the copier division at $P_T = 600$, the chip division earns an internal profit of $(\$600 - \$500)(400) = \$40,000$ per week. The copier division's average total cost is $AC_A = C_A/Q + \$600 = \$2,500$ per copier. At $P^* = 2,800$, the division makes a profit of $300 per copier, implying a total profit of $120,000 per week. The combined profit of the divisions is $40,000 + 120,000 = \$160,000$.

Now, suppose an external market for chips exists and a chip's current market price is $P_M = \$900$. For each additional chip produced and sold, the chip division's marginal revenue equals $900, the current market price. Setting $MR = MC$ implies $900 = 200 + Q_M$, where Q_M denotes the quantity of microchips. The solution is $Q_M = 700$. Next consider the copier division. The price it pays for chips is now $P_T = P_M = \$900$. Thus, its marginal cost (inclusive of the price of chips) is $MC_T = 1,000 + 900 = \$1,900$. Setting $MR = MC$ implies $4,000 - 6Q = \$1,900$. Thus, $Q^* = 350$ and $P^* = \$2,950$. To sum up, the chip division's total weekly output is 700 chips. Half of this output (350 chips) is transferred to the copier division; the other half is sold on the open market.

Questions and Problems

1. a. A senior manager argues that the chip division's main purpose is to serve the firm's final-product divisions. Accordingly, these services should be offered free of charge; that is, the transfer price for chips should be $P_T = 0$. Explain carefully what is wrong with this argument.
   b. Suppose the chip division treats the copier division as it would an outside buyer and marks up the transfer price above marginal cost. Explain what is wrong with this strategy.

2. In the numerical example, suppose the firm can purchase chips on the open market at a price of $300. What production decisions should the divisions make in this case?

Short-Run
and Long-Run Costs

This appendix takes a closer quantitative look at the cost setting of Spreadsheet Problem S1 and illustration in Figure 6.3. We start with the following economic facts. Let the firm's production function be given by

$$Q = 12L^{.5}K^{.5} = 12\sqrt{L} \cdot \sqrt{K} \qquad [6A.1]$$

where L and K are in thousands of units. The prices of labor and capital are $P_L = 36$ per unit and $P_K = 16$ per unit, respectively.

SHORT-RUN COSTS   We begin by deriving expressions for the firm's SAC and SMC. To do this, we fix the amount of capital at some level; call this $K°$. With capital fixed, we solve Equation 6A.1 for L:

$$L = Q^2/(144K°). \qquad [6A.2]$$

Total cost is

$$C = 16K° + 36L$$
$$= 16K° + Q^2/(4K°)$$

after substituting for L. In turn, short-run average cost is

$$SAC = C/Q = 16K°/Q + Q/(4K°) \qquad [6A.3]$$

259

and SMC = dC/dQ = Q/(2K°). It is easy to check that SAC is U-shaped. For instance, by setting K° equal to 9 thousand square feet, we obtain the SAC function:

$$SAC = 144/Q + Q/36.$$

This is the equation of the first SAC curve graphed in Figure 6.3. By setting K° = 18 thousand and K° = 27 thousand, we trace out the other SAC curves in the figure.

LONG-RUN COSTS   We can now confirm that the firm's LAC and LMC curves are constant, as shown in Figure 6.3. One way of doing so is to note that the level of LAC is given by the minimum point of each SAC curve. Returning to the SAC expression in Equation 6A.3, we can show that the point of minimum average cost occurs at output

$$Q = 8K°. \qquad [6A.4]$$

To see this, remember that the SMC curve intersects the SAC curve at its minimum point. Equating the preceding expressions for SAC and SMC, we find 16K°/Q + Q/4K° = Q/2K°. The solution is Q² = 64(K°)², or Q = 8K°. After substituting Q = 8K° into Equation 6A.3, we find the firm's minimum average cost to be min SAC = 16K°/8K° + 8K°/4K° = 4/unit. In turn, substituting Q = 8K° into Equation 6A.2 implies

$$L = (4/9)K°. \qquad [6A.5]$$

This equation specifies the necessary amount of labor to be used in conjunction with a plant of size K°.

In summary, Equation 6A.3 describes the short-run average cost of producing Q units of output using K° units of fixed capital, whereas Equation 6A.2 specifies the requisite amount of labor. For instance, the short-run average cost of producing 54 thousand units of output in a 9 thousand square-foot plant is SAC = 144/54 + 54/36 = $4.17. The necessary amount of labor is L = (54)²/[(144)(9)] = 2.25 thousand labor-hours. In turn, the LAC of producing Q units is $4 and is achieved using the amounts of capital and labor given by Equations 6A.4 and 6A.5. Thus, to produce 54 thousand units in the long run, the firm should use a 54,000/8 = 6.75 thousand square-foot plant and (4/9)(6.75) = 3 thousand labor-hours.

Questions and Problems

1. a. Using Equation 6A.3, find the short-run average cost of producing 108 thousand units in a 9 thousand square-foot plant. Determine the necessary quantity of labor.
   b. Would the same output be less expensive to produce using an 18 thousand square-foot plant?

CHAPTER 7

Perfect Competition

Everything is worth what its purchaser will pay for it.
Anonymous

There has been an ongoing debate between economists and ecologists for the past 30 years about whether or not the world is running out of resources. (This is a renewal of a centuries-old debate that began with Malthus.) Many ecologists have argued that resources are limited and that economic growth and unchecked population increases are draining these resources (a barrel of oil consumed today means one less barrel available tomorrow) and polluting the environment. Leading economists have pointed out that the cry about limited resources is a false alarm. Technological innovation, human progress, and conservation have meant that the supply of resources has more than kept pace with population growth and can do so indefinitely. Living standards around the globe are higher today than at any time in the past.

One example of this debate was a bet made in 1981 between Paul Ehrlich, a well-known scientist, and Julian Simon, an eminent economist.[1] Simon challenged ecologists to pick any resources they wished and any future date. He then made a simple bet: The prices of the chosen resources would be lower at the future date than they were at the present time. With the help of economists and other scientists, Ehrlich selected five resources (copper, chrome, nickel, tin, and tungsten) for which he

[1] This account is based on John Tierney, "Betting the Planet," *New York Times Magazine*, December 2, 1990, 52.

263

predicted increasing scarcity over the next decade. He hypothetically purchased $200 worth of each metal at 1981 prices. Then the two sides waited and watched price movements over the next 10 years.

What can the economics of supply and demand tell us about this debate (and this bet)? If the bet were to be made today, which side would you take?

This chapter and the three that follow focus on the spectrum of industry structures. Markets are typically divided into four main categories: perfect competition, monopolistic competition, oligopoly, and pure monopoly. Table 7.1 provides a preview of these different settings by considering two dimensions of competition: the number of competing firms and the extent of entry barriers. At one extreme (the lower right cell of the table) is the case of perfect competition. Such a market is supplied by a large number of competitors. Because each firm claims only a very small market share, none has the power to control price. Rather, price is determined by supply and demand. As important, there are no barriers preventing new firms from entering the market.

At the other extreme (the upper left cell of the table) lies the case of pure monopoly. Here a single firm supplies the market and has no direct competitors. Thus, as we shall see, the monopolist (if not constrained) has the ultimate power to raise prices and maximize its profit. Clearly, prohibitive entry barriers are a precondition for pure monopoly. Such barriers prevent rival firms from entering the market and competing evenhandedly with the incumbent monopolist.

Oligopoly (shown in the second row of Table 7.1) occupies a middle ground between the perfectly competitive and monopolistic extremes. In an oligopoly, a small number of large firms dominate the market. Each firm must anticipate the effect of its rivals' actions on its own profits and attempt to fashion profit-maximizing decisions in response. Again, moderate or high entry barriers are necessary to insulate the oligopolists from would-be entrants.

TABLE 7.1

Comparing Market Structures

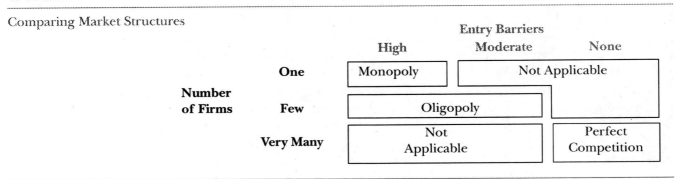

Finally, monopolistic competition (not shown in the table) shares several of the characteristics of perfect competition: many small firms competing in the market and an absence of entry barriers. In this sense, it would occupy the same cell as perfect competition. However, whereas perfect competition is characterized by firms producing identical standardized products, monopolistic competition is marked by product differentiation. In short, the two dimensions of competition shown in Table 7.1, although useful, do not do the full job in distinguishing different market structures.

THE BASICS OF SUPPLY AND DEMAND

A thorough knowledge of the workings of supply and demand, and how they affect price and output in competitive markets, is essential for sound managerial decision making. For example, if a product or service is sold in a perfectly competitive industry, top management is naturally concerned with a prediction of future prices in the market. Should the firm expand capacity with the expectation of price increases? Conversely, if price declines are expected, downsizing might be the proper response.

In a perfectly competitive market, price is determined by the market demand and supply curves. We will consider each of these entities in turn.

The **demand curve** for a good or service shows the total quantities that consumers are willing and able to purchase at various prices, other factors held constant.[2] Figure 7.1 depicts a hypothetical demand curve D for shoes in a local market. As expected, the curve slopes downward to the right. Any change in price causes a movement along the demand curve.

The **supply curve** for a good or service shows the total quantities that producers are willing and able to supply at various prices, other factors held constant. In Figure 7.1, the supply curve for shoes (denoted by S) is upward sloping. As the price of shoes increases, firms are willing to produce greater quantities because of the greater profit available at the higher price. Any change in price represents a movement along the supply curve.

The **equilibrium price** in the market is determined at point E where market supply equals market demand. Figure 7.1 shows the equilibrium price to be $25 per pair of shoes, the price at which the demand and supply curves intersect. At the $25 price, the quantity of output demanded by consumers exactly matches the amount of output willingly offered by producers. The corresponding equilibrium quantity is 8,000 pairs. To see what lies behind the notion of demand-supply equilibrium, consider the situation at different prices. Suppose the market price were temporarily greater than $25 (say,

[2]In Chapters 2 and 3, we already have presented an extensive analysis of the demand curve facing an individual firm. In the present discussion, we focus on total demand in the market as a whole. Except for this difference, all of the earlier analyses apply.

FIGURE 7.1

Supply and Demand

The intersection of supply and demand determines the equilibrium price ($25) and quantity (8,000 pairs).

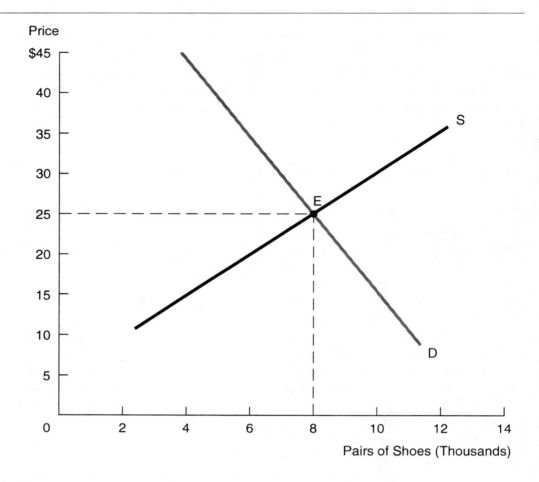

$35). At this higher price, the amount of shoes firms supply would greatly exceed the amount consumers would purchase willingly. Given the surplus of supply relative to demand, producers would be forced to reduce their prices to sell their output. Price reductions would occur until equilibrium was restored at the $25 price. Similarly, if the price were temporarily lower than $25, consumer demand would outstrip the quantity supplied. The result would be upward pressure on price until the equilibrium price was restored.

If we augment the demand and supply graph with quantitative estimates of the curves, we can pinpoint equilibrium price and quantity more precisely. Suppose the market demand curve in Figure 7.1 is described by the equation

$$Q_D = 13 - .2P,$$

where Q_D denotes the quantity of shoes demanded (in thousands of pairs) and P is the dollar price per pair. Let the market supply curve in the figure be given by

$$Q_S = .4P - 2.$$

Then, if we set supply equal to demand ($Q_S = Q_D$), we have $13 - .2P = .4P - 2$, or $.6P = 15$; therefore, $P = 15/.6 = \$25$. Inserting $P = \$25$ into either the demand equation or the supply equation, we confirm that $Q_D = Q_S = 8$ thousand units.[3]

Shifts in Demand and Supply

Changes in important economic factors can shift the positions of the demand and/or supply curves, causing, in turn, predictable changes in equilibrium price and quantity. For example, suppose the local economy is coming out of a recession and that consumer incomes are rising. As a result, a greater quantity of shoes would be demanded even at an unchanged price. An increase in demand due to any nonprice factor is depicted as a rightward shift in the demand curve. Shifting the entire curve means that we would expect an increase in the quantity demanded at *any* prevailing price.[4] Such a shift is shown in Figure 7.2a.

What is the result of the shift in demand? We see from the figure that the new equilibrium occurs at a higher price and greater quantity of output. This is hardly surprising. The increase in demand causes price to be bid up. In the process, the amount supplied by firms also increases. The change from the old to the new market equilibrium represents a movement along the stationary supply curve (caused by a shift in demand).

Now consider economic conditions that might shift the position of the supply curve. Two principal factors are changes in input prices and technology improvements. For instance, increases in input prices will cause the supply curve to shift upward and to the left. (Any effect that increases the marginal cost of production means that the firm must receive a higher price to be induced to supply a given level of output.) Technological improvements, however, allow firms to reduce their unit costs of production. As a consequence, the supply curve shifts down and to the right. Such a shift is shown in Figure 7.2b. The result is a greater market output and a lower price. The favorable shift in supply has moved the equilibrium toward lower prices and greater quantities along the unchanged demand curve.

[3]The same answer would be found if we began with the curves expressed in the equivalent forms $P = 65 - 5Q_D$ and $P = 5 + 2.5Q_S$. Setting these equations equal to one another, we find $65 - 5Q = 5 + 2.5Q$. It follows that $Q = 60/7.5 = 8$ thousand. Inserting this answer into either equation, we find $P = \$25$.

[4]It is important to distinguish between shifts in the demand curve and movements along the curve. The effect of a change in price is charted by a movement along the demand curve. (An increase in price means fewer units demanded, but the demand curve has not shifted.) By contrast, the demand curve shifts with a change in any *nonprice* factor that affects demand.

FIGURE 7.2

Shifts in Supply
and Demand

(a)   Price

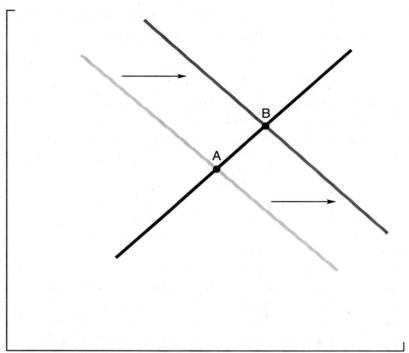

Quantity

(b)   Price

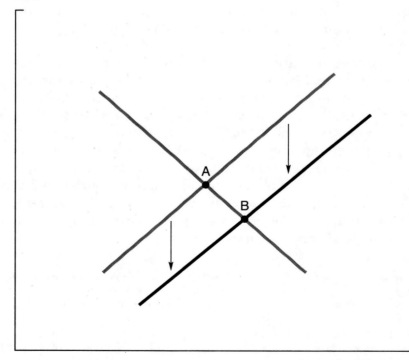

Quantity

268

**CHECK
STATION 1**

In 1999, the respective worldwide demand and supply curves for copper were $Q_D = 15 - 10P$ and $Q_S = -3 + 14P$, where Q is measured in millions of metric tons per year. Find the competitive price and quantity. Suppose that in 2000 demand is expected to fall by 20 percent, so $Q_D = (.8)(15 - 10P) = 12 - 8P$. How much are world copper prices expected to fall?

COMPETITIVE EQUILIBRIUM

Perfect competition is commonly characterized by four conditions.

1. *A large number of firms supply a good or service* for a market consisting of a large number of consumers.

2. *There are no barriers with respect to new firms entering the market.* As a result, the typical competitive firm will earn a zero economic profit.

3. *All firms produce and sell identical standardized products.* Therefore, firms compete only with respect to price. In addition, all consumers have perfect information about competing prices. Thus, all goods must sell at a single market price.

4. *Firms and consumers are price takers.* Each firm sells a small share of total industry output, and, therefore, its actions have no impact on price. Each firm takes the price as given—indeed, determined by supply and demand. Similarly, each consumer is a price taker, having no influence on the market price.

It is important to remember that these conditions characterize an ideal model of perfect competition. Some competitive markets in the real world meet the letter of all four conditions. Many other real-world markets are effectively perfectly competitive because they approximate these conditions. At present, we will use the ideal model to make precise price and output predictions for perfectly competitive markets. Later in this and the following chapters, we will compare the model to real-world markets.

In exploring the model of perfect competition, we first focus on the individual decision problem the typical firm faces. Then we show how firm-level decisions influence total industry output and price.

Decisions of the Competitive Firm

The key feature of the perfectly competitive firm is that it is a **price taker**; that is, it has no influence on market price. Two key conditions are necessary for price taking. First, the competitive market is composed of a large number of sellers (and buyers), each of which is small relative to the total market. Second, the firms' outputs are perfect substitutes for one another; that is, each firm's output is perceived to be indistinguishable from any other's. Perfect substitutability usually requires that all firms produce a standard, homogeneous, undifferentiated product, and that buyers have perfect information about cost, price, and quality of competing goods.

Together, these two conditions ensure that the firm's demand curve is perfectly (or infinitely) elastic. In other words, it is horizontal like the solid price line in Figure 7.3a. Recall the meaning of *perfectly elastic demand*. The firm can sell as much or as little output as it likes along the horizontal price line ($8 in the figure). If it raises its price above $8 (even by a nickel), its sales go to zero. Consumers instead will purchase the good (a perfect substitute) from a competitor at the market price. When all firms' outputs are perfect substitutes, the "law of one price" holds: All market transactions take place at a single price. Thus, each firm faces the same horizontal demand curve given by the prevailing market price.

THE FIRM'S SUPPLY CURVE   Part (a) of Figure 7.3 also is useful in describing the supply of output by the perfectly competitive firm. The cost characteristics of the typical firm in the competitive market are as shown in the figure. The firm faces a U-shaped, average cost (AC) curve and an increasing marginal cost (MC) curve. (Recall that increasing marginal cost reflects diminishing marginal returns.)

Suppose the firm faces a market price of $8. (For the moment, we are not saying how this market price might have been established.) What is its optimal level of output? As always, the firm maximizes profit by applying the MR = MC rule. In the case of perfectly elastic demand, the firm's marginal revenue from selling an extra unit is simply the price it receives for the unit: MR = P.

Here the marginal revenue line and price line coincide. Thus, we have the following rule:

> A firm in a perfectly competitive market maximizes profit by producing up to an output such that its marginal cost equals the market price.

In Figure 7.3, the intersection of the horizontal price line and the rising marginal cost curve (where P = MC) identifies the firm's optimal output. At an $8 market price, the firm's optimal output is 6,000 units. (Check for yourself that the firm would sacrifice potential profit if it deviated from this output, by producing either slightly more or slightly less.) Notice that if the price rises above $8, the firm profitably can increase its output; the new optimal output lies at a higher point along the MC curve. A lower price implies a fall in the firm's optimal output. (Recall, however, that if price falls below average variable cost, the firm will produce nothing.) By varying price, we read the firm's optimal output off the marginal cost curve. The firm's **supply curve** is simply the portion of the MC curve lying above average variable cost.

FIGURE 7.3

In part (a), the firm
produces 6,000 units
(where P = MC) and
makes a positive
economic profit. In
part (b), the entry of
new firms has reduced
the price to $6, and the
firm earns zero
economic profit.

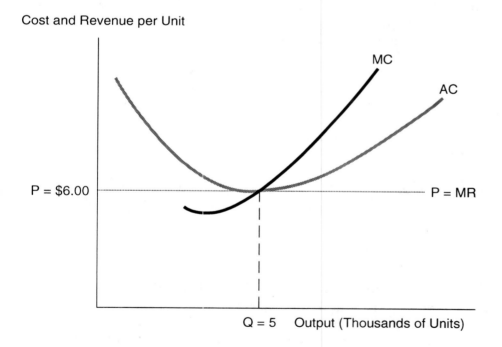

Cost and Revenue per Unit

MC

AC

P = $8.00

P = MR

AC = $6.50

Q = 6   Output (Thousands of Units)

(a) A Competitive Firm's Optimal Output

Cost and Revenue per Unit

MC

AC

P = $6.00

P = MR

Q = 5   Output (Thousands of Units)

(b) Long-Run Equilibrium in a Competitive Market

271

CHECK
STATION 2

The typical firm in a perfectly competitive market has a cost structure described by the equation

$$C = 25 - 4Q + Q^2,$$

where Q is measured in thousands of units. Using the profit-maximizing condition, P = MC, write an equation for the firm's supply curve. If 40 such firms serve the market, write down the equation of the market supply curve.

LONG-RUN EQUILIBRIUM Perfectly competitive markets exhibit a third important condition: In the long run, firms can freely enter or exit the market. In light of this fact, it is important to recognize that the profit opportunity shown in Figure 7.3a is *temporary*. Here the typical firm is earning a positive economic profit that comes to $\pi = (\$8.00 - \$6.50)(6,000) = \$9,000$. But the existence of positive economic profit will attract new suppliers into the industry, and as new firms enter and produce output, the current market price will be bid down. The competitive price will fall to the point where all economic profits are eliminated.

Figure 7.3b depicts the long-run equilibrium from the firm's point of view. Here the firm faces a market price of $6 per unit, and it maximizes profit by producing 5,000 units over the time period. At this quantity, the firm's marginal cost is equal to the market price. In fact, long-run equilibrium is characterized by a "sublime" set of equalities:

$$P = MR = LMC = \min LAC.$$

In equilibrium, we observe the paradox of profit-maximizing competition:

> The simultaneous pursuit of maximum profit by competitive firms results in zero economic profits and minimum-cost production for all.[5]

In short, the typical firm produces at the point of minimum long-run average cost (LAC) but earns only a normal rate of return because P = LAC.

Market Equilibrium

Let's shift from the typical firm's point of view to that of the market as a whole. Figure 7.4 provides this marketwide perspective. The current equilibrium occurs at E, where the market price is $6 per unit (as in Figure 7.3b) and the industry's total quantity of output is 200,000 units. This output is supplied by exactly 40 competitive firms, each producing 5,000 units (each firm's point of

---

[5]Remember that a zero economic profit affords the firm a normal rate of return on its capital investment. This normal return already is included in its estimated cost.

FIGURE 7.4

Competitive Price and
Output in the Long Run

An increase in demand
from D to D' has two
effects. In the short run,
the outcome is E'; in the
long run (after entry by
new firms), the outcome
is E*.

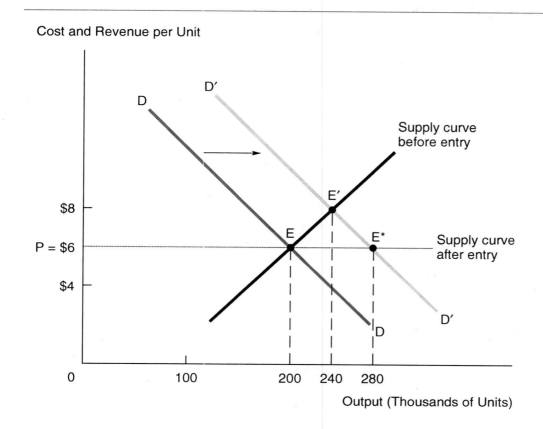

Cost and Revenue per Unit

minimum LAC). The market is in equilibrium. Industry demand exactly matches industry supply. All firms make zero economic profits; no firm has an incentive to alter its output. Furthermore, no firm has an incentive to enter or exit the industry.

In the perfectly competitive market described in Check Station 2, what is the equilibrium price in the long run? (*Hint:* Find the typical firm's point of minimum average cost by setting AC = MC.) Find the output level of the typical firm. Let industry demand be given by the equation $Q_D = 320 - 20P$. Find total output in the long run. How many firms can the market support?   **CHECK STATION 3**

Now consider the effect of a permanent increase in market demand. This is shown as a rightward shift of the demand curve (from DD to D'D') in Figure 7.4. The first effect of the demand shift is to move the market equilibrium from E to E'. At the new equilibrium, the market price has risen from $6 to $8 and industry output has increased to 240,000 units. The higher level of output is supplied by the 40 incumbent firms, each having increased its production to 6,000 units. (According to Figure 7.3a, this is precisely the firm's profit-maximizing response to the $8 price.) The equilibrium at E′ is determined by the intersection of the new demand curve and the total supply curve of the 40 firms currently in the industry. This supply curve also is shown in Figure 7.4 and is constructed by summing horizontally the individual firms' supply curves (i.e., marginal cost curves) in Figure 7.3. (Check Station 4 will ask you to derive the market equilibrium by equating demand and short-run supply.)

The shift in demand calls forth an immediate supply response (and a move from E to E′). But this is not the end of the story. Because the firms currently in the market are enjoying excess profits, new firms will be attracted into the industry. Price will be bid down below $8 and will continue to be bid down so long as excess profits exist. In Figure 7.4, the new long-run equilibrium result is at E*. Price is bid down to $6 per unit, its original level. At this price, total market demand is 280,000 units, a 40 percent increase above the 200,000 units sold at equilibrium E. In turn, industry supply increases to match this higher level of demand. How is this output supplied? With the price at $6 once again, each firm produces 5,000 units. Therefore, the total output of 280,000 units is supplied by 280,000/5,000 = 56 firms; that is, 16 new firms enter the industry (in addition to the original 40 firms). In the long run, the 40 percent increase in demand has called forth a 40 percent increase in the number of firms. There is no change in the industry's unit cost or price; both remain at $6 per unit.

CHECK STATION 4 Starting from the long-run equilibrium in Check Station 3, suppose market demand increases to $Q_D = 400 - 20P$. Find the equilibrium price in the short run (before new firms enter). (*Hint:* Set the new demand curve equal to the supply curve derived in Check Station 2.) Check that the typical firm makes a positive economic profit. In the long run—after entry—what is the equilibrium price? How many firms will serve the market?

LONG-RUN MARKET SUPPLY   The horizontal line in Figure 7.4 represents the case of a *constant-cost* industry. For such an industry, the long-run market supply curve is a horizontal line at a level equal to the minimum LAC of production. Recall that any long-run additions to supply are furnished by the entry of new firms. Furthermore, in a constant-cost industry, the inputs needed to produce the increased industry output can be obtained without bidding up their prices. This is the case if the industry in question draws its resources from large, well-developed input markets. (If the industry is a "small player" in these input markets, an increase in its demand will have a negligible effect on the inputs' market prices.) For instance, the market for new housing exhibits a nearly horizontal long-run supply curve. In the long run, the industry's two main inputs—building materials and construction labor—are relatively abundant and provided by nationwide markets.[6]

For an *increasing-cost* industry, output expansion causes increases in the price of key inputs, thus raising minimum average costs. Here the industry relies on inputs in limited supply: land, skilled labor, and sophisticated capital equipment. For instance, if U.S. drilling activity increased by 30 percent (perhaps due to increases in world oil prices), the typical oil company's average cost per barrel of oil could be expected to rise, for a number of reasons. First, the increase in drilling would bid up the price of drilling rigs and sophisticated seismic equipment. Second, skilled labor (such as chemical engineering graduates), being in greater demand, would receive higher wages. Third, because the most promising sites are limited, oil companies would resort to drilling marginal sites, yielding less oil on average. For an increasing-cost industry, the result of such increases in average costs is an upward-sloping long-run supply curve.

MARKET EFFICIENCY

You might be familiar with one of the most famous statements in economics—Adam Smith's notion of an "invisible hand":

> Every individual endeavors to employ his capital so that its produce may be of greatest value. He generally neither intends to promote the public interest, nor knows how much he is promoting it. He intends only his own security, only his gain. And he is in this led by an invisible hand to promote an end which was no part of his intention. By pursuing his own interest he frequently promotes that of society more effectively than when he really intends to promote it.[7]

One of the main accomplishments of modern economics has been to examine carefully the circumstances in which the profit incentive, as mediated by competitive markets, promotes social welfare.[8] Although economists are fond of proving theorems on this subject, the present approach is more pragmatic. Our aim is to examine the following proposition: *Competitive markets provide efficient amounts of goods and services at minimum cost to the consumers who are most willing (and able) to pay for them.* This statement is one expression of the notion of *market efficiency.* Of

---

[6]Here it is important to distinguish between long-run and short-run supply. In the short run, an increased local demand for new housing can bid up the wages of construction labor (and, to some extent, materials) until additional workers are attracted into the market. In addition, if available land is limited in rapidly growing metropolitan areas, its price may increase significantly.

[7]Adam Smith, *The Wealth of Nations* (1776).

[8]The study of the relationship between private markets and public welfare is referred to as *welfare economics.*

course, getting to the heart of market efficiency requires a careful explanation of what the "efficient" amount of a good or service means.

Private Markets: Benefits and Costs

The main step in our examination of market efficiency is the valuation (in dollar terms) of benefits and costs. We begin the analysis with a single transaction and move on to the thousands of transactions that take place within markets. Consider the following example.

THE DEMAND AND SUPPLY OF DAY CARE   A couple is seeking to obtain up to 10 hours of day care per week for their two-year-old. Through informal inquiries in their neighborhood, they have found a grandmother who has done babysitting and some day care in the past and comes highly recommended. The grandmother is not sure whether she is willing to commit to 10 hours. Before any discussion of price takes place, the couple has thought hard about their value for day care. They have decided that the maximum amount they are willing to pay is $8 per hour (i.e., they would be indifferent to the options of getting day care at this price and not getting it at all). For her part, the grandmother has decided that her minimum acceptable price is $4. (Thus, $4 is the best estimate of her "cost" based on the value of her time and the strain of taking care of a two-year-old. All things considered, she just breaks even at this price.) Can the couple and the grandmother conclude a mutually beneficial agreement? How can we measure the parties' gains from an agreement?

The answer to the first question clearly is yes. Any negotiated price between $4 and $8 would be mutually beneficial. What about the second question? If the parties are equally matched bargainers, we might expect the final price to be $6. The grandmother makes a profit of $2 per hour, or $20 per week. Similarly, the couple makes a $2-per-hour "profit"; that is, they pay only $6 for a day-care hour that is worth $8 to them. Their "profit" per week is $20. The couple's gain (or any consumer's gain in general) is customarily labeled **consumer surplus**. Although it goes under a different name, the couple's gain is identical in kind (and here in amount) to the grandmother's profit.

Figure 7.5 makes the same point in graphical terms. The couple's $8 value is drawn as a horizontal demand curve (up to a maximum of 10 hours per week). The grandmother's $4 cost line and a $6 price line are shown also. The grandmother's profit is depicted as the area of the rectangle between the price and cost lines. In turn, the couple's consumer surplus is shown as the area of the rectangle between the value and price lines. The areas of the profit and consumer surplus rectangles are both $20. The total gain from trade—the sum of consumer surplus and profit—is given by the area of the rectangle between the value and cost lines and comes to $40.

FIGURE 7.5

A Day-Care Transaction

This transaction provides the couple with a consumer surplus of $20 per week and the grandmother with a profit of $20 per week.

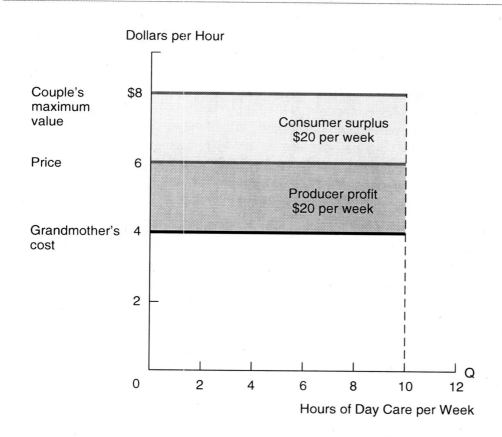

An agreement calling for 10 hours of day care per week delivers the maximum total gain to the parties together. For this reason, we call such a transaction *efficient.* In contrast, an agreement that called for only five hours of day care per week would furnish only $20 of total gain ($10 to each side). Although this agreement is better than nothing, it would rightly be labeled *inefficient* because it generates less than the maximum total gain. (More than 10 hours is infeasible because the grandmother is willing to supply 10 hours at most.)

We note two simple, but important, points about the efficiency concept. First, the actual price negotiated is *not* a matter of efficiency. An agreement calling for 10 hours of day care at a price of $7 (or at any other price between $4 and $8) would generate the same total profit, $40 per week. Of course, at $7 the total gain is redistributed. The grandmother's profit is $30 per week, and the couple's is $10. But the total gain has not changed. In algebraic terms, the total gain is

$$CS + \pi = (8 - P)Q + (P - 4)Q = 4Q.$$

In computing this total gain, the price paid by the buyer to the supplier just cancels out; that is, the terms involving the price P disappear. Note that for 10 hours of care (Q = 10), the total gain is $40.

Second, starting from any inefficient agreement, there is a different, efficient agreement that is better for both parties. In short, the best split of the proverbial pie for both parties is attained when the pie is made as big as possible in the first place. For instance, suppose the parties agreed on seven hours of day care per week at a price of $7. This inefficient agreement generates gains to the grandmother and couple of $21 and $7, respectively. Clearly, both parties would benefit from a 10-hour deal at an appropriate price. For instance, a price concession by the grandmother to $6.50 with a 10-hour deal would bring her $25 in profit and the couple $15 in consumer surplus. Both parties are better off than with the seven-hour agreement.

THE DAY-CARE MARKET   Let's now extend the previous analysis to the large day-care market that emerged in the last 25 years. Figure 7.6 shows the weekly demand curve for day care in a given geographical region. There is nothing remarkable about this bare-bones demand curve. Depending on the going hourly price for day care, more or less millions of day-care hours will be demanded. The lower the price, the greater the number of hours purchased. However, one aspect of this demand curve (or any demand curve) is important: Besides showing the quantity consumed at any price, *the demand curve shows the monetary value that consumers are willing to pay for each unit.* For instance, the "first" few units consumed are valued at roughly $12, the demand curve's price intercept. Even at a rate this high, some parents (with high incomes, rotten kids, or both) are willing to pay the high price for day care. But what about the 8-millionth hour of day care consumed? For this hour to be purchased, the hourly price must drop to $4. Put simply, the value of any unit of day care is given by the price the consumer is willing to pay for it.[9] (Thus, it is hard to claim that the 8-millionth hour is worth $4.50 because the would-be consumer of this hour is unwilling to pay that high a price.) In short, the value of a particular unit is given by the height of the demand curve at that quantity.[10] For this reason, the demand curve can be thought of as a **marginal benefit curve**.

Now suppose the going price for day care is in fact $4 per hour, with the result that 8 million hours are purchased per week. What is the *total* consumer surplus enjoyed by purchasers? The answer is straightforward: Consumer surplus

[9]This valuation method is based on the notion of *consumer sovereignty:* Each individual is the best judge of the value he or she derives from a purchase. When all the individual purchases are added together, we obtain a market demand curve—the best measure of aggregate value from day-care services. Thus, under the doctrine of consumer sovereignty, it would be improper for a government authority to place either an arbitrarily high value (say, $30 per hour) or low value (e.g., $.50 per hour) on day-care services.

[10]*Caution:* We are *not* saying that *each* of the 8 million day-care hours consumed at a price of $4 is *worth* $4. We mean only that the last, 8-millionth, unit is worth $4. The other hours are worth much more, as shown by the rising height of the demand curve as we move to smaller and smaller quantities.

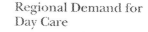

FIGURE 7.6

Regional Demand for Day Care

At a price of $4, the total demand for day care is 8 million hours per week. Parents receive a total consumer surplus of $32 million.

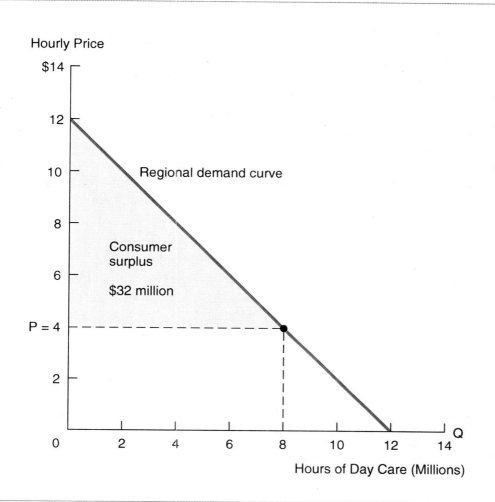

is measured by the triangle inscribed under the demand curve and above the price line. After all, the demand curve indicates what consumers are *willing* to pay, and the price line indicates what they *actually* pay, so the difference (added up over all units consumed) is their total surplus. Recall that the area of a triangle is given by one-half of its height times its base. Thus, the consumer surplus from 8 million hours demanded at a $4 price comes to $(.5)(12 - 4)(8) = \$32$ million.[11]

---

[11]An equivalent way to find consumer surplus is to reason as follows. The first unit consumed earns a surplus of $12 - 4 = 8$. The last (i.e., 8 millionth) unit consumed earns a surplus of $4 - 4 = 0$. Since demand is linear, the average surplus per unit is $(8 + 0)/2 = \$4$. We multiply this by 8 million units to arrive at a total surplus of $32 million.

To complete the description of the market, let's consider the supply of day care. A day-care supply curve is shown in Figure 7.7. Notice that the main part of the supply curve is provided by low-cost suppliers at $2.50 per hour. Let's say these suppliers enjoy significant economies of scale while maintaining quality day care. In fact, as we shall see, "grandmotherly" day care at $4 per hour will become a thing of the past. Less efficient, high-cost grandmothers will be priced out of the day-care market.

Now we are ready to take a closer look at market efficiency. To begin, we know that, in a competitive day-care market, the intersection of supply and demand determines price and quantity. In Figure 7.7, the competitive price is $2.50 and quantity is 9.5 million hours per week. Now we can make our key point: *This competitive outcome is efficient; that is, it delivers the maximum total dollar benefit to consumers and producers together.* This is particularly easy to see in

FIGURE 7.7

A Competitive Day-Care Market

The competitive price ($2.50) and output (9.5 million hours) are determined by the intersection of the supply and demand curves.

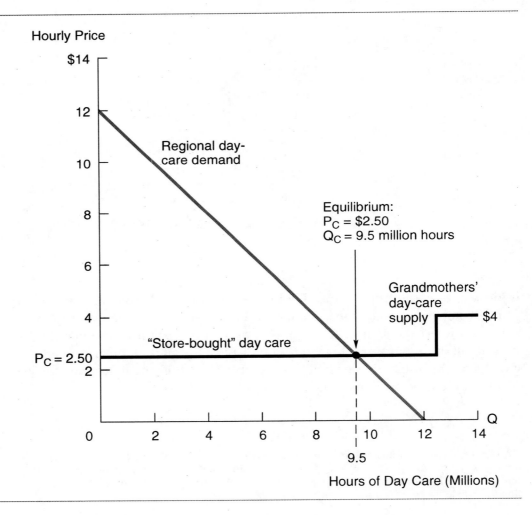

Figure 7.7, because day-care suppliers earn zero profits: Price equals average cost. All gain takes the form of consumer surplus. It is easy to check that the total surplus measures out to $(.5)(12 - 2.5)(9.5) = \$45.125$ million.

An equivalent way to confirm that the competitive level of output is efficient is to appeal to the logic of marginal benefits and costs. We have argued that the height of the demand curve at a given output level, Q, measures the marginal benefit (in dollar terms) of consuming the last (Qth) unit. Similarly, the height of the supply curve indicates the marginal cost of producing the Qth unit. At a competitive equilibrium, demand equals supply. A direct consequence is that marginal benefit equals marginal cost. Equating marginal benefits and marginal costs ensures that the industry supplies the "right" quantity of the good—the precise output that maximizes the total net benefits (consumer benefits minus supplier costs) from production.

In contrast, at a noncompetitive price—say \$4—only 8 million day-care hours would be demanded. At this reduced output, the marginal benefit (what consumers are willing to pay for additional day-care hours) is \$4, and this is greater than the marginal cost of supplying extra hours, \$2.50. Thus, there is a net welfare gain of $4.00 - 2.50 = \$1.50$ for each additional day-care hour supplied. More generally, so long as the demand curve lies above the supply curve (MB > MC), there is a net gain (MB − MC > 0) from increasing the output of day care. Conversely, at any output level beyond the competitive quantity (say, 11 million hours), the marginal benefit of extra hours falls short of the marginal cost of supply (MB < MC). Producing these units is a "losing" proposition. Thus, there is a net gain from cutting output back to the competitive level.[12]

Figure 7.7 provides a visual depiction of our original proposition:

> Competitive markets provide efficient levels of goods and services at minimum cost to the consumers who are most willing (and able) to pay for them.

Think of this statement in three parts, focusing on production, consumption, and total output in turn. First, in a competitive market, the active firms are

---

[12]In mathematical terms, consider the objective of maximizing the sum of consumer surplus and producer profit:

$$\text{Surplus} + \text{Profit} = (B - R) + (R - C) = B - C,$$

where B denotes the total consumer benefits associated with a given level of output, R is total revenue paid by consumers to producers, and C is the total cost of production. The revenue term is simply a transfer between consumers and producers and does not affect the objective. Thus, maximizing this sum is equivalent to maximizing net benefits, B − C. At the optimal level of output, it must be the case that MB = MC.

Furthermore, the competitive equilibrium achieves this optimal level of output. To see this, consider the demand and supply curves, denoted by the functions D(Q) and S(Q), respectively. The competitive price and output are determined by the intersection of supply and demand, $D(Q_C) = S(Q_C) = P_C$. By our earlier argument, $D(Q) \equiv MB(Q)$ and $S(Q) \equiv MC(Q)$ for all Q, where MB and MC denote the marginal benefit and cost functions, respectively. It follows that $MB(Q_C) = MC(Q_C) = P_c$. Thus, the competitive level of output is efficient.

necessarily least-cost suppliers; all other higher-cost would-be suppliers are priced out of the market. (In our example, grandmothers cannot compete; "store-bought" day care is more efficiently supplied than "home-made.") The supply curve in Figure 7.7 is not drawn arbitrarily; rather, it describes the *lowest* possible costs of production. In this sense, *production is efficient.*

Second, competitive markets obey the "law of one price"; that is, all buyers and suppliers face the same price. In particular, this means that only consumers who are most willing (and able) to pay this price (i.e., those who reside on the highest portion of the demand curve) will actually end up with the goods. In this sense, *consumption is efficient.*

Third, given the market selection of minimum-cost producers and maximum-value consumers, the optimal output is achieved at the competitive intersection of supply and demand. Since $P_C = MB = MC$, it is impossible to alter output—above or below the competitive level—and increase net benefits. In this sense, *the level of output is efficient.*

CHECK STATION 5   What are the efficiency implications of a government program to provide universal, *free* day care?

EFFICIENCY AND EQUITY   It is important to emphasize that efficient markets are not necessarily equitable or fair. The outcomes of competitive markets directly reflect the distribution of incomes of those who buy and sell in these markets. An inability to pay excludes many people from the economic equation. In trying to solve the problems of poverty, malnutrition, inadequate health care, and the like, the government has the responsibility of addressing equity issues (as well as efficiency issues).

DYNAMIC, MARKETWIDE EFFICIENCY   In our examination of competitive efficiency, we have focused on a *single* market and found that the efficient level of output occurs at the intersection of demand and supply, where $P_C = MB = MC$. Can this "invisible hand" result be extended to encompass at once all the innumerable markets in a modern economy? The generalization to multiple markets is more complicated than it might seem at first. When dealing with many markets, it is not quite correct to focus on them separately, one at a time. After all, demands for different goods and services in the economy are interdependent. Changing the price of one good affects not only its consumption but also the consumption of substitute and complementary goods. Similarly, any change in price and output in one market generates marginal benefits and costs not only for that good but also for other affected markets. Given these interdependencies, can we draw any conclusions about the workings of private markets and economic efficiency?

Modern economic theory provides an elegant and important answer to this question: *If all markets in the economy are perfectly competitive, the economy as a whole is efficient; that is, it delivers an efficient quantity of each good and service to consumers at least cost.* In short, a system of competitive markets in which all goods and services and all inputs (including labor) can be freely bought and sold provides a solution to the economic problem of resource allocation.[13] Indeed, no matter how well intentioned, government measures that interfere with competitive markets can cause welfare losses.

A final virtue of competitive markets is that they are dynamically efficient; that is, they respond optimally to changes in economic conditions. If a new product or service can be supplied at a cost below the price consumers are willing to pay, profit-seeking firms will create and supply a market where none formerly existed. If demand for an existing product rises, so will price, thus attracting new entrants and further supply. At the new equilibrium, the efficiency condition, P = MB = MC, will be restored. Alternatively, if costs decline, the efficient response is achieved via a fall in price, causing consumption to increase to a new, optimal level. Finally, markets encourage the pursuit of technological innovations. Firms have a continuous incentive to search for and adopt more profitable methods of production.

The "invisible hand" theorem—that perfectly competitive markets ensure maximum social benefits—is best thought of as a benchmark. Although many markets in the United States meet the requirements of perfect competition, notable cases of market failures also exist. Market failures usually can be traced to one of three causes: (1) the presence of monopoly power, (2) the existence of externalities, or (3) the absence of perfect information. In Chapter 11, we analyze each of these sources of market failure.

Is competition on the Internet one further step toward the textbook case of perfect competition?[14] The affirmative view holds that Internet competition, where consumers can easily find and identify the cheapest prices, should squeeze prices and profit margins to the bone. The early evidence suggests that the Internet can promote competition and efficiency in several respects. First, transacting online provides buyers and sellers much better information about available prices for competing goods. Clearly, the ability of customers to find better prices for standardized goods increases competition and induces more

Market Competition and the Internet

[13]The proof of the "efficiency theorem" is beyond the scope of this book. It can be shown that a perfectly competitive economy is *Pareto efficient;* that is, it is impossible to reorganize the economy to make some economic agent (an individual or a firm) better off without making some other agent worse off.

[14]For interesting discussions of market competition and the Internet, see G. Ellison and S. F. Ellison, "Lessons about Markets from the Internet," *Journal of Economic Perspectives* (Spring 2005): 139–158; "A Perfect Market: Survey of E-commerce," *The Economist,* May 15, 2004, special supplement; E. Brynjolfsson, Y. Hu, and M. D. Smith, "Consumer Surplus in the Digital Economy: Estimating the Value of Increased Product Variety at Online Booksellers," *Management Science* (November 2003): 1580–1596; M. E. Porter, "Strategy and the Internet," *Harvard Business Review* (March 2001): 63–78; S. Borenstein and G. Saloner, "Economics and Electronic Commerce," *Journal of Economic Perspectives* (Winter 2001): 3–12; and R. E. Litan and A. M. Rivlin, "Projecting the Economic Impact of the Internet," *American Economic Review,* Papers and Proceedings (May 2001): 313–317.

favorable prices. For instance, Internet prices for books and CDs tend to be 9 percent to 16 percent lower than traditional retail prices. New automobiles prices are about 2 percent lower on average to buyers who enlist online comparison and referral services. Online insurance fees and brokerage charges are lower than charges for similar storefront products and services (and over time tend to exert downward pressure on storefront prices). Internet prices also display less dispersion than do retail prices. (However, online price dispersion persists. Competition is not so intense that all sellers are forced to charge the same market price.)

Second, the Internet increases the geographic range of markets and the variety of items sold in those markets. Hundreds of fragmented transactions are readily enlisted in unified markets. For example, a consumer could expend the time and effort to find a used copy of a John Grisham legal mystery by going to several bookstores and paying about $4.50 (half the new price in paperback). Or the consumer could use the Internet's unified used book market, where scores of the same title sell for about $3.50, shipping included. The important point is that unified markets directly increase overall economic efficiency. However, unified markets need not always imply lower prices. For instance, with numerous buyers seeking scarce copies of original Nancy Drew mysteries (dust jackets intact), the Internet price averages $20 to $30 per copy. By comparison, the rare buyer who is lucky enough to find the same book on a bookstore shelf might pay only $5 to $15. As always the price effect of moving to a unified market depends on the relative increases in supply versus demand. An additional key benefit of online markets is greater product variety. One research study discovered that some 45 percent of all books sold online at Amazon were "rare" titles (ranked below the top 100,000). Using fitted demand curves, the study estimated the associated consumer surplus for these purchases with dramatic results. Consumer surplus averaged about 70 percent of the purchase price of each rare title. In total, the ability to find a wide variety of rare books was worth about $1 billion in 2000. By comparison, Amazon's low prices saved consumers about $100 million. Item variety proved to be worth 10 times more than price reductions.

Third, in many important instances, a firm's use of the Internet lowers costs: from finding and serving customers to ordering and procuring inputs, to lowering inventories. Selling online also may reduce the need for "bricks-and-mortar" investments, and online promotion and marketing may take the place of a direct sales force. Specific examples of cost savings abound: The cost of selling an airline ticket online is $20 cheaper than the cost of selling through a travel agent. Online automobile sales reduce the need for dealerships and vehicle inventories. Online stock trades are much less costly than brokered trades. Just as important, the Internet lowers the internal costs of the firm—by serving as a platform for sharing and disseminating information throughout the firm and for better managing all aspects of the supply chain. Of course, each firm is constantly in pursuit of lower costs—via online initiatives or in any other areas—as a way to gain a competitive advantage over its rivals. However, if all (or most) firms in a given market successfully exploit e-business methods to lower unit costs, the upshot is that the entire industry supply curve shifts downward. In a perfectly competitive market, these cost reductions are passed on, dollar for dollar, in lower prices to consumers. In the long run, only the most efficient firms will serve the market, and economic profits again converge to zero.

Fourth, by lowering barriers to entry, online commerce moves markets closer to the perfectly competitive ideal. The e-business environment frequently means a reduced need for capital expenditures on plant, equipment, and inventories as well as for spending on highly trained direct sales forces. Elimination or reduction of these fixed costs makes it easier for numerous (perhaps small) firms to enter the market and compete evenhandedly with current competitors.

What aspects of the online business environment are at odds with perfect competition? First, numerous e-business goods and services are highly differentiated. (They do not fit the standardized designation of perfect competition.) Differentiation allows the firm to raise price without immediately losing all sales. (Its demand curve is downward sloping, not horizontal.) For example, the firm can potentially command higher prices for ease of use, better customer service and support, faster shipping, and customized offers and services. Even in cyberspace, a firm's ability to earn positive economic profits depends on how well it differentiates its product and how effectively it establishes a strong brand name. Thus, a loyal customer of Amazon.com will continue to shop there for the ease, convenience, and product selection, even if prices are somewhat higher than at other sites. (Moreover, information goods usually exhibit high switching costs: Consumers are reluctant to learn to use a new software system or to navigate through an unfamiliar Web site.) Second, network externalities and economies of scale confer market power. The firm with the largest user network (e.g., Google in search, Microsoft in PC operating systems, eBay in online auctions, America Online in instant messaging, and Oracle in database software) will claim increasing market share and be able to command premium prices. In addition, the presence of economies of scale (due to high fixed costs and low marginal costs) means that market leaders (such as Google and Apple's iTunes) will command a significant average-cost advantage relative to smaller rivals. All of these factors create barriers to entry, preventing new rivals from penetrating the market. Thus, shielded from price competition, the market leaders are able to earn positive economic profits.

Although e-business offers obvious avenues for increased competition, it does not eliminate the potential for claiming and exploiting market power in a number of traditional ways. As management expert Michael Porter puts it, "Because the Internet tends to weaken industry profitability, it is more important than ever for companies to distinguish themselves through strategy."

INTERNATIONAL TRADE

As noted in Chapter 6, international trade is based on mutually beneficial specialization among countries, that is, on comparative advantage. The final section of this chapter underscores two additional points. First, when free trade is the norm, patterns of trade follow the rules of worldwide supply and demand. If a country's demand outstrips its available supply, it will make up the difference via imports from the rest of the world. Second, the proposition that competitive markets are efficient applies not only to individual markets within a nation but also to all global markets. Free trade is the basis for worldwide efficient production. When nations erect trade barriers, economic welfare is diminished.

To see why perfectly competitive global markets are efficient, we use exactly the same arguments as before. Under free trade, firms from all over the world compete for sales to consumers of different nations. Free competition means that the good in question will sell at a single world price (net of transport costs). Only the most efficient lowest-cost firms will supply the good. Only consumers willing and able to pay the world price will purchase the good. Finally, exactly the right amount of the good will be supplied and consumed worldwide. In competitive equilibrium, global output occurs at a quantity such that P = MB = MC. The quantity of output is efficient. In a nutshell, this is the efficiency argument for free trade.

Tariffs and Quotas

In reality, worldwide trade is far from free. Traditionally, nations have erected trade barriers to limit the quantities of imports from other countries. Most commonly, these import restrictions have taken the form of tariffs, that is, taxes on foreign goods, or direct quotas. The usual rationale for this is to protect particular industries and their workers from foreign competition. Since World War II, the industrialized nations of the world have pushed for reductions in all kinds of trade barriers. Under the General Agreement on Tariffs and Trade (GATT), member nations meet periodically to negotiate reciprocal cuts in tariffs. In the last decade, there has been a rise in protectionist sentiment in the United States, aimed in part at insulating domestic industries from competition and, in part, as retaliation against alleged protectionist policies by Japan and Europe.

Although there are a number of strategic reasons why a country might hope to profit from trade barriers, the larger problem is the efficiency harm imposed by these restrictions. To illustrate this point, we return to the digital watch example introduced in Chapter 6.

RESTRICTED TRADE IN WATCHES   Figure 7.8a depicts hypothetical U.S. demand and supply curves for digital watches. Suppose that the world price is $12.50 per watch (shown in the figure by the horizontal price line at P = $12.50).

FIGURE 7.8

Trade Restrictions

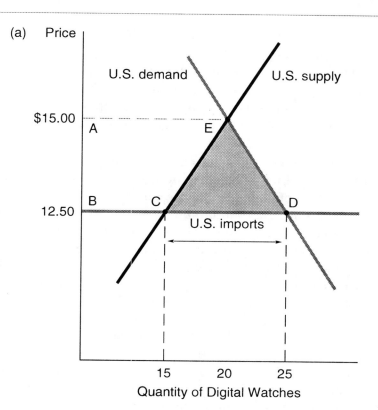

Figure (a) shows a
complete restriction on
trade. Figure (b) shows
a tariff.

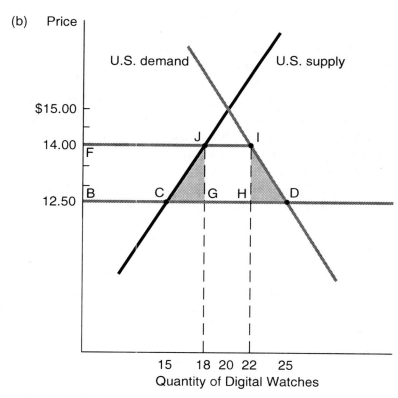

With free trade, the United States can import an unlimited number of watches at this price. At P = $12.50, domestic demand is 25 million watches, which outstrips the domestic supply of 15 million watches. Therefore, the U.S. imports 10 million watches. In Figure 7.8a, the length of the line segment CD measures this volume of imports, the difference between U.S. consumption and U.S. production.

Now suppose the United States enacts trade restrictions prohibiting the import of watches altogether. Then, the no-trade equilibrium price would occur at the intersection of domestic supply and demand. In the figure, this price is $15, and total output is 20 million watches.

What is the net effect of prohibiting watch imports? Domestic watch producers benefit, while domestic consumers are harmed. We now show that the cost to consumers exceeds the benefit to producers, thus causing a net loss in the aggregate. To see this, note that the extra profits earned by domestic producers due to the price increase (from $12.50 to $15) are given by the area of trapezoid ABCE. (The extra profit lies between the old and new price lines and above the industry supply curve.) However, the increase in price has sliced into the total surplus of consumers. The reduction in consumer surplus is measured by trapezoid ABDE. (This is simply the area between the two price lines and under the demand curve.) When we compare trapezoids ABDE and ABCE, we see that consumer losses exceed producer gains by the shaded triangle ECD. This triangle measures the harm done to society, or the so-called deadweight loss attributable to the trade prohibition.[15]

Figure 7.8b depicts the effect of a less dramatic trade restriction. In this instance, U.S. trade authorities have imposed a 12 percent tariff on Japanese imports, raising the price of watches to (1.12)($12.50) = $14. As shown in the figure, the tariff reduces total U.S. consumption to 22 million watches, while increasing domestic production to 18 million watches. Thus, U.S. imports are $22 - 18 = 4$ million watches. Although less extreme, the impact of the tariff is qualitatively similar to that of a complete trade prohibition. Compared to free trade, consumer surplus is reduced by trapezoid FBDI (the area between the two price lines). Producer profits are increased by trapezoid FBCJ. The trade authority also collects tariff revenue, given by rectangle JGHI, on the 4 million watches imported. Comparing the loss in consumer surplus to these twin gains, we see that the nation as a whole suffers a net loss measured by the areas of the two shaded deadweight loss triangles.

We make two final observations. First, a tariff is superior to the alternative of a quota that achieves an equivalent reduction in imports. A quota of 4 million units would have exactly the same result as the 12 percent tariff, except that it would raise no revenue. After eliminating the revenue rectangle JGHI, we find the total dead-weight loss of the quota to be trapezoid CDIJ. Second, moves to higher and higher tariffs steadily diminish imports, increase deadweight

---

[15]For more on deadweight loss, see the discussion of market failure in Chapter 11.

losses, and ultimately raise little revenue. In the present example, as the tariff is raised toward 20 percent, the price of watches approaches $15, and imports fall closer and closer to zero. Obviously, tariff rates that eliminate nearly all imports generate very little revenue.

Betting the Planet
Revisited

Simon's bet rested on the simple economics of supply and demand. If ecologists were correct in their assertion that the world was running out of essential resources, then the prices of these scarce resources should rise. Basing his opinion on his own research, Simon was confident that the ecologists were wrong and that resources would be more abundant tomorrow than today so that their prices would fall.

Who was right? When the bet was settled in 1991, the prices of all five metals had declined over the decade. The same quantities of the metals that were worth $1,000 in 1981 had a total market value of only $618 in 1991. The explanations? Increases in supply kept up with increases in demand; mining companies found new deposits and used more efficient methods to recover and refine ores; the metals often were replaced by cheaper substitutes; and the tin cartel collapsed and tin prices collapsed with it. Ehrlich wrote Simon a check for the difference between the prices then and now—$382 plus accumulated interest over the decade. Using price as the market test, the "boomster" had won his bet with the "doomster."

Of course, the result of such a bet hardly settles the larger debate about the depletion of resources.[16] Although supplies of many resources are more abundant now than in the past, this does not mean that resource supplies will outstrip demand indefinitely. Indeed, dramatic economic growth in the developing world has greatly raised demand for essential resources. The emergence of high-consuming middle classes in China and India means exponential increases in food consumption, automobile purchases, and energy use *per capita*. Higher living standards per capita constitute a greater demand on resources than population growth per se.

Are we entering an era of markedly higher resource prices and greater scarcity? The last few years have seen significant price increases for oil, food, and many commodities. In the longer term, much will depend on (1) technological innovations that enable the extraction of greater output from limited resources, (2) success in finding substitutes for today's most important scarce resources, and (3) better management and conservation. No doubt some combination of alternative fuels, wind, solar, and nuclear power will take the place of oil and coal in global energy supplies. A greater concern is the increasing scarcity of water (often wasted because it is priced much too low) and arable land and the long-term risks posed by global warming. Thus, the resource debate continues.

[16]For discussions of the resource debate, see J. Lahart, P. Barta, and A. Batson, "New Limits to Growth Revive Malthusian Fears," *Wall Street Journal*, March 24, 2008, A1; J. Diamond, "What's Your Consumption Factor?" *Wall Street Journal*, March 24, 2008, A19; and K. Arrow, et al., "Are We Consuming too Much?" *Journal of Economic Perspectives* (Summer 2004): 147–172.

SUMMARY

Decision-Making Principles

1. Whatever the market environment, the firm maximizes profit by establishing a level of output such that marginal revenue equals marginal cost.

2. In perfect competition, the firm faces infinitely elastic demand: Marginal revenue equals the market price. Thus, the firm follows the optimal output rule $P = MC$. In long-run equilibrium, the firm's output is marked by the equalities $P = MR = MC = AC_{min}$, and the firm earns zero profit.

3. Economic transactions are voluntary. Buyers and sellers participate in them if and only if the transactions are mutually beneficial.

4. Competitive markets provide the efficient amounts of goods and services at minimum cost to the consumers who are most willing (and able) to pay for them. Worldwide competition and free trade promote global efficiency.

Nuts and Bolts

1. In a perfectly competitive market, a large number of firms sell identical products, and there are no barriers to entry by new suppliers. Price tends toward a level where the market demand curve intersects the market supply curve. In the long run, price coincides with minimum average cost, and all firms earn zero economic profits.

2. The total value associated with an economic transaction is the sum of consumer and producer surplus. Consumer surplus is the difference between what the individual is willing to pay and what she or he actually pays.

3. For any market, the height of the demand curve shows the monetary value that consumers are willing to pay for each unit. Consumer surplus in the market is given by the area under the demand curve and above the market price line.

4. In equilibrium, a competitive market generates maximum net benefits. The optimal level of output is determined by the intersection of demand and supply, that is, where marginal benefit exactly equals marginal cost.

Questions and Problems

1. The renowned Spaniard, Pablo Picasso, was a prolific artist. He created hundreds of paintings and sculptures as well as drawings and sketches

numbering in the thousands. (He is said to have settled restaurant bills by producing sketches on the spot.)
   a. What effect does the existence of this large body of work have on the monetary value of individual pieces of his art?
   b. Might his heirs suffer from being bequeathed too many of his works? As the heirs' financial adviser, what strategy would you advise them to pursue in selling pieces of his work?

2. Consider the regional supply curve of farmers who produce a particular crop.
   a. What does the supply curve look like at the time the crop is harvested? (Show a plausible graph.)
   b. Depict the crop's supply curve at the beginning of the growing season (when farmers must decide how many acres to cultivate).
   c. Depict the crop's supply curve in the long run (when farmers can enter or exit the market).

3. Potato farming (like farming of most agricultural products) is highly competitive. Price is determined by demand and supply. Based on Department of Agriculture statistics, U.S. demand for potatoes is estimated to be $Q_D = 184 - 20P$, where P is the farmer's wholesale price (per 100 pounds) and Q_D is consumption of potatoes per capita (in pounds). In turn, industry supply is $Q_S = 124 + 4P$.
   a. Find the competitive market price and output.
   b. Potato farmers in Montana raise about 7 percent of total output. If these farmers enjoy bumper crops (10 percent greater harvests than normal), is this likely to have much effect on price? On Montana farmers' incomes?
   c. Suppose that, due to favorable weather conditions, U.S. potato farmers as a whole have bumper crops. The total amount delivered to market is 10 percent higher than that calculated in part (a). Find the new market price. What has happened to total farm revenue? Is industry demand elastic or inelastic? In what sense do natural year-to-year changes in growing conditions make farming a boom-or-bust industry?

4. In a competitive market, the industry demand and supply curves are $P = 200 - .2Q_d$ and $P = 100 + .3Q_s$, respectively.
   a. Find the market's equilibrium price and output.
   b. Suppose the government imposes a tax of $20 per unit of output on all firms in the industry. What effect does this have on the industry supply curve? Find the new competitive price and output. What portion of the tax has been passed on to consumers via a higher price?
   c. Suppose a $20-per-unit sales tax is imposed on consumers. What effect does this have on the industry demand curve? Find the new competitive price and output. Compare this answer to your findings in part (b).

5. The Green Company produces chemicals in a perfectly competitive market. The current market price is $40; the firm's total cost is $C = 100 + 4Q + Q^2$.
   a. Determine the firm's profit-maximizing output. More generally, write down the equation for the firm's supply curve in terms of price P.
   b. Complying with more stringent environmental regulations increases the firm's fixed cost from 100 to 144. Would this affect the firm's output? Its supply curve?
   c. How would the increase in fixed costs affect the market's long-run equilibrium price? The number of firms? (Assume that Green's costs are typical in the market.)

6. Firm Z, operating in a perfectly competitive market, can sell as much or as little as it wants of a good at a price of $16 per unit. Its cost function is $C = 50 + 4Q + 2Q^2$. The associated marginal cost is $MC = 4 + 4Q$, and the point of minimum average cost is $Q_{min} = 5$.
   a. Determine the firm's profit-maximizing level of output. Compute its profit.
   b. The industry demand curve is $Q = 200 - 5P$. What is the total market demand at the current $16 price? If all firms in the industry have cost structures identical to that of firm Z, how many firms will supply the market?
   c. The outcomes in parts (a) and (b) cannot persist in the long run. Explain why. Find the market's price, total output, number of firms, and output per firm in the long run.
   d. Comparing the short-run and long-run results, explain the changes in the price and in the number of firms.

7. In a perfectly competitive market, industry demand is given by $Q = 1,000 - 20P$. The typical firm's average cost is $AC = 300/Q + Q/3$.
   a. Confirm that $Q_{min} = 30$. (*Hint:* Set AC equal to MC.) What is AC_{min}?
   b. Suppose 10 firms serve the market. Find the individual firm's supply curve. Find the market supply curve. Set market supply equal to market demand to determine the competitive price and output. What is the typical firm's profit?
   c. Determine the long-run, zero-profit equilibrium. How many firms will serve the market?

8. In a competitive market, the industry demand and supply curves are $P = 70 - Q_D$ and $P = 40 + 2Q_S$, respectively.
   a. Find the market's equilibrium price and output.
   b. Suppose that the government provides a subsidy to producers of $15 per unit of the good. Since the subsidy reduces each supplier's marginal cost by 15, the new supply curve is $P = 25 + 2Q_S$. Find the

market's new equilibrium price and output. Provide an explanation for the change in price and quantity.

   c. A public-interest group supports the subsidy, arguing that it helps consumers and producers alike. Economists oppose the subsidy, declaring that it leads to an inefficient level of output. In your opinion, which side is correct? Explain carefully.

9. Demand for microprocessors is given by $P = 35 - 5Q$, where Q is the quantity of microchips (in millions). The typical firm's total cost of producing a chip is $C_i = 5q_i$, where q_i is the output of firm i.

   a. Under perfect competition, what are the equilibrium price and quantity?

   b. Does the typical microchip firm display increasing, constant, or decreasing returns to scale? What would you expect about the real microchip industry? In general, what must be true about the underlying technology of production for competition to be viable?

   c. Under perfect competition, find total industry profit and consumer surplus.

10. a. When a best-selling book was first released in paperback, the Hercules Bookstore chain seized a profit opportunity by setting a selling price of \$9 per book (well above Hercules' \$5 average cost per book). With paperback demand given by $P = 15 - .5Q$, the chain enjoyed sales of $Q = 12$ thousand books per week. (Note Q is measured in thousands of books.) Draw the demand curve and compute the bookstore's profit and the total consumer surplus.

   b. For the first time, Hercules has begun selling books online—in response to competition from other online sellers and in the quest for new profits. The average cost per book sold online is only \$4. As part of its online selling strategy, it sends weekly emails to preferred customers announcing which books are new in paperback. For this segment, it sets an average price (including shipping) of \$12. According to the demand curve in part (a), only the highest-value consumers (whose willingness to pay is \$12 or more) purchase at this price. Check that these are the first 6 thousand book buyers on the demand curve. In turn, because of increased competition, Hercules reduced its store price to \$7 per book.

     At P = \$7, how many book are bought in Hercules' stores? (Make sure to exclude online buyers from your demand curve calculation.) Compute Hercules' total profit, then compute the sum of consumer surplus from online and in-store sales. Relative to part (a), has the emergence of online commerce improved the welfare of book buyers as a whole? Explain.

11. The market for rice in an East Asian country has demand and supply given by $Q_D = 28 - 4P$ and $Q_S = -12 + 6P$, where quantities denote millions of bushels per day.

a. If the domestic market is perfectly competitive, find the equilibrium price and quantity of rice. Compute the triangular areas of consumer surplus and producer surplus.

b. Now suppose that there are no trade barriers, and the world price of rice is \$3. Confirm that the country will import rice. Find Q_D, Q_S, and the level of imports, $Q_D - Q_S$. Show that the country is better off than in part (a) (by again computing consumer surplus and producer surplus).

c. The government authority believes strongly in free trade but feels political pressure to help domestic rice growers. Accordingly, it decides to provide a \$1 per bushel subsidy to domestic growers. Show that this subsidy induces the same domestic output as in part (a). Including the cost of the subsidy, is the country better off now than in part (b)? Explain.

Discussion Question   Over the last 30 years in the United States, the *real* price of a college education (i.e., after adjusting for inflation) has increased by almost 70 percent. Over the same period, an increasing number of high school graduates have sought a college education. (Nationwide college enrollments almost doubled over this period.) While faculty salaries have barely kept pace with inflation, administrative staffing (and expenditures) and capital costs have increased significantly. In addition, government support to universities (particularly research funding) has been cut.

a. College enrollments increased at the same time that average tuition rose dramatically. Does this contradict the law of downward-sloping demand? Explain briefly.

b. Use supply and demand curves (or shifts therein) to explain the dramatic rise in the price of a college education.

Spreadsheet Problems

S1. In a perfectly competitive market, the cost structure of the typical firm is given by $C = 25 + Q^2 - 4Q$, and industry demand is given by $Q = 400 - 20P$. Currently, 24 firms serve the market.

a. Create a spreadsheet (similar to the given example) to model the short-run and long-run dynamics of this market. (*Hint*: Enter numerical values for the Price, # Firms, and QF cells; all other cells should be linked by formulas to these three cells.)

b. What equilibrium price will prevail in the short run? (*Hint*: Use the spreadsheet's optimizer and specify cell F8, the difference between demand and supply, as the target cell. However, instead of maximizing this cell, instruct the optimizer to set it equal to zero. In addition, include the constraint that $P - MC$ in cell F14 must equal zero.)

	A	B	C	D	E	F	G	H
1								
2				EQUILIBRIUM IN A PERFECTLY				
3				COMPETITIVE MARKET				
4								
5				The Industry				
6		Price	# Firms	Supply	Demand	D − S	Tot. Profit	
7								
8		10	24	192	200	8	552	
9								
10								
11				The Typical Firm				
12		Q_F	MC	Cost	AC	P − MC	Firm Profit	
13								
14		8	12	57	7.13	−2	23	
15								
16								
17		SR: (1) D − S = 0 and (2) P = MC; Adjust: P & Q_F						
18		LR: (1) and (2) and (3) P = AC; Adjust: P & Q_F & # Firms						
19								

    c. What equilibrium price will prevail in the long run? (*Hint*: Include cell C8, the number of firms, as an adjustable cell, in addition to cells B8 and B14, and add the constraint that total profit in cell G8 must equal zero.)

S2. The industry demand curve in a perfectly competitive market is given by the equation P = 160 − 2Q, and the supply curve is given by the equation P = 40 + Q. The upward-sloping supply curve represents the increasing marginal cost of expanding *industry* output. The total *industry* cost of producing Q units of output is C = 800 + 40Q + .5Q². (Note that taking the derivative of this equation produces the preceding industry MC equation.) In turn, the total benefit associated with consuming Q units of output is given by the equation B = 160Q − Q². (Total benefit represents the trapezoidal area under the demand curve. It is also the sum of consumer surplus and revenue. Note that taking the derivative of the benefit equation produces the original industry demand curve MB = 160 − 2Q.)

    a. Create a spreadsheet similar to the given example. Only the quantity cell (C5) contains a numerical value. All other cells are linked by formulas to the quantity cell.

b. Find the intersection of competitive supply and demand by equating the demand and supply equations or by varying quantity in the spreadsheet until MB equals MC.

c. Alternatively, find the optimal level of industry output by maximizing net benefits (cell F9) or, equivalently, the sum of consumer and producer gains (cell F10). Confirm that the perfectly competitive equilibrium of part (b) is efficient.

	A	B	C	D	E	F	G
1							
2			EFFICIENCY OF				
3			PERFECT COMPETITION				
4							
5		Quantity	32		Price	96	
6							
7		Benefit	4,096		Con Surplus	1,024	
8		P = MB	96				
9					B − C	1,504	
10		Revenue	3,072		CS + Profit	1,504	
11		MR	32				
12					Profit	480	
13		Cost	2,592				
14		MC	72				
15							

Suggested References

Adams, W., and J. R. Brock (Eds.). *The Structure of American Industry.* New York: Prentice-Hall, 2000, especially Chapter 1.

This volume devotes separate chapters to describing the market structures of the major sectors in the American economy—from agriculture to banking, from cigarettes to beer, from automobiles to computers.

The following readings discuss Internet and e-commerce competition:

Borenstein, S., and G. Saloner. "Economics and Electronic Commerce." *Journal of Economic Perspectives* (Winter 2001): 3−12.

Brynjolfsson, E., Y. Hu, and M. D. Smith. "Consumer Surplus in the Digital Economy: Estimating the Value of Increased Product Variety at Online Booksellers." *Management Science* (November 2003): 1580−1596.

The following volume assesses the effects of airline deregulation in promoting competition and lowering prices. It also estimates the increase in consumer surplus resulting from airline deregulation.

Morrison, S. A., and C. Winston. *The Evolution of the Airline Industry.* Washington, DC: Brookings Press, 1995.

The following book and articles provide readable treatments of competitiveness, free trade, and protectionism.

Bagwhati, J. *In Defense of Globalization.* Oxford, UK: Oxford University Press, 2004.

Baldwin, R. E. "Are Economists' Traditional Trade Policy Views Still Valid?" *Journal of Economic Literature* (June 1992): 804−829.

Bhagwati, J. "Free Trade: Old and New Challenges." *Economic Journal* 104 (March 1994): 231−246.

"Research on Free Trade." *American Economic Review* 83, Papers and Proceedings (May 1993): 362−376.

Samuelson, P. A. "Where Ricardo and Mill Rebut and Confirm Arguments of Mainstream Economists Supporting Globalization." *Journal of Economic Perspectives* 18 (Summer 2004): 135−146.

"A Survey of Globalization." *The Economist* (September 29, 2001).

The best Internet sources for analyzing free trade are the writings of Professor Jagdish Bhagwati of Columbia University: http://www.columbia.edu/~jb38/.

CHECK STATION ANSWERS

1. Equating $Q_D = 15 - 10P$ and $Q_S = -3 + 14P$ implies $18 = 24P$, or $P = 18/24 = \$.75$ per pound. Given the drop in demand, we equate $12 - 8P = -3 + 14P$, implying the new price $P = \$.68$. Although demand has fallen 20 percent, price has declined by just some 10 percent.

2. Setting $P = MC$ implies $P = 2Q_F - 4$, or $Q_F = (P + 4)/2$. With 40 firms, the supply curve is $Q_S = 40(P + 4)/2 = 20P + 80$.

3. To find the point of minimum average cost, we set $AC = MC$. This implies $25/Q + Q - 4 = 2Q - 4$, or $25/Q = Q$. After multiplying both sides by Q, we have $Q^2 = 25$ or $Q_{min} = 5$. Thus, each firm will produce 5 thousand units. In turn, $AC_{min} = 6$. Thus, the long-run price is also $P = \$6$. At this price, $Q_D = 320 - (20)(6) = 200$ thousand units. The requisite number of firms to supply this demand is $200/5 = 40$. (This exactly matches the number of current firms.)

4. From Check Station 2, the short-run supply curve is $Q_S = 20P + 80$. Setting Q_D equal to Q_S implies $400 - 20P = 20P + 80$. Therefore, we have $P = \$8$. In turn, $Q_F = (8 + 4)/2 = 6$ thousand units and $Q_S = (40)(6) = 240$ thousand units. With price greater than average cost, each firm is making a positive economic profit. In the long run, $P = AC_{min} = \$6$, implying $Q_D = 400 - (20)(6) = 280$ thousand units, supplied by $280/5 = 56$ firms.

5. If day care is free ($P = \$0$), the outcome will be inefficient: Too much day care will be demanded and consumed. The marginal benefit of the last hours consumed will be nearly zero, that is, much less than the hours' marginal cost, $MB < MC$. (However, there may be beneficial distributional consequences.)

CHAPTER **17**

Linear Programming

Management is the art of doing the best one can within constraints and occasionally getting around them.

ANONYMOUS

An Investment Problem

A portfolio manager has $20 million to invest in a fund consisting of the following bonds:

Bond Category	Quality Rating	Maturity (Years)	Yield (Percent)
Treasury bills	5	.4	4.0
Treasury bonds	5	4.0	6.0
Corporate bonds	3.5	3.2	4.4
Municipal bonds	3	2.0	5.6
Junk bonds	1	2.5	8.0

He has listed the bonds in descending order of quality rating (Treasury securities carry the lowest risk, junk bonds are most risky). The second column lists average maturity (in years) for each category. The final column shows the expected return or yield (in percent per year, after tax) for each bond. Junk bonds have the greatest expected return, followed by treasury bonds.

660

The manager intends to create a bond fund by investing proportions of the $20 million in the different securities and has announced an investment goal of a high-quality, medium-maturity portfolio. In particular, the fund's average quality rating should be at least 3.5, and its average maturity should be no shorter than 1.5 years and no longer than 2.5 years.

The portfolio manager seeks to create a bond fund that offers the highest expected return subject to the quality and maturity requirements given. To accomplish this goal, what proportion of the $20 million should she invest in each bond?

In the investment problem, the analyst seeks to maximize the portfolio return subject to various constraints. Constrained optimization problems of this sort form the core of a distinct managerial field known as *operations research* (O.R.). Indeed, we all enjoy the benefits of operations research applications in our everyday lives although we may not know it. Suppose you decide to take your family to Disney World[1]:

Operations research will be your invisible companion, scheduling the crews and aircraft, pricing the plane tickets and hotel rooms, even helping to design capacities on the theme park rides. If you use Orbitz to book your flights, an O.R. engine sifts among millions of options to find the cheapest fares. If you get directions from MapQuest, another O.R. engine spits out the most direct route. If you ship souvenirs home, O.R. tells UPS which truck to put the packages on, exactly where on the truck the packages should go to make them fastest to load and unload, and what route the driver should follow to make his deliveries efficiently.

All of these operations involve maximizing or minimizing subject to constraints. The most basic and important tool of operations research is linear programming.

Linear programming (LP) is a method of formulating and solving decision problems that involve explicit resource constraints. Analysts use the LP method to solve problems such as the investment problem and a host of other decision questions: How should a firm allocate its advertising expenditure among various media? What quantities of two jointly manufactured goods should a firm produce with a fixed amount of labor and inputs? How should a federal agency allocate its limited budget between two competing safety programs? What quantities of output should a consumer-products firm transport from each of its factories to each of its retail outlets to minimize transportation cost?

What do these problems have in common? First, all seek to find the best values of certain variables: the right advertising mix, the most profitable product quantities, the appropriate budget allocation. These values, which the decision

---

[1]This account comes from V. Postrel, "Operation Everything," *Boston Globe*, June 27, 2004, D1.

maker controls, are **decision variables**. Second, each decision has an explicit objective, be it maximum profit, minimum cost, or maximum number of lives saved. Third, constraints limit the possible values of the decision variables. For example, limited labor supply may constrain the quantity of output. Similarly, the federal agency cannot spend more than its available budget, and the consumer-products firm must supply the quantities to its retail outlets subject to its factories' production capacities. Thus, in each case, the heart of the problem is finding (calculating) values for the decision variables that best meet the given objective while satisfying various constraints.

With respect to the first two features, decision variables and objectives, the LP method resembles the optimization methods we have encountered already. Like the pricing and output decisions of Chapters 2 and 3, LP decisions rely on marginal analysis (of a special kind) for their solution. Unlike those decisions, however, LP problems incorporate explicit resource constraints. The interplay of these constraints creates new and interesting economic trade-offs.

In this chapter, we take a systematic approach to managerial decisions involving economic constraints. First, we describe a number of constrained decision problems and show how they can be formulated and solved mathematically as linear programs. Next, we examine the important concept of shadow prices for resources. Then we introduce more complex linear programming decisions and illustrate the kinds of solutions furnished by computer programs.

LINEAR PROGRAMS

We can analyze a host of managerial decisions using linear programming. Here is a representative example.

FINDING AN OPTIMAL COMPUTER MIX   Consider a personal computer (PC) manufacturer that produces two versions of its popular desktop computer. The standard version has a high-capacity (80-gigabyte) hard disk, a conventional disk drive, and a rewritable DVD drive. The economy version, which sells at a lower price, has a 40-gigabyte hard drive and a conventional rewritable CD drive. The prices, variable costs, and contributions of the models are shown in the table.

	Standard PC	Economy PC
Price	$1,600	$1,000
Variable cost	1,100	700
Contribution	500	300

The firm has ample components (such as monitors and keyboards) from which to assemble PCs, but a limited capacity (given available factory space and necessary equipment) for producing DVD drives and hard-disk drives. The firm's maximum weekly outputs are 200 DVD drives and 20,000 gigabytes of hard-drive capacity. The firm can split its hard-drive capacity in any way between the two models. For instance, it could devote all of its hard-drive capacity to 250 standard models or, alternatively, to 500 economy models. Or it could produce other combinations—for instance, 200 standard models and 100 economy models.

In addition, the firm assembles computers using a 50-person labor force that supplies 2,000 hours of labor per week. The two models require roughly equal assembly time—an average of five labor-hours each. How many computers of each type should the firm produce to maximize its profit? Answering this question requires two steps: (1) formulating the firm's decision as a linear program, that is, a set of mathematical equations that precisely describe the firm's available options; and (2) solving these mathematical equations.

The formulation stage begins with the identification of the relevant decision variables. The firm must determine two key quantities: the number of standard models (S) and the number of economy models (E). The firm seeks to maximize the total contribution (π) it obtains from these products. We can express this contribution algebraically as

$$\pi = 500S + 300E. \qquad \text{[OF]}$$

The goal to be maximized—in this instance, total contribution—is the **objective function (OF)**.

Next we identify the production constraints. The company cannot produce an unlimited number of computers. It faces three principal constraints. First, the firm can produce only 200 DVD drives a week. This means that, at most, it can produce 200 standard models. Also, it can produce a maximum of 20,000 gigabytes of hard drives. Finally, the firm has only 2,000 hours of labor to devote to production of PCs. The algebraic representations of these constraints are

$$S \leq 200 \qquad \text{[D]}$$
$$80S + 40E \leq 20,000 \qquad \text{[H]}$$
$$5S + 5E \leq 2,000. \qquad \text{[L]}$$

As the labels in brackets indicate, the inequalities correspond to the DVD drive, hard-disk drive, and labor constraints, respectively. The right-hand side of each inequality lists the total capacity (or supply) of the particular input. The left-hand side shows the total amount used of each resource if the firm produces quantities S and E of the models. For instance, producing S standard models requires S number of DVD drives—one drive per machine. Thus, according to the first constraint, DVD capacity limits the weekly output of standard models to 200.

Next consider the hard-disk constraint. Production of the models in the quantities S and E together requires 80S + 40E gigabytes of hard-disk capacity. For instance, producing 100 of each model per week would require a total of (80)(100) + (40)(100) = 12,000 gigabytes of capacity, which is safely within the 20,000 gigabytes available. Finally, consider the labor constraint. Here, the firm uses a total of 5S + 5E hours of labor. The total amount of labor cannot exceed 2,000.

The complete mathematical description of the problem consists of the objective function (to be maximized), the three resource constraints, and two nonnegativity constraints, S ≥ 0 and E ≥ 0. These last two constraints simply reflect the impossibility of producing negative quantities. Although obvious (even trivial) to the decision maker, we must include them to get the right answer. (Computer programs don't have the same intuition as managers.)

We now have a fully formed linear program. What makes it linear? All of the expressions, for both the objective function and the constraints, are linear. In a linear expression, we can multiply the variable by a constant, we can add or subtract these multiplied variables, and we can add a constant to the expression. But this is all; we cannot multiply two variables together, we cannot raise variables to powers, we cannot take square roots of variables, or anything else. Roughly speaking, the linearity assumption requires that the key quantities in the actual managerial problem—revenues, costs, and profits—vary proportionally with changes in the firm's decision variables. For instance, if the firm can sell its product at fixed prices, its revenue is proportional to output, thus satisfying linearity. However, if the firm faces a downward-sloping demand curve (the usual circumstance in Chapters 2 and 3), revenue is a nonlinear function of output; that is, the revenue graph is curved. The linear programming method cannot handle this case. (Instead, we can use a related method, nonlinear programming.)

Graphing the LP Problem

We can solve small-scale linear programs, like the PC example, using graphical methods. This approach provides the numerical solution and offers insight as to the factors that determine the optimal decision. The method consists of the following steps:

1. Construct a graph, placing a decision variable on each axis.
2. Graph each constraint as though it were binding, that is, as if it held with strict equality.
3. Find the feasible region, the area of the graph that simultaneously satisfies all constraints.
4. Superimpose contours of the objective function on the feasible region to determine the optimal corner of the region.

5. Solve the appropriate equations of the LP problem to determine the optimal values of the decision variables at the corner solution.

Let's apply this procedure to solve the computer company's production problem. Figure 17.1 plots the firm's decision variables, S and E, on the horizontal and vertical axes, respectively, and plots the three resource constraints as straight lines. The area OABCD represents the "feasible region" of all *possible* combinations of the two computer models. For each resource, the constraint line in the graph depicts model combinations that use up exactly the available resource. Any point lying to the right of any of the resource constraint lines represents quantities that the firm cannot produce. For example, if the point lies to the right of the DVD constraint, it represents an output combination that requires more than 200 DVD drives. Any point to the left of this line requires fewer than 200 drives. In turn, the equation $80S + 40E = 20,000$

FIGURE 17.1

Production Constraints for a PC Manufacturer

The feasible combinations of standard and economy model PCs lie within the region OABCD.

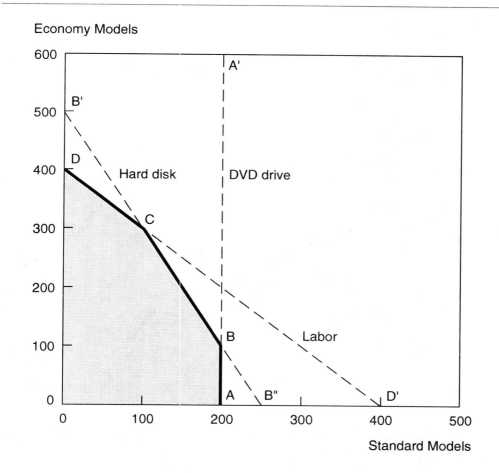

describes the binding hard-disk constraint and appears on the graph as the line B′B″.[2] Finally, the binding labor constraint is given by the equation 5S + 5E = 2,000 and is graphed as DD′. The firm's feasible region of production consists of S and E combinations that simultaneously satisfy all three constraints: the shaded area bounded by OABCD.

The company still has to determine the output combination (the point in the feasible region) that maximizes total contribution. To find this point, we draw in contribution contours—lines indicating combinations of S and E that yield a fixed value of contribution. For instance, we can graph the contour corresponding to a contribution of $75,000 by using the equation 500S + 300E = 75,000. This contour is shown in Figure 17.2. (Check this by noting that the

FIGURE 17.2

Production Constraints with Contribution Contours

The firm's profit-maximizing combination of computers occurs at point C, where the highest contribution contour touches the feasible region.

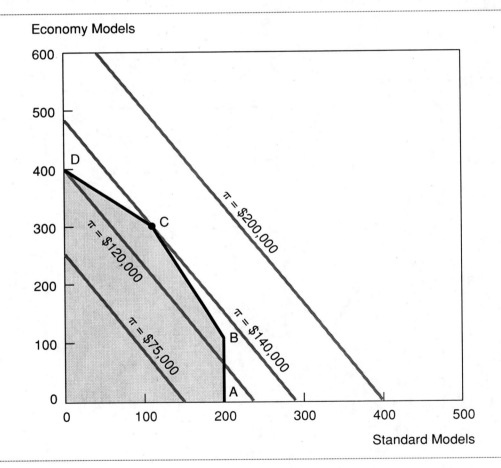

[2]The easiest way to graph any constraint line is to pinpoint its two intercepts, that is, set one of the decision variables equal to zero and solve for the other. Doing this for the hard-disk equation, we find E = 0 with S = 250 and, in turn, S = 0 with E = 500. Thus, the horizontal intercept is 250 (at B″) and the vertical intercept is 500 (at B′).

horizontal intercept is S = 150, since the firm can earn $75,000 by producing only standard models. In turn, the vertical intercept is E = 250.) Figure 17.2 also depicts contours corresponding to contributions of $120,000, $140,000, and $200,000. Note that increasing the contribution causes a parallel (northeast) shift in the contour. Obviously, larger production quantities are necessary to generate the greater contribution. Note, however, that the contour slopes do not change because the ratio of contributions is always $500 to $300.

The optimal solution is found at the corner of the feasible region that touches the highest contribution contour. In Figure 17.2, this occurs at point C. Here, the contour corresponding to $140,000 contribution just touches the feasible region. As the figure shows, this is the best the firm can do. The firm can consider other feasible production plans, but any such plan lies on a lower contribution contour. For instance, point B's plan (200 standard models and 100 economy models) produces only $130,000 in contribution (i.e., lies on a lower contour). At point D the firm earns even less. However, "pie in the sky" production plans are irrelevant. The firm cannot attain a higher contribution—say, $200,000—because such a contour lies wholly outside the feasible region.

We can reinforce the visual solution to the LP problem by using marginal analysis. Suppose the firm takes point D as a candidate for its optimal production plan. Using marginal analysis, the firm asks whether it could increase its contribution by moving to some other point on the edge of the feasible region. Suppose it considers moving in the direction of C, producing more standard models and fewer economy models. (Note that segment DC portrays the binding labor constraint.) To produce an extra standard model requires five additional hours of labor; with all labor utilized, this means producing one fewer economy model (which frees up five labor-hours). Would such a move improve the firm's profit? It certainly would! The net increase in contribution is $200. (The gain is $500 in contribution for the extra standard unit minus $300 in lost contribution from the economy unit that is no longer produced.) Thus, the firm should make the one-unit switch. But, having switched one unit, it can increase its profit by switching a second unit (by exactly the same logic). It can continue to increase its profit by moving along segment DC until it attains the production plan corresponding to point C. Here, it can no longer improve its profit because it runs up against the hard-disk capacity constraint. Having exploited all its options for increasing its profit, the firm has arrived at its optimal product mix.[3]

What are the precise model quantities at point C? Since point C lies on the constraint lines corresponding to hard disks and labor, we know that these constraints are binding; that is, the optimal mix uses up all available hard-disk capacity and labor. Thus, S and E satisfy the constraints, $80S + 40E = 20,000$ and $5S + 5E = 2,000$. Solving these two equations in two unknowns, we find

[3]Check for yourself that, starting from point B, the firm also profits by moving toward point C. How much does contribution increase if it produces an extra economy unit?

that S = 100 and E = 300. Total contribution is π = (500)(100) + (300)(300) = \$140,000 after inserting the optimal quantities into the objective function.

　A farmer raises two crops, wheat and barley. Wheat sells at \$1.60 per bushel and barley at \$1.00 per bushel. The production of each crop requires land and labor in differing amounts. Each 1,000 bushels of wheat requires 1 acre of farmland and four labor-hours per week. An equal quantity of barley also requires 1 acre but requires only two hours of labor per week. The farmer has 10 acres of land and an average of 32 hours of labor per week to devote to wheat and barley production. How much of each crop should the farmer produce? In your answer, formulate and graph the appropriate LP problem.

A Minimization Problem

The production problem the PC company faces is typical of a large class of profit-maximization problems. A second important class of decisions involves cost minimization. The next example illustrates the point.

REGULATION AT LEAST COST　An environmental regulatory agency is launching a program to reduce water pollution in one of the region's major rivers. As a first step, it has set standards for two key measures of water quality. It seeks (1) to increase the level of dissolved oxygen (essential to fish and other life in the estuary) by 6 milligrams (mg) per liter and (2) to reduce the concentrations of chlorides by 70 mg per liter. Its aim is to meet both these standards at minimum cost by allocating funds between two programs.

> Program 1: Direct treatment of effluents. Each \$1 million spent in this program will increase dissolved oxygen by 3 mg/liter and reduce chlorides by 10 mg/liter.
>
> Program 2: Flow regulation. Each \$1 million spent in this program will increase dissolved oxygen by 1 mg/liter and reduce chlorides by 20 mg/liter.

How much should the agency spend on one or both programs to meet its goals?

Let's formulate and solve the agency's problem. As always, we begin by identifying the decision variables. Here, the agency must choose how much to spend on direct treatment and how much to spend on flow regulation. We label the spending (in millions of dollars) on the respective programs by D and F. The agency seeks to minimize the total cost (C) of the programs, subject to meeting its goals.

$$\text{Minimize: } C = D + F. \qquad [OF]$$

The goals it must meet can be expressed by the following inequalities.

$$\text{Subject to: } 3D + F \geq 6 \qquad [O]$$

$$10D + 20F \geq 70. \qquad [C]$$

The first inequality reflects the fact that the programs together must increase oxygen by 6 mg/liter. The right-hand side lists this minimum requirement. The left-hand side shows the total amount of oxygen generated by the programs. For instance, spending $2 million on each program ($D = F = 2$) would increase oxygen by $(3)(2) + 2 = 8$ mg/liter, which would more than meet the goal. In turn, the left-hand side of the second constraint shows the reduction in chlorine: 10 mg per million spent on the first program plus 20 mg per million on the second. The nonnegativity constraints, $D \geq 0$ and $F \geq 0$, complete the formulation.

Figure 17.3 shows the graph of the feasible region. The main point to observe is the impact of the "greater than or equal to" constraints. The feasible region lies above the two-sided boundary AZB. (Make sure you understand that the constraint lines are properly graphed. Check the intercepts!) Obviously, large values of F and D (i.e., greater spending on the programs) will make it easier to meet the dual improvement goals, but the point is to do it at *minimum* cost. When it comes to cost contours, the object is to get to the lowest one (i.e., the one farthest to the southwest) while meeting both goals. Figure 17.3 shows the relevant part of the "least-cost" contour. Note that it touches the feasible region at point Z, the corner formed by the binding oxygen and chlorine constraints. The precise amounts to spend on each program are found by solving the equations $3D + F = 6$ and $10D + 20F = 70$. The solution $D = 1$ and $F = 3$ is the result.[4] In short, $1 million and $3 million should be spent on the respective programs. The least-cost total outlay is $4 million.

ALGEBRAIC SOLUTIONS   The mathematics for solving small-scale linear programs involves two main steps: (1) identifying the correct set of simultaneous equations and (2) solving these equations for the optimal values of the decision variables. In the preceding example we used simple graphics to solve the first step. (*Caution:* We cannot simply assume certain constraints will be binding and go ahead and solve them. In the computer example, there are five

---

[4]Recall that there are two equivalent ways to solve simultaneous equations. The first method is by *substitution*. For instance, in the regulator's problem, we transform the equation $3D + F = 6$ to the form $F = 6 - 3D$. Then we insert this expression for F into the second equation, $10D + 20F = 70$. We are left with one equation in one unknown: $10D + 20(6 - 3D) = 70$. The solution is $D = 1$. Putting this value back into the first equation, we find $F = 6 - (3)(1) = 3$. The second method is by *elimination*. It is easiest to eliminate F by multiplying both sides of the first equation by 20 to obtain $60D + 20F = 120$. Then we subtract the second equation from this expression. Note that 20F in each equation cancels out, leaving $60D - 10D = 120 - 70$; this implies $D = 1$ and $F = 3$. Either method works equally well.

FIGURE 17.3

Clean-Water Funding

At point Z, $1 million is spent on program D and $3 million on program F. This plan meets the oxygen and chloride constraints at minimum total cost.

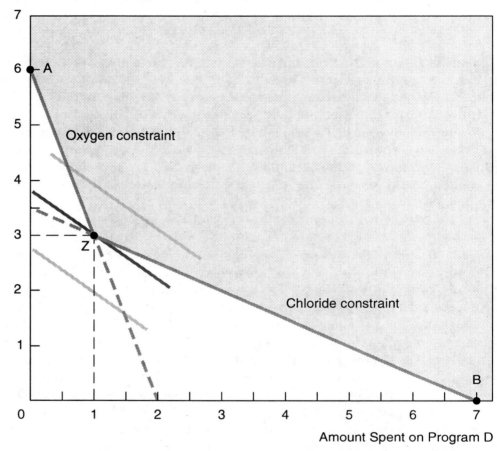

inequalities, including the nonnegativity constraints, only two of which are binding equalities in the optimal solution. Without a graph or other analysis, which two constraints will be binding is a pure guess.)

Once you understand the general points of the graphical method, you may be interested in a quick way of finding the optimal corner. The method relies on a comparison of slopes:

> The optimal corner is formed by the constraints whose slopes most closely bracket the slope of the objective function.

To apply this rule, we simply note the slope of each constraint from the graph. In the computer problem, the slopes of the labor constraint, hard-disk constraint, and DVD constraint are −1, −2, and −∞, respectively. The slope of the contribution contour is $-5/3$, and this falls between the first two slopes. Accordingly, the optimal output in Figure 17.2 occurs at point C, where the labor and hard-disk constraints are binding. Similarly, in the regulator's problem (Figure 17.3), point Z is optimal because the slope of the cost contour (-1) falls between the slope of the oxygen constraint (-3) and the chlorine constraint ($-1/2$).

FORMULATION ISSUES   In some cases, LP problems have no solution or the solution is unbounded. Consider the following formulation:

$$\text{Maximize: } 3x + y$$

$$\text{Subject to: } x + 2y \leq 12$$

$$x + y \geq 15.$$

The difficulty here lies in the constraints. It is impossible to find values of the decision variables that simultaneously satisfy both inequalities. (Graph the constraints to confirm this.) In short, the problem itself is infeasible. It lacks a feasible region and, therefore, has no possibility of an optimal solution.[5]

A different formulation difficulty arises if we make a slight modification in the preceding example. Suppose that the variable y is omitted in the first constraint so that the inequality reads $x \geq 12$. The new problem has a feasible region—in fact, too large a region. The feasible region consists of all points to the left of the vertical line $x = 12$ and above the downward-sloping line $x + y = 15$. Now the feasible region is unbounded; it extends vertically indefinitely. Clearly, we can make the value of the objective function as large as we like by making y as large as possible—all the while keeping x below 12. This linear program has an unbounded solution, which tells us that we have poorly formulated the problem. After all, in the real world, no firm has the opportunity to make an infinite profit. Somehow we have omitted the real constraints that limit the firm's profitability.

SENSITIVITY ANALYSIS AND SHADOW PRICES

The solution of the basic linear program provides management with its optimal decision. The solution is also the starting point for considering a range of related decisions and what-if questions. For instance, managers of the computer firm recognize that changing market prices are a fact of life in the PC

[5]This kind of infeasibility can arise quite naturally. In this problem, for instance, let the decision variables denote the quantity of two products. Total production is limited due to fixed capacity (the first constraint). At the same time, the firm has contracted to deliver a minimum of 15 total units to a buyer (the second constraint). Here, there is no solution, because the firm has contracted to deliver more than it possibly can supply.

industry. How might the firm change its production mix in response to changes in product prices? As a second example, the firm might consider increasing (at a cost) one or more of its production capacities (labor or hard-drive capacity, for instance). How much would such an increase in capacity be worth, and would it be worth the cost?

Sensitivity analysis is important in almost all decision contexts, but especially so in LP problems. As we shall see, analysts use computers to solve almost all medium- and large-scale LP problems. Standard computer output provides not only the numerical solution to the problem in question but also a wide variety of sensitivity analyses. Thus, a solid understanding of sensitivity analysis is essential in order to take full advantage of the power of linear programming.

Changes in the Objective Function

It is natural to ask how changes in the coefficients of the objective function affect the optimal decision. In the computer firm's production problem, for instance, the current contributions are $500 and $300 per unit of each model type. Obviously, if market prices or variable unit costs change, so will the contributions. How would such changes affect the firm's optimal production mix?

As a concrete example, suppose the firm anticipates that the current industry price for an economy model, $1,000, will fall to $900 in the coming months. Thus the firm expects that contribution per unit of the economy model will fall to $900 − 700 = \$200$ as a result. Assuming an unchanged contribution for model S, the firm's new objective function is

$$\pi = 500S + 200E.$$

With the sizable drop in E's contribution per unit, intuition suggests that the firm should reduce the output of E and increase the output of S. Figure 17.4 indicates that this is indeed the case. It shows the same feasible region as Figure 17.2. But, the slopes of the contribution contours change. In Figure 17.4, the highest contribution contour touches the feasible region at point B, where the hard disk and DVD constraints are binding. (The slope of the new contribution contour is $-500/200 = -2.5$, and this falls between the slopes of these two constraint lines, -2 and $-\infty$.) We find the values of the decision variables at optimal corner B by solving the equations $S = 200$ and $2S + E = 500$. The resulting values are $S = 200$ and $E = 100$, and maximum contribution is $120,000. In contrast, if the firm were to maintain its old production mix, $S = 100$ and $E = 300$ (at point C), it would earn a contribution of only $110,000. To sum up, the firm should respond to the fall in economy model contribution by shifting to a greater quantity of standard models.

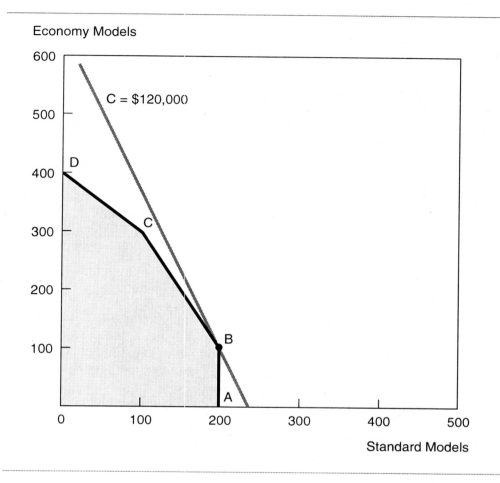

FIGURE 17.4

Production Constraints with New Contributions

A fall in the unit contribution of economy PCs causes the contribution contour to steepen and the optimal mix of PCs to move from point C to point B.

A general conclusion emerges from this example: The optimal production plan depends on the *relative* contributions of the two models. To see this, write the objective function in the form $\pi_S S + \pi_E E$, where π_S and π_E denote the contribution per unit for the respective models. The slope of the contribution contour is $\Delta E/\Delta S = -\pi_S/\pi_E$. Depending on the ratio of model contributions, one of the following three plans is optimal:

Point B (S = 200, E = 100) provided $\quad -\infty < -\pi_S/\pi_E \leq -2$

Point C (S = 100, E = 300) provided $\quad -2 \leq -\pi_S/\pi_E \leq -1$

Point D (S = 0, E = 400)   provided $\quad -1 \leq -\pi_S/\pi_E \leq 0$

Note that a small change in the contribution ratio has no effect on the optimal plan so long as the requisite inequality continues to hold. For instance, if the price cut is to $960 (only 4 percent), the new contribution ratio will be 500/260. Production plan C will continue to be optimal because the second inequality still will be satisfied. (Of course, with the fall in price, the firm's profit will drop; nonetheless, the firm should stick to plan C.) If the contribution of model E falls below half that of model S, production plan B will become optimal.[6] Finally, if the contribution of E exceeds that of S, producing model E exclusively will produce the most total contribution. In other words, as production of one model becomes relatively less and less profitable, the optimal plan shifts to increasing amounts of the other model.

CHECK STATION 2   How will the farmer's mix of crops be affected if the price of wheat increases to $2.25? If it falls to $.90? What if both crop prices fall by 15 percent? How high would the ratio P_W/P_B have to be to induce the farmer to produce only wheat? How low would the ratio have to be for him to produce only barley?

Shadow Prices

Let's return to the original version of the computer firm's problem. Management is operating according to its optimal production plan: 100 standard models and 300 economy models per week, which together generate $140,000 in contribution. At this solution, production uses 100 percent of hard-disk capacity and all of the firm's current labor supply. This prompts some natural questions for management to contemplate: How much would profits increase by increasing hard-disk capacity? What about by increasing the labor force? As we shall see, the notion of shadow prices for resources provides the answers to these questions.

The **shadow price** of a resource measures the change in the value of the objective function associated with a unit change in the resource. To illustrate, let's compute the shadow price associated with hard-disk capacity. Suppose the firm increases this capacity from 20,000 to 22,000. Figure 17.5 shows the capacity increase as a rightward shift in the hard-disk constraint line. With the increase in capacity, point C moves to the southeast. Nonetheless, (the newly positioned) point C remains the optimal corner; that is, the firm should continue to utilize all of its disk capacity and labor. The hard-disk and labor constraints are $80S + 40E \leq 22,000$ and $5S + 5E \leq 2,000$, respectively. Solving these as binding constraints, we find the optimal production plan to be $S = 150$ and $E = 250$. The firm's new contribution is $(500)(150) + (300)(250) = \$150,000$. The 2,000-unit increase in disk capacity has resulted in a $10,000 profit increase. Thus, the shadow price of an extra unit of capacity is $10,000/2000 = \$5$.

---

[6]If the slope of the objective function contour happens to be identical to the slope of a given constraint, any production point along the constraint is optimal. For instance, if $-\pi_S/\pi_E = -2$, maximum total contribution is attained at points B and C and any other point along segment BC.

FIGURE 17.5

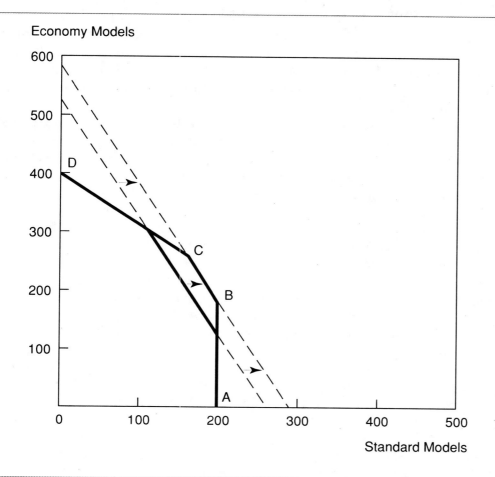

The Shadow Price of Hard Disks

If the firm can increase its hard-disk capacity by 2,000, it will operate at point C and increase its profit by $10,000.

To find the shadow price associated with additional hours of labor, we set up an analogous calculation. Suppose the firm expands its labor force to 2,100 hours per week. The binding constraint equations are now $5S + 5E = 2,100$ and $80S + 40E = 20,000$. Thus, the optimal production plan is $S = 80$ and $E = 340$. The new contribution is $(500)(80) + (300)(340) = \$142,000$. The addition of 100 labor-hours per week increases contribution by $2,000. (Remember, the old contribution was $140,000.) Therefore, the shadow price of labor (per hour) is $2,000/100 = \$20$.

Each individual resource constraint has a shadow price. Each shadow price measures the change in the objective function from a change in that resource *alone*, that is, with the amounts of all other resources held constant. As is usual in sensitivity analyses, we trace the impact of one effect at a time. Also, *each shadow price is constant so long as the same constraints are binding in the optimal solution.* This price measures both the benefit of added capacity and the cost of reduced capacity. For instance, we saw that a 2,000-unit increase in hard-disk capacity raised profit by $10,000 (implying a shadow price of $5). By the same token, we can confirm that having 3,000 extra units of capacity raises profit by $15,000, whereas 1,000 extra units raises profit by $5,000. In fact, a 2,000-unit drop in capacity (a move from 20,000 to 18,000) causes a $10,000 fall in contribution (from $140,000 to $130,000). In each case, the shadow price per unit change in capacity is $5—a constant.

Now consider what happens if we expand hard-disk capacity beyond a total of 24,000 units—say, from 24,000 to 24,400 units. If we were to draw the new constraint in Figure 17.5, we would find that it lies entirely outside (i.e., to the right of) the downward-sloping labor supply constraint. Clearly, the hard-disk constraint is no longer binding. Instead, the DVD and labor constraints are binding, implying $S = 200$ and $5E + 5S = 2,000$. Thus, the optimal product mix is $S = 200$ and $E = 200$. The optimal mix remains the same when hard-disk capacity is increased beyond 24,000 or any higher amount. Any additions to capacity beyond 24,000 go unused. What is the shadow price of each extra unit of capacity beyond 24,000? Zero! The extra capacity has no effect on the feasible region, the firm's optimal plan, and its maximum profit. Because the change in profit from the extra units is zero, the shadow price is zero as well.

Thus, we have demonstrated a third property concerning shadow prices: *Any resource that is not used fully in the optimal solution (i.e., has a nonbinding constraint) has a shadow price of zero.* For example, in the original version of the problem (Figure 17.2), C is the optimal corner, where $S = 100$ and $E = 300$. Because this production plan uses only 100 DVD drives, and 200 units of capacity are available, the shadow price of DVD capacity is zero. Clearly, the firm would be no worse off with less capacity (unless capacity were reduced below 100, in which case the shortage of capacity would affect the optimal production plan).

To sum up, a constraint's shadow price measures the improvement in the objective that results from relaxing the constraint or, conversely, the decline in the objective from tightening the constraint.

CHECK STATION 3   For the farmer's problem, compute the shadow prices of land and labor. How many additional hours would the farmer have to expend before the shadow price of labor fell to zero?

OPTIMAL DECISIONS AND SHADOW PRICES   Shadow prices that emerge from a linear program's optimal solution measure implicit values for the firm's limited resources. In the short run, these resources may be fixed. But in the longer run, the firm frequently can expand or contract its resources, usually at some cost. Shadow prices are essential for making these decisions. For instance, suppose the computer producer can hire extra labor at a cost of $15 per hour (wages plus fringe benefits). Should it do so? The answer is yes. The additional contribution per labor-hour is $20 (simply the shadow price for labor found earlier). Because the cost is only $15, the firm makes a net profit of $20 - 15 = \$5$ per labor-hour hired. It profitably can hire extra labor up to the point where labor's shadow price falls below

$15. This occurs at a total labor supply of 2,500 labor-hours. At this point, the labor constraint becomes nonbinding (lies just outside the DVD and hard-disk constraint lines); thus, its shadow price falls to zero. Therefore, starting from 2,000 labor-hours, the firm could profit from hiring as many as 500 extra hours.

Now, suppose the firm could engage a subcontractor to provide an extra 2,000 units of hard-disk capacity *and* 100 hours of labor for a fixed fee of $18,000. Should the firm accept this deal? Again, the answer is derived directly from knowledge of the resource shadow prices. The total value to the firm of the extra capacities is simply $(2,000)(5) + (100)(20) = \$12,000$. Here, the values of the separate capacity increases (using the respective shadow prices) are summed to arrive at the firm's total benefit. Because this benefit is less than the $18,000 cost, the firm should refuse the deal.

Finally, shadow prices play a crucial role in evaluating new activities. To illustrate, suppose the firm is contemplating the production and sale of a new super-turbo computer (T). Each unit of this model has an expected contribution of $700, contains a 120-gigabyte hard disk and one DVD drive, and requires 10 hours of labor. Should the firm produce this model? One way to answer this question is to formulate the new, larger LP problem as follows:

$$\text{Maximize:} \quad 500S + 300E + 700T$$

$$\text{Subject to:} \quad S + T \leq 200$$
$$80S + 40E + 120T \leq 20,000$$
$$5S + 5E + 10T \leq 2,000.$$

Using an LP computer program to solve this problem, we find that $S = 100$, $E = 300$, and $T = 0$. Despite the higher unit contribution, no units of the turbo model should be produced because its assembly would require a large quantity of "expensive" labor.

We can reach the same conclusion much more quickly using the shadow prices from our original problem. Suppose the firm considers producing one turbo unit, $T = 1$. The direct benefit is simply the unit's contribution, $700. What is the implicit cost of this unit? Because producing the unit uses the firm's limited resources, the firm will be able to produce fewer units of the other models, and total contribution from those models must fall. This loss in contribution is an opportunity cost. Measuring this cost is straightforward. Producing a single turbo unit uses 120 gigabytes of hard-disk capacity valued at $5 per unit (its shadow price), one unit of DVD capacity valued at $0 (remember, its shadow price is zero), and 10 hours of labor valued at $20 each. The total cost is

$$(120)(5) + (1)(0) + (10)(20) = \$800.$$

Thus, if the firm produced this turbo unit, the change in its total contribution would be $700 - 800 = -\$100$. Producing a single turbo unit (or indeed any number of units) is a losing proposition. (If the firm produced 10 units, it would generate 10 times the loss, $-\$1,000$.) Of course, if the unit contribution were predicted to be $900, a comparison of benefit and opportunity cost would show that the firm should introduce the turbo PC. This benefit-cost comparison would not indicate how many turbo units the firm should produce. The precise, optimal value of T can be determined only by solving the new linear program just illustrated.

Thus, we have the following general rule:

> A firm can profitably introduce a new activity if and only if the activity's direct benefit exceeds its opportunity cost, where opportunity cost is the sum of the resources used, valued at their respective shadow prices.

CHECK STATION 4   The farmer considers planting a third crop, soybeans. The price of soybeans is $1.75 per bushel. Growing 1,000 bushels of soybeans requires 2 acres of land and 4 hours of labor per week. Is soybean production profitable? Explain.

In closing this section, it is worth making one further point about the relationship between marginal analysis and the optimal solutions of linear programs. Earlier we saw that a new activity is excluded (its quantity is set equal to zero) if its unit benefit is less than its unit cost. What about activities that are *included* in the optimal solution? Recall that both standard and economy computers are part of the PC firm's optimal production mix. The marginal benefit of producing an extra standard model is $500 (its contribution). Using the resource shadow prices, its marginal cost is computed as

$$(80)(5) + (1)(0) + (5)(20) = \$500.$$

In the optimal solution, marginal benefit and marginal cost are identical. Similarly, for the economy model, marginal benefit is $300 and marginal cost is

$$(40)(5) + (1)(0) + (5)(20) = \$300.$$

Again marginal benefit and marginal cost are identical. The following general result holds for any linear program:

> For any decision variable that is positive in the optimal solution, its marginal benefit equals its marginal cost, where the latter is computed according to the resource shadow prices.

Thus, once again we find that the relationship, $M\pi = MB - MC = 0$, holds at the optimum solution.

Business Behavior —Allocating HIV Resources

In the fall of 1999, the Centers for Disease Control and Prevention called for a panel of health scientists, economists, and policy experts to formulate a frame-work and strategy for HIV prevention in the United States. A member of that panel, Edward Kaplan of Yale University, has described the work of the panel in analyzing the problem of HIV prevention.[7] The panel concluded that a key goal was "to prevent as many new HIV infections as possible within the resources available for HIV prevention." Although this broad goal might seem obvious, current health-care measures often pursue other ends. As Kaplan notes, formulating the problem as a constrained maximization problem was, at least at first, foreign to many on the panel who were not economists.

The panel modeled the strategy for HIV prevention as an LP problem. The key question was: How should the budget for prevention ($412 million in 1999) allocate funds across dozens of alternative prevention programs, with myriad constraints, to maximize the number of HIV cases prevented? Prevention programs range from counseling at-risk populations to screening blood donations to preventing mother-to-child transmissions to funding needle exchanges for intravenous drug users. The panel marshaled the available economic and medical data to solve a variety of LP problems under different scenarios (from pessimistic to optimistic). They found that an optimal resource policy could prevent about 3,900 new HIV infections per year at the $412 million funding level. Investigation of the relevant shadow prices showed that increasing funding would lead to greater HIV prevention but at a diminishing rate.

In contrast to the optimal plan, current U.S. prevention policy roughly allocates funds to different programs, regions, and targeted populations in proportion to reported AIDS cases and prevents only an estimated 3,000 infections. (Although spending more dollars where there are more AIDS cases probably makes sense for *treatment*, it is not the best plan for maximum *prevention*. Proportional allocation also contains a perverse incentive: The allocation should reward health authorities for preventing AIDS cases, not for reporting more numerous cases.) Overall, the most cost-effective prevention programs (derived with the LP approach) can increase prevention by some 30 percent compared to current programs. Kaplan also noted that if the allocation included funds for needle-exchange programs (at the time, federal law prohibited funding for such programs), annual preventions would increase to some 5,300. To sum up, Kaplan credits the resource allocation model with organizing the tough thinking needed to combat AIDS.

FORMULATION AND COMPUTER SOLUTION FOR LARGER LP PROBLEMS

Skill in recognizing, formulating, and solving linear programming problems comes with practice. This section presents four decision problems that represent a cross section of important management applications of linear programming. Once you are comfortable with these applications, the other decision problems you encounter will begin to look familiar, and their formulation and

---

[7]E. Kaplan, "Allocating HIV Resources," *OR/MS Today* (February 2001): 26–29.

solution will be almost automatic. In addition, you will be able to formulate larger-scale problems and then solve them using standard computer programs. The final two problems display the kinds of LP solutions such programs provide, with emphasis on interpreting the computer output.

PRODUCTION FOR MAXIMUM OUTPUT   A manufacturing firm can produce a good using three different production methods, each requiring different amounts of labor and capital—two inputs in fixed supply. The firm has 60 machine-hours and 90 labor-hours per day to devote to the product. The processes require the following inputs to produce one unit of output.

	Process 1	Process 2	Process 3
Machine-Hours	.5	1	2
Labor-Hours	2	1	.5

The firm seeks to maximize output by using the processes singly or in combination. How much output should it produce, and by which processes?

The LP formulation is as follows:

Maximize: $x_1 + x_2 + x_3$

Subject to: $.5x_1 + x_2 + 2x_3 \leq 60$

$2x_1 + x_2 + .5x_3 \leq 90.$

All decision variables are nonnegative.

The decision variables (x_1, x_2, and x_3) denote the quantities of output produced via each process. The firm wishes to maximize total output, the sum of the outputs produced by each process subject to the constraints that the total amounts of labor and capital used to produce total output cannot exceed available supplies of inputs.

This problem involves two constraints (plus three nonnegativity constraints) and three decision variables. Here, the previous graphical method will not work because there are more decision variables than axes of the graph. However, we can find the solution graphing the two *constraints* on the axes instead. The method is shown in Figure 17.6, where available input supplies—rather than decision variables—are placed on the axes. The rectangle OLMK represents the feasible region, whose sides indicate the available amounts of capital and labor (60 and 90 units, respectively).

The next step is to graph a contour of the objective function. Figure 17.6 shows two such contours. The inner contour shows combinations of inputs necessary to produce 40 units of output; the outer contour corresponds to producing 70 units. For instance, if the firm seeks to produce 40 units, it can do so

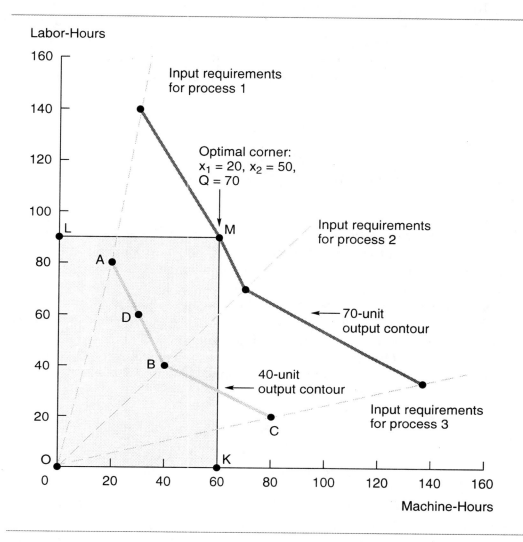

FIGURE 17.6

Maximum Output with
Limited Inputs

With 60 machine-hours and 90 labor-hours, the firm can produce its maximum output, 70 units, at point M by using processes 1 and 2 in combination.

via process 1, using 20 machine-hours and 80 labor-hours; this input combination is shown as point A in the figure. Alternatively, it could use process 2, using 40 units of each input (point B), or process 3, using 80 and 20 units (point C).

To complete the production contour we draw the segments connecting these points. For instance, the firm could produce the 40 units using a combination of processes 1 and 2. Consider the outputs $x_1 = 20$, $x_2 = 20$, and $x_3 = 0$. Total production is 40 units, using a total of $10 + 20 = 30$ machine-hours and $40 + 20 = 60$ labor-hours. This pair of inputs occurs at point D in Figure 17.6, halfway along the segment joining A and B. In general, by using processes 1 and 2 in various proportions to produce 40 units in total, we trace out the line segment AB. Similarly, combinations of processes 2 and 3 use inputs described by the line segment BC.

To complete the graphical solution, we find the highest production contour attainable given the fixed supply of inputs. The highest contour touches the corner of the feasible region at point M, where each input is fully utilized. At this point, the firm produces output using only processes 1 and 2. Returning to the mathematical formulation, we know from the graph that $x_3 = 0$ and that

$$.5x_1 + x_2 = 60$$
$$2x_1 + x_2 = 90$$

because both constraints are binding. Solving these equations simultaneously, we find $x_1 = 20$, $x_2 = 50$, and maximum total output is 70.

PRODUCTION AT MINIMUM COST   Suppose that we have the same production processes as in the previous example, but inputs are variable rather than fixed. In particular, the firm can rent machine time at a price of $8 per machine-hour and can hire labor at a wage of $10 per hour. How should the firm use the available processes to produce 40 units of output at minimum cost?

To find the optimal decision, we must formulate correctly the objective function. The cost of producing a single unit via process 1 is $(.5)(\$8) + (2)(\$10) = \$24$. (The cost is simply the sum of inputs used multiplied by their prices.) The total input costs per unit for processes 2 and 3 come to $18 and $21, respectively. Therefore, the formulation is

Minimize: $24x_1 + 18x_2 + 21x_3$

Subject to: $x_1 + x_2 + x_3 = 40.$

All decision variables are nonnegative.

This problem is simple enough that it can be solved by just looking at it. To minimize cost, the firm should produce exclusively via process 2, because it has the lowest cost per unit ($18). Thus, the optimal production plan is $x_2 = 40$, $x_1 = x_3 = 0$.

REMARK   The solution to the minimum-cost problem features a single binding constraint. Furthermore, the optimal production plan uses only a single process. In the solution to the maximum-output problem, two of the three constraints are binding. The optimal production plan involves two processes (whose values are found by solving the two binding constraints simultaneously). The findings for these examples illustrate a general result:

> In any linear programming problem, the number of decision variables that take nonzero values in the optimal solution always is equal to the number of binding constraints.

Therefore, in decision problems in which the number of decision variables (call this number N) greatly exceeds the number of constraints (call this M), at least N − M decision variables will be zero in the optimal solution.

Computer Solutions

Solving LP problems graphically is impractical for problems in which the decision variables and constraints number three or more. Fortunately, many computer programs are available to solve large-scale LP problems. Indeed, a major airline routing its aircraft can find itself facing an LP problem involving thousands of decision variables and hundreds of constraints. Computers can efficiently solve even problems this large. In its broad description, the computer solution is much the same however large the problem. Typically, the user inputs a mathematical formulation of the problem, that is, the objective function and all constraints. The computer program then produces optimal values of all decision variables, the optimal value of the objective function, and the shadow prices associated with the constraints.

The last 15 years have seen the development of dozens of *spreadsheet-based* linear programming packages.[8] The user enters basic data, including constraints, directly into a spreadsheet. The program then carries out all arithmetic calculations and displays the optimal solution and shadow prices in the original spreadsheet. A key advantage is that this output can be used as inputs into larger, related spreadsheets. The following examples illustrate a typical spreadsheet-based LP program.

A STAFFING PROBLEM   A major city has minimum requirements for the number of police officers on duty during each four-hour period (see the following table). Because split shifts are prohibited, each officer must work eight consecutive hours.

Officers receive standard pay rates for shifts 1 and 2, time and a quarter for shifts 3 and 4, and time and a half for shifts 5 and 6. How can the police department find a daily work schedule that will minimize its total wage cost?

Shift	Time	Required Number of Police Officers
1	8 A.M.–12 P.M.	150
2	12–4 P.M.	100
3	4–8 P.M.	250
4	8 P.M.–12 A.M.	400
5	12–4 A.M.	500
6	4–8 A.M.	175

[8]For a review of these software packages, see R. Fourer, "Linear Programming Survey," *OR/MS Today* (June 2007): 42–51. (An updated version of this comprehensive survey of LP software packages is available online at http://lionhrtpub.com/orms.)

The formulation of this decision problem is as follows.

Minimize: $x_1 + 1.125x_2 + 1.25x_3 + 1.375x_4 + 1.5x_5 + 1.25x_6$

Subject to: $x_1 + x_6 \geq 150$

$x_2 + x_1 \geq 100$

$x_3 + x_2 \geq 250$

$x_4 + x_3 \geq 400$

$x_5 + x_4 \geq 500$

$x_6 + x_5 \geq 175$

All decision variables are nonnegative.

Here $x_1, x_2, \ldots, x_6$ denote the number of officers who *begin* duty with shift 1, 2, . . ., 6. The objective function lists the total number of regular-time salaries of the force. (The city pays an officer beginning duty in shift 1 regular time for eight hours. One beginning in shift 2 receives four hours of regular-time pay and four hours at time and a quarter; overall, he or she counts as a 1.125 officer. We similarly calculate the pay for officers beginning shifts 3 through 6.) The left-hand side of the first constraint lists the number of police on duty during the 8 A.M. to 12 P.M. period. (This is the sum of x_1 and x_6, the numbers of officers beginning shifts at 8 A.M. and ending shifts at noon.) This number must be no fewer than the 150-person requirement. We express the other five constraints in the same way.

The manager enters the objective function and the relevant constraints into the spreadsheet. Table 17.1 shows the completed spreadsheet (including the problem's optimal solution and shadow prices). In the table, the decision variables appear in row 6 and are in colored type for easy identification. We can vary these as we wish and observe the effect on the objective. The values shown here are the optimal values generated by executing Excel's optimization program, Solver. In actual practice, the user is free to enter any initial values. For instance, the user could begin by setting all six variables at 300 officers—values that far exceed required staffing levels. The manager can also experiment with other values. Cell I5 lists the objective, the total number of regular-time police officers (the value of which the manager wants to minimize). The value in this cell has been computed by using the objective function equation in the LP formulation.

Rows 8 and 10 represent the constraints. The fixed values in row 10 denote the required number of officers on the six shifts (the right side of the preceding inequalities). The computed values in row 8 list the numbers of officers actually present during the time periods. For instance, the value in cell C8 is the sum of cells B6 and C6, and so on. Finally, each value in row 12, the so-called extra officers, is the difference between the actual (row 8) and required (row 10) number of personnel.

To direct the computer to solve the LP problem, one must complete the Solver menu (shown below the spreadsheet in Table 17.1). In the menu, we

TABLE 17.1

Linear
Programming
Solution for Police
Staffing Problem

The department
meets its
hourly staffing
requirements at
minimum total
cost.

	A	B	C	D	E	F	G	H	I	J
1										
2		8 A.M.–12	12–4 P.M.	4–8 P.M.	8 P.M.–12	12–4 A.M.	4–8 A.M.			
3										
4	Shift Costs	1	1.125	1.25	1.375	1.5	1.25		Total Cost	
5									1,150	
6	# of Officers	150	175	75	325	175	0			
7										
8	# per 8-Hour Shift	150	325	250	400	500	175			
9										
10	Officers Required	150	100	250	400	500	175			
11										
12	Extra Officers	0	225	0	0	0	0			
13										
14	Shadow Price	1.0	0	1.125	0.125	1.25	0.25			

Solver Parameters [?] [X]

Set Target Cell: $I$5

Equal to: ◯ Max ⬤ Min

By Changing Cells:

$B$6 : $G$6

Subject to Constraints:

$B$12 : $G$12 ≥ 0
$B$6 : $G$6 ≥ 0

[Solve]
[Close]
[Options]
[Add]
[Change]
[Delete]

have entered target cell I5 (total cost) to be minimized by varying cells B6 to G6 (the numbers hired beginning in each time period). The constraints specify that cells B12 through G12 must be greater than or equal to zero, so cannot be a shortage of officers (i.e., a negative number of extra officers) on any shift. The final constraint states that all decision variables must be nonnegative.

Upon execution, the spreadsheet-based optimization program instantly computes all optimal values consistent with satisfying all constraints. From the spreadsheet solution in Table 17.1, we see that the minimum total number of regular-time officers is 1,150, as shown in cell I5. Note that the bare minimum number of officers is present on five of the six shifts; only the second shift has excess numbers. Moreover, officers begin work on five of the six shifts; no officers begin work on shift 6 at 4 A.M. (This illustrates the earlier general result: Since there are five binding constraints, there are exactly five nonzero decision variables.)[9]

The spreadsheet also lists the shadow price associated with each constraint. For instance, the shadow price of requiring an extra officer on the fourth shift (moving from 400 to 401 officers) is .125. How can this extra officer be obtained for only a *fractional* increase in the workforce? The answer is by hiring one fewer officer beginning in shift 2 (where we already have surplus personnel) and hiring one more officer beginning in shift 3. This trade satisfies the new constraints. The net increase in cost comes from the difference between the hourly costs on shifts 2 and 3: $1.25 - 1.125 = .125$. This confirms the shadow price.

A SCHOOL BUSING PROBLEM   Each year, a municipality contracts with a private bus company for the transportation of students in the primary grades to and from school. As a management consultant to the city, you must structure a busing plan. The city's annual payment to the bus company will depend on the number of "kid-miles" the company carries. (For instance, carrying 20 children 2 miles each amounts to 40 kid-miles, as does carrying 8 children 5 miles each.)

The city's three elementary schools draw students from four distinct geographic neighborhoods. The city's planning department has furnished figures on the number of students in each neighborhood, the capacity of each school, and the distance from each school to each neighborhood. Figure 17.7 shows a map of the school district and provides the pertinent data. You must formulate a busing plan that will minimize total transportation cost. Before turning to the LP formulation and the computer solution in Table 17.2, try coming up with an optimal bus plan on your own, using the information in Figure 17.7.

From the data in Figure 17.7, we can develop the following LP formulation:

Minimize: $2.0N1 + 3.0E1 + \cdots + 13.0W3 + 2.2S3$

Subject to: $N1 + E1 + W1 + S1 \leq 360$

$N2 + E2 + W2 + S2 \leq 400$ School capacities

$N3 + E3 + W3 + S3 \leq 260$

$N1 + N2 + N3 = 240$

$E1 + E2 + E3 = 120$ Neighborhood

$W1 + W2 + W3 = 400$ Enrollments

$S1 + S2 + S3 = 200$

All decision variables are nonnegative.

[9]This is not the only optimal plan. A second solution of the LP problem is $x_1 = 75$, $x_2 = 250$, $x_3 = 0$, $x_4 = 400$, $x_5 = 100$, and $x_6 = 75$. This plan also requires the minimum number of regular-time officers (1,150).

FIGURE 17.7

Data for a School Busing Problem

The number of elementary school children in the neighborhoods and the student capacities of the schools are listed in parentheses.

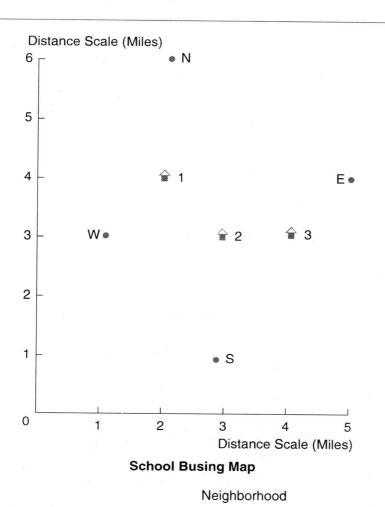

School Busing Map

Neighborhood

Distances *from* (in miles) *to*	(240) North	(120) East	(400) West	(200) South
(360) School 1	2.0	3.0	1.4	3.2
(400) School 2	3.2	2.4	2.0	2.0
(260) School 3	3.6	1.4	3.0	2.2

The formulation begins with recognizing that a busing plan has 12 decision variables: the number of children from each of four neighborhoods bused to each of three schools; for instance, the variable N1 denotes the number of students from the north neighborhood bused to school 1, and so on. Remember that the city wants to minimize the total number of kid-miles traveled. As the formulation shows, the objective function is found by multiplying the number of students along a given route by the distance along the route (2.0N1, for instance) and summing. The first three constraints pertain to school capacities:

TABLE 17.2

Linear Programming
Solution for Busing
Problem

The least-cost solution
shows the numbers
of children bused on
six routes between
neighborhoods and
schools.

	A	B	C	D	E	F	G	H	I
1									
2	Distances						Total		
3		North	East	West	South		Kid-Miles		
4	School 1	2.0	3.0	1.4	3.2		1,792		
5	School 2	3.2	2.4	2.0	2.0				
6	School 3	3.6	1.4	3.0	2.2				
7									
8									
9	Students					Total in	Capacity	Extra	Shadow
10		North	East	West	South	School	of School	Spaces	Prices
11									
12	School 1	240	0	120	0	360	360	0	0.8
13	School 2	0	0	280	120	400	400	0	0.2
14	School 3	0	120	0	80	200	260	60	0
15									
16	Total Kids Bused	240	120	400	200				
17	Students in District	240	120	400	200				
18	Difference	0	0	0	0				
19	Shadow Prices	2.8	1.4	2.2	2.2				
20									

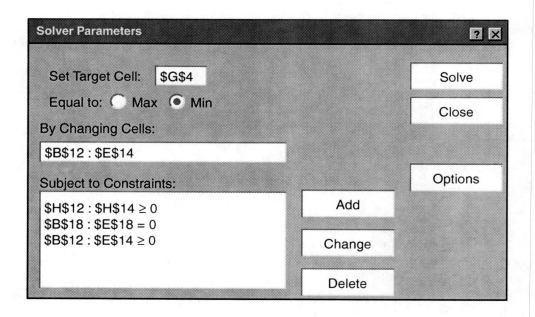

Solver Parameters   [?] [X]

Set Target Cell: $G$4

Equal to: ◯ Max ◉ Min

By Changing Cells:

$B$12 : $E$14

Subject to Constraints:

$H$12 : $H$14 ≥ 0
$B$18 : $E$18 = 0
$B$12 : $E$14 ≥ 0

Solve

Close

Options

Add

Change

Delete

The total number of students going to each school cannot exceed the school's capacity. The last four constraints pertain to neighborhood enrollments: For each neighborhood, all school-age children ride the bus to some school. (If the left-hand side of the equality fell short of the right-hand side, many happy children would be left on street corners without being picked up for school.)

Table 17.2 shows the computer solution. Note that the north and east children go to the schools closest to them, and the west and south students go to either their nearest and second-nearest schools. School 3 has extra spaces. The city pays for the minimum number of kid-miles: 1,792. The table also lists shadow prices associated with each school and each neighborhood. For instance, the shadow price associated with busing an extra child from the north neighborhood is 2.8; this results from busing the student to school 1 (2 miles). But, because school 1 already is at capacity, the extra north child displaces a west child who goes to school 2 instead of school 1 (an extra distance of .6 miles). In turn, the extra west child going to school 2 displaces a south child who now travels an extra distance of .2 miles to school 3. Thus, the listed shadow price represents a total increase in miles of: 2.0 + .6 + .2 = 2.8.

CHECK STATION 5

Confirm that the shadow prices associated with school 1 and the west neighborhood are correct.

An Investment Problem Revisited

Recall that the manager wants to construct a portfolio of securities that offers the highest expected after-tax return, subject to the following requirements: (1) The portfolio's average quality rating is at least 3.5, and (2) the portfolio's average maturity is at least 1.5 years but no greater than 2.5 years.

Bond Category	Quality Rating	Maturity (Years)	Yield (Percent)
Treasury bills	5	.4	4.0
Treasury bonds	5	4.0	6.0
Corporate bonds	3.5	3.2	4.4
Municipal bonds	3	2.0	5.6
Junk bonds	1	2.5	8.0

The LP formulation is

Maximize: $4.0B + 6.0T + 4.4C + 5.6M + 8.0J$

Subject to: $5B + 5T + 3.5C + 3M + 1J \geq 3.5$

$.4B + 4.0T + 3.2C + 2.0M + 2.5J \geq 1.5$

$.4B + 4.0T + 3.2C + 2.0M + 2.5J \leq 2.5$

$B + T + C + M + J = 1.0.$

All decision variables are nonnegative.

TABLE 17.3

Linear Programming Solutions for an Optimal Portfolio

By dividing funds among treasury bills, treasury bonds, and junk bonds, the investor earns a maximum expected return (6.23 percent) while meeting three investment requirements.

	A	B	C	D	E	F	G	H	I	J	K	L	M
1													
2		T-Bills	T-Bonds	Corp Bonds	Munis	Junk		Portfolio		Requirement	Gap	Shadow Price	
3													
4	Proportions	0.260	0.365	0	0	0.375		1					
5													
6	Returns	4	6	4.4	5.6	8		6.23					
7													
8	Ratings	5	5	3.5	3	1		3.5		3.5	0	0.708	
9													
10										1.5	1	0	
11	Maturities	0.4	4	3.2	2	2.5		2.5					
12										2.5	0	0.555	
13													

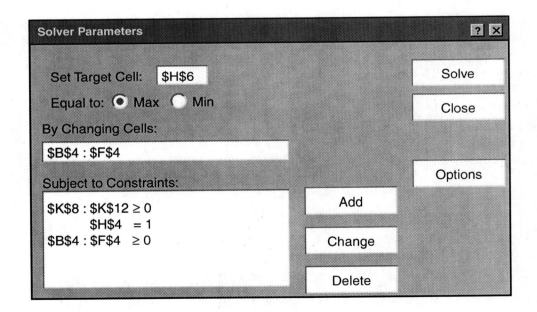

Solver Parameters

Set Target Cell: $H$6

Equal to: ● Max   ○ Min

By Changing Cells:

$B$4 : $F$4

Subject to Constraints:

$K$8 : $K$12 ≥ 0
$H$4 = 1
$B$4 : $F$4 ≥ 0

Solve
Close
Options
Add
Change
Delete

The portfolio manager must determine the proportions of the individual's total dollar investment to invest in the securities. These proportions are denoted by B, T, C, M, and J for the respective securities. (For instance, if the manager divided the portfolio equally among the five assets, the values would be B = T = C = M = J = .2.) The actual size of the manager's investment fund does not enter into the formulation. The optimal proportions will be the same whether the manager is investing $20,000 or $20 million.

The objective function lists the average (or expected) return of the portfolio. The first constraint indicates that the portfolio's average risk rating must be at least 3.5. The second and third constraints list the bounds on the portfolio's average maturity. The final constraint ensures that the portfolio proportions sum exactly to 1.

What portfolio will maximize the investor's expected return, subject to the risk and maturity constraints? From Table 17.3, we see that the optimal portfolio puts 26 percent of the individual's total dollar investment in Treasury bills, 36.5 percent in Treasury bonds, and the remainder in junk bonds. This portfolio has a risk rating of exactly 3.5 (which just meets this constraint), has a maturity of exactly 2.5 years (which just meets the upper maturity constraint), and delivers a maximum portfolio return of 6.23 percent.

The spreadsheet also lists the relevant shadow prices as calculated by the LP program. The shadow prices associated with the risk and maturity constraints are of some interest. The former shadow price shows that allowing a unit reduction in the portfolio's risk index (reflecting a tolerance for greater risk) would raise the portfolio's expected return by .708 percent. According to the latter shadow price, increasing the average maturity of the portfolio by a year would increase the expected return by .555 percent. (In either case, the portfolio would shift toward a greater share of junk bonds and a smaller share of Treasury bills.)

SUMMARY

Decision-Making Principles

1. Linear programming is a method of formulating and solving decision problems that involve explicit resource constraints. The range of LP problems includes product mix, cost minimization, transportation, scheduling, inventory, and financial and budgeting decisions.

2. To qualify as a linear program, all decision variables must enter linearly into the objective function and into all constraints. So long as the LP problem is feasible, an optimal solution always exists at one of the corners of the feasible region. The optimal corner can be found by graphical means or by computer algorithms.

3. The shadow price of a resource shows the change in the value of the objective function associated with a unit change in the resource. Thus, the shadow price measures the improvement in the objective from relaxing a constraint or, conversely, the decline in the objective from tightening a constraint. A nonbinding constraint has a shadow price of zero.

4. Decision makers should adopt a new activity if and only if the activity's direct benefit exceeds its opportunity cost. We measure this opportunity cost by the sum of the resources used in the activity valued at their respective shadow prices.

Nuts and Bolts

1. Formulating linear programs requires identifying the relevant decision variables, specifying the objective function, and writing down the relevant constraints as mathematical inequalities.
2. Solving linear programs requires identifying the binding constraints and solving them simultaneously for the optimal values of the decision variables.
3. For two-variable problems, the optimal solution can be found by graphing the feasible region (framed by the binding constraint lines) and superimposing contours of the objective function. The optimal corner is found where the highest contour (or, for minimization problems, the lowest contour) touches the feasible region. The optimal corner determines which constraints are binding.
4. The shadow price of a constraint is found by changing the right-hand side of the inequality by a unit, solving the binding constraints for the decision variables, and recomputing the objective function. The shadow price is simply the change between the new and old values of the objective.

Questions and Problems

1. Explain whether LP techniques can be used in each of the following economic settings.
   a. There are increasing returns to scale in production.
   b. The objective function and all constraints are linear, but the number of decision variables exceeds the number of constraints.
   c. The firm faces a downward-sloping linear demand curve. (To sell more output, it must lower its price.)
   d. The firm can vary the amounts of two basic chemicals in producing a specialty chemical, but, for quality control reasons, the relative proportions of chemicals must be between 40/60 and 60/40.
2. Which of the following formulations can be solved via the LP method?
   a. Maximize: $x + 2y$, subject to: $x + y \leq 2$ and $3x - y \geq 4$.
   b. Maximize: xy, subject to: $x + y \geq 2$ and $3x - y \geq 4$.
   c. Maximize: $x + 2y$, subject to: $x + y \leq 2$ and $3x - y \geq 4$.
   d. Maximize: $x + 2y$, subject to: $x + y \leq 2$ and $3x + y \geq 8$.
   e. Maximize: $x + 2y$, subject to: $x + y \leq 2$ and $x/(x + y) \leq .7$.

3. A manager has formulated the following LP problems. Use graphical methods to find the optimal solutions. (In each, all variables are nonnegative.)
   a. Maximize: $10x + 15y$, subject to: $2x + 5y \leq 40$ and $6x + 3y \leq 48$.
   b. Minimize: $.75x + y$, subject to: $x + .5y \geq 10$ and $x + y \geq 16$.

4. Consider an LP problem in which a firm produces multiple goods (A and B) using two inputs (X and Y) in limited supply. Suppose a technological advance increases the amount of good A that can be produced per unit of input X. How will this change the feasible region? How will this affect the quantities of the goods produced in the profit-maximizing solution to the LP problem? (To answer these questions, be sure to graph the two resource constraints.)

5. An athlete carefully watches her intake of calcium, protein, and calories. Her breakfast diet consists mainly of milk and cereal, whose prices and nutrient contents appear in the following table:

	Milk (1 oz)	Cereal (1 oz)
Calcium	2	2
Protein	2	6
Calories	6	2
Price	$.10	$.15

   She seeks a diet that supplies at least 50 units of calcium, 90 units of protein, and 66 calories at minimum cost.
   a. Formulate, graph, and solve this decision problem. What is the minimum cost of meeting the nutrient requirements?
   b. Calculate and provide an economic interpretation of the shadow price associated with calcium.

6. A firm produces tires by two separate processes that require different quantities of capital (K), labor (L), and raw materials (M). Process 1 requires one unit of K, four units of L, and two units of M to produce a tire yielding a $4 profit. Process 2 requires one unit of K, two units of L, and four units of M to produce a tire yielding a $6 profit. The available supply of capital is 10; of labor, 32; and of raw materials, 32.
   a. Formulate and solve (by graphing) the firm's profit-maximization problem.
   b. Find the shadow prices of raw materials and labor.

7. Consider again the investment problem that opened the chapter.
   a. Suppose the portfolio manager limits the portfolio to Treasury bills and Treasury bonds. Using a graph, find the proportions of each type of bond that maximize expected return subject to the risk and maturity constraints.

b. Now suppose the manager can invest in any of the five securities but cares only about the risk constraint. Determine the optimal portfolio.

c. Answer part (b), assuming the manager cares only about the maturity constraints.

8. A soft-drink producer must decide how to divide its spending between two forms of media: television advertising and magazine advertising. Each 30-second commercial on prime-time network television costs $120,000 and, by the company's estimate, will reach 10,000 viewers, 5,000 of whom are in the prime consumer age group, 15 to 25. A single-page ad in a leading human interest weekly magazine costs $40,000 and reaches 5,000 individuals, 1,000 of whom are in the 15 to 25 age group. In addition, the company plans to hold a sweepstakes contest to promote its new soft drink. (A requirement for entry is to enclose the coded label from the new drink.) The company believes the print ad will be more effective in generating trial purchases and entries. Each magazine spot is expected to produce 500 entries and each television spot 250 entries. Finally, the company's goal in its promotion campaign is to reach at least 600,000 total viewers and 150,000 young viewers and to produce 30,000 or more contest entrants.

How many spots of each kind should it purchase to meet these three goals and do so at minimum cost?

9. A lumber company uses labor (L) and capital (K) to produce joint products, hardwood (H) and plywood (P). These items can be produced by one of two processes:
Process 1: 1 unit of L and 2 units of K to yield 2 units of H and 1 unit of P
or
Process 2: 2 units of L and 2 units of K to yield 2 units of H and 4 units of P
Profit contribution is $2 per unit of H and $1 per unit of P. The firm has 110 units of L and 160 units of K available.

a. Formulate and solve the firm's profit-maximization problem. (*Hint:* Don't be distracted by the fact that the processes produce joint products. The correct decision variables are the levels of each process.)

b. Find the shadow price of labor.

c. Answer part (a), assuming the contribution of P rises to $3 per unit.

Discussion Question Following the example in the text, consider two HIV prevention programs: (1) intensive counseling of high-risk individuals and (2) instituting a needle-exchange program for intravenous drug users. Counseling has an estimated cost of $1,500 per individual per year and is expected to prevent .2 new HIV cases per individual helped. The needle-exchange program costs $500 per individual and prevents .1 new HIV cases per individual.

a. Which program is more effective at HIV prevention *per individual treated*? Which program is more cost effective, that is, more effective *per dollar spent*? Do your answers raise a dilemma as to which program to fund?

b. Suppose that a regional health organization has a total budget of $450,000 to spend on the two programs and has identified 1,000 high-risk individuals. In coordinating the two prevention programs, it sets two variables, C and N, for the respective numbers to be counseled or furnished clean needles. (Given their very different orientations, the programs are mutually exclusive; each individual is enrolled in a single program.) If the authority's goal is to prevent as many new HIV cases as possible, how many individuals should it enroll in each program?

c. What is the authority's optimal allocation if the at-risk population numbers only 250? Show that it will have unused funds.

d. Finally, what is authority's optimal allocation if the at-risk population numbers 500? Be sure to show the appropriate LP formulation.

Spreadsheet Problems

S1. An electronics firm has production plants in Oregon and Tennessee. It ships its products overseas from three ports: Los Angeles, New Orleans, and New York. Transportation costs between plants and seaports are shown in the table.

	Los Angeles	New Orleans	New York
Oregon	$14	$26	$30
Tennessee	24	10	12

The maximum capacity of the Oregon plant is 9,000 tons; the capacity of the Tennessee plant is 10,000 tons. The minimum daily quantities shipped overseas from Los Angeles, New Orleans, and New York are 5,000, 7,000, and 6,000 tons, respectively.

a. The company's objective is to minimize the cost of transporting its product from plants to ports while fulfilling its daily overseas shipping requirements. Formulate the appropriate LP problem.

b. Attempt to solve the LP problem by inspection. Find the company's minimum-cost transport plan using a standard LP computer program.

c. Find and interpret the shadow price associated with the 6,000 minimum daily shipment to New York.

S2. A manufacturer produces six products from six inputs. Each product requires different combinations and amounts of inputs. The following table shows the profit and raw materials requirements for each product. The last column shows the total amounts of raw materials available.

Products	1	2	3	4	5	6	Total Amounts of Inputs
Profits	60	70	48	52	48	60	
Inputs Required:							
Aluminum	.5	2	—	2	1	—	400
Steel	2	2.5	1.5	—	.5	—	580
Plastic	—	1.5	4	—	.5	—	890
Rubber	1	—	.5	1	.5	2.5	525
Glass	1	2	1.5	.4	1	2	650
Chrome	.5	2	.5	2	1.5	2	620

a. Formulate the appropriate linear program.
b. Find the company's most profitable production plan using a standard LP computer program.

Suggested References

The following reference is one of many fine, applied programming texts.

Kolman, B., and R. E. Beck. *Elementary Linear Programming with Applications.* New York: Academic Press, 1995.

The following articles describe typical managerial applications.

Kaplan, E. "Allocating HIV Resources." *OR/MS Today* (February 2001): 26–29. The panel's full report is available online at www.nationalacademies.org (search for "No Time to Lose" full text). The direct link is www.nap.edu/books/0309071372/html/

Higle, J. L., and S. W. Wallace. "Sensitivity Analysis and Uncertainty in Linear Programming." *Interfaces* (July–August 2003): 53–60.

Bollapragada, S., et al. "NBC's Optimization Systems Increase Revenues and Productivity." *Interfaces* (January–February 2002): 47–60.

LeBlanc, L. J., et al. "Nu-kote's Spreadsheet Linear Programming Models for Optimizing Transportation." *Interfaces* (March–April 2004): 139–146.

Kimes, S. E., and J. A. Fitzsimmons. "Selecting Profitable Sites at La Quinta Motor Inns." *Interfaces* (March–April 1990): 12–20.

Linear programming software is surveyed by

Fourer, R. "Linear Programming: Software Survey." *OR/MS Today,* (June 2007), 42–51.

CHECK STATION ANSWERS

1. The formulation of the farmer's problem is

Maximize: $R = 1.6W + 1.0B$

Subject to: $W + B \leq 10$ (land)

$4W + 2B \leq 32$ (labor),

where W and B denote the amounts (in thousands of bushels) of wheat and barley, respectively. Graphing the problem reveals that both constraints are binding. Solving simultaneously the equations $W + B = 10$ and $4W + 2B = 32$, we find $W = 6$ thousand bushels and $B = 4$ thousand bushels. The resulting revenue is \$13,600.

2. So long as P_W/P_B is between 1 and 2, the crop mix $W = 6$ and $B = 4$ is optimal. (For instance, a 15 percent fall in both prices has no effect on the ratio.) A rise in the price of wheat to \$2.25 puts the ratio outside this range, causing the farmer to produce only wheat. The new solution is $W = 8$ and $B = 0$, with only the labor constraint binding. A fall in the price of wheat to \$.90 causes the farmer to produce only barley. Now the solution is $B = 10$ and $W = 0$.

3. To find the shadow price of land, solve the equations $W + B = 11$ and $4W + 2B = 32$ to arrive at $W = 5$ thousand bushels and $B = 6$ thousand bushels. The farmer's new revenue is \$14,000. Land's shadow price is the difference between the old and new revenues, $\$14,000 - \$13,600 = \$400$. To find the shadow price of labor, solve the equations $W + B = 10$ and $4W + 2B = 33$ to arrive at $W = 6.5$ and $B = 3.5$. Labor's shadow price is $\$13,900 - \$13,600 = \$300$. Labor's shadow price becomes zero when the supply of labor increases to 40 hours per week. At this level, the labor constraint line lies (just) outside the land constraint line.

4. Producing 1,000 bushels of soybeans has an opportunity cost of

$$(2)(\$400) + (4)(\$300) = \$2,000.$$

The direct revenue from selling the 1,000 bushels is \$1,750. Since this revenue falls short of the cost, soybeans (in this or any other amount) should not be grown.

5. a. *School 1's shadow price:* The extra spot in school 1 will be filled by a west student who was attending school 2. This saves .6 kid-miles, because school 1 is this much closer to the west neighborhood than is school 2. In turn, the freed space in school 2 is filled by a south student (who was attending school 3) for a .2 kid-mile savings. The total gain in kid-miles is $.6 + .2 = .8$.

   b. *West neighborhood's shadow price:* The extra west student attends school 2 (an extra 2.0 kid-miles), displacing a south student who now moves to school 3 (an extra .2 kid-miles). Thus, the total increase in kid-miles is 2.2.

CHAPTER 12

Decision Making
under Uncertainty

If Hell is paved with good intentions, it is largely because of the impossibility of foreseeing consequences.

ALDOUS HUXLEY

Gearing Down for a Recession

Selling yachts is a very cyclical industry. In a booming economy, large increases in personal disposable income greatly expand the demand for this high-priced luxury item. In the midst of a recession, sales of yachts sink and a sizable percentage of yacht dealers go out of business. You have owned a yacht dealership for the last two years and have made handsome profits during the good times. Currently you are in the process of deciding on the number of yachts to order from the manufacturer for the coming season. If the economy continues to grow as in the past, your order will be roughly the same as in the previous year. However, a number of economic forecasters are predicting a significant chance—40 percent—of a recession in the next six months. If a recession occurs, you can expect to sell no more than half the number of yachts sold in the past. Should you order for a rising economy or scale back for a recession? A wrong decision means large losses (in an unexpected recession) or forgone profits (in an unexpected boom).

In this chapter, we focus on decisions involving risks—situations in which the consequences of any action the decision maker might take are uncertain because unforeseeable events may occur that will affect his or her final situation. To analyze this type of problem, the decision maker should begin by

1. Listing the available alternatives, not only for direct action but also for gathering information on which to base later action;

465

2. Listing the outcomes that can possibly occur (these will depend on chance events as well as on his or her own actions);

3. Evaluating the chances that any uncertain outcome will occur; and

4. Deciding how well he or she likes each possible outcome.

As this list indicates, decision making under certainty and uncertainty share a number of features. Whatever the setting, the manager should be aware of all available actions, determine the consequences of each action, and formulate a criterion for assessing each outcome. The introduction of uncertainty, however, requires additional analysis and judgment. First, the manager must be aware of these uncertain events and how they will affect the outcome of any action he or she chooses. Moreover, after accounting for these uncertainties, the manager must assess or estimate the likelihood of alternative outcomes. Second, in decisions under risk, the manager has a course of action that is missing in decisions under certainty: the option to acquire additional information about the risks before making the main decision. Third, the manager must carefully assess the firm's attitude toward risk, that is, formulate a criterion that determines which risks are acceptable. This criterion then can serve as a guide for choosing among risky alternatives.

In this chapter, we begin our study of decision making under uncertainty. First, we review the fundamentals of uncertainty, probability, and expected value. Then we examine the use of decision trees as a guide for managerial choices, especially in sequential decisions. Finally, we explore the effect of risk aversion on managerial decisions: how a manager can assess attitudes toward risk and apply the expected-utility criterion as a decision guide.

UNCERTAINTY, PROBABILITY, AND EXPECTED VALUE

Uncertainty lies at the heart of many important decisions. Managers are often uncertain about outcomes that have a direct bearing on the firm's profit. For example, introducing a new product entails a multitude of risks, including the cost and timetable of development, the volume of sales in the product's first and subsequent years, and competitors' possible reactions. The example that opens this chapter suggests that uncertainty concerning the future course of the macroeconomy—consumer and business spending, price inflation, interest rate movements—is an important factor for many industries and firms.

Uncertainty (or *risk*) is present when there is more than one possible outcome for a decision.[1] Roughly speaking, the greater the dispersion of possible outcomes, the higher the degree of uncertainty. The key to sound decision making under uncertainty is to recognize the range of possible outcomes and

---

[1]Throughout the discussion, we use the terms *risk* and *uncertainty* interchangeably.

assess the likelihood of their occurrence. Uncertainty is acknowledged in expressions such as "it is likely," "the odds are," and "there is an outside chance." The difficulty with such qualitative expressions is that they are ambiguous and open to different interpretations. One is prompted to ask, "How likely is likely?" The essential means for quantifying statements of likelihood is to use *probabilities*. It is far more useful for a meteorologist to state that there is a 60 percent chance of rain tomorrow than to claim that rain is likely. Probability has been described as the mathematical language of uncertainty. The key is to have a sound understanding of what probabilities mean.

The **probability** of an outcome is the odds or chance that the outcome will occur. In the usual parlance, we speak of probabilities as ranging between 0 and 1. (An event having a probability of 1 is a certainty; an event having a probability of 0 is deemed impossible.) Whatever the probability, the relevant question is, What is the basis for this assessment? Frequently there is an *objective* foundation for the probability assessment. The chance of heads on a single toss of a fair coin is 50 percent, or one-half. In a random draw, the chance of picking the lone black ball from a hat containing five balls is one in five, and so on.

When viewed closely, the main basis for assessments such as these is the notion of a probability *as a long-run frequency*. If an uncertain event (like a coin toss or a random draw) is repeated a very large number of times, the frequency of the event is a measure of its true probability. For instance, if a fair coin is tossed 1,000 times, the frequency of heads (i.e., the number of heads divided by the total number of tosses) will be very close to .5. If the actual long-run frequency turned out to be .6, we would be justified in asserting that the coin was unfair. The frequency interpretation applies to most statistical data. For example, if annual employment in the mining industry totals 40,000 workers and 80 workers die in mining accidents each year, the annual probability of a representative mine worker dying on the job is 80/40,000 or .2 percent.

It should be evident that in many (and perhaps most) situations, there is no chance that a situation will be repeated and therefore no way to assess probabilities on frequency grounds. In its development of a new product (one that is unique to the marketplace), a firm knows that the product launch is a one-shot situation. The firm may believe there is a 40 percent chance of success, but there is no way to validate this by launching the product 100 times and watching for 40 successes. Similarly, a company about to enter into patent litigation faces the problem of predicting the likely outcome of a one-time legal suit. Still another example is a business economist attempting to put odds on the likelihood of a new oil price "shock" (say, a 50 percent rise in oil prices) over the next 18 months.

In dealing with such situations, decision makers rely on a *subjective* notion of probability. According to the *subjective* view, the probability of an outcome represents the decision maker's degree of belief that the outcome will occur. This is exactly the meaning of a statement such as "The chance of a successful product launch is 60 percent." Of course, in making a probability assessment, the manager should attempt to analyze and interpret all pertinent evidence and information that might bear on the outcome in question.[2] For the new product, this would include consumer surveys, test market results, the product's unique qualities, its price relative to prices of competing products, and so on. The point is that a subjective probability is not arbitrary or ad hoc; it simply represents the decision maker's best assessment, based on current information, of the likelihood of an uncertain event. In this sense, all probabilities—even those based on frequencies or statistical data—represent the decision maker's degree of belief.

Expected Value

The manager typically begins the process of analyzing a decision under uncertainty by using a probability distribution. A **probability distribution** is a listing of the possible outcomes concerning an unknown event and their respective probabilities. As we saw earlier, assessing relevant probability distributions is the first step in the manager's analysis. For example, the manager might envision the probability distribution shown in the table for the first year's outcome of a new-product launch.

Outcome	First-Year Sales Revenue	Probability
Complete success	$10,000,000	.1
Promising	7,000,000	.3
Mixed response	3,000,000	.2
Failure	1,000,000	.4

This probability distribution provides the best available description of the uncertainty surrounding the market's reception of the product. Note the considerable range of outcomes and the high likelihood of failure. (Revenue of $1 million is not enough to justify continuing the product.) Failure is the norm for even the most promising new products.

[2]Any probability forecast is based on the decision maker's currently available information. Consequently, if this information changes, so will the probability assessment. Thus, a disappointing market test would lead management to lower its probability assessment of product success. The point is that probability assessments are not engraved in stone; rather, they are constantly being revised in light of new information. In addition, various "experts" often hold different subjective probability assessments about an event based on different information or different interpretations of common information. (In contrast, the objective probability of heads in a single coin toss is immutable; that is, it is always one-half. Assuming there is no doubt about the fairness of the coin, this probability will not change with new information, nor will it be subject to dispute.) We take up the subjects of information acquisition and probability revision in Chapter 13.

From the probability distribution, we can compute the expected value of the uncertain variable in question. In the preceding example, expected revenue is $(.1)(\$10) + (.3)(\$7) + (.2)(\$3) + (.4)(\$1) = \$4.1$ million.

More generally, suppose the decision maker faces a risky prospect that has n possible monetary outcomes, $v_1, v_2, \ldots, v_n$, predicted to occur with probabilities $p_1, p_2, \ldots, p_n$. Then the expected monetary value of the risky prospect is

$$E(v) = p_1v_1 + p_2v_2 + \cdots + p_nv_n.$$

In the preceding numerical example, we have applied exactly this formula with respect to the four possible outcomes.

DECISION TREES

The **decision tree** is a convenient way to represent decisions, chance events, and possible outcomes in choices under risk and uncertainty. In fact, this simple diagram can incorporate all the information needed to "solve" the decision problem once the specific objectives of the decision maker have been established. The method is extremely versatile. When first encountered, choices under risk appear messy, ill defined, and puzzling. The actual choices, the potential risks, and the appropriate objective to pursue may all be far from clear. The individual should not be blamed for regarding his or her choice as "a riddle wrapped in a mystery inside an enigma," to borrow a phrase from Winston Churchill. However, sketching a crude decision tree almost always will clarify the options. The very structure of the tree emphasizes the ingredients (choices, outcomes, and probabilities) necessary for making an informed decision. The more precise the tree becomes (after drawing and redrawing), the more precise one's thinking becomes about the problem. The "finished" tree can then be evaluated to solve the decision problem. Probably more important, the decision tree provides a visual explanation for the recommended choice. One easily can pinpoint the "why" of the decision: which circumstances or risks weighed in favor of which course of action. And one can undertake any number of sensitivity analyses, altering the facts of the decision to determine the impact on the recommended course of action.

Decision trees can be simple or complex, spare or "bushy," small enough to evaluate by hand or large enough to require a computer. To illustrate the method, we start with a concise example.

An Oil Drilling Decision

An oil wildcatter must decide whether to drill at a given site before his option period expires. The cost of drilling is $200,000. This sum will be completely lost if the site is "dry," that is, contains no oil. The wildcatter estimates that, if

FIGURE 12.1

The Wildcatter's Drilling Problem

By drilling, the wildcatter earns an expected profit of $120,000.

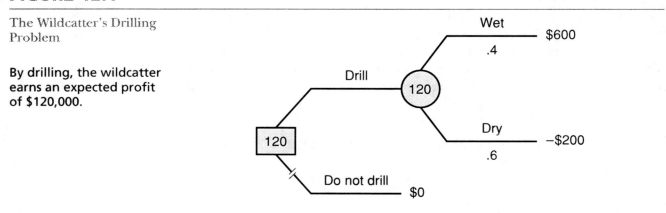

he strikes oil, the total profit (before drilling costs) over the well's life will be $800,000. Thus, if there is a strike, the wildcatter will earn a $600,000 profit.

Figure 12.1 shows the decision tree for the wildcatter's problem. The tree depicts the sequence of events in the decision, reading from left to right. The problem starts with a point of decision, by convention represented by a square, from which emanate two branches: the decisions to drill or not to drill. If the choice is not to drill, the story ends there. The final profit outcome is $0, as indicated at the tip of the branch. If the choice is to drill, a chance event, represented by a circle, occurs. The chance event summarizes the risk associated with drilling. The two possible outcomes, a strike or a dry well, are shown on the branches emanating from the circular chance node. The respective monetary outcomes, $600,000 and −$200,000, are listed next to the branch tips.

We need one final piece of information to complete the description of the decision problem. This is the probability, in the wildcatter's best judgment, that the site will have oil. Suppose this probability is .4 (or a 40 percent chance). This is listed on the chance branch corresponding to "wet." Obviously, the probability of dry must be .6, because wet and dry sites are the only two outcomes. For the moment, let us suppose the wildcatter's probability assessment is based on a completed geological survey of the site, his judgment of how this site compares with other sites (with and without oil) that he has drilled in the past, and any other pertinent information. (In Chapter 13, we will say much more about interpreting, estimating, and revising probability projections of uncertain outcomes.)

All that remains is to specify a criterion by which the decision maker can choose a course of action under uncertainty. The criterion we employ at the outset of this chapter is expected value.

> The **expected-value criterion** instructs the manager to choose the course of action that generates the greatest expected profit.

Let's apply the expected-value criterion to determine the wildcatter's best course of action. The "do not drill" option results in a certain outcome of $0. The expected profit from the "drill" option is

$$(.4)(600,000) + (.6)(-200,000) = \$120,000.$$

Note that this expected profit is a weighted average of the possible outcomes, the weight for each outcome being its probability. The greater an outcome's probability, the more weight it has in determining the overall expected profit (i.e., the expected profit moves closer to it). For instance, if the strike chances were .5, the expected value would be a straight average of the possible profit and loss, or $200,000. Better strike odds produce a higher expected profit.

In Figure 12.1, the expected profit of $120,000 has been recorded at the chance node of the tree. This indicates that, before the chance event has been resolved (i.e., before the true outcome, oil or no oil, has been revealed), the expected value of the risky drilling prospect is $120,000. According to the expected-value criterion, the wildcatter's optimal decision is to drill. The double slashes through the decision tree's "do not drill" branch show that this choice has been ruled out.

A firm supplies aircraft engines to the government and to private firms. It must decide between two mutually exclusive contracts. If it contracts with a private firm, its profit will be $2 million, $.7 million, or −$.5 million with probabilities .25, .41, and .34, respectively. If it contracts with the government, its profit will be $4 million or −$2.5 million with respective probabilities .45 and .55. Which contract offers the greater expected profit?

CHECK STATION 1

GOOD AND BAD DECISIONS AND OUTCOMES   Suppose the wildcatter follows the expected-value criterion and drills the site. Unfortunately, the site turns out to be dry. The resulting $200,000 loss is a *bad outcome*. But this does not mean that the choice to drill the site was a *bad decision*. Given what the wildcatter knew then, the risk was worth taking. Roughly speaking, the chance of a very large profit outweighed the chance of a smaller (although sizable) loss. Drilling was a good decision that happened (unluckily) to end in a bad outcome. Alternatively, suppose the wildcatter chooses to drill a second site instead of the first. At the second, the outcomes are $550,000 and −$220,000, with probabilities .3 and .7, respectively. The expected profit of the second site, $11,000, is barely positive. Upon drilling the second site, the wildcatter strikes oil. Certainly this is a good outcome. But even a lucky outcome cannot turn this into a good decision. In fact, the second site offers uniformly worse outcomes and worse odds than the first. Accordingly, it never should be chosen over the first site. (If the wildcatter has sufficient resources, both sites could be drilled profitably.)

The point is that a good decision must be judged on the basis of the information available before the fact, that is, at the time the choice must be made.

Of course, hindsight is 20-20, but this is of no avail to the manager. Moreover, 20-20 hindsight is misleading when it comes to evaluating past decisions. A bad outcome does not brand the decision as bad, nor does a good outcome mark a decision as good. What matters are the chances of the foreseeable good and bad outcomes at the point of decision. No matter how basic this point, it is surprising how often it is forgotten by decision makers in business and government. Perhaps the greatest virtue of using decision trees in evaluating and comparing risks is that it reminds us of the difference between good decisions and good outcomes.

Features of the Expected-Value Criterion

The depiction of the risk in Figure 12.1 hardly could be simpler. Thus, it comes as no surprise that the expected-value calculation is automatic, indeed, almost trivial. Nonetheless, it is important to recognize the general properties of this criterion, properties that apply equally to simple and complex risks.

The first (and most basic) feature of the expected-value standard is that it values a risky prospect by accounting not only for the set of possible outcomes but also for the probabilities of those outcomes. For instance, suppose the wildcatter must decide whether to drill on one site or another. (There are insufficient resources to drill on both.) The first site's possible monetary outcomes are 800, 600, 160, −60, and −200 (all in thousands of dollars); these outcomes occur with probabilities .05, .15, .2, .25, and .35, respectively. Consequently, the expected profit from drilling this site is (.05)(800) + (.15)(600) + (.2)(160) + (.25)(−60) + (.35)(−200), or $77,000. The second site has the same five possible outcomes as the first but with probabilities .05, .2, .25, .2, and .3. Notice that the second site offers higher probabilities of "good" outcomes than the first site. Clearly, then, the second site should have a higher value than the first. The expected-value standard satisfies this commonsense requirement. Performing the appropriate computation will show that the second site's expected profit is $128,000, a significantly higher figure than the expected profit of the first site.

Second, the expected value of a risky prospect represents the average monetary outcome if it were repeated indefinitely (with each repeated outcome generated independently of the others). In this statistical sense, the expected-value standard is appropriate for playing the long-run averages. Indeed, many managers employ the expected-value criterion when it comes to often-repeated, routine decisions involving (individually) small risks. For instance, suppose you have the chance to bet on each of 100 tosses of a coin. You win a dime on each head and lose a nickel on each tail. This, you'll no doubt agree, is the epitome of a routine, often-repeated, low-risk decision. Here the expected-value criterion instructs you to bet on each toss. If you choose this profitable (albeit somewhat boring) course of action, your expected gain in the 100 tosses is $2.50. Your actual profit will vary in the neighborhood of $2.50, perhaps coming out a little above, perhaps a little below. The statistical "law of large numbers" applied to the independent tosses ensures that there is no real risk associated with the bet.

Third, in decisions involving multiple and related risks, the expected-value criterion allows the decision maker to compute expected values *in stages.* Figure 12.2 makes this point by presenting a "bushier" (and more realistic) tree for the wildcatter's drilling decision. The tree incorporates three risks affecting drilling profits: the cost of drilling and recovery, the amount of oil discovered, and the price of oil per barrel. As the tree depicts, the cost of drilling and recovery is the first uncertainty to be resolved and depends on the depth at which oil is found (or not found). In the wildcatter's judgment, oil may be struck at one of two depths or not at all. Thus, the tree depicts three branches emanating from the initial chance node. As an example, let's consider the second branch: oil found at 5,000 feet. This branch ends in a chance node from which three new branches emerge. These branches show the possible amounts of oil (barrels per year) that might be recovered; the third branch, for instance, has a total recovery of 16,000 barrels. Finally, each recovery branch ends in a chance node from which three new branches sprout. These indicate the possible different values of average oil prices over the life of the well. For example, the third branch lists a $55-per-barrel price. At the end of this branch, the last uncertainty is resolved and the wildcatter's profit, in this case $180,000, is finally determined. (Simply take the profit figures at face value. We have not supplied the revenues and costs on which they are based.)

The path from the leftmost chance node to the $180,000 profit outcome indicates one particular scenario that might occur: finding a 16,000-barrel oil field at 5,000 feet and selling it at a two-year average price of $55 per barrel. However, this outcome is but one of many possible outcomes contingent on the resolution of the multiple risks. In all there are $(2)(3)(3) + 1 = 19$ possible profit outcomes, one for each branch tip. The combination of multiple risks, each with multiple outcomes, means that the corresponding decision tree will be bushy indeed.

The bushy tree also requires a lengthier process of probability assessment, because the wildcatter must evaluate probabilities for three distinct risks. The first three branches of the tree show his chances of striking (or not striking) oil at different depths. If he finds some oil at a given depth, the next question is how much. The secondary branches of the tree list the chances of finding different oil quantities. Note that the likelihood of different recovery amounts depends on the depth at which oil is first found, and the likelihood of very large deposits is better at 3,000 feet than at 5,000 feet. (Remember that these recovery probabilities are conditional on some oil being found at all. Shallow fields are likely to be large fields, but the chance of finding oil at 3,000 feet is only .13 in the first place.) Finally, once the recovery quantity is ascertained, the sole remaining uncertainty concerns the market price of oil. The chances listed on the third-level branches have been obtained from an expert's prediction of future prices. Note that the chances of different market prices per barrel are

FIGURE 12.2

A More Complicated
Drilling Decision

This decision tree contains
multiple risks that generate
19 possible outcomes.

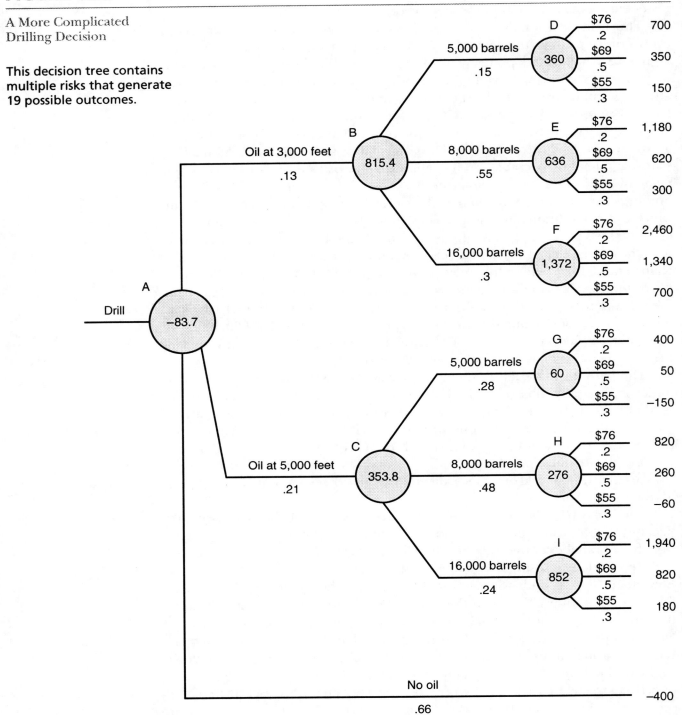

independent of the quantity of oil recovered (i.e., the chances are the same regardless of the recovery amount).

What is the wildcatter's expected value from drilling in the face of these multiple risks? To answer this question, we calculate the expected value in stages by "averaging back" the tree, starting at the branch tips and working to the left. To illustrate, consider the chance node D on the tree: a 5,000-barrel-per-year oil reserve at a depth of 3,000 feet. The three branches list the profit outcomes for this field depending on the (uncertain) oil price. The expected profit from such a field is simply the average of the possible profit outcomes weighted by the respective probabilities. Thus, the expected profit is $(.2)(700) + (.5)(350) + (.3)(150) = \$360$ thousand, listed in chance node D. But what if the field had yielded 8,000 barrels per year? By an analogous calculation, we find the expected profit to be $636 thousand in this case, as shown in chance node E. The expected profits for the chance nodes F through I (corresponding to different-sized fields at different depths) have also been computed and listed on the tree. At this point, we have "averaged out" the price uncertainty.

In the next step, we average over the possible quantities of oil found. Chance node B shows the expected profit if oil is found at 3,000 feet, computed by averaging the expected profits at nodes D through F:

$$(.15)(360) + (.55)(636) + (.3)(1,372) = \$815.4 \text{ thousand.}$$

Node C lists the expected profit ($353.8 thousand) for a field found at 5,000 feet.

The last step is to compute the overall expected profit of drilling. This is shown in the initial chance node A and is the average of the expected profits at B and C and the $400 thousand loss if no oil is found. As always, this expected value is computed using the branch probabilities as weights. Therefore, the expected profit from drilling is

$$(.13)(815.4) + (.21)(353.8) + (.66)(-400) = -\$83.7 \text{ thousand.}$$

The wildcatter has solved his decision problem by calculating the expected profit of drilling in stages. Since this is negative, the wildcatter should choose not to exercise his option on the site.

CHECK STATION 2

Suppose the chief executive of an oil company must decide whether to drill a site and, if so, how deep. It costs $160,000 to drill the first 3,000 feet, and there is a .4 chance of striking oil. If oil is struck, the profit (net of drilling expenses) is $600,000. If oil is not struck, the executive can drill 2,000 feet deeper at an additional cost of $90,000. Her chance of finding oil between 3,000 and 5,000 feet is .2, and her net profit (after all drilling costs) from a strike at this depth is $400,000. What action should the executive take to maximize expected profit?

The Perils of International Business

For the last 30 years, globalization of business has been an enduring trend. Consumers in all parts of the world buy an increasing proportion of foreign goods, and a growing number of firms operate across national boundaries. The prospects of rapid growth and high profits from untapped foreign markets are attractive to large firms. Telecommunication companies vie for shares of the Chinese market, expecting to quintuple the number of phone lines from 5 per hundred people to 25 (still only about one-third of the U.S. average). Ford has invested $6 billion in developing a "world" car to be marketed and sold all over the globe. Procter & Gamble and Kimberly-Clark compete for the disposable diaper market in Brazil. A parade of U.S. mutual fund companies are rushing to Europe, Japan, and Australia in pursuit of those nations' retirement savings.

However, if opportunity is one side of the international business coin, the other side is risk. Leveraging successes enjoyed in local markets to far-flung foreign operations is far from certain. These risks come in many categories.

ECONOMIC CONDITIONS   The 1990 recession in Europe and the late 1990s financial crisis in Southeast Asia caused dramatic falls in business and consumer spending. Global firms with sales concentrated in these regions saw profits evaporate and losses mount.

UNCERTAIN COSTS   Because of low-skilled workforces, lack of capital, and primitive distribution systems, the costs of doing business in developing countries are frequently high and uncertain. Foreign firms assembling electronics goods in Russia have been plagued by low worker productivity, vandalism, and crime.

DIFFERENT CULTURES   Brazilians spend a higher percentage of income on their children than do citizens of neighboring countries. They are eager for disposable diapers, while Argentines are largely indifferent. Consumers in Southeast Asia are accustomed to buying light meals from street vendors, not from fast-food restaurants. To cite an extreme case of cultural miscalculation, General Motors introduced its popular Nova car model into South America. Only after disastrous sales did the company realize that *no va* means "does not go" in Spanish.

POLITICAL RISK   Tax and regulatory burdens, government bureaucracy and even corruption, and changing political parties and governments all contribute to the risk of doing business abroad. Over the past 50 years, international businesses have been decimated by unrest and civil war in places such as Cuba, Lebanon, El Salvador, Vietnam, and the Balkans. Today, outright expropriation is much less frequent but remains a risk.

EXCHANGE-RATE RISK   A firm that earns a significant part of its revenues abroad is subject to exchange-rate risk when converting these to its home currency. For instance, a depreciating Japanese yen means lower dollar profits from revenues earned in Japan. Similarly, the costs incurred by a foreign subsidiary are subject to exchange-rate risk. Thus, the depreciating currencies of Southeast Asia (by lowering the dollar-equivalent costs) make production in that part of the world more attractive to global firms.

Even the most experienced international firms face unforeseen risks and suffer missteps in foreign markets. Despite its marketing muscle and well-tested formula for operating stores, McDonald's has gained little market share in South Africa and the Philippines. Instead, it has been humbled by well-established local competitors catering to local tastes. In 1977, Coca-Cola was the leading soft drink in India before the company pulled up stakes refusing to divulge its secret formula to the Indian government. Returning in 1993, the company found itself a distant second to Thums Up, an imitation cola in a similar glass bottle, that won the allegiance of Indian consumers in Coke's absence. Admitting that its tried and true business formula was the wrong one for India, Coca-Cola's management purchased Thums Up and now aggressively markets that drink alongside "The Real Thing."

The lesson to take from these companies' experience is that international businesses, if they are to be successful, must be especially vigilant in identifying myriad risks and capturing them in carefully conceived, bushy decision trees.

SEQUENTIAL DECISIONS

Some of the most interesting and important business and economic problems call for a sequence of decisions to be made over time. For example, suppose a chemical firm is considering a large capital investment in a new petrochemical facility. The profitability of such an investment depends on numerous uncertain factors: future market demand, reactions of close competitors, and so on. Profits also depend on the future product and pricing decisions of the firm itself. It is not simply that the firm faces many decisions over time; the more important point is that the sequence of decisions is interdependent. A correct investment decision today presupposes that the company will make optimal (i.e., profit-maximizing) pricing decisions tomorrow if the plant is built. The following example illustrates this general point about sequential decisions.

In Chapter 1, we sketched a decision problem facing a pharmaceutical firm that must choose between two R&D approaches. Suppose the profits and probabilities of the competing methods are summarized in the following table.

An R&D Decision Revisited

R&D Choice	Investment	Outcomes	Profit (Excluding R&D)	Probability
Biochemical	$10 million	Large success	$90 million	.7
		Small success	50 million	.3
Biogenetic	$20 million	Success	$200 million	.2
		Failure	0 million	.8

All profit figures are expressed in terms of present discounted values and thus are directly comparable to investment figures.

We observe that the biogenetic (G) approach requires a greater initial investment and is significantly riskier than the biochemical (C) alternative. In the worst case, the firm will write off the R&D effort, earning no commercial profit and therefore losing its $20 million investment. The biochemical approach is also uncertain but far less risky. A commercially viable drug is guaranteed. Even in its worst case, the firm makes a $40 million net profit. Straightforward calculations show that

$$E(\pi_C) = (.7)(90) + (.3)(50) - 10 = \$68 \text{ million,}$$

whereas

$$E(\pi_G) = (.2)(200) - 20 = \$20 \text{ million,}$$

where $E(\pi)$ denotes expected profit. Of the two methods, the company should pursue the biochemical approach.

However, the firm's decision analysis should not end here. It has a considerably wider range of options than first appears. Resources permitting, the firm might do well to hedge its bet by pursuing *both* R&D programs simultaneously. Depending on the results, the firm can decide which method to commercialize.

The decision tree in Figure 12.3 depicts the simultaneous R&D option. The tree lists four distinct possible R&D outcomes: one, both, or neither effort

FIGURE 12.3

Simultaneous R&D Investments

By investing in both R&D methods, the company earns an expected profit of $72.4 million.

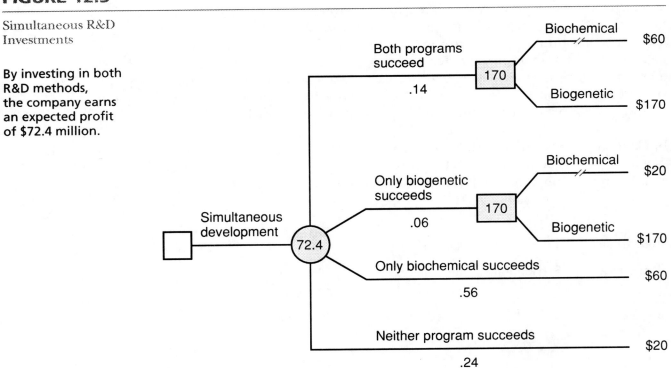

may be successful. The probability of each joint outcome is the product of the probabilities of the individual outcomes because these risks are assumed to be independent. Thus, the chance that both methods will succeed is $(.7)(.2) = .14$, and so on. Note that the probabilities of the four possible outcomes sum to 1, as they must.

When the results of both R&D programs are in, the firm must decide which method to commercialize. If the biogenetic research effort fails (the lower two branches), the firm has no choice; it must go the biochemical route. If the biogenetic research is successful, the firm should commercialize this method because it offers the greater profit. (Note that the firm will produce the drug with only a *single* method—whichever is more profitable.) Thus, in the upper two branches, the drug is produced biogenetically. The profit is $200 million minus $30 million (the total investment on both methods), or $170 million. The other profit outcomes are computed in analogous fashion.

What is the firm's expected profit at the start of the simultaneous R&D effort? Multiplying the possible monetary outcomes by their respective probabilities, we compute this to be

$$(.14)(70) + (.06)(70) + (.56)(60) + (.24)(20) = \$72.4 \text{ million.}$$

Simultaneous development offers a larger expected profit than the next-best alternative, pursuing the biochemical approach exclusively. By undertaking both, the firm enjoys the security of biochemical's "sure thing" profits while still testing the biogenetic waters—a long shot that could provide a huge profit. Even in the likely event that the biogenetic option fails, the firm makes a profit. The decision tree instructs us that pursuing both approaches simultaneously increases the firm's expected profit by $72.4 - 68 = \$4.4$ million vis-a-vis pursuing the biochemical method alone.

However, the firm has not yet exhausted its options. Now it considers pursuing the R&D methods sequentially: one first, then (if necessary) the other. This raises an obvious question: Which method should it pursue first?

The decision tree in Figure 12.4 depicts the sequential strategy: biochemical R&D first, then biogenetic R&D. After the outcome of the first R&D effort is known, the firm can choose to commercialize it or invest in the second program. (If the biogenetic program is subsequently pursued and fails, the firm goes back and completes development of the biochemical approach.) The top square shows the firm's decision in the event the biochemical program is successful. Contrary to one's intuition, the firm should *not* proceed to immediate development; rather, its best course of action is to invest in the second R&D program, see the result, and, if it fails, fall back on the biochemical approach. The resulting expected profit from making this second R&D investment is $82 million—$2 million better than from immediately commercializing a biochemically based drug. What if the biochemical program is less successful? The lower decision square provides the answer. As we might expect, the firm's best action

FIGURE 12.4

Sequential R&D:
Biochemical First

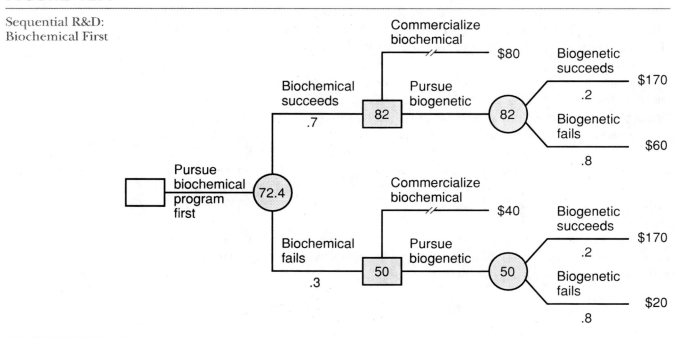

is to invest in the second R&D program; the expected profit of $50 million is $10 million greater than the alternative. Thus, regardless of the outcome of the biochemical program, the biogenetic program also should be pursued.

The drug company's overall expected profit at the outset—that is, at the tree's initial chance node—is $(.7)(82) + (.3)(50) = \$72.4$ million. The expected profit from this sequential strategy is exactly the same as under simultaneous development. This result may seem surprising until we note that the two strategies call for the company to take exactly the same actions. Even under sequential development, the company's best strategy is to pursue both R&D methods, just as under simultaneous development. Despite the apparent differences in the decision trees, the strategies must have the same expected profit because they call for the same actions in all cases. Thus, this sequential strategy offers no advantage over committing to simultaneous development in the first place.

In contrast, the reverse sequential strategy—pursue the biogenetic program first, then the biochemical program if necessary—is advantageous. Figure 12.5 depicts this strategy. The tree shows that if the biogenetic program is successful, it should be commercialized (for an expected profit of $180 million). Otherwise, the biochemical program should be pursued and brought to market (for an expected profit of $48 million). To calculate the firm's expected profit when it first embarks on this sequential program, we average

FIGURE 12.5

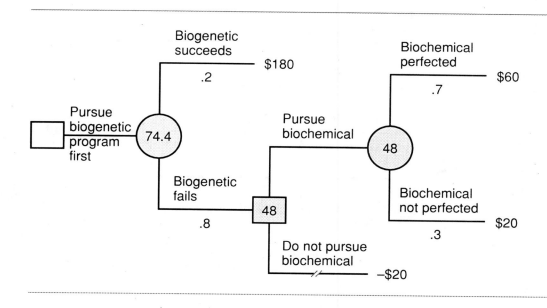

Sequential R&D:
Biogenetic First

By trying the
biogenetic program
first (and following
with the other
program if necessary),
the drug company
maximizes its expected
profit.

these two results. Thus, the overall expected profit is (.2)(180) + (.8)(48) = $74.4 million. This sequential strategy provides $2 million more profit on average than the next-best alternative.

How do we account for the superiority of first pursuing the biogenetic method? To answer this question, let's compare the actions under the sequential and simultaneous programs. The actions are the same in each case, except when the biogenetic program achieves immediate success. Here the company need not pursue the biochemical program and so saves the $10 million investment—a sum it would have spent under simultaneous development. This saving occurs 20 percent of the time (when the biogenetic program is successful). Therefore, the company's expected savings from sequential development (relative to simultaneous development) is (.2)(10) = $2 million. This accounts for the expected profit difference, 74.4 − 72.4, between the two strategies. By postponing pursuit of the biochemical method, the firm is able to profit from the information concerning the success or failure of the risky biogenetic approach. The condensed decision tree in Figure 12.6 summarizes the expected profits for all of the company's possible actions.

Firm A is deliberating whether to launch a new product. If firm B (its main competitor) does not bring out its own product (a 40 percent probability), firm A expects to earn $20 million over the product's life. If firm B introduces its own product, there is a 50 percent chance that the market will view it as superior to A's, in which case firm A will lose $30 million on the launch. If A's product is superior, its profit will be $10 million. Presuming its goal is to maximize expected profit, should firm A launch the product?

CHECK STATION 3

FIGURE 12.6

Summary of
Pharmaceutical
Company's R&D
Options

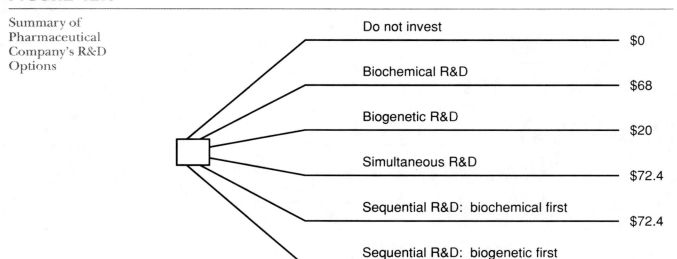

**Risking a
New York
Blackout**

On a July evening in 1977, separate lightning strikes hit two electrical transmission towers carrying power to New York City. It was clear that the city's electricity demand that evening, even with emergency generating capacity, would require the remaining transmission lines to carry power in excess of their short-term emergency rating. This presented a terrible dilemma to the systems operator in the control center of the Consolidated Edison Company of New York. If the demand-supply imbalance was not corrected, and quickly, the overload would cause the circuit breakers on the remaining lines to open, causing a citywide blackout. (After the 1965 blackout of much of the Northeast, circuit breakers were redesigned to open automatically so as to isolate transmission trouble spots.)

The operator's available information about the severity of the disaster was incomplete at best. He could communicate by phone with a limited number of controllers and operators in the system. Most important, the operator had only 15 to 25 minutes to take action! Careful consideration, extensive analysis, and exhaustive deliberation were out of the question. He could not follow "normal operating procedure" or turn to a page of instructions in an emergency operating manual. What should he have done?

One option was to do nothing, relying on the system to weather the imbalance. (Perhaps the city's demand for power would decline in the course of the evening.) Another option was to try to get more power generated within New York City. Should he have ordered circuit breakers on the damaged lines to be manually closed to restore limited transmission capacity? Unfortunately, there was a common difficulty with all of these alternatives. Even if the operator ordered the given measure immediately, he would not know whether it would be successful until after the fact.

The operator had another (albeit more drastic) alternative. In all likelihood, he could solve the demand-supply imbalance by "shedding load," that is, deliberately blacking out a portion of the city. Was this his best option? If so, how much load should he shed: enough (70 percent) to ensure against a complete disaster, or a minimum amount (25 percent)? If you were in the operator's place, what kind of decision analysis would you undertake in 20 minutes? In his place, what would you have done?[3]

Research shows that individuals have difficulties identifying and evaluating risks. Too often they rely on intuition, rules of thumb, and experience to make risky decisions. Managers' most common pitfalls include

Business Behavior —Risky Decisions

1. **Seeing too few possibilities.** That is, they take too narrow or a "myopic" view of the future. While successful firms astutely foresee possible future consequences and act appropriately, many firms suffer losses by failing to foresee coming events. Too often managers simply extrapolate the current status quo into their forecasts for the future, thus ignoring upside and downside possibilities alike. Professor Max Bazerman of Harvard Business School calls these risks "predictable surprises" (the disasters you should have seen coming). It is like drawing a decision tree with whole sections of chance branches missing (because those possibilities have been overlooked) but not knowing it.

2. **Relying on verbal expressions of probability.** Losing the patent case is *unlikely*. There is a *reasonable chance* that our product will beat our rival's to market. Although expressions such as these come naturally, they are surprisingly imprecise. Researchers have asked scores of individuals, including business people, what a host of such expressions mean in terms of probability. For instance, "unlikely" conveys a probability of anywhere between 11 percent and 39 percent, with a median response of 25 percent. In turn, a "reasonable chance" can mean a probability as high as 80 percent or as low as 50 percent. As decision trees remind us, determining reasonable probabilities for the risks that matter is crucial for crafting profit-maximizing decisions. A pessimistic view of "unlikely" could well lead to a very different decision than an optimistic view. It's far better to try to pinpoint and agree on reasonable probability estimates in the first place.

[3]This account is based on Robert Behn, "The Shed Load Decision," *Management Case* (Duke University, 1983) and "Con Ed Control Had Fifteen Minutes to Pull Switch," *New York Times,* July 18, 1977. A short description of Con Ed's actions and their results follows the Check Station Answers at the end of the chapter.

3. **Holding optimistic beliefs.** Here, optimism means overstating the probability of favorable outcomes and downplaying the chances of unfavorable ones. By nature confident, many managers unconsciously engage in wishful forecasting: What they want to have happen they believe is likely to happen. Clearly, overoptimistic, unrealistic beliefs can lead to poor or even disastrous decisions. A constructive remedy to unfounded optimism is to insist on realistic assessments based on external benchmarks. Nobel prize winner Daniel Kahneman calls this "taking the outside view." For instance, a management team might believe and claim a 60 percent chance of success for a new product, based purely on an internally focused assessment. But, of all new product launches surveyed each year, only about 10 to 15 percent are successfully being sold two years later. Even if impressive internal factors justify elevating the product's success rate to, say, three times this base rate, a realistic revised probability is only 30 to 45 percent—a far cry from 60 percent.

RISK AVERSION

Thus far, we have used the concept of expected monetary value as a guide to making decisions under uncertainty. A decision maker who follows the expected-profit criterion is said to be **risk neutral**. This standard is appropriate for a manager who is willing to play the averages. The evidence suggests, however, that individuals and firms are not neutral toward risks that are large relative to their financial resources. When it comes to significant risks, individuals and institutions adopt an attitude that is conservative toward losses. Thus, the use of the expected-profit criterion must be qualified.

A COIN GAMBLE You are offered the following choice: You can receive $60 for certain (the money is yours to keep), or you can accept the following gamble. A fair coin is tossed. If heads come up, you win $400; if tails come up, you lose $200. Would you choose the sure $60 or accept the gamble on the coin toss? In answering, imagine that real money (your own) is at stake.

When given this choice, the majority of individuals prefer the sure $60 to the gamble. This is not surprising given the magnitude of the risk associated with the coin toss. Notice, however, that choosing $60 is at odds with maximizing expected profit. The expected profit of the coin toss is $(.5)(400) + (.5)(-200) = 100. Thus, a risk-neutral decision maker would prefer the gamble to the sure $60. Refusing the bet shows that you are not risk neutral when it comes to profits and losses of this magnitude.

A precise way to express one's evaluation of the coin toss (or any risky prospect) is to name a certainty equivalent. The **certainty equivalent (CE)** is the amount of money for certain that makes the individual exactly indifferent to the risky prospect. Suppose that, after some thought, you determine you would be indifferent to the options of receiving $25 for certain or facing the risk of the coin toss. You are saying that your CE for the coin toss is $25. This CE is significantly smaller than the expected value of the bet, $100. This being the case, we would say that you are *risk averse*. An individual is **risk averse** if his or her certainty equivalent for a given risky prospect is less than its expected value.

Loosely speaking, the magnitude of one's aversion to risk is indicated by the shortfall of the CE below the expected value of the risky prospect; this difference (sometimes referred to as a *discount for risk*) measures the reduction in value (below expected value) due to a prospect's riskiness. Here the risk discount is $100 - 25 = 75. The discount depends on individual preferences as well as on the size of the risk. For instance, a second individual might prefer to avoid the coin toss altogether; that is, in a choice between the coin toss and receiving $0 for certain, this individual prefers $0. This preference makes good sense for someone who does not wish to bear the downside risk of the coin toss. Suppose this individual is indifferent to the options of *paying* $20 for certain or taking the coin toss. (He or she is willing to pay $20 to avoid the risk of the gamble.) Here the CE is -$20, and the risk discount is $100 - (-20) = 120. Clearly, the second decision maker is more risk averse than the first.

THE DEMAND FOR INSURANCE   Risk aversion provides a ready explanation concerning the demand for insurance. Insurance companies stand ready to compensate their policyholders in the event of losses (specified in the insurance contract) at a price in the form of the premium paid by the customer to the company. Risk-averse individuals are willing to give up monetary income to avoid risks. In effect, this is what they do when they purchase insurance.

To make the argument concrete, consider a couple who is about to purchase fire insurance to protect their home (which is valued at $150,000). The risk of a fire destroying their house is very small—about 1 in 300 in any given year. Nevertheless, the loss of their house would mean financial ruin. Thus, the couple finds it prudent to purchase insurance. In return for payment of a $500 annual premium, a 100 percent fire policy promises to pay whatever amount is necessary to rebuild and replace the house in the event of fire. In purely financial terms, the couple faces the following options. If they do not buy the policy, their wealth at the end of the year will be $150,000 if there is no fire or $0 if a fire occurs (a 1-in-300 chance). Their expected wealth is $149,500. (Check this for yourself.) By purchasing the policy, their net wealth is $150,000 - $500 = $149,500 at the end of the year. Their wealth is certain. Regardless of whether a fire occurs, they will have their house (or the money to rebuild it). Notice that whether or not they purchase insurance, the couple's expected wealth is the same, $149,500. Because they are risk averse, the couple prefers the certain $149,500 provided by insurance to the alternative of bearing the risk of fire. Thus, they purchase full insurance.

In this example, the company has offered the couple "actuarially fair" insurance; that is, the couple's premium ($500) just covers the company's expected payout under the policy: $(1/300)(\$150,000) = \$500$. Because of their large size and ability to pool different risks, insurance companies generally behave as though they are risk neutral. To illustrate, suppose the company insures 300,000 houses in a state against fire. Although it is impossible to predict which houses will be struck by fire, the law of large numbers indicates that very close to 1,000 homes in total will have fire losses. Thus, the total premiums ($150 million) will closely match the company's actual payout. Because of administrative costs in writing the policies, insurance companies typically charge premiums that exceed their expected losses. (Of course, competition among insurance companies limits the premiums any one company can charge.) But higher premiums do not eliminate (although they may reduce) the demand for insurance. Even if the fire insurance premium were $1,000 per year, the risk-averse couple might leap at the chance to buy coverage rather than go unprotected.[4]

Risk Management at Microsoft

"Microsoft sees risk everywhere, in a dozen broad categories: financial, reputational, technological, competitive, customer, people (employees and contractors), operations, distributions, business partners, regulatory and legislative, political and strategic."[5] This might seem an unusual statement. After all, what could be more secure than the company's near-monopoly position in PC operating systems?

Yet, Microsoft's risk managers see things quite differently. Their job is to identify, quantify, and manage literally hundreds of risks, of which 20 to 30 may be most important at a given time. Of particular importance are regulatory risks (government antitrust actions) and uncertainties surrounding intellectual property rights. In the longer term, the emergence of new software markets and Microsoft's ability to influence or control the accompanying standards and platforms are crucial. Once managers have identified key risks, they can address the best way to manage them: via insurance, or via a shared-risk joint venture, by diversification, or (in the extreme case) by ceasing the risky activity all together.

Risk management is becoming a pervasive part of big business. When faced with enormous uncertainties, management's stance is decidedly not risk neutral. Invariably, it is risk averse. Beyond the expected monetary

---

[4]The general rule is that a risk-averse individual always will insure fully against a risk if offered actuarially fair insurance. At higher premiums, a range of outcomes is possible: full insurance, partial insurance, or no insurance. A popular type of partial insurance involves provision for deductibles. With a deductible, the company pays only for the portion of losses above a specified monetary threshold. Thus, the policyholder buys insurance (at a reduced premium) for large losses but self-insures for small ones.

[5]This quotation and the synopsis in the text is drawn from E. Teach, "Microsoft's Universe of Risk," *CFO Magazine* (March 1997): 69–72.

returns associated with the separate risks on its radar screen, management must be concerned about its combined risk exposures. As noted earlier, it is wise to diversify by pursuing multiple risky R&D initiatives, instead of putting all eggs in one basket. Firms operating in "dirty" industries must continuously assess the risks posed by changing environmental regulations. In the wake of the monumental losses associated with Hurricane Katrina, disaster insurers have been taking a microscope to their risk portfolios. Using computer models, they sift through decades of data on storm patterns and earthquakes to estimate risk probabilities. While looking out for excessive geographic concentration of insurance coverage, the insurers are also reassessing shoreline properties, scrutinizing building codes, raising premiums, dropping policies, reinsuring portions of their risks, and even offloading risks by selling "catastrophic" (CAT) bonds to investors. (With CAT bonds, an investor obtains a high-interest return in "normal" circumstances but loses a portion, or all, of the principal if yearly hurricane damage claims exceed specified thresholds.)

An important insight offered by risk management is that many risks are interdependent. Decisions made in one area create (or mitigate) risks in another. Alerted to the risks of mass tort litigation for repetitive stress injury, Microsoft incorporated this cost ($2.82 per unit) when setting the licensing fee for its new innovative keyboards, thereby providing a prudent monetary reserve for this risk.

Expected Utility

How can a manager formulate a criterion, reflecting the firm's attitude toward risk, to guide his or her decisions? The formal answer to this question was developed some 50 years ago by mathematical economists John Von Neumann and Oscar Morgenstern, and is called the expected-utility rule. (At the same time, Von Neumann and Morgenstern developed the field of game theory, which we encountered in Chapter 10.)

The use of expected utility proceeds in two steps. First, the decision maker must think carefully about the firm's preferences concerning risks: what risks it is willing to accept and how to value those risks. In the process, the manager constructs a utility scale that describes this risk tolerance. Second, the manager analyzes the decision problem in much the same way as before, that is, constructs a decision tree showing relevant probabilities and possible monetary outcomes and then evaluates the tree. However, there is one crucial difference: In contrast to the risk-neutral manager, who averages *monetary values* at each step, the risk-averse decision maker averages the *utilities* associated with monetary values. At each point of decision, the manager selects the alternative that supplies the maximum expected utility. With this summary in hand, let's see exactly how the method works.

FIGURE 12.7

The Wildcatter's
Drilling Problem
Revisited

**Given his degree of
risk aversion, the
wildcatter chooses
not to drill.**

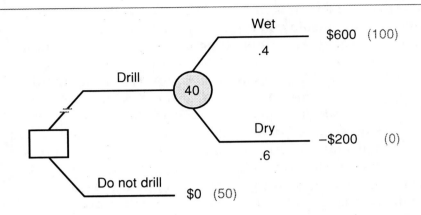

A RISK-AVERSE WILDCATTER   Once again, let's consider the wildcatter's basic decision problem, reproduced in Figure 12.7. Now suppose the wildcatter is risk averse; he is unwilling to rely on expected profits as his choice criterion. Instead, he seeks to determine a criterion for choosing among risky prospects that reflects his own attitude toward risk. We now show how he can construct a utility function that measures his own degree of risk aversion and how he can use this function to guide his choices.

The wildcatter begins by attaching a utility value to each possible monetary outcome. Let's start with the decision to drill. Here the outcomes are $600,000 and −$200,000; these are the best and worst possible outcomes, respectively. The wildcatter is free to set these utility values arbitrarily so long as the best outcome receives the higher value. The usual choice is to assign the worst outcome a utility value of zero. Thus, we would write $U(-200) = 0$; that is, the utility associated with a loss of $200,000 is zero. In turn, let's arbitrarily set $U(600) = 100$. This establishes a range of utility values from 0 to 100 for monetary outcomes between the worst and best possible outcomes.

Using these utility values, the wildcatter evaluates the option to drill by computing its expected utility. The **expected utility** is the probability of each outcome times its utility, summed over all outcomes. Thus, the expected utility of drilling is

$$E(U_{drill}) = (.4)U(600) + (.6)U(-200)$$
$$= (.4)(100) + (.6)(0) = 40.$$

Now consider the "do not drill" option. In this case, the wildcatter's monetary result is $0 for certain. What utility value should the wildcatter assign this outcome? To determine $U(0)$, the wildcatter compares $0 for certain with a gamble offering $600,000 (with probability p) and −$200,000 (with probability

1 − p). The wildcatter measures his relative preference for $0 by finding the probability, p, that leaves him indifferent to the options of $0 and the gamble. Suppose that, after some mental trial and error, he judges his indifference probability to be p = .5; that is, he is indifferent to a certain $0 and to a 50-50 risk between $600,000 and −$200,000. The fact that he is indifferent (at p = .5) allows us to find U(0). The expected utility of the 50-50 gamble is

$$(.5)U(600) + (.5)U(-200) = (.5)(100) + (.5)(0) = 50.$$

Since the wildcatter is indifferent to $0 for certain and this gamble, the two alternatives must have the same utility; that is, U(0) = 50.

Finally, the wildcatter uses expected utility as a guide for his decision. The simple rule is this:

> The decision maker should choose the course of action that maximizes his or her expected utility.

The expected utility of drilling is 40, whereas the utility of not drilling is 50. Thus, the wildcatter should elect not to drill the site. The decision tree in Figure 12.7 shows how the expected utility rule is applied. Beside each monetary value in the tree is its associated utility. The expected utility of drilling is computed and listed by the chance circle. Finally, the "drill" decision branch has been crossed out because it has the lesser expected utility. The wildcatter's preferred option is not to drill.

In the more complicated examples to come, there will be many opportunities to practice the mechanics of expected utility. For the moment, the key point to remember is this: The decision maker's job is to assess utilities that express his or her attitude toward risk. There is no formula for determining the "right" utilities; they are purely personal and subjective.

In the preceding example, the wildcatter's key assessment is that $0 for certain is equivalent (in terms of his preferences) to a 50-50 risk between $600,000 and −$200,000. Notice that this assessment reflects risk aversion on his part. The 50-50 risk has an expected value of $200,000. Yet the wildcatter's stated CE for this risk is $0; this is a considerable risk discount. With this assessment in hand, it becomes a simple matter to compare expected utilities: 40 for drilling versus 50 for not drilling. We also should note an equivalent way to explain the decision not to drill. Given his degree of risk aversion, the wildcatter prefers to drill only if the chances of striking oil are greater than .5. Because the actual probability of an oil strike on this site is only .4, he naturally chooses not to drill.

A MORE COMPLICATED OIL-DRILLING PROBLEM Figure 12.8a depicts a more complicated drilling prospect involving four possible monetary outcomes and associated probabilities. In addition, the wildcatter's utility value is listed

FIGURE 12.8

A More Complicated
Drilling Prospect

The decision tree in
part (a) summarizes the
risks of drilling. The
wildcatter chooses to
drill because the
expected utility of this
option exceeds the
utility of not drilling.
Part (b) reduces the
drilling decision tree to
an equivalent tree.

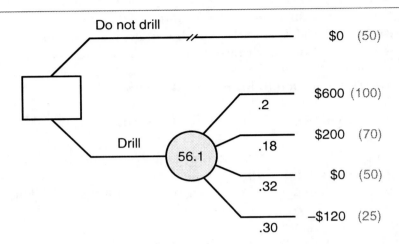

(a) Basic Decision Tree

(b) Reducing the Drill Option to an Equivalent Risk

beside each monetary outcome. He continues to set U(600) = 100 and
U(−200) = 0. Accordingly, U(0) remains 50. The wildcatter also has assessed
U(200) = 70 and U(−120) = 25. In other words, he is indifferent to the options
of $200,000 for certain and a 70-30 risk between the outcomes, $600,000 and
−$200,000. Similarly, he is indifferent to *losing* $120,000 for certain or a 25-75

risk between the same two outcomes.[6] Therefore, these utilities are U(200) = (.7)(100) + (.3)(0) = 70 and U(−120) = (.25)(100) + (.75)(0) = 25.

Now the wildcatter is ready to compare his two options. The expected utility of drilling is (.2)(100) + (.18)(70) + (.32)(50) + (.3)(25) = 56.1. The utility of not drilling is U($0) = 50. Thus, drilling offers the higher expected utility and should be elected.[7]

WHY THE EXPECTED-UTILITY METHOD WORKS   The preceding discussion shows how the expected-utility rule works. It is also worth checking *why* it works. Figure 12.8b demonstrates the reasoning behind the expected-utility rule. Beside each monetary outcome is listed an equivalent (in terms of preference) risk over the best and worst outcomes. By his own admission, the wildcatter is indifferent to a given monetary outcome versus the equivalent risk. Therefore, we can substitute the equivalent risk for each monetary outcome in the decision tree. Substituting equivalent risks will not change how the wildcatter feels about the drill option. (This assumption usually is called the *substitution principle.*) We make the substitution by (mentally) deleting the monetary outcome and, in its place, connecting the equivalent risk to the branch tip. Although the decision tree looks very bushy, the substitution has an important implication: Now the only outcomes in the tree are $600,000 and −$200,000—the best and worst outcomes. If we add up the *total* probability of obtaining $600,000, we obtain the reduced tree on the right. The probability is computed as

$$(.2)(1.0) + (.18)(.7) + (.32)(.5) + (.30)(.25) = .561.$$

(Note that four branch paths on the tree end in $600,000. Each path involves a pair of chance branches, so we use the product rule for probabilities.) Thus, the actual drilling risk is equivalent (has been reduced) to a simpler risk offering a .561 chance at $600,000 and a .439 chance at −$200,000.

Now the wildcatter's decision is straightforward: Drilling is preferred to not drilling because, by his own admission, the wildcatter rates $0 for certain as equivalent to a .5 chance of the best outcome, and this is less than the .561 equivalent chance offered by drilling. We have gone to some trouble to see through the logic of the wildcatter's choice. But notice that applying the

---

[6]Notice that −$200,000 is not an actual drilling outcome. (The worst actual outcome is −$120,000.) However, this fact makes no substantive difference in assigning utilities. The wildcatter is free to assign any outcome as the lowest or "zero-utility" value so long as this monetary outcome is lower than all actual outcomes.

[7]We note in passing that the original drilling site and the second drilling site have identical expected profits: $120,000. (Check the expected value of the second site.) Loosely speaking, the original site is more risky than the second. (It has a greater upside potential as well as greater downside risk.) Here the risk-averse wildcatter rejects the first site while choosing to drill the second.

expected-utility rule determines the decision in *exactly* the same way (albeit more compactly). We found the expected utility of drilling to be 56.1. Since this is greater than the utility of not drilling (50), drilling is the better option. Henceforth we can apply the expected-utility rule with confidence that it properly evaluates the relative risks of different courses of action.

Expected Utility and Risk Aversion

Figure 12.9 shows the wildcatter's utility curve over a range of monetary outcomes. This curve is constructed by plotting utilities for particular monetary values and then drawing a smooth curve through those points. As pictured, the utility curve is concave, that is, becomes less and less steep. The concavity of the curve reflects the wildcatter's risk aversion. To see this, consider a simple two-outcome risk—say, a 50-50 chance of $600,000 or −$200,000. By

FIGURE 12.9

The Wildcatter's
Utility Curve

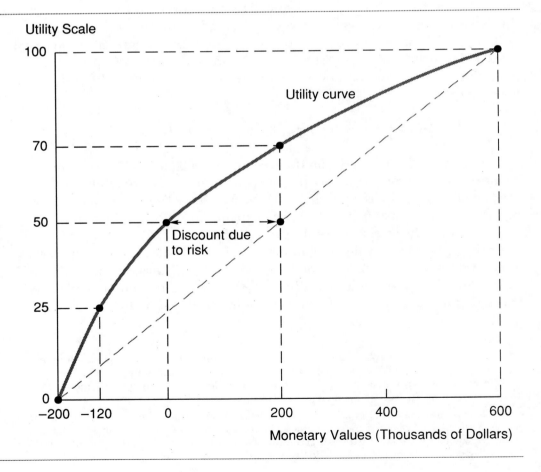

definition, the expected utility of this risk is $(.5)(100) + (.5)(0) = 50$. Pinpoint 50 on the vertical utility scale, read over to the curve, and then read down to the certainty equivalent value. As we saw earlier, this is $0. Now, instead of reading off the curve at $U = 50$, read over to the dashed line connecting the endpoints of the curve. Reading down, we arrive at the monetary value $200,000. This is exactly the expected value of the risky prospect: $(.5)(600) + (.5)(-200) = \$200$ thousand. The point is that the expected value of any risky prospect always lies along a straight-line utility curve. *A risk-neutral manager has a linear utility graph.* In fact, the horizontal gap between the CE (read off the curve) and the expected value (read off the line) exactly measures the discount due to risk aversion. For any concave curve, it is always true that the CE falls to the left of (i.e., is lower than) the corresponding expected value.

Figure 12.10 shows three typical utility curves. The concave curve reflects risk aversion, and the linear graph reflects risk neutrality. The third curve is convex, that is, becomes steeper and steeper. It is easy to check that an individual displaying such a curve is risk loving and prefers to bear risk. More precisely, the individual's CE for any risk is greater than (lies to the right of) its expected value.

With the utility graph in hand, the decision maker can supply requisite utility values and routinely evaluate decision trees. Besides assigning utility values to outcomes, the decision maker can use the graph in reverse. For instance, the expected utility of the second oil site (56.1) merits drilling. A direct expression of how much the site is worth to the wildcatter is given by its certainty equivalent. To find the CE, start at a utility of 56.1 in Figure 12.9, read over to the utility curve, and then read down to the corresponding monetary value—in this case, about $50,000. This is the value the wildcatter places on the site. Thus, he would not sell out if offered $30,000 but would do so readily if offered a certain $60,000 (or any sum greater than $50,000).

Consider a 50-50 risk between $600,000 and $0. Check that the expected utility of this risk is 75. Using the utility graph, find the CE of this risk. Compare the risk's CE and its expected value. Why is the gap between the two relatively small?   **CHECK STATION 4**

Once a utility curve has been assessed, the manager can use the expected-utility rule repeatedly and routinely to guide his or her decisions. Each particular decision carries accompanying profits and losses. But what ultimately matters is the impact of the firm's many decisions on its monetary wealth position. As a general rule, it is best to assess a utility function over final monetary wealth. For example, suppose the wildcatter begins the year with $1.8 million. He thinks about the potential range of his realized *wealth* two years from now. (This range depends on the number and riskiness of sites he might explore.) In a worst-case scenario he

FIGURE 12.10

Three Utility Functions

A risk-averse individual (part [a]) has a concave utility function. A risk-neutral individual (part [b]) has a linear utility function. A risk-loving individual (part [c]) has a convex utility function.

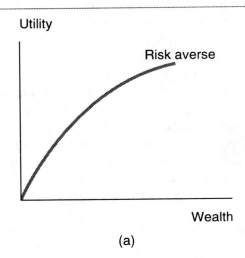

(a)

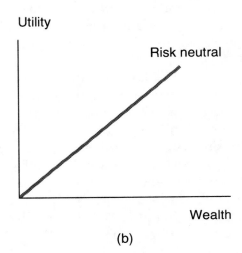

(b)

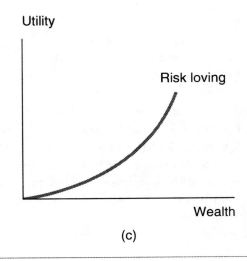

(c)

might end with debts of $1.5 million. In the best case, his wealth might reach $5 million. Thus, he should assess his utility curve over this wide range.

To sum up, the manager must think hard about tolerance for risks over different final wealth positions. In doing so, the manager assesses a utility graph that best represents his or her attitude toward risk.[8] Once the utility curve is in hand, the manager can analyze the problem by means of the usual decision tree after supplying utility values for possible final monetary wealth positions. Finally, the manager averages back the tree and selects the course of action that has the highest expected utility.

To solve the yacht dealer's problem posed at the beginning of the chapter, we supply the following information. The dealer incurs fixed costs amounting to $150,000 per year and obtains yachts from the manufacturer at an average cost of $10,000 each. In a growing economy, the demand for yachts is described by $P = 20 - .05Q$; in a slumping economy, demand is $P = 20 - .1Q$, where P is measured in thousands of dollars.

Gearing Down for a Recession Revisited

Let's start by finding the dealer's profit-maximizing yacht order for each type of economy. Setting MR = MC, we find the dealer's optimal quantity and price to be $Q_G = 100$ and $P_G = \$15,000$ for a growing economy; the resulting profit is $\pi_G = \$350,000$. For the recession economy, we find $Q_R = 50$, $P_R = \$15,000$, and $\pi_R = \$100,000$. Of course, the dealer must place the order now, before knowing the true direction of the economy. Let's suppose the dealer must choose to order a round lot of either 50 or 100 yachts. (Other possibilities are considered in Problem 13 at the end of the chapter.) In light of a 60 percent chance of growth, which order, 50 or 100, has the higher expected profit?

The decision tree in Figure 12.11 answers this question. If 100 yachts are ordered, the dealer's profit is either $350,000 or $-$150,000$. Under slumping demand, the best the dealer can do is sell all 100 yachts at a price of $10,000 each. (At this quantity, revenue is maximized; that is, MR = 0.) If 50 yachts are ordered, the possible outcomes are $225,000 and $100,000. The first outcome occurs when the dealer plans for a recession but is pleasantly surprised by growing demand and sells the 50 yachts at a price of $17,500 each. (Note that this price is obtained from the demand curve for a growing economy.)

Direct calculation shows that ordering 50 yachts generates an expected profit of $175,000, whereas ordering 100 yachts produces only $150,000. Thus, a risk-neutral dealer prefers the smaller (50-yacht) order. (A risk-averse dealer shares this preference, because ordering 50 yachts is less risky than ordering 100.) This result might conflict with one's intuition. After all, a growing economy is more likely than not, and ordering 100 yachts is optimal in this case; therefore, one would judge 100 yachts to be the better choice. What's wrong

---

[8]There are a variety of methods decision makers can use to assess utility curves. One such method is presented in Problem 11 at the end of this chapter. In the process of utility assessment, the manager can gain considerable insight about his or her risk preferences. For instance, a common finding is that decision makers become considerably less risk averse when starting from a high (rather than a low) financial wealth base.

FIGURE 12.11

Ordering Yachts under
Uncertainty

The dealer's better
course of action is
to order 50 yachts.

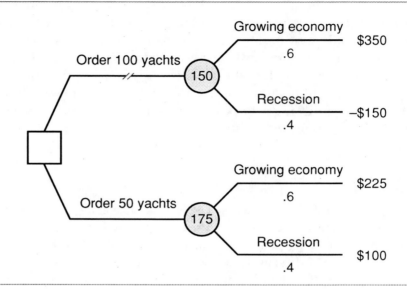

with this reasoning? The key point is that the cost of making a wrong decision differs across the two actions. Taking a large yacht order is very costly (generates a large loss) if a slumping economy causes inventory to be sold at bargain prices. The "cost" of placing a limited order and having too little inventory to accommodate a growing economy is relatively small. (At least the dealer can raise prices.) As a result, the expected profit associated with the small order is significantly greater than that of the large order.

SUMMARY

Decision-Making Principles

1. In choices among risky prospects, sound decision making means assessing the foreseeable good and bad outcomes and their respective chances. Thus, decisions must be judged according to the information available at the time the choice is made, not with the benefit of 20-20 hindsight.

2. When a series of related decisions are to be made, an optimal initial choice depends on foreseeing and making optimal choices for the decisions that follow.

3. To make sound decisions, the manager must also assess his or her own (or the company's) attitude toward risk. A risk-averse decision maker assesses a (certainty equivalent) value for a risky prospect that is smaller than the prospect's expected value.

Nuts and Bolts

1. The decision tree is the basic tool for making decisions under uncertainty. The tree must include branches for (a) all possible actions of the decision maker and (b) all chance events that can affect outcomes. Each chance branch should be assigned a probability. In decisions involving profits and losses, each branch tip should be assigned a monetary value.

2. The decision tree should accurately depict the chronology of the decision setting, that is, the sequence of decision nodes and chance nodes.

3. The expected-value criterion values a risky prospect by taking a weighted average of the possible monetary outcomes, the weight for each outcome being its probability:

$$E(v) = p_1 v_1 + p_2 v_2 + \cdots + p_n v_n.$$

The expected-value criterion is appropriate for a risk-neutral decision maker who is willing to play the averages.

4. More generally, the principle of expected-utility maximization provides a consistent guide to decisions. In applying this principle, the manager constructs a utility graph that portrays his or her attitude toward risk. If the manager is risk neutral, this graph will be linear; if risk averse, it will be concave.

5. Whatever his or her attitude toward risk, the manager "solves" the decision tree by a process of "averaging and eliminating"—starting from the right and moving left. The expected utility (profit) at any chance node is found by averaging, that is, by multiplying branch utilities (or profits) by probabilities. At any decision node, the decision maker selects the alternative having the greatest expected utility (profit). All inferior decision branches are eliminated. The movement from right to left means that the last uncertainties are averaged first and the last decisions are evaluated first.

Questions and Problems

1. a. Average back the decision tree below, supplying expected monetary values for points A through E.
   b. One of your fellow managers is worried that there are no probabilities given for the branches leading from point D. In order to solve the tree, he decides to assign a .5 probability to each branch. Do you agree with this procedure or not? Explain.

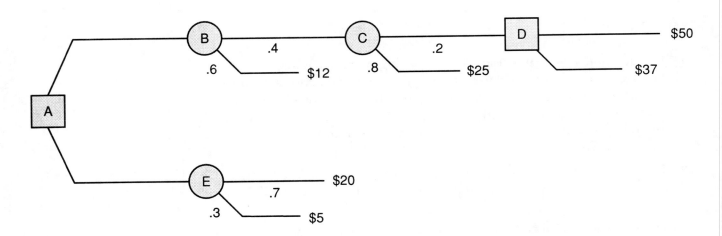

2. In 1976 the parents of a seven-year-old boy sued a New York hospital for $3.5 million. The boy was blinded shortly after he was born two weeks premature. His parents claimed that hospital doctors administered excessive oxygen to the baby and that this caused the blindness. The case went to trial, and just as the jury announced they had reached a verdict, the lawyers for the two sides arrived at an out-of-court settlement of $500,000.
   a. If you were the parents, how would you decide whether to accept the settlement or wait for the jury's decision? What probability assessments would you need to make? Would you have accepted the settlement?
   b. Answer the questions in part (a), taking the hospital's point of view.

3. For five years, a firm has successfully marketed a package of multitask software. Recently, sales have begun to slip because the software is incompatible with a number of popular application programs. Thus, future profits are uncertain. In the software's present form, the firm's managers envision three possible five-year forecasts: maintaining current profits in the neighborhood of $2 million, a slip in profits to $.5 million, or the onset of losses to the tune of −$1 million. The respective probabilities for these outcomes are .2, .5, and .3.

   An alternative strategy is to develop an "open," or compatible, version of the software. This will allow the firm to maintain its market position, but the effort will be costly. Depending on how costly, the firm envisions four possible profit outcomes: $1.5 million, $1.1 million, $.8 million, and $.6 million, with each outcome considered equally likely.
   a. Which course of action produces greater expected profit?
   b. Roughly speaking, which course of action appears to be less risky? If management were risk averse, would this fact change its preferred course of action?

4. A European consortium has spent a considerable amount of time and money developing a new supersonic aircraft. The aircraft gets high marks on all performance measures except noise. In fact, because of the noise, the consortium's management is concerned that the U.S. government may impose restrictions on some of the American airports where the aircraft can land. Management judges a 50-50 chance that there will be some restrictions. Without restrictions, management estimates its (present discounted) profit at $125 million; with restrictions, its profit would be only $25 million. Management must decide now, before knowing the government's decision, whether to redesign parts of the aircraft to solve the noise problem. The cost of the redesign program is $25 million. There is a .6 chance that the redesign program will solve the noise problem (in which case, full landing rights are a certainty) and a .4 chance it will fail.

   Using a decision tree, determine the consortium's best course of action, assuming management is risk neutral.

5. A firm faces uncertain revenues and uncertain costs. Its revenues may be $120,000, $160,000, or $175,000, with probabilities .2, .3, and .5, respectively. Its costs are $150,000 or $170,000 with chances .6 and .4, respectively. (Revenues and costs are independent.)
   a. How many possible profit outcomes exist? Draw a decision tree listing these profit outcomes at the branch tips. Compute the firm's expected profit by folding back the tree. (It does not matter which uncertainty, demand or cost, is resolved first in the tree.)
   b. Without a decision tree, calculate *separately* the firm's expected revenue and expected cost. What is the firm's expected profit? (This result underscores a great computational convenience of the expected-value criterion. Expected profit is equal to expected revenue minus expected cost; that is, expectations can be taken separately.)

6. Global Studios is thinking of producing a megafilm, *Aqua World*, which could be a megahit or a megaflop. Profit is uncertain for two reasons: (1) the cost of producing the film may be low or high, and (2) the market reception for the film may be strong or weak. There is a .5 chance of low costs (C), and a .5 chance of high costs. The probability of strong demand (D) is .4; the probability of weak demand is .6. The studio's profits (in millions of dollars) for the four possible outcomes are shown in the table.

Low C/Strong D	Low C/Weak D	High C/Strong D	High C/Weak D
80	10	0	−70

    a. Should the studio produce the film? Use a decision tree to justify your answer.

    b. The studio is concerned that Kevin Costmore, the film's director and star, might let production costs get out of control. Thus, the studio insists on a clause in the production contract giving it the right to terminate the project after the first $30 million is spent. By this time, the studio *will know for certain* whether total production costs are going to be low (i.e., under control) or high (out of control). How much is this termination clause worth to the studio vis-a-vis the situation in part (a)?

7. In 1996, McDonald's (MD) launched Campaign 55, reducing the prices of its "flag-ship" sandwiches with the objective of regaining market share. Before the launch, suppose MD's management envisioned two possible outcomes: a strong customer response or a weak response. Industry experts were not very optimistic about the campaign. They assessed the probability of a strong response to be .25. MD forecasted an expected profit of $50 million if the response proved to be strong. If the immediate customer response was weak, management believed that all was not lost. If MD could persuade the majority of its franchisees to back and help fund the campaign, the resulting profit would be $20 million. However, if the majority rose up against the campaign, the red ink would fly, and McDonald's profit would be −$100 million. MD considered these two outcomes to be *equally likely*.

    a. Given these assessments, construct a decision tree to determine MD's expected-profit-maximizing course of action.

    b. Suppose that MD has the flexibility to try the campaign but to terminate it if the initial response is weak, thereby limiting its total loss to $20 million. (It must pull the plug before knowing whether the franchisees are for or against the campaign.) Again, construct a decision tree to determine MD's expected-profit-maximizing strategy.

8. Firm A is facing a possible lawsuit by legal firm B. Firm B represents the family of Mr. Smith, who was killed in a motel fire (allegedly caused by faulty wiring). Firm A was the builder of the motel. Firm A has asked its legal team to estimate the likely jury award it will be ordered to pay in court. Expert legal counsel anticipates three possible court outcomes: awards of $1,000,000, $600,000, or $0, with probabilities .2, .5, and .3, respectively. In addition to any awards, firm A's legal expenses associated with fighting the court case are estimated to be $100,000.

    Firm A also has considered the alternative of entering out-of-court settlement negotiations with firm B. Based on the assessments of its lawyers, A envisions the other side holding out for one of two settlement amounts: $900,000 (a high amount) or $400,000 (a more reasonable amount). Each demand is considered equally likely. If presented with one of these settlement demands, firm A is free to accept it (in which case firm B agrees to waive any future right to sue) *or* reject it and take its chances in court. The legal cost of pursuing a settlement (whether or not one is reached) is $50,000.

Determine the settlement or litigation strategy that minimizes firm A's expected total cost (any payment plus legal fees).

*9. Filene's Basement, a Boston-based department store, has a policy of marking down the price of sale items each week that they go unsold. You covet an expensive brand of winter coat that is on sale for $100. In fact, you would be willing to pay as much as $120 for it. Thus, you can buy it now (for a profit of $120 − $100 = $20) or wait until next week, when the price will be reduced to $75 if the coat is still available. The chances of its being available next week are 2/3. If it is available in week 2, you can buy or wait until week 3. There is a 1/2 chance it will be sold between weeks two and three and a 1/2 chance it will be available at a reduced price of $60. Finally, if it is available in week 3, you can buy or wait until week 4. There is a 1/4 chance it still will be available, at a price of $50 (and a 3/4 chance it will be sold in the mean-time). Week four is your last chance to buy before the coat is withdrawn.

a. How long should you wait before buying? Illustrate via a decision tree.

b. Filene's has 120 of these winter coats for sale. What is its expected total revenue from the pricing scheme in part (a)? (One-third of the coats sell in the first week, one-half of the remaining coats in the second week, and so on. All coats in week 4 are sold for $50.)

c. Alternatively, Filene's can set a single price for all coats. Its demand curve is P = 180 − Q. Would it prefer a common-price method or the price-reduction method in part (b)? Explain.

10. As CEO of firm A, you and your management team face the decision of whether to undertake a $200 million R&D effort to create a new mega-medicine. Your research scientists estimate that there is a 40 percent chance of successfully creating the drug. Success means securing a worldwide patent worth $550 million (implying a net profit of $350 million). However, firm B (your main rival) has just announced that it is spending $150 million to pursue development of the same medicine (by a scientific method completely independent of yours). You judge that B's chance of success is 30 percent. Furthermore, if both firms are successful, they will split equally the available worldwide profits ($275 million each) based on separate patents.

a. Given its vast financial resources, firm A is risk neutral. Should firm A undertake the $200 million R&D effort? (Use a decision tree to justify your answer.)

* Starred problems are more challenging.

b. Now suppose that it is feasible for firm A to delay its R&D decision until after the result of B's R&D effort (success or failure) is known. Is it advantageous for firm A to have this "second move"? (Use a decision tree to justify your answer.)

c. Instead, suppose that firm A and firm B can form a joint venture to pursue either or both of their R&D programs. What is the expected profit of simultaneously pursuing *both* programs? *Hint:* Be sure to compute the probability that *both efforts fail* (in which case the firms' combined loss is 200 + 150 = $350 million.). Could the joint venture profitably pursue a *single* program?

11. Consider once again the R&D strategies of the pharmaceutical company. Suppose the company's management is risk averse and has assessed the following utility values for the set of possible outcomes (in millions of dollars).

Outcome	Utility	Outcome	Utility
$200	100	$70	59
180	95	60	55
170	92	50	50
100	71	40	44
80	64	20	32
		0	0

Compute the expected utility of pursuing the biochemical approach alone. Next, find the expected utility of pursuing the biogenetic approach first, then continuing with the biochemical approach if necessary. In light of these calculations, what action do you recommend for the company? How has the company's risk aversion influenced its decision?

12. Consider once again the dilemma facing Consolidated Edison's system operator. To keep things simple, we focus on one of the decisions before him: to shed or not to shed load. Suppose his choices are to shed 50 percent of the load (which will solve the problem at the cost of blacking out 50 percent of New York City) or maintain full load (risking the chance of a total blackout).

a. The operator envisions three possible scenarios by which the system might weather the demand-supply imbalance at full load. The first scenario he considers "improbable," the second is a "long shot," and the third is "somewhat likely." How might he translate these verbal assessments into a round-number estimate of the probability that 100 percent load can be maintained? What probability estimate would you use?

b. Consider the three outcomes: 100 percent power, 50 percent power, and 0 percent power (i.e., a total blackout). It is generally agreed that 0 percent power is "more than twice as bad" as 50 percent power. (With 50 percent power, some semblance of essential services, police, fire, hospitals, and subways, can be maintained; moreover, with a deliberate 50 percent blackout, it is much easier to restore power later.) What does this imply about the utility associated with 50 percent power? (For convenience, assign 100 percent power a utility of 100 and 0 percent power a utility of 0.)

c. Construct a decision tree incorporating your probability estimate from part (a) and your utility values from part (b). What is the operator's best course of action? Explain.

*13. Put yourself in the yacht dealer's shoes. You currently are considering other order quantities in addition to 50 and 100. Find the optimal order quantity, that is, the exact quantity that maximizes your expected profit. (*Hint:* From the two demand curves, find the expected price equation, that is, the expected sale price for any given quantity of yachts. Given this expected-price equation, apply the MR = MC rule to maximize expected profit.)

14. In attempting to quantify its attitude toward risk, top management of the pharmaceutical company has reported certainty equivalent values for a variety of 50-50 risks. These are summarized in the following table.

Outcome of 50-50 Risk	Certainty Equivalent
$200 and $0	$ 50
$200 and $50	112
$50 and $0	13
$200 and $112	153
$112 and $50	70
$50 and $13	28
$112 and $13	50

For instance, the company's CE for a 50-50 risk between $200 million and $0 is $50 million, and so on.

a. Use these responses to determine utility values for each of the monetary values in the second column. (*Hint:* Set $U(\$200) = 100$ and $U(\$0) = 0$. Show that $U(\$50) = 50$, $U(\$112) = 75$, and so on.) Construct a utility graph by plotting points and drawing a smooth curve. (You may wish to check the utility values in Problem 11 against your curve.)

*b. Consider the mathematical utility function $U = 7.1\sqrt{y}$, where U is the utility value corresponding to monetary outcome y. Check that this function is an accurate description of the pharmaceutical company's attitude toward risk. Is the company very risk averse?

Discussion Question   In 1997, after spending more than one-half billion dollars in development and after extensive test marketing, Procter & Gamble in partnership with Frito-Lay and Nabisco launched a series of snack food products made with Olestra, a "no fat" substitute. The campaign launch promised that consumers would enjoy the same flavor of potato chips or crackers, but with zero fat. Although touted as a miracle product, Olestra faced a number of uncertainties: ultimate consumer demand, willingness to pay, and pricing; product cost, quality, and shelf life; regulatory approval; and, most important, medical side effects (stomach cramps and the ugly specter of diarrhea in some consumers).

Use this example and other management cases discussed most every week in the business press to make a list of the many categories of risks faced by managers. In particular lines of business, what categories of risks are the most crucial for the firm's profit? Provide examples of firm strategies to eliminate, mitigate, or insure against these risks.

Suggested References

The following texts are among the best and most complete treatments of decisions under uncertainty.

Brown, R. *Rational Choice and Judgment: Decision Analysis for the Decider.* Hoboken, NJ: John Wiley and Sons, 2005.

Keeney, R. L. "Making Better Decision Makers." *Decision Analysis* (December 2004): 193–204.

Raiffa, H. *Decision Analysis.* New York: McGraw-Hill, 1997 (paperback).

Savage, S. *Decision Making with Insight.* Belmont, CA: Thomson Learning, 2003.

The next two references survey the experimental evidence on decision making under uncertainty.

Camerer, C. "Individual Decision Making" in J. H. Kagel and A. E. Roth (Eds.). *The Handbook of Experimental Economics.* Princeton, NJ: Princeton University Press, 1995.

Davis, D. D., and C. A. Holt. *Experimental Economics,* Chapter 8. Princeton, NJ: Princeton University Press, 1993.

The following reference is the fascinating account of the many risks and decisions involved in Ford's redesign of its popular Taurus model.

Walton, M. *Car Wars.* New York: Norton, 1999 (paperback).

The following two references offer comprehensive guides to decision-tree applications and software:

Keefer, D. L., C. W. Kirkwood, and J. L. Corner. "Perspective on Decision Analysis Applications, 1990–2001." *Decision Analysis* (March 2004): 4–22.

Maxwell, D. T. "Improving Hard Decisions: Decision Analysis Software Survey." *OR/MS Today* (December 2006): 51–61.

Internet sites dealing with decision making under uncertainty include

Sam Savage's wonderful guide to risk at www.analycorp.com/uncertainty/, and

Decision-tree software published by Decision Support Services, www.treeplan.com/.

1. The firm's expected profit under the private contract is (.25)($2) + (.41)($.7) + (.34)(−$.5) = $.617 million. Under the government contract, the firm's expected profit is (.45)($4) + (.55)(−$2.5) = $.425 million. In terms of expected value, the private contract is the better alternative.

2. The executive's expected profit of drilling to *only* 3,000 feet is (.4)(600) + (.6)(−160) = $144 thousand. By quitting after 3,000 feet, the executive takes a loss of $160,000. What is her expected profit it she drills deeper? It is (.2)(400) + (.8)(−250) = −$120 thousand. The expected loss from drilling deeper is smaller than that from quitting. Finally, the expected profit from drilling 5,000 feet (if necessary) is (.4)(600) + (.6)(−120) = $168 thousand. This is the executive's best course of action.

3. We calculate firm A's expected profit from launching the product in two steps. If firm B brings out its own product (probability 60 percent), A's expected profit is (.5)($10) + (.5)(−$30) = −$10 million. If B does not bring out a product (probability 40 percent), A's profit is $20 million. Thus, firm A's overall expected profit is (.4)($20) + (.6)(−$10) = $2 million. To maximize expected profit, the firm should launch the product.

4. The expected utility of a 50-50 risk between $600,000 (U = 100) and $0 (U = 50) is (.5)(100) + (.5)(50) = 75. From Figure 12.9, we see that the CE of this risky prospect is about $220,000. In contrast, the expected value of this risk is $300,000. To determine this expected value using the figure, draw a line between the $600,000 and $0 points on the graph. Then find .75 on the utility scale, read over to the line, and read down to the monetary value of $300,000. Note that the risk discount (the horizontal gap between the utility curve and the dashed line) is smaller here than for the $600,000 versus −$200,000 risk. This illustrates a general principle: The smaller the range of risk, the closer the CE is to the expected value.

**Con Ed
Revisited**

What decision did the Con Ed operator take, and what was the result? The operator initially attempted to reroute power, thinking that only one transmission line was down. He also reduced voltage and called for added emergency power from city generators. About 30 minutes into the emergency, he shed about 25 percent of the system's load. Unfortunately, this proved to be too little, too late. Eleven minutes after load was shed, New York City blacked out completely. It took 25 hours to restore power to all parts of the city.

Index

SECOND EDITION, Excel 2007 Update

MANAGEMENT SCIENCE
The Art of Modeling with Spreadsheets

STEPHEN G. POWELL

Dartmouth College

KENNETH R. BAKER

Dartmouth College

WILEY

John Wiley & Sons, Ltd.

PUBLISHER   *Susan Elbe*
EXECUTIVE EDITOR   *Beth Lang Golub*
SENIOR PRODUCTION EDITOR   *Nicole Repasky*
SENIOR MARKETING MANAGER   *Amy Scholz*
ASSISTANT MARKETING MANAGER   *Carly DeCandia*
SENIOR DESIGNER   *Hope Miller*
SENIOR MEDIA EDITOR   *Allie K. Morris*
SENIOR EDITORIAL ASSISTANT   *Maria Guarascio*
PRODUCTION MANAGEMENT SERVICES   *Thomson Digital*
COVER DESIGN   *David Levy*

This book was set in Times Ten by Thomson Press and printed and bound by Courier/Westford. The cover was printed by Phoenix Color.

This book is printed on acid free paper. ∞

ISBN-13: 978-0-470-39376-5

Printed in the United States of America

10 9 8 7 6 5 4 3 2 1

To Becky and Judy,
for all their encouragement and support

1 Introduction

1.1 MODELS AND MODELING

Modeling is the process of creating a simplified representation of reality and working with this representation in order to understand or control some aspect of the world. While this book is devoted to *mathematical* models, modeling itself is a ubiquitous human activity. In fact, it seems to be one of just a few fundamental ways in which we humans understand our environment.

As an example, a map is one of the most common models we encounter. Maps are models because they simplify reality by leaving out most geographic details in order to highlight the important features we need. A state road map, for example, shows major roads but not minor ones, gives rough locations of cities but not individual addresses, and so on. The map we choose must be appropriate for the need we have: a long trip across several states requires a regional map, while a trip across town requires a detailed street map. In the same way, a good model must be appropriate for the specific uses intended for it. A complex model of the economy is probably not appropriate for pricing an individual product. Similarly, a back-of-the-envelope calculation is likely to be inappropriate for acquiring a multibillion-dollar company.

Models take many different forms: mental, visual, physical, mathematical, and spreadsheet, to name a few. We use mental models constantly to understand the world and to predict the outcomes of our actions. Mental models are informal, but they do allow us to make a quick judgment about the desirability of a particular proposal. For example, mental models come into play in a hiring decision. One manager has a mental model that suggests that hiring older workers is not a good idea because they are slow to adopt new ways; another manager has a mental model that suggests hiring older workers is a good idea because they bring valuable experience to the job. We are often unaware of our own mental models, yet they can have a strong influence on the actions we take, especially when they are the primary basis for decision making.

While everyone uses mental models, some people routinely use other kinds of models in their professional lives. Visual models include maps, as we mentioned earlier. Organization charts are also visual models. They may represent reporting relationships, reveal the locus of authority, suggest major channels of communication, and identify responsibility for personnel decisions. Visual models are used in various sports, when a coach sketches the playing area and represents team members and opponents as X's and O's. Most players probably don't realize that they are using a model for the purposes of understanding and communication.

Physical models are used extensively in engineering to assist in the design of airplanes, ships, and buildings. They are also used in science, as, for example, in depicting the spatial arrangement of amino acids in the DNA helix or the makeup of a chemical compound. Architects use physical models to show how a proposed building fits within its surroundings.

Mathematical models take many forms and are used throughout science, engineering, and public policy. For instance, a groundwater model helps determine where flooding is most likely to occur, population models predict the spread of infectious disease, and exposure-assessment models forecast the impact of toxic spills. In other settings, traffic-flow models predict the buildup of highway congestion, fault-tree models help reveal the causes of an accident, and reliability models suggest when equipment may need replacement. Mathematical models can be extremely powerful, especially when they give clear insights into the forces driving a particular outcome.

1.1.1 Why Study Modeling?

What are the benefits of building and using formal models, as opposed to relying on mental models or just "gut feel?" The primary purpose of modeling is to generate *insight*, by which we mean an improved understanding of the situation or problem at hand. While mathematical models consist of numbers and symbols, the real benefit of using them is to make better *decisions*. Better decisions are most often the result of improved understanding, not just the numbers themselves.

Thus, we study modeling primarily because it improves our thinking skills. Modeling is a discipline that provides a structure for problem solving. The fundamental elements of a model—such as parameters, decisions, and outcomes—are useful concepts in all problem solving. Modeling provides examples of clear and logical analysis and helps raise the level of our thinking.

Modeling also helps improve our quantitative reasoning skills. Building a model demands care with units and with orders of magnitude, and it teaches the importance of numeracy. Many people are cautious about quantitative analysis because they do not trust their own quantitative skills. In the best cases, a well-structured modeling experience can help such people overcome their fears, build solid quantitative skills, and improve their performance in a business world that demands (and rewards) these skills.

Any model is a laboratory in which we can experiment and learn. An effective modeler needs to develop an open, inquiring frame of mind to go along with the necessary technical skills. Just as a scientist uses the laboratory to test ideas, hypotheses, and theories, a business analyst can use a model to test the implications of alternative courses of action and develop not only a recommended decision but, equally important, the rationale for why that decision is preferred. The easy-to-understand rationale behind the recommendation often comes from insights the analyst has discovered while testing a model.

1.1.2 Models in Business

Given the widespread use of mathematical models in science and engineering, it is not surprising to find that they are also widely used in the business world. We refer to people who routinely build and analyze formal models in their professional lives as **business analysts**. In our years of training managers and management students, we have found that strong modeling skills are particularly important for consultants, as well as for financial analysts, marketing researchers, entrepreneurs, and others who face challenging business decisions of real economic consequence. Practicing business analysts and students intending to become business analysts are the intended audience for this book.

Just as there are many types of models in science, engineering, public policy, and other domains outside of business, many different types of models are used in business. We distinguish here four model types that exemplify different levels of interaction with and participation by the people who use the models:

- **One-time decision models**
- **Decision-support models**
- **Models embedded in computer systems**
- **Models used in business education**

Many of the models business analysts create are used in one-time decision problems. A corporate valuation model, for example, might be used intensively during merger negotiations but never thereafter. In other situations, a one-time model might be created to evaluate the profit impact of a promotion campaign, or to help select a health insurance provider, or to structure the terms of a supply contract. One-time models are usually built by decision makers themselves, frequently under time pressure. Managerial judgment is often used as a substitute for empirical data in such models, owing to time constraints and data limitations. Most importantly, this type of model involves the user intensively, because the model is usually tailored to a particular decision-making need. One major benefit of studying modeling is to gain skills in building and using one-time models effectively.

Decision-support systems are computer systems that tie together models, data, analysis tools, and presentation tools into a single integrated package. These systems are intended for repeated use, either by executives themselves or by their analytic staff. Decision-support systems are used in research and development planning at pharmaceutical firms, pricing decisions at oil companies, and product-line profitability analysis at manufacturing firms, to cite just a few examples. Decision-support systems are usually built and maintained by information systems personnel, but they represent the routine use of what were once one-time decision models. After a one-time model becomes established, it can be adapted for broader and more frequent use in the organization. Thus, the models within decision-support systems may initially be developed by managers and business analysts, but later streamlined by information systems staff for a less intensive level of human interaction. An additional benefit of studying modeling is to recognize possible improvements in the design and operation of decision-support systems.

Embedded models are those contained within computer systems that perform routine, repeated tasks with little or no human involvement. Many inventory replenishment decisions are made by automated computer systems. Loan payments on auto leases or prices for stock options are also determined by automated systems. Routine real estate appraisals may also be largely automated. In these cases, the models themselves are somewhat hidden in the software. Many users of embedded models are not aware of the underlying models; they simply assume that the "system" knows how to make the right calculations. An ancillary benefit of studying modeling is to become more aware, and perhaps more questioning, of these embedded models.

1.1.3 Models in Business Education

Models are useful not only in the business world, but also in the academic world where business analysts are educated. The modern business curriculum is heavily dependent on models for delivering basic concepts as well as for providing numerical results. An introductory course in Finance might include an option-pricing model, a cash-management model, and the classic portfolio model. A basic Marketing course might include demand curves for pricing analysis, a diffusion model for new-product penetration, and clustering models for market segmentation. In Operations Management, we might encounter inventory models for stock control, allocation models for scheduling production, and the newsvendor model for trading off shortage and surplus outcomes. Both micro- and macroeconomics are taught almost exclusively through models. Aggregate supply-and-demand curves are models, as are production functions.

Most of the models used in education are highly simplified, or *stylized*, in order to preserve clarity. Stylized models are frequently used to provide insight into qualitative phenomena, not necessarily to calculate precise numerical results. In this book, we frequently use models from business education as examples, so that we can combine learning about business with learning about models. In fact, the tools presented in this book can be used throughout the curriculum to better understand the various functional areas of business.

1.1.4 Benefits of Business Models

Modeling can benefit business decision making in a variety of ways.

- Modeling allows us to make inexpensive errors. Wind-tunnel tests are used in airplane design partly because if every potential wing design had to be built into a full-scale aircraft and flown by a pilot, we would lose far too many pilots. In a similar way, we can propose ideas and test them in a model, without having to suffer the consequences of bad ideas in the real world.

- Modeling allows us to explore the impossible. Many companies have policies, procedures, or habits that prevent them from making certain choices. Sometimes these habits prevent them from discovering better ways of doing business. Modeling can be used to explore these "impossible" alternatives and to help convince the skeptics to try a different approach.

- Modeling can improve business intuition. As we have said, a model is a laboratory in which we perform experiments. We can usually learn faster from laboratory experiments than from experience in the real world. With a model, we can try thousands of combinations that would take many years to test in the real world. We can also try extreme ideas that would be too risky to test in the real world. And we can learn about how the world works by simulating a hundred years of experience, all in a few minutes.

- Modeling provides information in a timely manner. For example, while a survey could be used to determine the potential demand for a product, effective modeling can often give useful bounds on the likely range of demand in far less time.

- Finally, modeling can reduce costs. Data collection is often expensive and time-consuming. An effective modeler may be able to provide the same level of information at much lower cost.

Even among those who do not build models, skill in working with models is very important. Most business students eventually find themselves on a team charged with recommending a course of action. If these teams do not build models themselves, they often work with internal or external consultants who do. Experience in building and analyzing models is, in our minds, the best training for working effectively on problem-solving teams. People who have not actually built a few models themselves often accept model results blindly or become intimidated by the modeling process. A well-trained analyst not only appreciates the power of modeling but also remains skeptical of models as panaceas.

We believe that modeling skills are useful to a very broad range of business-people, from junior analysts without a business degree to senior vice presidents who do their own analysis. Many recent graduates have only a superficial knowledge of these tools because their education emphasized passive consumption of other people's models rather than active model building. Thus, there is considerable potential even among master's-level graduates to improve their modeling skills so that they can become more capable of carrying out independent analyses of important decisions. The only absolute prerequisite for using this book and enhancing that skill is a desire to use logical, analytic methods to reach a higher level of understanding in the decision-making world.

1.2 THE ROLE OF SPREADSHEETS

Because spreadsheets are the principal vehicle for modeling in business, spreadsheet models are the major type we deal with in this book. Spreadsheet models are also mathematical models, but, for many people, spreadsheet mathematics is more accessible than algebra or calculus. Spreadsheet models do have limitations, of course, but they allow us to build more detailed and more complex models than traditional mathematics allows. They also have the advantage of being pervasive in business analysis. Finally, the spreadsheet format corresponds nicely to the form of accounting statements that are used for business communication; in fact, the word "spreadsheet" originates in accounting and only recently has come to mean the electronic spreadsheet.

It has been said that the spreadsheet is the *second best* way to do many kinds of analysis and is therefore the *best* way to do most modeling. In other words, for any one modeling task, a more powerful, flexible, and sophisticated software tool is almost certainly available. In this sense, the spreadsheet is the Swiss Army knife of business analysis. Most business analysts lack the time, money, and knowledge to learn and use a different software tool for each problem that arises, just as most of us cannot afford to carry around a complete toolbox to handle the occasional screw we need to tighten. The practical alternative is to use the spreadsheet (and occasionally one of its sophisticated add-ins) to perform most modeling tasks. An effective modeler will, of course, have a sense for the limitations of a spreadsheet and will know when to use a more powerful tool.

Despite its limitations, the electronic spreadsheet represents a breakthrough technology for practical modeling. Prior to the 1980s, modeling was performed only by specialists using demanding software on expensive hardware. This meant that only the most critical business problems could be analyzed using models, because only these problems justified the large budgets and long time commitments required to build, debug, and apply the models of the day. This situation has changed dramatically in the past 15 years or so. First the personal computer, then the spreadsheet, and recently the arrival of add-ins for specialized analyses have put tremendous analytical power at the hands of anyone who can afford a laptop and some training. In fact, we believe the 1990s will come to be seen as the dawn of the "end-user modeling" era. End-user modelers are analysts who are not specialists in modeling, but who can create an effective spreadsheet and manipulate it for insight. The problems that end-user modelers can solve are typically not the multibillion-dollar, multiyear variety; those are still the preserve of functional-area specialists and sophisticated computer scientists. Rather, the end user can apply modeling effectively to hundreds of important but smaller-scale situations that in the past would not have benefited from this approach. We provide many illustrations throughout this book.

Spreadsheet skills themselves are now in high demand in many jobs, although experts in Excel may not be skilled modelers. In our recent survey of MBAs from the Tuck School of Business (available at http://mba.tuck.dartmouth.edu/spreadsheet/), we found that 77 percent said that spreadsheets were either "very important" or "critical" in their work. Good training in spreadsheet modeling, in what we call **spreadsheet engineering**, is valuable because it can dramatically improve both the efficiency and effectiveness with which the analyst uses spreadsheets.

1.2.1 Risks of Spreadsheet Use

Countless companies and individuals rely on spreadsheets every day. Most users assume their spreadsheet models are error-free. However, the available evidence suggests just the opposite: many, perhaps most, spreadsheets contain internal errors, and more errors are introduced as these spreadsheets are used and modified. Given this evidence, and the tremendous risks of relying on flawed spreadsheet models, it is critically important to learn how to create spreadsheets that are as close to error-free as possible and to use spreadsheets in a disciplined way to avoid mistakes.

It is rare to read press reports on problems arising from erroneous spreadsheets. Most companies do not readily admit to these kinds of mistakes. However, the few reports that have surfaced are instructive. The European Spreadsheet Risks Interest Group (EUSPRIG) maintains a website (http://www.eusprig.org/stories.htm) that currently documents dozens of verified stories about spreadsheet errors that have had a quantifiable impact on the organization. Here is just a small sample:

- Some candidates for police officer jobs are told they passed the test when in fact they have failed. Reason: improper sorting of the spreadsheet.
- An energy company overcharges consumers between $200 million and $1 billion. Reason: careless naming of spreadsheet files.
- A think-tank reports that only 11 percent of a local population has at least a bachelor's degree when in fact the figure is 20 percent. Reason: a copy-and-paste error in a spreadsheet.
- Misstated earnings lead the stock price of an online retailer to fall 25 percent in a day and the CEO to resign. Reason: a single erroneous numerical input in a spreadsheet.
- A school loses £30,000 because its budget is underestimated. Reason: numbers entered as text in a spreadsheet.
- The Business Council reports that its members forecast slow growth for the coming year when their outlook is actually quite optimistic. Reason: the spreadsheet shifted, so the wrong numbers appeared in the wrong columns.
- Benefits of unbundling telecommunication services are understated by $50 million. Reason: incorrect references in a spreadsheet formula.

These cases suggest that spreadsheets can lead to costly errors in a variety of ways. But are spreadsheets themselves properly *built* in the first place? Apparently not, at least according to the evidence cited by Ray Panko. He summarizes the results of seven field audits involving 367 real-world spreadsheets. Overall, 24 percent were found to contain material errors. Considering only the more recent studies, 91 percent of the 54 spreadsheets tested contained errors, presumably because our ability to find errors has improved.[1] This evidence serves notice that errors in spreadsheets are rampant and insidious.

Why are errors in spreadsheets so common? Traditional computer programming, which is much older than spreadsheet programming and carried out largely by trained professionals, typically uses elaborate and formalized development methods. One aspect of these methods is **code inspection**, which involves a line-by-line audit of finished computer code by a separate team from the one that originally created the code. A typical code inspection finds errors in 5 percent of the lines of code written (and tested) by professional programmers. If this error rate characterizes professional programmers, how much more prevalent are errors among end-user programmers building spreadsheets?

Despite this evidence, very few corporations (and even fewer individuals) employ even the most basic design and inspection procedures. These procedures take time and effort, whereas one of the great appeals of spreadsheet modeling is that it is quick and easy for business analysts who are not professional programmers. But this ease of use is a delusion if the spreadsheets that result contain significant errors.

Drawing on various field studies, Panko offers the following summary of the current state of spreadsheet model building.

> Overall, these studies show that many spreadsheets are large, complex, important, and affect many people. Yet [spreadsheet] development tends to be quite informal, and even trivial controls such as cell protection are not used in most cases. In [traditional] programming, code inspection and data testing are needed to reduce error rates after a module is developed. Yet code inspection is very infrequent [in spreadsheet programming], and while data testing is done, it lacks such rigors as the use of out-of-bounds data. *In general, end-user development in spreadsheeting seems to resemble programming practice in the 1950s and 1960s.*[2] [emphasis added], p.19.

---

[1]Panko, R. "What We Know about Spreadsheet Errors," *Journal of End User Computing* 10, (Spring 1998): 15–21.

[2]Ibid.

1.2.2 Challenges for Spreadsheet Users

Spreadsheets represent the ubiquitous software platform of business. Millions of spreadsheet models are used each day to make decisions involving billions of dollars, and thousands of new spreadsheets come into being each day. Given this usage pattern, we might think that spreadsheet engineering is a well-developed discipline and that expertise in spreadsheet modeling can be found in just about any company. Amazingly, the opposite is true.

What is the current state of spreadsheet use by end-user modelers? The evidence available from audits of existing spreadsheets, laboratory experiments, surveys of end users, and field visits suggests that, despite widespread use, the quality with which spreadsheets are engineered generally remains poor. There are four major problem areas:

- End-user spreadsheets frequently have major bugs.
- End users are overconfident about the quality of their own spreadsheets.
- The process that end users employ to create their spreadsheets is inefficient at best and chaotic at worst.
- End users fail to employ the most productive methods for generating insights from their spreadsheets.

We mentioned previously the research studies that have attempted to determine the error rate in existing spreadsheets. These studies range over many companies and many industries. The methods used in these studies differ as well. One major shortcoming of these studies is that only certain types of errors can be identified. In particular, careful audits can uncover errors in specific cells but cannot reveal conceptual errors in the modeling behind the spreadsheet. We might wonder, for example, how many existing spreadsheets were designed to solve the wrong problem. Nevertheless, an estimated error rate of 90 percent is noteworthy. It seems fair to conclude that most spreadsheets in actual use contain bugs.

Our own auditing research, conducted as part of the Spreadsheet Engineering Research Project (http://mba.tuck.dartmouth.edu/spreadsheet/), suggests that errors in individual cells may be only the tip of the iceberg. We have found that a substantial majority of spreadsheets in use contain at least one error. However, some of these errors do not materially change the overall results of the model. But many of the spreadsheets we have studied involve a very high degree of complexity, even when the underlying problem being modeled is rather simple. Complexity arises in many ways:

- Individual cell formulas that are excessively long and involved
- Poorly designed worksheets that are difficult to navigate and understand
- Poorly organized workbooks whose underlying structure is concealed

Spreadsheets that are overly complex and difficult for anyone other than the designer to use, even if they are technically correct, may be the cause of some of the costly mistakes attributed to spreadsheets.

Laboratory experiments have uncovered another disturbing fact about spreadsheet modeling: end users appear to be overconfident about the likelihood of errors in their own spreadsheets. In these experiments, undergraduate volunteers were asked to build a spreadsheet for a well-defined problem. After they were done, the volunteers were given time to review and audit their models. Finally, they were asked to evaluate the likelihood that their model contained one or more bugs. While 18 percent of the subjects thought their models had one or more bugs, the actual proportion proved to be 80 percent. That is, 80 percent of these spreadsheets actually had bugs but only about 18 percent of those who built them suspected they had bugs. This finding of overconfidence is consistent with the findings of other studies: people tend to underestimate the possibility that they might make mistakes. Unfortunately, this overconfidence translates directly into a casual attitude toward spreadsheet design and ultimately into a disturbingly high error rate among spreadsheets in actual use.

Our observations and research into how end users actually construct spreadsheets suggest that the process is often inefficient:

- End users typically do not plan their spreadsheets. Instead, they build them live at the keyboard and are drawn into endless rework. (In our survey of MBA graduates, we found that about 20 percent sketched a spreadsheet on paper first, whereas about 50 percent started by entering data and formulas directly into the computer.)

- End users do not use a conscious prototyping approach, which involves building a series of models starting with the simplest and gradually adding complexity.

- End users rarely spend time debugging their models, unless the model performs in such a counterintuitive manner that it demands intervention.

- End users almost never subject their spreadsheets to review by another person. In general, end users appear to trust that the model they *thought* they had built is actually the model they see on their screens, despite the fact that spreadsheets show only numbers, not the relationships behind the numbers.

- Finally, many end users, even some who are experts in Excel, do not consistently use tools that can help generate the insights that make modeling worthwhile. Excel's Data Table and Goal Seek tools, to cite just two examples, are overlooked by the majority of end users. Without these tools, the end user either fails to ask questions that can provide telling insights, or else wastes time generating results that could be found more easily.

The evidence is strong that the existing state of spreadsheet design and use is generally inadequate. This is one reason we devote a significant portion of this book to spreadsheet engineering. Only with a solid foundation in spreadsheet engineering can the business analyst effectively generate real insights from spreadsheet models.

1.2.3 Background Knowledge for Spreadsheet Modeling

Many people new to modeling fear it because modeling reminds them of painful experiences with mathematics. We do not wish to downplay the essentially mathematical nature of modeling, even modeling using spreadsheets. However, an effective modeler does not need to know any really advanced math. Knowledge of basic algebra (including functions such as the quadratic, exponential, and logarithmic), simple logic (as expressed in an IF statement or the MAX function), and basic probability (distributions and sampling, for example) will usually suffice. When we find it necessary to use any higher math in this book, we provide explanations. But our focus here is less on the mathematical details of models than on the creative process of constructing and using models.

We assume throughout this book that the reader has a basic familiarity with Excel. This includes the ability to build a simple spreadsheet, enter and format text and data, use formulas and simple functions such as SUM, construct graphs, and so on. We do not assume the reader is an expert in Excel, nor do we assume knowledge of the advanced tools we cover, such as Solver and Crystal Ball. We have found that, in many situations, advanced Excel skills are not required for building effective models. And we believe that the main purpose of modeling is to improve the insight of the modeler. Thus, it is appropriate for a modeler with only basic Excel skills to build a model using only basic tools, and it is appropriate for a modeler with advanced skills to draw on advanced tools when needed. We have also found that too much skill in Excel can sometimes distract from the essential modeling tasks, which are almost always more about finding a simple and effective representation of the problem at hand than about finding some Excel trick.

For easy reference we have included two chapters that deal specifically with Excel. In Chapter 3 we give an overview of Excel, from the basics of entering text and data to charting. Chapter 4 presents some advanced Excel skills that are particularly useful to modelers, including range names, advanced formulas and functions, macros, and Visual Basic. We expect most readers to already know Excel to some degree, and to use these chapters as needed to hone specific skills. We believe that, by working through the examples in the book, the reader's Excel skills will improve naturally and painlessly, just as ours have improved over years of building models and teaching modeling to students whose Excel skills often exceeded ours.

1.3 THE REAL WORLD AND THE MODEL WORLD

We stated at the outset that modeling provides a structure for problem solving. It does this through a process of abstraction, in which the essence of the problem is captured in a simplified form. Because of this abstraction process, modeling does not come naturally to most people but must be learned. Because it does not come naturally, it can appear to be artificial and counterintuitive, causing many students of modeling to become uncomfortable with the process. This section attempts to reduce that discomfort by placing modeling in the context of problem solving in the real world.

A model is an abstraction, or simplification, of the real world. It is a laboratory—an artificial environment—in which we can experiment and test ideas without the costs and risks of experimenting with real systems and organizations. Figure 1.1 is a schematic showing how modeling creates an artificial world. We begin in the real world, usually with a messy problem to solve. If we determine that modeling is an appropriate tool, we then move across an invisible boundary into the model world.

In order to move into the model world, we abstract the essential features of the real world, leaving behind all the inessential detail and complexity. We then construct our laboratory by combining our abstractions with specific assumptions and building a model of the essential aspects of the real world. This is the process of **model formulation**. It is an exercise in simplifying the actual situation and capturing its

FIGURE 1.1 The Real World and the Model World

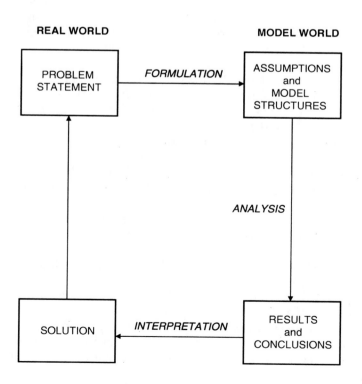

essence, with a specific purpose in mind. The model formulation process typically forces us to confront four features of a model:

- Decisions
- Outcomes
- Structure
- Data

Decisions refers to possible choices, or courses of action, that we might take. These would be controllable variables, such as quantities to buy, manufacture, spend, or sell. (By contrast, uncontrollable variables such as tax rates or the cost of materials are not decision variables.) **Outcomes** refers to the consequences of the decisions—the performance measures we use to evaluate the results of taking action. Examples might include profit, cost, or efficiency. **Structure** refers to the logic and the mathematics that link the elements of our model together. A simple example might be the equation $P = R - C$, in which profit is calculated as the difference between revenue and cost. Another example might be the relationship $F = I + P - S$, in which final inventory is calculated from initial inventory, production, and shipments. Finally, **data** refers to specific numerical assumptions. That may mean actual observations of the real world (often called "raw" or "empirical" data), or it may mean estimates of uncontrollable variables in the problem's environment. Examples might include the interest rate on borrowed funds, the production capacity of a manufacturing facility, or the first-quarter sales for a new product.

Once it is built, we can use the model to test ideas and evaluate solutions. This is a process of **analysis**, in which we apply logic, often with the support of software, to take us from our assumptions and abstractions to a set of derived conclusions. Unlike model formulation, which tends to be mostly an art, analysis is much more of a science. It relies on mathematics and reason in order to explore the implications of our assumptions. This exploration process leads, hopefully, to insights about the problem confronting us. Sometimes, these insights involve an understanding of why one solution is beneficial and another is not; at other times, the insights involve understanding the sources of risk in a particular solution. In another situation, the insights involve identifying the decisions that are most critical to a good result, or identifying the inputs that have the strongest influence on a particular outcome. In each instance, it is crucial to understand that these insights are derived from the *model* world and not from the *real* world. Whether they apply to the real world is another matter entirely and requires managerial judgment.

To make the model insights useful, we must first translate them into the terms of the real world and then communicate them to the actual decision makers involved. Only then do *model* insights turn into useful *managerial* insights. And only then can we begin the process of evaluating solutions in terms of their impact on the real world. This is a process of **interpretation**, and here again, the process is an art. Good modelers can move smoothly back and forth between the model world and the real world, deriving crisp insights from the model, and translating the insights, modifying them as needed, to account for real-world complexities not captured in the model world.

This schematic description of the modeling process highlights some of the reasons it can be a challenge to incorporate modeling into problem solving. Powerful in competent hands, modeling is also somewhat esoteric. It involves deliberate abstraction and simplification of a situation, which appears to many people as a counterproductive exercise. Modeling requires a willingness to temporarily set aside much of the richness of the real world and to operate in the refined and artificial world of models and model insights. It also requires confidence that whatever insights arise in the model world can be translated into useful ideas in the real world. In addition, it requires an ability to mix art with science in order to exploit the modeling process to its full potential. Until we have some experience with this process, we may be resistant and skeptical. And it is always easy to criticize a model as being too simple. Good models are as simple as they can possibly be. But this very simplicity can appear to be a fatal flaw to skeptics. Nevertheless, modeling is one of the most powerful tools in the problem solver's tool kit, simply because there is no more practical way to arrive at the insights modeling can provide.

1.4 LESSONS FROM EXPERT AND NOVICE MODELERS

Perhaps the best way to become a good modeler is to serve an apprenticeship under an expert. Unfortunately, such opportunities are rare. Moreover, experts in all fields find it difficult to express their expertise or to teach it. While narrow, **technical** skills are relatively easy to teach (e.g., how to use the NPV function in Excel), expertise consists largely of **craft** skills that are more difficult to teach (e.g., what to include and exclude from the model). In the arts, there is a tradition of studio training, where a teacher poses artistic challenges to students and then coaches them as they work through the problems on their own. This is one way for students to acquire some of the difficult-to-articulate craft skills of the master. There is no comparable tradition in the mathematical fields; in fact, there is a long-standing belief that modeling cannot be taught but must simply be acquired by experience.

One way to improve modeling skills is to understand what expert and novice modelers actually do when they build and use models. From closely observing experts, we can attempt to articulate a set of modeling best practices. From observing novices we can understand the reasons for their relatively lower level of modeling accomplishment: the blind alleys, counterproductive behaviors, misperceptions, and cognitive limitations that keep them from attaining expert performance. In this section we summarize research studies on both expert and novice modelers.

1.4.1 Expert Modelers

An alternative to an apprenticeship under an expert is to study experts in a laboratory setting. Tom Willemain did this in a series of experiments with 12 expert modelers. He gave each expert a short problem description as it would come from a client and observed the subject working for one hour on the problem. The subjects were asked to think out loud so that their thought processes could be recorded. Willemain's results concerning the "first hour in the life of a model" are highly suggestive of some of the ingredients of good modeling practice.[3]

Willemain was interested in determining the issues to which expert modelers devote attention as they formulate their models. He identified five topics important to modelers:

- Problem context
- Model structure
- Model realization
- Model assessment
- Model implementation

Problem context refers to the situation from which the modeler's problem arises, including the client, the client's view of the problem, and any available facts about the problem. In this activity, the modeler tries to understand the problem statement as provided by the client and to understand the messy situation out of which the problem arises.

Model structure refers to actually building the model itself, including issues such as what type of model to use, where to break the problem into subproblems, and

[3]Thomas R. Willemain, "Insights on Modeling from a Dozen Experts," *Operations Research* 42, No. 2 (1994): 213–222; "Model Formulation: What Experts Think About and When," *Operations Research* 43, No. 6 (1995): 916–932.

how to choose parameters and relationships. In Figure 1.1, this would be the process of moving into the model world, making abstractions and assumptions, and creating an actual model.

Model realization refers to the more detailed activities of fitting the model to available data and calculating results. Here, the focus is on whether the general model structure can actually be implemented with the available data and whether the type of model under development will generate the hoped-for kinds of results. This topic corresponds to the analysis process in Figure 1.1.

Model assessment includes evaluating the model's correctness, feasibility, and acceptability to the client. Determining the correctness of a model involves finding whether the model assumptions correspond well enough to reality. Feasibility refers to whether the client has the resources to implement the developed model, whether sufficient data are available, and whether the model itself will perform as desired. Client acceptability refers to whether the client will understand the model and its results and whether the results will be useful to the client. In this phase, we can imagine the modeler looking from the model world back into the real world and trying to anticipate whether the model under construction will meet the needs of the client.

Finally, **model implementation** refers to working with the client to derive value from the model. This corresponds to the interpretation activity in Figure 1.1.

One of Willemain's interesting observations about his experts was that they frequently switched their attention among these five topics. That is, they did not follow a sequential problem-solving process, but rather moved quickly among the various phases—at one moment considering the problem statement, at another considering whether the necessary data would be available, and at yet another thinking through whether the client could understand and use the model. A second significant finding was that model structure, presumably the heart of a modeler's work, received a relatively small amount of attention (about 60 percent of the effort) when compared to the other four topics. Finally, it turned out that experts often alternated their attention between model structure and model assessment. That is, they would propose some element of model structure and quickly turn to evaluating its impact on model correctness, feasibility, and acceptability. Willemain suggests that the experts treat model structuring as the central task, or backbone, of their work, but they often branch off to examine related issues (data availability, client acceptance, and so on), eventually returning to the central task. In effect, model structuring becomes an organizing principle, or mental focus, around which the related activities can be arrayed.

The overall picture that emerges from this research is one in which craft skills are as essential to the effective modeler as technical skills. An effective modeler must understand the problem context, including the client, or modeling will fail. Similarly, a model that is technically correct but does not provide information the client can use, or does not gain the trust of the client, represents only wasted effort. Experts approach modeling with a general process in mind, but they move fairly quickly among the different activities, creating, testing, and revising constantly as they go. The experts appear to be comfortable with a high degree of ambiguity as they approach the task of structuring a model. They do not rush to a solution, but patiently build tentative models and test them, always being ready to revise and improve.

1.4.2 Novice Modelers

Novices have been studied in many domains, from solving physics problems to playing golf. In general, novice problem solvers can be expected to show certain kinds of counterproductive behaviors. One is that they focus on just one approach to a problem and devote all their time to it, while experts are likely to try many different approaches. Novices also do not evaluate their performance as frequently or as critically as expert problem solvers do. Finally, novices tend to attempt to solve a problem using only the information given in that problem, while experts are more likely to draw on experience with other problems for useful analogies or tools.

In an attempt to better understand how our own students model problems, we conducted an experiment similar in most respects to Willemain's experiment with experts.[4] We audiotaped 28 MBA students while they worked through four ill-structured modeling problems. Thus, this experiment did not focus on building a spreadsheet model for a well-defined problem, as might be assigned in a course for homework, but rather on formulating an approach to an ill-structured problem of the kind that consultants typically encounter. (Some of these problems will be presented in Chapter 2.) The students were given 30 minutes to work on each problem. The task was to begin developing a model that could ultimately be used for forecasting or for analysis of a decision.

We observed five behaviors in our subjects that are not typical of experts and that limit their modeling effectiveness:

- Overreliance on given numerical data
- Use of shortcuts to an answer
- Insufficient use of abstract variables and relationships
- Ineffective self-regulation
- Overuse of brainstorming relative to structured problem solving

In the study, some of the problems included extensive tables of numerical data. In these problems, many subjects devoted their time to examining the data rather than building a general model structure. Having data at hand seemed to block these students from the abstraction process required for effective modeling. In other problems, very little data was provided, and in these cases, some students attempted to "solve" the problem by performing calculations on the given numbers. Again, the data seemed to block the abstraction process. Many subjects complained about the lack of data in problems in which little was given, seeming to believe that data alone could lead to a solution. In general, then, our subjects appear to rely more on data than do experts, who build general model structures and only tangentially ask whether data exist or could be acquired to refine or operationalize their model structures.

Another problematic behavior we observed in our subjects was taking a shortcut to an answer. Where experts would consider various aspects of a problem and try out several different approaches, some students rushed to a conclusion. Some would simply rely on intuition to decide that the proposal they were to evaluate was a good or bad idea. Others would use back-of-the-envelope calculations to come to a conclusion. Still others would claim that the answer could be found by collecting data, or performing marketing research, or asking experts in the industry. (We call this behavior "invoking a magic wand.") All of these approaches seem to avoid the assigned task, which was to structure a *model* for analyzing the problem, not to come to a conclusion.

Expert problem solvers generally use abstract variables and relationships in the early stages of modeling a problem. We saw very little of this in our subjects, who appeared to think predominantly in concrete terms, often using specific numbers. Expert modelers tend to be well trained in formal mathematics, and they naturally think in terms of variables and relationships. Our subjects were generally less well trained in mathematics but tended to have extensive experience with spreadsheets. Their approach to spreadsheet modeling involved minimal abstraction and maximal reliance on numbers. Our subjects did not often write down variables and functions, but they fairly often sketched or talked about a spreadsheet in terms of its row and column headings.

[4]Stephen G. Powell and Thomas R. Willemain, "How Novices Formulate Models. Part I: Qualitative Insights and Implications for Teaching," *Journal of the Operational Research Society*, forthcoming 2007; Thomas R. Willemain and Stephen G. Powell, "How Novices Formulate Models. Part II: A Quantitative Description of Behavior," *Journal of the Operational Research Society*, forthcoming 2007.

As we noted earlier, experts pause frequently during problem solving to evaluate the approach they are taking. They are also willing to try another approach if the current one seems unproductive. By contrast, many of our subjects did little self-evaluation during the experiment. Some focused more on the problem we had given them as a business problem than a modeling problem. So the special features that a model brings to analyzing a situation seemed lost on them. Without a clear goal, a typical subject would launch into a discussion of all the factors that might conceivably influence the problem. Only rarely did we observe a subject stopping and asking whether progress was being made toward a *model*.

Finally, the predominant problem-solving strategy we observed our subjects using could be described as unstructured problem exploration. For example, they would list issues in a rambling and unstructured manner, as if they were brainstorming, without attempting to organize their thoughts in a form that would support modeling. Structured problem solving, as used by experts, seeks to impose an organized plan on the modeling process.

In general our subjects failed to think in modeling terms—that is, by deciding what the outcome of the modeling process was to be and working backwards through variables and assumptions and relationships to the beginning. Instead, they explored a variety of (usually) unrelated aspects of the problem in a discursive manner.

What can a business analyst who wants to improve modeling skills learn from this research? First, expertise takes time and practice to acquire, and the novice should not expect to perform like an expert overnight. However, some expert behaviors are worth imitating from the start. Don't look for quick answers to the problem at hand, and don't expect the data to answer the problem for you. Rather, use what you know to build a logical structure of relationships. Use whatever language you are most comfortable with (algebra, a spreadsheet, a sketch), but work to develop your ability to abstract the essential features of the situation from the details and the numbers. Keep an open mind, try different approaches, and evaluate your work often. Most important, look for opportunities to use modeling, and constantly upgrade both your technical and craft skills.

1.5 ORGANIZATION OF THE BOOK

This book is organized around the three skills we believe business analysts most need in their modeling work:

- Spreadsheet engineering
- Modeling craft
- Management science and statistics

Spreadsheet engineering deals with how to design, build, test, and perform analysis with a spreadsheet model. Modeling craft refers to the nontechnical but critical skills that an expert modeler employs, such as abstracting the essential features of a situation in a model, debugging a model effectively, and translating model results into managerial insights. Management science covers optimization and simulation. Along with statistics, a basic knowledge of these tools is important for the well-rounded analyst. Figure 1.2 provides an overview of the organization of the book.

The heart of this book is the material on building spreadsheet models and using them to analyze decisions. However, before the analyst can build spreadsheet models successfully, certain broader skills are needed. Therefore, we begin in Chapter 2 with a discussion of the various contexts in which modeling is carried out and the role that modeling plays in a structured problem-solving process. We also introduce in this chapter the craft aspects of modeling—the tricks of the trade that experienced and successful modelers employ. These are not Excel tricks, but rather approaches to dealing with the ambiguities of analysis using models. Chapters 3 and 4 provide the basic and advanced Excel skills needed by effective modelers. Chapters 5 and 6 provide the essential tools of spreadsheet engineering. Along with Chapters 1 and 2,

FIGURE 1.2   Outline of the
Book

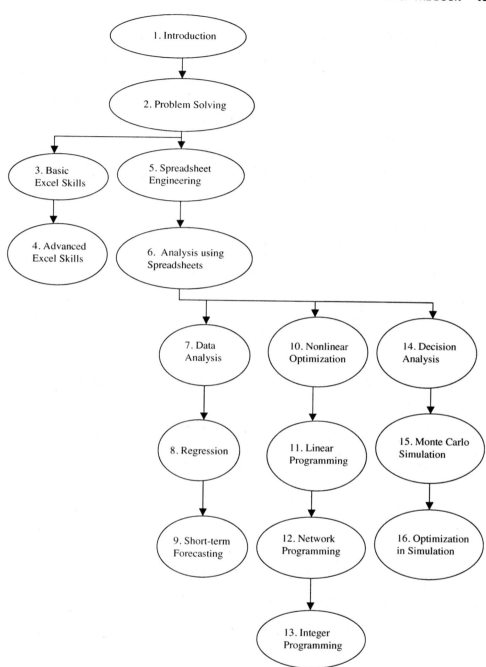

these chapters should be studied by all readers. Chapter 5 provides guidelines for designing effective spreadsheets and workbooks, while Chapter 6 provides an over-view of various tools available for analyzing spreadsheet models. Chapters 7 through 16 cover the advanced tools of the management scientist and their spreadsheet implementations. Chapters 7–9 deal with data analysis, regression, and forecasting. Chapters 10–13 explore optimization, and Chapters 15 and 16 cover simulation. Numerous examples throughout the text illustrate good modeling technique, and most chapters contain exercises for practice. Many of these exercises relate to a set of case problems, which are included at the end of the book. These problems provide an opportunity to gain experience with realistic modeling problems that build on concepts in different chapters.

1.6 SUMMARY

The following statements summarize the principles on which this book is based.

• *Modeling is a necessary skill for every business analyst.*
Models are encountered frequently in business education and in the business world. Furthermore, analysts are capable of formulating their own models.

• *Spreadsheets are the modeling platform of choice.*
The wide acceptance and flexibility of the spreadsheet make it the modeling platform of choice for most business situations. Since familiarity with spreadsheets is required for almost everyone in business, the basis for learning spreadsheet-based modeling is already in place.

• *Basic spreadsheet modeling skills are an essential foundation.*
While basic knowledge about spreadsheets is usually assumed in business, spreadsheet skills and spreadsheet modeling skills are not the same. Effective education in business modeling begins with training in how to use a spreadsheet to build and analyze models.

• *End-user modeling is cost-effective.*
In an ever-growing range of situations, well-trained business analysts can build their own models without relying on consultants or experts.

• *Craft skills are essential to the effective modeler.*
Craft skills are the mark of an expert in any field. The craft skills of modeling must gradually be refined through experience, but the process can be expedited by identifying and discussing them and by providing opportunities to practice their use.

• *Analysts can learn the required modeling skills.*
Modeling skills do not involve complex mathematics or arcane concepts. Any motivated analyst can learn the basics of good modeling and apply this knowledge on the job.

• *Management science/statistics are important advanced tools.*
Extensive knowledge of these tools is not required of most business analysts; however, solid knowledge of the fundamentals can turn an average modeler into a power modeler.

SUGGESTED READINGS

Many books are available on Excel, although most of them cover its vast array of features without isolating those of particular relevance for the business analyst. In the chapters on Excel, we provide several references to books and other materials for learning basic Excel skills. A working business analyst should probably own at least one Excel guide as a reference book. Two such references are:

Stinson, C., and M. Dodge. 2003. *Microsoft Excel Version 2003 Inside Out.* Bellingham, WA: Microsoft Press.
Walkenbach, J. 2003. *Excel 2003 Bible.* New York: John Wiley and Sons.

Several textbooks present the tools of management science using spreadsheets. We recommend these for a more detailed treatment of management science than we provide here.

Ragsdale, C. 2001. *Spreadsheet Modeling and Decision Analysis.* 4th ed. Cincinnati: South-Western.
Winston, W., and C. Albright. 2004. *Practical Management Science.* 2d ed. Pacific Grove, CA: Duxbury.

The standard reference on the mathematics of management science is:

Hillier, F., and G. Lieberman. 2004. *Introduction to Operations Research.* 8th ed. Oakland, CA: McGraw-Hill.

While this text does not rely on spreadsheets, it does provide in a relatively accessible form the methods behind much of the management science we present in this book.

The following two references are more narrowly focused books that apply spreadsheet modeling to specific business disciplines.

Benninga, S. 2000. *Financial Modeling.* 2d ed. Cambridge, MA: MIT Press.
Lilien, G., and A. Rangaswamy. 2004. *Marketing Engineering.* State College, PA: Decision Pro.

Finally, for stimulating books on modeling and problem solving, we recommend:

Casti, J. 1997. *Would-be Worlds: How Simulation Is Changing the Frontiers of Science.* New York: John Wiley and Sons.
Koomey, J. D. 2001. *Turning Numbers into Knowledge: Mastering the Art of Problem Solving.* Oakland, CA: Analytics Press.
Starfield, A., K. Smith, and A. Bleloch. 1990. *How to Model It.* New York: McGraw-Hill.

2 Modeling in a Problem-Solving Framework

2.1 INTRODUCTION

Modeling is an approach that helps us develop a better understanding of business situations. As a result, it helps us make better decisions. Thus, we don't view modeling as an end in itself, but rather as part of the broader process of business decision making. In this chapter, we discuss how modeling contributes to that broader process. We refer to the decision-making process generically as a **problem-solving** process, although specific instances could involve making forecasts, evaluating business opportunities, or allocating resources.

Any successful problem-solving process begins with recognition of a problem and ends with implementation of a proposed solution. All the work that comes between these two points is the problem-solving process. In some cases, this process is highly structured and planned, perhaps involving a large team working over several months; in other cases, it is informal and unstructured, perhaps involving only one person for a couple of hours. Modeling is just one of many tools or strategies that can be used within problem solving. An effective problem solver knows when and how to use modeling effectively within the broader context of problem solving.

Modelers can play different roles in the problem-solving process. Primarily, these roles are:

- End user
- Team member
- Independent consultant

When the entire team consists of one person, then problem owner (or client) and modeler are one and the same. We refer to this role as the **end-user** modeler. The end user is often a small-business owner or an entrepreneur, who has no staff and no budget for consultants. In large firms, many managers are also end users at times, when there is no time to brief the staff or bring in consultants, or when the problem is too sensitive to share with anyone else. The end user carries out all of the activities in modeling: identifying a problem worthy of attention, developing a model, using the model to develop insights and practical solutions, and implementing the results. There is an enormous untapped potential for end-user modeling, because there are so many relatively small problems for which modeling can provide insight, and because there are so many end users who have (or can acquire) the spreadsheet and modeling skills necessary to develop useful models.

In addition to the end-user role, modelers are often assigned to the role of **team member** on an internal committee or task force. In many cases, the problem-solving process may have begun before the committee was formed, and the modeler may or may not have been part of that process. Although chosen for expertise in modeling, the team-member modeler's role also requires good inter-personal and communication skills. A critical part of the work is communicating with nonmodelers on the team about the assumptions that go into the model and the intuition behind the model's results. Of course, the team-member modeler must also have the necessary technical skills to apply modeling successfully, but communication skills are more important for the team-member than for the end-user modeler.

A third role for the modeler is that of **independent consultant**. This role differs from the role of team member because there is usually a client—someone who identifies the problem and ultimately manages the implementation of any solution. The role of consultant modeler also requires excellent communication and interpersonal skills. Despite being an organizational outsider, the consultant modeler must understand the client's problem deeply and translate the client's understanding of the problem into modeling terms. This role also requires the ability to translate model insights back into a language the client can understand, so that the client can implement a solution.

As we build our formal modeling skills we need to have an overall concept of the problem-solving process and where modeling fits into that process. Thus, we begin this chapter by describing a widely used problem-solving process and the role that formal modeling plays in this process.

Influence charts, which are the second topic in this chapter, help to bridge the gap between a qualitative understanding of a fuzzy problem and a formal model with numbers and equations. Influence charts help the modeler construct a logical structure within which to represent the parameters, relationships, and outcomes of a model without excessive detail or precision. They are an essential tool for both novice and expert modelers.

The final topic of the chapter is the craft of modeling. The technical side of modeling concerns the specific and well-defined tasks necessary to build a model, such as how to use an IF statement. The craft side of modeling, on the other hand, represents the artistry that experts bring to bear. Craft skills are harder to learn than technical skills, but they are just as important for successful modeling. We describe some of the most important craft skills and discuss the role these skills play in modeling. The modeling cases that appear later in the book provide opportunities to practice these skills in ill-structured problem situations.

2.2   THE PROBLEM-SOLVING PROCESS

While problem solving is an almost universal aspect of life, very few individuals follow a structured approach to it. This could indicate that effective problem solving is instinctive and intuitive and that the only way to improve in this area is through experience. We do not, however, subscribe to this point of view. In our experience, some degree of conscious attention to the process pays off in improved results and efficiency, even for experienced modelers and managers. This is especially true for problem-solving teams, where intuitive methods often fail because what is intuitive to one member makes no sense to another. While the end-user modeler can perhaps get by with shortcuts, team members and independent consultants are more effective when they carefully manage the problem-solving process.

The problem-solving process is often described as a sequential, step-by-step procedure. While this makes for easy description, there is, in fact, no simple plan that represents the universal problem-solving process. Moreover, when people look back on their own problem-solving activities, they tend to remember more structure than was really there. Thus, a sequential description of problem solving should not be taken literally. As we described in the previous chapter, even modeling experts appear to jump around from one aspect of a problem to another as they attempt to formulate models. Any process must be flexible enough to accommodate different work styles, unexpected discoveries and disappointments, and inevitable fluctuations in effort and creativity. The process we discuss later in this chapter helps focus attention on some of the critical aspects of effective problem solving, without providing a straitjacket that will cramp a problem solver's style. Our description comes from what experts tell us, from what we observe in our students, and from what we have experienced in our own problem solving.

2.2.1 Some Key Terms

We begin by making an important distinction between a **problem** and a **mess**. On the one hand, a mess is a morass of unsettling symptoms, causes, data, pressures, shortfalls, and opportunities. A problem, on the other hand, is a well-defined situation that is capable of resolution. Why is the concept of a mess important in problem solving? Simply because problems do not come to us fully defined and labeled. Rather, we operate in a world full of confusion: causes and effects are muddled, data exist but there is little relevant information, problematic shortfalls or inadequacies appear alongside attractive opportunities, and so on. Where are the problems in this mess? Identifying a problem in the mess is itself a creative act that will do much to determine the quality of any solutions we propose. In most situations, a number of problems could be extracted from a given mess. Which one we choose depends on our understanding of the situation and on our insight into where analysis and action could be most effective. Our first piece of advice on problem solving, then, is to recognize that defining the problem to be solved is a critical step in the process— one that deserves considerable attention.

One way to focus attention on the problem definition is to use a problem statement of the form "In what ways might ..." Imagine the situation facing a manufacturing company whose costs are rising sharply due to increasing wages. Here are some possible problem statements the company could use:

- In what ways might we increase the productivity of our workforce?
- In what ways might we reduce the labor content of our products?
- In what ways might we shift our manufacturing to lower-cost regions?
- In what ways might we increase revenues to keep pace with costs?
- In what ways might we change our product line to maintain profit margins?

This is just a sample of the problem statements that could apply to a given situation. It should be obvious that the approach taken to resolving the "problem" will be very different depending on which of these statements is adopted. Our advice is to pay close attention to the problem definition, take any problem definition as tentative, and prepare to alter it if evidence suggests that a different problem statement would be more effective.

The appropriate problem-solving approach depends, of course, on the problem at hand. Some problems are simple and require only a rudimentary approach, while others are complex and require a much more elaborate and thought-out process. It is useful to distinguish **well-structured** from **ill-structured problems**.

Well-structured problems have the following characteristics:

- The objectives of the analysis are clear.
- The assumptions that must be made are obvious.
- All the necessary data are readily available.
- The logical structure behind the analysis is well understood.

Algebra problems are typically well-structured problems. Consider this problem: Solve the following system of equations for X and Y:

$$3X + 4Y = 18$$
$$9X + Y = 21$$

The solution to this problem consists of the values $X = 2$, $Y = 3$. Not only can we easily demonstrate that these values actually do solve the problem, but we can prove that this is the only solution to the problem. Once we have found these values for X and Y, there is nothing more to be said about the problem.

By contrast, in a typical ill-structured problem, to varying degrees, the objectives, assumptions, data, and structure of the problem are all unclear. Here are several examples of ill-defined problems:

- Should the Red Cross institute a policy of paying for blood donations?
- Should Boeing's next major commercial airliner be a small supersonic jet or a slower jumbo jet?
- Should an advertiser spend more money on the creative aspects of an ad campaign or on the delivery of the ad?
- How much should a midcareer executive save out of current income toward retirement?

Unlike well-structured problems, ill-structured problems require *exploration* more than *solution*. Exploring a problem involves formulating hypotheses, making assumptions, building simple models, and deriving tentative conclusions, all with an inquiring mind and in a spirit of discovery. Problem exploration is a more creative and open-ended process than problem solving. It often reveals aspects of the problem that are not obvious at first glance. These discoveries can become useful insights.

At any stage in the problem-solving process, there are two quite different styles of thinking: **divergent** and **convergent**. Divergent thinking stresses generating ideas over evaluating ideas. It involves thinking in different directions or searching for a variety of answers to questions that may have many right answers. Brainstorming, in which the evaluation process is strictly prohibited, promotes divergent thinking and allows many ideas to flourish at the same time, even ideas that contradict each other. Convergent thinking, on the other hand, is directed toward achieving a goal, a single solution, answer, or result. It involves trying to find the one best answer. In convergent thinking, the emphasis shifts from idea generation to evaluation: Which of these ideas leads to the best outcomes? In many cases, this evaluation is carried out using a model.

Why is this distinction between divergent and convergent thinking useful? One reason is that some individuals naturally prefer, enjoy, or are skilled at one or the other type of thinking. When working as end users, these individuals should be conscious of their preference or skill and take steps to ensure that they devote sufficient time and energy to the other approach. Good evaluators need to encourage themselves to generate more ideas; good idea generators need to encourage themselves to test their ideas thoroughly. Since end users do it all, they must ensure that the balance between divergent and convergent thinking is appropriate throughout the problem-solving process.

An understanding of these concepts is just as important to members of a problem-solving team. In this situation, members can afford to specialize in their preferred thought process: idea generators can take a lead role in that phase, while strong evaluators can take a lead role when that becomes the primary activity of the group. But people need to understand their own strengths and the strengths of others on the team and need to appreciate that the other types make an important contribution. Finally, teams work best when they are aware of which type of thinking they are stressing at each point in the process. It is disruptive and inefficient to have one member of a team evaluating ideas during a brainstorming session; it is just as disruptive to have someone offering great new ideas during the preparation of the final presentation to the client.

2.2.2 The Six-Stage Problem-Solving Process

We now describe a six-stage problem-solving process (Figure 2.1) that begins with a mess and ends with implementation of a solution. This process can be used to solve (or explore) almost any problem, from the most well structured to the most ill structured. Since not all problem solving involves the use of formal models, we first describe the

FIGURE 2.1   The Creative
Problem-Solving Process
Source: After Couger, *Creative
Problem Solving and
Opportunity Finding*

Exploring the mess
    Divergent phase
        Search mess for problems and opportunities.
    Convergent phase
        Accept a challenge and undertake systematic efforts to respond to it.

Searching for information
    Divergent phase
        Gather data, impressions, feelings, observations; examine the situation from many
        different viewpoints.
    Convergent phase
        Identify the most important information.

Identifying a problem
    Divergent phase
        Generate many different potential problem statements.
    Convergent phase
        Choose a working problem statement.

Searching for solutions
    Divergent phase
        Develop many different alternatives and possibilities for solutions.
    Convergent phase
        Select one or a few ideas that seem most promising.

Evaluating solutions
    Divergent phase
        Formulate criteria for reviewing and evaluating ideas.
    Convergent phase
        Select the most important criteria. Use the criteria to evaluate, strengthen, and
        refine ideas.

Implementing a solution
    Divergent phase
        Consider possible sources of assistance and resistance to proposed solution.
        Identify implementation steps and required resources.
    Convergent phase
        Prepare the most promising solution for implementation.

process in its most general form. Subsequently, we discuss how formal modeling fits within this overall framework. Throughout this section, we illustrate the stages of the process with the following example.

EXAMPLE
Invivo Diagnostics

Invivo Diagnostics is a $300M pharmaceutical company built on the strength of a single product that accounts for over 75 percent of revenues. In 18 months, the patent for this product will expire, and the CEO wants to explore ways to plug the expected $100–$200M revenue gap as revenues from this product decline. ∎

The six stages in the problem-solving process are:

- Exploring the mess
- Searching for information
- Identifying a problem
- Searching for solutions
- Evaluating solutions
- Implementing a solution

Divergent thinking tends to predominate early in this process, while convergent thinking comes to dominate later on, but there is a role for each type of thinking in every stage of the process.

Stage 1: Exploring the Mess   As we have said, problems do not appear to us in the form of well-posed problem statements. Rather, we find ourselves in various messes, out of which problems occasionally emerge. It often takes a special effort to rise above the press of day-to-day activities and begin a problem-solving process. In this sense, the most important aspect of this phase may be more psychological than intellectual. The divergent thinking in this phase involves being open to the flow of problems and opportunities in the environment; the convergent phase distills a specific problem out of the mess. During this phase, we ask questions such as the following:

- What problems (or opportunities) do we face?
- Where is there a gap between the current situation and the desired one?
- What are our stated and unstated goals?

This stage will be complete when we have produced a satisfactory description of the situation and when we have identified (although not necessarily gathered) the key facts and data.

In the Invivo example, management in the pharmaceutical company is well aware that one drug has provided the bulk of their profits over the past decade. Nevertheless, most of their day-to-day attention is devoted to tactical issues, such as resolving conflicts with suppliers or allocating R&D funds to the development of new drugs. As the date approaches on which their major drug loses its patent protection and alternative drugs can begin to compete, the managers gradually shift attention to the situation facing them. While the threat is obvious, the problem is not well defined. Each member of management probably explores this mess individually, in an informal way. They might make rough estimates of the magnitude of the threat (how much will profits fall when the patent expires?), and they might consider alternatives to improve outcomes (should we institute a cost-cutting program in manufacturing?). Eventually, management as a whole realizes the importance of the issue and creates a task force to address it. All of this activity comes under the heading of *exploring the mess*.

Stage 2: Searching for Information   Here we mean information in the broadest sense: opinions, raw data, impressions, published literature, and so on. In this phase we cast about widely for any and all information that might shed light on what the problem really is. Examining the situation from many different points of view is an important aspect of this phase. We might survey similar companies to determine how they approach related problems. We might search the literature for related academic research. The search itself at this stage is divergent. Eventually, we begin to get a sense that some of the information is more relevant, or contains suggestions for solutions, or might otherwise be particularly useful. This is the convergent part of this phase. In this stage, we should expect to be using diagnostic skills, prioritizing, and constructing diagrams or charts. During this phase, we ask questions such as the following:

- What are the symptoms and causes?
- What measures of effectiveness seem appropriate?
- What actions are available?

This stage will be complete when we have found and organized relevant information for the situation at hand and when we have made some initial hypotheses about the source of the problem and potential solutions.

The task force at Invivo holds several meetings to get to know each other and to get organized. They also hire a consultant to gather information and to bring an outside perspective to the discussion. The CEO charges the group to "find a strategy to deal with the patent situation;" the task force recognizes, however, that this is not a problem statement, but only a vague indication of senior management's discomfort about the future of the company. The consultant, meanwhile, begins interviewing key managers inside the firm and gathering information externally. She collects information on general trends in the pharmaceutical industry as well as case studies on the transition off patent for other drugs. A rough picture emerges of the rate at which generics have invaded a market once patent protection has been lost. She also collects specific information on strategies that other market-dominating firms have used to limit their losses during similar transitions. The consultant interviews economists specializing in industry structure. Inside the firm, she interviews the scientists who develop new drugs, and she begins to formulate a picture of how the firm's portfolio of new drugs will contribute to future revenues. If the problem-solving process is to work well here, a broad search for information must precede any effort to close in on a specific problem that can be resolved. However, even while this search goes on, the members of the task force are beginning to form opinions as to the real problem they face and the solutions they prefer.

Stage 3: Identifying a Problem   In the divergent portion of this phase, we might pose four or five candidate problem statements and try them on for size. We will eventually choose one of these statements, perhaps somewhat refined, as our working problem statement. As mentioned before, there is a significant benefit for any problem-solving group to have an unambiguous statement of the problem they are solving. This is not to say that we can't modify or even replace one problem statement with another if the evidence suggests this is necessary. All problem statements should be viewed as tentative, although as time passes, the cost and risk of changing the problem statement increase. In this stage, we should be asking whether the situation fits a standard problem type, or whether we should be breaking the problem into subproblems. During this phase, we ask questions such as the following:

- Which is the most important problem in this situation?
- Is this problem like others we have dealt with?
- What are the consequences of a broad versus narrow problem statement?

This stage will be complete when we have produced a working problem statement.

The consultant to Invivo holds a series of meetings with the task force to present and discuss her preliminary research. The group now has a shared understanding of the financial state of their own firm, as well as a general idea of the state of the industry. They discuss how other firms fared when major drugs came off patent and what strategies were used to smooth the transition. At this point, the consultant leads an effort to define a problem statement that can serve as an organizing theme for the future efforts of the task force. In the discussion that ensues, two major points of view emerge. One group focuses on preserving the revenue-generating power of the patent drug as long as possible. They ask whether it would be possible to extend the patent, slow the introduction of generic competitors, or perhaps make an alliance with competitors that would share the profits from this category of drugs without significantly reducing its revenues. The other group focuses on a different issue: how to generate more revenue from other drugs now in the development pipeline. They ask whether the firm should increase its R&D spending, narrow its efforts to just the most promising drugs, or look for quicker ways to get regulatory approval. The consultant recognizes that no one is looking at reducing costs or shrinking the firm as possible strategies.

The task force has reached a critical stage in the problem-solving process. How they define the problem here will determine in large measure the solutions they eventually recommend. The consultant, recognizing this, makes an effort to have the group debate a wide range of problem statements. Here are some candidate problem statements they may consider:

- In what ways might we slow the decline in revenues from our patented drug?
- In what ways might we increase the chances of success of R&D on new products?
- In what ways might we increase market share for our existing products?

- In what ways might we resize the firm to match declining profits?
- In what ways might we develop more products with the same investment?
- In what ways might we partner with other firms?

Eventually, the task force comes to the conclusion that protecting the revenues from the existing drug is both difficult and risky. The most effective strategy probably involves developing a portfolio of new drugs as quickly and effectively as possible. Accordingly, they adopt the problem statement: "In what ways might we reduce the time to market for the six drugs currently under development?"

Stage 4: Searching for Solutions Again, there is a divergent aspect to this phase, in which a deliberately open-ended process searches for good, even radical, solutions. Brainstorming or other creativity-enhancing techniques might be particularly useful, since the team has a well-considered problem statement to serve as a focal point for the creation of solutions. Prior to this point, it is premature to consider solutions. It can even be dangerous to do so, since superficially appealing solutions often gain support on their own, even if they solve the wrong problem. The convergent part of this phase involves a tentative selection of the most promising candidate solutions. The selection process must be tentative at this point, because criteria have not yet been established for a careful comparison of solutions. Nonetheless, there are costs to considering too many solutions, so some pruning is often necessary. During this phase, we ask questions such as the following:

- What decisions are open to us?
- What solutions have been tried in similar situations?
- How are the various candidate solutions linked to outcomes of interest?

This stage will be complete when we have produced a list of potential solutions and perhaps a list of advantages and disadvantages for each one.

Having decided to focus their efforts on improving the R&D process, the task force at Invivo first forms a subcommittee composed mainly of scientists from the R&D division, along with a few business experts. The consultant conducts extensive interviews within the R&D group to uncover inefficiencies and possible ways to improve the process of bringing drugs to market. The subcommittee eventually develops a list of potential solutions, along with an evaluation of their advantages and disadvantages. Three areas for potential improvement stand out:

- Hire outside firms to conduct clinical trials and develop applications for Food and Drug Administration (FDA) approvals. This will speed up the approval process, although it will also increase costs.
- Invest a higher percentage of the R&D budget in drugs with the most promise of winning FDA approval. This should reduce the time required for the most promising drugs to reach the market, but it may also reduce the number of drugs that do so.
- Focus the drug portfolio on drugs in the same medical category. This should help develop an expertise in just one or two medical specialties, rather than spreading efforts over many technical areas and markets.

Stage 5: Evaluating Solutions This stage can be considered the culmination of the process, as it is here that a preferred solution emerges. Any evaluation of the candidate solutions developed in the previous phase requires a set of criteria with which to compare solutions. Usually, many criteria could be relevant to the outcome; some divergent thinking is useful in this phase to ensure that all relevant criteria, even those that are not obvious, are considered. Once the most important criteria are identified, the various solutions can be evaluated and compared on each criterion. This can lead directly to a preferred alternative. More often, this process leads to changes—and improvements—in the solutions themselves. Often, an aspect of one solution can be grafted onto another solution, or a particularly negative aspect of a generally attractive solution can be removed once the weakness has been recognized. So this phase, while generally stressing convergent thinking, still involves considerable creativity. During this phase, we ask questions such as the following:

- How does this solution impact each of the criteria?
- What factors within our control could improve the outcomes?
- What factors outside our control could alter the outcomes?

This stage will be complete when we have produced a recommended course of action, along with a justification that supports it.

During this phase, the Invivo task force develops a set of criteria with which to evaluate each of the previously proposed solutions. The overall goal is to ensure that the firm remains profitable into the future, even as the main drug goes off patent and its revenues are lost. However, it is difficult to anticipate how any one solution will impact profits directly. For example, how much additional profit will the firm realize if it saves two months in the development process for a particular drug? For this reason, each solution is measured against many criteria, and the results are synthesized by the task force. Here are some of the criteria they develop:

- R&D cost reduction
- Increase in market share
- Months of development time saved
- Increase in probability of FDA approval

After extensive discussion, the task force finally decides that the one most critical area for improvement is how R&D funds are allocated over time. In the past, the firm has generally been very slow to cancel development of any particular drug. Each drug has the passionate support of the scientists working on it, and the commitment of this group to its own drug has superseded the business judgment needed to recognize that other drug-development teams can make better use of scarce R&D resources. With a more business-oriented allocation process, fewer drugs will be developed, but each will get increased R&D funding. Hopefully, more drugs will then come to market quickly.

Stage 6: Implementing a Solution   This stage is included to remind us that a solution is useless if it cannot be implemented. Political resistance, departures from established tradition, and high personal cost or risk are some of the many reasons apparently rational solutions do not get implemented in real organizations. In the divergent portion of this phase, the problem-solving team identifies potential sources of resistance and support. As this phase proceeds and specific implementation plans for the proposed solution are developed, the thinking style turns from divergent toward convergent. In this stage, we should expect to perform change management and focus on communication. During this phase, we ask questions such as the following:

- What are the barriers to successful implementation?
- Where will there be support and motivation, or resistance and conflict?
- Are the resources available for successful implementation?

This stage will be complete when we have produced an implementation plan and executed enough of it to begin evaluating how well it is succeeding.

To implement its plan, the task force at Invivo must first convince senior management to support its recommended solution. The consultant has a major role to play here in developing an effective presentation and in convincing both scientists and executives that this solution will work. The task force's role ends when it has won approval and has appointed a new committee to manage the implementation of the new R&D budget allocation process. Of course, the problem-solving process does not really end here, as the new committee must carry the plan forward, monitor its impacts, modify it as needed, and solve a new set of problems as they arise. To this extent, no problem-solving process ever really ends; it just flows into a subsequent process.

Every successful problem-solving effort starts with a mess and concludes with an implemented solution. Sometimes the cycle will be repeated more than once, so that the implementation itself creates a new situation and paves the way for follow-on problems to be identified. Nevertheless, the process passes through the stages we have outlined here. Knowledge of these stages is helpful in planning the overall tasks and resources, allocating effort, and setting expectations about progress. Within each stage, an awareness of the contributions from divergent and convergent thinking is helpful in balancing the need for creativity with the need for closure.

It is worth repeating that only rarely are these six stages followed in a strict sequence. Most problem-solving processes move back and forth from one stage to another, perhaps rethinking the problem statement while evaluating solutions, or returning to an information-gathering mode while searching for solutions. As in any creative endeavor, it is important for a problem-solving team (or individual) to remain flexible. That means remaining open to discoveries and to evidence that past work needs to be rethought.

2.2.3 Mental Models and Formal Models

The problem-solving process described earlier is generic in that it does not specifically address how formal modeling is used within the overall framework. Informal modeling, often called *mental modeling*, goes on constantly during problem solving. That is, problem solvers construct quick, informal mental models at many different points in the process. For example, when a potential solution is proposed, everyone on the team runs that idea through a mental model to get a quick first impression of its attractiveness. As an example, consider the following question:

> Would a tax on carbon emissions in developed countries significantly reduce global warming?

What mental models do you use to evaluate this question? How do you think a tax would affect actual emissions of carbon? What effect would it have on economic growth and quality of life? How would developing countries react to such a policy, and what would be the long-term impact on global temperature? Usually, when we consider questions like this, we use mental models to link causes (the tax) with their effects (changes in global temperature).

Mental models help us to relate cause and effect, but often in a highly simplified and incomplete way. Mental models also help us to determine what might be feasible in a given situation, but our idea of what is possible is often circumscribed by our personal experiences. Finally, mental models are always influenced by our preferences for certain outcomes over others, although those preferences may not be acknowledged or even understood. One source of confusion and debate on topics such as global warming is that we all use different mental models, based on different assumptions and preferences for outcomes, and we have limited means of sharing those models because they are informal and hidden from view. So, while mental models may be useful, even necessary, they can also be extremely limiting. A common pitfall is to reject an unusual idea because it appears at first to be unworkable. Effective divergent thinking can help overcome this pitfall and allow unusual ideas to persist long enough to get a thorough hearing. But in some circumstances, mental models are simply not robust enough to provide sufficient insight, and formal models are called for.

Formal models (see Figure 2.1) provide the same kind of information as mental models. In essence, they link causes to effects and help us evaluate potential solutions. Once a set of potential solutions and a set of criteria have been identified, a formal model can be used to measure how well each solution performs according to the criteria. Formal models are undoubtedly costlier and more time-consuming to build than mental models, but they have the great advantage of making our assumptions, logic, and preferences explicit and open to debate.

Mental models were used extensively during the problem-solving process in our pharmaceutical company example. Every member of the task force was experienced in the industry, so each of them had developed mental models to think through the implications of the various proposals. For example, they each had some idea of the development and testing protocols for new drugs, the current process used to allocate R&D funds, and the profit streams new drugs typically generate. Using this experience, they were able to make rough, qualitative assessments of the impact the new R&D-allocation process would have on new-drug success, as well as the profit impact of introducing fewer drugs sooner. However, given the complexity of the drug-development process and the interaction of the various competing companies in the market, mental models would simply not support quantitative estimates of the overall profit impact of the proposed solution.

How could Invivo use formal modeling in its problem-solving process? With a formal model, it could track the progress of each of the six drugs through the various stages of development. One of the key assumptions it needs to agree on is how the new R&D process affects the completion time and probability of success at each stage. They would probably want to add to this basic model a module that projects the introduction of competing products in each medical category. This requires discussion and agreement on a set of assumptions about the plans of their competitors. Finally, they can complete the model by adding a financial component to determine their profits under any scenario. Taken as a whole, this model projects a stream of new-drug introductions by the firm and its competitors, then determines the price and market share for each drug, and ultimately calculates the resulting profits. Unlike mental models, a formal model built along these lines can help analyze whether the firm will be able to generate enough revenues from new drugs to offset the loss in revenues from its blockbuster drug.

2.3   INFLUENCE CHARTS

As we have pointed out, model building and analysis are used within the broader context of problem solving. To be successful, this process must begin with recognition of a problem and end with implementation of a solution. At a minimum, modeling should help in evaluating alternative solutions, but it also can provide the analyst with an enhanced intuitive understanding of the problem and the forces at work within it.

A key challenge modelers face in the problem-solving process is how to translate an initial, vague understanding of a problem into a concrete model. A mathematical model, of course, requires specific numerical inputs and outputs along with the precise relationships that connect them. Many modelers make the mistake of plunging into the details of a model before they think through the role the model will play in the overall process. We recommend a different approach, using the power of visualization to develop a broad understanding of the critical inputs, outputs, and relationships in a chart before building an initial model. An **influence chart** is a simple diagram that shows what outcome variables the model will generate and how these outputs are calculated from the necessary inputs. Influence charts are not designed to provide numerical results or insights into which particular solutions are desirable. Rather, they can help to bring clarity to the initial stages of the model formulation process.

Influence charts are particularly powerful in the early, conceptual stages of a modeling effort. They encourage the modeler or modeling team to focus on major choices, such as what to include and what to exclude from the model, rather than on details that may ultimately turn out to be unimportant. Influence charts provide a high-level view of the entire model that can be comprehended at one glance. This high-level perspective, in turn, supports modeling in teams by facilitating communication among team members. As a result, areas of agreement and disagreement among team members surface early. Influence charts can also be highly effective in communicating the essence of the modeling approach to clients.

Influence charts are flexible, so they support the frequent revision that effective modeling requires. We often encourage our student teams to devote the first hour in the life of a model to working out an influence chart. In addition, we ask them not to turn on the computer until all members of the team agree that their chart represents a suitable initial description of their model.

2.3.1 A First Example

To illustrate how influence charts are built, we begin with a highly simplified example.

EXAMPLE
A Pricing Decision

Determine the price we should set for our product so as to generate the highest possible profit this coming year.

∎

Since our plan will ultimately be measured by its profitability, we define Profit as the outcome measure and enclose it in a hexagon to distinguish it from other variables in the chart (Figure 2.2a). Next we ask what we need to know to determine Profit. The major components of Profit, Total Revenue and Total Cost, are drawn as variables enclosed in circles to the left of Profit and connected to it by arrows (Figure 2.2b). These arrows identify which variables are required to calculate the outcome. Next, Total Cost is determined by Fixed Cost and Variable Cost, which are drawn to the left of Total Cost (Figure 2.2c). Variable Cost in turn is the product of Quantity Sold and Unit Cost (Figure 2.2d). Now we turn to Total Revenue, which is the product of Quantity Sold and Price. We add Price and enclose it in a box to show it is our decision variable (Figure 2.2e). Finally, Price Elasticity, along with the price we set, determines Quantity Sold, so in Figure 2.2f, we add the Price Elasticity variable and an arrow from Price to Quantity Sold.

Traditionally, influence charts are built from right to left, using diagrammatic conventions that distinguish the roles of different types of variables (Figure 2.3). For example, we use hexagons to represent outputs and boxes to represent decisions, as indicated in our example. We also use circles to represent other variables. As we complete the layout, we can identify certain of the variables as inputs. These are shown in the diagram as triangles. Later, we will also use double circles to represent variables that are random.

While this is a highly simplified example, its development does involve a number of modeling choices. For example, we can see in the influence chart that Fixed Cost is assumed to be a known quantity, because there are no variables that are needed to determine Fixed Cost. In another situation, we might face a set of choices as to which production technology to choose for the coming year. In that case, Fixed Cost would not be known but would be influenced by our technology choices, and the chart would have to reflect those complexities. Another modeling choice is evident in how Quantity Sold is determined. In our chart, both Price and Price Elasticity influence Quantity Sold. This reflects our modeling judgment that we face a price-dependent market. In many situations, we might assume instead that Sales are independent of Price, at least within a reasonable range of prices. One final modeling decision is evident in our chart: because Quantity Sold determines Revenue, we are assuming

FIGURE 2.2a Start the Influence Chart with the Objective (Profit)

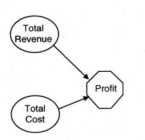

FIGURE 2.2b Decompose Profit into Total Revenue and Total Cost

FIGURE 2.2c Decompose Total Cost into Variable Cost and Fixed Cost

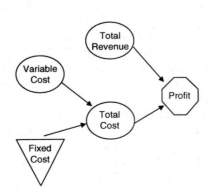

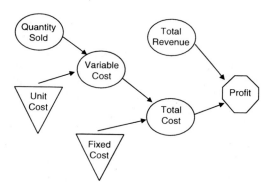

FIGURE 2.2d Decompose Variable Cost into Quantity Sold and Unit Cost

that production and sales are simultaneous. If, on the other hand, it were our practice to produce to stock and to sell from inventory, we would need to modify the chart to reflect this practice. This example illustrates that influence charts help the modeler make explicit decisions about what is included in the model and how the variables interact to determine the output.

2.3.2 An Income Statement as an Influence Chart

An income statement is a standard accounting framework that is widely used for reporting on the past performance of a company. The bottom line in an income statement is Retained Earnings, which is roughly the difference between revenue and costs, adjusted for taxes and dividends. A simple income statement is shown in the form of an influence chart in Figure 2.4.

If our purpose were simply to record the historical performance of a company, then the relationships depicted in Figure 2.4 would be sufficient. Moreover, the related spreadsheet would consist entirely of numbers; no formulas would be needed

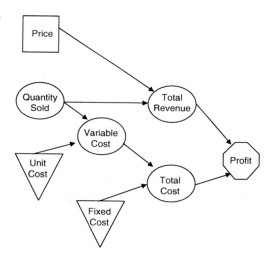

FIGURE 2.2e Decompose Total Revenue into Quantity Sold and Price

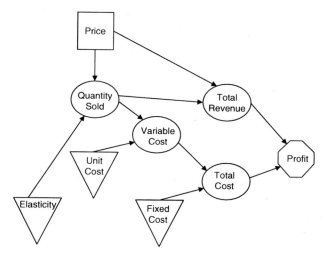

FIGURE 2.2f Decompose Quantity Sold into Price and Price Elasticity

FIGURE 2.3 Symbols Used in Influence Charts

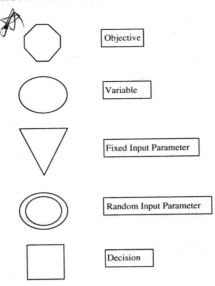

Objective

Variable

Fixed Input Parameter

Random Input Parameter

Decision

because all variables are already determined. However, Figure 2.4 would be inadequate if our purpose were to make projections into the future because it reveals nothing about how critical variables such as Sales Revenue and Cost of Goods Sold will be determined. (A projected income statement is known as a *pro forma* income statement; the Latin phrase *pro forma* literally means "as a formality," but the meaning in accounting is "provided in advance.") In other words, Figure 2.4 represents only a static accounting framework and not a *model* of the future. To convert a static income statement into a model, we need to determine how underlying variables such as Quantity Sold evolve over time. In a simple model, we could assume that Unit Cost and Price are constant and that Quantity Sold is determined by Initial Sales and Sales Growth Rate. Figure 2.5 shows an influence chart for this model.

Even in this case, where accounting rules determine much of the model structure, an influence chart is useful for depicting the underlying forces that drive the results.

2.3.3 Principles for Building Influence Charts

An influence chart is not a technical flowchart that must conform perfectly to a rigid set of rules. Rather, it is a somewhat free-form visual aid for thinking conceptually about a model. We offer the following guidelines for constructing such charts:

- Start with the outcome measure. To decide which variable this is, ask what single variable the decision maker will use to measure the success of a plan of action.
- Decompose the outcome measure into a small set of variables that determine it *directly*. Each of these influencing variables should be independent of the others, and together they should be sufficient to determine the result.
- Take each variable in turn and repeat this process of decomposition. For each variable, ask, "What do I need to know to determine... ?"
- Identify input data and decisions as they arise.
- Make sure that each variable appears only once in the diagram.
- Highlight special types of elements with consistent symbols. For example, we use squares for decision variables and double circles for random variables, but any consistent code will work.

FIGURE 2.4 Influence Chart for a Static Income Statement

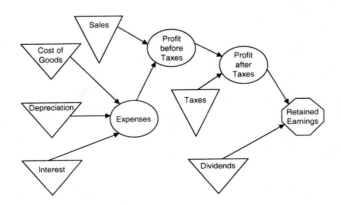

FIGURE 2.5 Influence Chart for an Income Statement Model

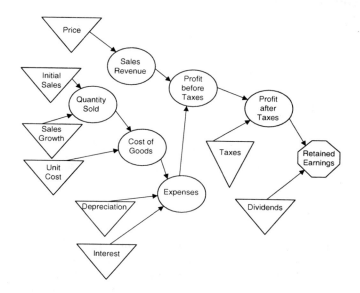

The most common error in drawing influence charts is to draw an arrow from the output back to the decisions. The thinking here seems to be that the outcome will be used to determine the best decisions. Remember, however, that an influence chart is simply a *description* of how we will calculate outcomes for *any* set of decisions and other parameters. It is not intended to be used to find the best decisions. That is a separate process, requiring an actual model, not simply a diagram.

2.3.4 Two Additional Examples

In this section, we present two detailed exercises in building influence charts for unstructured problems. Read each case and draw an influence chart before proceeding. We will then describe the process of building an influence chart and discuss some of our modeling choices. Keep in mind, however, that there is no one correct diagram, just as there is no one correct model.

EXAMPLE
The S.S.
Kuniang

In the early 1980s, New England Electric System (NEES) was deciding how much to bid for the salvage rights to a grounded ship, the S.S. *Kuniang*.[1] If the bid was successful, the ship could be repaired and outfitted to haul coal for the company's power-generation stations. But the value of doing so depended on the outcome of a U.S. Coast Guard judgment about the salvage value of the ship. The Coast Guard's judgment involved an obscure law regarding domestic shipping in coastal waters. If the judgment indicated a low salvage value, and if NEES submitted the winning bid, then NEES would be able to use the ship for its shipping needs. If the judgment was high, the ship would be considered too costly for use in domestic shipping. The Coast Guard's judgment would not be known until after the winning bid was chosen, so there was considerable risk associated with submitting a bid. If the bid were to fail, NEES could purchase either a new ship or a tug/barge combination, both of which were relatively expensive alternatives. One of the major issues was that the higher the bid, the more likely that NEES would win. NEES judged that a bid of $2 million would definitely not win, whereas a bid of $12 million definitely would win. Any bid in between was possible. ■

The goal here is to select an amount to bid for the S.S. *Kuniang* that will allow NEES to supply coal to its plants in the most economical way. We assume that the amount of coal to be shipped is fixed and that NEES will either use the *Kuniang* or buy a new ship or a tug/barge combination. That is, we explicitly rule out the possibility that NEES can avoid meeting the demand for shipped coal. We further assume that

[1]D. E. Bell, "Bidding for the S.S. *Kuniang*," *Interfaces* 14 (1984): 17–23.

FIGURE 2.6 S.S. *Kuniang*
Influence Chart

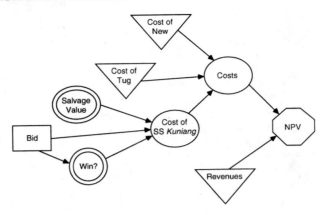

the outcome measure is the Net Present Value (NPV) of profits from this shipping operation over an appropriate time period (in the case of a ship, perhaps 20 years).

Our influence chart starts with an outcome measure for NPV and two influences: Costs and Revenues (Figure 2.6). Since the revenues are independent of the ship chosen, that part of the diagram does not need to be developed further. The costs incurred in coal shipping depend on which option is chosen. Apparently, NEES can always buy a new ship or a tug/barge combination, and it may have the option to buy the *Kuniang* if its bid wins. The costs of the *Kuniang* are the essential part of the model. These costs are dependent on the salvage value set by the Coast Guard, which is unpredictable and is therefore shown as a random variable (a double circle). The cost is also influenced by the size of the bid and by whether it wins the auction. In Figure 2.6, we have shown the outcome of the auction as the random variable "Win?" We have in mind a simple model in which the probability of winning increases as our bid increases. But this is an area of the diagram where further elaboration could be productive. We could, for example, add modules for the bids of our competitors. We could also add a module for the auction process itself. Whether to add further detail is always the modeler's judgment. But this simple influence chart is sufficiently detailed to support the building of a prototype model.

One additional point to notice here is that the numerical information in the problem statement, which places some limits on reasonable bids, plays no role at all in constructing the influence chart. In fact, we routinely ignore all available numerical data when we build influence charts because the goal is to develop a problem *structure*, not to solve the problem. Problem structure is not influenced by the values of parameters. This principle conflicts with another that many of us learned in early math classes, which was to use all the given data to solve the problem. This may be an appropriate problem-solving heuristic for simple math problems in school, but it is not necessarily helpful in structuring real business decisions.

EXAMPLE
Automobile Leasing

During the 1990s, leasing grew to 40 percent of new-car sales. Nowadays, the most popular leases are for expensive or midrange vehicles and terms of 24 or 36 months. The most common form of leasing is the closed-end lease, where the monthly payment is based on three factors:

• *Capitalized Cost*: the purchase price for the car, net of trade-ins, fees, discounts, and dealer-installed options.

• *Residual Value*: the value of the vehicle at the end of the lease, specified by the leasing company (the "lessor") in the contract. The customer has the right to purchase the vehicle at this price at the end of the lease.

• *Money Factor*, or *Rate*: the interest rate charged by the leasing company.

A lower residual value results in higher monthly payments. Therefore, a leasing company with the highest residual value usually has the lowest, and most competitive, monthly payment. However, if the actual end-of-lease market value is lower than the contract residual value, the customer is likely to return the car to the lessor. The lessor then typically sells the vehicle, usually at auction, and realizes a "residual loss."

On the other hand, if the actual end-of-lease market value is greater than the contract residual, the customer is more likely to purchase the vehicle. By then selling the vehicle for the prevailing market value, the customer in essence receives a rebate for the higher monthly payments. (Of course, the customer may also decide to keep the car.) When customers exercise their purchase option, the lessor loses the opportunity to realize "residual gains." ∎

The primary challenge for companies offering a closed-end lease is to select the residual value of the vehicle. Intelligent selection means offering competitive monthly payments on the front end without ignoring the risk of residual losses on the back end. In approaching this problem from a modeling perspective, the first task is to find ways to cut it down to size. After all, any leasing company offers leases on dozens of vehicles at any one time. Furthermore, unless it is just starting to do business, the company has an existing portfolio of hundreds of leases on its books, and the risk characteristics of this portfolio may influence the terms offered on new leases. We can become overwhelmed by complexity if we start by trying to model the entire problem. It is vital in modeling an ill-structured problem of this type to start simple and add complexity sparingly.

One reasonable approach is to develop an influence chart for a specific lease on a single type of vehicle. Once a prototype model based on this diagram is tested and proved, we can expand on it by bringing in excluded aspects of the problem.

An example will make the problem more concrete. Consider new Honda Accord models, which sell for $25,000. Also consider only three-year leases, and assume the money rate is fixed at 5 percent. Given these assumptions, our goal is to determine the best contract residual value (CRV) for a single lease on this single class of vehicles.

The CRV is clearly our decision variable. How will we determine whether we have made a good choice? Once we have chosen the CRV (and the other terms of the lease), we will offer it to the leasing market. Some number of customers will purchase our lease and pay us the monthly lease payments for three years. (A few will default during this period, but we ignore that factor in our initial prototype.) Our monthly lease revenues will be the product of the monthly payment and the number of leases sold. The monthly payment, in turn, will depend on the term, the money factor, and the CRV.

At the end of three years, all our leases will expire. Some customers will buy their vehicles at the CRV; others will return their vehicles and take a new lease with us; still others will return their vehicles and not purchase another lease with us. (We ignore the value of follow-on leases in our initial prototype.) When all is said and done, we will have made some level of profit. Profit, then, is our outcome measure, and it is influenced by three factors: lease revenues, our cost of borrowing (to pay for new vehicles), and the residual value of vehicles at the end of the lease (Figure 2.7).

So far, this is a rather straightforward influence chart. But two parts of it deserve additional attention. First, what determines how many leases are sold? Presumably,

FIGURE 2.7 National Leasing Influence Chart

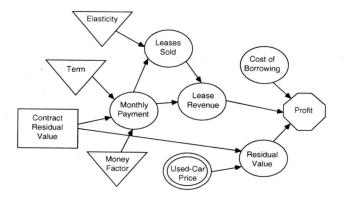

customers are sensitive to the monthly payment, and that influence is shown in the diagram, but what else influences volume? One simple approach is to assume a value for demand elasticity: volume increases (or decreases) by x percent when our monthly payments decrease (or increase) by 1 percent. This relationship is sufficient to generate some realistic aspects of the lease market—namely, a decline in volume with increasing payments—and it may be sufficient for a prototype model. But it does not explicitly include any information about our competitor's monthly payments. In particular, the elasticity is probably different when our payments are above the competition than when they are below. This may be a fertile area for refinement in later prototypes.

We should also consider what factors determine the residual value of the vehicle to the leasing company. When a lease expires, the contract allows the customer to purchase the vehicle for the CRV or to return it to the leasing company. The customer's decision at this point is crucial to determining the profitability of the lease. If used-car prices are high relative to the CRV, it is in the customer's interest to buy the car at the CRV and then sell it for the higher market price. But if used-car prices are low, customers will tend to return their leased vehicles and buy a cheaper equivalent used car. In this case, the leasing company will have to sell the vehicle at the low market price. And, of course, some customers will lease a new vehicle regardless of used-car prices, and some may not behave in an economically rational manner at all. Should we include all of these factors in our influence chart?

One approach would be to assume that all vehicles will be purchased if used-car prices exceed the CRV, and none will be purchased if the reverse holds. But how do we know how much used cars will be worth three years from now? In our chart, we model used-car prices as a random variable—for example, a normal distribution with a mean of $15,000 and a standard deviation of $2,000. Alternatively, we might assume that this class of vehicles loses a random amount of its value each year, where the annual loss is uniformly distributed between 8 and 12 percent. This slightly more detailed model will also generate a distribution of values three years from now. In further refinements of the chart, we might expand on these ideas and model the fundamental determinants of used-car values: new-vehicle quality, the macro economy, and so on. In any case, a random value for used-car prices captures one of the essential features of this problem—namely, the uncertainty surrounding residual losses and residual gains. This influence chart is probably sufficiently detailed to support construction of a prototype model. Working with this model will help us discover whether we have captured the essential trade-offs in the problem.

As we have stressed before, the influence chart documents the simplifying assumptions made during the modeling process. Here are some of the critical assumptions embodied in Figure 2.7:

- One vehicle/one lease term
- No lease defaults
- No follow-on leases
- Rational behavior of customers at lease end
- Random used-car prices

We recommend that the modeler or one member of the modeling team record each assumption as it is made during the process of developing an influence chart. This is useful for two reasons. First, it focuses attention and discussion on assumptions as they are being made. Second, each assumption should be viewed as a potential area for later refinement of the model.

2.4 CRAFT SKILLS FOR MODELING

Successful modelers can draw on both technical and craft skills in their work. **Technical skill** refers to the ability to carry out specific, narrow, well-defined tasks in the modeling process. This includes, for example, calculating present values, or linking balance sheets and income statements correctly, or identifying a tail probability in the results of a simulation model. Proper use of technical skill leads to a correct result and allows little room for creativity. In contrast, **craft skill** does not lead to a single correct result and does require creativity. Some examples of craft skill are making useful simplifications in a complex problem, designing a prototype, or brainstorming ways to increase demand for a new product. Craft skills develop slowly, over time and with experience, whereas technical skills can be learned at one pass. In playing the piano, technical skill is developed by practicing scales, while real craft is needed to interpret the music while playing it. Craft skills are harder to describe and teach than technical skills, but they are just as important to successful modeling. In fact, it is the high level of craft skill that distinguishes the expert modeler from the journeyman. In this section, we describe some of the most important craft skills and discuss the role that these skills play in modeling. The modeling cases that appear later in the book provide opportunities to practice these skills in ill-structured problem situations.

Craft skills are rarely discussed in books on spreadsheets or management science. One reason may be the common perception that modeling is an art that cannot be taught, only learned through long experience. Another reason may be that expert modelers, like experts in all fields, are largely unconscious of their own craft skills. There is also no well-accepted theory or classification for the craft skills in modeling. Nevertheless, we have found that awareness of these skills is essential to the successful development of truly skilled modelers. We commonly encounter highly skilled spreadsheet users whose craft skills are weak. As a consequence, they cannot successfully employ modeling in new and ill-structured situations. On the other hand, we rarely encounter analysts with good craft skills who cannot learn enough Excel to become good modelers. Furthermore, craft skills *can* be learned, despite the impediments we have cited. The first step in this process is to identify the skills themselves so that the modeler-in-training can begin to develop an awareness of modeling on a higher level than the merely technical.

It is helpful to classify craft skills into useful rules of thumb, or **modeling heuristics**. In general, a heuristic is an approach, a strategy, or a trick that has often proved effective in a given situation. A widely cited example from general problem solving is to write down everything we know about a problem. Heuristics are thought to be one of the most common ways humans deal with the complexities of the world around them, so it should not be surprising to find that modelers have their own. A modeling heuristic is a rule of thumb that experienced modelers use to help them overcome the inevitable difficulties that arise in modeling. We believe that novices can improve their modeling abilities by observing how these heuristics are used in a number of different situations. However, the only way to acquire these skills is to practice them on new problems.

In this section, we describe eight fundamental heuristics and illustrate how they can be used in practice. For the novice modeler, our purpose here is to raise awareness of the role these skills play so that they can be called on routinely in modeling work. With practice and refinement they can become as familiar as technical skills. Implementing these ideas will lead to a stronger personal tool kit of modeling skills. The modeling cases provide an opportunity to begin practicing these skills. In fact, we initiate that process in this chapter.

Throughout this section, we will refer to four modeling cases that describe ill-structured problems. One involves assisting a friend in planning for retirement, another deals with determining how many draft TV commercials to commission, the third requires evaluating the feasibility of towing icebergs to Kuwait for drinking water, and the fourth involves determining the profitability of a new production process. Short synopses of these cases are given here, while the complete versions can be found in the collection of modeling cases at the end of the book. Before proceeding any further, it would be helpful to read these synopses and give some thought to how to model them.

EXAMPLE
Retirement Planning

The client currently is 46 years old, with an income of about $126,000 per year. His goal is to retire between ages 62 and 67 and to have enough savings to live comfortably in about the same fashion he does now (with some money available for expanded travel). The client's accumulated savings for retirement total $137,000. His employer contributes around $10,000 per year into the retirement fund, while he has been contributing $7,500. How much should he be saving? ∎

EXAMPLE
Draft TV Commercials

The client directs TV advertising for a large corporation. His budget for a single ad campaign is typically around $10 million. Under current procedures, a single TV advertisement is commissioned for about $500,000, and the remainder of the budget is spent on airing the ad. The client is considering a new approach, in which two or more draft commercials (at about the same cost) would be commissioned from different agencies. The best of these drafts would then be aired using the remainder of the budget. Is this new plan more effective than the old procedure? ∎

EXAMPLE
Icebergs for Kuwait

Drinking water is in short supply in Kuwait and is therefore very expensive. One suggested remedy is to tow icebergs from Antarctica to Kuwait (a distance of about 9,600 kilometers) and melt them for freshwater. The volume of an iceberg ranges from about 500,000 cubic meters to more than 10 million cubic meters. Theoretical analysis suggests that an idealized spherical iceberg would lose about 0.2 meter of radius per day during transport, although this amount increases with the speed of towing and the distance from the pole. Fuel costs for towboats depend on the size of the boat, the speed, and the volume of the iceberg being towed. Would it be cost-effective to tow icebergs to Kuwait for freshwater, and, if so, how should this be done? ∎

EXAMPLE
The Racquetball Racket

A new and cheaper process has been invented for manufacturing racquetballs. The new ball is bouncier but less durable than the major brand. Unit variable costs of production for the new process will run about $0.52, while the current process costs $0.95. A new plant would cost between $4 million and $6 million. We have 14 years of data on the number of racquetball players in the United States, the average retail price of balls, and the number of balls sold. The number of players is expected to increase about 10 percent per year for 10 years and then level off. In a recent survey, 200 players were asked to use both balls over several months, and their preferences were assessed at several different prices for the new ball. What is the net present value of an investment in a new plant to manufacture balls using this new process? What is the best price for the new ball, and how might the competitor react to introduction of a new ball? ∎

2.4.1 Simplify the Problem

Without a doubt, the most important heuristic in all modeling is to *simplify*. Simplification is the very essence of modeling. We should never criticize a model for being simple, only for being too simple for the purposes at hand. Remember: a model that is too simple can often be modified to better suit the desired purposes.

A model that is more complex than necessary, however, already represents a waste of some modeling effort. Worse yet, a model may be so complex that it cannot be simplified effectively. It is, in fact, much harder to detect when a model is more complex than needed than it is to detect when a model is too simple. Overly simple models make us uncomfortable and motivate us to improve them; overly complex models may simply confuse and overwhelm us.

In discussing the importance of simplicity in models, Michael Pidd offers the following aphorism: [2] "Model simple, think complicated." By this, he reminds us that models are not independent of their users. So the right question to ask about a model is not whether the model by itself is adequate, but whether the user can discover helpful insights with the model. Simple models can support rigorous, critical thinking on the part of the user. Simple models are also more transparent and therefore easier to understand and apply. Users (and their managers) are more likely to trust simple

[2]Michael Pidd, *Tools for Thinking: Modelling in Management Science* (Chichester: John Wiley and Sons, 1996), p. 95.

models and implement the recommendations that are developed from their analysis. A modeling team will find that a simple model facilitates communication within the team, while only the modeling experts may understand a complex model.

There is no more useful tool in the modeler's kit than "keeping it simple." Thus, we try to cut away all complexity that is not essential. Never stop asking whether any particular aspect of a model is necessary for achieving the goals at hand. Novice modelers are often amazed at the simplicity of experts' models, particularly the simplicity of an expert's *first* model. Two other heuristics we will discuss later, decomposition and prototyping, are themselves powerful tools for keeping models simple.

How does one go about simplifying situations for modeling? One approach is to focus on the connections between the key decisions and the outcomes that result from those decisions. Then, ask what central trade-offs make these decisions difficult and build a model to explore those trade-offs. In the Retirement Planning case, for example, increasing one's savings rate reduces current disposable income but increases one's assets at retirement. If that trade-off makes the problem difficult, focus the modeling effort on that issue and leave out anything that seems peripheral.

In the Draft TV Commercials case, money spent on creative work will increase the quality of the advertisement, while money spent on buying airtime will increase the number of consumers who see the advertisement. If the budget is limited, there is an inevitable trade-off between spending money on creative work and spending money on airtime. Focus the modeling effort on illuminating this trade-off.

In the Icebergs for Kuwait case, we know that large icebergs will provide more water, but they may take longer and cost more to transport. Small icebergs provide less water but may be more efficient to move. Here is an essential trade-off to capture in the model.

The goal in the Racquetball Racket case is not to make a highly accurate forecast of profits from the venture, but rather, to understand the risks introduced by various factors such as the competitor's response to our entry. This argues for a simple but highly flexible model. Obviously, the pricing decision will be a key one. A high price may provide attractive margins but also limit our market share. On the other hand, a low price may provide a large market share but leave us with very tight margins. The relationship between price and profitability is one important aspect of the problem, but it helps to keep this relationship simple because we are interested in understanding how it is affected by the competitive response.

Simplification by its nature involves making assumptions. Boldness and self-confidence in making assumptions is a mark of an experienced modeler. Many modelers, however, make assumptions but do not recognize that they are doing so. For example, in the Racquetball Racket case, many student modelers assume that sales will immediately reach a steady state. But if they don't realize this is an assumption, they miss the opportunity to test the sensitivity of their results to it. Thus, it is important both to make assumptions and to recognize them as they are being made. Every assumption should be revisited at some point in the analysis, to see if an alternative assumption would substantially change the results or provide new insights.

This discussion is summarized well by Morgan and Henrion:

> There are some models, especially some science and engineering models, that are large or complex because they need to be. But many more are large or complex because their authors gave too little thought to why and how they were being built and how they would be used.[3]

2.4.2 Break the Problem into Modules

One of the fundamental ways to approach any type of problem solving is to decompose the problem into simpler components. The decomposition approach is basic to Western science and, some would say, to Western thought itself.

[3]M. G. Morgan and M. Henrion, *Uncertainty: A Guide to Dealing with Uncertainty in Quantitative Risk and Policy Analysis* (Cambridge, UK: Cambridge University Press, 1992), p. 289.

The challenge, of course, is to know where to draw the lines; that is, which are the most productive components to create? One approach is to divide the problem into components that are as *independent* of each other as possible.

In the Retirement Planning case, it is natural to decompose the problem into a working-life module and a retirement module. Within the working-life module, we will want to keep track of salary and other income as well as accumulating retirement assets. In the retirement module, we will follow the accumulated assets as they are drawn down for consumption. We may also track certain aspects of consumption, such as travel expenses. These modules are nearly independent: the only necessary connection is that the final assets from the working-life module become the initial assets in the retirement module.

In the Draft TV Commercials case, one module can be devoted to determining the quality of the advertisement that is ultimately aired, while another can be devoted to determining the impact of a budget for airing an advertisement of a given quality. These modules are largely independent: the quality of the advertisement chosen depends on the distribution of quality in the population from which advertisements are drawn, as well as on the number of drafts purchased. Meanwhile, the impact of a given budget in creating audience impressions depends on the size of the budget and the quality of the ad being aired. This latter module requires some assumption about the influence of incremental advertising dollars on incremental impact. The simplest assumption would be that impact is proportional to advertising spending, although we might expect diminishing returns to set in eventually.

In the Icebergs for Kuwait case, a productive approach would be to create three modules. The first determines the supply of icebergs at the edge of the ice cap in Antarctica (by size, shape, etc.). The second module determines how large the iceberg is when it arrives in Kuwait, given its size and shape at the start of the trip, the speed at which it is towed, melting rates, and other factors. Finally, the third module converts the iceberg into a certain quantity of drinking water and a corresponding economic value.

In the Racquetball Racket case, a typical decomposition is to determine annual dollar sales of our ball by multiplying the number of users by the average number of balls purchased per year. The number purchasing our ball is the total number of users multiplied by our share of the market. Our share, in turn, is a function of our price and quality relative to the competitor's price and quality. There are, of course, other ways to decompose sales: by geographic region, by age of buyer, by product type, and so on. Choosing among these methods in a given situation depends on two things: how effective it is to build a model of one component and how easy it is to extend the model for one component to cover all the other components.

Why does the decomposition heuristic work? The great advantage of decomposing a problem is that the components are simpler to deal with than the whole. In addition, the process provides a natural structure for the analysis, thereby allowing the analyst to focus effort on one area at a time. Finally, this heuristic naturally leads us to think in terms of modules, and from there, it is a short step to discover the *interchangeability* of modules. For example, we can change our approach to modeling market share in the Racquetball Racket case without changing any other module. This leads us naturally to another powerful heuristic: *prototyping*.

2.4.3 Build a Prototype and Refine It

A **prototype** is just a working model. A prototype of a new car, for example, is a working model of the car, built to test design concepts prior to high-volume manufacturing. A prototype of a computer program is a working model that can be used to test whether the program works as intended. It can also be used to test the reactions of the users, who may not be able to specify their needs in the abstract but may discover their needs through experimenting with the prototype. A prototype of a model (in our sense) is nothing more than a working version of a model. As a working model, it should take data and inputs from the user and produce key outputs in response. However, the prototype is very likely to need further refinements, since

FIGURE 2.8 Sketch of Results for the Retirement Planning Case

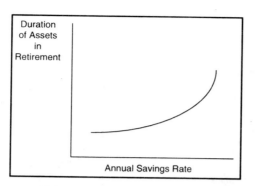

there will probably be gaps between its current performance and the desired results. These gaps describe the tasks that remain, either in terms of interaction with the user or in terms of analysis yet to be done, if the prototype is to be elevated to a finished model. Prototyping is an essential part of an effective modeling approach, especially when modeling is performed under tight limits on the available time and budget.

What would a prototype for the Retirement Planning case look like? In this case, the essential concern is to explore the relationship between working life savings and retirement assets. We might take as our objective the number of years that we can live off our retirement assets before they are exhausted. In order to estimate this result, it will be useful to simplify at the start some of the many complexities of the problem. For a first prototype, we could make the following assumptions:

- Income grows at a constant rate during the working years.
- The savings rate is a constant percentage of annual income in the working years.
- Retirement assets provide a fixed rate of return.
- The retirement date is fixed.
- Postretirement consumption is a fixed percentage of income in the final year of work.

Using these assumptions, we can rather easily build a model that accomplishes the following tasks:

- Project our income (at some assumed growth rate) from the present to retirement.
- Calculate our retirement contributions (given a constant savings rate).
- Accumulate our retirement assets (at some assumed rate of return).
- Project our assets as they are drawn down during retirement (at the assumed consumption rate).
- Determine the year in which they are exhausted.

This simple model allows us to create a plot that shows how long our assets last as a function of our savings rate (Figure 2.8). If that relationship is the essential summary of our analysis, we have completed our first prototype. We can now test the model, varying decisions and parameters in an attempt to gain insight into the problem. Eventually, we may want to build a refined model, if the first prototype proves inadequate in some way.

In an initial approach to the Draft TV Commercials problem, we might avoid the complexities of sampling from a population of potential drafts and simply assume that advertisement quality increases with the number of draft ads, but with diminishing returns. We might implement this relationship using a power function:

$$Quality = a(Number\ of\ drafts)^b$$

We might also assume that the total budget is fixed and that each draft advertisement costs a fixed percentage of the budget. It follows that each additional draft advertisement reduces the budget available for airing by the same amount. If we assume that the total impact created by an advertisement is the product of the quality of the advertisement (in impressions per dollar spent on airing) and the airing budget, we have the basis for a prototype. From this simple model, we can plot a graph that relates the total number of impressions created to the number of draft advertisements (Figure 2.9).

FIGURE 2.9 Sketch of Results for the Draft TV Commercials Case

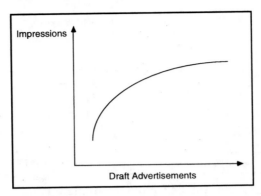

Are we content with this first prototype? Probably not. Assuming that we have or can acquire some data on the variability of ad quality, we might later refine the portion of the model in which the quality of the best draft is determined. Sampling from a distribution of ad quality will give us the average quality of the best advertisement as a function of the number of drafts. We expect this function to have the same concave shape as the power function in our first prototype. But it will be better in at least two ways: first, it more closely resembles the actual process by which the best advertisement is created; second, it allows us to test the sensitivity of the results (total impressions created) to the variability in the distribution of quality.

A prototype for the Icebergs for Kuwait problem could be a model for the radial shrinking of a spherical iceberg of fixed initial size being towed at constant speed from the ice pack to Kuwait. If we calculate the final volume of the iceberg and multiply by the price of water, then we can compute an initial estimate of the value of the project.

This is the information the client wants, so our simple model is a legitimate prototype. Is this approach highly simplified? Of course it is. But the model's simplicity is its strength, not its weakness. If we have built our prototype quickly, we have time left over to refine it. Rather than having a number of separate pieces to integrate, we can work with one unified model.

Before refining this model, we would want to use it to explore the problem. For example, we would want to test the sensitivity of the final cost to the initial size of the iceberg, the towing speed, and the size of the boat. These tests will give us ideas not only about the ultimate results the model will generate, but also about where improvements might be warranted. We might, for example, want to test towing strategies that involve changes in speed over the trip. On the other hand, perhaps the weakest part of the model is the assumption that the iceberg is spherical and melts with a constant radius. Does the submerged portion of an iceberg melt faster or slower than the visible part? Does the ratio of these parts change with size? Every assumption is an opportunity to improve the analysis. The trick to effective prototyping is to find those improvements that lead to significant improvements in the results, not merely to a more elegant, more complex, or more "realistic" model.

In the Racquetball Racket case, the objective is to help the client make a go/no-go decision. A highly accurate forecast of the NPV is not necessarily required, especially if the estimated NPV is clearly positive or negative. Thus, a prototype should give us a first, rough estimate of project NPV. It will move us closer to that goal if we assume that

- our competitor will price at its current level,
- our price and our competitor's price both remain constant over the life of the product,
- no third competitor will enter, and
- total demand for balls will grow at a constant percentage rate, independent of prices.

The only remaining component involves our market share, which we could model as an S-shaped function of our price. The following function is useful in this context:

$$Share = b + (a - b)(Price^c/(d + Price^c))$$

We can use the market research data to help us determine plausible values for the parameters a, b, c, and d. With this module in place, we have a full prototype, because the model can generate an NPV for any price we choose. With the model, we

FIGURE 2.10 Sketch of Results for the Racquetball Racket Case

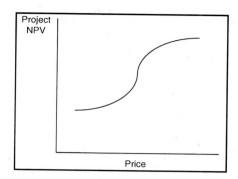

can develop a chart showing how project NPV varies with our price and whether there is a price we can charge at which the project looks attractive (Figure 2.10). Once again, we are not done with the analysis. These results are only the first in what will most likely be a long sequence of estimates for project NPV, but this prototype supports the next stage in the analysis, which involves testing the sensitivity of our results to our assumptions.

In general, how do we know when we have a completed prototype? If we have

- decomposed the problem into modules,
- built at least a simple model for every module, and
- coordinated the modules so that they work together to generate results in the form we think the client wants,

then we have a prototype. If we cannot provide at least a tentative answer to the client's major questions, we don't have a prototype. If one or more modules are missing, we don't have a prototype. But once our ideas come together in a working model, the event marks a key milestone, for then the emphasis will shift from creation to refinement, in collaboration with the client.

The cyclic nature of prototyping is worth some elaboration. Many people think that prototyping involves building one model after another until we are satisfied that we have the final model, and *then* carrying out the analysis. This is a fundamental misconception. It is essential to use each successive prototype to answer the managerial questions in the problem before refining the model further. This discipline helps keep the modeler's attention on the *problem*, and not exclusively on the model or the modeling process. One reason modelers sometimes hesitate to use prototypes in this way is that they are embarrassed by the shortcomings of their early models and don't want to see them being used "for real." But it is only in this way that a modeler can see the value of each successive refinement.

Why is prototyping such a powerful idea? One reason is that a prototype keeps the entire problem in the mind of the modeler. It is impossible to perfect a module in isolation because it has value only as part of the entire model. In most situations, we cannot know how well a module works until it is integrated with the others, so it is vital to build prototypes in which every major component is represented. Prototyping also helps avoid the seduction of modeling for its own sake. Remember that the task is to provide management with *insight*. Modeling is merely a means to that end. One way to maintain focus on the managerial question at hand is to use a series of prototypes to generate tentative answers to the client's questions. By using each model to provide an answer and by performing sensitivity analysis on each model, the focus will remain, appropriately, on the problem rather than on the model.

Prototyping is a particularly critical tool for novice modelers, who often struggle psychologically with the vagaries of the creative process. Many of our students have never struggled as hard as they do in modeling ill-structured problems. Some of them suffer from all the symptoms of depression when they have worked for a week and feel they have nothing to show for it. For these students, as for most modelers, having a working prototype, *no matter how primitive*, is a great psychological boost. Once we have a prototype, we have not only a tentative answer for the client, but also a road map for future work.

Finally, prototyping is an essential tool for the practicing analyst who operates under severe time constraints. Once a prototype is up and running, the analyst should ask this question: Where would my model benefit most from additional work? Or, to put it more precisely: Where should I focus my efforts to most improve the quality of my advice to the client? This is an impossible question to answer in the abstract. But with a prototype and some skill in sensitivity analysis, we can get a fair idea of which modules or which components within a given module have the biggest impact on the results. Thus, the prototype is itself a necessary tool in the analyst's efforts to use time effectively.

2.4.4 Sketch Graphs of Key Relationships

One of the reasons modeling is so difficult for many people is that it appears to be highly abstract or mathematical, and they cannot find a way to express their thoughts in these terms. Most people have good intuitions about the modeling challenges they face, but they lack the skills to represent those intuitions in a useful way. The ability to change representation systems is one of the powerful heuristics that experts suggest for general problem solving. Good problem solvers can look at a problem from many angles—inventing analogies, drawing pictures, hypothesizing relationships, or perhaps carrying out suggestive physical experiments.

Novice modelers rarely use drawings or sketches to represent their understanding of a problem. They haven't discovered that visual depictions of models are often much easier to work with than verbal or mathematical ones. When it comes to creating a relationship between variables, sketching a graph is a very useful first step.

The inability to visualize the relation between variables is a common stumbling block in modeling. Ask a manager whether the relation between advertising and sales is linear or concave, and you may get a puzzled look. Yet if we draw coordinate axes and label the horizontal axis "Advertising," and the vertical "Sales," most anyone will say the graph slopes up and probably "bends over" at some point. So the *intuition* for a concave relation in this case is widely shared; what many people lack is a representation system within which they can express their intuition. Such people lack the mathematical sophistication to select a plausible family of functions to represent a given graphical relation.

Here is another example of the power of visualization. When one of our students is completely stuck about how to start a modeling problem, we might draw a simple diagram (Figure 2.11) consisting of a box with one arrow coming in from the top and another going out to the right. Along with the drawing, we'll say that the way we see the problem, we have some decisions to make (arrow going into box), then the future will evolve in some way (inside the box), and in the end, we'll have some outcomes (arrow going out of box). The model we need to build is going to transform alternative decisions into outcomes we can evaluate. This simple picture does wonders—it focuses the novice on three key issues:

- What *decisions* do we have?
- How will we evaluate *outcomes*?
- What system of *relationships* connects the decisions to the outcomes?

To an experienced modeler, this picture would seem trivial. To a struggling novice, however, it can be a revelation. Somehow, the picture itself is far more powerful than an equivalent verbal or algebraic description.

Why does this visualization heuristic work? We suspect one reason has to do with the power of looking at a problem from different viewpoints. Somehow, changing how we look at a problem often helps us overcome a sense of being stuck, of having no useful knowledge about a particular issue. (Novice modelers usually are able to sketch a graph for a relation, even when they say they know nothing about the mathematical function involved.)

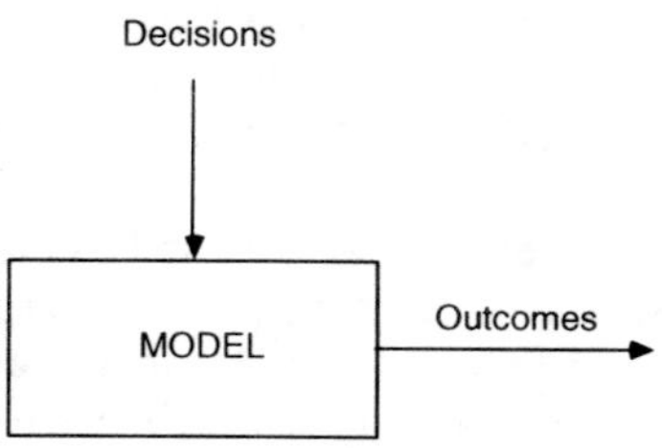

Visualization probably works by *externalizing* the analysis—that is, by moving the focal point of analysis from inside the mind to an external artifact

FIGURE 2.11 Visualization of the Modeling Process

Decisions

MODEL

Outcomes

FIGURE 2.12   Useful
Functions for Modeling

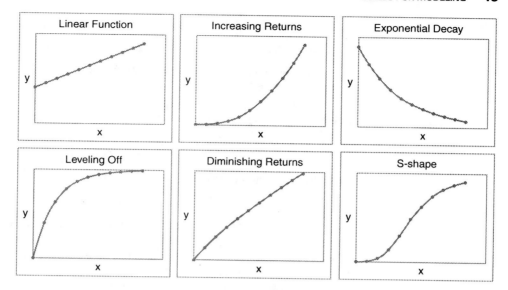

(such as a graph or equation). This is clearly essential for modeling in groups, where thoughts in the mind cannot be debated unless they are represented outside the mind. But it is also crucial for the solo modeler, because it is far easier to test and refine an external artifact than an inchoate idea in the mind.

Sketching graphs is also a powerful heuristic because there is only a small set of possible relations between two variables that are useful in a typical modeling problem, and common sense can rule out most of them. The most often used is the simple straight line (with either positive or negative slope). In the spirit of prototyping, we often suggest that the *first* relation we would propose between *any* variables is a linear one. Build a working prototype first and gain some experience with it. Come back later and refine the linear relation if theory or intuition suggests a more complex relation and if model testing suggests that the results will be sensitive to this relation.

In order to make full use of this heuristic, the modeler also needs to know a few useful families of functions. Here is a basic list. (These families are also depicted in Figure 2.12.)

- Linear function, showing constant returns (positive or negative), $y = a + bx$.
- Power function with increasing returns, $y = ax^b$ with $(b > 1)$.
- Exponential function, representing decline and decay, $y = ae^{-bx}$.
- Exponential function, representing leveling off at an asymptote, $y = a(1 - e^{-bx})$.
- Power function, with diminishing returns, $y = ax^b$ with $(b < 1)$.
- The S-shaped curve, for rapid, then slowing growth, $y = b + (a - b)(x^c/(d + x^c))$.

This use of graphs to select a family of curves to represent a relation is closely related to the parameterization heuristic discussed next.

2.4.5   Identify Parameters and Perform Sensitivity Analysis

We have seen that sketching a graph is a powerful way to express one's intuitions about the relationship between two variables. (The idea could be extended to three variables, although it gets more complicated.) But there is no direct way as yet to enter a sketch into a spreadsheet. Some explicit formula must be created to stand for the sketch in the model itself. This could take the form of a traditional mathematical function, for example:

$$D5 = \$A\$1 + \$A\$2 * D4$$

or it could be a complex combination of spreadsheet functions, for example:

D5= IF(D2-D1 > $E$4,VLOOKUP(E7,Data,3),VLOOKUP(E7,Data,2))).

In either case, the relations involve input numbers, and these parameters play an essential role in spreadsheet modeling and analysis.

For example, we might hypothesize that there is a downward-sloping relation between the quantity we sell and the price we can charge. This assumption is consistent with the linear demand curve

$$Price = a - b \times (Quantity)$$

and also with the constant-elasticity demand curve

$$Price = a \times (Quantity)^b (b < 1)$$

In each of these functions, the symbols a and b are parameters that stand for as-yet-undetermined numbers. Each of these functions represents a *family* of relations having the common property of sloping downward; the linear family declines at a constant rate, while the constant-elasticity family declines at a decreasing rate. When we implement one of these families in a spreadsheet model, we choose particular values of the parameters; that is, we select one from among the family of curves. Rarely will we know the values of these parameters exactly. This is where sensitivity analysis comes in. With sensitivity analysis, we can determine plausible ranges for the parameters and test the impact of changing parameter values on model outputs. In fact, we will recommend in Chapter 6 that testing the sensitivity of the critical outputs to model parameters is an essential step in any modeling activity. One reason we can be creative in the functional relationships we put in our models is that we have confidence that we can eventually test our results with respect both to the functions we have used and to the parameters that drive those functions.

Parameterization plays a key role in one of our favorite short modeling problems, called *Hot and Thirsty*.[4] The goal is to model the temperature of a warm beer as it cools over time in a refrigerator. Common sense leads to a difference equation of the form

$$T_{t+1} = T_t - Heat\ loss\ over\ the\ interval(t, t + 1)$$

where T_t represents the temperature of the beer at time t. What factors influence the heat loss? Clearly, the type of beer may be relevant, as are the material used in its container, the shape of the container, the humidity of the refrigerator, how frequently it is opened, and so on. So many factors influence heat loss that one might think the only feasible approach is to gather data on all of them, a daunting task. However, there is an easier way.

A little understanding of thermodynamics (or some experience with refrigerators) will suggest that heat loss is proportional to the temperature difference between the beer and the air in the refrigerator, with the constant of proportionality depending on all the factors cited above; that is:

$$T_{t+1} = T_t - k \times (T_t - T_{fridge})$$

If, for the moment, we assume some arbitrary value for the constant of proportionality k, it is straightforward to build a spreadsheet model for this relation. Then, as we choose different values of the parameter k, we can graph different decline curves for the temperature (see Figure 2.13). It is surprising but true that we can use common sense and a little experience with beer to determine plausible values for k within a rather narrow range, just based on the time it takes to cool to refrigerator temperature. We could also determine k rather accurately by cooling a beer for, say, 15 minutes and then determining its temperature. We can then use the family of curves in Figure 2.13 to read off the value of k that gives us this temperature.

---

[4]A. Starfield, K. Smith, and A. Bleloch, *How to Model It* (New York: McGraw-Hill, 1990), 54–69.

FIGURE 2.13 Temperature of Beer over Time

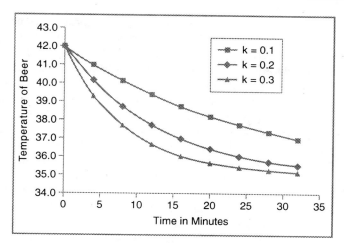

This looks like sleight of hand, as if we were manufacturing knowledge out of ignorance. After all, we know that k depends on a long list of factors, none of which is known in this problem. Yet here we lump all these influences into a single number. What really has happened is that we have used intuition and common sense to build a structure (or model) that is more general than needed for the immediate purpose, and then we have specialized it to the case at hand by varying the single number k. We have also saved a lot of effort by building a model structure before we tried to collect data, because, using this approach, we never have to know the type of beer, its container, or anything about the refrigerator.

Why is parameterization such a powerful heuristic? We believe its power comes, as the previous example suggests, from our ability to select one from a family of curves by using sensitivity analysis. Parameterization also reduces the vagueness in relation to a single dimension, which itself is a great simplification. Then, if we can find ways (such as the graphical approach described earlier) to display the implications of a particular choice for the parameter, we can bring to bear our usually considerable intuition about the problem. So the power of parameterization, in part, lies in building links between our rational knowledge and our intuition.

2.4.6 Separate the Creation of Ideas from Their Evaluation

Jim Evans, who has written extensively on the role of creativity in management science, points out in his book *Creative Thinking*[5] that one of the important emotional blocks to creativity is the tendency to judge ideas before they receive an adequate hearing. Many modelers we have worked with show a marked *preference* for judging ideas over generating them, especially if generating ideas means coming up with wild notions that probably will not work. But some wild notions actually do work, and others spark the mind to generate additional creative solutions. It is, therefore, essential to have methods available that help *quiet the critical voice* during the most creative phases of the problem-solving process.

The "quiet the critic" heuristic is based on the distinction, discussed earlier, between divergent and convergent thinking. Divergent thinking involves generating alternative problem statements, approaches, and possible solutions, with a minimum of evaluation. Convergent thinking, on the other hand, involves the rational analysis of these alternatives, with the goal of choosing the best (and rejecting the rest). Each stage of the problem-solving process involves both divergent and convergent thinking. However, it is generally most effective to stress divergent types of thinking early in the modeling process and to gradually shift to more convergent thinking as the model and analysis take shape.

[5]James R. Evans, *Creative Thinking* (Cincinnati: South-Western, 1991).

The quintessential divergent-thinking process is **brainstorming**, in which a group generates as many ideas on an issue as possible, without any critical evaluation. The most effective brainstorming sessions involve a facilitator, who can set the ground rules and remind participants not to criticize the ideas of others. The purpose of not criticizing ideas is to prevent premature selection of obvious or mundane approaches to a problem. Some participants always seem to have difficulty refraining from evaluating their own ideas or those of others during such a session. It is often equally difficult for them to show overt enthusiasm for ideas, from whatever source. Fostering a climate in which ideas are celebrated, regardless of their source or their apparent usefulness, should be a goal of modeling teams and individuals.

It's difficult to appreciate the power of brainstorming without seeing it in action. We recall a class session in which we were analyzing the problem of how to configure a highway tunnel to accommodate the maximum traffic volume. We had determined the optimal speed and heading for cars to follow, but were stuck on how to ensure that drivers would actually follow our solution. We then had a short brainstorming session focused on how to accomplish this. Among many other creative ideas, one student suggested installing rows of lights in the tunnel that would blink on and off at a speed set by the traffic engineers to guide drivers to the correct speed. This student was from another country, and the other students' first reaction was that this solution must be something she had seen in use in her home country. Once they began to realize it was not a known solution but something she had invented on the spot, they were more willing to think of alternatives beyond their own experience.

Why does this heuristic work? Apparently, our educational systems encourage students to criticize their own ideas and those of others, but not to create ideas or to appreciate their own and others' creative ideas. This imbalance can be so extreme that an open-ended project such as modeling becomes overwhelming because the pitfalls of every approach seem so clear to the modeler. When the critical faculty is so strong, the modeler needs reassurance that mistakes and blind alleys are a necessary part of the creative process. By finding ways to "quiet the critic," the novice modeler gains time to find a solution that eventually will stand up to their own scrutiny and to the scrutiny of others.

2.4.7 Work Backward from the Desired Answer

Most modeling projects proceed from the ground up: make assumptions, gather data, build a prototype, and so on. This is a reasonable approach in many ways, and to some extent, there is no alternative. But the bottom-up approach can lead to difficulties, especially in the hands of creative individuals. Creative exploration of a problem with a succession of models sometimes leaves the modeling team in a quandary about which approach among many to take and which results to show the client.

One way to break through this dilemma is to *work backward from the desired answer*. That is, imagine the *form* the answer will take, and then work backward from that point to select the model and analysis necessary to generate the chosen form of answer. An example will clarify this point.

It is clear in the Retirement Planning case that the client wants to know how his savings during his working life will influence his retirement years. But there are many ways to measure the quality of retirement living; which ones are best suited to this client? Would he like to know his asset level at retirement, or the number of years his assets will hold out, or the maximum amount he can afford to spend if he lives to 75, or the probability of running out of money before he is 90? Before we can focus our modeling, we must have an answer (even a tentative one) to this question. We also need to know how the client thinks about his savings decision—in terms of a constant percentage of his income or a constant dollar amount, or perhaps a percentage rising at a certain rate. Until we settle this question, we are also not ready to think about how we are going to present our results. If, after sufficient thought, we decide we want to show the client how his final assets depend

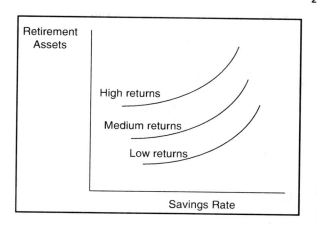

FIGURE 2.14 Sketch of Results for Retirement Analysis

on his (constant percentage) savings rate and how this relationship itself depends on the returns he can earn on his assets, we can sketch the chart shown in Figure 2.14. Notice that we do not need a model, nor do we need any data, to sketch this chart because it is only an illustration. But the chart has considerable value because it focuses our modeling effort on a clear end product.

We sometimes facetiously call this the "PowerPoint heuristic." Here's the idea: most decision makers are very busy, so they cannot sit through a long-winded presentation. In fact, we like to imagine that our client is so busy that we have to condense our entire presentation to *one* PowerPoint slide. If that's all we have, that one slide must contain the essential message we have to deliver. What is that message? Is it a number, a table, a chart, a procedure, a recommendation? Sketching out what that one slide might look like involves making decisions about the critical outputs, thus focusing the modeling effort on the essential message.

The power of this heuristic lies not just in being able to organize one's thoughts at the end of a modeling effort, but also in organizing the work itself by asking periodically: What will our final results look like?

2.4.8 Focus on Model Structure, not on Data Collection

As we mentioned in Chapter 1, novice modelers often spend a high proportion of their time searching for and analyzing *data*. Expert modelers, however, spend most of their time working on the *structure* of their models. This contrast has significant implications for the appropriate conduct of a modeling project.

Why do novices emphasize data analysis over model structure? This attitude appears to be based on three beliefs. First, novices assume that the available data are an accurate indicator of the information needed in the modeling process. Second, they believe that obtaining data moves the process forward in a productive direction. Third, they believe that the available data will ultimately improve the quality of the recommendations developed as a result of modeling. From these beliefs, it seems to follow logically that data collection and analysis should be an important and early activity in any modeling project. But these beliefs are not supported by experience. As Mosteller, Fienberg, and Rourke state it, "Although we often hear that data speak for themselves, their voices can be soft and sly."[6]

Novice modelers tend to accept, without critical screening, any data provided to them. By contrast, expert modelers know that most data contain hidden biases and errors. Perhaps the biggest single problem with empirical information is that it reports on the *past*, whereas modeling looks to the *future*. Even if we have accurate data on the growth in sales over the past 10 years, can we be sure next year's growth will follow the same pattern? Other common sources of biases and errors in empirical data include:

- *Sampling error* (e.g., a phone survey does not contact the homeless)
- *Differences in purpose* (e.g., accounting profits do not correspond to economic profits)

[6]Frederick Mosteller, Stephen E. Fienberg, and Robert E. K. Rourke, as quoted in Jonathan G. Koomey, *Turning Numbers into Knowledge* (Oakland, CA: Analytics Press, 2001), p. 86.

- *Masking* (e.g., actual sales may not reflect underlying customer demand)
- *Inappropriateness* (e.g., growth rates on one product may not predict those on another)
- *Definitional differences* (e.g., demand histories do not reveal price elasticity)

Experts look at all data skeptically, asking where the information came from and who gathered it (and with what motivations). They try to determine all the ways in which it may be flawed for the purpose they have in mind. Even when high-quality data are available, the modeler must use judgment before incorporating the data into a model. Sometimes, good judgment involves discarding parts of the data as irrelevant or misleading; sometimes it involves choosing how to summarize the data (whether to use the average or the worst case, for example). Experts, then, are much more skeptical than novices about the accuracy and appropriateness of data, and therefore more skeptical about the usefulness of data in a modeling effort.

While novices believe that collecting data will move the modeling process forward beneficially, they seldom recognize that data collection can also be distracting and limiting. For example, if the corporate database records sales by industry and by company size, most likely a model for sales will relate it to these two driving variables, rather than to less readily available, but perhaps more important, factors. A better model results in most cases if it is built up from first principles, without being overly influenced by the available data.

The Racquetball Racket case provides another example of how the availability of data can limit modeling creativity. The market research firm has given us information on the percentage of people who would buy our ball at various prices. They present the data in the form of a ratio of our competitor's price to our price. Does this imply that we should use the price *ratio* as the driving variable in our model of market share? The implication of such an approach would be that consumers do not react to the actual level of prices but only to relative prices. In other words, our share would be the same if we charged $5 and the competition $10, or if we charged $1 to their $2. Is this a plausible model, or might consumers react instead to the *difference* in prices? If we focus first on the data as presented, we may not even recognize the relevance of this question.

Thus, experts first build an appropriate model structure and use data to refine that model. The principle, in essence, is to let the model tell us what data we need rather than letting the data dictate our model.

Novice modelers often think they cannot build a useful model without acquiring good data first. Worse, they often feel that collecting good data, or at least better data than they currently have, is necessary before they even begin to *think* about a model. In either case, their premise is that data hold the key to a successful analysis. Some companies foster this attitude by emphasizing "data-driven decision making." A popular textbook even offers the advice that "one of the *first jobs* of an analyst is to gather exactly the *right data* and summarize the data appropriately." [Emphases added.] But how can a modeler identify the right data before building an initial model within which these questions can be answered? Most important, how can the modeler know what data will have the biggest impact on the ultimate recommendations that flow out of the modeling process? As Clifford Stoll says: "Minds think with ideas, not information. No amount of data, bandwidth, or processing power can substitute for inspired thought."[7]

Inexperienced modelers appear to believe that the quality of a model's recommendations depends critically on the quality of the model's data. But the managerial recommendations that evolve from modeling and analysis are often driven far more by the structure of the model than by the specific parameters in it. Therefore, it is imperative to get the model structure right, but it may be quite acceptable to work with rough parameter estimates. Once the modeling process has

[7] As quoted in Jonathan G. Koomey, *Turning Numbers into Knowledge: Mastering the Art of Problem Solving.* (Oakland, CA: Analytics Press, 2001), p. 101.

begun and a prototype provides us a basis for determining which data would be desirable, we can address the question of whether rough parameter estimates will work. The precision needed for the numerical inputs can be determined only through testing the model itself. This is an additional benefit from sensitivity analysis, beyond the plausibility tests that we mentioned earlier. Sensitivity tools can help identify which parameters require precise values—that is, the ones for which data analysis would be most beneficial. Experts, then, focus on getting model structure right and on acquiring only data that they anticipate will materially affect their conclusions.

Based on our observations of expert modelers, we believe that data collection should rarely be the main concern in modeling. It is quite possible to build models, analyze models, and draw insights from models without relying on data analysis or statistical methods at all. In fact, we endorse that approach as a first cut. Data collection should ideally be undertaken only after a model-based determination has been made as to precisely which data are needed and with what level of precision. We have come to this point of view after observing problem-solving teams waste large amounts of precious time and effort on poorly conceived data collection expeditions, and observing novice modelers in a research setting become distracted from model structuring by the lack of data or by an excess of data. This is not to say that data collection is irrelevant; there are circumstances in which empirical data have a major impact on the quality of model-based recommendations. However, most business analysis takes place under a fairly severe time constraint. In such circumstances, modelers seldom have the luxury to search for the best possible data. Sometimes, we can find only data that were collected for other purposes and may not be tailored to our needs. At other times, very little data are available at all. Nevertheless, we must remember that *modeling* is central, not data.

2.5 SUMMARY

Effective modeling takes place within a larger problem-solving process. Modeling can be useful both in finding a good solution and in facilitating communication as the solution is developed, refined, and implemented. Therefore, it is important to recognize the larger context in which modeling occurs. We organize the problem-solving process into six stages.

1. Exploring the mess
2. Searching for information
3. Defining the problem
4. Searching for solutions
5. Evaluating solutions
6. Implementing a solution

Although it's convenient to describe these stages as if they were separate and occurred in a strict sequence, that is seldom the case. In fact, we can't always identify the specific activities at each stage until after the fact. Nevertheless, every implemented solution comes about through some version of this problem-solving process. Generally speaking, the bigger the problem at hand or the larger the team working on it, the more important it is to use a structured problem-solving process.

Mental modeling is an essential tool in problem solving. A mental model allows us to trace the consequences of a course of action without actually implementing it. In that way, mental models save us the time and cost, not to mention the occasionally disastrous consequences, of actually trying out alternative solutions to a problem.

Formal models provide the same kind of benefits as mental models. A formal model is a laboratory within which we can search for the best solution, without incurring the time and cost of trial-and-error approaches. Formal models are costlier and more time-consuming to build than mental models, but they have the great advantage that they make our assumptions, logic, and preferences explicit. They also allow us to search among many more solutions than would otherwise be possible. Finally, an effective formal model can help communicate the reasoning behind a solution and in that way help to motivate an individual or organization to act.

Influence charts offer the modeler a bridge between an ill-structured problem and a formal model. A formal model is usually precise and quantitative, but an influence chart is conceptual, abstract, and nonnumerical. It helps the modeler decide what is to be included in the model and what is to be excluded. It also helps focus attention on outputs, inputs, and the logic that connects them. Finally, it helps a modeler or modeling team to surface and recognize the assumptions behind the model and its limitations.

Modeling heuristics are rules of thumb that help in the design and use of models. They enhance pure technical skill by enabling us to invent models for new and unfamiliar situations. They also play a major role in the craft of modeling. Our list of modeling heuristics includes:

1. Simplify the problem.
2. Break the problem into modules.
3. Build a prototype and refine it.
4. Sketch graphs of key relationships.

5. Identify parameters and perform sensitivity analysis.
6. Separate the creation of ideas from their evaluation.
7. Work backward from the desired answer.
8. Focus on model structure, not on data collection.

Some of the items on the list are useful to help a modeling effort get off to a good start. If we think in terms of the chronological steps in a typical modeling project, the last heuristic may be the first one to apply: focus first on structuring a model rather than on obtaining data. The first model ought to be simple. It should be guided mainly by the desire to capture an essential trade-off in the problem. Simplification, by its nature, involves making assumptions about the problem, and these should be explicit. In any stage of model development, there should be a companion phase in which those assumptions are subjected to sensitivity analysis so that we can determine which ones need refinement. Devising a model structure made up of modules enables us to focus on the components of the model as a means of overcoming complexity in the overall problem. An ideal structure contains independent modules and allows interchangeable substitutes for the original module.

In building an initial model structure, we might start with visual representations, such as diagrams or graphs, for the inputs and also for the outputs. Visualizing the outputs, in the sense of working backward, keeps us focused on the precise requirements of the problem. Then, in order to convert graphical representations to mathematical representations, we might want to draw on a small family of familiar functions, specifying parameters as needed. Parameters used in this way are numerical assumptions, and, as with structural assumptions, they deserve sensitivity analysis. Sensitivity testing will tell us which parameters or which functional relationships are most critical to the ultimate outcomes.

Some of the heuristics on our list may be applied repeatedly during a modeling project. Developing a good model is a multistep process involving successive refinement. We start with a first prototype, and we test it to determine how well it addresses the problem. This testing may suggest we do some data collection, and it might stimulate our thinking about enrichments to the model. At various stages in the process, especially when the project is team-based, we may need some creative input from brainstorming activity. However, with the repeated cycles of model enhancement and model testing, we will have compiled some analysis, perhaps overly simple, that we can bring to bear on the problem. As we improve the model, we continually add to our store of knowledge and insight about the problem, so that at every stage in the process, we have an answer for the client and a sense of whether our analysis is adequate. Prototyping thus creates an important dialogue with the client and helps assure that the focus remains on the problem rather than the model.

SUGGESTED READINGS

For more information on problem solving and creativity, consult the following books:

Adams, J. L. 2001. *Conceptual Blockbusting*. Reading, MA: Addison-Wesley.
Couger, J. D. 1995. *Creative Problem Solving and Opportunity Finding*. Danvers, MA: Boyd & Fraser.
Evans, J. R. 1991. *Creative Thinking*. Cincinnati: South-Western.

Very little has been written on the craft aspects of modeling, whether in business or science. The original work on heuristics in problem solving is the following:

Polya, G. 1971. *How to Solve It*. Princeton, NJ: Princeton University Press.

This little classic, which is still in print 60 years after it was written, is focused on problem solving in mathematics, but it still provides worthwhile reading.

Two more recent books that discuss some of the ideas in this chapter are:

Pidd, M. 1996. *Tools for Thinking: Modelling in Management Science*. Chichester: John Wiley and Sons.
Koomey, J. G. 2001. *Turning Numbers into Knowledge: Mastering the Art of Problem Solving*. Oakland, CA: Analytics Press.

The following classic articles are still relevant after many years and remain worth reading:

Geoffrion, A. M. 1976. "The Purpose of Mathematical Programming Is Insight, Not Numbers." *Interfaces* 7, 81–92.
Little, J. D. C. 1970. "Models and Managers: The Concept of a Decision Calculus." *Management Science* 16, B466–B485.
Morris, W. T. 1967. "On the Art of Modeling." *Management Science* 13, B707–717.
Urban, G. L. 1974. "Building Models for Decision Makers." *Interfaces* 4, 1–11.

EXERCISES

PROBLEM FORMULATION

The four short cases we have analyzed in this chapter (Retirement Planning, Draft TV Commercials, Icebergs for Kuwait, and Racquetball Racket) are reproduced with full details toward the end of this book. For each of these cases, prepare for building a model by reading the full case and answering the following questions.

1. Explore the mess by answering the following questions:

   (a) What do we know?
   (b) What can we assume?
   (c) What could the results look like?
   (d) What information can be brought to bear?

(e) What can we ask the client?

(f) Are there any similar situations or problems?

2. Formulate one or more problem statements.

3. What are the decisions, outcomes, and relationships in the problem?

4. Draw an influence chart for the problem.

5. In what ways could we simplify the problem?

6. What modules will we need to build?

7. What are the key relationships in the problem? Draw their graphs.

8. What are the parameters of the problem?

INFLUENCE CHARTS

Draw influence charts for each of the following problems.

1. The Boeing Company faces a critical strategic choice in its competition with Airbus Industries for the long-haul flight segment: should it design and build a super-747 model that can carry 550 passengers at speeds around 350 mph, or a plane that can fly at 95 percent of the speed of sound but carry only about 350 passengers? As a member of Boeing's Planning Group, your task is to build a model to investigate the trade-offs involved in this decision.

2. The Red Cross provides about 40 percent of the replacement blood supply for the United States. The available donor base has been shrinking for years, and although increased advertising has kept Red Cross supplies adequate, the time is approaching when demand will outstrip supply. For many years, the Red Cross has refused to pay donors for blood, because to do so would "put the blood supply of the country at risk." However, Red Cross management has begun to consider changing its policy. Evaluate the impacts of a policy under which the Red Cross would pay each of its donors a set fee.

3. Your client is the planning office of a major university. Part of the job of the planning office is to forecast the annual donations of alumni through the university's long-established giving program. Until now, the forecast has been made subjectively. The client wants you to develop a more objective approach. The Planning Office can make data available for the past 10 years that shows for each alumni class in that year:

• The number of living alumni in the class
• The number of givers

• Total direct donations from the class
• Other gifts for the class (e.g., employer matching)

4. Congress is considering a new law that will grant amnesty to the roughly 11 million illegal aliens in the United States. Under this law, anyone who has entered the country illegally in the past can apply for permanent residence status and a green card, which conveys the right to work. This law, if passed, can be expected to have significant impacts on industries that currently rely on illegal workers (such as hospitality, meat packing, and construction). It may also have impacts on wages, school enrollments, healthcare costs, and the future rate of illegal immigration.

5. A major pharmaceutical manufacturer is facing a difficult decision concerning one of its hearing-enhancement products. The product has been on the market less than two years, and reports have recently begun to come in that the product may cause serious hearing loss in certain users. The number and severity of these reports are not sufficiently high to warrant a recall order from the FDA, but if the reports continue this could eventually happen. In the meantime, management is considering issuing a voluntary recall to limit the potential damages. However, any such recall will probably destroy the future market for this product, which may be entirely safe, and it will also hurt sales of all other products sold by this company and depress its stock price.

SKETCHING GRAPHS

Sketch graphs for the relationships described in each of the following problems and select one or more of the families of functions discussed in Section 4 to represent it.

1. The relationship between the effectiveness of a new drug and the amount spent on R&D.

2. The relationship between the cost of manufacturing a product and the cumulative quantity produced.

3. The relationship between the time it takes to complete a project and the number of people assigned to work on it.

4. The relationship between the probability the FDA will approve a given drug and the number of patients enrolled in the clinical trials of the drug.

5. The relationship between the sales of a given brand of cereal in a grocery store and the amount of shelf space devoted to displaying it.

3 Basic Excel Skills

3.1 INTRODUCTION

Excel may be the most versatile software program ever created. It is used daily by millions of people in every conceivable walk of life. Some of its users are simply adding up short columns of numbers, while others are creating sophisticated applications in which Excel is performing complex numerical calculations while interacting with several other software systems. With such a versatile and flexible tool, it is difficult for any user to determine just which of the thousands of features in Excel are really worth knowing. In this chapter, we describe the basic Excel skills we think are important for every business analyst.

This chapter is not intended to serve as a beginner's tutorial on Excel. Those who are new to Excel and who need a tutorial should work through a book or a CD, or take an online course. Several of these are listed in the suggested readings. Those who have a working knowledge of Excel will find in this chapter some reminders about familiar tools and perhaps pointers to some new ones as well. We have found that many experienced users have never taken the time to explore Excel systematically, so their skills are deep in some areas but shallow in others. We recommend that you skim this chapter for Excel features that are new to you and add them to your skill set. A few minutes spent in learning how to use Excel more efficiently, even if you are an experienced user, can pay dividends in the future every time you build a spreadsheet model.

3.2 EXCEL PREREQUISITES

What spreadsheet skills are prerequisites for an analyst who would like to learn to *model* in Excel? The most basic skill, and one that doesn't show up in the books, is the ability to *learn by trial and error*. Few successful users of software learn primarily from manuals or help facilities. Most have learned to scan the menus and search in a partly random, partly intelligent fashion for the tool they need and to experiment freely, knowing that (almost) nothing they do cannot be undone. In fact, the Undo command is one of the most important features in Excel!

Getting down to Excel, the first necessary skill is to be able to *navigate* around a worksheet and between worksheets in a workbook. This includes moving the cursor, scrolling, using the Home and End keys, and so on. Even the novice modeler needs to *enter text* and *enter data* and to choose the *format* of these entries. It is handy to be able to change the font name, style, and size; to use bold and italics; and to color a cell or its contents. The ability to *edit* the contents of a cell is important. Other necessary skills include *inserting* and *deleting* rows or columns and entire worksheets; *cutting*, *copying*, and *pasting*; *printing*; and *drawing charts*.

Skillful use of *formulas* and *functions* separates the novice spreadsheet user from the advanced user. To create formulas effectively, users must understand both *relative cell addressing* and *absolute cell addressing*. Excel has innumerable built-in functions that can drastically simplify calculations. Some of the most useful are SUM,

FIGURE 3.1 Office Building Spreadsheet

	A	B	C	D	E	F	G
1	Office Building						
2							
3	Parameters	Rate of increase	Year 1	Year 2	Year 3	Year 4	Year 5
4	Building cost per sq ft		$80.00				
5	Size of building		180,000				
6	Rent per sq ft	5%	$15.00	15.75	16.54	17.36	18.23
7	Operating expense per sq ft	6%	$1.20	1.27	1.35	1.43	1.51
8	Vacancy rate	-4%	30%	0.26	0.22	0.18	0.14
9	Percent financed		85%				
10	Mortgage rate		12%				
11	Sale multiple		12				
12	Cost of capital		10%				
13							
14			Year 1	Year 2	Year 3	Year 4	Year 5
15	Cash Flow						
16		Gross income	1,890,000	2,097,900	2,321,865	2,562,982	2,822,406
17		Operating expense	216,000	226,960	242,696	257,259	272,695
18		Net operating income	1,674,000	1,868,940	2,079,167	2,305,722	2,549,710
19		Interest cost	$1,464,720	$1,464,720	$1,464,720	$1,464,720	$1,464,720
20		Before-tax cash flow	$209,280	$404,220	$614,447	$841,002	$1,084,990
21							
22		Down payment (at time 0)	$2,160,000				
23		Sale price					$30,596,526
24		Mortgage cost					$12,240,000
25		End of year cash flows	$209,280	$404,220	$614,447	$841,002	$19,441,516
26							
27	NPV	$11,472,032					

IF, MAX, MIN, AVERAGE, and NPV. The Insert Function window not only lists all the available functions by category, but also specifies the syntax of each function, explaining what inputs each requires and in what order.

Beyond these basic tools, Excel contains literally hundreds of specialized features. Few modelers use more than several dozens of these routinely, and even fewer can remember all of them between uses. It is *not* necessary to master all of these specialized tools in order to succeed at modeling.

We will use a simple spreadsheet model as an example throughout this chapter. The reader should open this model and use it to test out the features described below. The spreadsheet itself is shown in Figure 3.1[*].

EXAMPLE
Office Building Planning

Potential investors in an office building construction project have asked us to evaluate this opportunity. Our task is to predict the after-tax cash flows resulting from constructing and operating this proposed office building over a five-year period. At a planned size of 180,000 square feet, the expected construction cost is $80 per square foot. The investors plan to take out a mortgage for 85 percent of the cost of the building (paying the remainder in cash), and they have been guaranteed a rate of 12 percent for a term of 30 years. The owners must also pay for the cost of operating the building, which includes taxes, insurance, maintenance, and certain utilities. They assume that the average operating cost per square foot will be $1.20. They have also estimated that they can charge a rental rate of $15 per square foot, with an occupancy rate of 70 percent. The cost of capital is 10 percent. Rents in the future are expected to grow 5 percent per year, while operating expenses grow 6 percent and the occupancy rate drops 4 percentage points yearly as the building ages. The owners plan to sell the building at the end of the fifth year for 12 times the final year's net operating income. ∎

3.3 THE EXCEL WINDOW

Each Excel file is called a *workbook*. A workbook consists of a number of individual *worksheets*. We will use the word "spreadsheet" to refer to both workbooks and worksheets.

The basic spreadsheet layout consists of a grid of rows and columns of cells (see Figure 3.2). The rows are labeled with numbers and the columns are labeled with letters. The maximum number of rows in a single worksheet is 1,048,576; the maximum number of columns is 16,384. The address of a cell corresponds to its column and row label—for example, C3 or AB567.

[*]To download spreadsheets for this chapter, go to the Student Companion Site at www.wiley.com/college/powell.

FIGURE 3.2 Features of
the Excel Window

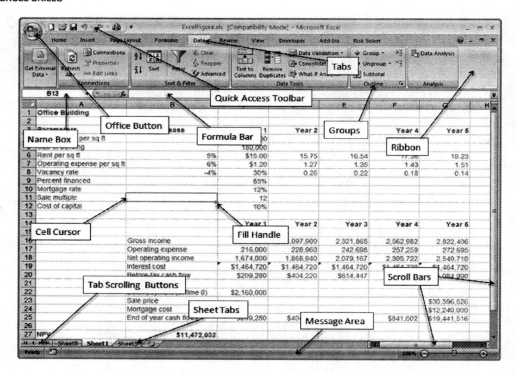

Excel displays on the computer screen a portion of this grid surrounded by other information. Some of the important features of the Excel window are described here and noted in Figure 3.2.

Office Button The Office Button, which is located at the upper left corner of the window, provides access to the most commonly used commands such as New, Open, Close; Save, Save As; and Print. It also provides access to Excel Options.

Quick Access Toolbar Just to the right of the Office Button is the Quick Access Toolbar. This toolbar provides a set of icons that provide shortcuts to frequently used commands. You can customize this toolbar by selecting the downward pointing arrow to the right of the icons.

Tabs The main Excel commands are organized across the top row into the following *tabs*:

- Home
- Insert
- Page Layout
- Formulas
- Data
- Review
- View
- Add-ins

Additional tabs may, under certain conditions, appear to the right of the eight listed above.

Ribbons and Groups Each tab gives access to a *ribbon* in which *commands* are organized into *groups*. For example, the Home tab has the following groups of commands:

- Clipboard
- Font
- Alignment
- Number
- Styles
- Cells
- Editing

The Font group includes the following commands:

- Font
- Font size (increase and decrease)
- Bold, italics, underline
- Borders
- Fill color
- Font color

In addition, the Font group includes a small downward-pointing arrow icon (↘) that opens the Format Cells window.

Message Area   When Excel performs lengthy calculations, a message will appear in this area giving information on the progress of the procedure.

Scroll Bars   These bars allow the user to change the portion of the spreadsheet displayed on the screen.

Sheet Tabs   These tabs allow the user to select which worksheet is displayed. The selection allows the user to move from sheet to sheet within a workbook.

Tab-Scrolling Buttons   These small triangles allow the display of different tabs in workbooks where not all of the tabs are visible at once.

Name Box   This box displays the cell address where the cursor is located, as well as the list of any named ranges. (Named ranges are covered in Chapter 4.)

Formula Bar   This box displays the contents of the cell where the cursor is located, whether a number, formula, or text. This is usually the area in which the user enters information into a cell.

Mouse Cursor   The location of the cursor is shown with an open cross symbol.

Cell Cursor   When a cell has been selected, it is outlined with a dark border. When a range of cells has been selected, it is colored blue and outlined with a dark border.

Fill Handle   At the lower right-hand corner of the cell border is a cross that can be selected for copying the contents of the cell to adjacent cells. When this cross is selected, the mouse cursor changes to a darkened cross.

3.4   CONFIGURING EXCEL

Many users are not aware that they can control the look and behavior of their spreadsheets by setting certain parameters. Select Office Button▶Excel Options, and a window appears with nine tabs listed in a column on the left (see Figure 3.3).

FIGURE 3.3 The Excel Options Window

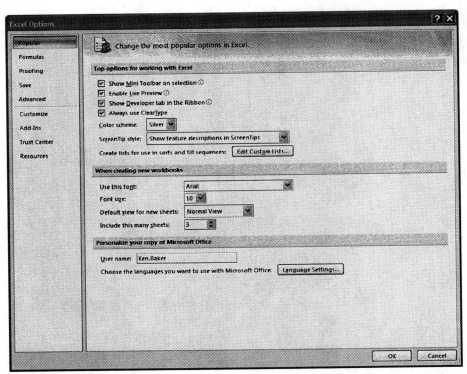

Except where noted below, most of the choices provided on these tabs can safely be left at their default values.

Popular Tab   Select an appropriate font and font size.

Formulas Tab   In most uses, it is preferable to have the spreadsheet calculate all formula cells each time a change is made to any cell. This updating occurs if `Automatic Calculation` is selected under `Calculation` options. On occasion, it is useful to turn this feature off. To do so, check `Manual Calculation`. When the manual calculation option is chosen, the spreadsheet can be recalculated at any time by pressing F9, but it will not recalculate automatically when a cell is changed. The message "Calculate" will appear in the Message area when a cell has been changed but the spreadsheet has not been recalculated.

When a spreadsheet contains simultaneous relationships, calculations cannot be made in the usual manner. This situation typically generates an error message warning of a *circular reference*. This error message is useful because circular references usually occur when there is a mistake in the logic. However, there are circumstances where a circular reference is sensible (for example, when linking income statement and balance sheet models). In these cases, it is necessary to specify a number of iterations to calculate the desired values. Check the box labeled `Enable iterative calculation` to implement an iterative approach.

Under `Error Checking` check the box labeled `Enable background error checking`. Check all nine `Error checking` rules.

Proofing Tab   Select the preferred options for the AutoCorrect feature in Excel.

Save Tab   Check the box labeled `Save AutoRecovery information` so that Excel will automatically save your spreadsheets as often as specified.

Advanced Tab   Under `Editing` options, check the boxes labeled `Enable fill handle and cell drag and drop`, and `Allow editing directly in cells`.

Under Cut, copy, and paste, check the boxes labeled Show Paste Options buttons and Show Insert Options buttons.

Customize Tab   Customize the Quick Access Toolbar. Experienced Excel users will recognize that they use some commands quite frequently and instead of hunting for the commands in the ribbon, they can place the corresponding icon in the Quick Access Toolbar for convenience.

Add-ins Tab: View and manage add-ins.

Trust Center Tab: Information on privacy and security.

Resources Tab: Access to software updates and other information.

3.5   MANIPULATING WINDOWS AND SHEETS

Since most workbooks contain far more information than can be displayed on a computer screen, it is important to know how to display the most useful portion of the worksheet. The Zoom level (or magnification) of the worksheet can be set with a slider located at the lower right corner of the Excel window (see Figure 3.2). Alternatively, click on the 100% button to the left of the slider and the Zoom window opens (Figure 3.4). This window allows you to choose a preset or custom level of magnification. (The Zoom window can also be opened by selecting View▶Zoom▶Zoom.)

The View▶Window command makes it possible to simultaneously display more than one worksheet on the screen. These sheets may be from the same workbook or from different workbooks. This command can be particularly useful when we are building formulas in one sheet using cells located in another. Select Window▶New Window to add a spreadsheet window, and then resize the new window and select the sheets to display, as in Figure 3.5.

Excel provides an option to split the screen horizontally, vertically, or both in order to display two sets of rows or columns in the same spreadsheet. If, for example,

FIGURE 3.4   The Zoom Window

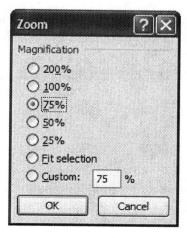

we wish to enter formulas in row 100 that reference cells in rows 1–10, we highlight row 10 and select View▶Window▶Split. Excel will open a second pane of rows with its own scroll bar, splitting the window horizontally. We can then display row 100 in the bottom pane while displaying rows 1–10 in the upper pane. The window can also be split vertically by highlighting a column. The window can even be split both horizontally and vertically by highlighting a cell. Figure 3.6 shows the worksheet split both horizontally and vertically at cell B13. (The screen can also be split by dragging the horizontal or vertical split bars, which are located just above and to the right of the row and column scroll bars, respectively.)

3.6   NAVIGATION

There are several ways to move the display from one portion of a spreadsheet to another. The horizontal and vertical scroll bars move the display of the portion of the entire spreadsheet that contains cell entries left and right or up and down,

FIGURE 3.5 Two Excel Windows Displayed Simultaneously

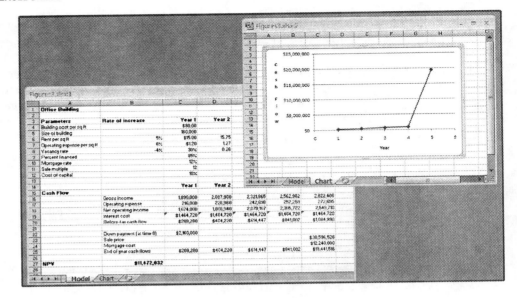

respectively. However, the scroll bars cannot move the display to blank areas. This can be done by clicking on the scroll arrows above and below the vertical scroll bar and to the left and right of the horizontal scroll bar. We can also shift the display by clicking on a cell and highlighting a range that extends outside the display area.

The display area also can be moved by using the arrow keys ($\uparrow\downarrow\leftarrow\rightarrow$). If we hold one of these keys down, the cursor moves in the direction indicated until it reaches the limit of the display area, at which point the display shifts to keep the cursor on the screen. The Page Up and Page Down keys also shift the display up or down by a fixed number of rows. These keys are useful for quickly scanning the contents of a spreadsheet. (Other more complex ways of navigating a spreadsheet are covered in Chapter 4.)

Another way to navigate around a spreadsheet is to type a cell address into the Name Box (just above column A). When we press the Enter key, the cursor moves to the cell address we have entered and the display shifts to accommodate the

FIGURE 3.6 Using Split Screen to Fix Row and Column Headings

	A	B	C	D	E	F	G
1	Office Building						
2							
3	**Parameters**	**Rate of increase**	**Year 1**	**Year 2**	**Year 3**	**Year 4**	**Year 5**
4	Building cost per sq ft		$80.00				
5	Size of building		180,000				
6	Rent per sq ft	5%	$15.00	15.75	16.54	17.36	18.23
7	Operating expense per sq ft	6%	$1.20	1.27	1.35	1.43	1.51
8	Vacancy rate	-4%	30%	0.26	0.22	0.18	0.14
9	Percent financed		85%				
10	Mortgage rate		12%				
11	Sale multiple		12				
12	Cost of capital		10%				
13							
14			Year 1	Year 2	Year 3	Year 4	Year 5
15	Cash Flow						
16		Gross income	1,890,000	2,097,900	2,321,865	2,562,982	2,822,406
17		Operating expense	216,000	228,960	242,698	257,259	272,695
18		Net operating income	1,674,000	1,868,940	2,079,167	2,305,722	2,549,710
19		Interest cost	$1,464,720	$1,464,720	$1,464,720	$1,464,720	$1,464,720
20		Before-tax cash flow	$209,280	$404,220	$614,447	$841,002	$1,084,990
21							
22		Down payment (at time 0)	$2,160,000				
23		Sale price					$30,596,526
24		Mortgage cost					$12,240,000
25		End of year cash flows	$209,280	$404,220	$614,447	$841,002	$19,441,516
26							
27	NPV		$11,472,032				

change. (If we use Names for cells or ranges of cells, they will appear in this box, and we can click on them to move the cursor. Range Names are covered in Chapter 4.) We can also use the Home▶Editing▶Find & Select▶Go To command to shift the cursor and display within a worksheet or to another worksheet.

3.7   SELECTING CELLS

There are many ways to select some or all of the cells in a spreadsheet. Here are the essentials. (More specialized methods are covered in Chapter 4.)

Selecting All Cells in a Worksheet   Click on the box immediately to the left of column A and above row 1.

Selecting a Column or a Row   Click on a single column label or a row label (for example, A or 1). To select several adjacent columns or rows, click on the first label and drag the cursor to the last label.

Selecting Rectangular Ranges   Any rectangular range of cells can be selected by selecting one of its four corner cells and dragging the cursor across to the diagonal corner. The same effect can be achieved by selecting a corner, dragging across the columns to the opposite corner and then across the rows to the diagonal corner, or vice versa.

Selecting Noncontiguous Ranges   To select two distinct rectangles of cells, select the first range, hold down the Control key, and select the second range. This method can be used to select three or more ranges as well.

3.8   ENTERING TEXT AND DATA

Information typed into a cell appears in two places: in the cell itself and in the formula bar. After we have clicked on Enter, we can edit the contents of the cell either by moving the cursor to the formula bar or by double-clicking on the cell and editing directly in the cell.

When we type letters into a cell, Excel automatically understands that the contents are text, and it left-justifies the contents in the cell. When we type in numbers, it recognizes the contents as numerical and right-justifies the contents.

To copy the contents of one cell to adjacent cells, we can either drag the Fill handle (the solid square at the lower right corner of the selected cell) over the adjacent cells, or else use Home▶Editing▶Fill▶Down (or Right, Up, Left).

FIGURE 3.7   The Series Window

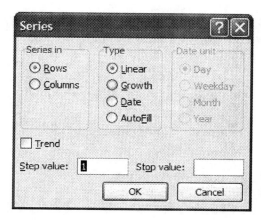

We often need to enter a series of numbers or dates. Examples include the numbers of successive customers (1, 2, 3, 4, ...) or successive quarters in a year (Q1, Q2, Q3, ...). Excel provides several ways to enter these series quickly. The Home▶Editing▶Fill▶Series command will enter various kinds of series (see Figure 3.7). The same effect can be accomplished by entering the first two cell entries, highlighting them, and copying to the rest of the range using the Fill handle. Excel can usually guess the pattern correctly. For example, enter 1 and 2 in one column. Highlight the two cells. Fill down to the next eight cells using the Fill handle, and the remainder of the series (3, 4, 5, 6, 7, 8, 9, 10) will appear. To enter the numbers between 10 and 50 in steps of 5, enter 10 and 15 in adjacent cells and fill down until 50 is reached.

3.9 EDITING CELLS

There are several ways to edit the information in cells. Here are the most useful alternatives:

Formula Bar   The simplest way to edit is to click on the Formula bar. A vertical cursor will appear in the Formula bar, and information can be entered or modified using all the normal Windows typing options. If the selected cell is not empty, its contents will appear in the Formula bar. Clicking on the text there will make the editing cursor appear.

Double-Click   A handy alternative approach is to double-click on a cell, or equivalently, to press the F2 key. This allows editing in the cell itself. If the selected cell is not empty, any cells referred to in the formula will be highlighted in color, a useful debugging device. See Figure 3.8, where we have double-clicked on cell E19 and the formula in the cell is displayed. The four cell references used to calculate the result in cell E19 (C4, C5, C9, and C10) are highlighted in color, and a border with the matching color is drawn around each of those cells. Finally, the function used in the formula (ISPMT) is displayed below the cell, along with its arguments. If we click on the function name, the Help page for that function will appear.

We can modify the cell contents by inserting the vertical cursor where it is needed and typing directly into the cell or by moving the vertical cursor to the Formula bar and typing there. Alternatively, we can alter any cell reference in a formula by dragging the highlighted outline to another location. This option provides a visual device for editing, which is convenient when the formula is based on distinctive reference patterns.

Insert Function   An alternative for editing a formula is Insert Function (the f_x icon to the left of the Formula bar). If we click on this icon when the cursor is on a cell that does not contain a function, it will bring up the Insert Function window, which lists all available functions. If a specific function is then selected, it will be entered into the

FIGURE 3.8 Double-Clicking on a Cell Containing a Formula

	A	B	C	D	E	F	G
1	Office Building						
2							
3	Parameters	Rate of increase	Year 1	Year 2	Year 3	Year 4	Year 5
4	Building cost per sq ft		$80.00				
5	Size of building		180,000				
6	Rent per sq ft	5%	$15.00	15.75	16.54	17.36	18.23
7	Operating expense per sq ft	6%	$1.20	1.27	1.35	1.43	1.51
8	Vacancy rate	-4%	30%	0.26	0.22	0.18	0.14
9	Percent financed		85%				
10	Mortgage rate		12%				
11	Sale multiple		12				
12	Cost of capital		10%				
13							
14			Year 1	Year 2	Year 3	Year 4	Year 5
15	Cash Flow						
16		Gross income	1,890,000	2,097,900	2,321,865	2,562,982	2,822,406
17		Operating expense	216,000	228,960	242,698	257,259	272,695
18		Net operating income	1,674,000	1,868,940	2,079,167	2,305,722	2,549,710
19		Interest cost	$1,464,720	$1,464,720	=-12*ISPMT($C$10/12,1,360,$C$9*$C$4*$C$5)		
20		Before-tax cash flow	$209,280	$404,220	ISPMT(rate, per, nper, pv) 2		$1,084,990
21							
22		Down payment (at time 0)	$2,160,000				
23		Sale price					$30,596,526
24		Mortgage cost					$12,240,000
25		End of year cash flows	$209,280	$404,220	$614,447	$841,002	$19,441,516
26							
27	NPV	$11,472,032					
28							

formula, and its own window will appear, which facilitates entering the inputs properly. If we click on the f_x icon when the cursor is on a cell that already contains a function, it will bring up the corresponding function window, allowing the definition of the function to be verified or the arguments of the function to be revised. (More information on functions can be found in Section 3.12.)

Absolute and Relative Cell References   A relative reference to cell C3 is simply "C3," whereas an absolute reference is $C3. These types of references are useful primarily to make copying of complex formulas easy and reliable. Rather than typing in the appropriate dollar signs, it can be easier to enter all addresses in relative form (without dollar signs), highlight one or more addresses, and then press F4 repeatedly until the desired combination of absolute and relative references appears. (More information on formulas can be found in Section 3.11.)

3.10   FORMATTING

We can change individual column widths and row heights by moving the vertical or horizontal lines between the column and row labels. Widths or heights common to multiple columns or rows can be set using the Home▶Cells▶Format▶Cell Size▶Row Height/Column Width commands after highlighting the appropriate rows or columns. Alternatively, change one column width or one row height after highlighting the appropriate columns or rows.

Any range of cells can be formatted by highlighting the range and then selecting Home▶Cells▶Format▶Format Cells (or by selecting Home▶Font▶↘). This opens a window with the following six tabs (see Figure 3.9):

Number   Choose a type of formatting—for example, Currency or Date—and specify parameters such as the number of decimal places displayed.

Alignment   Align text horizontally and vertically, and choose Wrap Text to fit long text labels into cells.

FIGURE 3.9   The Format Cells Window

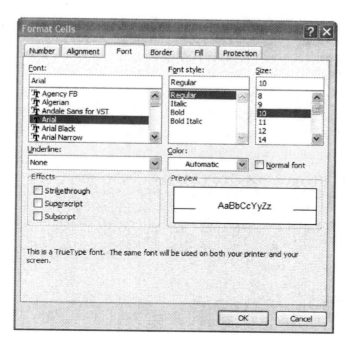

Font   Specify font, size, color, and superscript or subscript for the cell contents.

Border   Set various borders around a range of cells.

Fill   Set a background pattern or a color shade for the cell (but not its contents).

Protection   Lock or hide cells for safety.

Many of these options are also available on the Home ribbon. The most frequently used icons on this ribbon are Increase Decimal and Decrease Decimal, which change the number of decimals displayed in selected cells by one decimal place each time they are clicked.

3.11   BASIC FORMULAS

Formulas in Excel provide the basic mechanism for entering the relationships in a model. In modeling terms, every cell in a spreadsheet that involves a formula is either an output of the model or an intermediate calculation needed to calculate an output.

With very few exceptions, well-written formulas contain no numbers, only cell references. Although it is often permissible to use numbers that never change in a formula, like the value 24 for the number of hours in a day, it is dangerous to embed parameters that may change in formulas. (In Chapter 5 we will see that isolating parameters is a feature of well-built spreadsheets.) Because formulas are built up from the values in other cells, they are written in terms of references to the contents of those cells.

Excel uses the following symbols for the basic arithmetic operations:

- Addition   +
- Subtraction   −
- Multiplication   *
- Division   /
- Raise to a power $^\wedge$

Excel formulas start with the equal sign (=) and are evaluated from left to right. However, arithmetic operations will be carried out in a specified order unless parentheses are used to control the calculation order. The basic arithmetic operations are calculated in the following order:

- Negation (as in −1)
- Exponentiation ($^\wedge$)
- Multiplication and division (* and /)
- Addition and subtraction (+ and −)

If a formula involves both multiplication and division (or both addition and subtraction), the leftmost of these operations is performed first.

Here are some examples that show how the calculation order and the use of parentheses can determine the outcome of a calculation.

- $2 + 3/10 = 2.3$
- $(2 + 3)/10 = 0.5$
- $(2 + 3)/10^\wedge 2 = 0.05$
- $(2 + 3)/(10^\wedge 2) = 0.05$
- $2 + 3/10^\wedge 2 = 2.03$

It is generally a good practice to use parentheses to make the meaning of a calculation clear and to ensure that it is calculated correctly.

When a formula is to be entered into just one cell, the references to its inputs can simply specify column and row, as for example, (D2+D3)/D5. The cell reference D2 is an example of a **relative reference**. If the formula above was entered in cell E3, then the reference to cell D2 would be interpreted by Excel as referring to the cell one column to the left and one row above the current cell. That is, the cell reference is interpreted *relative to the current cell*. Likewise, from cell E3, a reference to J14 is interpreted as a reference to the cell 5 columns to the right and 11 rows down.

Many spreadsheets are built by copying formulas from one cell to a range of cells. For example, row 18 in the Office Building spreadsheet (Net Operating Income) requires subtracting Operating Income from Gross Income each year. Thus the formula entered into cell C18 (C16–C17) is the same formula that we need in the following years, cells D18:G18. We can fill these four cells efficiently by entering the formula once in cell C18 and then copying it to the other cells. Because Excel interprets the cell addresses C16 and C17 relative to the current cell, when we copy the formula, it continues to apply correctly.

However, this same procedure will not work for row 17, in which we calculate Operating Expense. The Operating Expense for Year 1 is the size of the building in square feet (C5) times the cost per square foot (C7). Thus we could calculate the correct value in C17 using the formula C5*C7. But the Operating Expense in the next year, Year 2, is not calculated in the same way. The size of the building is fixed for all time in C5, but the cost per square foot grows each year as given in cells D7:G7. So the correct formula in cell D17 is C5*D7. In other words, one of the addresses in the original formula (C5) needs to remain fixed, while the other (D7) needs to shift from year to year. Clearly, we need a way to write a cell address so that Excel will interpret it not in a relative fashion but as fixed. This is done using dollar signs before the column letter and row number, as in $C$5. The first dollar sign fixes the column during copying; the second dollar sign fixes the row. So, if we write the original formula in cell C17 as $C$5*C7, which does not change the value in C17, we can then copy it across the row correctly. The reference to the size of the building in C5 will remain fixed, and the reference to the cost will change as needed. Addresses with fixed columns or rows are known as **absolute addresses**. Examine all the formulas in the Office Building spreadsheet to see how relative and absolute addresses are used to make copying easy.

3.12 BASIC FUNCTIONS

Excel provides hundreds of built-in functions for calculating almost anything. No matter how complex or unusual the calculation we have in mind, Excel almost always has a function (or perhaps several functions) that can accomplish the task. Using Excel functions presents three challenges:

- Identifying the appropriate function or functions
- Using the function correctly
- Testing that the results match what was intended.

An efficient way to locate useful functions is to open the Insert Function window by clicking f_x next to the formula bar. (The Insert Function window can also be accessed from the Formulas ribbon.) Figure 3.10 shows the Insert Function window with the category Financial selected. The drop-down menu displays a list of function categories. The major categories are as follows:

- Most Recently Used
- All

FIGURE 3.10 The Insert
Function Window

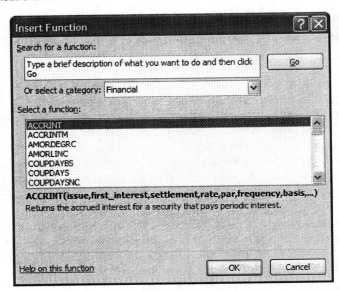

- Financial
- Date & Time
- Math & Trig
- Statistical
- Lookup & Reference
- Database
- Text
- Logical
- Information

To find a function, first identify the category it is likely to fall into, and then scan the alphabetical list of functions in this category. Each time a function is highlighted, the Insert Function window displays a brief description of the function and its inputs. For example, in Figure 3.11 we have highlighted the financial function ISMPT. The window displays its inputs (rate, per, nper, pv) and gives a short description: Returns the interest paid during a specific period of an investment.

FIGURE 3.11 The ISPMT
Function

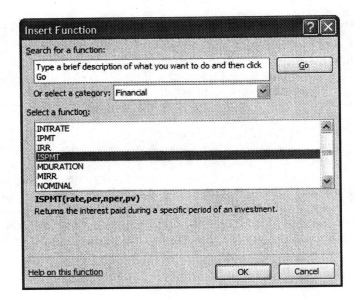

FIGURE 3.12 The Function Arguments Window for the ISMPT Function

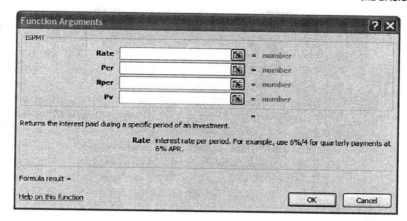

FIGURE 3.12 The Function Arguments Window for the ISMPT Function

At this point, click on OK and the Function Arguments window opens (Figure 3.12). This window displays a reference box for each of the arguments of the function (four in this case). We can either enter numbers directly in these boxes or (better) enter cell addresses (click on the icon at the right end of the box and identify the inputs by selecting them in the spreadsheet). The Function Arguments window shows the numerical value of each input as it is entered, and when enough inputs are entered, the window shows the value of the function. This allows us to see if we are getting plausible results before entering the function in the spreadsheet. (Help on this specific function is also available directly from the link at the bottom of this window.) Figure 3.13 shows the Function Arguments window with all four inputs entered and the result calculated (−122,060). Click on OK and the function will be entered in the cell we are editing.

Business analysts make heavy use of just a few of the hundreds of functions in Excel. We will describe six of the most important of these functions here. Other useful functions are described in Chapter 4.

The SUM function is used to add a set of numbers. Its arguments can simply be a list of cell references. For example, SUM(C1, C3, C5) adds the contents of the three cells listed, where the cell references are set off by commas. Alternatively, SUM(C1:C5) adds the contents of the cells in the range C1:C5. The SUM function can also be used to add a list of noncontiguous ranges, for example, SUM(C1:C5, D2:D6, E3:E7).

The MAX and MIN functions are used to find the largest and smallest values in a range. Thus MAX(1, 3, 5) yields 5, and MIN(C1:C5) calculates the smallest value in the range C1:C5.

The AVERAGE function calculates the average of the values in a range. The range can be in a column, in a row, or in an array (a rectangular range extending over

FIGURE 3.13 The ISMPT Function Evaluated

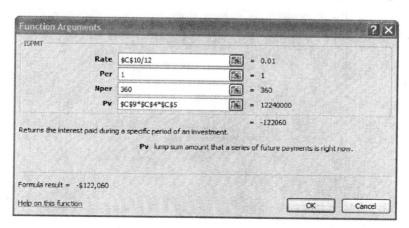

multiple columns and/or rows). If we are averaging a column of data that contains empty cells, does the AVERAGE function include those cells in the calculation? Click on Help in the Function Arguments window and note that the AVERAGE function ignores cells containing text, logical values (True or False), and empty cells, but does include cells containing the value zero.

The NPV function calculates the net present value of a stream of payments at a given discount rate. We illustrate the use of the NPV function in the Office Building spreadsheet. In this example, we make a down payment of $2,160,000 at the present time, the *start* of Year 1 (cell C22). Then we receive cash inflows at the *end* of the next five years (cells C25:G25). To calculate the net present value of this set of payments (cell B27), we discount the cash inflows to the present, using the discount rate given in cell C12, and subtract the down payment (since it occurs at the present time, it is not discounted). The formula is

$$NPV(C12,C25:G25)-C22$$

The Function Arguments window (Figure 3.14) shows the cell addresses of the arguments of the NPV function as well as their numerical values. It also shows the resulting value of the NPV calculation ($13,632,032.03), as well as the value of the entire formula ($11,472,032).

It is important to remember that the NPV function discounts the first payment in a stream of payments. Thus in the Office Building example, we discounted the cash inflow in Year 1 because according to the model, it comes in at the *end* of the year and the date of the evaluation is the *beginning* of the year. If, instead, the first cash inflow occurred at the beginning of the year, at the same time as the down payment, we would discount with the NPV function starting with Year 2 and add the undiscounted cash inflow from Year 1.

The IF function is used to perform a logical test and calculate one value if the test is true and another if it is false. The syntax for the IF function is

$$IF(logical\ test, value-if-true, value-if-false)$$

The first argument, the logical test, is an expression that Excel can evaluate as TRUE or FALSE. For example, the expression $100 > 0$ evaluates as TRUE, while $100 > 200$ evaluates as FALSE. (For practice, go to the Office Building spreadsheet and enter the formula $= C4 > 0$ in an empty cell. The result should be TRUE. The formula $= E16 > 5,000,000$ should be FALSE.)

If the logical test in an IF statement is TRUE, the *second* argument (value-if-true) is calculated and placed in the cell. If the logical test is FALSE, the *third* argument (value-if-false) is calculated and placed in the cell. For example, IF $(100 > 0, 25, 50)$ evaluates as 25, and IF $(100 < 0, 25, 50)$ evaluates as 50. Each of the three arguments in

FIGURE 3.14   The NPV Function

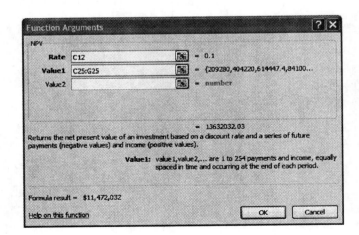

an IF function can be as complex as needed, as long as Excel can evaluate the logical test as TRUE or FALSE. So we could write the following function to choose one of two column sums, depending on the relative values of two other cells:

IF(D36>G76, SUM(A1:A100), SUM(B1:B100))

This example illustrates the **nesting of functions**. Nesting involves using one function within another. So in the example above, we have nested two SUM functions within an IF function. Excel imposes no practical limit on the number of functions that can be nested. However, nested functions can become complex and difficult to debug. It is good practice to calculate the components of a complex nested function separately to ensure that the logic is correct before bringing them together. And remember that future users of the model will appreciate documentation of formulas like the following one, whose meaning is not transparent:

IF(D345<I87, OFFSET(G118, MAX(I87:J129) − I86), −H45)

3.13 CHARTING

Charting is an essential skill for the business analyst, because model results can often best be understood in graphical terms. Excel provides tools that automate much of the detailed work involved in developing a chart. Charts are created by selecting the Insert tab and the Charts group.

The first step in creating a chart is to highlight the relevant data on the spreadsheet. Then select Insert▶Charts. Next select the type of chart (Column, Line, Pie, Bar, Area, Scatter, or Other Charts). A window then opens showing a variety of ways to depict that type of chart. Select one of these and Excel will plot the data in that format.

Note that when Excel displays a chart, it adds three Chart Tools tabs to the ribbon (Design, Layout, and Format). These tabs also appear whenever an existing chart is selected. The Design tab includes the following groups:

- Type
- Data
- Chart Layouts
- Chart Styles
- Location

The Type group allows a change in the chart type or saves the current chart as a template. The Data group allows data rows and columns to be swapped or the data range to be modified. Chart Layouts includes a variety of chart layouts for titles, axes, and so on. Chart Styles offers a variety of colors and shades. Finally, the Location group helps move the chart to a desired location.

We illustrate two types of frequently used charts: **line charts** and **scatter charts**. The data involve advertising and sales over the past 11 years, as given in the table. A line chart allows us to see how Advertising and Sales have changed over the past 11 years, while a scatter chart allows us to see whether Advertising and Sales are related to each other.

Year	Advertising	Sales
1995	56	600
1996	56	630

1997	59	662
1998	60	695
1999	61	729
2000	61	766
2002	65	844
2003	69	886
2004	68	931
2005	67	977

To create a line chart for Advertising and Sales over time, highlight all the data in the spreadsheet (including the column headings) and select Insert ▶ Chart. Choose the Line chart type and the 2D-Line subtype that shows each data point (Line with Markers), as shown in Figure 3.15. This chart is problematic because the years have been plotted as a data series rather than the X-axis values. To correct this, and to ensure that Years are on the horizontal axis, select Design ▶ Data ▶ Select Data. Under Legend Entries (Series) highlight Year and click on Remove. Also, under Horizontal (Category) Axis Labels click on Edit and enter the range for years: C5:C15. Click on OK and the chart will appear as in Figure 3.16. Clearly, Sales have increased steadily over this period. A close look reveals that the same is true for Advertising.

We can continue to refine this chart, using the options under Chart Layouts and Chart Styles. Our final version, shown in Figure 3.17, has an overall title, a Y-axis label, and a key showing the exact values for each data point. This is just one of the 11 predefined options under Chart Layouts.

FIGURE 3.15 Initial Line Chart for Advertising and Sales

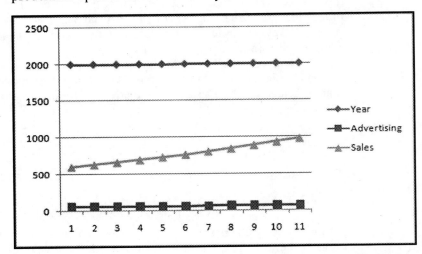

FIGURE 3.16 Entering Years as X-Axis Labels

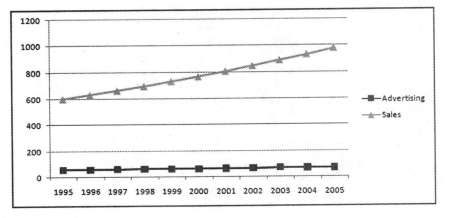

FIGURE 3.17   Final Line Chart for Advertising and Sales

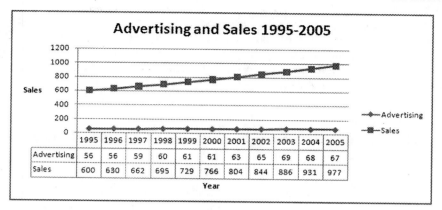

FIGURE 3.18   Initial Scatter Chart for Advertising and Sales

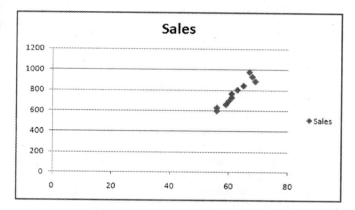

To create a scatter chart, highlight just the Advertising and Sales data and select Insert▶Chart▶Scatter▶Scatter with only Markers. The result is shown in Figure 3.18. This graph is correct, but it does not display the data in the clearest fashion because the axis scales are inappropriate. We change the horizontal axis scale by right-clicking in the Chart Area, selecting Format Chart Axis, and setting the minimum value under Axis Options to 50. Repeat this process for the vertical axis, setting the minimum to 500 and the maximum to 1,000. The improved chart is shown in Figure 3.19.

FIGURE 3.19   Final Scatter Chart for Advertising and Sales

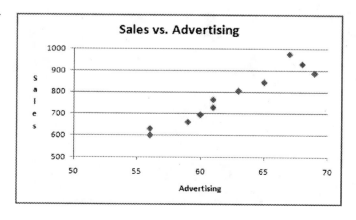

This chart conveys a different message from the line chart. Here, we see that higher levels of Advertising seem to be associated with higher levels of Sales, which perhaps suggests that Advertising is effective in increasing Sales. But the relationship may be influenced by other factors, since the scatter plot is not a straight line.

3.14 PRINTING

Printing in Excel is similar to printing in any Office application, with a few exceptions we discuss here.

First, many spreadsheets contain too much information to print on a single page. Depending on the column width and row height, Excel will select a range of cells to print on each page. Open the Office Building spreadsheet and select Office Button▶Print▶Print Preview. Excel displays the spreadsheet as it will look when printed. Click on Close Print Preview and note that Excel has divided the spreadsheet into pages with heavy dotted lines. The first page extends from A1 to E52, the second page from A53 to E104, and so on.

We can select certain cells for printing by highlighting the relevant range and selecting Page Layout▶Page Setup▶Print Area▶Set Print Area.

We display the Page Setup window by selecting Page Layout▶Page Setup ↘. Figure 3.20 shows the Page Setup window, which allows us to control other aspects of the printed page. For example, on the Page tab we can change the orientation of the printed spreadsheet from Portrait to Landscape. We can also change the scaling on this tab. A particularly useful option here is the button that fits a worksheet to a specified number of pages. Quite often, the number of pages is set to 1 for a scaled snapshot of the entire worksheet. On the Margins tab, we can alter the top, bottom, left, and right margins and the location of the contents on the page. Using the Header/Footer tab, we can enter text that will appear on every printed page, such as a page number or the name of the author of the workbook. Moreover, on the Sheet tab we can control whether gridlines and row and column headings will appear on the printed spreadsheet.

FIGURE 3.20 The Page Setup Window

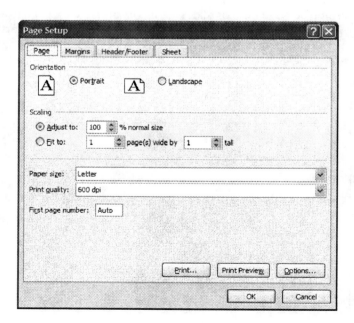

FIGURE 3.21 The Excel Help Window

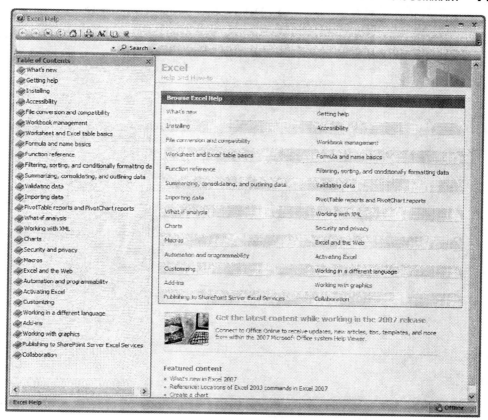

3.15 HELP OPTIONS

A great deal of useful information is available in Excel Help, which is opened by either pressing F1 or clicking on the question mark icon in the upper right corner of the spreadsheet (Figure 3.21).

Excel also offers access to targeted Help topics in a variety of specific situations. For example, some dialog boxes show a question mark at the right-hand end of the title bar. Click on the question mark and Excel opens the Help window for the operation controlled by the window. In other windows, there is a special link to Help. For example, the Insert Function window has a link to Help on this function, which opens the Help window for the function highlighted.

3.16 SUMMARY

Excel is both a highly versatile and a highly complex computer application. Not only can it be used for routine calculation, but it can also be used for complex decision support tasks. Each user must determine how many of the thousands of Excel features are needed on the job. This chapter presents the basic Excel skills every business analyst should have.

This chapter covers these basic features of Excel:

- The Excel window
- Configuring Excel
- Manipulating windows and sheets
- Navigation
- Selecting cells
- Entering text and data
- Editing cells
- Formatting
- Basic formulas
- Basic functions
- Charting
- Printing
- Help

SUGGESTED READINGS

Books

- Jacobs, K. 2007. *Microsoft Office Excel 2007: The L Line, The Express Line to Learning*. New York: John Wiley and Sons.

This book covers the fundamentals of Excel as well as some advanced features, such as macros and data analysis.

- Reding, E. and L. Wermers. 2007. *Microsoft Office Excel 2007—Illustrated Introductory*. Cambridge, MA: Course Technology.

This is an elementary workbook. Chapters A through E are essential. The remaining chapters are quite advanced and can be omitted by the beginner.

- Reding, E. and L. Wermers. 2007. *Microsoft Excel 2007—Illustrated Complete*. Cambridge, MA: Course Technology.

This book contains the previous one. Its additional chapters make it a handy reference manual.

Compact Disk

- Taylor, A. J. Hamish. 2002. *Excel Essentials: Using Microsoft Excel for Data Analysis and Decision Making*. Pacific Grove, CA: Duxbury Press.

This CD focuses on Excel skills useful in analyzing business problems. It consists of nine modules, starting with Excel menus and moving through more advanced topics, including Solver, graphing, regression, and pivot table.

Online Programs

Online courses in Excel 2007 are available from the following sources:

- ElementK: www.elementk.com
- CustomGuide: www.customguide.com
- Microsoft Office Online: http://office.microsoft.com
- RemoteCourse: http://www.remotecourse.com

4 Advanced Excel Skills

4.1 INTRODUCTION

Excel is a software application of almost unlimited depth and complexity. There is no way to count the number of features it offers, but they must run into the thousands, if not tens of thousands. Fortunately, most business analysts do not need to become experts in all aspects of Excel, but they often find that they need to develop expertise in a few specialized domains within Excel. Which domains are relevant depends on the job they perform as well as on their level of interest in Excel and spreadsheet modeling generally.

The previous chapter presented the Excel features we believe the great majority of business analysts should know. Even there our coverage was not exhaustive. For example, every analyst should know the basics of cell formatting, but only a few will need to learn and retain all the various ways to customize formats in a workbook.

In this chapter, we pursue several specialized topics in more depth. These are features of Excel that intermediate and advanced spreadsheet modelers use to make their work more efficient, to make their spreadsheets easier to use, or to make them more powerful. We suggest that novice modelers skip this chapter until they have developed at least a basic familiarity with the skills covered in Chapter 3. More advanced users can skim this chapter, focusing on topics of particular interest or relevance to their work.

The chapter covers the following topics:

- Keyboard shortcuts
- Controls
- Cell comments
- Naming cells and ranges
- Advanced formulas and functions
- Recording macros and using Visual Basic for Applications (VBA)

4.2 KEYBOARD SHORTCUTS

Most users of Windows are familiar with using the keyboard as an alternative to selecting commands or tools with the mouse. In Word, for example, using only the mouse to copy and paste a portion of text requires highlighting the text, selecting the Copy icon from the Home tab, clicking on the new location for the text, and selecting the Paste icon from the Home tab. Alternatively, and possibly more quickly, we can replace the first selection with the keystroke combination Ctrl + C and the second selection with the keystroke combination Ctrl + V. These keystroke combinations are examples of **keyboard shortcuts**. Since Ctrl + C and Crtl + V can be executed with two fingers of the left hand, we can keep the right hand on the mouse and use both hands almost simultaneously. (Most keyboard shortcuts are not case sensitive, so upper and lower cases give the same results.)

Excel shares many keyboard shortcuts with other Windows applications. For example, we can use Ctrl + C and Ctrl + V in Excel to copy and paste the contents of individual cells or ranges of cells just as we copy text in Word. Other shortcuts for familiar actions include

Ctrl + N	Office Button▶New
Ctrl + O	Office Button▶Open
Ctrl + S	Office Button▶Save
Ctrl + P	Office Button▶Print
Ctrl + X	Home▶Clipboard▶Cut
Ctrl + F	Home▶Editing▶Find & Select▶Find
Ctrl + H	Home▶Editing▶Find & Select▶Replace
Ctrl + G	Home▶Editing▶Find & Select▶Go To

These familiar shortcuts are only a small sample of the shortcuts available in Excel. Most of these use the special keys labeled F1–F12, Ctrl, Alt, or Shift. Here is a further sample:

Format cells	Ctrl + 1
Display Help	F1
Insert new worksheet	Shift + F11
Move cursor to cell A1	Ctrl + Home
Display the Find and Replace dialog box	Shift + F5
Switch to the next nonadjacent selection to the left	Ctrl + Left Arrow

In Figure 4.1 we list for handy reference some of the most useful of these keyboard shortcuts. (An exhaustive list is available under Help: search on "keyboard shortcuts" and select the topic Excel shortcut and function keys.) We recommend scanning this list for shortcuts that may have been forgotten or new ones for operations that have become routine. Whenever we regularly encounter a tedious and slow operation, it makes sense to search for a keyboard shortcut to save time.

4.3 CONTROLS

Excel controls allow the user to change the contents or behavior of a spreadsheet without interacting directly with individual cells. Controls such as boxes and buttons are familiar because they appear frequently in commonly used windows in the Excel user interface. Among the Excel Options, for example, the window for Formula options uses a button to select a Workbook Calculation mode (only one of the three available choices is allowed) and a check box (on or off) to Enable Iterative Calculation.

Controls can be inserted into a spreadsheet to assist users in choosing parameter inputs and to assist the analyst in performing sensitivity analysis. The controls available are displayed by selecting Developer▶Controls▶Insert, as in Figure 4.2. (If the Developer tab does not appear, choose Office Button▶Excel Options▶Popular and check the box Show Developer Tab in the Ribbon.) Each icon can be identified by holding the cursor above it. For example, the fourth icon in the top row (under Form Controls) is the Spin Button icon.

To place a control on a spreadsheet requires a sequence of steps. First, click on the desired control icon from the toolbar. Using the cursor, which now appears as a cross, drag and drop the control to the desired location in the spreadsheet. In doing so, use the cursor to set the size of the control as well as its location. With the control

FIGURE 4.1 Useful
Keyboard Shortcuts

For moving and scrolling	
Ctrl + arrow key	Move to the edge of the current data region
Home	Move to the beginning of the row
Ctrl + Home	Move to the beginning of the worksheet (A1)
Ctrl + End	Move to the bottom-right corner of the used area of the worksheet
PgDn	Move down one screen
PgUp	Move up one screen
Alt + PgDn	Move one screen to the right
Alt + PgUp	Move one screen to the left
F5	Display the Go To dialog box
For entering data on a worksheet	
Alt + Enter	Opens a new workbook, if one is already open
Shift + Enter	Complete a cell entry and move up one cell
Tab	Complete a cell entry and move to the right cell
Shift + Tab	Complete a cell entry and move to the left cell
Ctrl + Delete	Delete text to the end of the line
Shift + F2	Edit a cell comment
Ctrl + D	Fill down (a selected column of cells with the content of the first cell)
Ctrl + R	Fill to the right (a selected row of cells with the content of the first cell)
Ctrl + F3	Open the Define Name dialog box
For working in cells or the formula bar	
Ctrl + Shift + Enter	Enter a formula as an array formula
F2	Edit the active cell
F3	Open the Paste Name window
Shift + F3	Open the Insert Function (or Function Arguments) window
F9	Calculate all sheets in all open workbooks
Ctrl + Alt + F9	Calculate all worksheets in the active workbook
Shift + F9	Calculate the active worksheet
Ctrl + ;(semicolon)	Enter the current date
Ctrl + Shift + :(colon)	Enter the current time
Ctrl+ ~	Display all formulas
For inserting, deleting, and copying selection	
Ctrl + C	Copy the selection
Ctrl + X	Cut the selection
Ctrl + V	Paste the selection
Delete	Clear the contents of the selection
Ctrl + - (hyphen)	Delete (dialog box)
Ctrl + Z	Undo the last action
Ctrl + Shift + Plus sign	Insert (dialog box)
For selecting cells, columns, or rows	
Shift + arrow key	Extend the selection by one cell
Ctrl + Shift + arrow key	Extend the selection to the last nonblank cell in the same column or row
Ctrl + space bar	Select the entire column
Ctrl + A	Select the entire worksheet
For working with worksheets and macros	
Shift + F11	Insert a new worksheet
Alt + F8	Display the Macro dialog box
Alt + F11	Display the Visual Basic Editor (VBE)
Ctrl + PgDn	Move to the next sheet in the workbook
Ctrl + PgUp	Move to the previous sheet in the workbook
Miscellaneous	
Ctrl + S	Save an active workbook
Ctrl + N	Open new workbook
Ctrl + O	Open an existing workbook
Shift + F5 or Ctrl + F	Display the Find dialog box
Ctrl + H	Display the Replace dialog box
Note: In most cases, these shortcuts are not case sensitive.	

FIGURE 4.2 Form
Controls Window

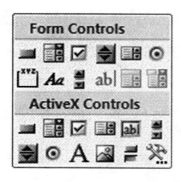

highlighted, right click and choose Format Control (or click Developer▶Controls▶Properties) and edit the inputs in this window to make the control work as desired. In some cases, preparations will involve entering input data for the control in a special section of the spreadsheet.

As an illustration, we demonstrate how the List Box and Spin Button controls work in a version of the Office Building model from Figure 3.1. (Other controls work in a similar fashion.) Figure 4.3 shows a version of the Office Building spreadsheet to which we have added a control panel in cells A2:B13. The purpose of the control panel is to make it easy to select two parameters: the building cost in cell C20 and the sale multiple in cell C27. The building cost is controlled by a List Box and the sale multiple by a Spin Button.

We input the List Box first. Imagine that we have three quotes from construction companies for the cost per square foot for the building: $78.50, $80.00, and $83.75. Because the building will be built by one of these three companies, we know that the cost will be one of these three numbers. Therefore, we do not want any numbers other than these three entered into cell C20, so we place a List Box on the spreadsheet that offers these three numbers as options.

In preparation for the construction of the List Box, enter the three allowable input parameters into a spare location in the spreadsheet such as F3:F5. Next, choose Developer▶Controls▶Insert and click on the List Box icon under Form Controls (not the one under ActiveX Controls). On the spreadsheet, select cell B4 to place the control there. With the List Box highlighted, right click and choose Format Control, then select the Control tab in the Format Control window, and enter F3:F5 for the Input range and F6 for the CellLink. These choices ensure that the options shown in the box come from F3:F5, and the result (1, 2, or 3) appears in F6. Finally, enter the formula =INDEX(F3:F5,F6) in A4 and revise cell C20 to reference A4.

We can test the control by selecting any one of the three inputs in the list box and verifying that the value in cell C20 changes appropriately. We can see that the ultimate NPV (displayed for convenience in cell A13) changes very little as the building costs change.

To install the Spin Button for the sales multiple, repeat the same procedure. From the Forms Control toolbar, click on the Spin Button icon and place it on cell B9.

FIGURE 4.3 Use of
Controls

	A	B	C	D	E	F	G
1	Control panel						
2							
3	Choose building costs	78.50				Cost quotes	
4	$80.00	80.00				78.50	
5		83.75				80.00	
6						83.75	
7						2	
8	Sale multiple						
9	12	▲					
10							
11		▼					
12	NPV						
13	$11,472,032						
14							
15							
16							
17	Office Building						
18							
19	Parameters	Rate of increase	2002	2003	2004	2005	2006
20	Building cost per sq ft		$80.00				
21	Size of building		180,000				
22	Rent per sq ft	5%	$15.00	15.75	16.54	17.36	18.23
23	Operating expense per sq ft	6%	$1.20	1.27	1.35	1.43	1.51
24	Vacancy rate	-4%	30%	0.26	0.22	0.18	0.14
25	Percent financed		85%				
26	Mortgage rate		12%				
27	Sale multiple		12				
28	Cost of capital		10%				
29							
30			2002	2003	2004	2005	2006

4.3

With the Spin Button highlighted, right click and choose Format Control, select the Control tab, and change `Current value` to 12, `Minimum value` to 5, `Maximum value` to 15, and `Incremental change` to 1. Then change the Cell link to A9. These choices allow the sales multiple to be any integer from 5 to 15, and the result appears in A9. Finally, revise cell C27 to reference A9. By clicking on the up and down arrows in the Spin Button, we can see that the NPV for this investment ranges from a low of about $400,000 to a high of $16 million over the allowable range for the sales multiple (with the cost quote at $80), indicating a high degree of sensitivity.

EXCEL TIP
Using
Controls

1. Open the Control toolbar on the screen (Developer▶Controls▶Insert).
2. Select the desired control icon (under Form Controls).
3. Click on the desired location for placement.
4. Click on Controls▶Properties (or right-click on the icon and select Format Control...).
5. Edit properties as needed.

4.4 CELL COMMENTS

With few exceptions, the spreadsheets we have seen in actual use are poorly documented. Most practicing analysts have experienced the frustration of trying to understand a complex formula or a model design six months after they built it, or two years after someone else built it. But while everyone agrees that spreadsheets should be documented, almost no one does it. The reason seems to be that most forms of documentation are too time-consuming. Cell comments are one easy way to document the details behind a cell or range of cells.

Inserting Comments   To insert a comment in a particular cell, highlight the cell and choose Review▶Comments▶New Comment. This opens a comment window to the side of the cell, linked to the cell by an arrow. The comment contains the user's name as a default. It also places a red triangle in the upper right corner of the cell, which is the indicator that the cell contains a comment.

The location or size of a comment can be changed after it is highlighted (by clicking on its border). It is good practice to size the comment box so that is does not extend beyond the contents and to place it on the spreadsheet where it will be visible but not cover up other important cells. Figure 4.4 shows a comment entered in cell C12 and sized to fit a blank portion of the spreadsheet.

Displaying Comments   All of the comments in a workbook can be displayed by choosing Review▶Comments▶Show All Comments. This command toggles back and forth between showing all of the comments and showing none of them. The command Show/Hide Comment applies only to the selected cell.

Editing Comments   Edit the comment by placing the cursor anywhere within the comment box. All the usual Excel text editing features can be used inside comment boxes.

Deleting Comments   To delete a comment, click on Review▶Comments▶ Delete. Another way to access these commands is to select a cell with a comment and then right-click. The menu that appears will contain the commands that manage cell comments.

Copying Comments   When a cell containing a comment is copied, the contents and the comment are both copied to the new cell. To copy *just* the comment in a cell, copy

FIGURE 4.4   Cell Comment

	A	B	C	D	E	F	G
1	Office Building						
2							
3	Parameters	Rate of increase	2002	2003	2004	2005	2006
4	Building cost per sq ft		$80.00				
5	Size of building		180,000				
6	Rent per sq ft	5%	$15.00	15.75	16.54	17.36	18.23
7	Operating expense per sq ft	6%	$1.20	1.27	1.35	1.43	1.51
8	Vacancy rate	-4%	30%	0.26	0.22	0.18	0.14
9	Percent financed		85%				
10	Mortgage rate		12%		This is the discount rate used		
11	Sale multiple		12		on all projects in this class.		
12	Cost of capital		10%				
13							
14			2002	2003	2004	2005	2006
15	Cash Flow						
16		Gross income	1,890,000	2,097,900	2,321,865	2,562,982	2,822,406
17		Operating expense	216,000	228,960	242,698	257,259	272,695
18		Net operating income	1,674,000	1,868,940	2,079,167	2,305,722	2,549,710
19		Interest cost	$1,464,720	$1,464,720	$1,464,720	$1,464,720	$1,464,720
20		Before-tax cash flow	$209,280	$404,220	$614,447	$841,002	$1,084,990
21							
22		Down payment (at time 0)	$2,160,000				
23		Sale price					$30,596,526
24		Mortgage cost					$12,240,000
25		End of year cash flows	$209,280	$404,220	$614,447	$841,002	$19,441,516
26							
27	NPV	$11,472,032					

the source cell, and then highlight the destination cell. Next, select Home▶ Clipboard▶Paste▶Paste Special, selecting Comments and clicking OK.

Printing Comments   Comments on the spreadsheet will be printed just as they appear on the screen. If the comments are extensive, we may want to print them in one place. Print all comments at the end of the worksheet by choosing Page Layout▶Page Setup ↘ Sheet tab and selecting Comments: At end of sheet from the pull-down menu.

4.5   NAMING CELLS AND RANGES

Individual cells and ranges of cells can be given names, and these names can be used in formulas to make them more readable. Named ranges are also used occasionally in other contexts, such as identifying a database for filtering or specifying input data for a Pivot Table (see Chapter 7). The use of range names is highly recommended in corporate settings for models that are used by many people. However, for the solo modeler, it is an open question whether the additional complexity of range names justifies their use.

Some examples of the use of range names will make their advantages clear. Here is a typical formula from a financial spreadsheet written in the standard manner, with cell addresses:

$$D20 = D13 + D14 + D15$$

Here is the same formula when written using range names:

Total_Expenses = Cost_of_Goods_Sold + Depreciation + Interest

Here are two equivalent formulas for calculating the actual quantity of a product sold depending on whether demand is more or less than the quantity available:

D14 = IF(D13 > D10, D10, D13)

Sales = IF(Demand > Quantity_Available, Quantity_Available, Demand)

In both of these cases, the formulas with range names are easy to read and easy to test against the underlying logic of the situation. In other words, when we see that Interest is included in the calculation of Total Expenses, we can mentally check whether this is the correct accounting treatment of interest costs. It is more difficult to do so when we see that D20 includes D15. Similarly, we can read and verify the logic of the IF statement more easily when it is written using range names than when it involves cell references.

However, there are some drawbacks to using range names. The most obvious is that entering range names takes time away from other work. Another drawback is that we must verify that each range name actually points to the correct cell or range. For example, it is not enough to check that Interest is *conceptually* part of Total Expenses; we must also verify that the range name "Interest" actually points to the cell where interest is calculated. Range names introduce an additional layer of complexity in a model, even as they simplify the look of formulas. Perhaps the best argument for their use is that they make a model more understandable for new users. Thus, if a model is expected to have a long lifetime and to be used and modified by a number of other users, range names are probably a worthwhile investment.

The simplest way to define a range name for a single cell is to place the cursor on that cell and note that the address of the cell appears in the Name box above column A. Click in the Name box and enter the name of the cell there. For example, place the cursor on cell C4 in the Office Building workbook, and its cell address appears in the Name box. Type "Building_cost" in the box and press Enter. (*Note*: Range names cannot contain blanks, so one common approach is to use the underscore character to turn a multiword name into a single word.) Now whenever we highlight cell C4, its range name appears in the Name box. When range names have been entered for all the parameters in cells B4:C12, we can click on the down arrow at the side of the Name box, and a list of all range names will appear. Highlight one of those names and the cursor will move to the named cell.

An alternative means for entering range names is to choose Formulas▶ Defined Names▶Define Name. This opens the New Name window, as shown in Figure 4.5. The cell address of the cursor appears in the lower portion of the window. Note that the cell address for this range name includes the sheet name (followed by an exclamation point) and an absolute reference to the cell location ($C$4). To enter the range name Size for cell B5, place the cursor on cell B5, choose Formulas▶Defined Names▶Define Name, and type "Size" in the upper box. Now when the cursor is placed on B5, "Size" will appear in the Name box. In the New Name window, the user has an option to select the scope of the name, determining whether it applies to the workbook or just to the worksheet. The default is workbook scope, which is the most common use because it avoids confusion. Note that when names are entered in the Name box, they are automatically assigned workbook scope.

Entering a name for a cell does not automatically change cell references in existing formulas to name references. For example, the original formula in cell D6, $C$6*(1+$B$6), does not change when we later assign range names to cells B6 and C6. We can rewrite this formula, however, using the range names, as Rent*(1+Rent_ growth). Similarly, we can rewrite the formula in E6 as D6*(1+Rent_growth) and copy this formula to the two cells to the right (because Rent_growth is specified by an absolute address). Alternatively, to insert newly created range names into existing formulas, we can highlight the range D6:G6 and select Formulas▶ Defined Names▶Define Name▶Apply Names... Then we select Rent_growth from the list of range names and click OK. When we look at the formulas in cells D6:G6, we will see that $B$6 has been replaced by its range name.

In the worksheet corresponding to Figure 4.6, we have entered range names for all the input parameters and

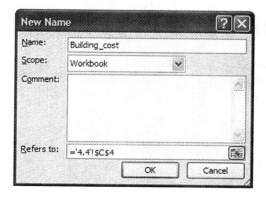

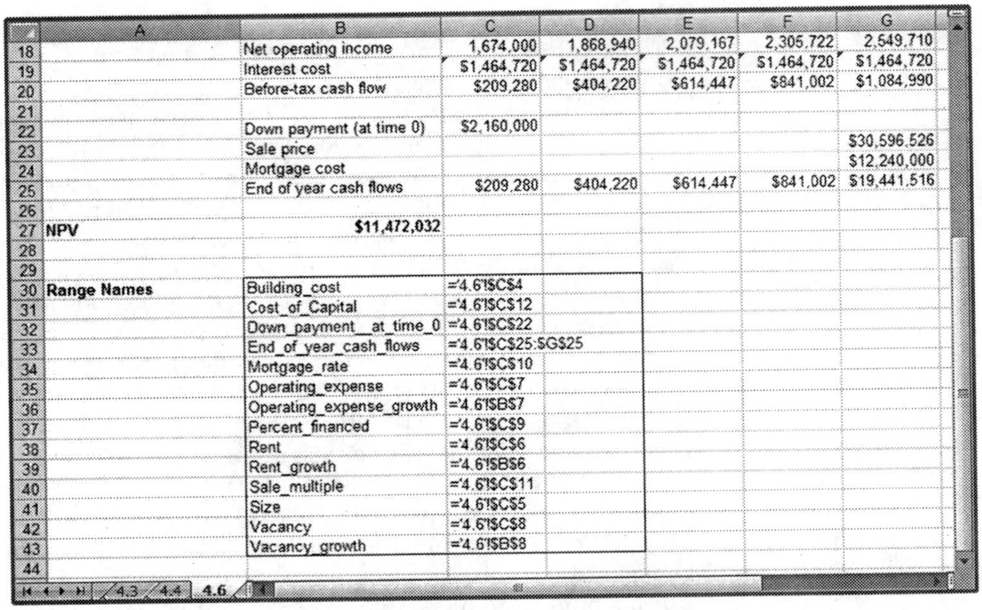

FIGURE 4.6 Documenting Range Names with the Paste List Command

	A	B	C	D	E	F	G
18		Net operating income	1,674,000	1,868,940	2,079,167	2,305,722	2,549,710
19		Interest cost	$1,464,720	$1,464,720	$1,464,720	$1,464,720	$1,464,720
20		Before-tax cash flow	$209,280	$404,220	$614,447	$841,002	$1,084,990
21							
22		Down payment (at time 0)	$2,160,000				
23		Sale price					$30,596,526
24		Mortgage cost					$12,240,000
25		End of year cash flows	$209,280	$404,220	$614,447	$841,002	$19,441,516
26							
27	NPV		$11,472,032				
28							
29							
30	Range Names	Building_cost	='4.6'!$C$4				
31		Cost_of_Capital	='4.6'!$C$12				
32		Down_payment__at_time_0	='4.6'!$C$22				
33		End_of_year_cash_flows	='4.6'!$C$25:$G$25				
34		Mortgage_rate	='4.6'!$C$10				
35		Operating_expense	='4.6'!$C$7				
36		Operating_expense_growth	='4.6'!$B$7				
37		Percent_financed	='4.6'!$C$9				
38		Rent	='4.6'!$C$6				
39		Rent_growth	='4.6'!$B$6				
40		Sale_multiple	='4.6'!$C$11				
41		Size	='4.6'!$C$5				
42		Vacancy	='4.6'!$C$8				
43		Vacancy_growth	='4.6'!$B$8				
44							

for many of the formulas. Examine this worksheet carefully to see how range names are used and how they improve the readability of formulas. Note that the formula for NPV in cell B27 reads

```
NPV(Cost_of_capital,End_of_year_cash_flows) - Down_payment_at_time_0
```

The range names Cost_of_capital and Down_payment_at_time_0 each refer to a single cell. However, the range name End_of_year_cash_flows refers to the range C25:G25. Range names can refer to ranges of any size and dimension and can be used in formulas and functions as long as the range itself is appropriate.

Range names often need to be edited, deleted, or redefined. All of these operations can be carried out in the Name Manager window. Another useful option within that window creates a table of names in the spreadsheet. To do this, move the cursor to an unused area of the spreadsheet. Choose Formulas▶Defined Names▶ Use in formula, and then select Paste Names ... and Paste List. Figure 4.6 shows the range names and their cell addresses pasted into cells B30:C43. This is one way to document range names and to make them easier to check. Note, however, that if we redefine the location of a range name, this list will *not* be updated automatically.

There are many more options for using range names; for more information refer to the references at the end of the chapter. But a warning is in order: range names are not a panacea for the problems arising from obscure and undocumented formulas. One limitation of range names is that in most cases copying and pasting formulas is easier with a mixture of relative and absolute addresses than it is using range names. Another limitation is the added complexity and possibilities for error that range names introduce. It is always a good idea to keep individual formulas as simple as possible and to document any formula whose logic is not self-explanatory.

EXCEL TIP
Advantages and Disadvantages

Advantages

- Formulas are easier to understand.
- Useful in Pivot Table and other applications.

of Range Names	***Disadvantages***
	• May reference incorrect cells or ranges.
	• Adds complexity to spreadsheet.
	• Requires additional effort.
	• Complicates copying.

■

4.6 ADVANCED FORMULAS AND FUNCTIONS

Sophisticated use of formulas and functions is a mark of an expert Excel modeler. Unfortunately, there are so many different ways to use these tools that no book can communicate them all. The exhaustive lists of functions that are commonly provided in Excel manuals are a useful reference, once the user knows what function to look up. But users who don't know the basics of creating complex formulas often cannot use such references effectively. In this section, we present some of the tools of advanced formulas and functions:

- R1C1 references
- Mixed addresses
- Nesting calculations
- Parameterization
- Advanced functions

4.6.1 R1C1 Reference Style

Most Excel users are familiar with the column-and-row style of cell references. Thus, D16 and $D$16 are two different ways to refer to the contents of the cell in the fourth column and 16th row. Although familiar, this system has some disadvantages. One is that the columns after column Z are designated AA, AB, and so on. Another is that when we copy a formula that employs a relative address, the relative cell reference changes in each successive cell. Thus, a formula like $C$6*(1+D6), when copied to the right, becomes $C$6*(1+E6), $C$6*(1+F6), $C$6*(1+G6), and so on, which makes debugging a challenge.

Excel makes available a different way to reference cell addresses that corrects some of these problems. In the **R1C1 style,** the columns are numbered from 1 to 16,384. Absolute cell references simply specify the row and column of the cell, as in R16C4 for D16. Relative references specify the number of rows above or below the current cell and the number of columns left or right of the current cell. For example, the relative address R[1]C[1] refers to the cell one row below the current cell and one column to the right. The address R[−1]C[−1] refers to the cell one row above and one column to the left. To refer to the cell one row above and in the same column, we simply use R[−1]C. To refer to the cell in the same row and one column to the right, we use RC[1].

To get an idea of what this style of cell references looks like in practice, open the Office Building model (Figure 4.4). The formula in cell C16, $C$5*C6*(1−C8), involves both absolute and relative addresses. It is constructed to allow copying to cells D16:G16. Now turn on the R1C1 reference style by selecting Office Button▶Excel Options▶Formulas. Then, under Working with formulas, check the box R1C1 reference style. The same formula now appears in the following way:

$$R5C3*R[-10]C*(1 - R[-8]C)$$

Instead of the absolute reference $C$5, we have the absolute reference R5C3. Instead of the relative reference C6, we have the relative reference R[−10]C. And instead of the relative reference C8, we have R[−8]C. Note that this formula can also be copied across the row. The biggest difference between these two approaches is that in the R1C1 style *all* the formulas from C16 to G16 are identical. This makes debugging a model much simpler. In fact, all of the formulas in this worksheet that are copied across the columns are identical (see rows 6–9, 16–20, and 25).

Since Excel allows us to switch back and forth from one style of addressing to the other, there is no reason not to use the system that is most convenient at the moment. Some modelers use the R1C1 style when developing their models but switch to the normal style when the model is complete. In this way, they enjoy the benefits of the more logical and more easily debugged R1C1 style without imposing this less well known style on users.

4.6.2 Mixed Addresses

We discussed in Chapter 3 using absolute and relative addresses like $C$5 and C5 to make the copy–paste operation easier. We can think of the dollar signs in absolute addresses as fixing the column and the row of the address during copying. Often, we wish to fix both column and row, but there are circumstances in which we want to fix just one. We do this with **mixed addresses**. In a mixed address, either the column is fixed and not the row, as in $C5, or the row is fixed and not the column, as in C$5.

Here is an example of a situation in which mixed addresses are useful. Refer to the workbook in Figure 4.7. In column B, we have input data on sales covering 12 months from January to December. In column C, we want to calculate cumulative sales from January to the current month. Can we enter a formula for cumulative sales in cell C2 that we can copy for the remaining 11 months? Each month we need a formula that sums the cells in column B from January (row 2) down to the current row. This can be accomplished with the formula SUM($B$2:$B2). Note that the absolute address $B$2 fixes the starting value for the sum, and the mixed address $B2 allows the row (but not the column) of the ending value to change as we copy. Enter this formula in cell C2; the result is 145 as expected. Then copy it down to row 13 and verify that it calculates the cumulative sales as required. The formula for December (C13), for example, becomes SUM($B$2:$B13).

Entering the dollar signs in cell addresses can be tedious, especially when using mixed addresses. The function key F4 is a useful hotkey in this situation. When editing a formula, place the cursor on a relative cell reference. Press F4 once and both dollar signs are added; press again, and only the column dollar sign appears; press a third time, and only the row dollar sign appears; press a fourth time and the original relative reference appears (with no dollar signs).

4.6.3 Nesting Calculations

We have seen before that Excel allows calculations within formulas, such as in

$$IF((D16+D17)>(E2/F7), F9*F10, G9*G10)$$

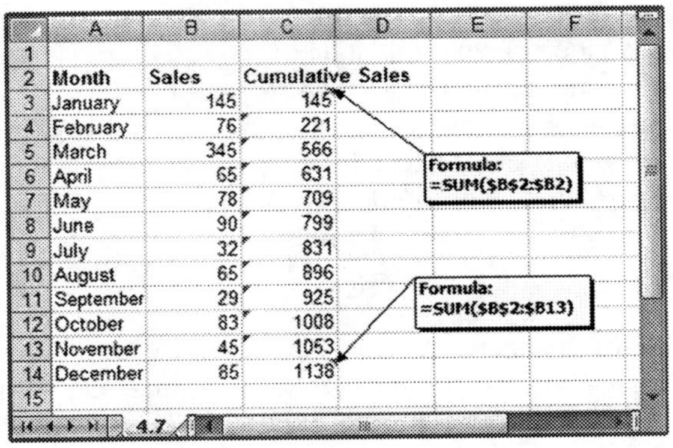

FIGURE 4.7 Using Mixed Addresses in Copying

Excel also allows functions to be used within other functions. This is referred to as **nesting**. So, for example, we could nest a SUM function within an IF function:

$$\text{IF(SUM(A1:A10)} > 0, \text{F9*F10, G9*G10)}$$

In fact, we can nest functions as many times as we like (in most cases), as long as the resulting calculations can be performed by the functions themselves. For example, we can nest IF functions within IF functions (although there is a limit of seven IFs in one formula), as in

$$\text{IF(D2} > \text{D3, G7, IF(B2} > \text{B3, G8, G9))}$$

Or we can nest several different functions:

$$\text{MIN(MAX(D4:D10), SUM(E4:E10), MIN(F4:F10))}$$

We demonstrate other ways to nest functions in the discussion of advanced functions.

4.6.4 Parameterization

We discussed in Chapter 2 the importance in effective modeling of well-parameterized functions, and we provided a set of useful mathematical functions for this purpose. A well-parameterized function is one that represents the relationship between two or more variables accurately, with parameters that have a natural meaning in the problem being modeled. For example, a linear function is a natural way to represent a supply contract in which a fixed charge is incurred for every order placed and a variable charge is incurred for every unit ordered. In this case, the slope of the linear function represents the variable charge and the intercept the fixed charge. When we vary either of these parameters during sensitivity analysis, the results are likely to be meaningful because the parameters themselves have a natural meaning.

Most relationships can be parameterized in alternative ways. Choosing the best parameterization for the problem at hand is part of the art of modeling. For example, a demand relationship between the price of a product and the quantity demanded could be modeled using the constant-elasticity function

$$Q = aP^b$$

In this function, the parameter b measures the *percentage* change in quantity that results from a *percentage* change in price.

An alternative is the linear relationship

$$Q = c - dP$$

The parameter d here represents the *unit* change in quantity for a *unit* change in price.

Yet another demand function might be used in a situation in which there is a reference price in the market, perhaps set by our major competitor's price. If we set our price above the reference price, we face one demand curve; if we price below the reference price, we face another demand curve. One way to model this is with an IF function, such as

$$Q = \text{IF}(\textit{Our Price} > \textit{Reference}, a - bP, c - dP)$$

These three functions represent three equally useful ways to relate demand to price. Which one works best in a given situation depends on the shape of the relationship we wish to create and on the parameters we wish to vary in sensitivity analysis.

Another application of parameterization is to create flexible functions for situations that are encountered often. A consulting company repeatedly found itself forecasting the market penetration of new products over time. After experimenting with many different parameterizations of the relationship between market share and time for new products, it settled on one that required four inputs: the initial share (*IShare*), the final share (*FShare*), the year in which share first starts to grow

FIGURE 4.8 A Flexible Four-Parameter Function for Market Share Growth

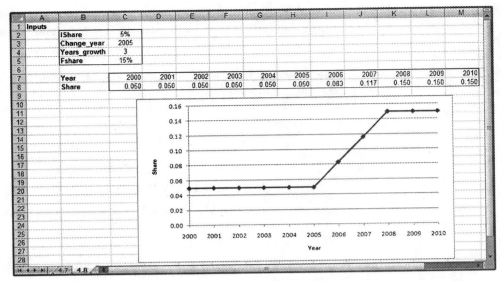

(*Change_year*), and the number of years of growth (*Years_growth*). The function takes the following form:

$$\text{Share in current year} = \text{IF}(\textit{Current year} < \textit{Change\_year}, \textit{IShare},$$
$$\text{IF}(\textit{Current\_year} > \textit{Change\_year} + \textit{Years\_growth}, \textit{FShare},$$
$$\textit{IShare} + (\textit{Current\_year} - \textit{Change\_year})^*((\textit{FShare} - \textit{Ishare})/\textit{Years\_growth}))$$

Before the *Change_year*, share is constant at *IShare*. After share has reached its limit (at *Change_year*+ *Years_growth*), it is constant at *FShare*. In between, the share is calculated by adding to *IShare* the annual growth ((*FShare*−*Ishare*)/*Years_growth*) times the number of years since *Change_year* (or *Current_year*−*Change_year*). Figure 4.8 shows a typical output from this function. Change any of the four input parameters and see how the function adjusts to show linear growth from *IShare* to *FShare*.

When we undertake sensitivity analysis with this function, we can easily vary the four parameters that appear explicitly: *IShare*, *FShare*, *Change_year*, and *Years_growth*. However, we cannot perform sensitivity analysis on parameters that appear implicitly, such as the *growth rate* of share. If the growth rate is an important parameter, we might want to create a different parameterization of this relationship in which this parameter appears explicitly. Here is an example of such a function:

$$\text{Share in current year} = \text{IF}(\textit{Current year} < \textit{Change\_year}, \textit{IShare},$$
$$\text{IF}(\textit{Current\_year} > \textit{Change\_year} + \textit{Years\_growth},$$
$$\textit{IShare}^*(1 + \textit{Growth\_rate})^{\wedge} \textit{Years\_growth},$$
$$\textit{IShare}^*(1 + \textit{Growth\_rate})^{\wedge} (\textit{Current\_year} - \textit{Change\_year}))$$

Neither of these alternatives is a simple function. If we were building only a single model involving growth in share, we would probably not go to the trouble of creating and debugging such a flexible function. But in a situation where this relationship is needed routinely, it may well be worth the effort.

4.6.5 Advanced Functions

AND and OR The logical functions AND and OR can be used to detect the relationship between values in various cells in a spreadsheet as it changes during analysis. For example, in the Office Building model we can determine whether the building cost is above $100 and the NPV is above $10,000,000 by using

```
AND(C4>100,B27>10000000)
```

The logical functions take on only two values: TRUE and FALSE. Thus in this spreadsheet

$$AND(C4>100, B27>10000000) = TRUE$$

$$OR(C4<100, B27<10000000) = FALSE$$

These functions can also be used to set flags, which are cells that warn the user when spreadsheet values are outside normal or acceptable ranges. (Flags are covered in more detail in Chapter 5.)

Truth tables are helpful for understanding how these logical functions operate. For example, the AND function is only true when *both* conditions are true, as shown in the table below.

Truth Table for AND

		Condition 1	
		True	False
	True	True	False
Condition 2			
	False	False	False

The OR function, by contrast, is true if one or the other or both conditions are true, as shown in the following table.

Truth Table for OR

		Condition 1	
		True	False
	True	True	True
Condition 2			
	False	True	False

Logical functions are particularly useful in combination with the IF function. When the logical test in an IF function depends on two conditions being true, such as D3>10 and D4<5, we could use two IF functions:

IF(D3>10, IF(D4<5, value_if_true, value-if-false), value-if-false)

or we can simplify using AND:

IF(AND(D3>10, D4<5), value_if_true, value-if-false).

If the logical condition were true if one or the other or both conditions were true, we would use the OR function:

IF(OR(D3>10, D4<5), value_if_true, value-if-false).

SUMIF and COUNTIF Two functions closely related to the IF function are SUMIF and COUNTIF. SUMIF adds all the cells in a range that satisfy a specified condition, while COUNTIF counts all the cells in a range that satisfy a specified condition. (COUNTIF is related to the COUNT function, which counts all the cells in a range that contain numbers.)

For example, if the range from D1 to D5 contains the following values

26

19

33

14

21

then SUMIF(D1:D5, "<20") = 33 and COUNTIF(D1:D5, "<22") = 3. (Note that the condition in the SUMIF and COUNTIF functions is enclosed in quotes.)

VLOOKUP and HLOOKUP The VLOOKUP (and HLOOKUP) functions are useful for capturing relationships based on tables. Suppliers, for example, typically offer discounts for larger order quantities. Here is an example of such a price schedule:

Order at least	Unit price
100	$39.50
200	38.00
300	37.00
400	36.00
500	35.00

We could capture this relationship using IF functions, but it would require nesting five IF functions. A simpler way is to use VLOOKUP, which takes three inputs: Lookup_value, Table_array, and Col_index_number. The Lookup_value is the value in the first column of the table. In this case, it is the order quantity for which we want to determine the price. The Table_array is the range in which the table is located. If the two columns of data in the above table were in cells C4:D8, the Table_array would be C4:D8. Finally, the Col_index_number is the number of the column in the table in which the result lies. In our example this is column 2. So

$$VLOOKUP(100, C4:D8, 2) = 39.50$$

and

$$VLOOKUP(425, C4:D8, 2) = 35.00$$

Note that the values in the first column of the table must be sorted, in either ascending or descending order. When the Lookup_value is not found in the first column, the VLOOKUP function finds the range in which it lies and chooses the next value in the table. Thus, all values above 400 but below 500 are treated as if they were 500. (Other options are available; see the Function Arguments window or Help.)

The HLOOKUP function performs the same function as the VLOOKUP function except that it is designed for horizontal tables.

INDEX, SMALL, and MATCH* The following example shows how three specialized functions, INDEX, SMALL, and MATCH, can be used in combination to carry out a sophisticated sequence of calculations. The example arises in power generation, where a large set of power plants must be brought into production in order from lowest cost to highest. Figure 4.9 shows part of the data in a workbook that contains cost and capacity data for 50 plants. The plants are numbered from 1 to 50 in column B. Plant capacities and costs are given in columns C and D, respectively. Our goal is to determine cumulative capacity when we employ only a certain number of plants in order of cost. Thus, we want to know, for example, how much capacity we have if we use the 35 cheapest plants.

The first step is to rank the costs from lowest to highest. We do this in column F using the SMALL function. The SMALL function calculates the kth smallest value in a range. So SMALL($D$6:$D$55,B6) returns the smallest cost; SMALL($D$6:$D$55,B7) the second lowest cost, and so on. Next, we need to find the relative position of a ranked cost in the cost range. For example, the lowest cost is 0.5; which plant has that cost, the 10th lowest, or the 25th lowest? We answer these questions in column G using the MATCH function, which gives the relative position

*This example is due to Jay Goldman of Strategic Decisions Group.

FIGURE 4.9   Using Nested Functions

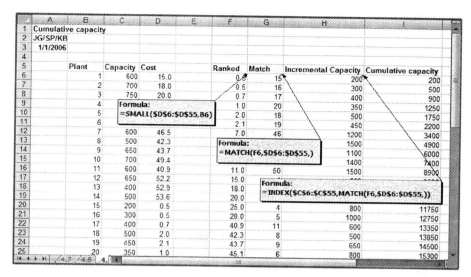

of an item in a sorted range. Thus MATCH(F6, $D$6:$D$55) = 15, which says that the lowest cost of 0.5, which appears in cell F6, is associated with the 15th plant. The next step is to determine the capacity of each plant as it appears in cost order. In other words, we know that the lowest cost plant is number 15; what is its capacity? We calculate this value using the INDEX function. The INDEX function gives the value at the intersection of a row and column index in a given range. So INDEX($C$6:$C$55, MATCH(F6, $D$6:$D$55,)) = 200. This function says, in effect, in the capacity range, find the value of the 15th entry. Column H thus gives the capacities of all the plants as they occur in cost order. Column I completes the calculation by adding up cumulative capacity. (Note that column G was included only for this explanation; it could be omitted from the final spreadsheet.)

Text and Date Functions   Excel offers a variety of functions for working with text and dates. These functions are often needed when working with information from databases. For example, if the first names of customers are in column A and the last names in column B, we can form their full names using the CONCATENATE function, which joins several text strings into one. Thus CONCATENATE("Sue", "Smith") = SueSmith. (To insert a space between the two names, we can use CONCATENATE("Sue", " ", "Smith")). Other useful text functions include EXACT, which compares two test strings, and LEFT, which returns a specified number of characters from the start of a string.

Date and time functions largely convert data from one format to another. Excel uses a date code in which years are numbered from 1900 to 9999. Thus if we enter the NOW function and format the cell as a date, the result is today's date, which happens to be 2/26/06. However, if we format it as a number, the result is 38774 in Excel's date code. Similarly, DATE(2006, 2, 26) = 2/26/06 as a date and 38774 as a number.

ROUND, CEILING, FLOOR, and INT   There are several ways to change the precision with which numbers are maintained in a spreadsheet. The CEILING function rounds up, and the FLOOR function rounds down, both to a given significance. The INT function rounds down to the nearest integer, and the ROUND function rounds to the specified number of digits. For example, ROUND(23.346,2)=23.35. Note that these functions actually _change_ the number that is stored in the cell, whereas formatting a cell does not change the number actually used in calculations. So we can format the number 23.346 to two digits and it will appear as 23.35, but any calculations based on this cell will use 23.346. By contrast, if we use ROUND(23.346,2), then both the display and the actual number are 23.35.

RAND and RANDBETWEEN Random numbers are often useful in modeling simple situations involving uncertainty (for more complex situations we use Crystal Ball, which is discussed in Chapters 15 and 16). The RAND() function returns a uniformly distributed random number between 0 and 1 each time the spreadsheet is calculated. To choose from a list of names randomly, we can create a random number for each student using this function and then sort students from the lowest to the highest value of the random number. RANDBETWEEN() returns a random number between two limits set by the user. For example, RANDBETWEEN(50,150) returns uniformly distributed random integers between 50 and 150.

Financial Functions Excel provides dozens of functions for financial calculations, some quite specialized. We have already discussed the NPV function, which is used frequently in evaluating investments. Some closely related functions are PV, which calculates the present value of a constant stream of payments; FV, which calculates the future value of a constant stream of payments; and IRR, which calculates the internal rate of return of a stream of payments. A couple of other functions that simplify complex calculations are PRICE, which calculates the price of a bond for given settlement date, redemption date, redemption value, rate and yield; and SYD, which gives the sum-of-years' digits depreciation for given cost, salvage value, life, and period.

4.7 RECORDING MACROS AND USING VBA[*]

Macros are small computer programs that automate frequently performed tasks. Macros are written in the Visual Basic for Applications language and stored in Visual Basic modules, so a deep understanding of macros requires knowledge of VBA. Fortunately, Excel provides a mechanism for creating macros simply by recording the steps involved, so many simple macros can be created by users who have little or no programming knowledge. We illustrate here how to *create* a macro by recording keystrokes, how to *edit* a macro using basic concepts from VBA so as to make it more powerful, and how to turn a macro into a *user-defined function*.

Any set of steps in Excel that an analyst repeats frequently is a good candidate for a macro. For example, some organizations require that every spreadsheet has a certain header and footer (containing date, author, and related information) and that the first several columns are formatted in a standard manner. To carry out these tasks manually might require 20–30 separate actions in Excel and take 10–15 minutes every time a new workbook must be created. If these actions can be captured in a macro, the entire sequence can be executed with one key combination that takes seconds to execute. Some firms provide such macros to employees as a way of ensuring compliance with corporate standards for good spreadsheet practice.

4.7.1 Recording a Macro

Financial analysts often need to calculate cumulative returns for a series of returns data over time. Consider, for example, the following daily returns on the stock of Apple Computer for December 2004. What is the cumulative return for each day, calculated from December 1?

Date	Daily Return
20041201	0.011
20041202	−0.038

[*]The assistance of Bob Burnham, Senior Research Computing Associate, Tuck School of Business at Dartmouth College, on this section is gratefully acknowledged.

20041203	−0.039
20041206	0.049
20041207	−0.044
20041208	0.006
20041209	0.011
20041210	0.018
20041213	−0.004
20041214	0.006
20041215	0.000
20041216	0.020
20041217	−0.024
20041220	−0.035
20041221	0.015
20041222	0.001
20041223	0.004
20041227	−0.013
20041228	0.016
20041229	0.004
20041230	0.006
20041231	−0.006

Since there is no single function in Excel for calculating cumulative returns, we need to proceed in steps. The first step is to add 1 to each return. Then we multiply these growth factors together over the period in question and subtract 1 from the total to calculate the cumulative return. For example, the cumulative return over the first two days is $(1 + 0.011)^*(1 - 0.038) - 1 = -0.027$. We have carried out this calculation in the workbook shown in Figure 4.10. The input data appear in columns A and B. In column C we have added 1 to each return; in column D we have multiplied the growth factors in column C. We use the PRODUCT function to do this; for example, the cumulative return from December 1 to December 31 is calculated in cell D25 using the formula `PRODUCT($C$4:$C25)-1`.

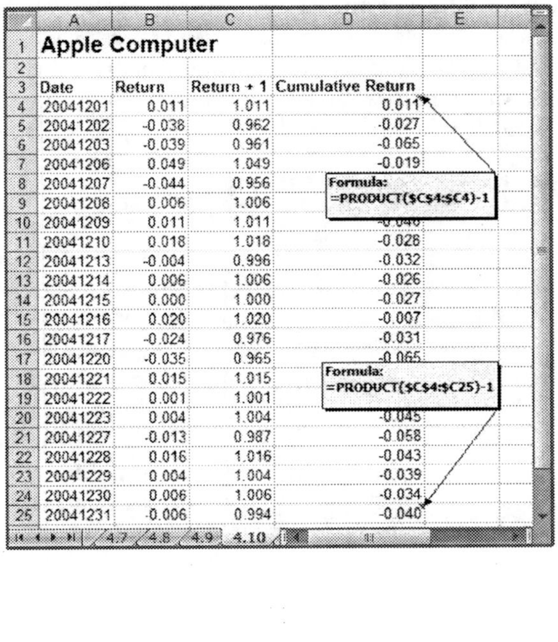

Date	Return	Return + 1	Cumulative Return
20041201	0.011	1.011	0.011
20041202	-0.038	0.962	-0.027
20041203	-0.039	0.961	-0.065
20041206	0.049	1.049	-0.019
20041207	-0.044	0.956	
20041208	0.006	1.006	
20041209	0.011	1.011	[illegible]
20041210	0.018	1.018	-0.028
20041213	-0.004	0.996	-0.032
20041214	0.006	1.006	-0.026
20041215	0.000	1.000	-0.027
20041216	0.020	1.020	-0.007
20041217	-0.024	0.976	-0.031
20041220	-0.035	0.965	-0.065
20041221	0.015	1.015	
20041222	0.001	1.001	
20041223	0.004	1.004	-0.045
20041227	-0.013	0.987	-0.058
20041228	0.016	1.016	-0.043
20041229	0.004	1.004	-0.039
20041230	0.006	1.006	-0.034
20041231	-0.006	0.994	-0.040

FIGURE 4.10 Calculating Cumulative Returns in Excel

There are several shortcomings to the procedure we have described. One is that we have to repeat these steps every times we want to calculate a cumulative return, which could be dozens of times a day. Second, we have to clutter up our spreadsheet with intermediate calculations in column C. Instead, we can use a macro to solve the first problem and a user-defined function to solve the second.

The first step in creating a macro is to document the steps that must be executed to create the desired outcome. Calculating cumulative returns for every period given a column of returns requires four steps:

Step 1: In the cell to the right of the first return, write a formula that adds 1 to the first return (e.g., =B4+1).

Step 2: Copy this formula down to the last time period.

Step 3: In the next column over, write a formula that calculates the cumulative return (e.g., =PRODUCT($C$4:$C4)-1).

Step 4: Copy this formula down to the last time period.

This procedure will work for the data in our example, but if we want our macro to be more useful, we should anticipate that the columns to the right of the returns data may in some instances not be empty. If this is the case, our first step should be to insert two blank columns to the right of the returns data.

To record a macro for this process, display the Returns data sheet. Then turn on the Macro Recorder, which is a device that will record every action performed on a workbook until the Recorder is turned off. The Recorder is turned on by selecting Developer▶Code▶Record Macro. This opens the window shown in Figure 4.11. Give the macro a descriptive name (such as Compound_growth), store it in This Workbook, and assign it a shortcut key that is not normally used (such as "a"). Click on OK and notice that the Stop Recording button has replaced the Record Macro button in the Code group. Next, proceed carefully through the steps outlined above. Then click on the Stop Recording button. Check that the macro works correctly by invoking it using Ctrl + a after deleting the contents of columns C and D. (It might be wise to make a copy of the worksheet beforehand.) The results should be the same as those obtained earlier by manual calculation.

4.7.2 Editing a Macro

The macro we have created is very efficient for calculating cumulative returns as long as the data are located in the range B4:B25. But we should expect to face situations in which we have a different number of returns and they are located somewhere else in the spreadsheet. Can we modify the existing macro so that it works more generally?

The first step in this direction is to open the Visual Basic Editor (VBE) and view the code that was created when we recorded the Compound_growth macro. Open the Visual Basic Editor by choosing Alt-F11 (see Figure 4.12). The large pane on the right is the **Code window**. The code for the macro can be viewed and edited here. The pane on the left is the **Project Explorer window**, which lists all the open workbooks and can be used to locate all the macros in a workbook.

Three toolbars are commonly used in the VBE: Standard, Edit, and Debug. The Standard toolbar allows for the usual Windows operations (Save, Help, and so on), but it also allows running and stopping a program as well as displaying various information in the Editor (such as

FIGURE 4.11 Record Macro Window

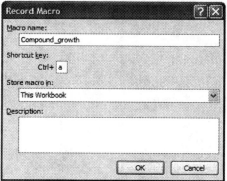

FIGURE 4.12 Visual Basic
Editor

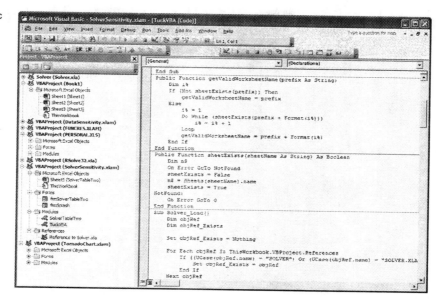

the Properties window or the Object browser). The Edit toolbar is helpful for working with the code itself. It has useful icons for indenting text, adding comments, and so on. Finally, the Debug toolbar makes it possible to run the program in steps and to add a watch window to keep track of variables during code execution.

The actual code for the Compound_ growth macro is shown in Figure 4.13. The first line of the macro starts with the word Sub followed by the name of the macro: Compound_growth(). The last line of the macro is EndSub. The second line of the code begins with a single quote ('); this is a comment line and is not executed by the code. The remainder of the code is reproduced below, along with a brief explanation of what each line accomplishes.

Columns("C:D").Select	select columns C and D
Selection.Insert shift:=xlToRight	insert two columns
Range("C4").Select	select C4
ActiveCell.FormulaR1C1 = "=RC[−1]+1"	enter formula = B4+1
Range("C4").Select	select C4
Selection.Copy	copy C4
Range("C5:C25").Select	select C5:C25
ActiveSheet.Paste	paste to C5:C25
Range("D4").Select	select D4
Application.CutCopyMode = False	exit copy mode
ActiveCell.FormulaR1C1 = "= PRODUCT(R4C3:RC3)−1"	enter formula = PRODUCT($C$4:$C4) −1
Range("D4").Select	select D4
Selection.AutoFill Destination:= Range("D4:D25"), Type:=xlFillDefault	autofill to D4:D25
Range("D4:D25").Select	select D4:D25

FIGURE 4.13 Compound
Growth Macro as Recorded

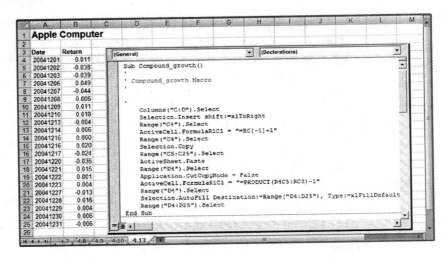

The major task in making this macro more general is to replace the references to specific cell locations with generic locations, to be specified by the user. The edited code for this more powerful macro is given in Figure 4.14. Comments have been added to this code to help explain the various changes.

The first part of the code uses Dim (Dimension) statements to create names for three ranges: userdata, plusOneRng, and cumRetRng. The first range, userdata, will be set by the user, who must highlight the range of returns before running this macro. The plusOneRng will contain the returns plus one; the cumRetRng will contain the cumulative returns.

The second block of code inserts two blank columns to the right of the returns data. The line ActiveSheet.Columns(userdata.Column + 1).Select highlights the column to the right of the returns data. The line Selection.Insert shift:=xlToLeft, which occurs twice, inserts a blank column.

The next block of code gives the names plusOneRng and cumRetRng to the first and second columns, respectively, to the right of the returns data.

The fourth block of code creates the column of returns with 1 added. First the range plusOneRng is selected. Then the formula RC[-1]+1 is used to add one to the return one cell to the left. Then this formula is copied to the bottom of the range.

FIGURE 4.14 Compound
Growth Macro as Edited

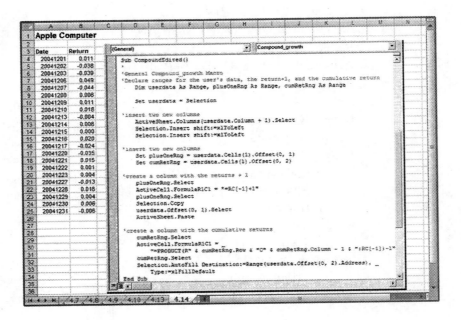

The fifth and final block of code calculates the cumulative returns. First the range cumRetRng is selected. Then the PRODUCT formula is entered. Finally, the formula is copied to the bottom of the range.

Test this macro by first highlighting the range B4:B25, then choosing Developer▶Code▶Macros (or Alt+F8), highlighting CompoundEdited, and selecting Run. The results should be identical to those obtained earlier. Now delete these results, highlight just the range B10:B20, and repeat the macro. This should add returns in columns C and D starting in 12/09 and running to 12/23. This demonstrates the increased generality of this version of the macro.

Most of the lines of code that appeared in the original macro have been changed in the edited version. Nonetheless, the overall flow of the logic as established in the recorded macro carries over to the edited version. It is usually the case that recorded macros are narrow in their scope and often contain superfluous details. With some knowledge of VBA, it is possible to edit these templates and make them both more general and more efficient.

4.7.3 Creating a User-Defined Function

The macros we have created to this point are powerful tools for analysts who frequently work with cumulative returns. Nevertheless, they still have limitations. One is simply that they require the use of macros, which are not familiar to the majority of Excel users. Another limitation is that we have to clutter the spreadsheet with intermediate calculations. It would be preferable if Excel itself had a built-in function for calculating cumulative returns. Then we could simply enter this function into any cell where it was needed, anywhere in a spreadsheet. Although Excel does not have such a function, we can create one in VBA.

There are two types of VBA programs: Sub procedures and Function procedures. Both perform actions in Excel. The macros we have created are examples of Sub procedures. A Function procedure differs from a Sub procedure in that it can return a value. The user-defined function we wish to create will return the cumulative return for a specified range of returns data. Figure 4.15 shows such a program written in VBA.

A user-defined function begins with the words Public Function, the function name (CumulativeReturn), and the type of inputs it accepts. Here our function requires one input: a range called "Returns." The next two lines create a variable called "cell" (a range) and another called TotalRet, a real number. Then the variable TotalRet is set to the value 1# (1# is equivalent to 1.0).

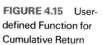

FIGURE 4.15 User-defined Function for Cumulative Return

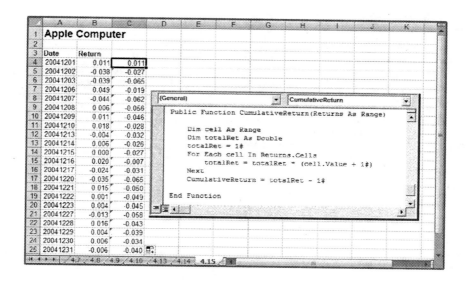

The core of this function is a For . . . Next loop. This loop takes each cell in the range Returns, adds 1, and multiplies by the current value of TotalRet. When we subtract 1 from the final value of TotalRet, we have the cumulative return over the range, which is assigned to the function value, CumulativeReturn.

How can this function be used in a spreadsheet? First, we can confirm that the function is available in a given spreadsheet by opening the Insert Function window and selecting User-defined functions. Then we can use the function just as we use any other Excel function. In the worksheet corresponding to Figure 4.15, we have entered the function CumulativeReturn($B$4:$B4) in cell C4. Then we copy that function down the column. The results are identical to those we have found using macros.

User-defined functions are preferable to macros in many ways. They are easier to use for those unfamiliar with macros. They can be used to calculate just the needed results without adding anything extraneous to the spreadsheet. And they can be made highly general.

We have not attempted to give a comprehensive overview of VBA in this section, but rather to convey a sense of what can be accomplished using macros and VBA. For those who spend a high percentage of their work life using Excel, many of whom create elaborate spreadsheets and perform highly repetitive tasks, macros and VBA represent the next frontier in power and efficiency.

4.8 SUMMARY

This chapter covers selected Excel features that are used by intermediate and advanced modelers to make their work with spreadsheets more efficient or to make their spreadsheets more powerful.

The chapter covered the following topics:

- Keyboard shortcuts
- Controls
- Cell comments
- Naming cells and ranges
- Advanced formulas and functions
- Recording macros and using Visual Basic for Applications

Keyboard shortcuts can make interacting with Excel easier and quicker. Controls and cell comments make spreadsheets easier to understand and easier to work with. Named ranges are generally used by sophisticated modelers to make formulas easier to read and less prone to error.

All Excel modelers must know how to create simple formulas, but some models require more advanced use of formulas. We show how to nest functions to create powerful formulas in a single cell and how to create reusable formulas using flexible parameterizations.

SUGGESTED READINGS

An interactive Excel tutorial that covers many of the topics in this chapter can be downloaded at no cost from http://www.kelley.iu.edu/albrightbooks/#Tutorial.

There are a number of excellent advanced books on Excel. Here are some of our favorites.

ALBRIGHT, S. C. 2007. *VBA for Modelers*. Belmont CA: Duxbury.

GROSS, D., F. AKAIWA, and K. NORDQUIST. 2006. *Succeeding in Business with Microsoft Excel 2003*. Boston MA:, Thomson Learning.

ROMAN, S. 2002. *Writing Excel Macros with VBA*. 2nd ed., Sebastopol CA: O'Reilly.

SENGUPTA, C. 2004. *Financial Modeling Using Excel and VBA*. Hoboken NJ: John Wiley and Sons.

WINSTON, W. 2004. *Microsoft Excel Data Analysis and Business Modeling*. 2nd ed. Redmond, WA: Microsoft Press.

5 Spreadsheet Engineering

Builders of ships, bridges, and skyscrapers all spend considerable time and money planning the structure before they order concrete and steel. Even the builder of a modest house starts with blueprints and a plan of activities. Without detailed planning, complex structures cannot be built efficiently, and they sometimes fail in use. The same is true of spreadsheet models. Spreadsheets can be as important to a business as bridges are to a road network. If a business relies on a spreadsheet, the business should devote sufficient resources to ensuring that the spreadsheet is suitably *engineered.*

Advance planning can speed up the process of implementing a complex design. Some years ago, the auto industry learned that investing more resources in pre-production activities saved a great deal of time and money when a new car was being prepared for manufacturing. One of the major sources of efficiency in this case was avoiding cycles of rework and redesign. Without good planning, the need for design improvements is detected only after implementation has begun, and much of the implementation effort is wasted. The same is true of spreadsheet models: extra time spent in planning can actually *reduce* the overall time required to perform a spreadsheet analysis.

Sometimes, at the outset, it seems as if a spreadsheet project will be fairly straightforward. The flexibility of the spreadsheet environment seduces us into believing that we can jump right in and start entering formulas. Then, as we move further into the process of building the spreadsheet, it turns out that the project is a bit more complicated than it seemed at first. We encounter new user requirements, or we discover obscure logical cases. We redesign the spreadsheet on the fly, preserving some parts of the original design and reworking others. The smooth logical flow of the original spreadsheet gets disrupted. Rather quickly, a simple task becomes complicated, driven by a cycle of unanticipated needs followed by rework and additional testing. Before long, we face a spreadsheet containing "spaghetti logic," and as a result, we have reason to worry that the spreadsheet contains errors.

In addition to speeding up the design process, advance planning can help the designer avoid critical errors in a design. A mistake in the design of a building or bridge can cause it to collapse; a bug in a spreadsheet can lead to poor decisions and substantial monetary losses. As we pointed out in Chapter 1, research suggests that many spreadsheets actually in use contain hidden errors. Learning how to avoid bugs is an essential aspect of spreadsheet modeling. Many analysts spend 80 percent of their time building (and fixing) models, and only 20 percent using them for analysis. With good design skills, this ratio can be reversed, so that analysts can spend the majority of their effort improving actual decisions.

In this chapter, we offer guidelines for the engineering of spreadsheets. Our motivation is to improve both the efficiency and the effectiveness with which spreadsheets are created. An *efficient* design process uses the minimum time and effort to achieve results. An *effective* process achieves results that meet the users' requirements. Although spreadsheet modeling is a creative process, and thus cannot be reduced to a simple recipe, every spreadsheet passes through a predictable series of stages. Accordingly, we organize our guidelines around these phases:

- Designing
- Building
- Testing

In this chapter, and several later chapters, we draw on the following example to illustrate our precepts and methods.

EXAMPLE
*The
Advertising
Budget
Decision*

As product-marketing manager, one of our jobs is to prepare recommendations to the Executive Committee as to how advertising expenditures should be allocated. Last year's advertising budget of $40,000 was spent in equal increments over the four quarters. Initial expectations are that we will repeat this plan in the coming year. However, the committee would like to know whether some other allocation would be advantageous and whether the total budget should be changed.

Our product sells for $40 and costs us $25 to produce. Sales in the past have been seasonal, and our consultants have estimated seasonal adjustment factors for unit sales as follows:

Q1 90%	Q3 80%
Q2 110%	Q4 120%

(A seasonal adjustment factor measures the percentage of average quarterly demand experienced in a given quarter.)

In addition to production costs, we must take into account the cost of the sales force (projected to be $34,000 over the year, allocated as follows: Q1 and Q2, $8,000 each; Q3 and Q4, $9,000 each), the cost of advertising itself, and overhead (typically around 15 percent of revenues).

Quarterly unit sales seem to run around 4,000 units when advertising is around $10,000. Clearly, advertising will increase sales, but there are limits to its impact. Our consultants several years ago estimated the relationship between advertising and sales. Converting that relationship to current conditions gives the following formula:

$$Unit\ sales = 35 \times seasonal\ factor \times \sqrt{(3,000 + Advertising)}$$ ∎

Although this problem is not ill structured in the terms we discussed in Chapter 2, it is still good practice to begin the process of building a spreadsheet model by drawing an influence chart. The key output measure is Profit, which decomposes readily into Revenue and Cost (see Figure 5.1). Revenue depends on

FIGURE 5.1 Influence Chart for the Advertising Budget Problem

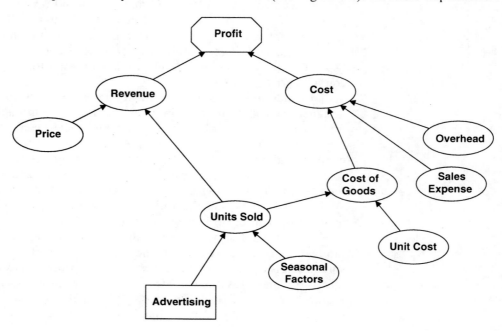

Price and Units Sold, while Cost depends on Overhead, Sales Expense, and Cost of Goods. The Cost of Goods depends on the Unit Cost and Units Sold. Finally, Units Sold depends on the Seasonal Factors and Advertising.

Drawing the influence chart helps us to clearly identify outputs (Profit) and decisions (Advertising). It also helps lay bare the essential relationships that connect the two. Finally, it should help us to recognize assumptions as we make them. Two assumptions in particular may be relevant later: one is that units sold are identical to units produced, so we ignore the timing of production and inventory; the second is that price is considered a parameter, not a decision variable, and it does not influence unit sales.

5.2 DESIGNING A SPREADSHEET

The essential first step in developing any spreadsheet model is to *design* it. In this section we offer some tips on good design practices for single-worksheet models. In the next section we discuss how to design an effective workbook composed of interconnected worksheets. We begin with eight guidelines for designing a worksheet.

5.2.1 Sketch the Spreadsheet

Carpenters have the saying, "Measure twice, cut once." That is, since planning is inexpensive and miscut wood is useless, plan carefully to avoid waste and rework. A similar piece of advice applies to spreadsheets: careful planning tends to result in far less time spent correcting mistakes.

Turn the computer *off* and *think* for a while before hitting any keys. This advice may seem harsh at the start, but we have seen many modelers create a spreadsheet in a flurry of keystrokes, only to discover at some later point that their design is flawed and in need of wholesale revision. To those who are relatively new to spreadsheet modeling, we recommend beginning with a sketch of their spreadsheet before entering anything into the computer. We also believe this is a good first step for experienced modelers. A sketch should show the physical layout of major elements and should contain at least a rough indication of the flow of calculations. Instead of laboriously writing out formulas with cell addresses, we use variable names to indicate how calculations will be performed. For example, we might write: *Profit = Total Revenue – Total Cost*. In order to show the logic for calculating unsold goods, we might write: IF(*Stock > Demand, Stock – Demand*, 0). The acid test for whether a sketch is sufficiently detailed is whether someone else could build a spreadsheet from it without any significant redesign.

An influence chart often provides a useful starting point for a spreadsheet design, as we illustrated earlier. The process of constructing an influence chart helps to identify the key outputs and inputs, as well as the logic that connects them. These are all critical ingredients in the spreadsheet model, but a spreadsheet provides a somewhat different view. For one thing, a spreadsheet has to be populated with numbers, while an influence chart involves only the *names* of parameters, variables, and relationships. Also, the physical design of the spreadsheet is usually different from that of the influence chart. Whereas an influence chart begins with outputs and works back to inputs, a spreadsheet typically starts with inputs and works toward outputs.

For the Advertising Budget example, a sketch of the spreadsheet might include four major sections (Parameters, Decisions, Outputs, and Calculations), row headings for the entries in the Calculations section, and a brief indication of how each row in the model will be calculated. For example, we could note the equation, *Gross Margin = Revenue – Cost of Goods*. Figure 5.2 shows an initial sketch along these lines. In this sketch we have not listed each of the parameters or the values of the decision variables. Nor have we shown specific cell addresses. The level of detail that

FIGURE 5.2 Sketch of Spreadsheet for the Advertising Budget Problem

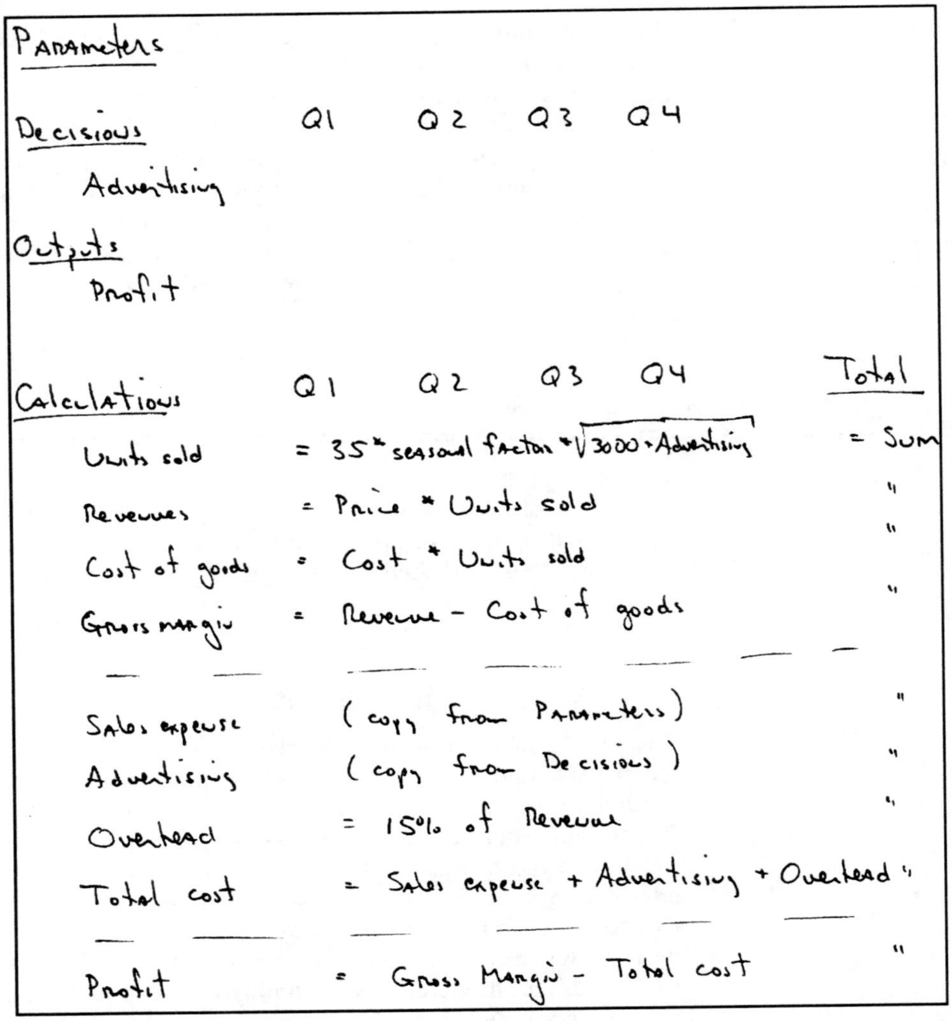

is appropriate for a sketch depends on the complexity of the problem and the preferences of the designer.

The normal logical flow would require calculations to precede outputs. Why have we placed calculations at the bottom of the spreadsheet? The reason has to do with the use we envision for the model. We expect to vary some of the decision variables, and we'll want to know the consequences for the output measure. Since we want to see the effects of varying decisions on the output, it makes sense to place these items close together in the spreadsheet. In addition, we may also want to alter one or more of the input parameters and revisit the relationship between decisions and output. Therefore, it also makes sense to have inputs in close proximity to output and decisions. The one part of the spreadsheet we won't be examining or altering, once we've tested it, is the set of calculations. Therefore, we place the calculations in a secondary location.

Part of the thinking process, then, is anticipating what use will be made of the model. We will return to this point later, but for now, the planning process should take this into consideration when the model structure is sketched.

5.2.2 Organize the Spreadsheet into Modules

Modules bring together groups of similar items, and they separate unlike items. Modularization is a basic principle of good design and a useful first step in organizing information. In spreadsheets, this means separating data, decision variables, outcome measures, and detailed calculations. If an influence chart has been constructed, as

FIGURE 5.3 The Advertising Budget Spreadsheet

	A	B	C	D	E	F	G	H	I	J
1	Advertising Budget Model									
2	SGP/KRB									
3	1/1/2006									
4										
5	PARAMETERS									
6				Q1	Q2	Q3	Q4			Notes
7		Price	$40.00							Current price
8		Cost	$25.00							Accounting
9		Seasonal		0.9	1.1	0.8	1.2			Data analysis
10		OHD rate	0.15							Accounting
11		Sales Parameters								
12			35							Consultants
13			3000							
14		Sales Expense		8000	8000	9000	9000			Consultants
15		Ad Budget	$40,000							Current budget
16										
17	DECISIONS							Total		
18		Ad Expenditures		$10,000	$10,000	$10,000	$10,000	$40,000		sum
19										
20	OUTPUTS									
21		Profit	$69,662							
22										
23	CALCULATIONS									
24		Quarter		Q1	Q2	Q3	Q4	Total		
25		Seasonal		0.9	1.1	0.8	1.2			
26										
27		Units Sold		3592	4390	3192	4789	15962		given formula
28		Revenue		143662	175587	127700	191549	638498		price*units
29		Cost of Goods		89789	109742	79812	119718	399061		cost*units
30		Gross Margin		53873	65845	47887	71831	239437		subtraction
31										
32		Sales Expense		8000	8000	9000	9000	34000		given
33		Advertising		10000	10000	10000	10000	40000		decisions
34		Overhead		21549	26338	19155	28732	95775		rate*revenue
35		Total Fixed Cost		39549	44338	38155	47732	169775		sum
36										
37		Profit		14324	21507	9732	24099	69662		GM -TFC
38		Profit Margin		9.97%	12.25%	7.62%	12.58%	10.91%		pct of revenue
39										

H ◀ ▶ H \5.3/ |◀

discussed in Chapter 2, then a lot of this work will already have been done. An influence chart will have identified the outcome measure (or measures) of major interest as well as the data and decisions that make up the inputs. Most importantly, the influence chart will also have organized the major steps in the calculations required to produce the outputs.

Along with grouping and separating, the next step is to consider the flow of information in the model—that is, to specify which information will need to pass from one group to another. Data and decisions will serve as inputs to some of the calculations, and a small number of the calculations will eventually be highlighted as outputs. After these key linkages are identified, the additional development of one module can go on somewhat independently of modifications in other modules. Keep in mind that formulas should generally reference cells located above and to the left.

Figure 5.3[*] displays our spreadsheet for the Advertising Budget example. Following the layout in our initial sketch, we use four modules and surround each one with a border for clarity. The detailed calculations are simple enough to include in a single block, but even here, we use blank lines to separate gross margin, costs, and profits. We highlight values of decision variables (the quarterly advertising expenditures) and the output measure (annual profit) with color shading. Models that are more complex may, of course, contain many more modules and require layouts that are more elaborate.

As planned, the modules for parameters, decisions, and outputs are in close proximity. Therefore, we can change the value of an input and immediately see the impact on the output in the same Excel window.

5.2.3 Start Small

Do not attempt to build a complex spreadsheet all at once. Isolate one part of the problem or one module of the spreadsheet; then design, build, and test that one part.

[*]To download spreadsheets for this chapter, go to the Student Companion Site at www.wiley.com/college/powell.

Once that part of the model is in good shape, go on to the next one. By making (and correcting) many little mistakes in each module, and thus keeping the mistakes local if they occur, it is possible to avoid making really large and complex mistakes that require much more effort to detect and correct.

If we were building a model to cover 100 customers, it would make sense to start with a model for one customer, or perhaps a few customers. If the model structure is the same or similar for each of the customers, it should be easy to replicate this initial building block. Then, when the basic building block is working, the model can be expanded to include the remaining customers. Similarly, if we were building a complex model to cover 12 months, we would start by building a model for the first month; then we would expand it to 2 months and ultimately to all 12.

In the Advertising Budget example, we start by creating the Parameters and Decisions modules, because those simply organize and display the information we have gathered. Since we do not know at the outset what values we will ultimately choose for the decision variables, we enter convenient values (last year's expenditures of $10,000 each quarter seem appropriate), simply to hold a place and to assist us in debugging the logic of the spreadsheet. When we begin work on the financial logic, we focus on the first quarter. Only when the profit in the first quarter has been calculated successfully should we move on to the rest of the year. (Recursive formulas, which use a previous value to calculate the current value, facilitate this process.)

5.2.4 Isolate Input Parameters

Place the numerical values of key parameters in a single location and separate them from calculations. This means that formulas contain only cell references, not numerical values. It also means that a parameter contained in several formulas appears only once as a numerical value in the spreadsheet, although it may appear several times as a cell reference in a formula.

Parameterization offers several advantages. First, placing parameters in a separate location makes it easy to identify them and change them. It also makes a particular scenario immediately visible. Parameterization ensures that changing a numerical value in one cell is sufficient to induce a change throughout the entire model. In addition, parameterization is required for effective sensitivity analysis, as we discuss in Chapter 6. Finally, it is relatively easy to document the assumptions behind parameters, or the sources from which they were derived, if those parameters appear in a single location.

In our audits of spreadsheets, we frequently observe a tendency to bury parameters in cell formulas and to replicate the same parameter in multiple cells. This makes identifying parameters difficult, because they are not immediately visible. It's also difficult to know whether all numerical values of a parameter have been changed each time an update is required. By contrast, the habit of using a single and separate location considerably streamlines the building and debugging of a spreadsheet.

In our sample spreadsheet, all the parameters are located in a single module (cells B6:G15). Notice, for example, that price is referenced in cells D28:G28. When price is changed in C7, it is automatically changed in these other cells as well.

5.2.5 Design for Use

While designing a spreadsheet, try to anticipate who will use it and what kinds of questions they will want to address. Make it easy to change parameters that can be expected to change often. Make it easy to find key outputs by collecting them in one place. Include graphs of the outputs to make it easier to learn from the spreadsheet.

In our example spreadsheet, we have anticipated that when we move into the analysis phase, we will primarily be changing one or more values in the Parameters module (or the Decisions module) and observing the effect on the key output, annual profits. That is why we have copied the value of profits from cell H37 to cell C21, where it can be read more conveniently. In a larger model, the outputs may be scattered over many locations in different worksheets. It is very helpful to gather them together and place them near the inputs so that the details of the model itself do not interfere with the process of analysis. We will have more to say about this principle when we discuss workbooks in the next section.

5.2.6 Keep It Simple

Just as good models should be simple, good spreadsheets should be as simple as possible while still getting the job done. Complex spreadsheets require more time and effort to build than simple ones, and they are *much* more difficult to debug. Some of our earlier guidelines, such as modularization and parameterization, help keep models simple.

Long formulas are a common symptom of overly complex spreadsheets. The most serious constraint on effective spreadsheet modeling is not computing power, but human brainpower. Therefore, there is little to be gained from minimizing the number of cells in a spreadsheet by writing a long formula in one cell. It is better to decompose a complex calculation into its intermediate steps and to display each step in a separate cell. This makes it easier to spot errors in the logic and to explain the spreadsheet calculations to others. Overall, it is a more efficient use of the combined human–computer team.

In the Advertising Budget example, we could calculate Gross Margin (cell D30) in a single row rather than use three rows to calculate its components (Units Sold, Revenue, and Cost of Goods). However, the detail helps in checking the logic, and it may eventually prove helpful during analysis. Later on, for example, we may decide that it would be more realistic to model sales as a function of price. Instead of modifying a complicated Gross Margin formula, we will find it easier to work with the formula for Units Sold.

5.2.7 Design for Communication

Spreadsheets are often used long after the builder ever thought they would be, and frequently by people who are not familiar with them. Logical design helps users understand what the spreadsheet is intended to accomplish and how to work with it effectively. The look and the layout of a spreadsheet often determine whether its developer or another user can understand it several months or years after it was built. Visual cues that reinforce the model's logic also pay dividends when the spreadsheet gets routine use in a decision-support role.

The use of informative labels and the incorporation of blank spaces can go a long way toward conveying the organization of a spreadsheet. The specialized formatting options in Excel (outlines, color, bold font, and so on) can also be used to highlight certain cell entries or ranges for quick visual recognition. This facilitates navigating around the spreadsheet, both when building the spreadsheet and when using it. However, formatting tools should be applied with care. If used to excess, formatting can confuse, obscure, and annoy rather than help. In our example spreadsheet, we use various formatting tools to improve readability, including bold font, borders, color shading, and capitalization. Within a team or an organization, or when creating a series of spreadsheets, it also helps to use these formatting tools consistently. For example, we use yellow shading and a border to designate cells that represent decision variables in virtually all of our spreadsheet models.

Sometimes large spreadsheets can be reorganized with the help of split windows. For example, if we were to display the Advertising Budget spreadsheet at normal size, it would not fit within one (laptop) window. As a result, the lower part of the Calculations module would drop out of view. If we wanted to preserve the top portion of the spreadsheet, but also view the quarterly profit levels and the profit-margin percentages, we could split the window vertically, as shown in Figure 5.4. (To split a screen, select a row or column and choose View▶Window▶Split.)

FIGURE 5.4 Split-Window Display in the Advertising Budget Spreadsheet

	A	B	C	D	E	F	G	H	I	J
1	Advertising Budget Model									
2	SGP/KRB									
3	1/1/2006									
4										
5	PARAMETERS									
6				Q1	Q2	Q3	Q4			Notes
7		Price	$40.00							Current price
8		Cost	$25.00							Accounting
9		Seasonal		0.9	1.1	0.8	1.2			Data analysis
10		OHD rate	0.15							Accounting
11		Sales Parameters								
12			35							Consultants
13			3000							
14		Sales Expense		8000	8000	9000	9000			Consultants
15		Ad Budget	$40,000							Current budget
16										
17	DECISIONS							Total		
18		Ad Expenditures		$10,000	$10,000	$10,000	$10,000	$40,000		sum
19										
20	OUTPUTS									
21		Profit	$69,662							
37		Profit		14324	21507	9732	24099	69662		GM -TFC
38		Profit Margin		9.97%	12.25%	7.62%	12.58%	10.91%		pct of revenue
39										

5.3 \ 5.4 /

5.2.8 Document Important Data and Formulas

Spreadsheets have become widespread in the business world because they are easy to build and use. Originally, many analysts learned to build spreadsheets because their corporate information technology departments could not serve their needs in a timely fashion. One reason for the lack of a timely response is that information technology professionals use a careful and time-consuming design process for creating computing applications, including extensive documentation. Spreadsheet users rarely apply the same level of effort to their applications. The question, then, is: How can we preserve the benefits of using spreadsheets, while also gaining the benefits of a careful design process?

One answer to this question is to find *practical* ways to document a spreadsheet. Creating separate documentation or user manuals is often impractical. But it is neither difficult nor time consuming to record the source of each important parameter and explain each important calculation in the spreadsheet itself. A design sketch or influence chart of the spreadsheet provides documentation, in a fashion, for every important relationship in the model. Transferring this information to the actual spreadsheet helps preserve the underlying logic of the model and ultimately helps convey that logic to users of the spreadsheet.

In our example spreadsheet, we have documented both input parameters and the model logic in column J (refer to Figure 5.3). We have noted the source of each of the parameters: the accounting department, consultants, and so on. For each formula, we have provided a short explanation of the arithmetic, such as *Revenue = Price*Units*.

At the detailed level, we can provide documentation within individual cells by inserting cell comments. The command Review▶Comments▶New Comment brings up a small window in which we can describe the contents of the cell where the cursor is located. Figure 5.5 shows an example in which the Comment window explains that last year the budget was distributed equally among the quarters. The format of the comment is controlled by a selection from the Excel Options▶Advanced menu. In the Display Section within this menu are three buttons controlling the display of cell comments. A comment can be displayed permanently by clicking on Comments and indicators. Or we can click on Indicators only, in which case there will be a red triangle in the upper right-hand corner of the cell, but the comment will be displayed only when the cursor is placed within that cell. If we click on No Comments, then neither the comment nor the indicator will be visible at all.

Finally, it may be worth creating a separate module to list the assumptions in the model, particularly the structural simplifications adopted at the outset of the model-building process. In the Advertising Budget example, we assumed that production

FIGURE 5.5 Comment Window for the Budget Parameter

	A	B	C	D	E	F	G	H	I	J
1	Advertising Budget Model									
2	SGP/KRB									
3	1/1/2006									
4										
5	PARAMETERS									
6				Q1	Q2	Q3	Q4			
7		Price	$40.00							Notes
8		Cost	$25.00							Current price
9		Seasonal		0.9	1.1	0.8	1.2			Accounting
10		OHD rate	0.15							Data analysis
11		Sales Parameters								Accounting
12			35							
13			3000							Consultants
14		Sales Expense		8000	8000	9000	9000			Consultants
15		Ad Budget	$40,000							Current budget
16										
17	DECISIONS									
18		Ad Expenditures		$10,000	$10,000	$10,000	$10,000	Total $40,000		sum
19										
20	OUTPUTS									
21		Profit	$69,662							
22										
23	CALCULATIONS									
24		Quarter		Q1	Q2	Q3	Q4	Total		
25		Seasonal		0.9	1.1	0.8	1.2			
26										
27		Units Sold		3592	4390	3192	4789	15962		given formula
28		Revenue		143662	175587	127700	191549	638498		price*units
29		Cost of Goods		89789	109742	79812	119718	399061		cost*units
30		Gross Margin		53873	65845	47887	71831	239437		subtraction
31										
32		Sales Expense		8000	8000	9000	9000	34000		given
33		Advertising		10000	10000	10000	10000	40000		decisions
34		Overhead		21549	26338	19155	28732	95775		rate*revenue
35		Total Fixed Cost		39549	44338	38155	47732	169775		sum
36										
37		Profit		14324	21507	9732	24099	69662		GM -TFC
38		Profit Margin		9.97%	12.25%	7.62%	12.58%	10.91%		pct of revenue
39										

Comment on Sales Parameters: "The budget was split equally among the quarters last year."

quantities would be equal to demand quantities each quarter and that there would be no inventory. That is, we assumed that we could ignore the detailed timing problems that might arise in the supply chain when we attempt to meet demand directly from production. These assumptions will not be obvious to another user of the model but may significantly influence the results. Thus, they should be noted on the spreadsheet itself.

Workbooks offer additional options for effective documentation, as they do for most of the other guidelines. We now turn to the question of how to design workbooks effectively.

5.3 DESIGNING A WORKBOOK

Although many effective spreadsheet models use only a single worksheet, it is often desirable to use multiple worksheets in a workbook. In fact, the multisheet format can be exploited to better accomplish many of the goals discussed in the previous section, such as modularization and ease of use. Most of the design principles described above apply equally well to the design of workbooks. However, some additional issues arise, as we discuss below. (The Northern Museum model is available with the book. We recommend that the reader open this model and explore it before reading on.)

EXAMPLE
Northern Museum Capital Campaign

The Northern Museum is a 115-year-old natural history museum located in northern New England. It houses extensive natural history, historical, and ethnological collections in a 20,000-square-foot building. It also houses a planetarium and weather station.

The physical plant of the Museum has grown increasingly inadequate for its programs and collections, and the Board has begun planning seriously for a major capital campaign. This campaign will attempt to raise several million dollars over a six-year period. In order to raise this money, the Board will have to authorize significant expenditures for consultants and other expenses. In a typical campaign, expenses exceed donations for at least the first two years. The Board is concerned that the campaign and ongoing revenue shortfalls from operations may have serious impacts on its endowment.

In order to better understand the financial implications of the capital campaign, the Board and the executive director asked the treasurer to construct a planning model. This model would link the short-term budgeting perspective the Board had traditionally taken to finances with a long-term planning perspective. It would allow the Board and the director to make explicit their assumptions about the future growth of the Museum in the context of the capital campaign and to evaluate the consequences of those assumptions on its financial health.

An early step in the process of developing this model was to construct an influence chart (Figure 5.6). This chart shows that a central purpose of the model was to track the evolution of the endowment and how it is influenced by both operating results and the capital campaign. The critical assumption that drives the model is that shortfalls between operating revenues and costs will be made up by withdrawals ("Drawdowns") from the endowment. This process had actually been going on at the Museum for several years, and the Board was concerned that expenses associated with the capital campaign not be allowed to reduce the endowment to a dangerous level before it could be built up from donations. ∎

5.3.1 Use Separate Worksheets to Group Similar Kinds of Information

Workbooks should be designed to make a model easy to understand and use. Individual worksheets should each have a well-defined purpose and be given descriptive names. They should also appear in a natural order. Assumptions, calculations, and results should be placed on separate worksheets whenever possible. This allows users to view assumptions and results without being distracted by the details of the calculations.

The Northern Museum workbook consists of 10 worksheets appearing in the following order.

Overview: Describes the purpose and assumptions behind the model

Instructions: Gives step-by-step instructions for using the model

Log of changes: Records the major changes made to the model over time

Guide to sheets: Shows the logical relationships among the worksheets and provides hyperlinks to navigate directly to any worksheet

Influence chart: Depicts the fundamental logic of the model itself

FIGURE 5.6 Influence Chart for Northern Museum Model

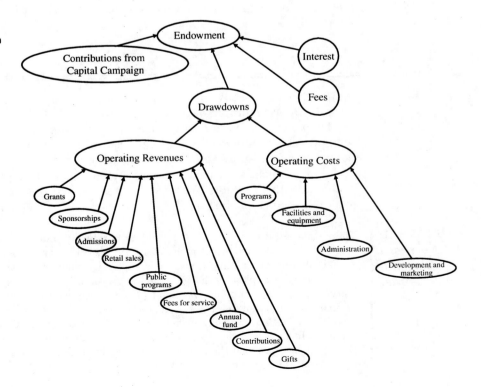

Assumptions: Provides some historical data and records assumptions used in the model

Long-term Model: Projects revenues, costs, endowment, and critical ratios from 2006 to 2016

Short-term results: Summarizes projections one and three years out in the same format as the Long-term Model worksheet

Historical data: Records historical data

Ratio charts: Provides graphical depiction of the ratios calculated in the Long-term Model worksheet

Figure 5.7 shows the Guide to sheets. This simple worksheet helps the user to understand the structure of the workbook and to determine which worksheets provide inputs to other sheets. For example, it shows that the Long-term Model sheet takes its inputs only from the Assumptions sheet. If we examine cell F30 in the Long-term Model sheet, we see that it references cell F30 on the Assumptions sheet (using the formula =Assumptions!F30). Note that a reference to a cell on another worksheet begins with the name of that worksheet followed by an exclamation mark. When using formulas that contain references to other worksheets, the references themselves begin to look complicated, and most users find it convenient to create these references by pointing and clicking. The complexity of multisheet references reinforces the importance of keeping formulas and worksheet names simple, so that someone examining the logic for the first time can follow the calculations. Another way to make formulas look simple is to use range names.

5.3.2 Design Workbooks for Ease of Navigation and Use

The purpose of a structured workbook is to facilitate understanding by users, so any form of structural help for finding their way around the workbook is beneficial. Using revealing names for individual worksheets is one helpful approach. (To change a worksheet name, double-click on the name tab at the bottom of the spreadsheet and edit the name, or right-click on the worksheet name and select Rename.)

The Northern Museum workbook illustrates a number of techniques for assisting with navigation and use. We pointed out previously that the worksheet named Guide to sheets (Figure 5.7) shows the logical relationships among the

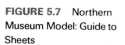

FIGURE 5.7 Northern Museum Model: Guide to Sheets

worksheets. It also provides an easy way to navigate to a particular worksheet. Each of the cells that displays a worksheet name also has a hyperlink, so that when the user clicks on the worksheet name, the display moves to the corresponding worksheet. (A hyperlink can be added to a cell by choosing Insert▶Links▶Hyperlink.) The Influence chart sheet also uses hyperlinks to take the user from a given variable such as Revenues to the exact location in the Long-term Model sheet where that variable is calculated (cell A26). Finally, the Long-term Model sheet illustrates another use of hyperlinks for navigation. The phrase `Return to Influence chart` appears near the upper left corner of the worksheet. This phrase is created using Word Art (Insert▶Text▶WordArt). A hyperlink can be associated with WordArt by highlighting the WordArt object and choosing Insert▶Links▶Hyperlink. Click on this phrase and Excel returns to the Influence chart sheet.

Another approach to navigation aids is to use buttons. A button is one of the Form Controls that can be selected from the Developer tab. Select Developer▶Controls▶Insert to display the menu of choices, as discussed in Chapter 4. For example, we can create a command button that will invoke a particular macro. (Macros are also covered in Chapter 4). In the Ratio charts sheet, we have created a Command Button called `Go to Guide`, whose purpose is to take the user back to the Guide to sheets. It calls on the following macro that was created using the Record Macro procedure (Developer▶Code▶Record Macro):

```
ActiveSheet.Shapes("CommandButton1").Select
Sheets("Guide to sheets").Select
ActiveSheet.Range("A1").Select
```

In worksheets with many rows it is often difficult to recognize the large-scale structure among all the details. The Excel Group and Outline option (Data▶Outline▶Group) can be used in these cases to help the user understand the structure and navigate to the desired location quickly. Grouping simply provides a display option in which the rows that provide details can be hidden in the display. Figure 5.8 shows how grouping is used in the Northern Museum Long-term Model sheet. The details behind the calculation of Revenues are grouped so that rows 10 to 25 are

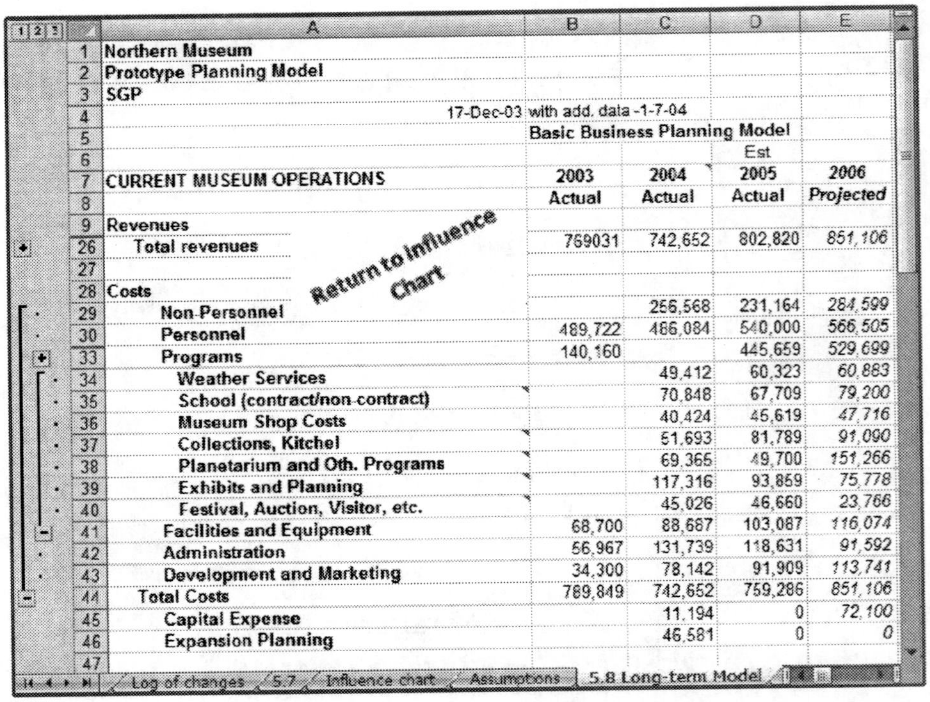

	A	B	C	D	E
1	Northern Museum				
2	Prototype Planning Model				
3	SGP				
4	17-Dec-03	with add. data -1-7-04			
5		Basic Business Planning Model			
6				Est	
7	CURRENT MUSEUM OPERATIONS	2003	2004	2005	2006
8		Actual	Actual	Actual	Projected
9	Revenues				
26	Total revenues	769031	742,652	802,820	851,106
27					
28	Costs				
29	Non-Personnel		256,568	231,164	284,599
30	Personnel	489,722	486,084	540,000	566,505
33	Programs	140,160		445,659	529,699
34	Weather Services		49,412	60,323	60,883
35	School (contract/non-contract)		70,848	67,709	79,200
36	Museum Shop Costs		40,424	45,619	47,716
37	Collections, Kitchel		51,693	81,789	91,090
38	Planetarium and Oth. Programs		69,365	49,700	151,266
39	Exhibits and Planning		117,316	93,859	75,778
40	Festival, Auction, Visitor, etc.		45,026	46,660	23,766
41	Facilities and Equipment	68,700	88,687	103,087	116,074
42	Administration	56,967	131,739	118,631	91,592
43	Development and Marketing	34,300	78,142	91,909	113,741
44	Total Costs	789,849	742,652	759,286	851,106
45	Capital Expense		11,194	0	72,100
46	Expansion Planning		46,581	0	0
47					

FIGURE 5.8 Northern Museum Model: Outlining

hidden. Similarly, the details under Personnel Costs have been grouped so that rows 31 and 32 are hidden. Other groupings have been created, but they are not active in the view shown in Figure 5.8. By selecting among the + and − symbols to the left of the worksheet, the user can tailor the display.

5.3.3 Design a Workbook as a Decision-Support System

Frequently, a spreadsheet evolves from a single use by its developer to repeated use by multiple users or a team. When this evolution takes place, the spreadsheet has become a decision-support system. A **decision-support system** is an integrated information system that provides data, analytics, and reporting capabilities over an extended period of time to multiple users. The Northern Museum model is a decision-support system because the Board and the executive director regularly use it to address a variety of budget and planning issues. In fact, one of the keys to its success is that it has helped the various interested parties at the Museum focus on a common way to think about and plan for the future.

Effective decision-support systems are designed to present information in a manner that is most useful to decision makers. Often, this means using graphs instead of tables of numbers, as in most Excel models. In the National Museum model, nine ratios are calculated in the Long-term Model sheet. These ratios indicate how the Museum is performing over time on important aspects of its operation, such as the ratio of general admission revenues to total expenditures (row 62). Museum professionals track this ratio carefully and compare it to the results of similar museums to understand the financial health of the operation. In order to make this information most useful, the tables in the Long-term Model sheet are displayed in the form of graphs in the Ratio charts sheet. While the treasurer, who is most familiar with the model, concentrates on the Assumptions and Long-term Model sheets, other users naturally concentrate on the graphical summaries in the Ratio graphs sheet.

If a workbook will be used by multiple users, it is important to protect the contents of the workbook from unwanted changes. In the Advertising Budget example, if we wanted to protect all the cells other than the decision variables, we would first lock all cells, then unlock the cells for the advertising allocation, and finally protect the entire worksheet. The details are as follows. First, we select the entire worksheet. Then, we select Home▶Font↘, choose the Protection tab, and check the box for Locked (Figure 5.9). Next, we repeat the process for the decision variables, first selecting the range C18:F18. Again, we select Home▶Font↘ and

FIGURE 5.9 The Protection Tab in the Format Cells Window

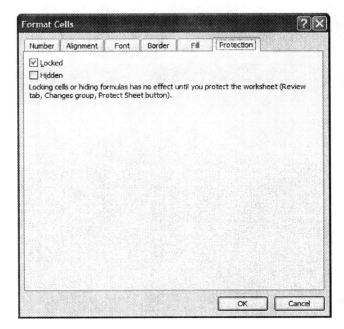

FIGURE 5.10   The Protect
Sheet Window

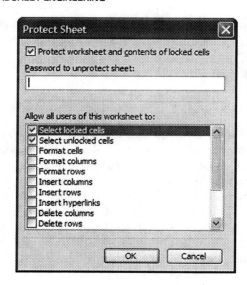

choose the Protection tab, but this time we uncheck the box for Locked. Finally, we protect the entire worksheet, using Review▶Changes▶Protect Sheet. At the top of the Protect Sheet window (Figure 5.10), we check the box for Protect worksheet. In the lower window, there is a list of actions that can be allowed users. If we check only the box for Select locked cells, then a user will be able to select and modify only the decision variable cells. It will not be possible to select other cells. On the other hand, if we check the boxes for Select locked cells and Select unlocked cells, then the user will be able to select any of the locked cells (e.g., to verify a formula) but will not be permitted to alter the contents of those cells.

It can also be useful to ensure that only legitimate values are used as inputs. This process is called **data validation**, a technique that is highly recommended for workbooks available to multiple users over an extended period. To invoke data validation, highlight the cells involved and click on Data▶Data Tools▶Data Validation. The Data Validation window contains three tabs, as shown in Figure 5.11. On the first tab, we can restrict the allowable inputs to a cell—for example, to require a number (as opposed to text) and one that lies between certain minimum and maximum values. In the Advertising Budget example, we require a user to enter a price that lies between unit cost (cell C8) and $100. On the second tab, we have an option of creating an input message that will appear whenever the cursor is placed on this cell. This message functions like a cell comment. On the third tab, we can design an error alert for the case of an invalid entry. An example for the Advertising Budget spreadsheet is shown

FIGURE 5.11   The Data
Validation Window

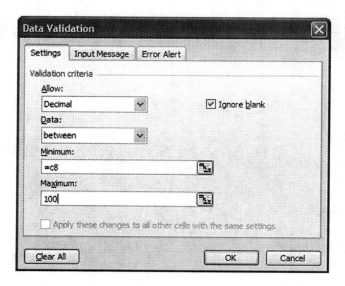

FIGURE 5.12 Error Alert
Produced by Data Validation

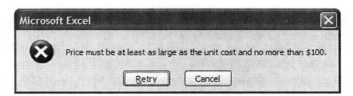

FIGURE 5.12 Error Alert
Produced by Data Validation

in Figure 5.12, which shows the error alert when we attempt to enter a price greater than $100 or less than the unit cost.

5.4 BUILDING A WORKBOOK

The second stage in creating a useful spreadsheet model is actually building it. Since most spreadsheet users do not consciously design their spreadsheets, they merge the designing and building processes. The usual result is that a great deal of time and energy are wasted fixing mistakes and redesigning a model that should have been designed once at the start.

A well-*designed* spreadsheet should be easy and quick to *build*. However, speed is not the only criterion here. Most bugs in spreadsheets are introduced during the building process. Therefore, learning to build spreadsheets without introducing errors is also vital. All of the guidelines in this section are designed to make the building process routine, repeatable, and error-free.

5.4.1 Follow a Plan

Having gone to the trouble of sketching the spreadsheet, we should follow the sketch when building. With a sufficiently detailed sketch, the building process itself becomes largely mechanical and therefore less prone to mistakes.

5.4.2 Build One Worksheet or Module at a Time

Rather than trying to build an entire workbook at one pass, it is usually more efficient to build a single worksheet or module and test it out before proceeding. For one thing, as we build the first module, we may discover that the design itself can be improved, so it is best to have made a limited investment in the original design before revising it. Another rationale for this advice is to localize the potential effects of an error. If we make an error, its effects are likely to be limited mainly to the module we're building. By staying focused on that module, we can fix errors early, before they infect other modules that we build later.

5.4.3 Predict the Outcome of Each Formula

For each formula entered, predict the numerical value expected from it before pressing the Enter key. Ask what order of magnitude to expect in the result, and give some thought to any outcomes that don't correspond to predictions. This discipline helps to uncover bugs: without a prediction, every numerical outcome tends to look plausible. At the same time, a prediction that is orders of magnitude different from the calculated number provides an opportunity for error. For example, if we predict $100,000 for annual revenue, and the calculated value comes to $100,000,000, then there is a flaw either in our intuition or in our formula. Either way, we can benefit: our intuition may be sharpened, or we may detect an error in need of fixing.

5.4.4 Copy and Paste Formulas Carefully

The Copy-and-Paste commands in Excel are not simply time-savers; they are also helpful in avoiding bugs. Instead of entering structurally similar formulas several times, we copy and paste a formula. Repetition can be a source of errors, and copying formulas can diminish the potential for this type of error. Careless copying is also a source of bugs. One of the most common errors is to select the wrong range for copying—for example, selecting one cell too few in copying a formula across a row. Recognizing this problem keeps us alert to the possibility of a copying error, and we are therefore more likely to avoid it.

5.4.5 Use Relative and Absolute Addressing to Simplify Copying

Efficient copying depends on skillful use of relative and absolute addressing. Remember that an address such as B7 is interpreted in a *relative* fashion in Excel: if the highlighted cell is A6, B7 is read as the cell one row down and one column to the right. When we include a cell with a relative address in a formula and then copy the formula, the cell address changes to preserve the relative position between the highlighted cell and the input cell. On the other hand, an *absolute* address, such as $B$6, refers to the cell B6 regardless of the location of the highlighted cell. When a formula with an absolute address is copied, the address remains $B$6. Absolute addresses are usually used when referring to a parameter, because the location of the parameter is fixed.

5.4.6 Use the Function Wizard to Ensure Correct Syntax

The button f_x on the standard toolbar brings up the Insert Function window, which contains a complete listing of all the functions built into Excel. It is not necessary to memorize the exact syntax of an occasionally used function, or to guess at the correct syntax, because help is available. For example, we might want to calculate the payment on a car loan once in a while, but it is difficult to memorize the exact form of the PMT function. Whenever this function is needed, click on the Insert Function button and select PMT. A window then appears that shows what inputs the function needs and in what order (see Figure 5.13). This window even calculates the value of the function when its inputs are specified, thus providing quick feedback on whether the results are as expected.

5.4.7 Use Range Names to Make Formulas Easy to Read

Any cell or range of cells in a spreadsheet can be given a name. This name can then be used in formulas to refer to the contents of the cell. If cell B6 is named VblCost, we can use either B6 or VblCost interchangeably in any formula. Obviously, it is easier to understand a formula that uses range names than one that uses cell addresses.

FIGURE 5.13 Function Arguments Window

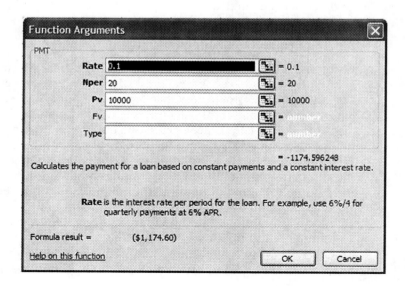

FIGURE 5.14   New
Name Window

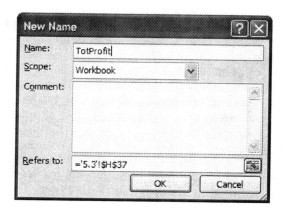

Formulas containing descriptive names are easier for the developer to debug and easier for new users to understand.

Range names require extra work to enter and maintain, so they may not be worth the effort in simple spreadsheets destined for one-time use. But in a spreadsheet that will become a permanent tool or be used by other analysts after the designer has moved on, it is a good idea to use range names to help subsequent users understand the details. Some firms require that all major spreadsheets use range names throughout.

We can assign a name to a cell or a range of cells by selecting Insert▶ Formulas▶Defined Names▶Define Name and specifying the relevant cell range (see Figure 5.14). For example, in the spreadsheet of Figure 5.3, we have assigned the name TotProfit to cell H37. This allows us to use the formula =TotProfit in C21, our main output cell. (To view all the range names in use, look in the pull-down window at the top of the spreadsheet, to the left of the formula window.) As a more ambitious example, we can assign the name Price to cell C7 and the name Sales to the range D27:G27 (by highlighting the four-cell range before defining the name). Then, the revenue formulas in cells D28:G28 can be entered as =Price*Sales. This makes the formulas easier to interpret and reduces the possibility for errors.

5.4.8   Choose Input Data to Make Errors Stand Out

Most modelers naturally use realistic values for input parameters as they build their spreadsheets. This has the advantage that the results look plausible, but it has the disadvantage that the results are difficult to check. For example, if the expected price is $25.99 and unit sales are 126,475, revenues will be calculated as $3,287,085.25. We could check this with a calculator, but it is not easy to check by eye. However, if we input arbitrary values of $10 for price and 100 for unit sales, we can easily check that our formula for revenue is correct if it shows a result of $1,000. Generally speaking, it saves time in the long run to input arbitrary but simple values for the input parameters (for example, 1, 10, and 100) during the initial building sequence. Once the spreadsheet has been debugged with these arbitrary values, it is then a simple matter to replace them with the actual input values.

5.5   TESTING A WORKBOOK

Even a carefully designed and built spreadsheet may contain errors. Errors can arise from incorrect references in formulas, from inaccurate copying and pasting, from lack of parameterization, and from a host of other sources. There is no recipe to follow for finding all bugs. When a bug is found late in the analysis phase, the user must backtrack to fix the bug *and* to repeat most or all of the previous analysis. This can be avoided by carefully testing the spreadsheet before using it for analysis.

The tips we offer here can help an end user test whether a model is correct. However, common sense and the experience of thousands of professional programmers suggest that one of the most effective ways to find errors in a model is to give it to an outsider to test. Another pair of eyes can often find errors that have eluded the builder, who is so immersed in the details that errors are no longer detectable. Finding another pair of eyes may be impractical for many end users who work on their own, but it should be feasible in almost any company, especially when the spreadsheet is large, complex, and important. Formal code inspection, as practiced by professionals, is rarely carried out for spreadsheet models. However, some sophisticated companies practice *peer review,* in which important spreadsheet models are examined in detail by individuals or teams other than the builders. We suspect this practice will become more common as the risks of spreadsheet errors become more widely appreciated.

5.5.1 Check That Numerical Results Look Plausible

The most important tool for keeping a spreadsheet error-free is a skeptical attitude. As we build the spreadsheet, we transform input parameters into a set of intermediate results that eventually lead to final outcomes. As these numbers gradually appear, it is important to check that they look reasonable. We offer three distinct ways to accomplish this:

- Make rough estimates.
- Check with a calculator.
- Test extreme cases.

Make Rough Estimates   In an earlier section, we recommended predicting the rough magnitude of the result of each formula before pressing Enter. This helps catch errors as they are made. Similarly, it is a good idea to scan the completed spreadsheet and to check that critical results are the correct order of magnitude. For example, in the Advertising Budget example, if we sell about 3,000 units in Q3 at $40 each, we should make about $120,000. This calculation can be made in our heads, and it helps to confirm that the value in cell F28 ($127,700) is probably accurate.

Check with a Calculator   A more formal approach to error detection is to check some portion of the spreadsheet on a calculator. Pick a typical column or row and check the entire sequence of calculations. Errors often occur in the last row or column due to problems in Copy-and-Paste operations, so check these areas, too.

Test Extreme Cases   If the logic behind a spreadsheet is correct, it should give logical results even with unrealistic assumptions. For example, if we set Price to $0, we should have zero revenues. Extreme cases such as this are useful for debugging because the correct results are easy to predict. Note, however, that just because a spreadsheet gives zero revenues when we set Price to $0 does not guarantee that the logic will be correct for all cases.

In the Advertising Budget example, if we price at cost, we should get a Gross Margin of zero. We can make this test by entering $25 for Price in C7 and then observing that Gross Margin in D30:G30 becomes zero. Testing extreme cases is one of the tools professional programmers use that end users can easily adopt as their own.

5.5.2 Check That Formulas Are Correct

Most spreadsheet errors occur in formulas. We can reduce the possibility of errors by making formulas short and using multiple cells to calculate a complex result. We can also reduce errors by using recursive formulas wherever possible, so that successive formulas in a row or column have the same form. Yet another good idea is to design the spreadsheet so that formulas use as inputs only cells that are above and to the left and are as close as possible. But having taken all these precautions, we still need to test that formulas are correct before beginning the analysis. We offer seven ways to perform this testing.

- Check visually.
- Display individual cell references.
- Display all formulas.
- Use the Auditing Tools.
- Use Error Checking.
- Use error traps.
- Use auditing software.

Check Visually Most end users check formulas one at a time, by highlighting each cell in a row or column in sequence and visually auditing the formula. This procedure can work fairly well, especially if the formulas are recursive so that many cell references change in a predictable way or do not change at all from cell to cell. A visual check also works best if range names are used. This method is extremely tedious, however, and tedious methods encourage carelessness. Several better methods are described in the following sections.

Display Individual Cell References Another way to check formulas is to use the cell-edit capability, invoked either by pressing the F2 key or by double-clicking on the cell of interest. This reveals the formula in the cell, displayed with color-coded cell references. Each cell that appears in the formula is highlighted by a selection border, which is color-coded to the cell reference in the formula. Often, the locations of the cell references in a formula give visual clues to whether a formula is correctly structured. When an error is found, it is often possible to drag a highlighted border to a different cell as a means of correcting the address in the formula. This method is preferred to scanning formulas because it provides stronger visual clues for locating logical errors.

Display All Formulas Another excellent device is to display all the formulas in the spreadsheet by holding down the Control key and pressing the tilde key ($\sim$) on the upper-left corner of the main keyboard (Control + $\sim$). This displays all the spreadsheet formulas, as shown in Figure 5.15, making them easier to scan. Usually, successive formulas in a row or column have some consistent pattern. For example,

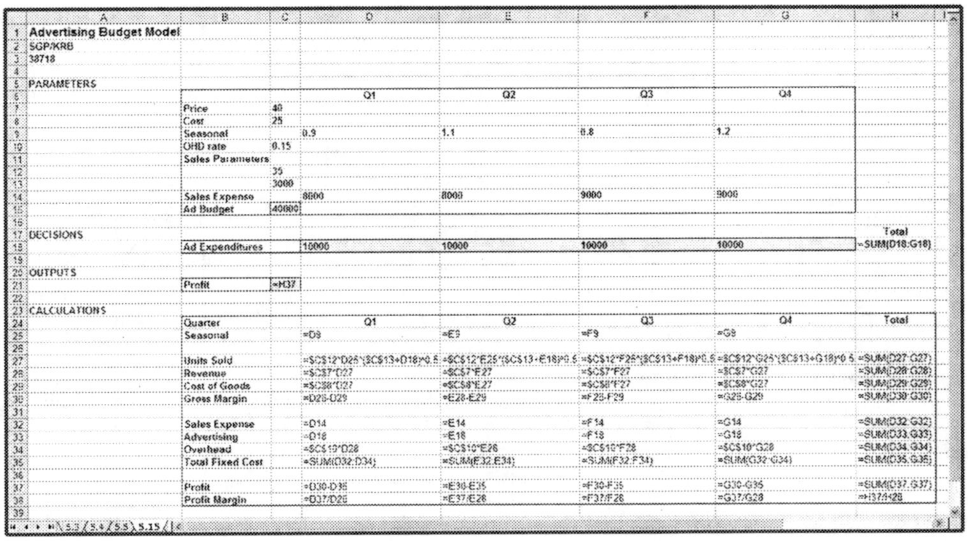

FIGURE 5.15 Displaying Formulas in the Advertising Budget Spreadsheet

one cell reference is absolute and does not change, while another is relative and changes from D28 to E28 to F28, and so on. If there is an error, it can often be detected as a break in a pattern. (Return the spreadsheet to its normal form by pressing Control + ~ again.)

In the spreadsheet for the Advertising Budget example, note the similar structure in the four formulas for Gross Margin in the range D30:G30. A copying error would show up as a break in the pattern here.

Use the Excel Auditing Tools Another useful and underutilized set of debugging tools in Excel is available on the ribbon under Formulas▶Formula Auditing. These options can be used to identify the cells used to calculate a given cell (its **predecessors**) or the cells it is used to calculate (its **dependents**). The `Trace Precedents` option draws colored arrows to the predecessors of a given cell. Invoking the `Trace Precedents` option again from this point will identify the predecessors of the predecessors, and so on, reaching backward into the logic of the calculations. The `Trace Dependents` option works similarly, but in the forward direction. The arrows convey a pattern of information flow, which should conform to the underlying logic of the model. For debugging purposes, the auditing tools can be used to display the information flows related to a group of cells. If these cells have a parallel or recursive structure, there should be a distinctive pattern in the arrows produced by the auditing tools. As with displaying formulas, bugs often show up as unexpected breaks in the pattern of these arrows.

In the spreadsheet for the Advertising Budget example, suppose we select cell H38. Next, we choose the option for `Trace Precedents` several times in succession. The cells that are used to calculate profit are highlighted, then their predecessors are highlighted, and so on, as shown in Figure 5.16. Again, an error in the formulas would show up as a break in these visual patterns. (Use the `Remove Arrows` option to erase the auditing arrows.)

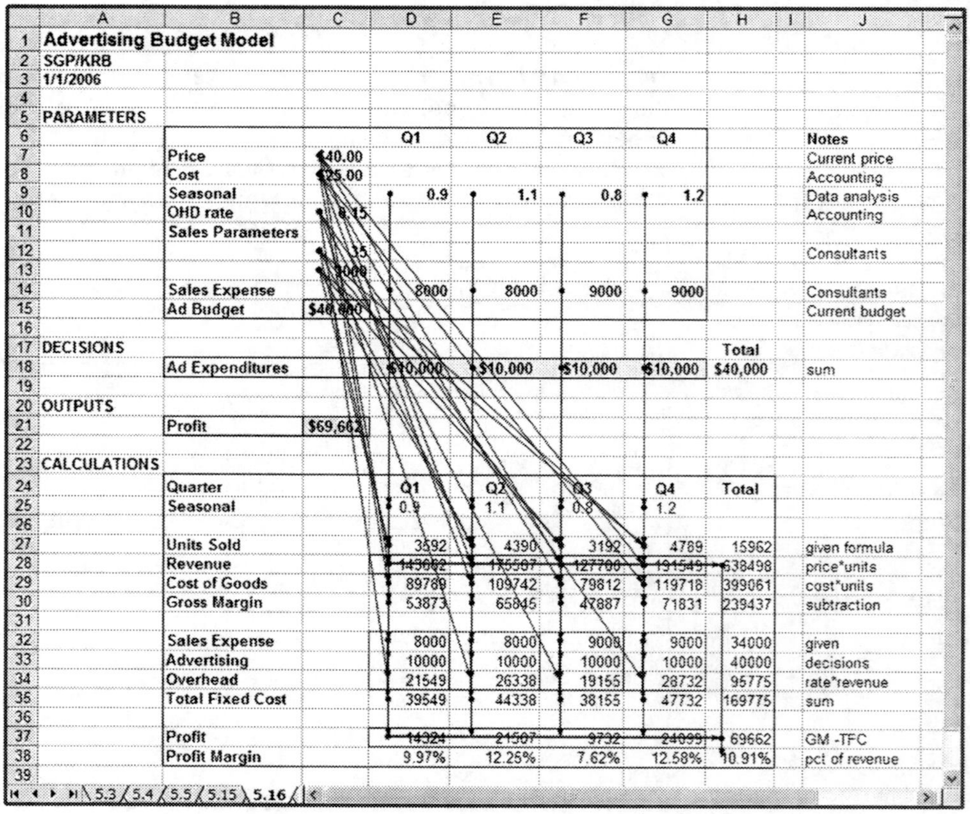

	A	B	C	D	E	F	G	H	I	J
1	Advertising Budget Model									
2	SGP/KRB									
3	1/1/2006									
4										
5	PARAMETERS									
6				Q1	Q2	Q3	Q4			Notes
7		Price	$40.00							Current price
8		Cost	$25.00							Accounting
9		Seasonal		0.9	1.1	0.8	1.2			Data analysis
10		OHD rate	0.15							Accounting
11		Sales Parameters								
12			35							Consultants
13			3000							
14		Sales Expense		8000	8000	9000	9000			Consultants
15		Ad Budget	$40,000							Current budget
16										
17	DECISIONS							Total		
18		Ad Expenditures		$10,000	$10,000	$10,000	$10,000	$40,000		sum
19										
20	OUTPUTS									
21		Profit	$69,662							
22										
23	CALCULATIONS									
24		Quarter		Q1	Q2	Q3	Q4	Total		
25		Seasonal		0.9	1.1	0.8	1.2			
26										
27		Units Sold		3592	4390	3192	4789	15962		given formula
28		Revenue		143662	175587	127700	191549	638498		price*units
29		Cost of Goods		89789	109742	79812	119718	399061		cost*units
30		Gross Margin		53873	65845	47887	71831	239437		subtraction
31										
32		Sales Expense		8000	8000	9000	9000	34000		given
33		Advertising		10000	10000	10000	10000	40000		decisions
34		Overhead		21549	26338	19155	28732	95775		rate*revenue
35		Total Fixed Cost		39549	44338	38155	47732	169775		sum
36										
37		Profit		14324	21507	9732	24099	69662		GM -TFC
38		Profit Margin		9.97%	12.25%	7.62%	12.58%	10.91%		pct of revenue
39										

5.3 / 5.4 / 5.5 / 5.15 / 5.16

FIGURE 5.16 Using the Auditing Toolbar in the Advertising Budget Spreadsheet

FIGURE 5.17   The Error
Checking Window

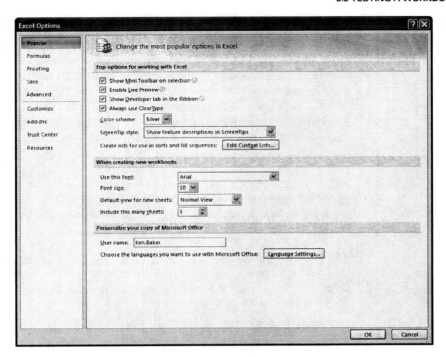

Use Excel Error Checking   This is the spreadsheet equivalent of grammar checking in word processing. Error checking is managed from the Formulas tab of the Excel Options menu. The single check box under Error Checking (See Figure 5.17) chooses whether the tool is enabled or disabled. If it is enabled, then all cells that are identified as possibly containing an error are flagged with a colored triangle. (The color can be chosen under Error Checking.) The Error checking rules comprise a list of nine types of checks. Although the user can choose which of these rules to activate, we generally recommend keeping all nine boxes checked.

Three of these categories of possible errors seem to be most prevalent: formulas inconsistent with other formulas in the region, formulas which omit cells in a region, and formulas referring to empty cells. Inconsistent formulas are those that violate a pattern. For example, a recursive formula that is copied across a row but that changes its pattern of references to absolute addresses would be flagged under this category. Often, these potential errors are consciously designed into the spreadsheet, and although they are not errors, they are nonetheless indicative of poor programming practice. Formulas that omit cells in a region also violate an expected pattern. Finally, formulas that refer to empty cells are either wrong outright or at least indicate dangerous programming practice. While this Error Checking capability can highlight only certain well-defined categories of potential errors (and the user can determine which categories by using the check boxes), it is a useful tool—one that should be employed during the design and testing phases of spreadsheet construction.

Use ErrorTraps   Error traps are formulas added to a spreadsheet that warn the user of potential errors. They can check for errors in input data or for errors in formulas.

A simple application is to check that row sums and column sums are consistent. For example, in cell H30 in the Advertising Budget spreadsheet we calculate total Gross Margin by adding up the four quarterly values for grow margin. But total Gross Margin can also be calculated by subtracting total Cost of Goods from total Revenue. If these two calculations do not give the same result, we have an error. An error trap can be set by entering an IF statement that checks the cells in question and returns a warning if an error occurs. For example, the statement

```
IF(SUM(D30:G30)<>(H28 - H29), "Warning: row and
      column totals do not match"," ")
```

returns the warning text when there is an error and returns a blank value otherwise.

The Long-term Model sheet of the Northern Museum workbook uses a different kind of error checking. In this situation there are two ways to calculate total costs, and both are of interest to important model users. One approach is to divide total costs into personnel and non-personnel costs. This is done in rows 29 and 30. The alternative is to break total costs down by programs, which is done in rows 34–40. The workbook designer decided that both approaches should be shown on the worksheet and even that inconsistent projections could be allowed. But to highlight these inconsistencies when they occur, the difference in total costs between the two methods is calculated in row 50.

Any number of error traps can be added to a workbook to improve its safety. It is important that the results of these error checks be clearly visible to the user. One way to do this is to create an overall error trap that checks whether *any one* of the individual traps is true, and returns a warning. This trap can be placed in a prominent place near the outputs, so a user will be unlikely to trust outputs that result from a model with errors.

Use Auditing Software   A number of Excel add-ins are available for auditing spreadsheets. These add-ins typically provide a set of tools for detecting errors and displaying model structure graphically. We describe one such tool, Spreadsheet Professional, in Section 5.6.

5.5.3 Test That Model Performance Is Plausible

For many end users, the analysis phase begins while testing is still in progress. This is natural and perhaps unavoidable, although we have stressed the importance of taking a careful and structured approach to designing, building, and testing a spreadsheet *before* using it for analysis. However, if analysis begins before testing is complete, it is at least desirable to retain a skeptical attitude toward the early results from using the model. Many minor bugs come to light during analysis. More importantly, actually using the model can reveal major logical flaws. These types of errors, which usually cannot be uncovered by the most meticulous checking of formulas, can destroy the credibility of the entire modeling process.

If a spreadsheet model is logically sound and built without errors, it should react in a plausible manner to a range of input values. Thus, sensitivity testing, which we discuss in Chapter 6, can be a powerful way to uncover logical and mechanical errors. In our Advertising Budget example, if profit were to go *down* as we increased the price, we could be fairly sure we had a bug in the model. But even if we have confirmed that profits rise with price, would we expect that relationship to be linear or nonlinear? We can test our intuition and the model by calculating profit for a range of prices and graphing the results. In this model as it is currently built, that relationship is in fact linear. We might conclude that this is as we expected and intended. On the other hand, we might decide that demand should instead depend on price (which, in our model, it does not) and that the model needs further refinement.

5.6* AUDITING SOFTWARE: SPREADSHEET PROFESSIONAL

Spreadsheet Professional is an add-in to Excel that assists the end user in building, testing, documenting, and using spreadsheets. It is one of a number of software products that have appeared in recent years that offer tools for building error-free spreadsheets. Some of these tools are specialized to a particular industry or range of applications. Spreadsheet Professional, which is available with this book, is a generic tool that can be used in any application.

Spreadsheet Professional, like most software, contains many tools and options. Here, we outline the major options and illustrate by example how to use the most important ones. More details can be found by reading Spreadsheet Professional Help or visiting the website www.spreadsheetinnovations.com.

5.6.1 Building tools

Spreadsheet Professional offers five tools to assist in building spreadsheet models.

Standard format: Formats the first three columns of a new spreadsheet to accept row titles, units, and source.

Build bar: Simplifies entering and copying formulas by allowing the user to copy the formula and its format to any number of cells in one step.

Translation bar: Translates formulas into English equivalents.

Spreadsheet Painter: Colors cells according to whether they are inputs, formulas, or labels.

Spreadsheet Formula Tracer: Displays the antecedents of a cell to any depth required. For example, in Figure 5.18 we use the Formula Tracer to show the antecedents of Profit in the Advertising Budget model. This display shows the cell address, its label (if any), its numerical value, and its formula.

5.6.2 Testing Tools

Spreadsheet Professional provides two related error-checking tools. The Spreadsheet Checker tests cells one by one for violations of any of 25 test conditions. The Spreadsheet Reports tool runs a batch test looking for violations in the entire workbook (or any selected worksheets) and writes the results to another workbook.

FIGURE 5.18 The Formula Tracer in Spreadsheet Professional

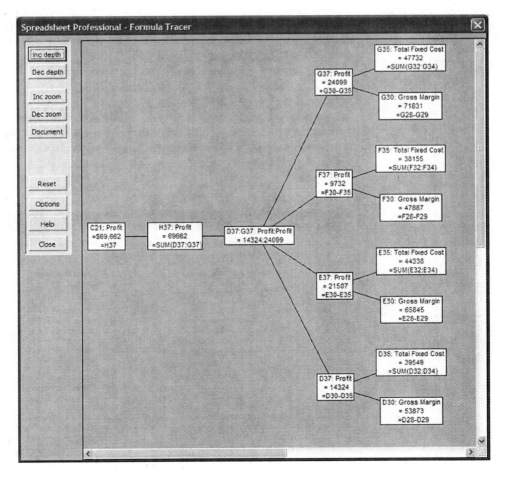

FIGURE 5.19 The Spreadsheet Checker in Spreadsheet Professional

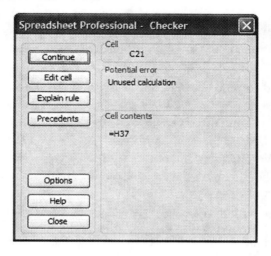

FIGURE 5.19 The Spreadsheet Checker in Spreadsheet Professional

Figure 5.19 shows the results of selecting the Checker when cell C21 is highlighted in the Advertising Budget model. The window displays the contents of the cell (=H37) and notes that it violates the test condition Unused calculation. Click Continue, and the Checker lists any additional error conditions the current cell violates and then moves on to the next cell in which a violation occurs. Click Precedents, and it lists all the cells used to calculate the current cell and their contents.

Figure 5.20 shows the 25 test conditions Spreadsheet Professional can identify. (Navigate to this window by selecting from the Spreadsheet Professional toolbar Test▶Spreadsheet Test Reports tool▶Options▶Test options.) Note that many of these conditions represent poor spreadsheet engineering but are not necessarily errors in the sense of cells producing wrong results. However, it is good practice to allow Spreadsheet Professional to test for all of these conditions.

The Spreadsheet Reports tool provides eight distinct analyses of a given workbook (see Figure 5.21). The most useful are the Map report and the Calculation test report, one of which is produced for each sheet. The Map report displays the structure of a worksheet by denoting the contents of each cell as a Label (L), Number (N), or Formula (F). The Calculations test report lists all the cells that violate any of the 25 test conditions.

Figure 5.22 shows the Map report for the Advertising Budget model. This report is best used to identify copying errors. The symbol "<" is used to denote a formula cell that has been copied from the left; the symbol "∧" is used to denote a cell copied from above. Note, for instance, cells H27, H32, and H37. These cells break a pattern of cell copying in their rows and may be problematic.

The Calculation test report for the Advertising Budget model is shown in Figure 5.23. This report provides a count of the number of cells that violate each test condition along with their cell addresses. For example, under the condition Unused input value, it describes the condition and explains why it may be problematic, and it notes that cell C15 violates this test. This report can be used to focus the debugging activity on just those cells that are most likely to cause problems.

FIGURE 5.20 Error Conditions in Spreadsheet Professional

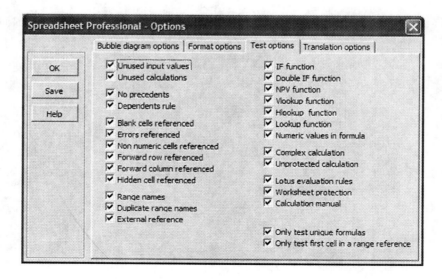

FIGURE 5.21   Report
Selection Window in
Spreadsheet Professional

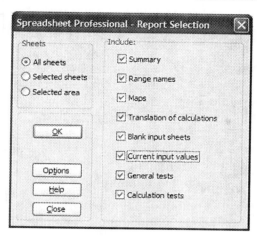

5.6.3   Documenting Tools

Many of the reports that are created by the Spreadsheets Reports tool can be used to document a spreadsheet. The following eight reports are provided:

> Summary: Provides background information on the workbook and its worksheets

> Range names: Lists all range names and external references

FIGURE 5.22   Map Report
for Advertising Budget

	A	B	C	D	E	F	G	H	I	J
1	L									
2	L									
3	N									
4										
5	L									
6				L	L	L	L			L
7		L	N							L
8		L	N							L
9		L		N	N	N	N			L
10		L	N							L
11		L								
12			N							L
13			N							
14		L		N	N	N	N			L
15		L	N							L
16										
17	L							L		
18		L		N	N	N	N	F		L
19		L		L		L				
20	L			L				L		
21		L	F		L	N		L		
22										
23	L									
24		L		L	L	L	L			
25		L		F	<	<	<			
26										
27		L		F	<	<	<	F		L
28		L		F	<	<	<	^		L
29		L		F	<	<	<	^		L
30		L		F	<	<	<	^		L
31										
32		L		F	<	<	<	F		L
33		L		F	<	<	<	^		L
34		L		F	<	<	<	^		L
35		L		F	<	<	<	^		L
36										
37		L		F	<	<	<	F		L
38		L		F	<	<	<	<		L
39										

5.21 5.22

FIGURE 5.23 Calculation
Test Report for Advertising
Budget

	A	B	
3	**Summary statistics**		
4	**Range analysed**	A1:K40	
5	**Number of numeric inputs**	20	
6	**Number of formulas**	56	
7	**Number of unique formulas**	22	
8	Unique cells are those that are not copies of the cell to their left.		
9	**Percentage of unique formulas**	39%	
10	**Number of labels**	63	
11			
12	**Potential errors summary**		
13	**Possible error condition**	**Frequency**	
14	Unused input value	1	
15	Unused calculation	10	
16	Forward row reference	1	
17	Forward column reference	1	
18	Numeric rule	1	
19			
20			
21	**Protection not enabled.**		
22	This sheet is not protected. Users can overwrite the		
23	contents of any cell even if the cell is locked.		
24	**Test notes.**		
25	Only unique cells have been tested.		
26	Remember to check cells that are a copy of the cells shown on this report.		
27			
28	Only the first cell in each range referenced by a formula has been tested.		
29			
30	**Unused input value**		
31	A number has been entered which is not used in any calculation. Potential errors to watch for:		
32	1. A calculation contains an incorrect reference.		
33	2. The writer of the spreadsheet may have forgotten that this input value exists and hard coded the value directly into subsequent calculations.		
34	C15		
35			
36	**Unused calculation**		
37	The results from this calculation are not used elsewhere on this worksheet Potential errors to watch for:		
38	1. The results should be used but there is an incorrect reference in a subsequent calculation.		
39	H18, C21, H27, H29:H30, H32:H35, D38		
40			

Maps: Codes cells as labels, numbers, or formulas (described above)

Translation of calculations: Translates calculations into English

Blank input worksheets: Provides a blank form for collecting all inputs

Current input values: Reports the current value of all inputs

General tests: Examines the workbook for problematic conditions, such as manual calculation

Calculation tests: Tests each formula for violations of 25 test conditions (described above)

5.6.4 Usage Tools

Spreadsheet Professional also provides several productivity tools. One is a sensitivity analysis tool, which is similar to the Data Sensitivity tool described in Chapter 6. Another is a breakeven tool, which is similar to Excel's Goal Seek tool, also described in Chapter 6. Finally, it provides the Spreadsheet Comparison tool, which allows a cell-by-cell comparison of two spreadsheets to find the differences.

5.7 SUMMARY

Spreadsheets are important throughout business, and important tools deserve careful engineering. Although spreadsheet modeling is not a science, we can enumerate a set of guidelines for designing, building, and testing our spreadsheets. Our guidelines have evolved from our observations working with both experienced and inexperienced model builders. These guidelines are designed to make the process of spreadsheet development both more efficient and more effective.

The available evidence suggests strongly that most spreadsheets in use contain errors and that their developers are overconfident about the reliability of their models. The implication is that we should be humble about our ability to develop spreadsheets that correctly implement the models we have conceived. Care and effort are required to build models successfully. Some useful lessons can be learned from professional programmers—most importantly, *be skeptical* and *test thoroughly.*

Here is a summary list of the guidelines given in this chapter.

Designing a Spreadsheet

1. Sketch the spreadsheet.
2. Organize the spreadsheet into modules.
3. Start small.
4. Isolate input parameters.
5. Design for use.
6. Keep it simple.
7. Design for communication.
8. Document important data and formulas.

Designing a Workbook

1. Use separate spreadsheets to group like information.
2. Design workbooks for ease of navigation and use.
3. Design a workbook as a decision support system.

Building a Workbook

1. Follow a plan.
2. Build one module at a time.
3. Predict the outcome of each formula.
4. Copy and Paste formulas carefully.
5. Use relative and absolute addressing to simplify copying.
6. Use the Function Wizard to ensure correct syntax.
7. Use range names to make formulas easy to read.
8. Choose input data to make errors stand out.

Testing a Workbook

1. Check that numerical results look plausible.
2. Check that formulas are correct.
3. Test that model performance is plausible.

SUGGESTED READINGS

The most thoughtful writing on spreadsheet design has appeared not in books but in journal articles. We list some useful articles here. More information can be found in references compiled in the Edwards and Panko articles.

Caine, D. J., and A. J. Robinson. 1993. "Spreadsheet Modeling: Guidelines for Model Development." *Management Decision* 31, 38–44.

Conway, D. G., and C. T. Ragsdale. 1997. "Modeling Optimization Problems in the Unstructured World of Spreadsheets." *Omega* 25, 313–322.

Edwards, J. S., P. N. Finlay, and J. M. Wilson. 2000. "The Role of OR Specialists in 'Do It Yourself' Spreadsheet Development." *European Journal of Operational Research* 127, 14–27.

Panko, R. R. 1999. "Applying Code Inspection to Spreadsheet Testing." *Journal of Management Information Systems* 16, 159–176.

The following short monographs and websites contain more detailed recommendations for best practices in spreadsheet design, building, and testing:

BPM Analytical. 2004. "Best Practice Spreadsheet Modelling Standards." http://www.bpmhome.com/bpm_standards.html.

Mailbarrow. Undated. "52 Ways to Prevent Spreadsheet Problems." http://www.mailbarrow.com/pdf/PreventingSpreadsheet- Problems_FULL_sample.pdf.

Raffensperger, J. F., 2002. "The Art of the Spreadsheet." http://www.SpreadsheetStyle.com.

Read, N., and J. Batson. 1999. "Spreadsheet Modeling Best Practice." http://www.eusprig.org/smbp.pdf.

EXERCISES

The following exercises refer to the cases in the back of this book. Read the case description carefully, sketch an appropriate spreadsheet on paper, then build and test a prototype model. The purpose of the model is specified in the question.

1. Refer to the XYZ Company case. Design a spreadsheet that will allow an analyst to predict the month in which the cash balance falls below zero, signaling a need to borrow money.

2. Refer to the Medical Supplies for Banjul case. Design a spreadsheet that will enable you to request the required funds from your team's finance officer, order supplies from the home office, and ensure dissemination of appropriate quantities to each village. Your final order to the home office should specify the number of packages required of each item.

3. Refer to the Reid's Raisins case. Design a spreadsheet that will allow the firm to project profit for base-case conditions; the open market grape price is $0.30.

4. Refer to the Big Rig Rental Company case. Design a spreadsheet that will allow the firm to determine the Net Present Value of cash flows over the five-year period.

5. Refer to the Flexible Insurance Coverage case. Design a spreadsheet that will allow an individual employee with estimated annual medical expenses of $400 to compare the total expenses under each plan.

6. Refer to the Snoey Software Company case. Design a spreadsheet that will determine the annual profit when the prices for the Educational, Large-Scale, and Professional versions are $100, $300, and $500, respectively.

7. Refer to the Cox Cable and Wire Company case. In the role of Meredith, design a spreadsheet with which to find a machine schedule and a corresponding inventory and shipment schedule that meets demand. What is the profit contribution of this schedule?

8. Refer to the BMW Company case. Design a spreadsheet that will allow the firm's managers to estimate what percentage of the firm's net income 10 years into the future will be devoted to disposal of vehicles, assuming there are no changes in trends and policies.

9. Refer to the ERP Decision case. Design a spreadsheet that will assist the Board in evaluating the net benefits of implementing the ERP system.

10. Refer to the Retirement Planning case. Review the problem statement and influence diagram that were generated for this case in conjunction with the corresponding exercise in Chapter 2. (If this has not yet been done, develop the problem statement and influence diagram as preliminary steps.) Design a spreadsheet to estimate the impact on Davidson's retirement of increasing his annual retirement savings by 10 percent.

11. Refer to the Draft TV Commercials case. Review the problem statement and influence diagram that were generated for this case in conjunction with the corresponding exercises in Chapter 2. (If this has not yet been done, develop the problem statement and influence diagram as preliminary steps.) Design a spreadsheet to determine the impact on ad quality of paying for three draft commercials.

12. Refer to the Icebergs for Kuwait case. Review the problem statement and influence diagram that were generated for this case in conjunction with the corresponding exercises in Chapter 2. (If this has not yet been done, develop the problem statement and influence diagram as preliminary steps.) Design a spreadsheet to estimate the economic value of the freshwater produced by towing the largest possible iceberg using the largest available boat.

13. Refer to the Racquetball Racket case. Review the problem statement and influence diagram that were generated for this case in conjunction with the corresponding exercises in Chapter 2. (If this has not yet been done, develop the problem statement and influence diagram as preliminary steps.) Design a spreadsheet to evaluate the Net Present Value of selling the new ball at $0.65, assuming the competitor does not change prices.

6 Analysis Using Spreadsheets

In the previous chapter, we pointed out that spreadsheet models often play a critical role in business planning and analysis. Because of their importance, spreadsheets should not be created haphazardly. Instead, they should be carefully engineered. We recommended a process for designing, building, and testing a spreadsheet that is both efficient and effective. Not only does this process minimize the likelihood that the spreadsheet contains errors, but it also prepares the user to investigate the business questions at hand in the analytic phase of the modeling process. In this chapter we provide a structure for this investigation and present the essential Excel tools that support analysis. Advanced methods, and the Excel tools that go with them, are elaborated in later chapters.

We have found that, over time, most analysts develop their own informal approaches to the analytic phase of modeling. Many of us have favorite tools that we tend to rely on, even when they are not really adequate to the task. But it is difficult to develop a *complete* set of analytic tools simply through experience. An analyst who does not know a particular tool generally does not think to ask the business question that the tool helps answer. By the same token, an analyst with a complete analytic toolkit would be more likely to ask the right questions.

Although Excel itself has thousands of features, most of the analysis done with spreadsheets falls into one of the following five categories:

- Base-case analysis
- What-if analysis
- Breakeven analysis
- Optimization analysis
- Risk analysis

Within each of these categories, there are specific Excel tools—such as the Goal Seek tool—and add-ins—such as Crystal Ball and Solver—which can be used either to automate tedious calculations or to find powerful business insights that cannot be found any other way. Some of these tools are quite complex and will be given more complete treatment in later chapters. Here, we provide only a brief introduction to these tools so as to give the reader an overview of the process of spreadsheet analysis. By contrast, some of the other tools we describe in this chapter are extremely simple, yet they seem to be underutilized by the majority of analysts.

Once again, we draw on the Advertising Budget example, which was introduced in Chapter 5, to illustrate the different kinds of analysis. Here is a sample of the kinds of questions we answer in this chapter:

- If we follow last year's plan to spend the same amount on advertising in each quarter, how much profit can we expect to make?
- How much will profit change if our product costs turn out to be 10 percent higher or lower than we have assumed?
- If our product costs rise, at what point will profit reach zero?

- What is the maximum profit we can make with an advertising budget of $40,000?
- How likely is it that we will lose money if price and cost are uncertain?

6.2 BASE-CASE ANALYSIS

Almost every spreadsheet analysis involves measuring outcomes relative to some common point of comparison, or **base case**. Therefore, it's worth giving some thought to how the base case is chosen. A base case is often drawn from current policy or common practice, but many other alternatives are available. Where there is considerable uncertainty in the decision problem, it may be appropriate for the base case to depict the most likely scenario; in other circumstances, the worst case or the best case might be a good choice.

Sometimes, several base cases are used during the course of analysis. For example, we might start the analysis with a version of the model that takes last year's results as the base case. Later in the analysis, we might develop another base case using a proposed plan for the coming year. At either stage, the base case is the starting point from which an analyst can explore the model using the tools described in this chapter, and thereby gain insights into the corresponding business situation. The base case also sets the tone for presenting results to decision makers.

In the Advertising Budget example, most of the input parameters such as price and cost are forecasts for the coming year. These inputs would typically be based on previous experience, modified by our hunches as to what will be different in the coming year. But what values should we assume for the decision variables in the base case? Our ultimate goal is to find the best values for these decisions, but that is premature at this point. A natural alternative is to take last year's advertising expenditures ($10,000 in each quarter) as the base-case decisions, both because this is a simple plan and because initial indications point to a repeat for this year's decisions.

6.3 WHAT-IF ANALYSIS

Once a base case has been specified, the next step in analysis often involves nothing more sophisticated than varying one of the inputs to determine how the key outputs change. Assessing the change in outputs associated with a given change in inputs is called **what-if analysis**. The inputs may be *parameters*, in which case we are asking how sensitive our base-case results are to forecasting errors or other changes in input values. Alternatively, the inputs may be *decision variables*, in which case we are exploring whether changes in our decisions might improve our results, for a given set of parameters. Finally, there is another type of what-if analysis, in which we test the effect on the results of changing some aspect of our model's *structure*. For example, we might replace a linear relationship with a nonlinear one. In these three forms of analysis, the general idea is to alter an assumption and then trace the effect on the model's outputs.

We use the term **sensitivity analysis** interchangeably with the term *what-if analysis*. However, we are aware that sensitivity analysis sometimes conveys a distinct meaning. In the optimization models of Chapters 10–13, we use the term sensitivity analysis more narrowly to mean the effect of changing a parameter on the *optimal* outcome. (In optimization models, the term *what-if analysis* is seldom used.)

When we vary a *parameter*, we are implicitly asking what would happen if there were an unexpected change in that parameter or if our forecast of that parameter were wrong. That is, what if we had made a different numerical assumption at the outset, but everything else remained unchanged? This kind of questioning is important because the parameters in our model represent assumptions or forecasts about the environment for decision making. If the environment turns out to be different from what we had assumed, then it stands to reason that the results will also be different. What-if analysis measures that difference and helps us appreciate the potential importance of each numerical assumption.

In the Advertising Budget model, for example, if unit cost rises to $26 from $25, then annual profit drops to $53,700. In other words, an increase of 4 percent in the unit cost will reduce profit by nearly 23 percent. Thus, it would appear that profits are quite sensitive to unit cost, and in light of this insight, we may decide to monitor the market conditions that influence the material and labor components of cost.

When we vary a *decision variable*, we are changing inputs that we control. First, we'd like to know whether changing the value of a decision variable would lead to an improvement in the results. If we locate an improvement, we can then try to determine what value of the decision variable would result in the largest improvement. This kind of questioning is different from asking about a parameter, because we can act directly on what we learn. What-if analysis can thus lead us to better decisions.

In the Advertising Budget model, if we spend an additional $1,000 on advertising in the first quarter, then annual profit rises to $69,882. In other words, an increase of 10 percent in the advertising expenditure during Q1 will translate into an increase of roughly 0.3 percent in annual profit. Thus, profits seem quite insensitive to small changes in advertising expenditures in Q1, all else being equal. Nevertheless, we have identified a way to increase profits. We might guess that the small percentage change in profit reflects the fact that expenditures in the neighborhood of $10,000 are close to optimal, but we will have to gather more information before we are ready to draw conclusions about optimality.

In addition to testing the sensitivity of results to parameters and decision variables, there are situations in which we want to test the impact of some element of model structure. For example, we may have assumed that there is a linear relationship between price and sales. As part of what-if analysis, we might then ask whether a nonlinear demand relationship would materially alter our conclusions. As another example, we may have assumed that our competitors will not change their prices in the coming year. If we then determine that our own prices should increase substantially over that time, we might ask how our results would change if our competitors were to react by matching our price increases. These what-if questions are more complex than simple changes to a parameter or a decision variable because they involve alterations in the underlying structure of the model. Nonetheless, an important aspect of successful modeling is testing the sensitivity of results to key assumptions in the model's structure.

In the Advertising Budget model, the nonlinear relationship between advertising and sales plays a fundamental role. In the spirit of structural sensitivity analysis, we can ask how different our results would be if we were to replace this relationship with a linear one. For example, the linear relationship

$$Sales = 3,000 + 0.1(Advertising \times Seasonal\ Factor)$$

lies close to the nonlinear curve for advertising levels around $10,000. When we substitute this relationship into the base-case model, holding advertising constant at $10,000 each quarter, we find that profit changes only slightly, to $70,000. But in this model, if we then increase Q1 advertising by $1,000, we find that profit *decreases*, while in the base-case model it increases. Evidently, this structural assumption does have a significant impact on the desired levels of advertising.

We have illustrated what we might call a "one-at-a-time" form of what-if analysis, where we vary one input at a time, keeping other inputs unchanged. We could, of course, vary two or more inputs simultaneously, but these more complex experiments become increasingly difficult to interpret. In many cases, we can gain the necessary insights by varying the inputs one at a time.

It is important not to underestimate the power of this first step in analysis. Simple what-if exploration is one of the most effective ways to develop a deeper understanding of the model and the system it represents. It is also part of the debugging process, as we pointed out in the previous chapter. When what-if analysis reveals something unexpected, we may have found a useful insight or perhaps discovered a bug.

Predicting the outcome of a what-if test is an important part of the learning process. For example, in the Advertising Budget model, what would be the result of doubling the selling price? Would profits double as well? In the base case, with a price of $40, profits total $69,662. If we double the price, we find that profits increase to $612,386. Profits increase by much more than a factor of two when prices double. After a little thought, we should see the reasons. For one, costs do not increase in proportion to volume; for another, demand does not decline as price increases. Thus, the sensitivity test helps us to understand the nature of the cost structure—that it's not proportional—as well as one possible limitation of the model—that no link exists between demand and price.

6.3.1 Benchmarking

During what-if analysis, we repeatedly change inputs and observe the resulting change in outputs. This can get confusing unless we keep a record of the results in some organized fashion. One simple solution to this problem is to **benchmark** sensitivity results against the base case by keeping a record of the base-case outcome on the spreadsheet.

In the Advertising Budget spreadsheet, we benchmark the base-case profit of $69,662 on the spreadsheet in cell F21, as shown Figure 6.1*. Note that this cell contains the *number* $69,662, not a cell reference to profit in C21. We construct this entry by selecting C21 and choosing Home▶Clipboard▶Copy, then selecting F21 and choosing Home▶Clipboard▶Paste▶Paste Special with the option `Values`, as shown in Figure 6.2. With this design, the result of any new sensitivity test appears in C21, while the base-case value is maintained in F21. If we wish, we can add a cell to measure the difference in profit between the base case and the sensitivity test, or the percentage difference, if that is more useful.

FIGURE 6.1 The Advertising Budget Spreadsheet

	A	B	C	D	E	F	G	H	I	J
1	**Advertising Budget Model**									
2	SGP/KRB									
3	1/1/2006									
4										
5	PARAMETERS									
6				Q1	Q2	Q3	Q4			Notes
7		Price	$40.00							Current price
8		Cost	$25.00							Accounting
9		Seasonal		0.9	1.1	0.8	1.2			Data analysis
10		OHD rate	0.15							Accounting
11		Sales Parameters								
12			35							Consultants
13			3000							
14		Sales Expense		8000	8000	9000	9000			Consultants
15		Ad Budget	$40,000							Current budget
16										
17	DECISIONS							Total		
18		Ad Expenditures		$10,000	$10,000	$10,000	$10,000	$40,000		sum
19							Base case value of			
20	OUTPUTS						profit recorded as a			
21		Profit	$69,662		Base case	$69,662	fixed number.			
22										
23	CALCULATIONS									
24		Quarter		Q1	Q2	Q3	Q4	Total		
25		Seasonal		0.9	1.1	0.8	1.2			
26										
27		Units Sold		3592	4390	3192	4789	15962		given formula
28		Revenue		143662	175587	127700	191549	638498		price*units
29		Cost of Goods		89789	109742	79812	119716	399061		cost*units
30		Gross Margin		53873	65845	47887	71831	239437		subtraction
31										
32		Sales Expense		8000	8000	9000	9000	34000		given
33		Advertising		10000	10000	10000	10000	40000		decisions
34		Overhead		21549	26338	19155	28732	95775		rate*revenue
35		Total Fixed Cost		39549	44338	38155	47732	169775		sum
36										
37		Profit		14324	21507	9732	24099	69662		GM -TFC
38		Profit Margin		9.97%	12.25%	7.62%	12.58%	10.91%		pct of revenue
39										

6.1

*To download spreadsheets for this chapter, go to the Student Companion Site at www.wiley.com/college/powell.

6.3.2 Scenarios

Up to this point, we have viewed each parameter in our model as independent of all the others. But it is often the case that certain *sets* of parameters go together in some natural way. For example, in the airline industry during a recession, we might expect passenger miles to be low and interest rates also to be low. Thus, in using a model to forecast future airline profitability, we might want to analyze a recession, and to do so, we would choose low values for these two inputs. Furthermore, when we perform what-if analysis, we would vary both parameters up and down *together*, not independently.

In general, we can think of a **scenario** as a story about the future decision-making environment translated into its effects on several of the model's parameters. More specifically, a scenario is a set of parameters that describes an internally consistent view of the future. In our airline example, the story involves a recession and the impact the recession has on specific parameters affecting demand and investment. In the oil industry, a scenario might depict the breakup of the OPEC cartel and its impacts on production and exploration worldwide. In the semiconductor business, a scenario might involve a breakthrough in optical technology that leads to the first chip powered by light. To translate these stories into useful terms, we would have to determine how such events influence specific parameters in a coordinated fashion.

In the Advertising Budget example, we can construct an optimistic scenario in which prices are high ($50) and costs are low ($20), yielding a profit of $285,155. Similarly, we can construct a pessimistic scenario, in which prices are low ($35) and costs are high ($30), leading to a loss of $77,991. Each scenario tells a coherent story that has meaning to the decision makers and is implemented in the model through a set of two or more parameters. Excel's Scenario Manager provides a way to record the inputs and outputs of multiple scenarios. We select Data▶Data Tools▶What-If Analysis▶ Scenario Manager and enter the first scenario by clicking on the Add button and entering the information required in the Add Scenario window and (after clicking OK) the Scenario Values window. Thereafter, we can use the Edit button to change the details, or the Add button to enter another scenario. Figure 6.3 shows the window for the Scenario Manager after the optimistic and pessimistic scenarios have been added. If we click on the Show button, the values corresponding to the selected scenario are placed in the spreadsheet. If we click on the Summary button, we obtain the summary table shown in Figure 6.4.

When scenarios involve a large number of parameters, it is convenient to switch from one set of parameters to another all at once. This can be accomplished using the Excel CHOOSE function. CHOOSE selects a value from a range based on an index number. The index number is the number of the scenario, and the range contains the inputs for a given parameter. This is illustrated in Figure 6.5. In cell C6 we enter the number of the scenario, 1, 2, or 3 in this case. In L7:N7 we enter the values for the price parameter for three scenarios: Optimistic (#1), Base Case (#2), and Pessimistic (#3).

FIGURE 6.2 The Paste Special Window

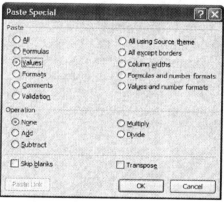

FIGURE 6.3 The Scenario Manager Window

FIGURE 6.4 The Summary Produced by the Scenario Manager

The CHOOSE function appears in cell C8, where the appropriate price is entered depending on the scenario chosen in C6. The appropriate value for cost is entered in cell C9 using the same approach. This method can be used to enter any number of parameters for a given scenario simply by changing the index number in cell C6.

As an application of scenario analysis, consider the Heineken Brewery case.[1] The modeling task in this case was to develop a forecast for Heineken profits over the five years 1999–2003. Because of uncertainty over the strategies that major players in the beer industry would pursue over this time period, no single base case was considered appropriate. Three scenarios were developed, as described in the following.

> *Business As Usual:* The industry avoids major price wars, and financial returns improve slightly. Heineken's performance is the same as in the late 1990s, and in the near future, the company makes two major acquisitions and some small ones. Heineken continues to globalize and augments its market share by 8 percent over the five years.
>
> *Price War:* The industry price wars started by Miller and Busch continue worldwide, dropping returns toward the cost of capital. Heineken's performance is stable but with weaker margins and no new acquisitions.
>
> *Market Discipline:* The industry consolidates and avoids price wars. Heineken improves gross margins through an aggressive mergers-and-acquisitions program. It becomes a leader in the drive for industry consolidation.

These alternative futures were then translated into appropriate sets of input parameters. For the Price War scenario, two adjustments were made to the Business As Usual assumptions: revenue growth would be 0 percent (rather than 2 percent), and 1 percent (rather than 3 percent) of revenue growth would come from acquisitions. In the Market Discipline scenario, growth by acquisitions was increased so that Heineken augments its market share by 15 percent.

The results of the Heineken scenario analysis are summarized below. To focus on just one result, we can see that equity per share is 19.3 guilders lower in the Price War scenario and 40.5 guilders higher in the Market Discipline scenario, relative to the Business As Usual scenario.

Result	Units	Price war	Business as usual	Market discipline
Average annual growth	Percentage	2.4	5.6	7.0
Average ROIC	Percentage	13.0	13.1	14.2
Company value	NLG Billion*	29.8	35.8	48.5
Equity value	NLG Billion	27.5	33.5	46.2
Equity value per share	NLG	87.6	106.9	147.4
Probability	Percentage	15.0	60.0	25.0

*Netherlands guilders

[1] T. Koller, M. Goedhart, and D. Wessels. *Valuation* (New York: John Wiley and Sons, 2005), 253.

FIGURE 6.5 Use of the
CHOOSE Function
to Implement Scenarios

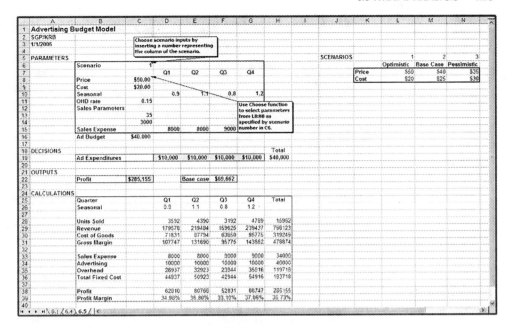

Several aspects of this case are noteworthy. First, scenarios should describe the major events that could impact the company or individual in the future. The story told in each scenario should be believable and coherent, although credible scenarios are not necessarily highly likely. (In fact, one of the strengths of scenario analysis is to focus attention on important but unlikely futures.) Second, the description of each scenario must be sufficiently complete to suggest plausible values for all the input parameters. Often, the parameters of a business-as-usual scenario are set first, and the parameters of the other scenarios are selected as changes from the base values.

6.3.3 Data Sensitivity

Simple what-if analysis requires changing one input and observing the resulting value of the output. But we often wish to understand how the output varies over a *range* of inputs. We could type in a series of input values and record the outputs manually, but an automatic procedure would be more efficient.

The **Data Sensitivity** tool was created to automate simple what-if analysis. It recalculates the spreadsheet for a series of values of an input cell and tabulates the resulting values of an output cell. This allows the analyst to perform several related what-if tests in one pass rather than entering each input value and recording each corresponding output.

The Data Sensitivity tool is one module in the **Sensitivity Toolkit,** which is an Excel add-in that is available with this book. Once the Toolkit is installed, the Sensitivity Toolkit option will appear on the far right of the menu bar. Data Sensitivity and the other modules can be accessed from this menu.

We illustrate the use of the Data Sensitivity tool in the Advertising Budget model by showing how variations in unit cost affect profit. We first select Add-ins▶Sensitivity Toolkit▶Data Sensitivity. The first window that appears (Figure 6.6) provides a choice for Table Type, which we leave at the default of One-Way Table. We also enter the address of the Result Cell, C21, which is the output cell in our model.

After pressing the Next button, a second window appears (Figure 6.7) that asks for information on the input parameter. The Cell to Vary is C8, which contains the unit-cost parameter. The Input Type has two options: Begin, End, Increment and Begin, End, Num Obs (Number of Observations). We most often use the default choice of Begin, End, Increment. To create a table in which the unit cost varies

FIGURE 6.6 Initial Inputs for a One-way Data Sensitivity

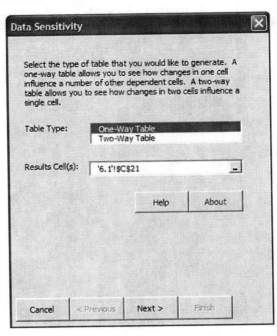

from \$20 to \$30 in steps of \$1, we enter 20 for the `First Value`, 30 for `Last Value`, and 1 for `Increment/N`.

Figure 6.8 shows the output generated by the Data Sensitivity tool. A worksheet has been added to the workbook, and the first two columns on the sheet contain the table of what-if values. In effect, the what-if test has been repeated for each unit-cost value from \$20 to \$30 in steps of \$1, and the results have been recorded in the table. In addition, the table is automatically converted to a graph, which can be edited at the user's discretion. As both the table and graph show, annual profits drop as the unit cost increases, and the cost-profit relationship is linear. We can also see that the breakeven value of the unit cost falls between \$29 and \$30, since profits cross from positive values to negative values somewhere in this interval.

Note that the Data Sensitivity tool requires that we provide a single cell address to reference the input being varied in a one-way table. The tool will work correctly only if the input has been placed in a single location. By contrast, if an input parameter had been embedded in several cells, the tool would have given incorrect answers when we tried to vary the input. Thus, the use of single and separate locations for parameters (or for decisions), which we advocated in Chapter 5, makes it possible to take advantage of the tool's capability.

We can also use the Data Sensitivity tool to analyze the sensitivity of an output to *two* inputs. This option gives rise to a two-way table, in contrast to the one-way sensitivity table illustrated in Figure 6.8. To demonstrate this feature, we build a table showing how profits are affected by both Q1 advertising and Q2 advertising. When we invoke the Data Sensitivity tool after using it for the one-way analysis, some of the values we specified remain visible. Thus, for example, the `Result Cell` remains C21 and does not need editing. In the Two-Way Inputs window, we ask for both cells to vary from \$5,000 to \$15,000 in steps of \$1,000, giving rise to the table shown in Figure 6.9 (after some modest reformatting), which appears on another newly added worksheet. A quick check that helps us confirm our work is to look up the profit value in the table corresponding to advertising expenditures of \$10,000 in both Q1 and Q2. In the center of the table, we see that this value is \$69,662, as expected.

FIGURE 6.7 Parameter Inputs for a One-way Data Sensitivity

By studying Figure 6.9, we can make a quick comparison between the effect of additional spending in Q1 and the effect of

FIGURE 6.8 One-way Data Sensitivity: Profit as a Function of Cost

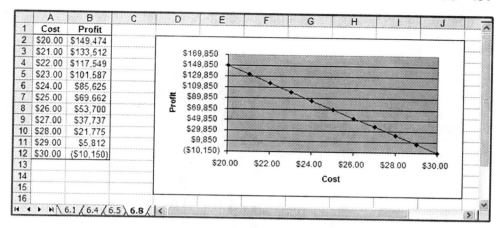

	Cost	Profit
2	$20.00	$149,474
3	$21.00	$133,512
4	$22.00	$117,549
5	$23.00	$101,587
6	$24.00	$85,625
7	$25.00	$69,662
8	$26.00	$53,700
9	$27.00	$37,737
10	$28.00	$21,775
11	$29.00	$5,812
12	$30.00	($10,150)

the same spending in Q2. As we can observe in the table, moving across a row generates more profit than moving the same distance down a column. This pattern tells us that we can gain more from spending additional dollars in Q2 than from the same additional dollars in Q1. This observation suggests that, starting with the base case, we could improve profits by shifting dollars from Q1 to Q2. We can also note from the table, or from the three-dimensional chart that automatically accompanies it, that the relationship between profits and advertising expenditures is not linear. Instead, profits show diminishing returns.

6.3.4 Tornado Charts

Another useful tool for sensitivity analysis is the **tornado chart**. In contrast to the information produced by the Data Sensitivity tool, which shows how sensitive an output is to one or perhaps two inputs, a tornado chart shows how sensitive the output is to several different inputs. Consequently, it shows us which parameters have a major impact on the results and which have little impact.

Tornado charts are created by changing input values one at a time and recording the variations in the output. The simplest approach is to vary each input by a fixed percentage of its base-case value, such as ±10 percent. For each parameter in turn, we increase the base-case value by 10 percent and record the output, then we decrease the base-case value by 10 percent and record the output. Next, we calculate the absolute difference between these two outcomes and display the results in the order of these differences.

The Sensitivity Toolkit contains a tool for generating tornado charts. For the Advertising Budget example, we select Add-ins ▶ Sensitivity Toolkit ▶ Tornado Chart and specify cell C21 as the Result Cell, just as we did when using the Data Sensitivity tool. Next, we designate the Input Parameters for the chart. Given the structure of our model (refer to Figure 6.1), we can simply enter the range C7:G15, since the tool will ignore blank cells and titles. However, it is also possible to enter a list of cells in the usual fashion, by holding down the Control key and pointing to each cell or cell range desired.

FIGURE 6.9 Two-way Data Sensitivity: Profit as a Function of Q1 and Q2 Advertising

Profit: $D$18 by $E$18

Q1 / Q2

Q1	$5,000	$6,000	$7,000	$8,000	$9,000	$10,000	$11,000	$12,000	$13,000	$14,000	$15,000
$5,000	$64,160	$65,060	$65,838	$66,529	$67,145	$67,695	$68,187	$68,625	$69,017	$69,366	$69,676
$6,000	$64,718	$65,598	$66,376	$67,067	$67,683	$68,233	$68,725	$69,164	$69,555	$69,904	$70,214
$7,000	$65,173	$66,053	$66,831	$67,522	$68,138	$68,688	$69,179	$69,618	$70,010	$70,359	$70,669
$8,000	$65,557	$66,437	$67,215	$67,906	$68,522	$69,072	$69,563	$70,002	$70,394	$70,743	$71,053
$9,000	$65,879	$66,759	$67,537	$68,228	$68,844	$69,394	$69,885	$70,324	$70,716	$71,065	$71,375
$10,000	$66,147	$67,027	$67,805	$68,496	$69,112	$69,662	$70,153	$70,592	$70,984	$71,333	$71,643
$11,000	$66,367	$67,247	$68,025	$68,716	$69,332	$69,882	$70,374	$70,813	$71,204	$71,553	$71,863
$12,000	$66,544	$67,424	$68,203	$68,894	$69,510	$70,060	$70,551	$70,990	$71,382	$71,731	$72,040
$13,000	$66,683	$67,563	$68,341	$69,033	$69,648	$70,198	$70,690	$71,129	$71,520	$71,869	$72,179
$14,000	$66,787	$67,667	$68,445	$69,136	$69,752	$70,302	$70,793	$71,232	$71,624	$71,973	$72,283
$15,000	$66,858	$67,738	$68,517	$69,208	$69,824	$70,374	$70,865	$71,304	$71,696	$72,045	$72,354

FIGURE 6.10 Tornado Chart Using the Constant Percentage Option

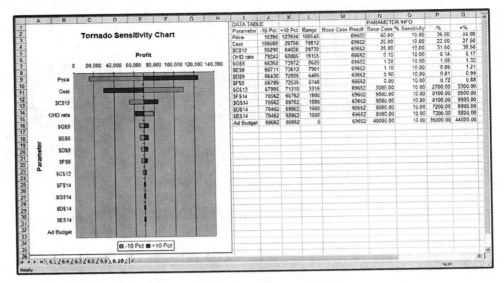

Parameter	-10 Pct	+10 Pct	Range	Base Case Result	Base Case	% Sensitivity	-%	+%
Price	15390	123934	108545	69662	45.00	10.00	36.00	44.00
Cost	109568	29756	79812	69662	25.00	10.00	22.50	27.50
$C$12	55295	84028	28732	69662	35.00	10.00	31.50	38.50
OHD rate	79240	60085	19155	69662	0.15	10.00	0.14	0.17
$G$9	65352	73972	8620	69662	1.20	10.00	1.08	1.32
$E$9	65711	73613	7901	69662	1.10	10.00	0.99	1.21
$D$9	66430	72895	6465	69662	0.90	10.00	0.81	0.99
$F$9	66789	72535	5746	69662	0.80	10.00	0.72	0.88
$C$13	67995	71310	3315	69662	3000.00	10.00	2700.00	3300.00
$F$14	70562	68762	1800	69662	9000.00	10.00	8100.00	9900.00
$G$14	70562	68762	1800	69662	9000.00	10.00	8100.00	9900.00
$D$14	70462	68862	1600	69662	8000.00	10.00	7200.00	8800.00
$E$14	70462	68862	1600	69662	8000.00	10.00	7200.00	8800.00
Ad Budget	69662	69662	0	69662	40000.00	10.00	36000.00	44000.00

The Tornado Chart tool provides a choice of three options:

- Constant percentage
- Variable percentage
- Percentiles

Suppose we select Constant Percentage and click the Next button. In the Constant Inputs window, we enter 10. In this instance, we vary the following parameters by ±10 percent of their base-case values: price, unit cost, overhead percentage, two sales parameters, four seasonal factors, four quarterly sales expenses, and the advertising budget. The final step is to click Finish.

The tornado chart appears on a newly inserted worksheet, as shown in Figure 6.10. The horizontal axis at the top of the chart shows profits, and the bars in the chart show the changes in profit resulting from ±10 percent changes in each input. After calculating the values (which are recorded in the accompanying table on the same worksheet), the bars are sorted from largest to smallest for display in the diagram. Thus, the most sensitive inputs appear at the top, with the largest horizontal spans. The least sensitive inputs appear toward the bottom, with the smallest horizontal spans. Drawing the chart using horizontal bars, with the largest span at the top and the smallest at the bottom, suggests the shape of a tornado, hence the name. If some of the information in the chart seems unclear, details can usually be found in the accompanying table, which is constructed on the same worksheet by the Tornado Chart tool. In our example, we can see in the table that price has the biggest impact (a range of more than $108,000), with unit cost next (a range of nearly $80,000), and the other inputs far behind in impact on profit.

The standardization achieved by using a common percentage for the change in inputs (10 percent in our example) makes it easy to compare the results from one input to another, but it may also be misleading. A 10 percent range may be realistic for one parameter, while 20 percent is realistic for another and 5 percent for a third. The critical factor is the size of the forecast error or uncertainty for each parameter. If these ranges are significantly different, we should assign different percentages to different inputs. This can be accomplished using the Variable Percentage option in the Tornado Chart tool.

To illustrate the Variable Percentage option in the Advertising Budget example, suppose we limit ourselves to seven parameters: price, cost, four seasonal factors, and overhead rate. Suppose that, based on a detailed assessment of the uncertainty in these parameters, we choose to vary price by 5 percent, cost by 12 percent, seasonal factors by 8 percent, and overhead rate by 3 percent. Before invoking the tool, we must enter this information into our spreadsheet. A reliable way to do so is to

FIGURE 6.11 Tornado
Chart Using the Variable
Percentage Option

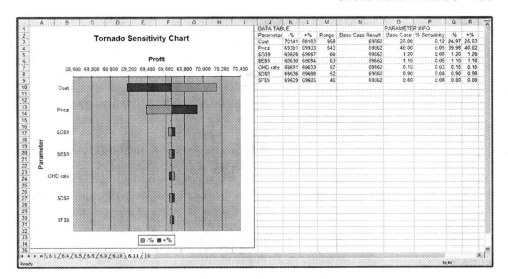

duplicate the range containing the input parameters in an unused region of the spreadsheet and then replace each parameter with the corresponding percentage. In this example, we can copy cells B6:G10 and paste into the range K6:P10. Then, we can replace the parameters we wish to vary with the corresponding percentages. (For more details on how to use these tools, click on the Help button on the first window under each option in the Sensitivity Toolkit.)

When we invoke the Tornado Chart tool, the Result Cell remains unchanged. For Input Parameters, we enter the range C7:G10 and select the Variable Percentage type of analysis. When we click on the Next button, we come to the Variable Inputs window, where we can enter the range L6:P10 and click Finish.

The resulting tornado chart is shown in Figure 6.11. As the results show, cost now has the biggest impact on profits, partly because it has a larger range of uncertainty than price.

Tornado charts are an extremely useful tool for determining quickly which parameters are most important in a model. Nevertheless, they have several drawbacks. We have already pointed out the potential pitfalls of assuming that every parameter varies by the same percentage of the base case. Models with significant nonlinearities present an additional pitfall. If the output is related to an input in a nonlinear fashion, the degree of sensitivity implied by a tornado chart may be misleading. An extreme example will make the point. Figure 6.10 suggests that profits are highly sensitive to costs. In particular, if costs increase by 10 percent, profit drops to around $30,000. This might suggest that cost increases alone could lead to losses. But suppose that costs are capped by a contract that specifies we will never pay more than $28 (at which value profits are still positive). Then cost increases cannot lead to losses, despite what the tornado chart suggests. In general, we must be cautious about drawing conclusions about the sensitivity of a model outside the range of the parameters tested in a tornado chart.

In Chapter 7, we discuss how to use confidence-interval information to guide the Variable Percentage analysis when some of our parameters are based on sample data. Later, in Chapter 15, we show how to use Monte Carlo simulation to fully account for uncertainty in spreadsheet models. There, we also explain how to use the Percentiles option in the Tornado Chart tool, and we show how a tornado chart can serve as a useful first step in simulation analysis.

6.4 BREAKEVEN ANALYSIS

Many managers and analysts throw up their hands in the face of uncertainty about critical parameters. If we ask a manager to directly estimate market share for a new product, the reply may be: "I have *no idea* what market share we'll capture." A powerful strategy in this situation is to reverse the sense of the question: instead of asking "What will our market share be?" ask, "How high does our market share have to get before we turn a profit?" The trick here is to look for a **breakeven,** or cutoff, level for a parameter—that is, a target value of the parameter at which some particularly interesting event occurs, such as reaching zero profits or making a 15 percent return on invested assets. Managers who cannot predict market share can often determine whether a particular breakeven share is likely to occur. This is why breakeven analysis is so powerful.

Even if we have no idea about the market share for the new product, we should be able to build a model that calculates profit given some *assumption* about market share. Once market share takes the role of a parameter in our model, we can use the Data Sensitivity tool to construct a graph of profit as a function of market share. Then, from the graph, we can find the breakeven market share quite accurately.

New capital investments are usually evaluated in terms of their net present value, but the appropriate discount rate to use is not always obvious. Rather than attempting to determine the appropriate discount rate precisely, we can take the breakeven approach and ask how high the discount rate would have to be in order for this project to have an NPV of zero. (The answer to this question is generally known as the **internal rate of return**.) If the answer is 28 percent, we can be confident that the project is a good investment. On the other hand, if breakeven occurs at 9 percent, we may want to do further research to establish whether the discount rate is clearly below this level.

FIGURE 6.12   The Goal Seek Window

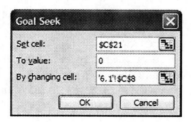

Breakeven values for parameters can be determined manually by repeatedly changing input values until the output reaches the desired target. This can often be done fairly quickly by an intelligent trial-and-error search in Excel. In the Advertising Budget model, suppose we want to find the breakeven cost to the nearest penny. Recall from

FIGURE 6.13   Using the Goal Seek Tool in the Advertising Budget Example

	A	B	C	D	E	F	G	H	I	J
1	Advertising Budget Model									
2	SGP/KRB									
3	1/1/2006									
4										
5	PARAMETERS									
6					Q1	Q2	Q3	Q4		Notes
7		Price	$40.00							Current price
8		Cost	$29.36	If the cost is set						Accounting
9		Seasonal		to $29.36...	0.9	1.1	0.8	1.2		Data analysis
10		OHD rate	0.15							Accounting
11		Sales Parameters								
12			35							Consultants
13			3000							
14		Sales Expense			8000	8000	9000	9000		Consultants
15		Ad Budget	$40,000							Current budget
16										
17	DECISIONS							Total		
18		Ad Expenditures		$10,000	$10,000	$10,000	$10,000	$40,000	sum	
19										
20	OUTPUTS									
21		Profit	$0		Base case	$69,662				
22				...then profit will hit						
23	CALCULATIONS			the target value of						
24		Quarter		$0.		Q3	Q4	Total		
25		Seasonal			0.9	1.1	0.8	1.2		
26										
27		Units Sold		3592	4390	3192	4789	15962	given formula	
28		Revenue		143662	175587	127700	191549	638498	price*units	
29		Cost of Goods		105463	128899	93745	140617	468724	cost*units	
30		Gross Margin		38199	46688	33955	50932	169775	subtraction	
31										
32		Sales Expense		8000	8000	9000	9000	34000	given	
33		Advertising		10000	10000	10000	10000	40000	decisions	
34		Overhead		21549	26338	19155	28732	95775	rate*revenue	
35		Total Fixed Cost		39549	44338	38155	47732	169775	sum	
36										
37		Profit		-1350	2350	-4200	3200	0	GM -TFC	
38		Profit Margin		-0.94%	1.34%	-3.29%	1.67%	0.00%	pct of revenue	
39										

6.1 / 6.4 / 6.5 / 6.8 / 6.9 / 6.10 / 6.11 \ 6.13 /

Figure 6.8 that profit goes to zero somewhere between $29 and $30. By repeating the search between these two costs in steps of $0.10, we can find the breakeven cost to the nearest dime. If we repeat the search once more, in steps of $0.01, we will obtain the value at the precision we seek.

Excel also provides a specialized tool called **Goal Seek** for performing this type of search. Three pieces of information are required: the output-cell address, the target level sought, and the input for which the search is conducted. To determine the breakeven cost in the Advertising Budget example, we select Data▶Data Tools▶What-If Analysis▶ Goal Seek. The Set Cell is Profit in C21; the To Value is the profit target of zero; and the Changing Cell is unit cost, in C7. With these three specifications, the Goal Seek window takes the form shown in Figure 6.12. The tool locates the desired unit cost as $29.36, and the corresponding results are displayed on the spreadsheet (see Figure 6.13). Choosing the OK button in the Goal Seek Status window preserves these values in the spreadsheet; choosing the Cancel button returns the spreadsheet to its base case.

Note that the Goal Seek tool searches for a prescribed level in the relation between a single output and a single input. Thus, it requires that the parameter or decision being varied resides in a single location, reinforcing one of the design principles we introduced in Chapter 5.

One warning should be added. If we invoke Goal Seek when there is more than one breakeven point, the value returned by the Goal Seek tool may depend on where we start. A simple example illustrates this feature. Suppose our model contains the formula $y = x^2 - 5x + 6$, and we want to find the value of x for which $y = 0$. If we set up this search on a spreadsheet and initially assign $x = 7$, then Goal Seek produces the result $x = 3$ as the desired value. However, if we initially assign $x = 1$, then Goal Seek returns the value $x = 2$. Thus, we may need to be alert to the possibility of more than one breakeven point, because Goal Seek can return only one value. If we suspect that there may be a second breakeven level, we may make a preliminary run with Data Sensitivity to see whether multiple breakeven points are a possibility.

6.5 OPTIMIZATION ANALYSIS

Another fundamental type of managerial question asks what decision variables achieve the best possible value of an output. In fact, we might claim that the fundamental management task is to make choices that result in optimal outputs. **Solver** is an important tool for this purpose. Solver is an add-in for Excel that makes it possible to optimize models with many decision variables and with constraints on the choice of decision variables. A basic version of Solver comes with Excel. A more powerful version is available with this book. Optimization is a complex subject, and we devote Chapters 10 to 13 to it and to the use of Solver. However, we can provide a glimpse of its power by demonstrating a simple application in the Advertising Budget example.

Suppose we wish to maximize total profits with an advertising budget of $40,000. We already know that, with equal expenditures in every quarter, annual profits come to $69,662. The question now is whether we can achieve a higher level of annual profits. By using Solver we can find that a higher level is, in fact, attainable. An optimal reallocation of the budget produces annual profits of $71,447. The chart in Figure 6.14 compares the allocation of the budget in the base case with the optimal allocation. As we can see, the optimal allocation calls for greater expenditures in quarters Q2 and Q4 and for smaller expenditures in Q1 and Q3.

FIGURE 6.14 Comparison of Base Case and Optimal Allocations

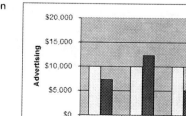

This is just one illustration of Solver's power. Among the many questions we could answer with Solver in the Advertising Budget example are these:

- What would be the impact of a requirement to spend at least $8,000 each quarter?
- What would be the marginal impact of increasing the budget?
- What is the optimal budget size?

Chapters 10–13 develop the techniques to answer these and a host of related questions for a variety of spreadsheet models.

6.6 SIMULATION AND RISK ANALYSIS

Uncertainty often plays an important role in analyzing a decision because with uncertainty comes risk. Until now, we have been exploring the relationship between the inputs and outputs of a spreadsheet model as if uncertainty were not at issue. However, risk is an inherent feature of all managerial decisions, so it is frequently an important aspect in modeling. In particular, we might want to recognize that some of the inputs are subject to uncertainty. In other words, we might want to associate probability models with some of the parameters. When we take that step, it makes sense to look at outputs the same way—with probability models. The use of probability models in this context is known as **risk analysis**.

One tool we use for risk analysis in spreadsheets is **Crystal Ball**, an add-in for Monte Carlo simulation that is available with this book. This tool allows us to generate a probability distribution for any output cell in a spreadsheet, given probability assumptions about some of the input cells. Simulation and risk analysis are the subjects of Chapters 15 and 16. Here, we simply illustrate how Crystal Ball can help us answer an important question about risk.

We return to the base case in the Advertising Budget example, in which we assumed equal expenditures of $10,000 for advertising each quarter. Our analysis, which assumed that all parameters are known exactly, showed an annual profit of $69,662. However, we might wonder about the distribution of profits if there's uncertainty about the unit price and the unit cost. Future prices depend on the number of competitors in our market, and future costs depend on the availability of raw materials. Since both the level of competition and raw material supply are uncertain, so, too, are the parameters for our price and cost. Suppose we assume that price is normally distributed with a mean of $40 and a standard deviation of $10, and that unit cost is equally likely to fall anywhere between $20 and $30. Given these

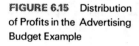

FIGURE 6.15 Distribution of Profits in the Advertising Budget Example

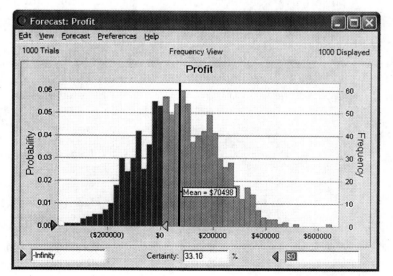

assumptions, what is the probability distribution of annual profits; specifically, what is the *average* profit? And how likely is it that profits will be *negative*?

Figure 6.15 shows the probability distribution for profits in the form of a histogram, derived from the assumptions we made about price and cost. The graph shows us that the estimated average profit is $70,498 under our assumptions. It also shows that the probability is about 33 percent that we will lose money. This exposure may cause us to reevaluate the desirability of the base-case plan.

Chapters 15 and 16 develop the techniques to address uncertain elements in the analysis, for a variety of spreadsheet models. There we show how to:

- Determine which inputs require probability models.
- Select appropriate probability models for those inputs.
- Configure Crystal Ball to generate a histogram for any output cell.

6.7 SUMMARY

The process of analyzing a spreadsheet model has several identifiable steps. The first step is to construct a base case, which becomes a key point of comparison for all of the subsequent analyses. The next step is what-if analysis: changing inputs and tracing the effects on one or more of the outputs. Early in the development of a spreadsheet, this step is an aid in debugging the model, as we mentioned in Chapter 5. Once the spreadsheet has been debugged and tested, what-if analysis helps us discover how sensitive an output is to one or more of the inputs. The Data Sensitivity tool helps us automate one-at-a-time sensitivity analysis. The information produced by this tool is also translated into a chart so that relationships can be portrayed visually.

A tornado chart provides another form of what-if analysis, treating several of the inputs at once. Scenario analysis can be used to analyze the outputs for a set of inputs that together tell a story. Whatever tool we use, probing for sensitivities helps provide useful insight to support management decisions. In the Advertising Budget example, our early probing revealed that profits respond in straight-line fashion to changes in the unit cost and that profits show diminishing returns to additional advertising expenditures.

A related step involves inverting the analysis, where we start with a target for a particular output and "back into" the input value that achieves that target level of performance. The most prominent form is breakeven analysis, which aims at a target of zero, but the concept can be applied to any target level. Excel provides the Goal Seek tool to automate the search for a single input value that achieves a desired output value. Breakeven analysis provides us with an early indication of risk: we can determine how much of a "cushion" there is in any one of our parameter forecasts. Should the actual value

turn out to be worse than our base-case assumption, breakeven analysis tells us how much of a difference we can tolerate before our output measure reaches a critical level. In the Advertising Budget example, we found that the $25 unit cost could grow to more than $29 before we would face negative profits.

The most ambitious forms of analysis are optimization and simulation. Optimization methods look for the best value of an output by searching through various combinations of the decisions. Simulation methods allow some of the inputs to be treated as probabilistic, tracing the implications for outputs. These two methods represent advanced techniques of modeling, and we devote several later chapters to them. In our analysis framework, they play the role of powerful tools capable of delivering further insights. In the Advertising Budget example, the insight obtained from optimization was that the allocation of advertising expenditures across the four quarters should not be equal, but rather should reflect the size of the seasonal factors. In fact, further optimization analysis reveals that the $40,000 budget itself is probably too small. A larger budget could increase profitability.

The progression from a base case to what-if and breakeven analysis, then to optimization and simulation analyses, represents a logical and increasingly sophisticated set of methods for *experimenting* with a spreadsheet model. This kind of experimentation provides the opportunity for the same kind of learning that a scientist derives from laboratory experiments. Indeed, the spreadsheet is an analyst's electronic laboratory, and in supporting management decisions with laboratory work, the analyst is serving as a *management scientist*. In the following chapters, we begin to develop the management scientist's advanced modeling tools.

EXERCISES

1. Refer to the XYZ Company case. From the corresponding exercise in Chapter 5, review the design of a spreadsheet that will allow an analyst to predict monthly cash needs and profitability for the first five months of the year.

a. In what month does the cash balance fall below zero, signaling a need to borrow money?

b. What is the profit, as a percentage of sales, in April?

c. Suppose the monthly increment in sales is 600—instead of 500, as in the base case. How does this change affect the answers in (a) and (b)? Construct a table to examine the month in which the cash balance disappears as a function of the monthly increment in sales.

d. Suppose the monthly increment in sales is 300—instead of 500, as in the base case. How does this change affect the answers in (a) and (b)? Construct a graph showing the profitability percentage in (b) as a function of the monthly increment in sales.

e. Starting with the base case, suppose that unit cost runs higher than originally thought. What level of unit cost will lead the firm to run out of cash by the end of March?

2. Refer to the Medical Supplies for Banjul case. Design a spreadsheet that will enable you to request the required funds from your team's finance officer, order supplies from the home office, and ensure dissemination of appropriate quantities to each village. Your final order to the home office should specify the number of packages required of each item.

a. The population figures will show that there are 3,000 children, 2,500 teenagers, 500 seniors, and 9,000 other adults in the population. If there were no stock on hand, what amount would be required for ordering supplies?

b. Using the parameters in (a), construct a graph showing how the amount required for the order would vary if the unit cost of a package of bandages rose by $0.25, $0.50, and so on, up to $3.00 per package.

c. Following up on (a), a check on stock shows an inventory of 124 packages of A-bandages, 16 packages of B-bandages, 82 packages of C-bandages, 72 rolls of tape, and 4 hearing aids. What amount will be required for ordering supplies?

3. Refer to the Reid's Raisins case. Design a spreadsheet that will allow the firm to determine how many grapes to buy under contract and how much to charge for the raisins they sell.

a. What is the profit projected for the base-case conditions, assuming a market price of $0.30 for the open-market grape price?

b. What is the breakeven value of the open-market grape price?

c. Construct a table showing how profit varies as a function of the price set for raisins. Cover a range from $1.80 to $2.80 in steps of $0.10.

d. Construct a tornado chart for the analysis in (a). List the relevant parameters in descending order of their impact on annual profit.

4. Refer to the Big Rig Rental Company case. Design a spreadsheet that will provide the owner with the five-year economic analysis requested.

a. What is the Net Present Value of the firm's cash flows over the five-year period?

b. Construct a tornado chart for the analysis in (a). List the relevant parameters in descending order of their impact on the Net Present Value.

c. What is the internal rate of return for the cash flows in (a)?

d. Construct a table to show how profit varies with the base rental rate, which is currently $1,000 per month.

5. Refer to the Flexible Insurance Coverage case. From the corresponding exercise in Chapter 5, review the design of a spreadsheet that will allow an individual employee to compare the annual expenses for each plan and thereby choose the cheapest alternative.

a. Consider the case of a single employee with estimated annual expenses of $400. What plan is the cheapest? What is the total annual cost associated with this plan?

b. For the analysis in (a), construct a table to show the best plan and the associated cost for annual expenses ranging from $100 to $1,200 in steps of $100.

c. Consider the case of a married employee with estimated annual expenses of $1,000 and an equal amount for the spouse. What plan is the cheapest? What is the total annual cost associated with this plan?

d. For the analysis in (c), construct a table to show the best plan and the associated cost for annual expenses ranging from $100 to $1,500 in steps of $100 for the employee, assuming that the employee's expenses and the spouse's expenses are the same.

e. For the analysis in (d), find the level of expenses at which the cost is the same under Plan 1 and Plan 2.

6. Refer to the Snoey Software Company case. Design a spreadsheet for the desired five-year economic analysis mentioned in the case.

a. Consider a recommendation that the prices for the Educational, Large-Scale, and Professional versions should be $75, $275, and $475, respectively. What annual profit would these prices achieve?

b. Construct three separate sensitivity analyses, starting from the base case in (a). For each analysis, vary the price above and below the base case, and find the best price for the version being analyzed. When these prices are used in combination, what annual profit is achieved?

c. For the pricing in (a), consider the set of prices that the five segments would be willing to pay for the three products. If each of these prices could vary by 15 percent, which one would have the greatest dollar impact on the annual profit?

7. Refer to the Cox Cable and Wire Company case. In the role of Meredith, design a spreadsheet that will evaluate the profitability of any particular production and delivery schedule.

a. Find a machine schedule and a corresponding inventory and shipment schedule that meets demand. What is the profitability of this schedule?

b. Suppose that material costs for both products were to rise by a specific percentage. At what percentage increase would profitability drop to zero?

c. Construct a table showing how profitability varies with changes in the selling price of Plastic reels. Repeat for Teflon reels. Which price has a greater effect on profitability?

8. Refer to the BMW Company case. From the corresponding exercise in Chapter 5, review the design of a spreadsheet that will allow BMW management to estimate the cost of disposal a decade into the future (i.e., in 1999) as a percentage of net income.

a. What percentage is predicted for 1999, assuming there are no changes in trends and policies?

b. How does the percentage change as a function of BMW's market share in 1999? (Consider a range from 5 to 8 percent.)

c. Construct a tornado chart for the analysis in (a). List the relevant parameters in descending order of their impact on the disposal cost.

d. Consider three scenarios, called Slow, Medium, and Fast, characterized by different landfill costs in 1999 (600, 1,200, and 1,800DM, respectively) and by different landfill percentages (60 percent, 50 percent, and 40 percent, respectively). For these scenarios, and assuming that incineration costs will run double landfill costs, construct a scenario table for BMW's disposal cost in 1999 and the percentage of its net income that this figure represents.

9. Refer to the ERP Decision case. Design a spreadsheet that will assist the Board in understanding the likely costs and benefits of implementing ERP.

a. Develop a base case. You may create any data you need for this purpose. Why is this base case appropriate for this situation?

b. How sensitive are the benefits of ERP in the base case to the efficiency gains?

c. Break the total benefits down into the contribution from efficiency gains, inventory turns, and CRM.

10. Refer to the Retirement Planning case. From the corresponding exercise in Chapter 5, review the design of a spreadsheet for this problem.

a. Develop a base case. You may create any data you need for this purpose. Why is this base case appropriate for this situation?

b. Perform an appropriate sensitivity analysis. Which parameters have the most significant impact on the results? Can you find applications for the Data Sensitivity, Tornado Chart, and Scenario Manager tools?

c. Identify applications of the Goal Seek tool in this situation. (For example, find the savings rate needed to ensure that assets do not run out before age 90.)

d. Identify potential applications of *optimization* in this case.

e. Identify potential applications of *simulation* in this case.

11. Refer to the Draft TV Commercials case. From the corresponding exercise in Chapter 5, review the design of a spreadsheet for this problem.

a. Develop a base case. You may create any data you need for this purpose. Why is this base case appropriate for this situation?

b. Perform an appropriate sensitivity analysis. Which parameters have the most significant impact on the results? Can you find applications for the Data Sensitivity, Tornado Chart, and Scenario Manager tools?

c. Identify applications of Goal Seek in this situation. (For example, what percentage of the overall budget should be devoted to draft commercials in order to achieve a preset target number of impressions?)

d. Identify potential applications of *optimization* in this case.

e. Identify potential applications of *simulation* in this case.

12. Refer to the Icebergs for Kuwait case. From the corresponding exercise in Chapter 5, review the design of a spreadsheet for this problem.

a. Develop a base case. You may create any data you need for this purpose. Why is this base case appropriate for this situation?

b. Perform an appropriate sensitivity analysis. Which parameters have the most significant impact on the results? Can you find applications for the Data Sensitivity, Tornado Chart, and Scenario Manager tools?

c. Identify applications of Goal Seek in this situation. (For example, how large an iceberg should they tow in order to break even at the current price for pure water?)

d. Identify potential applications of *optimization* in this case.

e. Identify potential applications of *simulation* in this case.

13. Refer to the Racquetball Racket case. From the corresponding exercise in Chapter 5, review the design of a spreadsheet for this problem.

a. Develop a base case. You may create any data you need for this purpose. Why is this base case appropriate for this situation?

b. Perform an appropriate sensitivity analysis. Which parameters have the most significant impact on the results? Can you find applications for the Data Sensitivity, Tornado Chart, and Scenario Manager tools?

c. Identify applications of Goal Seek in this situation. (For example, what percentage of the market must they achieve to break even on their investment?)

d. Identify potential applications of *optimization* in this case.

e. Identify potential applications of *simulation* in this case.

7 Data Analysis for Modeling

7.1 INTRODUCTION

In this chapter, we discuss the roles that data, data analysis, and statistics play in modeling, and we present a variety of relevant Excel tools. Data analysis and statistical techniques are used in many situations, not all of which are pertinent to the building of spreadsheet models for decision making. Since that is our focus in this book, we organize this chapter around tools that are most useful in the modeling context.

We emphasize that modeling is motivated by the existence of a problem to be resolved or a decision to be made. In the course of developing and testing a model for the purpose of shedding light on the problem, we may decide to collect empirical data to help determine either the value of a parameter or the structure of a relationship. However, the collection and analysis of that data is a means to an end, not a primary goal. Data analysis should be undertaken to improve the accuracy and usefulness of the conclusions drawn from the model, not to enhance the model for its own sake. In that sense, data analysis *supports* the modeling process, but modeling remains the primary focus.

Data analysis and statistical techniques are often used in contexts other than in modeling. Data analysis, for example, is often used to provide general background for managers. A marketing manager might ask for a report on company sales by geographic region and by product line—not to help make a specific decision, but simply to better understand the business environment. A credit card company might request a study to identify the predictors of overdue accounts, even though no specific decision is at hand. These uses of data analysis and statistical methods, while valuable in their own right, are not the focus of this chapter.

In Chapter 2, as part of our discussion of the craft of modeling, we recommended an emphasis on *structuring the model*, not on collecting data. Novice modelers generally place too much reliance on empirical data and fail to recognize biases, distractions, and irrelevancies in the data collection process. That is why we stress the importance of prototyping using readily available data, even roughly estimated data. Moreover, in Chapter 6, we noted the importance of using sensitivity analysis to determine which parameters have a significant impact on the results and may therefore be worthy of further refinement through data analysis.

We emphasize model structure over data analysis because we find that model structure almost always has a strong impact on the ultimate recommendations. Analysis of empirical data, by contrast, may or may not have such an impact. The modeling process itself, as described in earlier chapters, suggests what data to collect and how accurate these data must be for the purposes at hand.

As with the advanced techniques covered in later chapters, we have found that business analysts can themselves do much of the data analysis they need. To do so, they need an understanding of the fundamentals of data analysis and statistics. Most analysts will call on experts when their needs go beyond the fundamentals. With that in mind, our coverage in this chapter includes the basic methods for finding facts in databases: editing, searching, sorting, filtering, and tabulating. We then discuss sampling and making estimates of parameters using basic statistical techniques.

7.2 FINDING FACTS FROM DATABASES

One of the ways we encounter data is in the form of a database. For our purposes, a **database** is a table of information, with each row corresponding to a **record** in the database and each column corresponding to a **field** for the various records. For example, one record might correspond to a single customer order, and the fields might include the customer's name, items ordered, and total value of the order. Excel refers to a table of this type as a **list**. The first row of a list contains names for each of the fields. Each successive row contains one record. In this section, we cover some basic Excel commands that help us manipulate lists and thus seek out information in a given database. We consider commands that edit, search, sort, or filter information in a database, along with Pivot Table, which is used to build two- and three-way summary tables.

As examples, we'll work with three databases:

- Analgesics.xlsx, with data on retail sales of painkillers
- Applicants.xlsx, with data on MBA applicants from one year's pool
- Executives.xlsx, with data on executive compensation for a sample of companies

Figure 7.1 shows a portion of the Analgesics database. A second worksheet in the database provides definitions of the fields, in case the column titles are not self-explanatory. The information in the database describes more than 7,500 sales transactions for a variety of painkillers over a 10-week period at six different stores that form part of a retail chain. We might use this database to answer such questions as the following:

- What were the market shares of the various brands?
- What were weekly sales volumes at the different stores?

We use past tense here to emphasize that, although we are interested in projecting into the future, the data actually tell us something about the past.

FIGURE 7.1 First Portion of the Analgesics Database

	A	B	C	D	E	F	G	H
1	ID	ITEM	UPC	DESCRIPTION	SIZE	STORE	WEEK	SALES
2	1	6122741	2586610502	ALEVE CAPLETS	24 CT	101	383	0
3	2	6122741	2586610502	ALEVE CAPLETS	24 CT	101	384	0
4	3	6122741	2586610502	ALEVE CAPLETS	24 CT	101	385	0
5	4	6122741	2586610502	ALEVE CAPLETS	24 CT	101	386	0
6	5	6122741	2586610502	ALEVE CAPLETS	24 CT	101	387	0
7	6	6122741	2586610502	ALEVE CAPLETS	24 CT	101	388	0
8	7	6122741	2586610502	ALEVE CAPLETS	24 CT	101	389	0
9	8	6122741	2586610502	ALEVE CAPLETS	24 CT	101	390	0
10	9	6122741	2586610502	ALEVE CAPLETS	24 CT	101	391	0
11	10	6122741	2586610502	ALEVE CAPLETS	24 CT	101	392	0
12	11	6122741	2586610502	ALEVE CAPLETS	24 CT	103	383	0
13	12	6122741	2586610502	ALEVE CAPLETS	24 CT	103	384	0
14	13	6122741	2586610502	ALEVE CAPLETS	24 CT	103	385	0
15	14	6122741	2586610502	ALEVE CAPLETS	24 CT	103	386	0
16	15	6122741	2586610502	ALEVE CAPLETS	24 CT	103	387	0
17	16	6122741	2586610502	ALEVE CAPLETS	24 CT	103	388	0
18	17	6122741	2586610502	ALEVE CAPLETS	24 CT	103	389	0
19	18	6122741	2586610502	ALEVE CAPLETS	24 CT	103	390	0
20	19	6122741	2586610502	ALEVE CAPLETS	24 CT	103	391	0
21	20	6122741	2586610502	ALEVE CAPLETS	24 CT	103	392	0
22	21	6122751	2586610504	ALEVE CAPLETS	50 CT	102	383	0
23	22	6122751	2586610504	ALEVE CAPLETS	50 CT	102	384	0
24	23	6122751	2586610504	ALEVE CAPLETS	50 CT	102	385	0
25	24	6122751	2586610504	ALEVE CAPLETS	50 CT	102	386	0
26	25	6122751	2586610504	ALEVE CAPLETS	50 CT	102	387	0
27	26	6122751	2586610504	ALEVE CAPLETS	50 CT	102	388	0
28	27	6122751	2586610504	ALEVE CAPLETS	50 CT	102	389	0
29	28	6122751	2586610504	ALEVE CAPLETS	50 CT	102	390	0
30	29	6122751	2586610504	ALEVE CAPLETS	50 CT	102	391	0
31	30	6122751	2586610504	ALEVE CAPLETS	50 CT	102	392	0

7.1

FIGURE 7.2 First Portion of the Applicants Database

	A	B	C	D	E	F	G	H	I
1	ID	ROUND	AGE	SEX	CITZ CODE	1ST CONTACT	JOB MONTHS	INDUSTRY	INDUSTRY DESC.
2	1	1	30	M	U	Email	84	260	Finan Serv-Diversified
3	2	1	29	M	U	Phone call	86	370	Government
4	3	1	27	M	U	Phone call	40	260	Finan Serv-Diversified
5	4	1	30	M	U	Email	48		
6	5	1	32	M	U	Home Page	85	290	Finan Serv-Invest Mgt/Research
7	6	1	26	M	U	Home Page	32	280	Finan Serv-Invest Bk/Brokerage
8	7	1	29	M	U	Phone call	60	10	Accounting
9	8	1	27	F	U		44	220	Entertainment/Leisure/Media
10	9	1	29	M	U	Phone call	66	40	Agribusiness
11	10	1	31	M	U	Letter	78	420	Nonprofit
12	11	1	27	M	U	Phone call	24	460	Retail
13	12	1	27	M	U	Phone call	51	370	Government
14	13	1	28	M	U		26	230	Environmental Services
15	14	1	30	M	U	Phone call	72	20	Advertising/Marketing Services
16	15	1	27	F	U	Phone call	48	420	Nonprofit
17	16	1	25	M	U	Home Page	31	260	Finan Serv-Diversified
18	17	1	24	F	U	Phone call	24	210	Energy/Utilities
19	18	1	28	M	U	Phone call	31	400	Law
20	19	1	27	M	N	Home Page	54	80	Construction
21	20	1	26	M	U	Letter	32	230	Environmental Services
22	21	1	24	M	U	World Wide Web	24	580	Other Services
23	22	1	27	M	U	Phone call	46	260	Finan Serv-Diversified
24	23	1	28	M	U	Home Page	50	160	Consumer Gds-Food/Beverage
25	24	1	28	M	U	Home Page	60	10	Accounting
26	25	1	29	M	U	Phone call	30	370	Government
27	26	1	27	M	U		48	120	Consulting-Strategy/Management
28	27	1	26	M	U	Phone call	36	260	Finan Serv-Diversified
29	28	1	28	F	U	Home Page	44	260	Finan Serv-Diversified
30	29	1	35	M	U	Phone call	146	220	Entertainment/Leisure/Media
31	30	1	27	M	U	World Wide Web	50	120	Consulting-Strategy/Management

Figure 7.2 shows a portion of the Applicants database. Again, a second worksheet provides a glossary for the field names. The information was collected on nearly 3,000 MBA applicants, showing the status of the applicant pool on a date early in the summer. We might use this database to answer such questions as the following:

- What proportion of the applicants had nonprofit work experience?
- What was the average GMAT score for accepted applicants?

Figure 7.3 shows a portion of the Executives database. The information constitutes a sample of 100 records from a publicly available survey of executive compensation. We might use this database to answer such questions as the following:

FIGURE 7.3 First Portion of the Executives Database

	A	B	C	D	E	F	G	H	I
1	ID	EXECID	GENDER	SALARY	BONUS	OTHER	SHARES	CONAME	TICKER
2	2611	00006	MALE	683.462	412.768	0.000	207.828	ADC TELECOMMUNICATIONS INC	ADCT
3	4666	00029	MALE	750.000	1012.500	0.000	641.691	ALLTEL CORP	AT
4	2702	00074	MALE	875.000	1000.000	22.100	2234.402	ARROW ELECTRONICS INC	ARW
5	5562	00085	MALE	324.389	80.563	0.000	16632.050	ATMEL CORP	ATML
6	314	00111	MALE	750.000	825.000	294.770	183.031	BAXTER INTERNATIONAL INC	BAX
7	2766	00140	MALE	509.734	77.257	0.000	354.541	BOB EVANS FARMS	BOBE
8	2777	00152	MALE	700.000	317.665	0.000	39.928	KEYSPAN CORP	KSE
9	5588	00167	MALE	820.677	500.000	45.687	1208.415	CALLAWAY GOLF CO	ELY
10	516	00197	MALE	1350.000	1965.000	0.000		CHEVRON CORP	CHV
11	2962	00223	MALE	1000.000	0.000	0.000	255.198	CMS ENERGY CORP	CMS
12	2654	00246	MALE	1357.026	2162.508	91.721	1517.168	AFLAC INC	AFL
13	5865	00313	MALE	933.333	5554.350	300.034	6033.567	TRIARC COS INC -CL A	TRY
14	822	00315	MALE	771.018	463.200	0.000	224.861	EASTERN ENTERPRISES	EFU
15	9283	00393	MALE	1000.000	2750.000	143.698	643.966	FREEPRT MCMOR COP&GLD -CL B	FCX
16	5067	00398	MALE	205.000	0.000	56.891	9040.113	HUMANA INC	HUM
17	16384	00415	MALE	550.000	275.000	60.703	48.542	BARNES GROUP INC	B
18	1016	00418	MALE	620.000	952.468	0.000	334.430	GENUINE PARTS CO	GPC
19	10891	00474	MALE	410.004	400.000	0.000	1469.256	HORACE MANN EDUCATORS CORP	HMN
20	3296	00482	MALE	450.000	0.000	0.000	151.477	HUNT (JB) TRANSPRT SVCS INC	JBHT
21	3367	00522	MALE	750.000	0.000	46.067	740.528	KANSAS CITY SOUTHERN INDS	KSU
22	1329	00555	MALE	1185.577	3331.968	0.000	46497.711	LIMITED INC	LTD
23	4837	00563	MALE	1051.946	0.000	712.393	17308.998	LOEWS CORP	LTR
24	1459	00608	MALE	369.231	0.000	77.757	141.572	MCKESSON HBOC INC	MCK
25	1679	00705	MALE	730.769	0.000	159.776		OGDEN CORP	OG
26	5415	00731	MALE	800.000	10662.500	0.000	1185.531	PAINE WEBBER GROUP	PWJ
27	4903	00741	MALE	689.178	448.630	0.000	216.999	PPL CORP	PPL
28	9594	00749	MALE	990.000	698.465	128.496	1075.749	FORT JAMES CORP	FJ
29	586	00778	MALE	1000.000	8732.474	448.577	17500.746	CITIGROUP INC	C
30	10955	00791	MALE	773.085	975.000	0.000	4931.348	QUALCOMM INC	QCOM

FIGURE 7.4 Form for the Analgesics Database

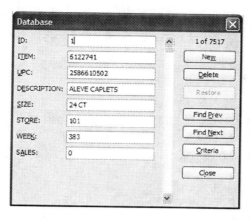

- What was the average salary among these executives?
- What proportion of compensation was due to annual bonuses?

These three databases contain what we might think of as "raw" data. That is, the databases were not necessarily compiled for the purpose of answering the questions we posed. They were likely built for other purposes, or in the hope that they might be generally helpful to unspecified users.

7.2.1 Searching and Editing

It is usually helpful to assign a range name to a list (see Chapter 4 for details on assigning range names). For example, we might assign the range name *Data* to our lists, so that we can easily select the entire database including column titles.

We can always search and edit a list directly, but Excel also provides a specialized tool for this purpose. To add this tool to the Quick Access Toolbar, choose Office Button▶Excel options▶Customize▶Choose commands from...▶ All Commands▶Form▶Add▶OK. With the database selected, we choose the Form icon on the Quick Access Toolbar. A window appears containing a form that is tailored to the structure of the database, as shown in Figure 7.4 for the Analgesics list. This form allows us to examine the records one at a time, using the Find Prev and Find Next buttons. We can also enter a record, using the New button, or delete a record, using the Delete button.

A simple way to search for a record in the database is to click on the form's Criteria button, type an identifying entry into one of the field windows, and then click on Find Next. A broader search of the entire database, which does not rely on the form, uses the Find command after the database has been selected. To access the Find command, choose Home▶Editing▶Find & Select▶Find. With this command, entries in the database can be edited from the Find and Replace window. One of the flexible aspects of the Find and Replace commands is the use of the symbols "?" and "*" to assist in these operations. The question mark stands for a single symbol, and the asterisk stands for any sequence of symbols.

> *Question*: In the Analgesics database, which transactions involve the brand Aleve?

The database contains entries for individual brands with tablets, caplets, gelcaps, and the like, each indicated in the Description field. For the purposes of investigating sales by brand name, we would like to combine all of these variations into a single descriptor for each brand. To accomplish this conversion, we use the Replace tab to locate Aleve* (where the asterisk stands for anything that may follow the brand name in the description of the item) and to designate the replacement as Aleve, as shown in Figure 7.5. By clicking on the Replace All option, we convert the

FIGURE 7.5 The Find and Replace Window

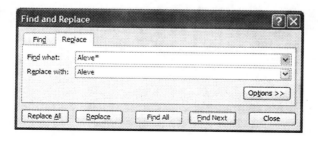

FIGURE 7.6 Replacing Compound Descriptions with a Simple Brand Name

	A	B	C	D	E	F	G	H	I
1	ID	ITEM	UPC	DESCRIPTION	SIZE	STORE	WEEK	SALES	UNITS
2	1	6122741	2586610502	Aleve	24	101	383	0	0
3	2	6122741	2586610502	Aleve	24	101	384	0	0
4	3	6122741	2586610502	Aleve	24	101	385	0	0
5	4	6122741	2586610502	Aleve	24	101	386	0	0
6	5	6122741	2586610502	Aleve	24	101	387	0	0
7	6	6122741	2586610502	Aleve	24	101	388	0	0
8	7	6122741	2586610502	Aleve	24	101	389	0	0
9	8	6122741	2586610502	Aleve	24	101	390	0	0
10	9	6122741	2586610502	Aleve	24	101	391	0	0
11	10	6122741	2586610502	Aleve	24	101	392	0	0
12	11	6122741	2586610502	Aleve	24	103	383	0	0
13	12	6122741	2586610502	Aleve	24	103	384	0	0
14	13	6122741	2586610502	Aleve	24	103	385	0	0
15	14	6122741	2586610502	Aleve	24	103	386	0	0
16	15	6122741	2586610502	Aleve	24	103	387	0	0
17	16	6122741	2586610502	Aleve	24	103	388	0	0
18	17	6122741	2586610502	Aleve	24	103	389	0	0
19	18	6122741	2586610502	Aleve	24	103	390	0	0
20	19	6122741	2586610502	Aleve	24	103	391	0	0
21	20	6122741	2586610502	Aleve	24	103	392	0	0
22	21	6122751	2586610504	Aleve	50	102	383	0	0
23	22	6122751	2586610504	Aleve	50	102	384	0	0
24	23	6122751	2586610504	Aleve	50	102	385	0	0
25	24	6122751	2586610504	Aleve	50	102	386	0	0
26	25	6122751	2586610504	Aleve	50	102	387	0	0
27	26	6122751	2586610504	Aleve	50	102	388	0	0
28	27	6122751	2586610504	Aleve	50	102	389	0	0
29	28	6122751	2586610504	Aleve	50	102	390	0	0
30	29	6122751	2586610504	Aleve	50	102	391	0	0

description of all Aleve brand items to the same description, as shown in Figure 7.6. The Find command is indifferent to case (i.e., whether Aleve is in capital letters or lower case.) When we want to be more precise about capital letters, we can click on the Options button for more detailed specifications.

7.2.2 Sorting

The Sort command can be used not only for database sorting but also for sorting any contiguous set of rows and columns on a spreadsheet. It is found by choosing Home▶Editing▶Sort & Filter. We give an example using the Executives database and another using the Applicants database.

Question: In the Executives database, are there any duplicate records?

Suppose we wish to determine whether any executive (identified by the number in column B) is represented more than once in the sample. We begin by selecting the database. (Exploiting the range name, we do this by clicking the pull-down menu of range names, located directly above column A, and selecting the name Data.) Then, we choose Home▶Editing▶Sort & Filter▶Custom Sort, which opens the Sort window (Figure 7.7). This window has three pull-down windows: Column (to Sort by), Sort On, and Order. Here we sort by the EXECID field, sort on Values, and sort in the order A to Z (note that this field is entered as text, so it must be sorted in alphabetical order). When we click on OK, the sorting procedure is carried out,

FIGURE 7.7 The Sort Window

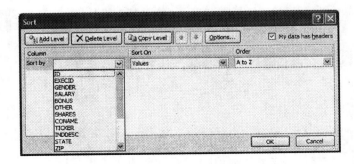

FIGURE 7.8 The Executives Database Sorted by the EXECID Field

	A	B	C	D	E	F	G	H	I
1	ID	EXECID	GENDER	SALARY	BONUS	OTHER	SHARES	CONAME	TICKER
2	2611	00006	MALE	683.462	412.768	0.000	207.828	ADC TELECOMMUNICATIONS INC	ADCT
3	4666	00029	MALE	750.000	1012.500	0.000	641.691	ALLTEL CORP	AT
4	2702	00074	MALE	875.000	1000.000	22.100	2234.402	ARROW ELECTRONICS INC	ARW
5	5562	00085	MALE	324.389	80.563	0.000	16632.050	ATMEL CORP	ATML
6	314	00111	MALE	750.000	825.000	294.770	183.031	BAXTER INTERNATIONAL INC	BAX
7	2766	00140	MALE	509.734	77.257	0.000	354.541	BOB EVANS FARMS	BOBE
8	2777	00152	MALE	700.000	317.665	0.000	39.928	KEYSPAN CORP	KSE
9	5588	00167	MALE	820.677	500.000	45.687	1208.415	CALLAWAY GOLF CO	ELY
10	516	00197	MALE	1350.000	1965.000	0.000		CHEVRON CORP	CHV
11	2962	00223	MALE	1000.000	0.000	0.000	255.198	CMS ENERGY CORP	CMS
12	2654	00246	MALE	1357.026	2162.508	91.721	1517.168	AFLAC INC	AFL
13	5865	00313	MALE	933.333	5554.350	300.034	6033.567	TRIARC COS INC -CL A	TRY
14	822	00315	MALE	771.018	463.200	0.000	224.861	EASTERN ENTERPRISES	EFU
15	9283	00393	MALE	1000.000	2750.000	143.698	643.966	FREEPRT MCMOR COP&GLD -CL B	FCX
16	5067	00398	MALE	205.000	0.000	56.891	9040.113	HUMANA INC	HUM
17	16384	00415	MALE	550.000	275.000	60.703	48.542	BARNES GROUP INC	B
18	1016	00418	MALE	620.000	952.468	0.000	334.430	GENUINE PARTS CO	GPC
19	10891	00474	MALE	410.004	400.000	0.000	1469.256	HORACE MANN EDUCATORS CORP	HMN
20	3296	00482	MALE	450.000	0.000	0.000	151.477	HUNT (JB) TRANSPRT SVCS INC	JBHT
21	3367	00522	MALE	750.000	0.000	46.067	740.528	KANSAS CITY SOUTHERN INDS	KSU
22	1329	00555	MALE	1185.577	3331.968	0.000	46497.711	LIMITED INC	LTD
23	4837	00563	MALE	1051.946	0.000	712.393	17308.998	LOEWS CORP	LTR
24	1459	00608	MALE	369.231	0.000	77.757	141.572	MCKESSON HBOC INC	MCK
25	1679	00705	MALE	730.769	0.000	159.776		OGDEN CORP	OG
26	5415	00731	MALE	800.000	10662.500	0.000	1185.531	PAINE WEBBER GROUP	PWJ
27	4903	00741	MALE	689.178	448.630	0.000	216.999	PPL CORP	PPL
28	9594	00749	MALE	990.000	698.465	128.496	1075.749	FORT JAMES CORP	FJ
29	586	00778	MALE	1000.000	8732.474	448.577	17500.746	CITIGROUP INC	C
30	10955	00791	MALE	773.085	975.000	0.000	4931.348	QUALCOMM INC	QCOM

7.1 / 7.2 / 7.3 / 7.4 / 7.5 / 7.6 / 7.7 / **7.8** /

producing the results shown in Figure 7.8. Then, when we scan the ID numbers in the sorted list, we can see that no two adjacent entries match. Therefore, no executive appears twice in the list.

EXCEL TIP
The Sort Command

When we sort a list with column headings, we check the box My data has headers in the Sort window. If we need to sort by columns instead of by rows, we click on the Options button and choose Sort left to right. Note also that although the Sort operation can be reversed by the Undo command, it is often a good idea to save the data to a new worksheet before sorting, so that the sorted data can be saved and analyzed separately. ∎

Question: In the Applicants database, how does work experience vary among the applicants in successive rounds?

In the previous example, we chose one basis for sorting—the executive identification. Sometimes we want to sort on a second or third criterion. When two sort criteria are specified, ties on the first criterion are broken by the second; and when three sort criteria are specified, ties on the second criterion are broken by the third. To sort on additional criteria, click on Add Level in the Sort window. In the Applicants database, for example, we can sort first by Round, then by Industry, and finally by Job Months (see Figure 7.9 for the entries in the Sort window) to get a sense of how applications arrive over time from people in different industries and with different lengths of service in their current job. The first portion of the result appears

FIGURE 7.9 Sorting by Three Fields

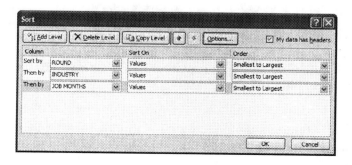

FIGURE 7.10   The Applicants Database Sorted by Round, Industry, and Job Months

	A	B	C	D	E	F	G	H	I
1	ID	ROUND	AGE	SEX	CITZ CODE	1ST CONTACT	JOB MONTHS	INDUSTRY	INDUSTRY DESC.
2	1637	1	25	M	U	Letter	22	10	Accounting
3	470	1	26	M	U	Letter	35	10	Accounting
4	91	1	26	F	U	Letter	36	10	Accounting
5	1694	1	27	M	U	Home Page	36	10	Accounting
6	1585	1	28	M	U	Phone call	37	10	Accounting
7	1638	1	27	M	U	Home Page	40	10	Accounting
8	392	1	24	F	U	Home Page	43	10	Accounting
9	1846	1	28	M	N	Phone call	44	10	Accounting
10	46	1	27	M	U	Phone call	45	10	Accounting
11	118	1	25	M	U	Phone call	48	10	Accounting
12	184	1	27	M	U	Test Score Tape (DNU)	48	10	Accounting
13	371	1	27	F	U	Phone call	48	10	Accounting
14	1793	1	27	F	U	Home Page	48	10	Accounting
15	1710	1	28	M	U	Phone call	49	10	Accounting
16	115	1	28	F	U	Phone call	56	10	Accounting
17	249	1	27	M	N	Home Page	56	10	Accounting
18	7	1	29	M	U	Phone call	60	10	Accounting
19	24	1	28	M	U	Home Page	60	10	Accounting
20	1906	1	29	M	U	Reapplicant	60	10	Accounting
21	1584	1	29	M	U	Phone call	66	10	Accounting
22	1626	1	29	M	U	Phone call	67	10	Accounting
23	504	1	29	M	U	Reapplicant	72	10	Accounting
24	1689	1	29	M	U	Home Page	75	10	Accounting
25	1518	1	29	M	N	Phone call	78	10	Accounting
26	1726	1	32	M	U	Email	82	10	Accounting
27	130	1	30	F	N	Phone call	100	10	Accounting
28	338	1	32	M	N	Email	102	10	Accounting
29	515	1	35	M	U	Reapplicant	120	10	Accounting
30	370	1	35	M	U	Home Page	144	10	Accounting

7.1 / 7.2 / 7.3 / 7.4 / 7.5 / 7.6 / 7.7 / 7.8 / 7.9 \ 7.10 /

in Figure 7.10. Looking deeper into this worksheet, we might observe, for example, that the applicants with relatively fewer months in advertising tend to apply in the first two rounds.

7.2.3 Filtering

The Filtering capabilities in Excel allow us to probe a large database and extract a portion of it that deals with the specific records in which we are interested. We may simply want to view the extracted portion temporarily, or we may want to store it separately, for further analysis. As an illustration, we use the Applicants database.

> *Question:* In the Applicants database, what are the characteristics of the applicants from nonprofit organizations?

Suppose we want to view only the applicants who worked in nonprofit organizations. We first select the database and then choose Home▶Editing▶Sort & Filter▶Filter. This adds a list arrow to the title of each column. If we click on the Industry Description list arrow, we see a list of all the possible entries in this column, each one next to a checked box. The first step is to uncheck the box for Select All; this step removes all the checks. Then we can check Nonprofit, and we see the subset of the database that contains Nonprofit entries (Figure 7.11). Filtering does not actually extract any records: it merely hides rows that do not match the filter criteria. Thus, in Figure 7.11, we see that applicants from the Nonprofit sector appear in rows 11, 16, 87, 103, and so on. We can copy and paste this subset to a different sheet if we wish. Alternatively, to restore the view of the entire database, we can either check Select All using the list arrow again, or we can choose Home▶Editing▶Sort & Filter▶ Filter▶Clear. While we are viewing a filtered subset of the database, the triangle marking the list arrow we had used shows up with the Filter symbol. This is a reminder that the information on the screen is filtered.

> *Question:* What is the average age of the applicants from the nonprofit sector?

Here we don't merely want to look at the subset of applicants from the nonprofit sector, but rather we want to describe one aspect of their characteristics

FIGURE 7.11 Filtering the
Applicants Database to
Highlight Nonprofit
Backgrounds

	ID	ROUND	AGE	SEX	CITZ CODE	1ST CONTACT	JOB MONTHS	INDUSTRY	INDUSTRY DESC.
11	10	1	31	M	U	Letter	78	420	Nonprofit
16	15	1	27	F	U	Phone call	48	420	Nonprofit
87	86	1	29	M	U	Test Score Tape (DNU)	4	420	Nonprofit
103	102	1	27	M	U	World Wide Web	30	420	Nonprofit
174	173	1	26	M	U	Home Page	37	420	Nonprofit
176	175	1	28	M	U	Phone call	60	420	Nonprofit
209	208	1	32	F	U	Home Page	108	420	Nonprofit
328	327	1	30	M	U	Phone call	62	420	Nonprofit
336	335	1	35	M	U	Phone call		420	Nonprofit
344	343	1	27	M	U	Phone call	44	420	Nonprofit
375	374	1	32	M	U	Home Page	88	420	Nonprofit
412	411	1	27	F	U	Phone call	48	420	Nonprofit
428	427	1	29	F	U	Phone call	52	420	Nonprofit
454	453	1	29	F	N	Test Score Tape (DNU)	56	420	Nonprofit
470	469	1	32	M	N	World Wide Web	51	420	Nonprofit
521	520	1	29	M	U	Home Page	72	420	Nonprofit
578	577	2	26	M	U	Test Score Tape (DNU)	26	420	Nonprofit
614	613	2	30	M	U	Home Page	6	420	Nonprofit
686	685	2	37	M	U	Letter	144	420	Nonprofit
748	747	2	28	F	U	Phone call	60	420	Nonprofit
825	824	2	29	M	N	Letter	58	420	Nonprofit
990	989	2	29	F	U	Phone call	67	420	Nonprofit
998	997	2	32	M	U	Reapplicant	98	420	Nonprofit
1120	1119	3	28	F	U	Phone call	35	420	Nonprofit
1172	1171	3	26	M	U	Home Page	36	420	Nonprofit
1184	1183	3	25	F	U	Phone call	38	420	Nonprofit
1202	1201	3	32	F	U	Email	84	420	Nonprofit
1229	1228	3	31	M	N	Home Page	15	420	Nonprofit

with a quantitative calculation. Intuitively, we might think of using the AVERAGE function. Suppose we place the cursor in cell U1, which lies immediately to the right of the database, and we enter the formula = AVERAGE (C2:C2917). The number that appears (28.97) is the average of the entire set of applicants. In other words, Excel's AVERAGE function does not adjust for the fact that we have done some filtering: it makes the calculation for the hidden cells as well as the visible cells. To make the calculation for just the visible cells, we move the cursor to cell V1 and enter the formula = SUBTOTAL (1,C2:C2917). This produces the desired value 29.48. The SUBTOTAL function ignores the hidden cells in its range.

The SUBTOTAL function is a general function that can be made to perform the calculations of one of Excel's more familiar functions, according to the first argument inside the parentheses. In our example, the argument 1 asks for the average value. The table below lists some of the most common functions that can be calculated with the SUBTOTAL function.

1	AVERAGE
2	COUNT
4	MAX
9	SUM

For a full list of the 11 functions that can be represented this way, invoke Help for the SUBTOTAL function.

One of the options on the arrow list is Number Filters. This allows us to use numerical criteria to sort a field. In a text field, the Text Filters option appears in the same place.

> *Question:* In the Applicants database, what are the ages of the oldest applicants?

For example, to find the 10 oldest applicants, we filter on Age and from its arrow list, we select Number Filters ▶ Top 10. The Top 10 AutoFilter window appears (see Figure 7.12). We could similarly create a list of the Top 10 percent by editing the Items entry in the right-hand window. By editing the middle window, we can restrict ourselves to the Top 5, or the Top 12, and so on, and by editing the left-hand window, we can obtain the Bottom 5, or the Bottom 15 percent, and so on.

> *Question:* Isolate the applicants who worked in either the Nonprofit or Government sectors.

FIGURE 7.12 The Top 10 Autofilter Window

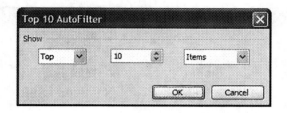

FIGURE 7.13 The Custom Autofilter Window

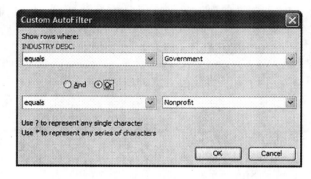

Another option under Number Filters or Text Filters is Custom Filter, which allows us to filter data using compound criteria. For example, to isolate the applicants who worked in *either* the Nonprofit or Government sectors, we select the Custom Filter option and click the Or button in the Custom AutoFilter window to set up the appropriate logical structure (see Figure 7.13).

> *Question:* Isolate the applicants who worked in either the Nonprofit or Government sectors and had GMAT scores above 700.

For more complicated compound criteria, we use the Custom filter on more than one field. Suppose, for example, that we wish to isolate the applicants who worked in either the Nonprofit or Government sectors and had GMAT scores above 700. We first filter the Industry Description field for Nonprofit and Government, and then we filter the GMAT field for scores above 700. The result of these filtering steps is shown in Figure 7.14.

7.2.4 Tabulating

Pivot Tables allow us to view summaries of the data in convenient tables, most often in formats known as **cross-tabulation tables** or **cross-tabs**. To appreciate how pivot tables work, we return to the Analgesics database and specifically to the edited version where we combined all of the item descriptions into single-word brand names. (The modified data are saved as a separate worksheet, with a new database name, such as BrandData.) In what follows, we describe the construction of three pivot tables, each an elaboration on the one before.

FIGURE 7.14 The Applicants Database After Filtering

	A	B	C	D	E	F	G	H	I	J	K
	ID	ROU	A	S	CITZ CO	1ST CONTACT	JOB MONT	INDUSTR	INDUSTRY DESC.	DECISION	GM
13	12	1	27	M	U	Phone call	51	370	Government	Cancel Enrollment	760
26	25	1	29	M	U	Phone call	30	370	Government	Deny	750
103	102	1	27	M	U	World Wide Web	30	420	Nonprofit	Deny	750
122	121	1	28	M	U	Letter		370	Government	Wait List Deny	720
209	208	1	32	F	U	Home Page	108	420	Nonprofit	Deny	740
263	262	1	32	M	U	Home Page	97	370	Government	Deny	770
323	322	1	32	M	U	Letter	76	370	Government	Wait List Deny	710
412	411	1	27	F	U	Phone call	48	420	Nonprofit	Wait List Deny	710
578	577	2	26	M	U	Test Score Tape (DNU)	26	420	Nonprofit	Deny	730
769	768	2	29	M	U	Email	82	370	Government	Deny	730
863	862	2	30	M	U	World Wide Web	84	370	Government	Deny	750
1128	1127	3	31	M	U	Phone call	78	370	Government	Deny	730
1184	1183	3	25	F	U	Phone call	38	420	Nonprofit	Deny	710
1229	1228	3	31	M	N	Home Page	15	420	Nonprofit	Deny	740
1251	1250	3	28	M	U	Home Page	61	370	Government	Deny	780
1259	1258	3	30	F	N	Letter	86	370	Government	Deny	720
1322	1321	4	28	M	N	World Wide Web	61	370	Government	Deny	730
1497	1496	1	30	F	U	Phone call	82	370	Government	Withdraw before Decision	770
1532	1531	1	26	F	U	Letter	50	370	Government	Withdraw after Decision	710
1561	1560	1	27	F	U	Phone call	48	420	Nonprofit	Deny	720
1574	1573	1	25	M	U	Email	38	420	Nonprofit	Deny	720
1609	1608	1	33	M	U	Phone call	115	420	Nonprofit	Withdraw after Decision	740
1654	1653	1	32	M	U	Home Page	98	370	Government	Enrolling	750
1809	1808	1	29	M	U	Phone call	24	370	Government	Deny	720
1834	1833	1	29	M	U	Home Page	63	370	Government	Wait List Deny	730
1844	1843	1	27	M	U	Home Page	46	420	Nonprofit	Withdraw after Decision	710
1846	1845	1	26	M	U	Home Page	38	420	Nonprofit	Deny	760
2101	2100	2	31	M	U	Phone call	48	420	Nonprofit	Wait List Deny	720
2113	2112	2	32	F	N	Test Score Tape (DNU)	89	370	Government	Deny	710
2116	2115	2	27	M	U	Phone call	60	370	Government	Wait List Deny	760
2199	2198	2	27	F	U	Home Page	40	420	Nonprofit	Wait List Deny	740
2200	2199	2	26	F	U	Email	28	370	Government	Deny	720

7.1 / 7.2 / 7.3 / 7.6 / 7.8 / 7.10 / 7.11 / 7.14 / 7.18 / 7.19

FIGURE 7.15 The Create
Pivot Table Window

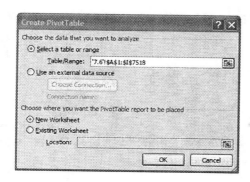

Question: What are total sales of painkillers, and how do they break down by brand name and by store?

First select the database and then choose Insert▶Tables▶Pivot Table▶ Pivot Table, which opens the Create Pivot-Table window (Figure 7.15). Place the Pivot Table report in a new worksheet and click OK. The new worksheet will have a template for the pivot table and a panel on the right (Pivot Table Field List) containing the field names (Figure 7.16).

FIGURE 7.16 The Pivot
Table Template

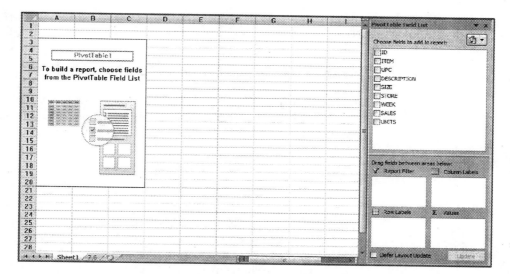

The Pivot Table Field List contains a drop-down menu that offers different layouts; we have shown the "stacked" layout in Figure 7.16. Next, drag the list item SALES to the Values box. A simple pivot table appears with the title Sum of SALES in cell A3 and the value 9432 in cell A4. (If a different title appears, such as Count of SALES, double-click on that name, and the Value Field Settings window appears, similar to the one in Figure 7.17. Select Sum in the main window of this option and click OK.) When the cursor is located on the pivot table (cells A3:A4), the Field List remains visible, otherwise it disappears.

FIGURE 7.17 The Value
Field Settings Window

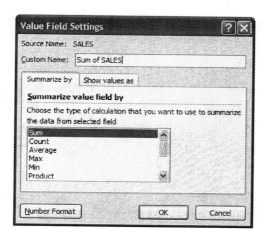

Extend the pivot table by dragging the list item DESCRIPTION to the Row Labels box. A more detailed pivot table appears in cells A3:B12, showing the breakdown of sales by brand name. Extend the pivot table again by dragging the list item STORE to the Column Labels box. The pivot table now shows a sales breakdown by both brand name and store, as shown in Figure 7.18.

Pivot tables can be modified easily after they are built. For example, we can use the filtering arrows in the row or column headings to limit our table to particular row and column entries. We can also edit the table using

FIGURE 7.18   Pivot Table
Showing Sales by Brand
Name and by Store Number

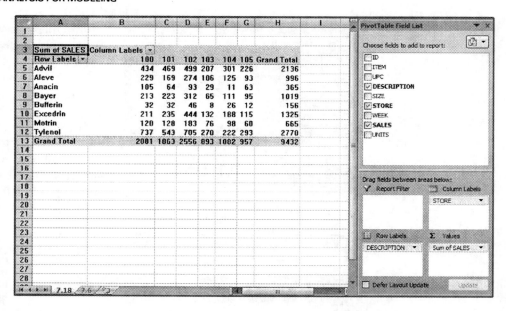

the Pivot Table Field List. (If the Pivot Table template and Field List are not visible, click anywhere in a pivot table to display them.) We can, for example, substitute WEEK for STORE in the Column Labels box to obtain a breakdown of sales by brand and by week.

> *Question:* In the Applicants database, how does the average GMAT score vary according to the round in which the application is filed?

The admissions process operates on a rolling basis, with a series of five decision periods (rounds). In developing a strategy for round-by-round selections, it is helpful to know whether there are systematic differences among the rounds. To probe this topic, we return to the Applicants database and set up a pivot table. The pivot table shows average GMAT score broken down by ROUND. Figure 7.19 displays the result. Evidently, there is a trend toward lower GMAT scores during the course of the overall admission period.

FIGURE 7.19   Pivot Table
Showing Average GMAT
Scores by Round

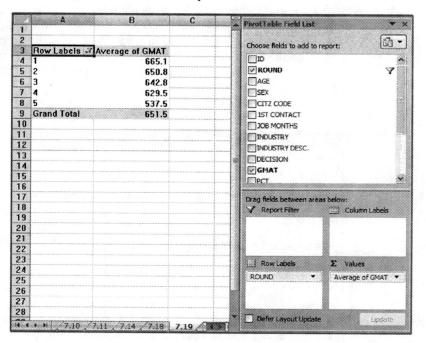

7.3 ANALYZING SAMPLE DATA

As explained earlier, our context for data analysis is determining parameters for our models. For example, we might want to determine the price parameter in the Advertising Budget model. If we have data on past prices—say, quarterly data for 10 years–we can expect to use this information to help determine the price parameter for next year. But next year's price could be different from any of the prices we have seen over the past 10 years. We think of the past data as a sample from some population of prices, just as next year's price is another sample, perhaps from the same or a related population.

We call the set of all possible values for a parameter the **population**. If we were to obtain data for the entire population, then we could build a comprehensive numerical picture of the parameter we are using in our model. Numerical features of populations are described by probability distributions, and, in modeling applications, we are often interested in three measures related to the probability distribution:

- The mean of the distribution
- The variance of the distribution
- A tail probability, or proportion, in the distribution

It is seldom the case, however, that we find ourselves with data covering an entire population. For one thing, the population may have infinite size, making it impossible to obtain all the data. But even with manageable populations, it may be prohibitively time-consuming or expensive to collect population data. Instead, we find ourselves working with information from a portion of the entire population; this portion is called the **sample**. In this situation, **statistics** are summary measures about the values in the sample, and the goal is to construct statistics that are representative of the overall population.

Terms Used in Sampling

Population: the set of all possible values of a parameter

Sample: a subset of the population

Statistic: a summary measure of sample values

■

When we were analyzing the Analgesics database, we assumed implicitly that our data were complete. In other words, the database contains data on *all* sales for the given stores and time periods. By contrast, the Executives database obviously does not cover all executives; it is a sample of 100 records drawn from a larger population.

The analysis of sample data provides a basis for estimating each of the three measures that help to describe a population (mean, variance, and tail probability). Ideally, the sample data points are drawn from the population of interest. As a practical matter, this may not be possible, but we might have a situation where the population from which samples are drawn is considered to be equivalent to the population of interest. For example, if we are interested in modeling customer demand for *next* month, we may use data on demand in the *previous* 12 months. At some level, observations from six months ago cannot be considered samples from the population of future demand levels, but there may be enough stability in the demand process that we can consider future populations to be essentially equivalent to six-month-old populations. This is an area where judgment is a crucial element in model building.

Samples can be generated in different ways, and the sampling process can determine whether the data are valuable or not. The most common forms of sampling are convenience sampling and random sampling. As its name implies, **convenience sampling** refers to a situation where we have easy access to information about a particular subset of the population. However, a convenience sample may not be representative. Suppose an insurance company wants a sample of customers to estimate family incomes, and it happens that one of its staff members is about to process the forms for all of this month's new customers. Can we use the income data from this group of customers as a sample? It is certainly convenient, because the processing will be taking place in any event. But new customers tend to be younger than the set of all customers, and their incomes tend to be lower. Thus, if we use the convenience sample to estimate income, we will be working with a sample that is not representative.

By contrast, **random sampling** refers to a situation where all values in the population have an equal chance of appearing in the sample. We assume random sampling in our examples unless we specify otherwise, because it is the simplest form of representative sampling. As an example, suppose we wish to take a random sample of 100 applicants from our Applicants database. One quick way to do so is to enter random numbers into the cells of column U by entering the random number function RAND() in the range U2:U2917. Then, using Paste Special to preserve the numbers generated, copy and paste the random values into column V. Next, sort the database by the values in column V. The first 100 applicants make up the desired random sample.

Classical methods in statistics deal with situations involving a random sample of observations. The data points in the sample are drawn from a population that can be described by a probability distribution, but the parameters of that distribution are unknown. Sampling and the analysis of sample information produce statistical data regarding the sample. Statistical data can be used in two ways—**descriptive** and **inferential**. Descriptive statistics summarize information in the sample. They have a limited purpose: they simply give a numerical picture of the observations. Inferential statistics have a different orientation. They use the information in the sample to make inferences about the population and thereby become the basis for estimating model parameters. However, we have to recognize that this type of estimation is subject to two important kinds of errors. First, there is **systematic error**, which occurs if the sample is not representative of the population. We can avoid systematic error by taking some time to design the sampling process and making sure that no unwanted patterns or biases occur in the sample. Second, there is **sampling error** (sometimes called statistical error), which occurs because the sample is merely a subset of the entire population. Because the subset is hardly ever a perfect representation of the population, sampling error is inevitable. The effects of sampling error can be mitigated (e.g., by taking larger samples), but they cannot be avoided entirely.

Sampling error is influenced by two factors—the size of the sample and the amount of variation in the population. Obviously, we can't do much about the latter; it is the nature of the population that we want to learn about, and we have to work with the extent of variation in it, whatever it may be. For example, there may be great variation in executive compensation, or there may be limited variation in applicants' GMAT scores. Whatever the case, we have to accept the level of variation in the population when we are devising our samples. By contrast, we can do something about the size of the sample. The larger the sample, the more it resembles the entire population, and so the smaller the chance for sampling error to occur. Moreover, when we're working on a computer and can obtain data in electronic form, it is only slightly more difficult to manage a large sample than a small one. Thus, a large sample can mitigate the effect of sampling error, even if we cannot overcome it completely.

Recall from our earlier remarks that it is a good idea to do some sensitivity analysis before collecting data. One of the outcomes of sensitivity analysis is insight into how precisely we need to determine certain parameters. From that information, we can estimate how large a sample we really need. The convenience of collecting data aside, we may often find that we need only a small sample to achieve the precision we desire.

7.4 ESTIMATING PARAMETERS: POINT ESTIMATES

As introduced in Chapter 2, parameters are numerical inputs, or uncontrollable variables, in a model. Parameters can be natural constants, such as the speed of sound or the density of water. These are numerical values that we would want to look up in a reference book. Parameters can also be quantitative phenomena in our environment, such as overhead rates, lead times, or process yields. These are numerical values that we might want to estimate from empirical data. When we are building a deterministic model, where we assume that all elements in the model are known with certainty, we want to use the most accurate values possible for our parameters. For such models, we are most likely to be interested in a single value to represent each parameter. When we are building a probabilistic model, and some parameters are described by probability distributions, we often want to estimate the means and variances of those distributions. The information on which estimates are based may come from a database or from a specialized study organized explicitly for the purpose of obtaining estimates. In either case, we can use standard statistical techniques to provide the estimates we seek.

A **point estimate** produces a single number that becomes our "best guess" for the value of the parameter. We then use this estimate in our model as the parameter's value. Following standard practice, we assume that the given data represent a random sample of observations. The ith observation in the sample has the value x_i, and the sample size is n. Three summary statistics for the sample are the sample average, the sample variance, and the sample standard deviation.

The **sample average** is calculated as

$$\bar{x} = \frac{1}{n} \sum_{i=1}^{n} x_i \tag{7.1}$$

The **sample variance** is calculated as

$$s^2 = \sum_{i=1}^{n} \frac{(x_i - \bar{x})^2}{n - 1} \tag{7.2}$$

and its square root is the **sample standard deviation**

$$s = \sqrt{\sum_{i=1}^{n} \frac{(x_i - \bar{x})^2}{n - 1}} \tag{7.3}$$

The sample average is the point estimate of the population mean. For example, in a production model, we might want to represent the time required for a product's final assembly. We might collect data on the 10 most recent assemblies to estimate the final assembly time. If we take the sample average of these 10 observations, using (7.1), that calculation gives us a point estimate of the assembly time to use in our model. The sample average is an estimate of the mean assembly time in the population.

The sample variance is the point estimate of the population variance. Consider an investment model in which we need to estimate the variance of week-to-week changes in a particular stock index. By creating a historical sample of the index and tracking its weekly changes, we can compute the sample variance as a point estimate, using (7.2), for the purposes of our model. The sample variance is an estimate of the variance of weekly values of the stock index in the population.

For purposes of illustration, we use our sample in the Executives database to estimate an average salary. If we select Data▶Analysis▶Data Analysis, we see a window listing a collection of Excel-based statistical analyses. (If the Data Analysis tool does not appear on the Analysis menu, load it by selecting Office Button▶Excel

FIGURE 7.20 The Descriptive Statistics Window

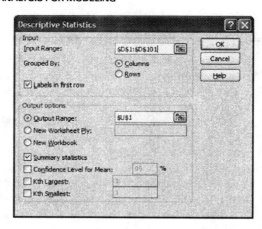

options ▶ Add-ins ▶ Analysis Toolpak.) If we select Descriptive Statistics, we see another window for this specific tool (see Figure 7.20). We select D1:D101 as the input range (because column D contains salaries) and cell U1 as the output range. Excel detects nonnumerical data in cell D1 unless we check the box for `Labels in first row`. When we click OK, Excel produces a standard table of descriptive statistics based on our sample, as shown in Figure 7.21. Some of the entries in this table involve advanced material beyond our present coverage, but a few of the items are worth noting. The sample average is listed as the Mean, with a value of 679.138. This result indicates that the average salary in our sample was slightly more than $679,000. The sample variance and the sample standard deviation are also shown as 118,307 and 343.9585, respectively. These calculations can also be made directly in a cell, using Excel's AVERAGE, VAR, and STDEV functions.

FIGURE 7.21 Descriptive Statistics for Executive Salaries

	T	U	V	W
1		SALARY		
2				
3		Mean	679.13806	
4		Standard Error	34.39584508	
5		Median	682.356	
6		Mode	750	
7		Standard Deviation	343.9584508	
8		Sample Variance	118307.4159	
9		Kurtosis	1.147135395	
10		Skewness	0.785424204	
11		Range	1908.296	
12		Minimum	91.704	
13		Maximum	2000	
14		Sum	67913.806	
15		Count	100	
16				

7.1 / 7.2 / 7.3

In some cases, we might be interested in **categorical**, or qualitative, information rather than numerical information. Examples might include good (versus defective) output items, in-the-money (versus worthless) stock options, or profitable (versus unprofitable) product introductions. We have two approaches for dealing with this kind of information. First, we can define the value x_i to be 1 or 0, according to whether the ith observation in the sample is, say, good or defective. Having created a quantitative measure out of the categorical information, we can use the above three formulas. A second approach is to use the proportion p observed in the sample as the summary statistic. Since this approach is often the most convenient, we treat the **sample proportion** as a fourth summary statistic of interest. We usually use p to denote the observed proportion in a sample. For example, we may be interested in the number of executives in our sample who received a bonus as part of their compensation. We can construct a small pivot table, based on column E in the Executives database, to verify that 81 of the 100 executives received bonuses that were larger than zero. Therefore, $p = 0.81$ is our sample proportion for positive bonuses. In the spirit of inferential statistics, the calculated proportion is an estimate of the proportion in the population.

7.5 ESTIMATING PARAMETERS: INTERVAL ESTIMATES

We can estimate parameters in two ways: with **point estimates** and with **interval estimates**. As we have seen, a point estimate is a single number that serves as the value of a parameter in our model. The interval estimate approach produces a range of values in which we are fairly sure that the parameter lies, in addition to a single-value point estimate. A range of values for a parameter allows us to perform sensitivity analysis in a systematic fashion, and it provides input for tornado charts or sensitivity tables, as described in Chapter 6.

7.5.1 Interval Estimates for the Mean

An interval estimate is expressed as the point estimate "plus or minus" some amount. In the case of our executive salaries, an interval estimate for the mean might be

$$679.138 \pm 58.525$$

In other words, the interval consists of a range on either side of the point estimate. The width of the range depends on how confident we wish to be at capturing the true value of the parameter. (Recall that, because of sampling error, the sample may not be perfectly representative of the population.) A wide range gives us considerable confidence that we've captured the true mean value, while a narrow range gives us less confidence.

We sometimes state an interval estimate in the form of a probability:

$$P(L \leq \mu \leq U) = 1 - \alpha$$

In this form, L and U represent the lower and upper limits of the interval, and $1 - \alpha$ (usually a large percentage) represents the **confidence level**. The symbol μ represents the true value of the parameter. The confidence level gives the long-run probability that the interval contains the true value of the parameter we're estimating. In other words, if we were to repeat the sampling process many times, about $(1 - \alpha)$ percent of our confidence intervals would contain the true value. However, given any one estimate, either the true value is within the confidence interval or it is not, with probability 1 or 0. In the case of our salary estimate, the interval estimate could be stated as

$$P(679 - 58 \leq \text{true mean salary} \leq 679 + 58) = 1 - \alpha$$

We discuss below how to determine the value of α.

To appreciate the reasoning that lies behind interval estimates, we return briefly to sampling theory. (See Appendix for background information on sampling theory.) Suppose, for the moment, that we are working with a population that is described by a normal probability model with mean μ and standard deviation σ. Imagine that we take repeated samples of n items from that population and calculate the sample average each time. How will this collection of sample averages be distributed? The answer is that the sample averages also follow a normal distribution, with a mean of μ and a variance of σ^2/n. As a specific illustration, suppose we start with a normal population with a mean of 100 and standard deviation of 10. In our experiment, we take samples of size 25 and calculate the sample average for each one. Figure 7.22

FIGURE 7.22 Simulated Distribution of Sample Averages Drawn from a Normal Population

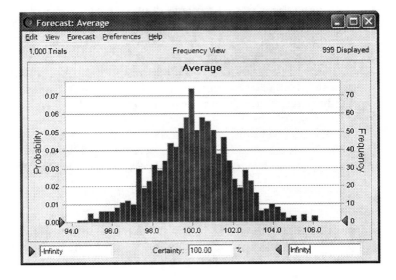

shows the sample averages in a histogram. Note that the histogram resembles the shape of a normal distribution and that, although most of the *population* lies between 70 and 130, the *sample averages* cluster in a much narrower range, from about 94 to 106. Sample averages show far less variability than the population they are drawn from because high outcomes in the sample tend to be balanced by low ones.

We use the term **standard error** to refer to the standard deviation of some function being used to provide an estimate. Here, the sample average (or sample mean) provides our estimate. Its standard deviation is called the **standard error of the mean**, defined as the square root of the variance of the sample average, or

$$\sigma_{\bar{x}} = \sigma/\sqrt{n}$$

We assume here that σ is known; later, we discuss how to proceed when it, too, must be estimated.

For a normal distribution, the *z*-score measures the number of standard deviations (in this case, standard deviations of the sample average) away from the mean. Here, the z-score corresponding to any particular sample average is the following:

$$z = \frac{\bar{x} - \mu}{\sigma_{\bar{x}}} = \frac{\bar{x} - \mu}{\sigma/\sqrt{n}} \tag{7.4}$$

The z-score tells us how many standard errors we are from the mean. For example, 90 percent of the sample averages will have z-scores between -1.64 and $+1.64$. In other words, they differ from μ by at most 1.64 standard errors. Stated another way, the chances that the sample average will fall no more than 1.64 standard errors from the true mean are 90 percent. In our example, the standard error is 2.0 ($\sigma/\sqrt{n} = 10/\sqrt{25} = 2.0$), so we expect 90 percent of the sample averages to fall between 96.72 and 103.28, which is confirmed in Figure 7.22.

Now imagine that we run the same experiment (calculating a sample average for a sample of size n), but without knowing the probability model that describes the original population. Even if the population does not follow a normal distribution, the sample averages will still follow a normal distribution with mean μ and variance σ^2/n, as long as n is sufficiently large. A value of $n > 30$ is considered large enough for the normal distribution to hold, but n can be a good deal smaller if the original population resembles the normal. (A value as small as $n = 6$ is large enough if the population is symmetric with a single peak.) Thus, for large samples, we can conclude that the chances are 90 percent that the sample average will fall no more than 1.64 standard errors from the true mean. The figure of 90 percent is the **confidence level**, and it helps determine the size of the relevant interval.

To continue our illustrative experiment, we take samples of size 25 from a uniform distribution with a range from 80 to 120. Again, we calculate sample averages and construct their histogram, as shown in Figure 7.23. As expected, the form of the histogram resembles the normal distribution. In addition, the standard error in this case turns out to be about 1.15, so that we expect 90 percent of the sample averages to fall between 96.1 and 103.8, which is confirmed in Figure 7.23.

To calculate a range for an interval estimate, then, we begin by expressing the confidence level as a percentage. A typical confidence level would be 90 percent, but other levels commonly used are 95 percent and 99 percent. Using (7.4), we can obtain the upper and lower limits of a 90 percent confidence interval for the mean:

$$\bar{x} \pm z(\sigma/\sqrt{n}) \tag{7.5}$$

The z-value in this formula corresponds to a tail probability of 0.05 in a normal distribution. (Including 90 percent of the area under a standard normal distribution in a particular interval is equivalent to 5 percent of the area in each tail.) The numerical value corresponding to a 90 percent confidence interval is $z = 1.64$, which can be verified using the Excel formula NORMSINV(0.95).

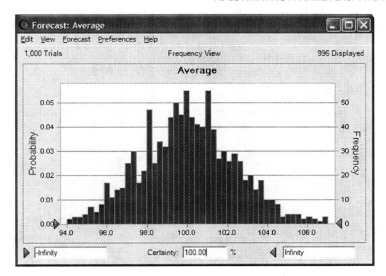

EXCEL TIP
Calculating
z-values

Excel's standard normal inverse function computes a *z*-value from a value of the cumulative distribution function (see Appendix). Because the confidence interval of 90 percent corresponds to 5 percent in each tail, the cumulative distribution function corresponds to 0.95 in this case. The Excel formula returns a value of approximately 1.645. Some common *z*-values are summarized in the table below:

confidence level	90%	95%	99%
z-value	1.645	1.960	2.576

■

We mentioned earlier that formula (7.5) for the interval estimate assumes that the standard deviation σ in the underlying population is known. But this will rarely be the case. When the standard deviation is not known, its value also must be estimated from the sample data. To do so, we replace σ by its point estimate, the sample standard deviation *s*, and then we can use (7.5), provided that our sample is larger than about $n = 30$. (When *n* is less than 30, other approaches are needed that are beyond the level of this book.) In the case of our sample of executive salaries, we have $s = 343.9585$. The form of a 90 percent confidence interval for the mean becomes

$$\bar{x} \pm z(s/\sqrt{n}) \tag{7.6}$$

Thus, our interval estimate for the population mean becomes

$$679.138 \pm 1.64(34.396) = 679.138 \pm 56.409$$

The 90 percent confidence interval for the true mean extends from \$622,729 to \$735,547. (In Excel's Descriptive Statistics tool, there is an option to calculate the half-width of the confidence interval and include it in the summary table. When Excel makes this calculation, it does not use the normal approximation mentioned earlier for sample sizes above 30, but instead uses a more precise formula. In the case of our example, the half-width is reported as 57.111, as compared to the approximate value of 56.409.)

Thinking back to our discussion of tornado charts in Chapter 6, an interval estimate calculated from (7.6) could provide a useful guideline for the high and low values of the parameter. If one of the parameters in our model is an executive's salary, then we can use \$679,138 as a point estimate; when we perform sensitivity analysis, we can use upper and lower limits of $622,729 and $735,547 to generate a tornado chart.

7.5.2 Interval Estimates for a Proportion

The confidence interval for a proportion takes a form very similar to that of the confidence interval for the mean. When we estimate the sample proportion p, the interval estimate takes the form

$$p \pm z\sqrt{\frac{p(1 - p)}{n}} \tag{7.7}$$

Usually, a sample size of at least 50 is needed for this formula to be reliable.

As an example, recall that 81 percent of our sample of executives received bonuses. The 90 percent confidence interval for this estimate becomes $0.81 \pm 1.64(0.0392)$ or 0.81 ± 0.06. The limits of the confidence interval are therefore 75 percent and 87 percent. The true proportion, of course, either lies in this interval or does not. But if we were to take many samples, we would capture the true proportion with (7.7) about 90 percent of the time.

7.5.3 Sample-Size Determination

Formulas for interval estimates—such as (7.5), (7.6), and (7.7)—express the range of the interval as a function of the sample size n. To this point, we have started with a sample of size n and proceeded to calculate an interval estimate. However, if we know the precision we want, we can use this same relationship to calculate the minimum necessary sample size. For example, suppose we wish to estimate the mean of a sample to within a range of $\pm R$. We can manipulate (7.5) algebraically to obtain

$$n = (z\sigma/R)^2 \tag{7.8}$$

This formula applies to the conditions associated with (7.5): sampling from a normal distribution with a known variance. When the standard deviation is unknown, we simply substitute its estimate. But where do we find an estimate if we haven't yet taken the sample? The solution is to take a fairly small sample (say, 10 or 20) to get an initial estimate s of the standard deviation, and then use (7.8), with s in place of σ, to determine more precisely how large the sample size should be.

For example, if we take our entire sample of 100 executives, we estimate the standard deviation of salaries to be 343.958. If we wish to estimate the mean salary to within $25,000 with 90 percent confidence, then the necessary sample size, from (7.8), must be

$$n = [(1.64)(343.958)/25]^2 = 509$$

Therefore, to produce an estimate with the desired precision, we need a sample more than five times as large as what we have. This assumes, of course, that our original estimate of the standard deviation is accurate.

The same reasoning applies to the case of estimating a proportion. Because the formula in (7.7) involves the sample size, we can solve for the minimum necessary sample size in terms of the proportion p. The algebra leads us to the following sample-size formula:

$$n = z^2 p(1 - p)/R^2 \tag{7.9}$$

If we have only a rough idea of the unknown proportion p, we can use that value in the formula, but if we have absolutely no idea at all about p, we can still proceed. The term $p(1 - p)$ is maximized when $p = 0.5$. So a conservative value would be obtained by substituting this value into (7.9) to obtain

$$n = (z/2)^2/R^2 \tag{7.10}$$

If we wish to estimate the proportion of executives who receive bonuses to within 0.02, at 90 percent confidence, then (7.9) tells us that we would need a sample size of 1,035, based on our estimate of the proportion p as 0.81. The more conservative formula in (7.10) prescribes a sample size of 1,681, using $p = 0.5$.

7.6 SUMMARY

Our premise in this chapter is that modeling is the central task; data collection and analysis support the modeling task where appropriate. Nevertheless, when early sensitivity testing indicates that certain parameters must be estimated precisely, we turn to data analysis for locating relevant information and for estimating model parameters.

The process of finding facts in data is aided by a facility with Excel and in particular with its database capabilities. As more data sets become available through public sources or on the Internet, it will become more valuable to be able to probe data sets quickly and intelligently. Excel provides an array of commands for searching, sorting, filtering, and tabulating data. Business analysts should be familiar with these tools in order to use data intelligently in spreadsheet modeling.

The basic numerical task involving data is to estimate model parameters. For this purpose, Excel provides statistically oriented tools that help make the process convenient. The Data Analysis tool for calculating descriptive statistics enables rapid construction of point estimates and interval estimates from raw data.

SUGGESTED READINGS

The popularity of spreadsheets, both in education and in industry, has influenced the writing of textbooks in several areas, including statistics. The list below contains textbooks on basic statistics, mostly with a classical treatment of the subject, except that they rely on a spreadsheet perspective.

Albright, S. C., W. L. Winston, and C. Zappe. 2006. *Data Analysis and Decision Making with Microsoft Excel.* 3rd ed. Mason, OH: South-Western.

Evans, J. R. 2007. *Statistics, Data Analysis, and Decision Modeling.* 3rd ed. Upper Saddle River, NJ: Prentice-Hall.

Levine, D. M., D. Stephan, T. C. Krehbiel, and M. L. Berenson. 2004. *Statistics for Managers using Microsoft Excel.* 4th ed. Upper Saddle River, NJ: Prentice-Hall.

Pelosi, M. K., and T. M. Sandifer. 2002. *Doing Statistics for Business with Excel.* 2nd ed. New York: John Wiley and Sons.

EXERCISES

1. The database Dish.xlsx contains a transaction history describing more than 4,000 purchases of detergent at a number of stores in a grocery chain over a period of several weeks.

a. Compile a pivot table that gives a tabulation of sales (in cases) by brand (Dove, Sunlight, and so on).

b. Compile a pivot table that gives a tabulation of sales broken down by brand and by week.

c. Compile a pivot table that gives a tabulation of sales broken down by brand, by week, and by store.

d. Compile a pivot table that gives a tabulation of the number of ounces purchased broken down by brand and by size of container. What is the sales volume in ounces for each brand?

2. The database Tissue.xlsx contains a transaction history describing more than 3,700 purchases of facial tissues at a number of stores in a grocery chain over a period of several weeks.

a. Compile a pivot table that gives a tabulation of the number of units sold by brand.

b. Compile a pivot table that gives a tabulation of sales units broken down by brand and by week.

c. Compile a pivot table that gives a tabulation of sales units broken down by brand, by week, and by store.

d. Compile a pivot table that gives a tabulation of sales units broken down by brand and by size of container. What is the sales volume in ounces for each brand?

3. The database Applicants.xlsx contains a description of an MBA applicant pool for an unspecified year in the 1990s. For each of the following requirements, create a separate worksheet and extract the data from the original database.

a. Among enrolling students, what is the average GMAT score? What is the average in the applicant pool as a whole?

b. How many in the applicant pool represented Financial Services in terms of job background? What was their average age? What was their average work experience (months)? What was their average GMAT score?

c. How many in the applicant pool represented Consulting in terms of job background? What was their average age? What was their average work experience (months)? What was their average GMAT score?

d. What proportion of the applicant pool had two or more degrees?

4. The database Population.xlsx contains data on the populations of the 50 states from 1990 to 1999. For each of the following requirements, create a separate worksheet and extract the data from the original database.

a. Sort the states by population in 1999, from highest to lowest.

b. Were the 10 states with the highest population the same in 1999 as in 1990?

c. Which state had the largest percentage increase in population from 1990 to 1999?

d. Which states had populations of more than 2 million or less than 1 million in 1995?

5. The database Executives.xlsx contains salary and company data on 100 executives. For each of the following requirements, create a separate worksheet and extract the data from the original database.

a. Among the top five executives in terms of Salary, how many work in the oil industry?

b. What is the total compensation (salary, bonus, and other) for each of the executives who rank in the top 10 on this dimension?

c. How many executives work for companies in California or New York and have sales less than 4,000?

d. How many executives who work for companies in California or New York have sales less than 4,000 or assets above 10,000?

6. The database Applicants.xlsx contains a description of an MBA applicant pool for an unspecified year in the 1990s. For each of the following requirements, create a separate worksheet and extract the data from the original database.

a. What percentage of the applicants were male?

b. How old was the youngest male applicant?

c. What was the GMAT score of the female with the highest score?

d. How many Economics majors are there among these applicants?

e. How many male Economics majors are there with Nonprofit experience?

f. How many males are there over the age of 28 who contacted the school with a phone call or letter?

7. Your company is changing its name, and you've been asked to study the impact of a name change announcement on the subsequent return generated by the firm's stock. In a sample of 400 companies that have made such announcements, you discover that over the 28-day period after a name change announcement, the average company experiences a 17 percent increase in price, with a standard deviation of 8 percent.

a. What is a 90 percent confidence interval for the mean stock price change for companies announcing a name change?

b. The range from 16 percent to 18 percent would constitute what (percentage) confidence interval for the mean change?

c. Do the data suggest that there is at least a 75 percent chance that a company's stock price will go up after a name change announcement?

8. Five years ago, an automobile manufacturer started offering an extended warranty to buyers of its sport-utility vehicle. The extended warranty covered defects occurring after the initial three-year warranty expired. Of the 10,000 people who bought the sport-utility vehicle in the first year of the program, 15 percent purchased the extended warranty.

In the Warranty Department, you have recently received data on a random sample of 200 of the cars sold in the first year that the extended warranty was available. For this sample, the average extended-warranty expenditure per car for the one-year period after the initial warranty elapsed was $350 with a standard deviation of $100.

a. What is a 95 percent confidence interval for the mean one-year extended-warranty expenditure per automobile?

b. At its introduction, the extended warranty was priced at $225 per year per automobile. Compute a 95 percent confidence interval for the one-year profitability of the extended warranty.

c. How large a sample would the Warranty Department require if it wanted its 95 percent confidence interval for the mean warranty expenditure to be no more than ±$5?

9. The Luxor Computer Company plans to introduce a pyramid-shaped desktop computer. The company is interested in the proportion of prospective customers who find the unusual shape a positive selling point. In a random sample of 350 potential customers, 203 of the respondents indicated that the shape was a positive selling point.

a. What is an estimate of the proportion of prospective customers who find the unusual shape a positive selling point?

b. What is a 90 percent confidence interval for the proportion of prospective customers who find the unusual shape a positive selling point?

c. How many prospective customers would have to be queried for Luxor to be 90 percent certain that its estimated proportion was within five percent of the true value?

10. The number of staff personnel needed to handle patients at a medical center is determined by the mean time that patients must wait before being attended to by a physician. For a random sample of 100 previously recorded emergencies, the sample mean waiting time was 72 minutes, with a standard deviation of 28 minutes.

a. What is a 50 percent confidence interval for the actual mean waiting time?

b. What is a 99 percent confidence interval for the actual mean waiting time?

11. Oxbridge University is contemplating a policy under which they would pay employees to not bring their vehicles to campus. Instead of paying an annual fee for on-campus parking, employees would receive a rebate from the university, provided that they found alternative means of getting back and forth to work. Since this idea is unusual, the university wants to estimate the proportion of its employees who would sign up. When the option was offered to a random sample of 40 employees, 5 signed up.

a. What is the estimated proportion that will sign up? What is the estimated standard deviation of the proportion that will sign up?

b. What is a 95 percent confidence interval for the proportion that will sign up?

c. How large a sample size is required to obtain a 95 percent confidence interval of ±0.05?

12. An engineer working on the auto assembly line is preparing to estimate the mean time required to install a dashboard. Assuming a required standard deviation of 10 seconds in the estimated mean, determine the sample size under the following conditions:

a. The desired confidence level of being in error by no more than one second (in either direction) is 0.99.

b. The desired confidence level is 0.95 for a tolerable error of one second.

c. A confidence level of 0.99 is desired with a tolerable error of two seconds. How does the sample size you obtain compare with your answer to (a)?

d. Repeat (a), assuming that $\sigma = 20$ seconds. By how much does the sample size decrease?

11 Linear Programming

11.1 INTRODUCTION

In Chapter 10, we introduced optimization with Solver, and we focused on nonlinear programming. The nonlinear solver is the default algorithm in Premium Solver,[1] and it can be applied to a variety of optimization problems. *Linear* programming is a special case for which certain mathematical conditions must hold, but it is much more widely used in practice than nonlinear programming. Because of the mathematical structure of a linear program, it is possible to harness a more powerful algorithm (called the *simplex method*) for linear problems than for nonlinear problems, and we can accommodate larger numbers of variables and constraints. In this chapter, we cover the use of the linear solver, and we examine several examples that illustrate the wide applicability of linear programming models. In the 50 years or so that computers have been available for this kind of decision support, linear programming has proven to be a valuable tool for understanding business decisions.

As in the previous chapter, our optimization models contain a set of decision variables, an objective function, and a set of constraints. But in the case of linear models, we can impose additional design guidelines on our worksheets that lead to a more standardized approach than we were able to adopt with nonlinear models. These additional guidelines help us develop models efficiently, debug our models quickly, and communicate our results effectively.

11.1.1 Linearity

The term *linear* in linear programs refers to a feature of the objective function and the constraints. A linear function exhibits three properties:

- Additivity
- Proportionality
- Divisibility

By **additive,** we mean that the contribution from one decision gets added to (or sometimes subtracted from) the contributions of other decisions. In an additive function, we can separate the contributions that come from each decision. By **proportional,** we mean that the contribution from any given decision grows in proportion to the value of the corresponding decision variable. When a decision variable doubles, then its contribution to the objective also doubles. By **divisible,** we mean that a fractional decision variable is meaningful.

As an example, suppose that we compute profit from the function

$$Profit = (Unit\ Revenue) \times (Quantity\ Sold) - (Unit\ Cost) \times (Quantity\ Purchased)$$

where *Unit Revenue* and *Unit Cost* are parameters known to be 100 and 60, respectively, whereas *Quantity Sold* and *Quantity Purchased* are decisions, which

---

[1]**Premium Solver for Education** is an advanced version of the Standard Solver in Excel and is available to users of this book. It should be installed before proceeding with this chapter.

we'll denote by x and y, respectively. In symbols, we can simply write:

$$\text{Profit} = 100x - 60y$$

where x and y are decision variables. Note that *Profit* separates into two additive terms, which we can call total revenue and total cost. The total revenue term ($100x$) is proportional to the decision variable *Quantity Sold*. Likewise, the total cost term ($60y$) is proportional to the decision variable *Quantity Purchased*. Fractional values for the decisions could well make sense. Suppose, for example, that the product is fuel and that the unit of measurement is gallons. Then certainly a fractional value such as $x = 72.4$ is plausible. Even if we think of discrete items, such as televisions, the unit of measurement could be dozens, in which case a fractional value such as $x = 15.5$ would also be meaningful. In summary, our *Profit* function exhibits all three of the linearity properties.

We turn now to an algebraic perspective. When we have several decision variables, we may give them letter names, such as x, y, and z, or we may number them and denote them by x_1, x_2, x_3, and so on. When there are n decision variables, we can write a linear objective function as follows:

$$z = c_1x_1 + c_2x_2 + \cdots + c_nx_n$$

where z represents the value of the objective function, and the c's are a set of given parameters called **objective function coefficients.** Note that the x's appear in separate terms (i.e., they are additive), they appear with exponents of 1 (i.e., their contributions to the objective function are proportional), and they are not restricted to integers (i.e., they are divisible). In a worksheet, we recognize the structure of z as a calculation that could be made by the SUMPRODUCT function. Thus, for spreadsheet purposes, we can recognize a linear function if it consists of a sum of pairwise products—where one of the pairs in each product is a parameter and the other is a decision variable.

For a constraint to be linear, its left-hand side must be a linear function. In other words, the left-hand side can be represented by a SUMPRODUCT function made up of a sum of pairwise products, where one element of each product is a parameter and the other is a decision variable. In most cases, we will actually use the SUMPRO-DUCT formula, although, as we will see in the next chapter, we sometimes prefer the SUM formula.

EXCEL TIP *The* *SUMPRODUCT* *Function*	The SUMPRODUCT function in Excel takes the pairwise products of two sets of numbers and sums the products. This operation is sometimes called the scalar product. For our purposes, the form of the function is the following: SUMPRODUCT(*Array1, Array2*) • *Array1* references the first set of numbers. • *Array2* references the second set of numbers. The two arrays must have identical layouts. Specifically, if *Array1* comprises a set of numbers in a single row, then *Array2* must also be a set of numbers in a single row. Both arrays must be of the same size. Suppose, for example, that we had three items with unit prices of 2, 3, and 4 and with sales volumes of u, v, and w, respectively. Then total revenue would come to $2u + 3v + 4w$, which could be computed from the formula SUMPRODUCT({2,3,4},{u,v,w}). When the volumes are $u = 30$, $v = 33$, and $w = 36$, the total revenue function takes on the value 303. ∎

11.1.2 Simplex Algorithm

The solution procedure for linear models is referred to as the **simplex algorithm,** or the linear solver. The simplex algorithm employs a strategy that shares some of the features of hill climbing, but it is able to exploit the special properties of linearity to find an optimal solution efficiently. For instance, if we can imagine a diamond that represents the set of feasible decision variables, then the simplex algorithm can be viewed as a procedure for moving along the edges of the diamond's surface until an optimal point is encountered. The simplex algorithm does not require a starting point in the worksheet; or to put it another way, it determines its own starting solution. This means that Solver ignores the initial information in the changing cells when solving a linear model. Once the solution procedure finds a **feasible solution**—one that satisfies all the constraints—it proceeds from there to an optimal solution. An **optimal solution** must satisfy all constraints, and its objective function must equal the best value that can be achieved. Moreover, the simplex method *guarantees* that it will find a global optimum (if there is one), and in that sense, the simplex method is completely reliable. We cannot say the same for the GRG algorithm except in special circumstances.

In mathematical terms, linear models are a special case of nonlinear models, and in principle, the GRG algorithm could be used as a solution procedure for the examples we present here. However, the simplex algorithm is especially suited to linear models, and it avoids numerical problems that sometimes affect the performance of the GRG algorithm. The linear solver is the preferred choice for any linear programming problem.

Linear programming models come in many sizes and shapes, but there are only a few standard types. It is helpful, therefore, to think in terms of a few basic structures when learning how to build and interpret linear programming models. In this chapter and the next, we present four different types. Most linear programming models are, in fact, combinations of these four types, but understanding the building blocks helps to clarify the key modeling concepts. In our framework, the four types are

- Allocation models
- Covering models
- Blending models
- Network models

We cover network models separately in Chapter 12.

11.2 ALLOCATION MODELS

The allocation model calls for maximizing an objective (usually profit) subject to less-than constraints on capacity. Consider the Veerman Furniture Company as an example.

EXAMPLE
Veerman Furniture Company

Veerman Furniture Company makes three kinds of office furniture: chairs, desks, and tables. Each product requires some labor in the parts fabrication department, the assembly department, and the shipping department. The furniture is sold through a regional distributor, which has estimated the maximum potential sales for each product in the coming quarter. Finally, the accounting department has provided some data showing the profit contributions on each product. The decision problem is to determine the product mix—that is, to maximize Veerman's profit for the quarter by choosing production quantities for the chairs, desks, and tables. The data shown in the accompanying table summarize the parameters of the problem:

Department	Hours per Unit			Hours Available
	Chairs	Desks	Tables	
Fabrication	4	6	2	1,850
Assembly	3	5	7	2,400
Shipping	3	2	4	1,500
Demand Potential	360	300	100	
Profit	$15	$24	$18	

11.2.1 Formulation

As recommended in the previous chapter, we approach the formulation of the optimization model by asking three basic questions. To determine the decision variables, we ask, "What must be decided?" The answer is the product mix, so we define decision variables as the number of chairs, desks, and tables produced. For the purposes of notation, we use C, D, and T to represent the number of chairs, desks, and tables in the product mix, respectively.

Next we ask, "What measure can we use to compare alternative sets of decision variables?" To choose between two different product mixes, we would calculate the total profit contribution for each one and choose the higher profit. To calculate profit, we add the profit from chairs, from desks, and from tables. Thus, an algebraic expression for total profit is:

$$\text{Profit} = 15C + 24D + 18T$$

To identify the model's constraints, we ask, "What restrictions limit our choice of decision variables?" In this scenario, there are two kinds of limitations: one due to production capacity and the other due to demand potential. In words, a production capacity constraint states that the number of hours *consumed* in the fabrication department must be less than or equal to the number of hours *available*. In symbols, we write:

Fabrication hours consumed $= 4C + 6D + 2T \leq 1{,}850$ (Fabrication hours available)

Similar constraints hold for the assembly and shipping departments:

Assembly hours consumed $= 3C + 5D + 7T \leq 2{,}400$ (Assembly hours available)

Shipping hours consumed $= 3C + 2D + 4T \leq 1{,}500$ (Shipping hours available)

Another type of constraint relates to demands. We require that the number of chairs *produced* must be less than or equal to the estimated demand *potential* for chairs. In symbols, we write:

Chairs produced $= C \leq 360$ (Chair demand potential)

Similar constraints hold for desks and tables:

Desks produced $= D \leq 300$ (Desk demand potential)

Table produced $= T \leq 100$ (Table demand potential)

We now have six constraints that describe the restrictions limiting our choice of decision variables C, D, and T. The entire model, stated in algebraic terms, reads as follows:

$$\text{Maximize } z = 15C + 24D + 18T$$

subject to

$$4C + 6D + 2T \leq 1{,}850$$
$$3C + 5D + 7T \leq 2{,}400$$
$$3C + 2D + 4T \leq 1{,}500$$
$$C \qquad\qquad \leq 360$$
$$\qquad D \qquad \leq 300$$
$$\qquad\qquad T \leq 100$$

11.2.2 Spreadsheet Model

This algebraic statement reflects a widely used format for linear programs. Variables appear in columns, constraints appear as rows, and the objective function appears as a special row at the top of the model. We will adopt this layout as a standard for spreadsheet display.

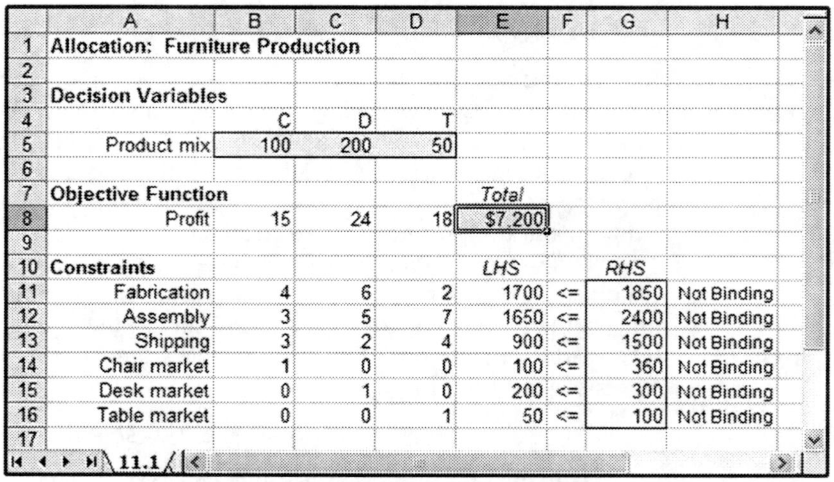

	A	B	C	D	E	F	G	H
1	**Allocation: Furniture Production**							
2								
3	**Decision Variables**							
4		C	D	T				
5	Product mix	100	200	50				
6								
7	**Objective Function**				*Total*			
8	Profit	15	24	18	$7,200			
9								
10	**Constraints**				*LHS*		*RHS*	
11	Fabrication	4	6	2	1700	<=	1850	Not Binding
12	Assembly	3	5	7	1650	<=	2400	Not Binding
13	Shipping	3	2	4	900	<=	1500	Not Binding
14	Chair market	1	0	0	100	<=	360	Not Binding
15	Desk market	0	1	0	200	<=	300	Not Binding
16	Table market	0	0	1	50	<=	100	Not Binding
17								

FIGURE 11.1 Spreadsheet Model for the Veerman Furniture Company Example

A worksheet for this allocation problem appears in Figure 11.1*. Notice the three modules in the worksheet:

- A highlighted row for the decision variables (B5:D5)
- A highlighted single cell for the objective function value (E8)
- A set of constraint relationships (rows 11–16).

In the Constraints module, cells containing the symbol $\leq$ have no function in the operation of the worksheet; they are intended as a visual aid, helping to convey a sense of the information in the constraints. We place them between the left-hand-side value of the constraint (a formula) and the right-hand-side value (a parameter). To the right of each constraint parameter, we construct a cell that displays the status of the constraint. In cell H11, for example, the formula is `IF(E11=G11, "Binding", "Not Binding")`. The constraint is **binding** if it is satisfied as an equality; otherwise, it is nonbinding. (Although this status indicator is a desirable feature of linear programming models for most beginners, we will often omit it, so that we can focus on the information in the constraints themselves.)

Figure 11.2 shows the formulas in this model. Note here that, aside from labels, the model contains only two kinds of cells: those containing a number (either a parameter or a decision variable) and those containing a SUMPRODUCT formula.

The set of values for the decision variables in Figure 11.1 was an arbitrary one. We could try different sets of three values in order to see whether we could come up with a good product mix by trial and error. Such an attempt might also be a useful debugging step, to provide some assurance that the model is correct. For example, suppose we start by fixing the number of desks and tables at zero and varying the number of chairs. For fabrication capacity, chairs consume 4 hours each, and there are 1,850 hours available, so we could put 1,850/4 = 462.5 chairs

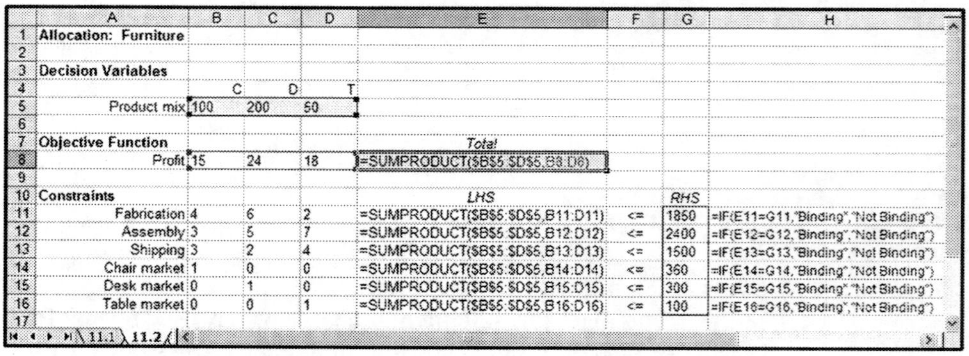

	A	B	C	D	E	F	G	H
1	**Allocation: Furniture**							
2								
3	**Decision Variables**							
4		C	D	T				
5	Product mix	100	200	50				
6								
7	**Objective Function**				*Total*			
8	Profit	15	24	18	=SUMPRODUCT($B$5:$D$5,B8:D8)			
9								
10	**Constraints**				*LHS*		*RHS*	
11	Fabrication	4	6	2	=SUMPRODUCT($B$5:$D$5,B11:D11)	<=	1850	=IF(E11=G11,"Binding","Not Binding")
12	Assembly	3	5	7	=SUMPRODUCT($B$5:$D$5,B12:D12)	<=	2400	=IF(E12=G12,"Binding","Not Binding")
13	Shipping	3	2	4	=SUMPRODUCT($B$5:$D$5,B13:D13)	<=	1500	=IF(E13=G13,"Binding","Not Binding")
14	Chair market	1	0	0	=SUMPRODUCT($B$5:$D$5,B14:D14)	<=	360	=IF(E14=G14,"Binding","Not Binding")
15	Desk market	0	1	0	=SUMPRODUCT($B$5:$D$5,B15:D15)	<=	300	=IF(E15=G15,"Binding","Not Binding")
16	Table market	0	0	1	=SUMPRODUCT($B$5:$D$5,B16:D16)	<=	100	=IF(E16=G16,"Binding","Not Binding")
17								

FIGURE 11.2 Formulas in the Veerman Furniture Company Worksheet

*To download spreadsheets for this chapter, go to the Student Companion Site at www.wiley.com/college/powell.

into the mix (that is, into cell B5), and the result would be feasible for the first constraint. However, we can see immediately—by comparing LHS and RHS values—that this solution violates the ceiling on chair demand. So we can reduce the number of chairs to 360, which will give us a feasible product mix and a profit of $5,400. (Recall that a feasible solution must satisfy *all* constraints.) Keeping the number of chairs fixed, we can now add desks to the product mix (by entering a number into cell C5). Using trial and error (or Excel's Goal Seek tool), we can determine that it is possible to raise the number of desks to 68, achieving a profit of $7,032. However, this choice consumes all of the remaining fabrication capacity, leaving no room for tables in the product mix. Similar kinds of explorations, with other values of the decision variables, can help us confirm that the model is working properly and give us a feel for the profit that might be achievable. Although we will not discuss this step as we build other models in this chapter, we wouldn't skip it unless we were dealing with a familiar type of problem.

11.2.3 Optimization

Once we are satisfied that the model is valid, we proceed to the optimization procedure. We invoke Solver, and in the Solver Parameters window, we specify:

Target cell	E8 (maximize)
Changing cells	B5:D5
Constraints	E11:E16 ≤ G11:G16

Note that in this last step, we reference parameters that have been entered in the worksheet. We usually do *not* enter the right-hand side constants in the Add Constraint window, even though Solver permits us to do so.

We select the linear solver (Standard LP Simplex) from the pull-down menu in the Solver Parameters window (see Figure 11.3). Next, we proceed to the Options menu and check the box for Assume Non-Negative, as in Figure 11.4. Our decision variables will be meaningful in this model only if they are nonnegative.

Before running Solver, we should create some hypotheses about the solution. For example,

- Do we expect the optimal solution to call for all three products?
- Will the optimal solution consume all of the available hours?
- Should desks, which have the highest profit margin, be produced at the maximum amount the market allows?

As we mentioned earlier, this is an excellent opportunity to test our intuition by posing and trying to answer such questions.

As we see in Figure 11.5, the optimal solution calls for no chairs, 275 desks, and 100 tables. Evidently, the profit margin on chairs is not sufficiently attractive for us to want to devote scarce resources to their production. The maximum profit contribution is $8,400, and the two binding constraints are fabrication hours and the demand ceiling

FIGURE 11.3 Solver Parameters Window

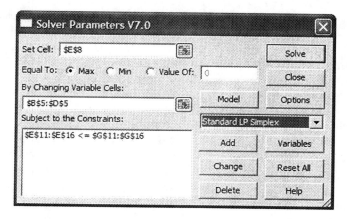

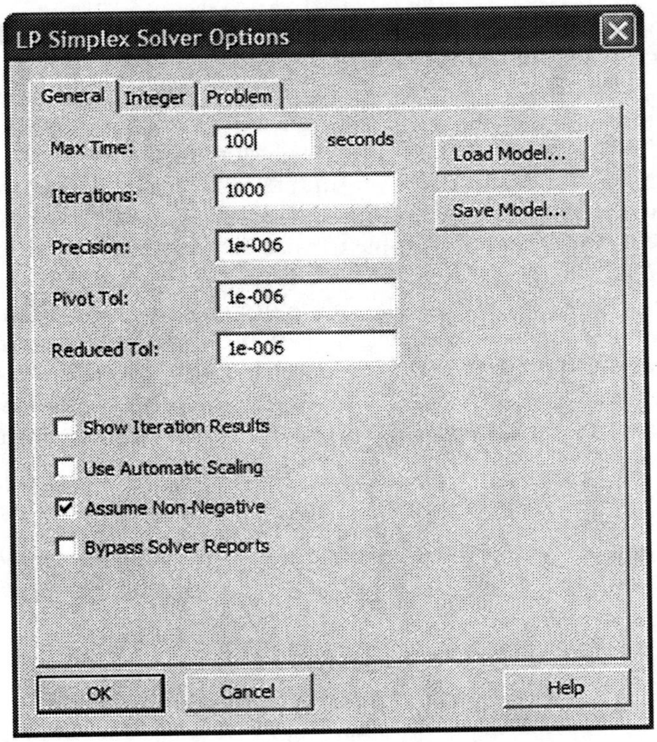

FIGURE 11.4 Solver Options Window

FIGURE 11.5 Optimal Solution for the Veerman Furniture Company Model

	A	B	C	D	E	F	G	H
1	**Allocation: Furniture Production**							
2								
3	**Decision Variables**							
4			C	D	T			
5	Product mix	0	275	100				
6								
7	**Objective Function**				*Total*			
8	Profit	15	24	18	$8,400			
9								
10	**Constraints**				*LHS*		*RHS*	
11	Fabrication	4	6	2	1850	<=	1850	Binding
12	Assembly	3	5	7	2075	<=	2400	Not Binding
13	Shipping	3	2	4	950	<=	1500	Not Binding
14	Chair market	1	0	0	0	<=	360	Not Binding
15	Desk market	0	1	0	275	<=	300	Not Binding
16	Table market	0	0	1	100	<=	100	Binding
17								

⏮ ◀ ▶ ⏭ \ 11.1 / 11.2 \ **11.5** / <

for tables. (We also have unused time in assembly and shipping and unmet demand in chairs and desks.) These results—decision variables, objective function, and binding constraints—are the three key pieces of information provided in the solution.

Recall the distinction made in Chapter 10 between tactical and strategic information in the solution to an optimization problem. If we are faced with implementing a production plan for the next quarter at Veerman Furniture, we would pursue the tactical solution, producing no chairs, 275 desks, and 100 tables. (We might first want to make sure that our marketing department approves the idea of bringing a limited range of products to the market in order to maximize short-term profits. This is one of the places where the simplifications in a model must be assessed against the realities of the actual situation.) On the other hand, if there is time to adjust the resources available at Veerman Furniture, we should explore the possibility of acquiring more fabrication capacity or expanding the demand potential for tables, as these are the binding constraints. In addition, if there is time to adjust marketing policies, we might also want to look into the possibility of raising the price on chairs.

11.3 COVERING MODELS

The covering model calls for minimizing an objective (usually cost) subject to greater-than constraints on required coverage. Consider Dahlby Outfitters as an example.

EXAMPLE
Dahlby Outfitters

Dahlby Outfitters wishes to introduce a packaged trail mix as a new product. The ingredients for the trail mix are seeds, raisins, flakes, and two kinds of nuts. Each ingredient contains certain amounts of vitamins, minerals, protein, and calories. The marketing department has specified that the product be designed so that a certain minimum nutritional profile is met. The decision problem is to determine the optimal product composition—that is, to minimize the product cost by choosing the amount for each of the ingredients in the mix. The data shown in the accompanying table summarize the parameters of the problem.

Component	Grams per Pound					Nutritional Requirement
	Seeds	Raisins	Flakes	Pecans	Walnuts	
Vitamins	10	20	10	30	20	20
Minerals	5	7	4	9	2	10
Protein	1	4	10	2	1	15
Calories	500	450	160	300	500	600
Cost/pound	$4	$5	$3	$7	$6	

■

11.3.1 Formulation

What must be decided? Here, the answer is the amount of each ingredient to put into a package of trail mix. For the purposes of notation, we use S, R, F, P, and W to represent the number of pounds of each ingredient in a package.

What measure will we use to compare sets of decision variables? This should be the total cost of a package, and our goal is the lowest possible total cost. To calculate the total cost of a particular composition, we add the cost of each ingredient in the package:

$$Cost = 4S + 5R + 3F + 7P + 6W$$

What restrictions limit our choice of decision variables? In this scenario, the main limitation is the requirement to meet the specified nutritional profile. Each dimension of this profile gives rise to a separate constraint. An example of such a constraint would state, in words, that the number of grams of vitamins *provided* in the package must be greater than or equal to the number of grams *required* by the specified profile. In symbols, we write:

$$Vitamin\ content = 10S + 20R + 10F + 30P + 20W \geq 20\ \text{(Vitamin floor)}$$

Similar constraints must hold for the remainder of the profile:

$$Mineral\ content = 5S + 7R + 4F + 9P + 2W \geq 10\ \text{(Mineral floor)}$$
$$Protein\ content = 1S + 4R + 10F + 2P + 1W \geq 15\ \text{(Protein floor)}$$
$$Calorie\ content = 500S + 450R + 160F + 300P + 500W \geq 600\ \text{(Calorie floor)}$$

In this basic scenario, no other constraints occur, although we could imagine that there might also be limited quantities of the ingredients available, expressed as less-than constraints, or a weight requirement for the package, expressed as an equality constraint. Putting the algebraic statement together in one place, we obtain the following model.

$$\text{Minimize } z = 4S + 5R + 3F + 7P + 6W$$

subject to

$$10S + 20R + 10F + 30P + 20W \geq 20$$
$$5S + 7R + 4F + 9P + 2W \geq 10$$
$$1S + 4R + 10F + 2P + 1W \geq 15$$
$$500S + 450R + 160F + 300P + 500W \geq 600$$

FIGURE 11.6 Worksheet
for the Dahlby Outfitters
Model

	A	B	C	D	E	F	G	H	I	J
1	Covering: Trail Mix Composition									
2										
3	Decision Variables									
4		S	R	F	P	W				
5	Amounts	0.50	0.40	0.30	0.70	0.20				
6										
7	Objective Function						Total			
8	Cost	4	5	3	7	6	$11.00			
9										
10	Constraints							LHS		RHS
11	Vitamins	10	20	10	30	20	41	>=	20	Not Binding
12	Minerals	5	7	4	9	2	13.2	>=	10	Not Binding
13	Protein	1	4	10	2	1	6.7	>=	15	Not Binding
14	Calories	500	450	160	300	500	788	>=	600	Not Binding
15										

⏮ ◀ ▶ ⏭ \ 11.1 / 11.2 / 11.5 \ **11.6** / | ◀   ▶

11.3.2 Spreadsheet Model

A worksheet for this model appears in Figure 11.6. Again, we see three modules:

- A highlighted row for the decision variables (B5:F5)
- A highlighted single cell for the objective function value (G8)
- A set of constraint relationships (rows 11–14).

If we were to display the formulas in this worksheet, we would again see that the model is made up of only numbers and cells containing the SUMPRODUCT formula.

11.3.3 Optimization

Once we are satisfied that the model is valid, we proceed to the optimization procedure. We invoke Solver and specify:

Target cell	G8 (minimize)
Changing cells	B5:F5
Constraints	G11:G14 ≤ I11:I14

We select the linear solver and, in the Options menu, check the box for Assume Non-Negative. After contemplating some hypotheses about the problem (for example, will the solution require all five ingredients?), we run Solver and obtain a solution. The optimal solution, shown in Figure 11.7, calls for 1.32 pounds of flakes, 0.33 pound of raisins, and 0.48 pound of seeds, with no nuts at all. Evidently, nuts are prohibitively expensive, given the nature of the required nutritional profile and the other ingredients available. The optimal mix achieves all of the nutritional requirements at a minimum cost of $7.54. The three binding constraints in this solution are the requirements for minerals, protein, and calories.

Of course, we might decide that a trail mix without nuts is not an appealing product. If we wish, we can amend the model in order to force nuts into the optimal mix. One way to do so is to specify a minimum amount of nuts. In Figure 11.8, we show an amended model that requires at least 0.15 pound of *each* ingredient. The value of

FIGURE 11.7 Optimal
Solution for the Dahlby
Outfitters Model

	A	B	C	D	E	F	G	H	I	J
1	Covering: Trail Mix Composition									
2										
3	Decision Variables									
4		S	R	F	P	W				
5	Amounts	0.48	0.33	1.32	0.00	0.00				
6										
7	Objective Function						Total			
8	Cost	4	5	3	7	6	$7.54			
9										
10	Constraints							LHS		RHS
11	Vitamins	10	20	10	30	20	24.642	>=	16	Not Binding
12	Minerals	5	7	4	9	2	10	>=	10	Binding
13	Protein	1	4	10	2	1	15	>=	15	Binding
14	Calories	500	450	160	300	500	600	>=	600	Binding
15										

⏮ ◀ ▶ ⏭ \ 11.1 / 11.2 / 11.5 / 11.6 \ **11.7** / | ◀   ▶

FIGURE 11.8 Worksheet for the Amended Dahlby Outfitters Model

	A	B	C	D	E	F	G	H	I	J
1	Covering: Trail Mix Composition									
2										
3	Decision Variables									
4		S	R	F	P	W				
5	Amounts	0.48	0.33	1.32	0.00	0.00				
6	Floor levels	0.15	0.15	0.15	0.15	0.15				
7	Objective Function						Total			
8	Cost	4	5	3	7	6	$7.54			
9										
10	Constraints						LHS		RHS	
11	Vitamins	10	20	10	30	20	24.642	>=	16	Not Binding
12	Minerals	5	7	4	9	2	10	>=	10	Binding
13	Protein	1	4	10	2	1	15	>=	15	Binding
14	Calories	500	450	160	300	500	600	>=	600	Binding
15										

◄ ◄ ► ►► \ 11.1 / 11.2 / 11.5 / 11.6 / 11.7 \ 11.8 / | ◄

FIGURE 11.9 Optimal Solution for the Amended Dahlby Outfitters Model

	A	B	C	D	E	F	G	H	I	J
1	Covering: Trail Mix Composition									
2										
3	Decision Variables									
4		S	R	F	P	W				
5	Amounts	0.39	0.15	1.36	0.15	0.15				
6	Floor levels	0.15	0.15	0.15	0.15	0.15				
7	Objective Function						Total			
8	Cost	4	5	3	7	6	$8.33			
9										
10	Constraints						LHS		RHS	
11	Vitamins	10	20	10	30	20	27.97	>=	16	Not Binding
12	Minerals	5	7	4	9	2	10.0791	>=	10	Not Binding
13	Protein	1	4	10	2	1	15	>=	15	Binding
14	Calories	500	450	160	300	500	600	>=	600	Binding
15										

◄ ◄ ► ►► \ 11.1 / 11.2 / 11.5 / 11.6 / 11.7 / 11.8 \ 11.9 / | ◄

0.15 is placed in row 6, just below the corresponding decision variable. In the Solver Parameters window, we add the constraint that the range B5:F5 must be greater than or equal to the range B6:F6. A requirement that a particular decision variable must be greater than or equal to a given value is called a **lower bound** constraint. Similarly, a requirement that a particular decision variable must be less than or equal to a given value would be called an **upper bound** constraint. It is usually convenient to locate the upper or lower bound on the worksheet in close proximity to the corresponding decision variable, as we have done in row 6.

After including the lower bound constraints, a new run of Solver produces the optimal solution shown in Figure 11.9. Note that the lower bounds create an optimal solution that contains all five of the ingredients, as expected. We might have anticipated that nuts would appear at their lower limit, because before we added the lower bound constraints, the optimization process kept nuts completely out of the mix. The cost is also higher in the amended model than in the original, at $8.33. This fact reflects an intuitive principle that complements the one we stated earlier: *When we add constraints to a model, the objective function cannot improve.* In most cases, as in this example, the objective function will get worse when we add a constraint.

11.4 BLENDING MODELS

Blending relationships are very common in linear programming applications, yet they remain difficult for beginners to identify in problem descriptions and to implement in spreadsheet models. Because of this difficulty, we begin with a special case—the representation of proportions. As an example, let's return to the product mix example of Veerman Furniture which was introduced earlier in this chapter. Recall from Figure 11.5 that the optimal product mix consisted of no chairs, 275 desks, and 100 tables. Suppose that this outcome is unacceptable because of the imbalance in volumes. For more balance, the marketing department might require that each of the products must make up at least 25 percent of the total units sold.

11.4.1 Blending Constraints

When we describe outcomes in terms of proportions, and when we place a floor (or ceiling) on one or more of those proportions, we are using blending constraints of a special type. Because the total number of units sold is $C + D + T$, a direct statement of the requirement for chairs is the following.

$$\frac{C}{C + D + T} \geq 0.25 \tag{11.1}$$

This greater-than constraint has a parameter on the right-hand side and all the decision variables on the left-hand side, as is usually the case. Although this is a valid constraint, it is not in *linear* form, because the quantities C, D, and T appear in both the numerator and denominator of the fraction. (In effect, the ratio divides decision variables by decision variables.) However, with a bit of algebra we can convert the nonlinear inequality to a linear one. First, multiply both sides of the inequality by $(C + D + T)$, yielding:

$$C \geq 0.25(C + D + T)$$

Next, collect terms involving the decision variables on the left-hand side, so that we get:

$$0.75C - 0.25D - 0.25T \geq 0 \tag{11.2}$$

This form conveys the same requirement as the original fractional constraint, and we recognize it immediately as a linear form. The coefficients on the left-hand side of (11.8) turn out to be either the complement of the floor $(1 - 0.25)$ or the floor itself (but with a minus sign). In a similar fashion, the requirement that the other products must respect the floor leads to the following two constraints.

$$-0.25C + 0.75D - 0.25T \geq 0$$
$$-0.25C - 0.25D + 0.75T \geq 0$$

Appending these three constraints to the product mix model (in rows 17–19) gives rise to the linear program described in Figure 11.10. Note that the first of the three new constraints is not satisfied by the existing solution. A Solver run produces the solution in Figure 11.11, where we can see that the new optimal mix becomes 100 chairs, 200 desks, and 100 tables. Thus, swapping chairs and tables for desks in the product mix, we can achieve the best possible level of profit, at \$8,100. Also, as we might have expected, chairs comprise exactly 25 percent of the optimal output in this solution.

Whenever we encounter a constraint in the form of a lower limit or an upper limit on a proportion, we can take the following steps:

FIGURE 11.10 Product Mix Model with Added Constraints

	A	B	C	D	E	F	G
1	Allocation: Furniture Production						
2							
3	Decision Variables						
4			C	D	T		
5	Product mix	0	275	100			
6							
7	Objective Function				Total		
8	Profit	15	24	18	\$8,400		
9							
10	Constraints				LHS		RHS
11	Fabrication	4	6	2	1850	<=	1850
12	Assembly	3	5	7	2075	<=	2400
13	Distribution	3	2	4	950	<=	1500
14	Chair market	1	0	0	0	<=	360
15	Desk market	0	1	0	275	<=	300
16	Table market	0	0	1	100	<=	100
17	Chair fraction	0.75	-0.25	-0.25	-93.75	>=	0
18	Desk fraction	-0.25	0.75	-0.25	181.25	>=	0
19	Table fraction	-0.25	-0.25	0.75	6.25	>=	0
20							

11.5 / 11.6 / 11.7 / 11.8 / 11.9 \ **11.10** /

FIGURE 11.11 Optimal Solution to the Product Mix Model with Added Constraints

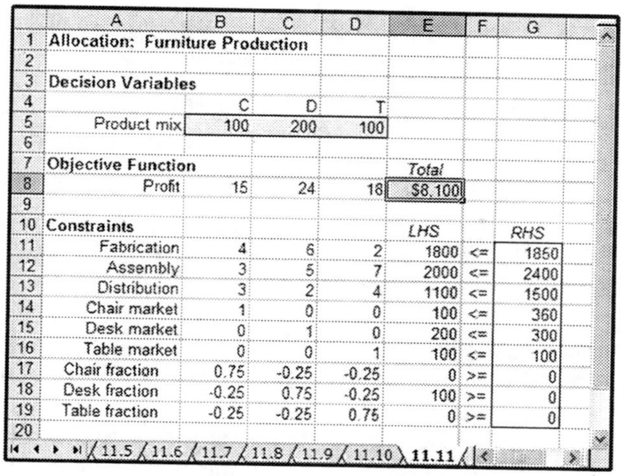

1. Write the fraction that expresses the constrained proportion.
2. Write the inequality implied by the lower bound or upper bound.
3. Multiply both sides of the inequality by the denominator and collect terms.
4. The result is a linear inequality, ready to incorporate in the model.

In Step 3, it is not actually necessary to collect terms because Solver allows us to leave a SUMPRODUCT formula on both sides of the inequality. However, we recommend collecting terms so that the variables appear on the left-hand side of the inequality and a constant appears on the right. This format is consistent with allocation and blending constraints and may make it easier to debug a model.

In general, the blending model involves mixing materials with different individual properties and describing the properties of the blend with weighted averages. We might be familiar with the phenomenon of mixing if we have spent time in a chemistry lab mixing fluids with different concentrations, but the concept extends beyond lab work. Consider the Diaz Coffee Company as an example.

EXAMPLE
The Diaz Coffee Company

The Diaz Coffee Company blends three types of coffee beans (Brazilian, Colombian, and Peruvian) into ground coffee to be sold at retail. Suppose that each kind of bean has a distinctive aroma and strength, and the company has a chief taster who can rate these features on a scale of 1 to 100. The features of the beans are tabulated as follows.

Bean	Aroma Rating	Strength Rating	Cost/lb.	Pounds Available
Brazilian	75	15	$0.50	150,000
Colombian	60	20	$0.60	120,000
Peruvian	85	18	$0.70	200,000

The company would like to create a blend that has an aroma rating of at least 78 and a strength rating of at least 16. Its supplies of the various beans are limited, however. The available quantities are specified above. All beans are delivered under a previously arranged purchase agreement. Diaz wants to make 4,000,000 pounds of the blend at the lowest possible cost. ∎

11.4.2 Formulation

Suppose, for example, that we blend Brazilian and Peruvian beans in equal quantities of 25 pounds each. Then we should expect the blend to have an aroma rating of 80, just halfway between the two pure ratings of 75 and 85. Mathematically, we take the weighted average of the two ratings:

$$\text{Aroma rating} = \frac{25(75) + 25(85)}{25 + 25} = 80$$

Now suppose that we blend the beans in amounts B, C, and P. The blend will have an aroma rating calculated by a weighted average of the three ratings, as follows:

$$\text{Aroma rating} = \frac{B(75) + C(60) + P(85)}{B + C + P}$$

To impose a constraint that requires an aroma rating of at least 78, we write:

$$\frac{B(75) + C(60) + P(85)}{B + C + P} \geq 78 \qquad (11.3)$$

This greater-than constraint has a parameter on the right-hand side of (11.2) and all the decision variables on the left-hand side, as is usually the case. Although this is a valid constraint, it is not in *linear* form, because the quantities B, C, and P appear in both the numerator and denominator of the fraction. If we were to include this form of the constraint in Solver, we would be forced to use the nonlinear solver to get a solution. However, we can convert the nonlinear inequality to a linear one by following the steps listed earlier and thus satisfy the linear solver. First, multiply both sides of the inequality by $(B + C + P)$, yielding:

$$75B + 60C + 85P \geq 78(B + C + P)$$

Next, collect terms on the left-hand side, so that we get:

$$-3B - 18C + 7P \geq 0 \qquad (11.4)$$

This form conveys the same requirement as the original fractional constraint in (11.3), and we recognize it immediately as a linear constraint. The coefficients on the left-hand side turn out to be just the *differences* between the individual aroma ratings (75, 60, 85) and the requirement of 78, with the signs indicating whether the individual rating is above or below the target. In a similar fashion, a requirement that the strength of the blend must be at least 16 leads to the constraint

$$-1B + 4C + 2P \geq 0$$

Thus, blending requirements are stated initially as fractions in (11.1) and (11.3), and in that form, they lead to nonlinear constraints. We are interested in converting these to linear constraints, as in (11.2) and (11.4), because with a linear model, we can harness the power of the linear solver. As discussed earlier, this means that we can find a global optimum reliably.

Now, with an idea of how to incorporate the blending requirements, we return to our scenario.

- What must be decided? The decision variables are the quantities to purchase, which we can continue to represent as B, C, and P. However, due to the scale of the model, it is convenient to take the dimensions of these three quantities to be thousands of pounds.

- What measure will we use? Evidently, it is the total purchase cost of meeting our 4 million pound requirement.

- What restrictions must we meet? In addition to the blending constraints, we need a constraint that generates a 4 million pound blend, along with three constraints that limit the supplies of the different beans.

11.4.3 Spreadsheet Model

Figure 11.12 shows the spreadsheet for our model, which contains a greater-than constraint and three less-than constraints, in addition to the blending constraints. In addition, the model has been scaled by taking the supply and output constraints, as well as the decision variables, to be in thousands of pounds. The three decision variables have been set arbitrarily to 100,000 in the figure. In a sense, the model has two key blending constraints, and it also has what we might think of as covering and

FIGURE 11.12 Worksheet for the Diaz Coffee Company Model

	A	B	C	D	E	F	G	H
1	Blending: Coffee beans							
2								
3	Decision Variables							
4		B	C	P				
5	Inputs	100	100	100			in '000	
6								
7	Objective Function				Total			
8	Cost	0.50	0.60	0.70	$180		in '000	
9								
10	Constraints				LHS		RHS	
11	Blend aroma	-3	-18	7	-1400	>=	0	Not Binding
12	Blend strength	-1	4	2	500	>=	0	Not Binding
13	Output	1	1	1	300	>=	4000	Not Binding
14	B-supply	1	0	0	100	<=	1500	Not Binding
15	C-supply	0	1	0	100	<=	1200	Not Binding
16	P-supply	0	0	1	100	<=	2000	Not Binding
17	Actual aroma	75	60	85	73.3		78	
18	Actual strength	15	20	18	17.7		16	
19								

⏮ ◀ ▶ ⏭ / 11.5 / 11.6 / 11.7 / 11.8 / 11.9 / 11.10 / 11.11 \ **11.12** / |◀ ▶

allocation constraints. Each of the constraints takes the same form: a SUMPRODUCT formula on the left-hand side and a parameter on the right-hand side. Note that this model contains both less-than and greater-than constraints, and it is helpful, when filling in the Solver Parameters window, to keep like constraints together.

Notice that the Output constraint requires that we produce *at least* 4 million pounds, not *exactly* 4 million pounds. Thus, as formulated here, there is some flexibility in the Output constraint. Although Diaz wishes to produce 4 million pounds, our model allows the production of a larger quantity if this will reduce costs. (Our intuition probably tells us that we should be able to minimize costs with a 400,000-pound blend, but we would accept a solution that lowered cost while producing more than this amount because we could simply throw away the excess and remain better off.) In many situations, it is a good idea to use the weaker form of a constraint, giving the model some additional flexibility and avoiding equality constraints. In other words, *we build the model with some latitude in satisfying the constraints of the decision problem, whenever possible.* The solution will either confirm our intuition (as this one does) or else teach us a lesson about the limitations of our intuition.

11.4.4 Optimization

We now invoke Solver and specify:

Target cell	E8 (maximize)
Changing cells	B5:D5
Constraints	E11:E13 ≥ G11:G13
	E14:E16 ≤ G14:G16

We select the linear solver and check the box for Assume Non-Negative. When we run Solver, we obtain the optimal blend of 1,500,000 pounds of Brazilian, 520,000 pounds of Colombian, and 1,980,000 pounds of Peruvian beans, for a total cost of $2.448 million (see Figure 11.13). Of the two blending constraints, only the first (aroma) constraint is binding; the optimal blend actually has better-than-required strength. The output constraint is also binding (consistent with our intuitive expectation), as is the limit on Brazilian supply.

In Figure 11.13, which displays the optimal solution, rows 17 and 18 on the worksheet are strictly speaking not part of our Solver model. (In other words, the model's constraints and objective function are not influenced by the calculations in these two rows.) Instead, they provide a more conventional calculation of the blended properties, and we include them simply for convenience when interpreting the results. Thus, where the first constraint of the model (row 11) is binding, the aroma calculation in row 17 shows that the weighted average exactly equals the requirement of 78. Although the second constraint (row 12) shows that the strength requirement is not binding, the comparison of the left-hand side (4,540) with the right-hand side

FIGURE 11.13 Optimal
Solution for the Diaz Coffee
Company Model

	A	B	C	D	E	F	G	H
1	Blending: Coffee beans							
2								
3	Decision Variables							
4		B	C	P				
5	Inputs	1500	520	1980			in '000	
6								
7	Objective Function				Total			
8	Cost	0.50	0.60	0.70	$2,448		in '000	
9								
10	Constraints				LHS		RHS	
11	Blend aroma	-3	-18	7	0	>=	0	Binding
12	Blend strength	-1	4	2	4540	>=	0	Not Binding
13	Output	1	1	1	4000	>=	4000	Binding
14	B-supply	1	0	0	1500	<=	1500	Binding
15	C-supply	0	1	0	520	<=	1200	Not Binding
16	P-supply	0	0	1	1980	<=	2000	Not Binding
17	Actual aroma	75	60	85	78.0		78	
18	Actual strength	15	20	18	17.1		16	
19								

| ◄ ◄ ► ►| ╲ 11.5 ╱ 11.6 ╱ 11.7 ╱ 11.8 ╱ 11.9 ╱ 11.10 ╱ 11.11 ╱ 11.12 ╲ 11.13 ╱ | ◄ | ► |

(zero) may not be very useful. However, the last row of the worksheet shows that the optimal blend's strength is 17.1 (see cell E18), giving us a clearer sense of the cushion between the strength achieved and the requirement of 16.

SOLVER TIP
Rescaling the Model

Rescaling the decisions and parameters of a model—using thousands or even millions as a unit of measure—has the virtue that it saves us the work of entering lots of zeros. As a consequence, we may avoid some data-entry errors, and the spreadsheet looks a little less crowded than it would with many large numbers on it. However, there is an important practical reason for rescaling. The way that Solver carries out its arithmetic sometimes makes rescaling desirable. As a guideline, the parameters in the objective function and the constraints should not differ from each other, or from the values of the decision variables, by more than a factor of 100,000. In the Diaz Coffee example, the ratio of the largest right-hand-side constant to the smallest constraint coefficient would be 4,000,000 if there were no rescaling. Although a model as simple as this one would likely run correctly, it is safer (as well as more convenient) to do the rescaling.

One symptom of a need for rescaling would be a response from Solver stating that there is no feasible solution to a problem in which we're sure that feasible solutions can be found. In these circumstances, we should try to multiply a constraint by some constant or redefine the decision variables using a different unit of measure. Sometimes, however, scaling problems are difficult to avoid completely when we're trying to keep the model easy for another user to understand. In these cases, we can ask Solver to perform some internal rescaling of the model if we check the option box for Use Automatic Scaling. The Automatic Scaling option may be helpful; however, it is always preferable for the model builder to do the rescaling. (Unfortunately, in some instances, the Automatic Scaling option causes the linear solver to go awry when it would otherwise have functioned perfectly.)

Finally, if we need to display our model results in units that are more natural for our audience, we can create a separate presentation worksheet. On this sheet, the numbers can be "unscaled" and displayed in any desired format without affecting the optimization process. ■

11.5 SENSITIVITY ANALYSIS FOR LINEAR PROGRAMS

As we stressed in Chapter 6, sensitivity analysis is a vital part of all spreadsheet modeling. In optimization modeling, some of the most valuable insights come not from the optimal solution itself, but from a sensitivity analysis around the optimal solution. As we will see, the special structure of linear programs gives rise to certain characteristic results. We again use the Solver Sensitivity option in the Sensitivity Toolkit.

We implement the Solver Sensitivity tool with the Veerman Furniture model to illustrate some of the features of sensitivity analysis in linear programs. Recall that the model allows us to find the profit-maximizing product mix among chairs, desks, and tables. The optimal product mix (see Figure 11.5) is made up of desks and tables, with no chairs. Two constraints are binding: fabrication hours and the tables market. The optimal total profit contribution in the base case is $8,400.

11.5.1 Sensitivity to Objective Function Coefficients

Suppose that we are using the Veerman Furniture model as a planning tool and that we wish to explore a change in the price of chairs. We might not yet know what the exact price will be, pending more information about the competition, but we want to explore the impact of a price change, which translates into a change in the profit contribution of chairs. For the time being, let's assume that if we vary the price, there will be no effect on the demand potential for chairs. We invoke Solver Sensitivity with the entries shown in Figures 11.14 and 11.15.

Objective Function	E8
Other Cell(s)	B5:D5
Cell to Vary	B8
First Value	12
Last Value	24
Increment	1

The Solver Sensitivity report appears on a new worksheet (see Figure 11.16). These results show how the optimal product mix and the optimal profit both change as the profit contribution on chairs increases. For the range of profit contributions we chose ($12 to $24), we see two distinct profiles. For values up to $16, the base-case solution prevails, but above $16, the optimal mix changes, as follows:

- Chairs stay at zero until the unit profit contribution on chairs reaches $16; then chairs enter the optimal mix at a quantity of 330.
- When the unit contribution reaches $21, the number of chairs in the optimal mix increases to 360.
- Desks and tables are not affected until the unit contribution on chairs reaches $16; then the optimal number of desks drops from 275 to 55. When the unit profit on chairs reaches $21, the optimal number of desks drops again, to 40.
- Tables stay level at 100 until the unit contribution on chairs reaches $21; then the optimal number of tables drops to 85.
- The optimal total profit remains unchanged until the unit contribution on chairs reaches $16; thereafter, it increases.

From this information, we can conclude that the optimal solution is insensitive to changes in the unit profit contribution of chairs, up to $16. Beyond that point, however, the profit contribution on chairs becomes sufficiently attractive that we want to have

FIGURE 11.14 First Input Window for Solver Sensitivity

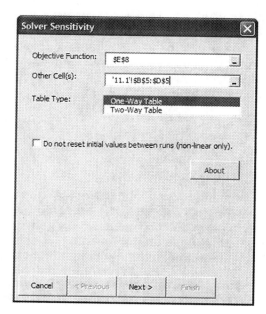

FIGURE 11.15 Second Input Window for Solver Sensitivity

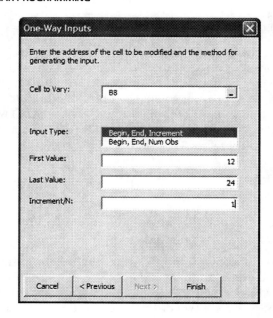

FIGURE 11.16 Solver Sensitivity Report for the Change in Price

	A	B	C	D	E	F
1	Unit Profit	Objective	Change	C	D	T
2	$12	$8,400		0	275	100
3	$13	$8,400	$0	0	275	100
4	$14	$8,400	$0	0	275	100
5	$15	$8,400	$0	0	275	100
6	$16	$8,400	$0	0	275	100
7	$17	$8,730	$330	330	55	100
8	$18	$9,060	$330	330	55	100
9	$19	$9,390	$330	330	55	100
10	$20	$9,720	$330	330	55	100
11	$21	$10,050	$330	360	40	85
12	$22	$10,410	$360	360	40	85
13	$23	$10,770	$360	360	40	85
14	$24	$11,130	$360	360	40	85
15						

all three products in the mix. In effect, chairs substitute for desks (though not at a ratio of 1:1) when the profit contribution exceeds $16. Subsequently, when the profit contribution exceeds $21, chairs substitute for both desks and tables and are limited only by their demand potential. Thus, if we decide to alter the price for chairs, we can anticipate the impact on our product mix from the information in the sensitivity table.

In all linear programs, there is a distinct pattern to the changes in the optimal solution when we vary a coefficient of a decision variable in the objective function. In some interval around the base-case value, there is no change at all in the optimal decisions, but the objective function value will change if the decision variable is positive. Outside of this interval, a different set of values for the decision variables becomes optimal. As we saw in this example, the change from one set of values to the other will not be gradual. Instead, it will often be dramatic, as illustrated by the optimal number of chairs changing from 0 to 330 when the profit contribution increases from $16 to $17.

11.5.2 Sensitivity to Constraint Constants

Turning to another question, we noticed in the optimal solution to the base case that two constraints are binding: fabrication hours and the demand for tables. If fabrication time is limiting our ability to increase profits, perhaps we should acquire more of it. How much should we pay for additional time? Notice that this is a sensitivity question that involves one of the right-hand side constants rather than an objective function coefficient. To obtain an answer, we can invoke Solver Sensitivity again. In this case, our entries are shown in Figures 11.17 and 11.18.

Objective Function	E8
Other Cell(s)	B5:D5
Cell to Vary	G12
First Value	1,500
Last Value	2,400
Increment	100

The Solver Sensitivity tool adds another new worksheet, as shown in Figure 11.19. The table shows how the optimal product mix and the optimal profit both change as the number of fabrication hours increases. Its columns correspond to the same outputs as in the first table, and its rows correspond to the values we designated for the input. Thus, we see the following changes in the optimal product mix:

- Chairs stay at zero until the number of fabrication hours reaches 2,000; then chairs enter the optimal mix and continue to increase thereafter.

FIGURE 11.17 First Input
Window for Solver
Sensitivity

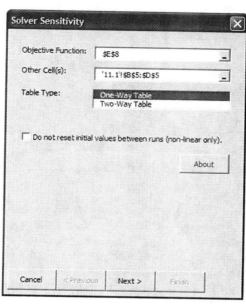

- Desks increase until the number of fabrication hours reaches 2,000; then desks stay level at 300.
- Tables stay level at 100 until the number of fabrication hours reaches 2,200; then tables drop.
- The optimal total profit increases as the number of fabrication hours increases, but not at a constant rate.

From this information, we can conclude that as we increase fabrication capacity, we should alter the product mix—first by increasing the number of desks, next by adding chairs to the mix, and then by swapping chairs for tables.

To determine how much we should be willing to pay for additional time, we examine the marginal value of additional fabrication hours. The **marginal value** is defined as the improvement in the objective function from a unit increase in the number available (i.e., an increase of 1 in the right-hand side of the fabrication constraint). We could calculate this marginal value by changing the number of fabrication hours to 1,851, re-solving the problem, and noting the improvement in the objective function. (It increases to $8,404, an improvement of $4.)

Marginal values are calculated automatically by the Solver Sensitivity tool and are displayed in the third column of the table, where we see that the marginal value of fabrication hours is $4.00 in the region of the base case. As the number of fabrication hours increases, the marginal value stays level for a while, then drops to $3.75, stays level at this value for a while, then later drops to about $2.32. This pattern is an instance of *diminishing marginal returns*: if someone were to offer us more and more of a scarce resource, its value would eventually decline. In this case, the scarce resource (or binding constraint) is fabrication capacity. Limited fabrication hours prevent us from achieving higher total profits; that is what makes fabrication hours economically scarce.

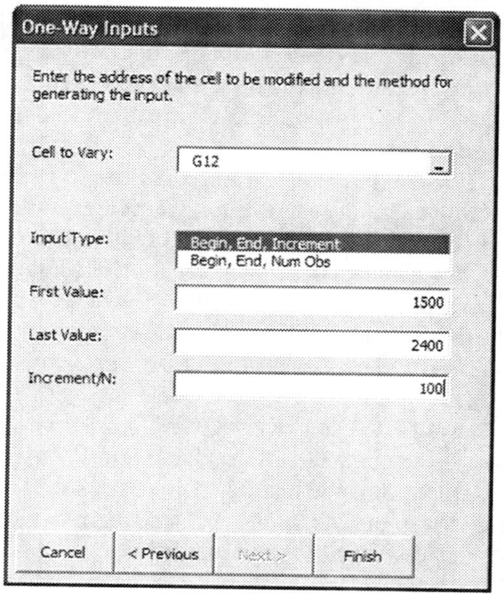

Starting with the base case, we should be willing to pay up to $4.00 for each additional fabrication hour because profit increases by this amount. This marginal value is also called the **shadow price**. In economic terms, the shadow price is the breakeven price at which it would be attractive to acquire more of a scarce resource. In other words, imagine that someone were to offer us additional fabrication hours (for example, if we could lease fabrication equipment). We can improve total profit by acquiring those additional hours, as long as their price is less than $4.00 each.

FIGURE 11.18 Second
Input Window for Solver
Sensitivity

FIGURE 11.19 Solver
Sensitivity Report for the
Change in Fabrication Hours

	A	B	C	D	E	F
1	RHS	Objective	Change	C	D	T
2	1,500	$7,000.00		0.00	216.67	100.00
3	1,600	$7,400.00	$4.00	0.00	233.33	100.00
4	1,700	$7,800.00	$4.00	0.00	250.00	100.00
5	1,800	$8,200.00	$4.00	0.00	266.67	100.00
6	1,900	$8,600.00	$4.00	0.00	283.33	100.00
7	2,000	$9,000.00	$4.00	0.00	300.00	100.00
8	2,100	$9,375.00	$3.75	25.00	300.00	100.00
9	2,200	$9,750.00	$3.75	50.00	300.00	100.00
10	2,300	$10,077.27	$3.27	77.27	300.00	95.45
11	2,400	$10,309.09	$2.32	109.09	300.00	81.82
12						

11.16 \ **11.19**

In this example, we observe that the marginal value of the scarce resource remains constant in a neighborhood around the base-case value. In particular, the $4.00 shadow price holds for additional fabrication hours until we reach 2,000; then it drops to $3.75. In the interval from 1,850 hours to 2,000 hours, the incremental hours allow more desks to be manufactured. In fact, we can see from Figure 11.19 that each additional 100 hours leads to an increment of 16.67 desks in the product mix. This increment, in turn, accounts for an increase of $400.00 in total profit, since desks contribute $24.00 each.

Above 2,000 fabrication hours, the pattern is a little different. With additional hours available, there are more chairs in the optimal product mix, and the optimal profit grows by $375.00 for each additional 100 hours. Thus, the shadow price is $3.75, and this value persists until around 2,200 hours. Actually, the shadow price changes at 2,266.67 hours, but our table is too coarse for us to see the precise change point. (We could see it more readily if we were to repeat the analysis with a step size of 1 hour.) Above 2,266.67 fabrication hours, the total profit increases at an even smaller rate ($2.32). In this interval, we see that chairs are added to the product mix, and tables are removed from it. Chairs consume more fabrication time than do tables. Therefore, with a relatively small amount of fabrication capacity (1,850 hours), we are better off not making chairs. As fabrication capacity increases (to, say, 2,300 hours), we are willing to swap chairs for tables, in light of other capacities available, in pursuit of optimal profits.

Linear programs typically exhibit a distinct pattern in sensitivity tables when we vary the availability of a scarce resource. The marginal value of capacity remains constant over some interval of increase or decrease. (This contrasts with the marginal value in nonlinear models, such as Figure 10.23, where we saw marginal values that changed continuously as we altered the availability of a scarce resource.) Within this interval, some of the decision variables change linearly with the change in capacity, while other decision variables stay the same. If someone were to continually give us more of a scarce resource, its value would drop and eventually fall to zero. In the case of our product mix problem, we could confirm that the value of additional hours drops to zero at a capacity level of 3,000.

The Solver Sensitivity tool has the limitation that we must specify in advance the grid over which we change the input parameter. If we choose too coarse a grid, we may not identify the precise point at which the solution changes. In that case, we can always refine the search and run the analysis again. An alternative is to use Solver's own Sensitivity Report, which provides information on the local sensitivity to both objective function coefficients and right-hand sides. (The chapter appendix provides some details on the information in the Sensitivity Report.)

We have illustrated the sensitivity of linear programs to two fundamental types of parameters: an objective function coefficient and a constraint constant. These cases are particularly interesting because each produces a characteristic pattern in the optimal solution. However, we should not lose sight of the fact that with the Solver Sensitivity tool, we can analyze the sensitivity of the optimal solution to *any* parameter in the model.

SOLVER TIP	Solver Sensitivity is a general-purpose tool for sensitivity analysis of optimization models. It is

SOLVER TIP
Solver Sensitivity and Shadow Prices

Solver Sensitivity is a general-purpose tool for sensitivity analysis of optimization models. It is used to determine the sensitivity of the optimal solution to *any* input parameter. It automatically calculates the change in the objective function per unit change in the input parameter, which we call the *marginal change* in the objective.

Solver Sensitivity can, of course, be used to assess the impact on the optimal solution of changes in the constraint constants, which typically represent resources. In this case, the marginal change in the objective can be interpreted as the marginal value of the resource. The marginal value of a resource is the change in the objective per unit change in the resource, which can usually be interpreted as the maximum amount we would be willing to pay to acquire additional resource.

The marginal value of a resource is given the special name **shadow price**. In linear programs, shadow prices are constant for some range of changes in the RHS. This feature is central to our interpretation of the economic patterns in the solutions to linear optimization models. In nonlinear models, by constrast, the marginal values of resources are typically not constant. ∎

11.6 PATTERNS IN LINEAR PROGRAMMING SOLUTIONS

In linear programming models, one form of insight comes from seeing a qualitative pattern in the solution. Stated another way, the optimal solution tells a "story" about a pattern of economic priorities, and it's the recognition of those priorities that provides useful insight. When we know the pattern, we can explain the solution more convincingly than when we simply read Solver results. When we know the pattern, we can also anticipate some of the answers to "what-if" questions without having to modify the worksheet. In short, the pattern provides a level of understanding that enhances decision making. Therefore, after we optimize a linear programming model, we should always try to discern the qualitative pattern in the optimal solution.

11.6.1 Identifying Patterns

Spotting a pattern involves observations about both variables and constraints. In the optimal solution, we pay special attention to which constraints are binding and which are not, as well as to which decision variables are positive and which are zero. Grasping the pattern of binding constraints and positive decision variables often allows us to reconstruct the solution in a step-by-step fashion. To the untrained observer, we seem to be solving the problem methodically, from scratch; in fact, we are only providing a retrospective interpretation of the solution, and we need to know that solution before we can devise the interpretation. Nevertheless, we are not merely reflecting information in the computer output. Rather, we are describing a set of economic imperatives at the heart of the model. When we can see those imperatives, and communicate them, then we have gained some insight. In the examples that follow, we show how to uncover these patterns.

While it can be extremely helpful to identify the pattern in the solution to a linear program, we should not assume that the pattern holds for anything other than small changes in the parameters. We can always check whether the pattern changes by rerunning Solver with new input parameters.

To illustrate the process of identifying a pattern, recall the solution of the product mix problem in Figure 11.5. The display in Figure 11.20 highlights the positive variables and the binding constraints. When we concentrate on these variables and constraints, we see that the problem becomes one of optimizing the choice of the variables D and T, subject to two constraints:

$$6D + 2T = 1,850$$

$$T = 100$$

The second equation dictates the value of T because it is a binding constraint containing only one variable. Once we know that $T = 100$, we can substitute into

	A	B	C	D	E	F	G
1	**Allocation: Furniture Production**						
2							
3	**Decision Variables**						
4		C	D	T			
5	Product mix	0	275	100			
6							
7	**Objective Function**				*Total*		
8	Profit	15	24	18	$8,400		
9							
10	**Constraints**				*LHS*		*RHS*
11	Fabrication	4	6	2	1850	<=	1850
12	Assembly	3	5	7	2075	<=	2400
13	Distribution	3	2	4	950	<=	1500
14	Chair market	1	0	0	0	<=	360
15	Desk market	0	1	0	275	<=	300
16	Table market	0	0	1	100	<=	100
17							

11.19 11.20

FIGURE 11.20 Optimal Product Mix Model, Highlighting Elements of the Pattern

the first constraint and deduce that $D = 275$. The solution is constructed as if we determine T first and then D. The construction of the solution goes like this:

- First, remove C from further consideration.
- Next, let the market ceiling for tables dictate the value of T.
- Finally (with T fixed), let the fabrication capacity dictate the value of D.

Note that this description describes the solution fully but does not use any numbers. In that sense, the pattern is a qualitative interpretation of the solution. However, once we supply the parameters of the constraints (here, that means 100 and 1,850), the pattern gives us a scheme for computing the optimal quantitative solution. It is almost as if Solver first spots the optimal pattern and then says, "Give me the numerical information in your problem." For any specification of the numbers (within certain limits), Solver could then compute the optimal solution by simply following the sequential steps in the pattern. In reality, of course, Solver cannot know the pattern until the solution is determined, because the solution is a critical ingredient in the pattern.

Let's return to the point that the patterns hold for any set of numbers within certain limits. What limits are we referring to? Suppose we make a change in the size of the market ceiling for tables and increment the ceiling by one, to 101. Then, the steps in the pattern lead us to a new optimal solution: $T = 101$ and $D = 274.667$. The impact on the objective function is an increment of $24(-0.333) + 18(+1) = 10$. In other words, a unit increase in the market ceiling for tables allows the optimal mix to increase profits by $10.

In effect, we have derived the shadow price for the market ceiling constraint. (We could confirm this result by rerunning Solver with a market ceiling of 101 for tables.) Thus, if we increment the ceiling by two units, the new optimal solution becomes $T = 102$ and $D = 274.333$, with an increase of $20 in the objective. How long can we continue incrementing the market ceiling for tables? To answer this question, we have to consider the impact on the constraints we have been ignoring, as well as on the decision variables. In the latter case, the optimal value of D drops 0.333 for every unit increase in the ceiling. At this rate, the ceiling could become as large as 825. But let's look at the nonbinding constraints.

- The Assembly constraint had a surplus of 325 hours in the original problem. Increasing T by one and reducing D by 0.333 consume an additional 5.333 Assembly hours. At this rate, there is room to increase the ceiling by at most $325/5.333 = 60.9375$.
- The Shipping constraint had a surplus 550 hours in the original problem. Increasing T by one and reducing D by 0.333 consume an additional 3.333

Shipping hours. At this rate, there is room to increase the ceiling by at most $550/3.333 = 165$.

- The chair ceiling is unaffected by the change.
- The desk ceiling had a surplus of 25 desks in the original solution, but because the change involves a reduction in the number of desks, the desk ceiling does not come into play.

Taking the tightest of the relevant limits, we conclude that the market ceiling for tables could be increased as much as 60.9375 without changing the pattern.

In the opposite direction, suppose we *reduce* the size of the market ceiling for tables.

- Reducing the ceiling for tables directly affects the variable T. There is room to decrease the ceiling by at most 100 tables.
- The desk ceiling had a surplus of 25 desks in the original solution. Decreasing T by one and increasing D by 0.333 consumes an additional 0.333 of the surplus in the constraint. At this rate, there is room to increase the ceiling by at most $25/0.333 = 75$ tables.

Taking the tighter of these two limits, we conclude that the market ceiling for tables could be reduced by as much as 75 without changing the pattern. Thus, the analysis of both directions leads to the conclusion that the shadow price holds for market ceilings from 25 to 160.9375. Beyond this range, the pattern changes: in particular, there is a change in the set of binding constraints or the set of nonzero variables (or both).

11.6.2 Further Examples

The following examples illustrate patterns in the optimal solution of other linear programs.

EXAMPLE
A Product Portfolio Decision

The product portfolio problem asks which products a firm should be making. If there are contracts that obligate the firm to enter certain markets, then the question is which products to make in quantities beyond the required minimum. Consider Grocery Distributors (GD), a company that distributes 15 different vegetables to grocery stores. GD's vegetables come in standard cardboard cartons that each take up 1.25 cubic feet in the warehouse. The company replenishes its supply of frozen foods at the start of each week and rarely has any inventory remaining at week's end. An entire week's supply of frozen vegetables arrives each Monday morning at the warehouse, which can hold up to 18,000 cubic feet of product. In addition, GD's supplier extends a line of credit amounting to $30,000. That is, GD is permitted to purchase up to $30,000 worth of product each Monday.

GD can predict sales for each of the 15 products for the coming week. This forecast is expressed in terms of a minimum and a maximum level of sales. The minimum quantity is based on a contractual agreement that GD has made with a few retail grocery chains; the maximum quantity represents an estimate of the sales potential in the upcoming week. The unit cost and unit selling price for each product are known. The given data are compiled in the following table.

Product	Cost	Price	Minimum	Maximum
Whipped Potatoes (WP)	2.15	2.27	300	1,500
Creamed Corn (CC)	2.20	2.48	400	2,000
Blackeyed Peas (BP)	2.40	2.70	250	900
Artichokes (AR)	4.80	5.20	0	150
Carrots (CR)	2.60	2.92	300	1,200
Succotash (SU)	2.30	2.48	200	800
Okra (OK)	2.35	2.20	150	600
Cauliflower (CL)	2.85	3.13	100	300
Green Peas (GP)	2.25	2.48	750	3,500
Spinach (SP)	2.10	2.27	400	2,000

Lima Beans (LB)	2.80	3.13	500	3,300
Brussel Sprouts (BS)	3.00	3.18	100	500
Green Beans (GB)	2.60	2.92	500	3,200
Squash (SQ)	2.50	2.70	100	500
Broccoli (BR)	2.90	3.13	400	2,500

■

GD solves the linear programming model shown in Figure 11.21. In this model, the objective is to maximize profit for the coming week. Sales for each product are constrained by a minimum quantity and a maximum quantity. In addition, constraints come from aggregate limits on warehouse space and purchase expenditures.

We invoke Solver and specify:

Target cell	R11 (maximize)
Changing cells	C9:Q9
Constraints	C9:Q9 $\geq$ C6:Q6
	C9:Q9 $\leq$ C7:Q7
	R14:R15 $\leq$ T14:T15

The solution shows that all of the decision variables are positive except for artichokes, and the minimum cost is $3,395.50.

Examining the variables in the solution in more detail, we notice that all but one of the purchase quantities match either the maximum or the minimum, with lima beans as the only exception. Any product that has a nonzero minimum must appear in the solution at a positive amount, but some products are purchased at even higher levels. These can be considered high-priority products. Products purchased at their minimum levels can be considered low-priority products. In either case, however, the values corresponding to high-priority products and low-priority products are dictated by one binding constraint containing one variable.

Examining the other constraints in the solution, we see that the credit limit is binding, but the space constraint is not. In effect, the credit limit serves as a bottleneck on purchases, but we can ignore the space constraint, because other constraints dictate how much space is used. A description of the pattern could take the following form:

- Set the volume of each high-priority product equal to its maximum level.
- Set the volume of each low-priority product equal to its minimum level.
- Use the entire credit limit.

In other words, we are actually solving a simpler problem than originally given: produce the highest possible value from the 15 products under a tight credit limit. To solve this problem, we can use a common-sense rule: pursue the products in the order of highest to lowest *profit-to-cost ratio*. Meanwhile, we must meet the given minimum quantities. Therefore, we can convert the pattern into a calculation scheme for the decision variables, as follows:

- Purchase each product at its minimum sales level.
- Rank the products from highest to lowest ratio of profit to cost.

	A	B	C	D	E	F	G	H	I	J	K	L	M	N	O	P	Q	R	S	T
1	**General Distributors**																			
2																				
3	**Data**	*Vegetable*	WP	CC	BP	AR	CR	SU	OK	CL	GP	SP	LB	BS	GB	SQ	BR			
4		*Cost*	2.15	2.20	2.40	4.80	2.60	2.30	2.35	2.85	2.25	2.10	2.80	3.00	2.60	2.50	2.90			
5		*Price*	2.27	2.48	2.70	5.20	2.92	2.48	2.20	3.13	2.48	2.27	3.13	3.18	2.92	2.70	3.13			
6		*Min*	300	400	250	0	300	200	150	100	750	400	500	100	500	100	400			
7		*Max*	1500	2000	900	150	1200	600	600	300	3600	2000	3300	500	3200	500	2500			
8																				
9	**Decisions**	*Cartons*	300	2000	900	0	1200	200	150	100	750	400	2150	100	3200	100	400			
10																				
11	**Objective**	*Profit $*	0.12	0.28	0.30	0.40	0.32	0.16	-0.15	0.28	0.23	0.17	0.33	0.16	0.32	0.20	0.23	$3,395.50		
12																				
13																		*LHS*		*RHS*
14	**Constraints**	*Credit*	2.15	2.20	2.40	4.80	2.60	2.30	2.35	2.85	2.25	2.10	2.80	3.00	2.60	2.50	2.90	30,000.00	<=	30,000
15		*Space*	1.25	1.25	1.25	1.25	1.25	1.25	1.25	1.25	1.25	1.25	1.25	1.25	1.25	1.25	1.25	14,937.50	<=	16,000
16																				
17	*Ratios*		1.056	1.127	1.125	1.083	1.123	1.078	0.936	1.098	1.102	1.081	1.118	1.060	1.123	1.080	1.079			
18																				

11.16 / 11.19 / 11.20 / 11.21

FIGURE 11.21 Optimal Solution for the GD Model

- For the highest-ranking product, raise the purchase quantity toward its maximum sales level. As we increase the purchase quantity, only two things can happen: either we reach the maximum for that product (in which case we go to the next highest priority product), or we use up the credit limit (in which case we are done).

The ranking mechanism prioritizes the products. Using these priorities, we essentially separate the products into three groups: a set of high-priority products, produced at their maximum levels; a set of low-priority products, produced at their minimum levels; and a *single* medium-priority product, produced at a level somewhere between its minimum and maximum. (This product is the one we are adding to the purchase plan when we use up the credit limit.) This procedure is complete and unambiguous, and this pattern describes the optimal solution without explicitly using any numbers. At first, the solution was just a collection of positive decision variables and binding constraints. But we were able to convert the solution into a prioritized list of allocations that establish the values of the decision variables one at a time.

Actually, Solver's solution merely distinguishes the three priority classes; it does not reveal the profit-to-cost ratio rule explicitly. That insight might come from reviewing the makeup of the priority classes, or from some intuition about how single-constraint problems are optimized. (The profit-to-cost ratios are shown for confirmation in row 17 of Figure 11.21.) But this brings up an important point. Solver does not usually reveal the economic reason why a variable should have high priority, and it is not always necessary (or even possible) for us to know why an allocation receives high priority. We simply notice a binding constraint containing just one positive variable, and that leads us toward a better understanding of the solution.

Again, we can alter the base-case model slightly and follow the consequences for the optimal purchase plan. For example, if we raise the credit limit, the only change in the solution will be the purchase of additional cartons of the medium-priority product. Thus, the marginal value of raising the credit limit by a dollar is equivalent to the incremental profit per dollar of purchase cost for the medium-priority product, or $0.118. We could confirm this result by rerunning Solver with one additional dollar of credit.

Suppose instead that we were to increase the amount of a low-priority product in the purchase plan. Then, following the optimal pattern, we would have to purchase less of the medium-priority product owing to the tight credit limit. Consider the purchase of more squash than the 100-carton minimum. Each additional carton of squash will cost $2.50, substituting for about 0.892 carton of lima beans in the credit constraint. The net effect on profit is as follows:

- Add a carton of squash (increase profit by $0.20).
- Remove 0.892 carton of lima beans (decrease profit by $0.2946).
- Therefore, net cost = $0.0946.

Thus, each carton of squash we force into the purchase plan, above the minimum sales level of 100, will reduce profits by 9.46 cents. If we were to rerun the model requiring 101 cartons of squash, we would confirm that profit declines by exactly this amount.

Comparing the analysis of GD's decision with the product mix example considered earlier, we see that the optimal pattern, when translated into a computational scheme, is complete and unambiguous in both cases. We can use the pattern to determine the shadow price on a binding constraint or to derive marginal costs of introducing nonoptimal decisions. A specific feature of GD's model is the focus on one particular bottleneck constraint. This feature helps us understand the role of a binding constraint when we interpret a pattern; however, in many problems, there is more than one binding constraint.

EXAMPLE
Production Planning

The production planning problem has several formulations. In one version, a company has contracted to meet a certain demand schedule and faces constraints on production capacity. The problem is to find a least-cost production plan. In our example, a company produces two products (A and B) using two types of machines (X and Y) over a planning period of three months. The products can be produced on either machine, and the following table describes the machine hours required to make a single unit of each product.

	Product A	Product B
Hours on Machine X	2.0	1.5
Hours on Machine Y	2.5	2.0

Machine capacities in hours on X and Y are given for each of the three months. In addition, the quantities to be delivered each month, according to the contract, are also given.

Month	X-Capacity	Y-Capacity	A-Demand	B-Demand
1	140	250	50	30
2	60	80	100	60
3	150	100	50	50

The relevant costs are labor on each machine ($30.00/hour) and inventory held ($10.00/unit/month, for either product). ■

Figure 11.22 provides a linear programming model for this problem, with the optimal solution shown. The variables in this model are of two kinds. One kind is the number of units of each product scheduled for production, broken down by machine and by month—for example, $AX1$. The other kind is the inventory of each product held from one month to the next—for example, $AI1$. The inventory variables allow us to express demand constraints using the basic accounting definition of inventory: Final inventory must be equal to starting inventory plus production minus shipments. One such equation applies to each product in each month (rows 21–26).

Our Solver parameters are as follows:

Target cell	R13 (maximize)
Changing cells	B10:Q10
Constraints	R15:R20 $\leq$ T15:T20
	R21:R26 $=$ T21:T26

A look at the optimal solution in Figure 11.22 leads us to the following description of the pattern:

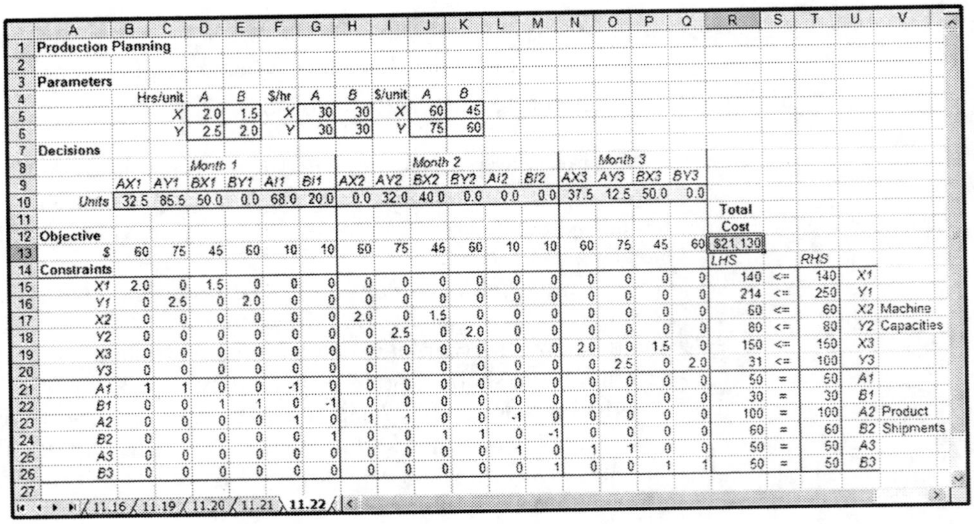

	A	B	C	D	E	F	G	H	I	J	K	L	M	N	O	P	Q	R	S	T	U	V
1	**Production Planning**																					
2																						
3	**Parameters**																					
4			Hrs/unit	*A*	*B*	$/hr	*A*	*B*	$/unit	*A*	*B*											
5			*X*	2.0	1.5	*X*	30	30	*X*	60	45											
6			*Y*	2.5	2.0	*Y*	30	30	*Y*	75	60											
7	**Decisions**																					
8				*Month 1*						*Month 2*					*Month 3*							
9		*AX1*	*AY1*	*BX1*	*BY1*	*AI1*	*BI1*	*AX2*	*AY2*	*BX2*	*BY2*	*AI2*	*BI2*	*AX3*	*AY3*	*BX3*	*BY3*					
10	*Units*	32.5	85.5	50.0	0.0	68.0	20.0	0.0	32.0	40.0	0.0	0.0	0.0	37.5	12.5	50.0	0.0					
11																		**Total**				
12	**Objective**																	**Cost**				
13	*$*	60	75	45	60	10	10	60	75	45	60	10	10	60	75	45	60	$21,130				
14	**Constraints**																	*LHS*		*RHS*		
15	*X1*	2.0	0	1.5	0	0	0	0	0	0	0	0	0	0	0	0	0	140	<=	140	*X1*	
16	*Y1*	0	2.5	0	2.0	0	0	0	0	0	0	0	0	0	0	0	0	214	<=	250	*Y1*	
17	*X2*	0	0	0	0	0	0	2.0	0	1.5	0	0	0	0	0	0	0	60	<=	60	*X2*	Machine
18	*Y2*	0	0	0	0	0	0	0	2.5	0	2.0	0	0	0	0	0	0	80	<=	80	*Y2*	Capacities
19	*X3*	0	0	0	0	0	0	0	0	0	0	0	0	2.0	0	1.5	0	150	<=	150	*X3*	
20	*Y3*	0	0	0	0	0	0	0	0	0	0	0	0	0	2.5	0	2.0	31	<=	100	*Y3*	
21	*A1*	1	1	0	0	-1	0	0	0	0	0	0	0	0	0	0	0	50	=	50	*A1*	
22	*B1*	0	0	1	1	0	-1	0	0	0	0	0	0	0	0	0	0	30	=	30	*B1*	
23	*A2*	0	0	0	0	1	0	1	1	0	0	-1	0	0	0	0	0	100	=	100	*A2*	Product
24	*B2*	0	0	0	0	0	1	0	0	1	1	0	-1	0	0	0	0	60	=	60	*B2*	Shipments
25	*A3*	0	0	0	0	0	0	0	0	0	0	1	0	1	1	0	0	50	=	50	*A3*	
26	*B3*	0	0	0	0	0	0	0	0	0	0	0	1	0	0	1	1	50	=	50	*B3*	
27																						

FIGURE 11.22 Optimal Solution for the Production Planning Model

- All product shipment constraints are binding (because they were cast as equations in the model).
- Capacity constraints on machine X capacity are binding in each period, but machine Y capacity is binding only in month 2.
- In the optimal production plan, the following variables are positive:

  $AX1, AX3$
  $AY1, AY3$
  $BX1, BX2, BX3$

- The positive inventory variables are $AI1$ and $BI1$.

To convert this pattern into a scheme for calculating the values of the decision variables, we again start by noticing which variables are positive and which are zero. If we focus on product–month combinations, we may not see a distinct pattern, although it becomes clear that the optimal schedule calls for overproduction in the first month, creating inventory that gets consumed in the second month ($AI2$ and $BI2$ are both zero). In the third month, production matches demand exactly. When we focus on product–machine combinations, on the other hand, a detailed pattern begins to take shape. We see that product B is never produced on machine Y ($BY1$, $BY2$, and $BY3$ are all zero), whereas product A is produced on both X and Y. Since machine X capacity is binding in each month, it is evidently important to produce B on X and to avoid producing B on Y. We see that it is also preferable to produce B on X in an earlier period, and to hold it in inventory, as compared to producing B on Y in the period when demand occurs. This observation suggests that the solution can be constructed by the following procedure:

- First, assign X-capacity in each month to make the number of units of B-demand in the same period.
- If X-capacity is inadequate to meet current B-demand, then assign X-capacity in the previous month and hold the items in inventory.
- If X-capacity is more than adequate for B-demand, then assign X-capacity to make the number of units of A-demand in the current period.
- If X-capacity is fully consumed, then assign Y-capacity to make the remaining number of units of A-demand in the current period.
- If Y-capacity is inadequate to meet current A-demand, then assign Y-capacity in the previous month and hold the items in inventory.

Clearly, machine X has a cost advantage over machine Y in making both products: Its hourly cost is the same, and it takes less time to produce either product. It is this relative cost advantage that leads to the pattern in the optimal solution. Here again, we have interpreted the optimal solution without explicitly using a number, yet we have provided a complete and unambiguous description of the solution. This description can be viewed as a system of priorities that determines the variables one at a time, in sequence.

Again, we can test our characterization of the optimal pattern by deriving the shadow prices. For example, suppose that the capacity of X were increased by one hour in month 1. Given the optimal pattern, we should want to transfer some production of A at the margin from machine Y to machine X. The extra hour of X would accommodate 1/2 unit of A. This would reduce production of A by 5/4 of an hour on Y. In cost terms, the extra hour of X incurs a cost of $30.00, while 5/4 of an hour on Y will be saved, at a benefit of $37.50. The net benefit is $7.50, which is the shadow price on the capacity constraint for machine X in month 1. We could, of course, confirm this result by rerunning Solver with one more hour of capacity on X.

As another example of altering the problem slightly, suppose that we increase by one unit the quantity of product A to be delivered in month 1. The marginal cost of meeting this shipment is just the cost of producing one more unit of product A on Y.

This amount is $75.00, which turns out to be the shadow price for the corresponding constraint. Suppose instead that we increase by one unit the quantity of product A to be delivered in month 2. In this case, the marginal cost is $85.00, since the marginal unit must be produced in month 1 (at a cost of $75.00) and held in inventory one month (at a cost of $10.00), because no capacity remains in month 2 under the optimal plan.

Suppose now that we increase by one unit the quantity of product B to be delivered in month 2. According to the pattern, we prefer to make this unit on machine X, but X is fully committed to product B during month 2. Following the pattern, we want to make product B on X during month 1 and hold it in inventory; to do so, however, we will have to transfer some production of A from machine X to machine Y. To find the marginal cost of this entire adjustment, we have to follow the economic implications of each element of the marginal change:

- Make one unit of B on X (time $= 1.5$ hrs; cost $= \$45.00$).
- Hold one unit of B one month (cost $= \$10.00$).
- Remove 1.5 hrs of A production from X (cost saved $= \$45.00; \frac{3}{4}$ unit).
- Add $\frac{3}{4}$ unit of A production to Y (time $= \frac{15}{8}$ hrs; cost $= \$56.25$).
- Therefore, net cost $= \$45.00 + \$10.00 - \$45.00 + \$56.25 = \$66.25$.

Once again, knowing the qualitative pattern in the optimal solution allows us to anticipate how that solution will change when the problem is modified. Moreover, we can calculate shadow prices by quantifying the implications of the pattern for changes in the constraint constants.

11.6.3 Review

The foregoing examples illustrate the process of extracting insight from the solution to a linear programming problem. By focusing just on positive variables and binding constraints, we try to rebuild the optimal solution from the given parameters, with the determination of one variable at a time, if possible. At the first step, we look for a binding constraint containing a single variable. That combination allows us to deduce the value of the variable immediately. Then, with that value known, we look for another binding constraint containing just one other variable, and we continue in this fashion. This construction can often be interpreted as a list of priorities, and those priorities reveal the economic forces at work.

Answers to two diagnostic questions help determine whether we have been successful at extracting a pattern:

- Is the pattern complete and unambiguous?
- Where do the shadow prices come from?

The answer to the first question takes us to a full solution of the problem, specifying all of the decision variables in the optimal solution uniquely. The second question invites us to alter one constraint constant in the original problem and trace the incremental changes in the variables, allowing us to derive the shadow price for the corresponding constraint. Note that this derivation is not necessary except to achieve a deeper interpretation of the results, because we can determine the value of the shadow price simply by running Solver Sensitivity.

Patterns, as we have suggested, have certain limits. If we test our specification of a pattern by deriving shadow prices, we have to recognize that a shadow price has a limited range over which it holds. (Recall from Figure 11.19 that the shadow price on fabrication time was $4.00 up to 2,000 hours and then dropped to $3.75.) Beyond this range, a different pattern prevails. As we change a right-hand side constant, there will eventually be a change in the shadow price. The same is true of the pattern: beyond the range in which the shadow price holds, the pattern may change. In the production planning example, however, we were able to describe the pattern in a fairly general way, so that it holds even when the shadow price changes.

Unfortunately, the pattern cannot always be reduced to a list of assignments in priority order. Occasionally it happens that, once we identify the positive variables and the binding constraints in the optimal solution, we might be able to say no more than that the pattern comes from solving a system of equations determined by the binding constraints and the positive variables. Nevertheless, in most cases, as the foregoing examples indicate, we can learn a great deal about the underlying economics by looking for patterns in the optimal solution.

11.7* DATA ENVELOPMENT ANALYSIS

Data Envelopment Analysis (DEA) is a linear programming application aimed at evaluating the efficiencies of similar organizational departments or *decision-making units* (DMUs, as they are called). The DMUs are characterized in terms of their inputs and outputs, but not in terms of their operating details. A DMU is considered **efficient** if it gets the most output from its inputs. In the diagram of Figure 11.23, for example, a DMU has three outputs (y_1, y_2, and y_3) and two inputs (x_1 and x_2). Its efficiency is defined as the value of its outputs divided by the value of its inputs. An inefficient DMU could potentially produce greater output value from the same inputs, or it could produce the same outputs from smaller input value. The purpose of DEA is to identify inefficient DMUs when there are multiple outputs and multiple inputs.

When inputs and outputs are treated as multidimensional, we need to use weighting factors to produce an overall efficiency measure. We compute the total value of two *inputs* x_1 and x_2 as $v_1 x_1 + v_2 x_2$. The input quantities are obtained from historical data, and the weights v_1 and v_2 are determined in the analysis. Similarly, we compute the total value of three *outputs* as $u_1 y_1 + u_2 y_2 + u_3 y_3$, where the output quantities (y_1, y_2, y_3) are historical data and the weights (u_1, u_2, u_3) are determined in the analysis. The efficiency measure is then the ratio of weighted outputs to weighted inputs:

$$E = \frac{u_1 y_1 + u_2 y_2 + u_3 y_3}{v_1 x_1 + v_2 x_2}$$

EXAMPLE
Burritoville
Restaurants

Juan Pimiento has been a successful entrepreneur, developing a chain of Mexican restaurants in the Southwest. A few years ago, he opened his first Burritoville store. When it became profitable and popular in its first two years, Juan built some new stores, bought similar competing stores, and eventually found himself the owner of a restaurant chain. Because some of the stores in the chain had been existing restaurants, and because he was inclined to experiment with store designs and menus, there were differences in the way the various stores operated. From his new vantage point, Juan thought that it might be a good idea to evaluate where in the chain things were going well and where they were not.

After reading up on DEA, Juan has come up with some historical data to summarize performance of his stores. The key outputs in his analysis are monthly profit and peak daily volume. The key inputs are labor hours and monthly facility cost. He has gathered the following data for the restaurants in the chain.

Store ID	Monthly Profit	Peak Volume	Labor Hours	Facility Cost
1	761	109	56	1,476
2	925	103	72	1,613
3	788	119	64	1,612
4	858	114	63	1,381
5	928	107	70	1,748
6	758	120	72	1,645
7	963	104	66	1,290
8	918	119	60	1,779
9	876	94	61	1,325
10	997	102	72	1,453

The data for monthly profit and facility cost have come directly from accounting records in the company. The average daily labor hours have been pulled together by store managers, working from daily personnel schedules. Peak volumes have been determined by having someone stand at the front door to count (and greet) customers coming into the store. With the data collection effort finished, Juan hopes that DEA can provide some insight into levels of efficiency at the various locations. ∎

Let's address the efficiency analysis for Store 1. Given the historical data, we know that the efficiency measure for Store 1 takes the following form

$$E_1 = \frac{u_1 y_1 + u_2 y_2}{v_1 x_1 + v_2 x_2} = \frac{761 u_1 + 109 u_2}{56 v_1 + 1476 v_2}$$

with the weights yet to be determined. The DEA method imposes two conditions on the analysis. First, to rescale the efficiency measure, the denominator is set equal to 1. Thus:

$$56 v_1 + 1476 v_2 = 1$$

Second, by convention, DEA requires that output value cannot exceed input value, for any of the DMUs, or:

$$761 u_1 + 109 u_2 - 56 v_1 - 1476 v_2 \leq 0 \quad \textit{for Store } 1$$
$$925 u_1 + 103 u_2 - 72 v_1 - 1613 v_2 \leq 0 \quad \textit{for Store } 2$$

and similarly for the eight remaining DMUs.

At this stage, the analysis turns to linear programming to find the weights that produce the largest efficiency value for Store 1. Because the denominator (input value) of E_1 is scaled to 1, the optimization problem for Store 1 simplifies to maximizing the output value, $761 u_1 + 109 u_2$.

Figure 11.24 shows the worksheet for the analysis, using the standard format for an allocation model. The objective function in this model corresponds to the output value of Store 1, computed by a SUMPRODUCT formula in cell G18. The equality constraint that fixes the value of inputs can be found in row 20, while the normalizing convention (requiring that output values never exceed input values) can be found in rows 21–30.

In the Solver Parameters window, we enter the following information.

Target cell	G18 (maximize)
Changing cells	C16:F16
Constraints	G20 = I20
	G21:G30 ≤ I21:I30

When we run Solver on this model, we obtain an objective function of 1.00, as shown in the figure, along with the following weights:

Output	Profit weight (u_1)	0.00027
Output	Volume weight (u_2)	0.00728
Input	Labor weight (v_1)	0.01199
Input	Facilities weight (v_2)	0.00022

With these weights, the input value is 1.0 and the output value is 1.0 for Store 1, resulting in an efficiency of 100 percent. In effect, we have imagined that the manager of Store 1 has been acting to optimize some measure of efficiency. Our model tells us that if that measure were based on weights of 0.00027, 0.00728, 0.01199, and 0.00022, then indeed, Store 1 would have the highest efficiency among the stores in the chain. In other words, there is at least one set of weights for which Store 1 performs as well as any other store in the set. In that sense, we can conclude that Store 1 is operating efficiently.

Figure 11.25 shows the analysis for Store 2. The format is the same as that for Store 1, and only two changes occur. First, the objective function now contains data for Store 2 in row 18. Second, the coefficients for the constraint on input value

FIGURE 11.23 Conceptual Description of a Decision Making Unit

Inputs   Outputs

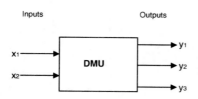

FIGURE 11.24 Analysis of Store 1 in the Burritoville DEA Model

	A	B	C	D	E	F	G	H	I
1	Restaurants								
2			*Outputs*		*Inputs*				
3	Data	*DMU*	*Profit*	*Volume*	*Hours*	*Cost*			
4		Store 1	761	109	56	1476			
5		Store 2	925	103	72	1613			
6		Store 3	788	119	64	1612			
7		Store 4	858	114	63	1381			
8		Store 5	928	107	70	1748			
9		Store 6	758	120	72	1645			
10		Store 7	963	104	66	1290			
11		Store 8	918	119	60	1779			
12		Store 9	876	94	61	1325			
13		Store 10	997	102	72	1453			
14									
15								DMU	1
16	Decisions	*Weights*	0.00027	0.00728	0.01199	0.00022			
17									
18	Objective	*Efficiency*	761	109	56	1476	1.000		
19									
20	Constraints	Input	0	0	56	1476	1.000	=	1
21		Store 1	761	109	-56	-1476	0.000	<=	0
22		Store 2	925	103	-72	-1613	-0.221	<=	0
23		Store 3	788	119	-64	-1612	-0.046	<=	0
24		Store 4	858	114	-63	-1381	0.000	<=	0
25		Store 5	928	107	-70	-1748	-0.198	<=	0
26		Store 6	758	120	-72	-1645	-0.150	<=	0
27		Store 7	963	104	-66	-1290	-0.060	<=	0
28		Store 8	918	119	-60	-1779	0.000	<=	0
29		Store 9	876	94	-61	-1325	-0.104	<=	0
30		Store 10	997	102	-72	-1453	-0.173	<=	0
31									

contain data for Store 2 in row 20. Otherwise, the parameters of the linear program remain unchanged from the analysis of Store 1. When we run Solver on this model, we obtain an objective function of 0.869, as shown in the figure, along with the following weights:

Output	Profit weight (u_1)	0.00094
Output	Volume weight (u_2)	0.0
Input	Labor weight (v_1)	0.01241
Input	Facilities weight (v_2)	0.00007

With these weights, the input value is 1.0, and the output value is 0.869, resulting in an efficiency of 86.9 percent. Note that cells G27 and G28 are zero. This means that the normalizing constraint is binding for Stores 7 and 8. In other words, Stores 7 and 8 have efficiencies of 100 percent, even at the most favorable weights for Store 2. In effect, we have imagined that the manager of Store 2 has been acting to optimize

FIGURE 11.25 Analysis of Store 2 in the Burritoville DEA Model

	A	B	C	D	E	F	G	H	I
1	Restaurants								
2			*Outputs*		*Inputs*				
3	Data	*DMU*	*Profit*	*Volume*	*Hours*	*Cost*			
4		Store 1	761	109	56	1476			
5		Store 2	925	103	72	1613			
6		Store 3	788	119	64	1612			
7		Store 4	858	114	63	1381			
8		Store 5	928	107	70	1748			
9		Store 6	758	120	72	1645			
10		Store 7	963	104	66	1290			
11		Store 8	918	119	60	1779			
12		Store 9	876	94	61	1325			
13		Store 10	997	102	72	1453			
14									
15								DMU	2
16	Decisions	*Weights*	0.00094	0.00000	0.01241	0.00007			
17									
18	Objective	*Efficiency*	925	103	0	0	0.869		
19									
20	Constraints	Input	0	0	72	1613	1.000	=	1
21		Store 1	761	109	-56	-1476	-0.078	<=	0
22		Store 2	925	103	-72	-1613	-0.131	<=	0
23		Store 3	788	119	-64	-1612	-0.161	<=	0
24		Store 4	858	114	-63	-1381	-0.067	<=	0
25		Store 5	928	107	-70	-1748	-0.113	<=	0
26		Store 6	758	120	-72	-1645	-0.290	<=	0
27		Store 7	963	104	-66	-1290	0.000	<=	0
28		Store 8	918	119	-60	-1779	0.000	<=	0
29		Store 9	876	94	-61	-1325	-0.022	<=	0
30		Store 10	997	102	-72	-1453	-0.053	<=	0
31									

some measure of efficiency. Our model tells us that if that measure were based on weights of 0.00094, 0.0, 0.01241, and 0.00007, then Store 2 would achieve the highest efficiency it could reach, 0.869. But even then, two other stores in the chain would achieve higher efficiency values. In that sense, we can conclude that Store 2 is operating inefficiently. When we analyze other stores in the chain, we can discover which ones are operating efficiently.

We could construct similar worksheets for the analysis of other stores following the same format. However, much of the content on those worksheets would be identical, so we can design a more streamlined approach to the analysis. Figure 11.25 contains a version of the model that actually handles the analysis for all 10 stores. The array in rows 4–13, as before, contains the problem data. Cell I15 contains the store number for the DMU being analyzed. Based on this choice, two adjustments must be made in the linear programming model. First, the outputs for the store being analyzed must be selected for use in the objective function, in cells C18:D18. Second, the inputs for the store being analyzed must be selected for use in the equality constraint, in cells E20:F20. These selections are highlighted in bold in Figure 11.25. The INDEX function uses the store number in cell I15 to copy the objective function coefficients from the data array into cells C18:D18. It also copies the input values from the data array into cells E20:F20. The four cells in bold format thus change when we enter a different selection in cell I15.

EXCEL TIP
The INDEX
Function

The INDEX function in Excel finds a value in a rectangular array according to the row number and column number of its location. The basic form of the function, as we use it for DEA models, is the following:

INDEX(*Array, Row, Column*)

- *Array* references a rectangular array.
- *Row* specifies a row number in the array.
- *Column* specifies a column number in the array. If *Array* has just one column, then this argument can be omitted.

In the example of Figure 11.25, suppose *Array* = C4:C13 and *Row* = I15. When cell I15 contains the number 4, the function INDEX(C4:C13, $I$15) finds the element in the fourth row of the array in cells C4:C13. In this case, the function returns the Profit output value for Store 4, or 858. This calculation would be suitable for cell C18, and the formula could be copied to cell D18, producing the entry INDEX(D4:D13, $I$15) and the corresponding value of 114. ∎

The analysis of the stores in the chain requires that we solve the model in Figure 11.25 several times, once for each DMU. In our example, we vary the contents of cell I15 from 1 to 10. For each value, we save the essential results in some other place before switching to a new DMU. In particular, we want to save the weights and the value of the objective function. Figure 11.26 shows a worksheet containing a summary of the 10 optimizations for the 10-store example (one from each choice of cell G16). This summary can be generated automatically with one run of the Solver Sensitivity tool.

As we can see in Figure 11.26, there are four efficient stores in our example: Stores 1, 4, 7, and 8. The other stores are inefficient, at levels ranging from 87 to 97 percent.

FIGURE 11.26 Sensitivity Report for the Allocation Example

	A	B	C	D	E	F	G
1	DMU	Efficiency	*Profit*	*Volume*	*Hours*	*Cost*	
2	1	1.000	0.00027	0.00728	0.01199	0.00022	
3	2	0.869	0.00094	0.00000	0.01241	0.00007	
4	3	0.973	0.00000	0.00818	0.00927	0.00025	
5	4	1.000	0.00012	0.00786	0.00000	0.00072	
6	5	0.885	0.00095	0.00000	0.01261	0.00007	
7	6	0.907	0.00000	0.00756	0.00856	0.00023	
8	7	1.000	0.00104	0.00000	0.00000	0.00078	
9	8	1.000	0.00109	0.00000	0.01440	0.00008	
10	9	0.974	0.00111	0.00000	0.01470	0.00008	
11	10	0.946	0.00095	0.00000	0.01254	0.00007	
12							

11.26

This means that the inefficient stores could probably learn something by examining the way that the efficient stores are run. For this reason, DEA is often used to organize benchmarking visits within the divisions or branches of a large organization.

11.8 SUMMARY

Linear programming represents the most widely used optimization technique in practice. In this chapter, we have taken note of the special features of a linear program: a linear objective function and linear constraints. Linearity in the optimization model allows us to apply the simplex method as a solution procedure, which in turn guarantees finding a global optimum whenever an optimum of any kind exists. Therefore, when we have a choice, we are better off with a linear formulation of a problem than with a nonlinear formulation.

To develop facility with the linear solver, it helps to practice formulating, solving, and interpreting linear programming problems. The spreadsheet layout can be somewhat standardized, and a number of additional guidelines become helpful.

- Follow a standard form whenever possible, relying on the SUMPRODUCT function.
- Enter cell references in the Solver windows; keep numerical values in cells.
- Use a linear model in preference to a nonlinear model.
- If the model contains simple bounds, place them near the decision variable cells.
- Show constraint relationships ($\leq, =, \geq$) on the worksheet.
- Group like constraints together (i.e., similar in logical direction.)
- Align data with decisions when appropriate.

- Use the weak form of a constraint and give the model maximum flexibility.
- For blending models, add redundant but more intuitive calculations of blending constraints, outside of the Solver model.
- Explore some feasible (and infeasible) possibilities as a way of debugging the model.
- Test intuition and suggest hypotheses before running Solver.
- Identify the patterns of economic priorities that appear in the solution.

Along with the technical information that we have covered, these guidelines help accelerate the process of building and applying linear programming models successfully.

One last caveat: While optimization is a powerful technique, we should not assume that a solution that is optimal for a model is also optimal for the real world. Because every model is a simplification, any optimal solution from a model must be interpreted before it can be applied in the real world. Often, the realities of the application will force changes in the optimal solution determined by the model. One powerful method for making this translation is to look for the pattern, or the economic priorities, in the optimal solution. These economic priorities are often more valuable to decision makers than the precise solution to a particular instance of the model.

SUGGESTED READINGS

Some advanced perspectives on optimization techniques, along with some guidance in constructing optimization models, can be found in the following books:

Baker, K. R. 2006. *Optimization Modeling with Spreadsheets.* Belmont, CA: Duxbury Press.

Fourer, R., D. F. Gay, and B. W. Kernighan. 2003. *AMPL: A Modeling Language for Mathematical Programming.* Belmont, CA: Duxbury Press.

Rardin, R. L. 1998. *Optimization in Operations Research.* Upper Saddle River, N J: Prentice–Hall.

Schrage, L. 1997. *Optimization Modeling with LINDO.* 5th ed. Belmont, CA: Duxbury Press.

Williams, H. P. 1999. *Model Building in Mathematical Programming.* 3d ed. Chichester: John Wiley & Sons.

EXERCISES

1. *Production Planning.* The Bogard Corporation produces three types of bookcases, which it sells to large office supply companies. The production of each bookcase requires two machine operations, trimming and shaping, followed by assembly, which includes inspection and packaging. All three types require 0.4 hour of assembly time, but the machining operations have different processing times, as shown here, in hours per unit:

	Standard	Narrow	Wide
Trimmer	0.2	0.4	0.6
Shaper	0.6	0.2	0.5

Each machine is available 150 hours per month, and the current size of the assembly department provides capacity of 600 hours. Each bookcase produced yields a unit profit contribution as follows:

	Standard	Narrow	Wide
Profit	$8	$6	$10

a. What are the optimal production quantities for the company?

b. What is the pattern in the optimal allocation?

2. *Fertilizing the Lawn.* The facilities manager at Oxbridge University is planning to apply fertilizer to the grass in the quadrangle area in the spring. The grass needs nitrogen, phosphorus, and potash in at least the amounts given in the following table.

Mineral	Minimum Weight (lb)
Nitrogen	12
Phosphorus	14
Potash	18

Three kinds of commercial fertilizer are available, with mineral content and prices per 1,000 pounds as given in the following table. There is virtually unlimited supply of each kind of fertilizer.

Fertilizer	Nitrogen Content (lb)	Phosphorus Content (lb)	Potash Content (lb)	Price ($)
A	20	10	5	10
B	10	5	15	8
C	15	10	5	7

How much of each fertilizer should be purchased to satisfy the requirements at minimum cost?

3. *Coordinating Production and Marketing.* The Andrews Apple Products Company purchases apples from local growers and makes applesauce and apple juice. It costs $0.80 to produce a jar of applesauce and $0.60 to produce a bottle of apple juice. The company has a policy that at least 20 percent but not more than 60 percent of its output must be applesauce.

The company wants to meet but not exceed the demand for each product. The marketing manager estimates that the demand for applesauce is a maximum of 5,000 jars, plus an additional 3 jars for each $1 spent on advertising for applesauce. The maximum demand for apple juice is estimated to be 4,000 bottles, plus an additional 5 bottles for every $1 spent on advertising for apple juice. The company has $16,000 to spend on producing and advertising its two products. Applesauce sells for $1.75 per jar; apple juice sells for $1.75 per bottle. The company wants to know how many units of each product to produce, and how much advertising to spend on each product, in order to maximize profit.

a. What are the optimal quantities of applesauce and apple juice for Andrews to produce? (Rounding off is acceptable.)

b. What is the optimal amount to spend on advertising? What is the optimal profit?

c. Describe the qualitative pattern in the solution.

4. *Managing a Portfolio.* A local bank wants to build a bond portfolio from a set of five bonds with $1 million available for investment. The expected annual return, the worst-case annual return on each bond, and the "duration" of each bond are given in the following table. (The duration of a bond is a measure of the bond's sensitivity to interest rates.)

	Expected Return	Worst Case Return	Duration
Bond 1	12.5%	8.0%	8
Bond 2	11.5%	7.5%	7
Bond 3	10.5%	6.8%	6
Bond 4	9.5%	7.0%	5
Bond 5	8.5%	7.4%	3

- The average worst-case return for the portfolio must be at least 7.2 percent.
- The average duration of the portfolio must be at most 6.
- Because of diversification requirements, at most 40 percent of the total amount invested can be invested in a single bond.

a. What is the maximum return on the $1 million investment? How should the investment be distributed among the bonds to achieve this return? (Assume that bonds can be purchased in fractional amounts.)

b. What is the qualitative pattern in the optimal solution?

c. What is the marginal rate of return on the investment amount? That is, what would be the percentage return on an additional dollar invested? (Give the percentage to four significant figures.)

5. *Planning Automobile Production.* The Auto Company of America (ACA) produces four types of cars: subcompact, compact, intermediate, and luxury. ACA also produces trucks and vans. Vendor capacities limit total production capacity to at most 1.2 million vehicles per year. Subcompacts and compacts are built together in a facility with a total annual capacity of 620,000 cars. Intermediate and luxury cars are produced in another facility with capacity of 400,000; and the truck/van facility has a capacity of 275,000. ACA's marketing strategy requires that subcompacts and compacts must constitute at least half of the product mix for the four car types. The Corporate Average Fuel Economy (CAFE) standards in the Energy Policy and Conservation Act require an average fleet fuel economy of at least 27 mpg.

Profit margins, market potential, and fuel efficiencies are summarized as follows:

Type	Profit Margin ($/vehicle)	Market Potential (sales in '000)	Fuel Economy (mpg)
Subcompact	150	600	40
Compact	225	400	34

Intermediate	250	300	15
Luxury	500	225	12
Truck	400	325	20
Van	200	100	25

a. What is the optimal profit for ACA?

b. What is the pattern in the optimal allocation?

c. How much would optimal annual profits drop if the fuel economy requirement were raised to 28 mpg?

6. *Making Beer.* The Schutzberg Brewery has received an order for 1500 gallons of 3 percent beer (that is, 3 percent alcoholic content). This is a custom order because Schutzberg does not produce a 3 percent product. They do brew the following products.

Product	Percent Alcohol	Cost per Gallon
Free	0.25	0.55
Light	2.50	0.65
Amber	4.50	0.80
Dark	6.00	0.75

There are 500 gallons of each of these products on hand. Rather than brewing a 3 percent beer from scratch, the brewmaster has decided to mix existing stocks, perhaps with some water (0 percent alcoholic content), to satisfy this small order in the shortest possible time, hoping that the taste will be adequate. In case the taste is bad and he has to throw the mixture out, he would like to minimize the cost of the mix.

a. What are the components of the least-cost blend that will result in a 3 percent beer?

b. What is the total cost for the 1,500 gallons of product?

c. Use the pattern in (b) to trace the effects of increasing the order by 10 percent. How will the optimal mix change? How will the optimal cost change?

7. *Make or Buy.* A sudden increase in the demand for smoke detectors has left Acme Alarms with insufficient capacity to meet demand. The company has seen monthly demand from its retailers for its electronic and battery-operated detectors rise to 20,000 and 10,000, respectively. Acme's production process involves three departments: fabrication, assembly, and shipping. The relevant quantitative data on production and prices are summarized as follows.

Department	Monthly Hours Available	Hours/Unit (Electronic)	Hours/Unit (Battery)
Fabrication	2,000	0.15	0.10
Assembly	4,200	0.20	0.20
Shipping	2,500	0.10	0.15
Variable cost/unit		$18.80	$16.00
Retail price		$29.50	$28.00

The company also has the option to obtain additional units from a subcontractor, who has offered to supply up to 20,000 units per month in any combination of electric and battery-operated models, at a charge of $21.50 per unit. For this price, the subcontractor will test and ship its models directly to the retailers without using Acme's production process.

a. What are the maximum profit and the corresponding make/buy levels? (Fractional decisions are acceptable.)

b. Describe the qualitative pattern in the solution.

c. Use the pattern in (b) to trace the effects of increasing the fabrication capacity by 10 percent. How will the optimal make/buy mix change? How will the optimal profit change?

d. For how much of a change in fabrication capacity will the pattern persist?

8. *Leasing Warehouse Space.* Cox Cable Company needs to lease warehouse storage space for five months at the start of the year. Cox knows how much space will be required in each month, and the company can purchase a variety of lease contracts to meet these needs. For example, Cox can purchase one-month leases in each month from January to May. The company can also purchase two-month leases in January through April, three-month leases in January through March, four-month leases in January and February, or a five-month lease in January. In total, the company could use 15 possible leases. Cox must decide which leases to purchase and how many square feet to purchase on each lease.

Since the space requirements differ month to month, it may be economical to lease only the amount needed each month on a month-by-month basis. On the other hand, the monthly cost for leasing space for additional months is much less than for the first month, so it may be desirable to lease the maximum amount needed for the entire five months. Another option is the intermediate approach of changing the total amount of space leased (by adding a new lease and/or having an old lease expire) at least once, but not every month. Two or more leases for different terms can begin at the same time.

The space requirements (in square feet) are shown in the following table.

	Month				
	Jan	Feb	Mar	Apr	May
Required space	15,000	10,000	20,000	5,000	25,000

Leasing costs (in dollars per thousand square feet) are given in the next table.

	Length of Lease				
	1	2	3	4	5
Cost ($/TSF)	$280	450	600	730	820

The task is to find a leasing schedule that provides the necessary amounts of space at the minimum cost.

a. Determine the optimal leasing schedule. What is the optimal total cost and the corresponding schedule?

b. Describe the qualitative pattern in the solution.

c. Use the pattern in (b) to trace the effects of increasing the space required for January. How will the leasing schedule change? How will the total cost change?

d. For how much of a change in January's requirement will the pattern persist?

9. Oil Blending. An oil company produces three brands of oils: Regular, Multigrade, and Supreme. Each brand of oil is composed of one or more of four crude stocks, each having a different viscosity index. The relevant data concerning the crude stocks are:

Crude Stock	Viscosity Index	Cost ($/barrel)	Supply per day (barrels)
1	20	7.10	1,000
2	40	8.50	1,100
3	30	7.70	1,200
4	55	9.00	1,100

Each brand of oil must meet a minimum standard for viscosity index, and each brand thus sells at a different price. The relevant data concerning the three brands of oil are:

Brand	Minimum Viscosity Index	Selling Price ($/barrel)	Daily Demand (barrels)
Regular	25	8.50	2,000
Multigrade	35	9.00	1,500
Supreme	50	10.00	750

a. The daily demands represent potential sales. In other words, the model should contain demand ceilings (upper limits). What is the optimal profit under these assumptions?

b. The daily demands are to be met precisely. In other words, the model should contain demand constraints in the form of equalities. What is the optimal profit under these assumptions?

c. The daily demands represent minimum sales commitments, but all output can be sold. In other words, the model should permit production to exceed daily demand. What is the optimal profit under these assumptions?

10. Coffee Blending and Sales. Hill-O-Beans Coffee Company blends four component beans into three final blends of coffee: one is sold to luxury hotels, another to restaurants, and the third to supermarkets for store-label brands. The company has four reliable bean supplies: Robusta, Javan Arabica, Liberica, and Brazilian Arabica. The following table summarizes the very precise recipes for the final coffee blends, the cost and availability information for the four components, and the wholesale price per pound of the final blends. The percentages indicate the fraction of each component to be used in each blend.

Component	Hotel	Restaurant	Market	Cost per Pound	Max Weekly Availability (lbs)
Robusta	20%	35%	10%	$0.60	40,000
Javan Arabica	40%	15%	35%	$0.80	25,000
Liberica	15%	20%	40%	$0.55	20,000
Brazilian Arabica	25%	30%	15%	$0.70	45,000
Wholesale Price Per Pound	$1.25	$1.50	$1.40		

The processor's plant can handle no more than 100,000 pounds per week, but there is virtually unlimited demand for the final blends. However, the marketing department requires minimum production levels of 10,000, 25,000, and 30,000 pounds, respectively, for the hotel, restaurant, and market blends.

a. In order to maximize weekly profit, how many pounds of each component should be purchased?

b. What is the economic value of an additional pound's worth of plant capacity?

c. How much (per pound) should Hill-O-Beans be willing to pay for additional pounds of Liberica in order to raise total profit?

d. Construct a graph to show how the optimal profit varies with the minimum weekly production level of the hotel blend.

e. Construct a graph to show how the optimal profit varies with the unit cost of Robusta beans.

11. Coordinating advertising and production. The Hawley Lighting Company manufactures four families of household lighting at its factory. The product families are table lamps, floor lamps, ceiling fixtures, and pendant lamps. The following table shows the average material costs for each of the products.

Product	Table	Floor	Ceiling	Pendant
Material cost	$66	85	50	80

Each product is made in one of two production processes by purchasing components, assembling and testing the product, and finally packaging it for shipping. Table lamps and floor lamps go through the assembly and finishing process in Department 1, while ceiling fixtures and pendant lamps go through the process in Department 2. Variable production costs and capacities (measured in units of product) are shown in the following table. The capacities are measured in units of product. Note that there are regular and overtime possibilities for each department.

Process	Regular Time		Overtime	
	Unit Cost	Capacity	Unit Cost	Capacity
Department 1	$16	100,000	18	25,000
Department 2	12	90,000	15	24,000

Average selling prices for the four products are known, and estimates have been made of the market demand for each product at these prices. These figures are shown in the following table.

	Table	Floor	Ceiling	Pendant
Selling price	$120	150	100	160
Potential sales (000)	60	20	100	35
Advertising effect	12%	10%	8%	15%

Sales levels can also be affected by advertising expenditures. Starting with the demand levels in the table, an increase of up to $10,000 in advertising raises the demand by the percentage shown in the last row. An expenditure of less than $10,000 in advertising will lead to a proportional effect on demand. For example, an increase in advertising of $5,000 for table lamps would raise demand by 6 percent, or 3,600 units. However, there is a budget limit of $18,000 on the total amount to be spent on advertising among all four products.

a. What is an optimal output plan for the company?

b. For each department, what is the marginal value of additional overtime capacity?

c. What is the marginal value of additional advertising dollars?

d. What is the marginal value of additional sales for each product?

12. *Scheduling staff.* You are the director of the Computer Center for Gaillard College and responsible for scheduling the staffing of the center, which is open from 8 A.M. until midnight. You have monitored the usage of the center at various times of the day and determined that the following number of computer consultants are required:

Time of Day	Minimum Number of Consultants Required to Be on Duty
8 A.M. – noon	4
Noon – 4 P.M.	8
4 P.M. – 8 P.M.	10
8 P.M. – midnight	6

Two types of computer consultants can be hired: full-time and part-time. The full-time consultants work for eight consecutive hours in any of the following shifts: morning (8 A.M. – 4 P.M.), afternoon (noon – 8 P.M.), and evening (4 P.M. – midnight). Full-time consultants are paid $14 per hour.

Part-time consultants can be hired to work any of the four shifts listed in the table. Part-time consultants are paid $12 per hour. An additional requirement is that during every time period, at least one full-time consultant must be on duty for every part-time consultant on duty.

a. Determine a minimum-cost staffing plan for the center. How many full-time and part-time consultants will be needed? What is the minimum cost?

b. After thinking about this problem for a while, you have decided to recognize meal breaks explicitly in the schedul-ing of full-time consultants. In particular, full-time consultants are entitled to a one-hour lunch break during their eight-hour shift. In addition, employment rules specify that the lunch break can start after three hours of work or after four hours of work, but those are the only alternatives. Part-time consultants do not receive a meal break. Under these conditions, what staffing schedule minimizes costs? What is the minimum cost?

13. *Project Scheduling.* A construction contractor is responsible for a project with seven key tasks. Some of the tasks can begin at any time, but others have predecessor tasks that must be completed previously. The individual tasks can be carried out at standard times, or they can be expedited ("crashed"). The cost of executing the task increases by a certain cost per day if its time is shortened. The following table shows the information describing the tasks of the project, their standard and minimum times (in days), their standard costs, the crashing cost per day shortened, and the predecessor(s).

Task Number	Minimum Time	Standard Time	Standard Cost	Cost/Day to Shorten	Predecessor Tasks
1	6	12	$ 1,600	$100	None
2	8	16	2,400	75	None
3	16	24	2,900	120	2
4	14	20	1,900	100	1, 2
5	4	16	3,800	140	3
6	12	16	2,900	165	3
7	2	12	1,300	60	4

The project has a deadline of 40 days, which the contractor is committed to meet.

a. If no crashing is done, how long will the project take, and what will be its cost?

b. Which activities should be crashed to achieve the least-cost schedule that meets a 40-day deadline? What is the difference between its cost and the cost in part (a)?

14. *Cargo Loading.* You are in charge of loading cargo ships for International Cargo Company (ICC) at a major East Coast port. You have been asked to prepare a loading plan for an ICC freighter bound for Africa. An agricultural commodities dealer would like to transport the following products aboard this ship:

Commodity	Tons Available	Volume per Ton (cu ft)	Profit per Ton ($)
1	4,000	40	70
2	3,000	25	50
3	2,000	60	60
4	1,000	50	80

You can elect to load any or all of the available commodities. However, the ship has three cargo holds with the following capacity restrictions:

Cargo Hold	Weight Capacity (tons)	Volume Capacity (cu ft)
Forward	3,000	100,000
Center	5,000	150,000
Rear	2,000	120,000

More than one type of commodity can be placed in the same cargo hold. However, because of balance considerations, the weight in the forward cargo hold must be within 10 percent of the weight in the rear cargo hold, and the center cargo hold must be between 40 and 60 percent of the total weight on board.

a. Determine a profit-maximizing loading plan for the commodities. What is the maximum profit and the loading plan that achieves it?

b. Suppose each one of the cargo holds could be expanded. Which holds and which forms of expansion (weight or volume) would allow ICC to increase its profits on this trip, and what is the marginal value of each form of expansion?

15. *Evaluating Performance.* Fidelity Savings & Loans (FS&L) operates a number of banking facilities throughout its region of the country. The officers of FS&L would like to analyze the efficiency of the various branch offices using DEA. The following data set has been selected to represent appropriate input and output measures of each banking facility. (Labor hours and Operating costs are considered inputs; Customer Satisfaction, New Loans and Return on Assets (ROA) are considered outputs.)

Branch	Labor Hrs.	Op. Costs	ROA	New Loans	Customer Satisfaction
1	3.73	6.34	5.32	770	92
2	3.49	4.43	3.39	780	94
3	5.98	6.31	4.95	790	93
4	6.49	7.28	6.01	730	82
5	7.09	8.69	6.40	910	98
6	3.46	3.23	2.89	860	90
7	7.36	9.07	6.94	880	89
8	6.38	7.42	7.18	970	99
9	4.74	6.75	5.98	770	94
10	5.04	6.35	4.97	930	91

a. Which branches are efficient?

b. Which branches are inefficient? For each inefficient branch, which other branches would be good benchmarking targets?

APPENDIX 11.1 THE SENSITIVITY REPORT

The Solver Sensitivity tool duplicates for optimization models the functionality of the Data Sensitivity tool for basic spreadsheet models. That parallelism makes Solver Sensitivity the vehicle of choice for most of the sensitivity analyses we might want to perform with optimization models. However, it is sometimes useful to draw on Excel's own sensitivity tool. The Sensitivity Report is one of three reports offered after a Solver run, once the optimal solution has been found. The other two reports are completely superfluous if a model has been constructed effectively, but the Sensitivity Report sometimes provides additional insight or efficiency.

To provide access to the Sensitivity Report, we must uncheck the box for Bypass Solver Reports in the Solver Options menu. After the optimal solution has been produced, we highlight Sensitivity in the Reports list in the Solver Results window. The Sensitivity Report for linear programs has two sections. The top section (titled Adjustable Cells) deals with the objective function and, in particular, with the coefficients in the objective function corresponding to each of the decision variables. The bottom section (titled Constraints) deals with the values of the constants on the right-hand sides. Figure 11A1 shows the Sensitivity Report for the Veerman Furniture (allocation) example.

In the top section, the report provides the values of the decision variables in the optimal solution (under Final Value) and the values of the coefficients in the objective function (under Objective Coefficient). The Allowable Increase and Allowable Decrease show how much we could change any one of the objective function coefficients without altering the optimal product mix—that is, without altering any of the decision variables. For example, the objective function coefficient for desks is $24.00 in the base case. This figure could rise to $54.00 or drop to $22.50 without having an impact on the optimal product mix. (Of course, the optimal profit would change because the number of desks remains fixed.) A similar range is provided for the other two variables, with 1E+30 symbolizing infinity in the report's output. Finally, there is a column labeled Reduced Cost. Entries in this column are zero for variables that are not at their bound (in this case, the bounds are zero). For chairs, the reduced cost of −1 reflects the fact that the objective function coefficient of $15 would have to improve by more than $1 before there would be an incentive to use chairs in the optimal mix. However, this same information is available in the Allowable Increase column for chairs. In most cases, the Reduced Cost information in the report is redundant.

In the bottom section, the report provides the values of the constraint left-hand sides (under Final Value) and the right-hand-side constraint constants (under Constraint R.H. Side), along with the shadow price for each constraint. The Allowable Increase and Allowable Decrease show how much we could change any one of the constraint constants without altering any of the shadow prices. For

FIGURE 11A1 Sensitivity Report for the Allocation Example

Cell	Name	Final Value	Reduced Cost	Objective Coefficient	Allowable Increase	Allowable Decrease
$B$5	Product mix C	0	-1	15	1	1E+30
$C$5	Product mix D	275	0	24	30	1.5
$D$5	Product mix T	100	0	18	1E+30	10

Constraints

Cell	Name	Final Value	Shadow Price	Constraint R.H. Side	Allowable Increase	Allowable Decrease
$E$11	Fabrication LHS	1850	4	1850	150	1650
$E$12	Assembly LHS	2075	0	2400	1E+30	325
$E$13	Shipping LHS	950	0	1500	1E+30	550
$E$14	Chair market LHS	0	0	360	1E+30	360
$E$15	Desk market LHS	275	0	300	1E+30	25
$E$16	Table market LHS	100	10	100	60.9375	75

FIGURE 11A2 Sensitivity
Report for the Covering
Example

	A	B	C	D	E	F	G	H
1	Microsoft Excel 11.0 Sensitivity Report							
2	Worksheet: [Sheets11.1W.xls]11.9							
3								
4	Adjustable Cells							
5				Final	Reduced	Objective	Allowable	Allowable
6		Cell	Name	Value	Cost	Coefficient	Increase	Decrease
7		$B$5	Amounts S	0.39	0.00	4	1.064766839	3.7
8		$C$5	Amounts R	0.15	0.65	5	1E+30	0.849173554
9		$D$5	Amounts F	1.36	0.00	3	2.651612903	1.72
10		$E$5	Amounts P	0.15	4.35	7	1E+30	4.351239669
11		$F$5	Amounts W	0.15	2.00	6	1E+30	2
12								
13	Constraints							
14				Final	Shadow	Constraint	Allowable	Allowable
15		Cell	Name	Value	Price	R.H. Side	Increase	Decrease
16		$G$11	Vitamins LHS	27.97004132	0	16	11.97004132	1E+30
17		$G$12	Minerals LHS	10.079913223	0	10	0.079132231	1E+30
18		$G$13	Protein LHS	15	0.17768595	15	7.29375	0.319166667
19		$G$14	Calories LHS	600	0.007644628	600	5836.5	8.326086957
20								

example, the number of Fabrication hours (1,850 in the base case) could change from 200 to 2,000 without affecting the shadow price of $4.00.

The ranging analysis for right-hand side constraint constants is omitted for constraints that involve a simple lower bound or upper bound. That is, if the form of the constraint is Variable ≤ Ceiling or else Variable ≥ Floor, then the sensitivity analysis will not appear. But, if the same information is incorporated into the model using the standard SUMPRODUCT constraint form, as in the case of the product mix model, then the Sensitivity Report will treat the constraint in its usual fashion and include it in the Constraints table. As an example, consider the modified version of the Dahlby Outfitters (covering) example, with a floor of 0.15 for each of the decision variables. Although there are four original constraints and five additional constraints limiting the decision variables to values no less than 0.15, the Sensitivity Report shows information for only the four original constraints (see Figure 11A2).

Compared to the Solver Sensitivity output, the Sensitivity Report is more precise but less flexible. The Sensitivity Report is more precise than Solver Sensitivity with respect to the question of where the decision variables change or where a shadow price changes. For our allocation example, recall that we could not tell precisely when the shadow price drops from $3.75 to $2.32. Only by searching on a smaller grid could we detect where the change takes place, and even that would require some careful interpolation in the table to obtain the exact value. By contrast, if we were to solve a base-case model in which there were 2,200 Fabrication hours, and if we asked for the Sensitivity Report, we would be able to see from the Allowable Increase on Fabrication hours that the shadow price holds up to 2,666.67 hours.

The Sensitivity Report is less flexible than Solver Sensitivity output with respect to the user's ability to tailor the analysis. The Sensitivity Report cannot "see" beyond the Allowable Increase or the Allowable Decrease. However, a coarse grid search using Solver Sensitivity can show how values in the model change beyond these ranges. In addition, Solver Sensitivity can track the effect of varying a parameter on any cells in the spreadsheet. The Sensitivity Report, by contrast, does not tell us explicitly how the objective function changes when we vary one of the objective function coefficients, nor does it tell us how the decision variables change when we vary one of the constraint constants. Solver Sensitivity can even track the effect of varying a parameter that is not, strictly speaking, within the model itself. For example, suppose there were several constraint constants that represented capacities and that these capacities could all be increased by a common percentage. Solver Sensitivity could be set up to track the decision variables and the objective function as functions of this percentage.

In addition, Solver Sensitivity can perform two-way analyses, in the same spirit as the two-way analysis in the Data Table tool. When we also consider the user's ability to tailor the analysis, something that is lacking in the Sensitivity Report, we conclude that the Solver Sensitivity is usally the preferred way of doing sensitivity analysis, in spite of the loss in precision.

Index